ENGLISH
MORALITY PLAYS
AND
MORAL INTERLUDES

ENGLISH
MORALITY PLAYS
AND
MORAL INTERLUDES

Edited by
Edgar T. Schell, University of California, Irvine
J. D. Shuchter, University of Colorado

HOLT, RINEHART AND WINSTON, INC.

NEW YORK · CHICAGO · SAN FRANCISCO · ATLANTA · DALLAS

MONTREAL · TORONTO · LONDON · SYDNEY

Acknowledgments

We wish to thank the following societies and institutions upon whose texts we have drawn in preparing this collection:

The Council of the Early English Text Society for *The Castle of Perseverance*

The Malone Society for *Wit and Science*

The Henry E. Huntington Library for *Enough Is as Good as a Feast*

Richard Southern and his publisher Faber & Faber, Ltd., have kindly given us permission to reproduce Professor Southern's sketch of the stage for *The Castle of Perseverance*, originally printed in *Medieval Theater in the Round*.

Mrs. Mary Gazley assisted in preparing the manuscript.

Deborah Schell and Deborah Shuchter have assisted in more ways than we can acknowledge. To them we dedicate this book.

Introductions and Notes copyright © 1969 by Holt, Rinehart and
Winston, Inc.

Library of Congress Catalog Card Number: 69-13430

03-073875-X
Printed in the United States of America
90123 68   987654321

INTRODUCTION

I

In 1639 one R. Willis, by then an old man, set down his recollections of a play he had seen in his youth. The play has since been lost, but it lived in Willis' memory for about sixty years:

The play was called *The Cradle of Security*, wherein was personated a King or some great Prince with his courtiers of several kinds, amongst which three Ladies were in special grace with him; and they, keeping him in delights and pleasures, drew him from his graver counsellors, hearing of sermons and listening to good counsel and admonitions, that in the end they got him to lie down in a cradle upon the stage, where, these three Ladies joining in a sweet song, rocked him asleep, that he snorted again; and in the meantime closely conveyed under the clothes where withall he was covered, a vizard like a swine's snout upon his face, with three wire chains fastened thereunto, the other end whereof being holden severally by those three Ladies, who fall to singing again, and then discovered his face that the spectators might see how they had transformed him, going on with their singing. Whilst all this was acting, there came forth of another door at the farthest end of the stage two old men, the one in blue with a sargeant at arms, his mace upon his shoulder, the other in red with a drawn sword in his hand and leaning with his other hand upon the other's shoulder. And so they two went along in a soft pace around about by the skirt of the stage till at last they came to the Cradle, when all the court was in greatest jollity; and then the foremost old man with his mace struck a fearful blow upon the Cradle, whereat all the courtiers with the three Ladies and the vizard all vanished, and the desolate Prince, starting up barefaced and finding himself thus sent for to judgment, made a lamentable complaint of his miserable case, and so was carried away by wicked spirits. This Prince did personate in the moral the wicked of the world, the three Ladies Pride, Covetousness and Luxury, the two old men the end of the world and the last judgment. This sight took such impression on me that when I came towards man's estate it was as fresh in my memory as if I had seen it newly acted.[1]

The Cradle of Security, like all of the plays in this volume, is a morality play. The fact that some sixty of these plays survive from a period spanning about two hundred years attests to their popularity during the fifteenth and sixteenth centuries. Willis' vivid memory of one he had seen more than half a century before suggests their dramatic effectiveness. But while Willis was setting down his impressions of *The Cradle of Security* the drama around him had changed considerably, and since then it has changed even more. Now plays of the sort that so moved Willis are buried in the histories of the drama between the mystery plays of the middle ages and the "regular" drama of Shakespeare and his contemporaries—often with a sense that they deserve no more than a valedictory nod.

Perhaps that will be our judgment as well; although we are beginning to recognize that the moralities were not replaced by a superior form of drama but rather absorbed into a different form. It may be that after all the historical assessment has been finished, we will conclude that these plays are simply not worth reading. It is true that without some spur we are disinclined to read them, and perhaps the term *morality* is in some measure at fault.[2] We instinctively resent the notion that someone is setting out to teach us how to behave, particularly when we suspect that he has a well-formed idea of how we should behave, and especially when he intends to do so in a place where we expect amusement, excitement, or at most the raising and quieting of pity and fear. And the prospect

---

[1] *Mount Tabor*, quoted in David Bevington, *From Mankind to Marlowe* (Cambridge, Mass., 1962), pp. 13–14.
[2] William Roy Mackenzie complained that "it would not be much worse for them if they were termed, instead, 'Respectability plays,' " *The English Moralities from the Point of View of Allegory* (Boston, 1914), p. 257.

of these plays getting a hearing is even worse if we add to the term *morality* the adjective *allegorical* and admit that the moral lessons are conveyed by "bloodless abstractions" such as Charity, Freewill, and Pity. It might on the whole be better to call them moral interludes, or perhaps just interludes—both names given to them in their heyday. We could then at least cloak these allegorical sermons in pleasant vagueness.[3]

But the term *morality* has the advantage of forcing us to confront squarely their nature and their intentions. If we are to read them, we ought to read them for what they are rather than for what we would like them to be. Nothing is more misleading than to set them in a scheme of inappropriate teleology, assuming that they aspired to be like the plays of the Shakespearian period. Morality plays are *sermones corporei*, embodied sermons aimed without equivocation or evasion at the moral betterment of their audiences. Their roots lie in the sermons of medieval preachers,[4] and while they turn during the sixteenth century toward secular issues, they do so with a strong religious bias. Thus success for a morality play is always some form of salvation, religious for the early plays, sectarian, political, or broadly social for the later plays.

Bernard Spivack has pointed out that the structural principle of plays of this sort rests upon "a sequential thesis in fulfillment of an instructive purpose."[5] The action of a particular play derives from those postulates of moral psychology developed over centuries of biblical exegesis and moral analysis which produced comprehensive schemes of man's life known as the Ages of Man, and which produced as well detailed and subtle analyses of the processes of man's soul. The larger pattern is clearly illustrated in *The Castle of Perseverance*, where the whole course of man's moral life is delineated, his youthful inclination toward worldly pleasure and toward sin, his

---

[3] The term *interlude* was used so indiscriminately during the Middle Ages (*Interludium de Clerico et Puella*) and the Renaissance (*The Interlude of Youth*, *Respublica*, a "merry interlude") that it is extremely difficult to circumscribe the sort of play to which it applies. It has sometimes been taken to refer to plays short enough to be presented between the courses of a banquet. At other times it has been used to distinguish didactic moralities from wholly secular entertainment. E. K. Chambers, after surveying the wide variety of works which included "interlude" in their titles, concluded that it could "apply to any kind of dramatic performance whatever": *The Mediaeval Stage* (Oxford, 1903), II, p. 183.

[4] See G. R. Owst, *Literature and the Pulpit in Medieval England* (New York, 1961), pp. 525-45.

[5] *Shakespeare and the Allegory of Evil* (New York, 1958), p. 102.

return to virtue in maturity, his lapse back into sin with the coming of age, and finally his salvation. Almost every morality play follows this pattern or a recognizable variation of it, for the pattern itself conforms to the natural shape of an admonitory sermon. ("If you do things of this sort, this is what will happen to you. But you can avoid that fate by behaving in these ways.") Within the framework of this larger pattern each play explores the moment-by-moment sequence of the soul's growth and change in a particular moral situation. As Covetous observes in the *Castle*, "every sin tilleth in other,/And maketh Mankind to be a fool"; and so, of course, every virtue draws others after it. The action of *The Interlude of Youth*, to choose a brief example, clearly derives from such a sequential thesis. It might be stated in this form: the natural vanity of youth leads to sins which inhibit charity (selfless love), but humility frees charity, causes youth to abstain from self-indulgent sins, and leads to salvation. In conformity with that thesis the play begins with Youth's rejection of Charity and his promise of salvation. Instead Youth calls for Riot, his "natural" companion. Riot brings in Pride, and Pride introduces Youth to his sister Lechery. When Charity tries to prevent Youth from going off with his new companions, Pride and Riot bind him in chains. Humility enters to free Charity; and when Youth returns, swollen with pride, Humility persuades him to renounce the vices and to take the name of Good Contrition. In the late Protestant morality *Lusty Juventus*, Juventus sums up his temptation and fall in a similar formula: "Under the title of Friendship to me [Satan] spake,/And so to Wicked Fellowship did me bring,/Which brought me clean to Abhominable Living."

There is nothing particularly unusual about such a sequence of action. We would not be surprised to find it at the heart of a modern play. Clifford Odets' *Golden Boy* is built on a similar scheme. What is unusual from our point of view is that the action is presented naked, without the covering of a fable purporting to show the actions of real people. Instead of Joe and Charley and Fred, we have "the motives and impulses of man's own heart, . . . clothed in flesh and blood and given him for companions."[6] And recognizing that, we

---

[6] E. N. S. Thompson, "The English Moral Play," *Transactions of the Connecticut Academy of Art and Sciences*, XIV (1910), p. 315.

are led to recognize that the landscape of the play is the soul itself. Thus the central character in a morality play is in the curious position of being at once the ground of the action and the principal actor upon that ground. That is why, particularly in the early plays, his fall into sin or his repentance may seem so abrupt and unmotivated. When Covetousness tempts him or Humility admonishes him, they do not touch answering chords within his soul, they are themselves the stirring of those impulses.

What has been said thus far may suggest that the plays are solemn and unfailingly serious. They are not. *Respublica* announces itself as "a merry interlude," and *Enough Is as Good as a Feast* is described as "a comedy full of pleasant mirth." In almost every play —*Everyman* is the sole exception—the solemn lessons of virtue must war with the raucous taunts of the vices and their elaborate buffoonery. We may easily recognize the broad comedy as a form of theatrical bait used to induce an audience to sit still for the sermons that are sure to come. But what we may not so easily recognize is that the comic passages are generally used in service of the plays' homiletic aims.[7] The butts of almost all of the jokes are ultimately the vices themselves, who are thereby characterized as grotesque, vain, divisive, or futile, depending upon the form the jokes take. Seen from a secure Christian perspective, vice is comic in the way that any ultimately useless activity is comic. And if the vices themselves become theatrically attractive through their involvement in the "leavening" humor of the plays, that is just as it should be. There is no point in denying the attractions of evil, or in warning an audience against vices to which they may not be expected to assent. So Shakespeare in *Richard III*, a play which owes a great deal to the moralities, induces the audience to assent to Richard's activities through the first half of the play by making him an audaciously comic character, and then forces them to awake with a shock to the evil at which they laughed.

For some time it was customary to regard the comic elements in the moralities as their saving grace, just as the medieval mysteries were read for indications of a developing secular spirit. In consequence discussions of the morality drama tended to be at once

7 See Spivack's discussion of the "comedy of evil," pp. 113-123.

apologetic and cajoling, admitting that the plays do not seem very promising, but arguing that they have a sort of rough vitality, and that besides a knowledge of them is essential to an accurate understanding of the achievement of the Elizabethans. But in recent years our emphasis has shifted toward the positive terms of that argument, and we have begun to see that if we grant the plays their intentions and methods they are capable of creating coherent and even exciting theatrical experiences. Thus we have moved away from Chambers' rather puzzled admission that a turn of the century production of *Everyman* was "quite unexpectedly impressive,"[8] and toward T. W. Craik's assertion that "no plays—those of Shakespeare's period not excepted—more thoroughly exploit their theatrical setting" than do the sixteenth-century moral interludes.[9] Most of us are not likely to get practical confirmation of that claim; performances even of *Everyman* are rare. But we can begin to recognize its justice if we read the plays with some exercise of the theatrical imagination, attending particularly to the ways in which they acknowledge their audiences, and involve them in the action.

The close relationship between morality drama and sermon literature practically guarantees that it will be a drama of direct address; but the conditions under which it was performed in effect sealed that guarantee. In the medieval drama at large there is no such division between the stage and the auditorium as the one we tend to enforce. Indeed, of course, the plays were not performed in auditoriums at all but alongside churches, in market squares, at street corners or in the middle of large fields. The stage might be a platform set on wheels and drawn from place to place around the town (the pageant wagon), or it might simply be an open space in some convenient locality with platforms or small structures set around it. The open space (called the *place*) could, like the Shakespearian stage, represent any place, while the platforms or mansions defined particular locations.[10] Some of the great mystery cycles, those in Chester and York certainly, used the pageant wagons; while the morality plays, performed by traveling professional companies,

[8] *Mediaeval Stage*, II, p. 201.
[9] *The Tudor Interlude* (London, 1962), p. 2.
[10] For a discussion of the various forms of the medieval stage see Glynne Wickham, *Early English Stages 1300 to 1660* (London, 1959), Vol. I.

preferred the place and mansion stage. But in either case the actors and playwrights had always to take account of the fact that the audience was not confined to its own area. Members of the audience could, and apparently did, drift into the acting area itself in search of better vantage points. And thus we find in both mystery and morality plays such phrases as "aback, fellows, and give me room." Richard Southern has argued convincingly that the great circular space within which *The Castle of Perseverance* was performed served also as the place where the spectators stood to watch the play.[11] He has led us to see the plan for the *Castle* not as a plan for a sort of medieval arena, with the audience kept at a safe distance from the actors, but rather as a plan for a theatre in the round, with the actors set in the midst of the audience and made to pass through the audience on their way from scaffold to scaffold. By the beginning of the fifteenth century, then, medieval drama had evolved a highly articulated and sophisticated idea of its physical theatre—an idea different from our own, to be sure, but not therefore more crude or less workable. When the plays began to move indoors during the sixteenth century, into the great banquet halls of noblemen or into the common rooms of the universities, they merely adapted their idea to their new circumstances. The halls became place and mansion stages, often quite complex. And there is abundant evidence from the plays themselves that the actors had still to recognize that they and their audience shared the same space.[12]

Thus the conditions under which the plays were performed, the theatres for which they were written, tended to prevent the development of a sharp distinction between the world of the play and the real world of the audience. The morality drama breaches that imaginary line with verve and freedom. The spectators are regularly absorbed into the plays, exhorted by the virtues, mockingly tempted by the vices, sometimes set to hold props for the actors, often drawn upon for illustrations of the moral qualities represented onstage. At times in the moral plays of the sixteenth century this habit of

[11] *The Medieval Theater in the Round* (London, 1957). See Southern's reconstruction of the theatre for which the *Castle* seems to have been written, Plate 2.
[12] Their relationship, however, began to change during the sixteenth century in ways that led finally to an absolute break between spectator and actor. See Anne Righter, *Shakespeare and the Idea of the Play* (London, 1964), pp. 13–86.

playing to and with the audience, rather than merely before them, is trivial, a matter of tricks and knockabout comedy to sustain interest. But its purpose is often more serious, for in drawing the audience into the plays, it extends the plays into the lives of the audience, making each man and woman Mankind tugged at by vices and virtues, in danger of hell and in hope of heaven. When Satan turns at the end of *Enough Is as Good as a Feast* to give his ironic advice to those worldly men in the audience we hear not merely the idiom of the sermon, but the sermon rendered, translated if you will, into precisely theatrical terms:

> All you worldly men, that in your riches do trust,
> Be merry and jocund, build palaces and make lusty cheer;
> Put your money to usury, let it not lie and rust;
> Occupy yourselves in my laws while ye be here.
>
> . . . .
>
> Oh, if you will after my laws behave,
> You shall have all things as this Worldly Man had.
>
> . . . .
>
> Yea, and after death I will provide a place
> For you in my kingdom forever to reign.
> You shall fare no worse than doth mine own grace—
> That is, to lie burning forever in pain.

(1451–66)

Satan's grotesque appearance, the limp body of Worldly Man, the death agonies through which he has passed, the arrogant flaunting of his wealth a moment before—all these things speak in the language of the theatre as eloquently as Satan's words.

Indeed in the sense that the theatre is a place where things are seen we might want to say, not merely that the morality drama exploits the conditions of its performance, but that it is precisely theatrical in its intentions. Like allegory in general, it is engaged in finding ways to embody, to make visible in action, invisible moral processes. Often these take the relatively undramatic form of debates, but just as often they issue in what we might call metaphors of action. So Mankind's induction into the service of the World in *The Castle of Perseverance* is represented in the covering of his original nakedness with rich clothing; and later in the same play his perseverance in virtue during his middle years is shown in the siege of the Castle by the forces of the World, the Flesh, and the Devil. Charity, locked up and ignored in the heart of Youth, is on the stage of *The Interlude of Youth* put into the stocks by Youth and Riot. In John Bale's moral history play *King John* (not included in this volume), the vice Sedition is very careful that the logic of theatrical representation be observed. He insists that his fellow vices carry him in upon their backs,

> That it might be said that, first, Dissimulation
> Brought in Private Wealth to every Christian nation!
> And that Private Wealth brought in Usurped Power;
> And he Sedition, in city, town and tower;
> That some man may know the fetch of all our sort.
>
> (1643–67)

For the moment Sedition functions as both actor and author, at once the presenter and the interpreter of action. At one time or another almost every major morality character plays this dual role, turning aside from the immediate action of the play to explain its significance to the audience. They thus betray their roots in the literature and logic of the preacher. But their rhetoric is not solely the rhetoric of speech, as his is; Sedition recognizes that in the theatre it is not enough merely to say what you mean, you must show it in action. Thus in attending to these plays, we need to attend to the rhetoric of the theatre, to the language of action, of movement and gesture, of costume and color, of spectacle.[13] It was, remember, the *sight* of *The Cradle of Security* that remained in Willis' memory.

Our growing recognition of the fundamental theatricality of the morality drama roughly parallels the growing theatricality and didacticism of our own drama. We may understand Chambers' surprise that *Everyman* was effective in performance because almost everything about the theatre of the turn of the century conspired to tell him that a frankly theatrical play which made almost no attempt to convince the audience of the reality of its fiction was not properly dramatic. But since then we have seen a great number of plays in a

---

[13] Craik's *Tudor Interlude* presents such information as we have about the theatrical resources of the sixteenth-century moralities. For the resources of the medieval theatre, consult Chambers and Wickham.

variety of dramatic modes which make little attempt to sustain the appearance of reality onstage, but which rather use the theatre in service of ideas, and even of messages. In a curious way we have been taught to appreciate a play like *The Castle of Perseverance* by such unlikely playwrights—unlikely for that purpose—as Genet, and Brecht, and Clifford Odets, playwrights whose theatres alternate between stage and secular pulpit. The morality they advance is by no means as simple or assured as the Christian morality of the *Castle*. And we might not want to push the resemblance between Brecht and, say, William Wager very far—their differences are as great as or greater than their similarities. But granting differences in poetic power, in idiom and ideology, and in the theatrical resources each had at his command, we can catch echoes of the theatrical logic which animates those lines from *Enough Is as Good as a Feast* quoted above in such things as the "Song of Mother Courage":

> Dangers, surprises, devastations—
> The war takes hold and will not quit.
> But though it last three generations
> We shall get nothing out of it.
> Starvation, filth, and cold enslave us.
> The army robs us of our pay.
> Only a miracle can save us.
> And miracles have had their day.
> Christians awake! The winter's gone!
> The snows depart, the dead sleep on.
> And though you may not long survive
> Get out of bed and look alive.[14]

If we are finally to base our judgment of the worth of the moralities on their contribution to the theatre of Shakespeare and his contemporaries, then, we ought at least to consider them first in light of our own homiletic theatre. For then we can recognize that the moralities were not—merely because they were moralities—predramatic or extradramatic plays, but that they were rather an expression in the theatrical language of the fifteenth and sixteenth centuries of a legitimate and long-lived mode of theatre.

[14] Translated by Eric Bentley. *Seven Plays by Bertolt Brecht* (New York: Grove Press, Inc., 1961), p. 330.

II

The history of the morality drama is at once complex and somewhat murky, complex because it shared the public's attention with so many other forms of drama and was, at least during its last half-century, the principal form, murky because we simply do not know very much about its genesis and development. We do not know what percentage of the actual corpus of plays is represented by the surviving texts. We do not understand what relationship the appearance of a printed text in a given year has to either the time of the writing of the play or to its performance, if there was a performance. We do not know the background or loyalties of the authors, and, in spite of a number of recent exploratory studies,[15] we still do not know how to understand the plays' relationships to the intellectual, theological, and social currents of their times. Criticism is a little ahead of scholarship here, for what led to the new wish to understand their external circumstances was a sudden new appreciation of the plays *as dramas*. Such a sequence is perhaps appropriate, but the scholarly lag makes it necessary to say that little written here about dates, texts, and allusions can be taken as final truth.

One of the few things we can be reasonably certain of is the relationship of the moralities to the great popular education movement launched by the Catholic church in the early thirteenth century. As the program of bringing a working knowledge of basic Christianity to priest and peasant spread, written works of two sorts began to appear: (1) collections of various kinds—sermons, doctrines, *exempla*, saints' lives, *casus viri illustrii* (Richard II's "sad stories of the death of kings");[16] and (2) moral narratives, in verse and prose, making use of such other literary forms as romance, and setting

---

[15] These are named above, in notes 1, 5, 9, 10 and 11. In addition, there is A. P. Rossiter, *English Drama from Early Times to the Elizabethans* (London, 1950). Somewhat ahead of its time was Willard Farnham, *The Medieval Heritage of Elizabethan Tragedy* (Berkeley, 1936).

[16] The body of work alluded to here is so enormous that no footnote could begin to refer to it. The reader is therefore directed to the following studies which deal with segments of the popular literary tradition in relation to drama: Farnham, *Medieval Heritage* (note 15); Eleanor Prosser, *Drama and Religion in the English Mystery Plays* (Stanford, 1961); V. A. Kolve, *The Play Called Corpus Christi* (Stanford, 1966). In addition, a useful survey is Louis B. Wright, *Middle Class Culture in Elizabethan England* (Ithaca, N.Y., 1963).

forth, in more-or-less fully realized fictions, the Christian interpretation of the life of man. It is from the latter writings, debates, dia-
logues, psychomachic epics, and just plain moral tales, that the
Mankind character, the morally educable person, emerges, as do
such other standard morality figures as the good counsellors and
the evil tempters. And from them the morality drama also derived
its characteristic structural formulas, the Three Ages of Man and
the Pilgrimage of Human Life.[17] The best guess about the genesis of
the morality drama is that at some point not very far from the year
1400 someone simply dramatized one of these moral narratives.
That assumption is given some weight both by the clear tendency
of these works to go toward dramatic form,[18] and by the extremely
close relationship, in terms of characters, incidents, and allegorical
machinery, between *The Castle of Perseverance*, the earliest surviving
full-length morality, and *The Pilgrimage of Human Life*, an enormous
poem which had been around in French for about 100 years before
it was translated into English in 1426.[19] (We should note that non-
dramatic moral allegory shows no signs of dying as it seeks dramatic
form, but that on the contrary the morality period itself is also the
flowering time of such works, culminating in *The Faerie Queene*.[20])

With due regard to the exaggeration inherent in such formulas,
it appears that the morality drama falls into four more-or-less distinct periods. The first period encompasses almost a whole century,
from approximately 1390 to about 1475, but from it we have only
three plays and a fragment surviving. The three plays, preserved in

[17] The doctrine of man embodied in the moralities belongs to a rather liberal and humanistic strain of
Catholic theology that grew up as a reaction against some of the rather terrible implications of the Augustinian theological tradition. The anti-Augustinian or popular tradition received additional support in the
later Middle Ages from Scholastic philosophy, which stressed the role of reason in religion and implied a
strong belief in man's ability to control his behaviour and to arrive by reason at an understanding of the
nature of things. In the popular tradition man is injured or infected by Original Sin not wholly depraved
by it. It is believed that the purgative power of repentance could enable man to attain the good, pious life
in this world. In vol. IV of *History of the Christian Church* (New York, 1930), D. Schaff suggests that the
popular theology was a practical necessity to the church for the high, or Augustinian theology "seemed
in its logical consequences to neutralize the appeal to the conscience of the sinner, to cut off the powerful
inducement of merit and reward, to limit the efficacy of the sacraments . . . and to weaken the hierarchy of
the Catholic Church" (pp. 535–536).
[18] See, for instance, E. C. York, "Dramatic Form in a Late Medieval English Narrative," *Modern Language
Notes* LXXII (1957). pp. 484–485.
[19] By John Lydgate; edited for the Early English Text Society by F. J. Furnivall and Katherine Locock
(London, 1899–1904), Extra Series Nos. 77, 92.
[20] The tradition is traced by C. S. Lewis in *The Allegory of Love* (Oxford, 1936).

a single manuscript once owned by Cox Macro and called therefore the Macro Moralities, are *The Castle of Perseverance* (c. 1390–1405), *Mankind* (c. 1460), and *Wisdom, Who is Christ* (c. 1475). The range of these pieces suggests something of the direction taken by moral drama. *The Castle*, as the reader will see, takes for its subject nothing less than the whole life of its hero, Humanum Genus, plus his afterlife, when his soul (played by a different actor) is judged and deemed worthy to join God in perpetual bliss. The play *Mankind* also treats of fall and redemption, but it is vastly different from *The Castle*. It is broad farce, focusing on the attempts of a comic devil, Titivillus, to prevent Mankind, who is a sort of downright English fellow, from leading the moral life, which consists for him, as it had for Piers the Plowman, in tilling his land and worshipping God. Mankind swerves from his duties twice, and the play ends as he is rescued the second time by Good Counsel and set back on the path of virtue. The play *Wisdom* is, again, utterly different from the others and unique in that it is the only morality in which the Mankind character appears on stage as three characters—Mind, Will, and Understanding—the three faculties of the human personality according to Aristotelian and Christian psychology. Lucifer successfully tempts the three to sin, but they recover when Wisdom appears. The play is very stately and dignified, and is concerned with fine points of theology. The fragment from this first period is *The Pride of Life* (c. 1390), which is of great interest not only because it is so very early but because it has a well-articulated social setting. The central character is the King of Life, a great boaster who ignores the good advice of his Queen and his Bishop and sends his court messenger out to challenge King Death to a duel, at which point the text breaks off. The play is strangely powerful, and the characters, who speak a deliciously colloquial English in driving rhymed alliterative verse, emanate a kind of mad intensity.

From about 1490 to approximately 1535 there is a second fairly distinct period, giving us four of the finest fruits of the morality style, John Skelton's *Magnificence* (1517), *Everyman* (c. 1490), John Redford's *Wit and Science*, and John Bale's *King John* (both 1530s). Here the later stages of the popular literary movement we have already mentioned merge effortlessly with the sophisticated but pious Humanism of the age of Erasmus and Colet, Cardinal Morton and Sir Thomas More. *Nature* (1490), by Henry Medwall, Morton's chaplain, extols Man as the flower of creation, minimizes his corruption and fall, and sets him on the right path at the end with the clear sense that he *deserves* another chance. *The Nature of the Four Elements* (c. 1510) consists almost entirely of the Mankind character being given a liberal education, as it was understood at the time. *Magnificence*, a history play in every respect except for the characters' names, teaches the Nichomachean Ethics as the surest way to achieve the Christian monarchy. Bale's play, focusing on the chronicle history of King John's battle with the Pope, does not share the large vision of the Humanist plays, but it does take a step beyond Skelton toward what came to be the Elizabethan history play, for real historical persons and allegorical characters out of the moral tradition walk Bale's stage together and interact. *King John* also provides an object lesson in the nature of tragedy, for Bale's fanatical Protestantism causes him to make the Pope into Antichrist and John into a perfectly virtuous proto-protestant martyr, and so the play attains only to the heights of melodrama.

The reader of this volume will find that Redford's *Wit and Science* is a delightful play, but it is also an important one, for it is the first of three plays embodying the Humanist trope of the wooing by *euphues* of *sophia* (pure intellectual wit and pious wisdom), one of the key metaphors of all of Renaissance literature, and one which ingeniously uses the literal facts of courtship and marriage as metaphors of the spiritual pilgrimage to perfection.

These plays are concerned with the problems of how to be a Christian, and they preach neither espousal of worldly values nor monastic withdrawal, but rather moderation in behavior and the development of the whole personality. Thus they are precisely secular in the sixteenth-century meaning, which involves no denial of the pressing reality of the afterlife. They are manifestly not "otherwordly" as they have been accused of being.[21] Their secularism takes such forms as the tendency to remove God from the stage and make the "presiding deity" of the play sometimes Nature,

---

[21] By Farnham in *Medieval Heritage;* by F. J. Furnivall in Introduction to *The Macro Plays* (London, 1904), E.E.T.S. Extra Series No. 91; by W. R. Mackenzie and E. N. S. Thompson, notes 2 and 6.

as in *Nature*, sometimes Mundus, as in *The World and the Child*, and sometimes only a feeling of what H. D. F. Kitto has called the "cosmic background,"[22] as in *Magnificence*.

During the second period we can also detect a move away from treating the whole life story of the central figure, and toward smaller plays dealing with one or another of Man's "Ages." Thus it is that in *The World and the Child* the time from Man's birth to his adulthood is dispensed with in a few score lines. And it is from this impulse that comedy, the earliest of the major subtypes to develop out of the morality, emerges; first, perhaps in *Mankind*, in the fore-shortening of fall and redemption to back-sliding and reform, but clearly in the early prodigal-son plays *Youth* and *Hickscorner* (between 1510 and 1515—the former in this volume).

The third period of the moral drama, from about 1535 to the accession of Elizabeth I in 1558, is distinguished by being a virtual lacuna in dramatic activity (publishing of plays, that is). Perhaps the terrible crisis of the Reformation is the cause. This is the time of the Catholic martyrs of Henry VIII and the Protestant martyrs of Mary Tudor and the energies of everyone must have been caught up in the national agony. Such plays as appear during these years tend to be religious polemic; we give *Respublica* here as an example.

What happens in the publication of plays after the accession of Elizabeth can only be described as an explosion. It is during the years from about 1558 to 1585, the years when Marlowe, Shakespeare, and Jonson may, as children, have been seeing plays, that the morality really flourishes and the tendencies glimpsed in the earlier plays crystallize.

Christian comedy is mainly redemptive in intention, but during this fourth period a not-so-latent satiric strain comes into its own. From the time of *The Castle of Perseverance*, morality plays had satirized the manners and morals of contemporary society, but generally in ways that rendered their satiric thrusts structurally subordinate to the moral careers of their heroes. *The Castle* might show that Backbiter is the guide to worldly success, or that new fashions are created only at the urging of Pride, but the play is built upon the progress of mankind through sin to repentance and

---

[22] *Form and Meaning in the Drama* (London, 1956).

salvation. In the sixties and seventies, however, plays that are built in rather different ways begin to appear. The Mankind figure is displaced by a reigning vice of some sort, Money or Folly perhaps, and we see not how a representative man fares during life's journey, but rather how vice spreads throughout society to corrupt a variety of men. The structural formula of these plays is simple and almost endlessly adaptable. The vice sets up a sort of confidence game, and proceeds to fleece a series of willing victims, "gulls," who come before him to beg favors. In addition to *All for Money* (1577) and *The Tide Tarrieth No Man*, the examples of the type which are given in this volume, variations of the satiric morality are to be found in *The Longer Thou Livest, The More Fool Thou Art* (1560–1568), and *Like Will to Like* (1562–1568). The finest instance of it however, and certainly one of the handful of truly great English comedies, is Ben Jonson's *The Alchemist* (1610).

Redemptive comedy too has a field-day during the fourth period, in wit-and-wisdom plays and prodigal-son plays. *The Marriage of Wit and Science* and *The Marriage Between Wit and Wisdom* are neither of them very good plays, being chiefly interesting for their distortions of the basic metaphor of Redford's play. Their substitution of elegant language and decoration for basic moral allegory is perhaps an ominous hint of the end of the morality style (*Wit and Wisdom* is an Inns of Court play, which is a world away from the popular morality tradition). The prodigal-son plays on the other hand do very well, showing the strong tendency of the playwrights to take irreducibly basic stories like that of the prodigal (understood since the twelfth century as a parable of the fall and redemption of mankind[23]) and graft them onto related and imported dramatic types. The prodigal son play first appears in the trappings of Roman comedy.[24] In the 1560s it becomes religious polemic—the "far country" to which the prodigal travels is Catholicism in *Lusty Juventus*. Experimentation in the sixties

---

[23] St. Bernard's interpretation of the parable of the prodigal son replaced earlier interpretations in which the prodigal and the older brother represented, variously, the Jew and the Gentiles. St. Bernard's treatment is found, in Latin, in Volume 183 of J. P. Migne, *Patrologia Cursus Completus, Series Latina* (Paris, 1875).
[24] In John Palsgrave's *Acolastus*, ed. P. L. Carver (London, 1937), E.E.T.S. Original Series No. 202; and in a fragment of a prodigal-son morality from the 1530s, published in *Malone Society Collections*, Vol. I, Part 1 (London, 1907).

produces a crude tragedy in *The Nice Wanton*, when the prodigal fails to be redeemed. And in *The Disobedient Child* the prodigal strays not into the arms of a Terentian *meretrix*, but into those of a wife! The author inveighs against marriage and the play ends inconclusively as the father only partially accepts his son's return.

The most interesting of the prodigal plays is one that never got out of manuscript—*Misogonus* ("The Hater," 1577). The author had the rather ingenious idea of combining the prodigal plot with the long-lost-brother motif from Italian comedy[25] with the result that the central figure of the play is actually the older brother in the parable. The author imagines him to be even more wicked than the prodigal, who comes in only in the last scene. This is a powerful play, especially in the wild comic viciousness of Misogonus and his terrifying shock and attempt at repentance when his brother comes home.

If the morality form might be said to have grown into comedy during the 16th century, it might also be said that it was from the beginning historical drama—in germ at least. Moralities tended to find court settings congenial and useful, largely because they were engaged in dramatizing moral issues which find their clearest temporal expression in the affairs and problems of kings. And more importantly Mankind is, metaphorically, a prince temporal if only because at some point in his life he acquires power over something. Whether nominally a king or merely a powerful man, he thus poses the problem of the use and abuse of power. And in this respect even a character like Humanum Genus in *The Castle*, neither a king nor a clearly placed social type, strikes a note characteristic of tyrants from Herod to Cambises:

> What caitiff of all my kende
>> Will not bow, he shall abyn;   *suffer*
> With my vengeance I shall him schende,   *injure*
>> And wrekyn me, by God's eyen.   *avenge*

It is only in the sixteenth century, however, under the stimulus of the various collections of cautionary tales for governors, that the

[25] The play is printed, with explanatory introduction, by R. W. Bond, *Early Plays from the Italian* (Oxford 1911).

incipient political themes of the moralities find expression in plays that may be called historical moralities or moral histories.[26]

We have already noted the steps taken by *Magnificence* and *King John* in mingling actual history and allegory. To these may be added David Lindsay's *Satire of the Three Estates,* performed in the 1550s. During the fourth period of the moral drama we find playwrights experimenting with the morality treatment of the lives of specific characters out of English chronicle history, ancient history, and Scripture. Of these prdouctions *Gorboduc* (1560-1561) and *Cambises* (1560-1569) are the most worthy of note, and to these we may add a play of the eighties, *The Famous Victories of Henry V*. It covers much the same material as Shakespeare's Hal plays, but the morality structure that has been argued for Shakespeare's play is patent in *The Famous Victories*.

Less frequently, the playwright shifts emphasis away from the corrupted leader and onto the suffering nation, which becomes in a sense the central figure of the play. This sense of the ravaged country is also imminent in the satiric comedies, where a cross-section of the country is represented by the parade of the vice's victims. *Respublica* is a play of this sort, and so are *A Looking Glass for London and England* (1590) and *Histriomastix* (c. 1598).

While we may speak of such plays as *Cambises* and *Gorboduc* as histories, they present themselves as tragedies. That term applies to them in the only meaning it had during the Middle Ages and the Renaissance: they are plays that end in the fall of their central characters, the fall because of the failure, for one reason or another, of the redemptive machinery of Christianity to operate. In the sixteenth century, as the universalized type of Mankind began to give way to more particularized social or moral types, playwrights became increasingly fascinated not only with narrow escapes from damnation but, more importantly, with the psychology of impenitence. The former produces tragicomedy, as when the hero of *Liberality and Prodigality* is brought to the very foot of the gallows before his sincere repentance is believed and he is pardoned, or when Marquis Walter in *Patient Grissell* (from Chaucer's *Clerk's Tale*) tells us that he hates what he is doing to Griselda and then

---

[26] These terms are Irving Ribner's, in *The English History Play in the Age of Shakespeare* (Princeton, 1957).

proceeds to do it (actually, tragi-comedy is visible even in *Everyman*, which is structurally a thriller, the race against Death).

But when the playwright focuses squarely on the sinning personality, we have the morality tragedies. This is what happened after mid-century, probably under the influence of the Calvinist doctrine of election. There were some men who, it seems, simply could not be saved. The prologue to *The Longer Thou Livest* explains that

> Bringing up is a great thing, so is diligence;
> But nothing, God except, is so strong as nature,
> For neither counsel, learning nor sapience
> Can an evil nature to honest manners allure;
> Do we not see at these days so many past cure,
> That nothing can their crookedness rectify,
> Till they have destroyed them utterly?

The careers of those who destroy themselves tend to be balanced off in the so-called homiletic tragedies against the careers of those elected to salvation. Worldly Man, in *Enough Is as Good as a Feast,* is finally irredeemable, although he may toy with the idea of repentance: "It will not out of the flesh that is bred in the bone verily. The Worldly Man will needs be a worldly man still." His counterpart, Heavenly Man, is unswervingly virtuous.

Enough Is as Good as a Feast is perhaps the best of that group of tragedies which divide mankind into good and bad men, a group which includes *Nice Wanton, The Trial of Treasure* (1567), and George Gascoigne's *The Glass of Government* (1575). Worldly Man and Heavenly Man, polarizing, represent limited spiritual conditions and thus they can neither change nor develop significantly, as the earlier Mankind figure could because he was both good and evil. With Worldly Man and Heavenly Man we are back to melodrama. Almost alone among the plays before Marlowe to escape this limitation is *The Conflict of Conscience* (1581), which, as the reader will see, looks forward in many ways to the work of the far greater historian of Dr. John Faustus of Wittenberg.

All our talk about the influence of the moralities on later drama must be conditioned by the undoubted fact that their eclipse in the 1580s is not just another critical myth (though of course we hear of moralities being performed down to the turn of the century, and Jonson's ironic use of them in his late plays suggests fresh viewing perhaps into the 1620s.)

The moralities were quickly supplanted as the dominant dramatic style for many reasons. Mobility was of their essence. Many of the plays were performed by traveling troupes of five or six (regardless of the number of roles in the play), in almost any sort of playing space and with the costumes and props that could be carried in a trunk. When the Burbages shrewdly guessed that there was money to be made out of plays in London, and began in 1576 the building of the great theatres, they automatically called forth a less ephemeral sort of play. The morality is *theatre intime* in a much stricter sense than is the Shakespeare play, and few of them would look better than slight on the stage of the Globe.

But the building of the theatres is only symptomatic of a truly momentous shift in the social order and the order of thought that had begun at least as early as the accession of Elizabeth. Humanism is always a delicate balance, and the Christian Humanism represented by the fusion of late medieval popular religion with the critical spirit of the English Erasmians was especially fragile. The Puritan attacks on the supposed immorality of the stage, dating from the 1560s, were only one of the signs of doom coming, as it were, from the "left." From the "right," the aristocratic side, came the repudiation of the popular drama by the influential Sir Phillip Sidney, and then the momentary leaning, during the 1570s, of powerful figures in the Church of England away from the old popular religious tradition and toward Calvinism. (This was short-lived, and within a few years playwrights were enlisted to take the part of the Church in the celebrated Marprelate controversy, but the shift had apparently been enough to help cut the ground from under the dramatic wing of the popular tradition, the morality).[27] Finally, the men who rushed to fill the new stages with characters between 1580 and 1590, John Lyly, Thomas Kyd, George Peele,

[27] Sidney's *Defense of Poesy*, with its attack on the unpolished native drama, was probably written in 1579–80, that is, just at the end of the morality period. The puritan party within the Anglican Church was of course just as dangerous to the theatre as were the Puritans who controlled the City of London. It is generally agreed by historians or the Tudor period that the turbulent decade of the 1570s was crucial in the Elizabethan religious and political settlement. See Lawrence Stone, *The Crisis of the Aristocracy* (Oxford, 1965), Ch. XIII.

Robert Greene, Christopher Marlowe, and William Shakespeare, were not only men of genius but had, all of them, either university or courtly connections, or both. The few morality writers about whom we know anything seem to have been beneficed clergymen.

After 1570 the split between court and town was decisive. The moral drama was perhaps one of its victims as were, ultimately, the great theatres. Only by casting their lot with the court and aristocratic values did they survive at all, and perhaps they were lucky to have lasted until 1642.

It is possible, of course, to trace specific points of influence from one form to another. The King's "vizard," in *The Cradle of Security* has its counterpart in *Wit and Science* when Wit looks at himself in a mirror and finds that his face is unrecognizably deformed. This dramatizes the concept of *dissimilitudo,* the "unlikeness" resulting from marring through sin what is made in God's image.[28] It is suggested in the mirror scene in *Richard II* and the pictures scene in *Hamlet*. Certain elements in the conception of Falstaff are traceable to Riot, the vice in *Youth*, whose tag lines are quoted as late as 1600. The devils and personifications in *Doctor Faustus* show a general awareness of morality conventions. But we do not offer the plays which follow as a collection of putative influential sources for Elizabethan drama. We offer them rather as examples of one form the drama took in that period from the development of a popular English drama in the fourteenth century to the closing of the theatres in 1642. It is a time which might profitably be conceived as a single unbroken period of secularized religious drama whose central dramatic action involves the moral career of the Christian Mankind figure. Looked at from that point of view the mystery cycles, the moralities, and the Elizabethan plays can be thought of as different styles for the representation of a fundamentally unchanging subject matter. So conceived, the mainspring of these earlier productions becomes not the dulling process of forcing doctrines into allegories but the lively experimentation with dramatic form; and dramatic history becomes not a matter of influences but the natural process of an "idea of a theatre" realizing itself according to the best lights of its own time and place.

[28] The basic reference here is again Bernard's interpretation of the parable of the prodigal son, note 23.

CONTENTS

✳ *THE CASTLE OF PERSEVERANCE*

(c. 1350–1399)

The Castle of Perseverance is the longest, most comprehensive, perhaps the oldest, and certainly one of the best morality plays in English. In it the whole scheme of man's life is played out, from birth to death, from innocence to salvation. Largely because of the range of its subject matter, the *Castle* develops in its greatest detail the fundamental pattern of action of the morality drama, as its hero moves through the moral stages of Innocence, Temptation and Fall, Life in Sin, Realization and Repentance, and comes at last to Salvation. The length and prolixity of the play may stand as a barrier to the reader; but the one is a consequence of its theme, the need for moral perseverance throughout man's life, the other a consequence of the conditions under which it was performed.

The *Castle* was written to be played in a great circular space, with the Castle itself erected in the center of the circle and scaffolds for the principal vices and virtues set around its perimeter. This arrangement is represented in a sketch affixed to the manuscript (see Plate 1). The sketch also calls for a moat or ditch to be dug around the outside of the circle, apparently to keep those who had not paid from seeing the play. Those who had may have sat or stood on earthen mounds built up between the scaffolds from earth dug out of the ditch, or they may have stood within the playing area, perhaps in triangular spaces so as to leave room for the actors to

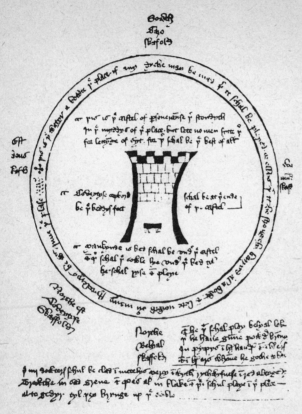

Plate 1. The stage plan for *The Castle of Perseverance* appended to the Macro manuscript. Right: A modernized version of the plan.

cross between scaffolds (see Plate 2). Those actors who played near the Castle would thus have been surrounded by their audience; and even those who played upon the scaffolds would have had to recognize that speeches directed to one part of the audience would have been inaudible to the rest of it. All of the actors needed speeches, then, which developed their ideas at sufficient length, or perhaps repeated them in different ways, so that the actors could make them clear to all parts of their audience. That need—and it is

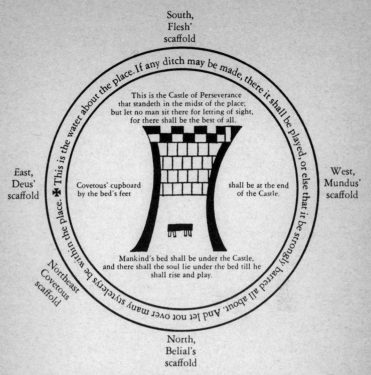

South,
Flesh'
scaffold

This is the water about the place. If any ditch may be made, there it shall be played, or else that it be strongly barred all about. And let not over many stytelers be within the place.

This is the Castle of Perseverance
that standeth in the midst of the place;
but let no man sit there for letting of sight,
for there shall be the best of all.

East,
Deus'
scaffold

Covetous' cupboard
by the bed's feet

shall be at the end
of the Castle.

West,
Mundus'
scaffold

Mankind's bed shall be under the Castle,
and there shall the soul lie under the bed till he
shall rise and play.

Northeast
Covetous
scaffold

North,
Belial's
scaffold

He that shall play Belial, look that he have gunpowder burning in pipes in his hands and in his ears and in his ars when he goeth to battle. The three daughters shall be clad in mantles: Mercy in white, Righteousness in red all together, Truth in sad green, and Peace all in black; and they shall play in the place all together till they bring up the soul.

a pressing one even today—is met by the play's leisurely and at times repetitive style.

The place and date of the play are matters of conjecture. Walter Smart has argued that it belongs to the area around the city of Lincoln because of its dialect and because of some local references (the gallows of Canwick, l. 2433).[1] Smart's findings were confirmed by Jacob Bennett, who went on to argue that the play as it stands is really a compilation of three different parts. On the basis of a stylistic analysis of the handling of the play's thirteen line stanza, Bennett concluded that the Banns of the play were added to the original version by another author and that the debate

[1] "*The Castle of Perseverance*: Place, Date and Source," *The Manly Anniversary Studies in Language and Literature* (Chicago, 1923), pp. 42–53.

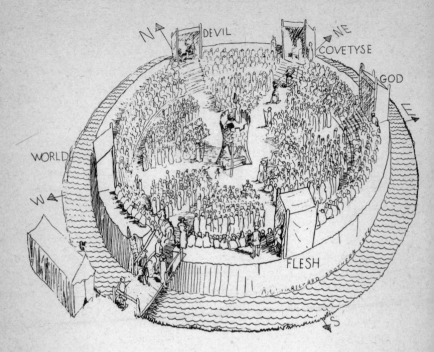

Plate 2. Tentative reconstruction of a medium-large theatre of the hill and ditch variety for *The Castle of Perseverance*. The sketch shows many elements of staging, but does not illustrate any particular scene in the play. Reproduced from Richard Southern's *Medieval Theatre in the Round* by permission of Faber and Faber, Ltd.

among the Four Daughters of God was a still later addition. Because of the relatively conservative language of the play, Bennett would date it in the latter part of the fourteenth century.[2]

The only text of the play is the so-called Macro Manuscript, which was edited by F. J. Furnivall and Alfred Pollard in 1904 for the Early English Text Society. We have followed that edition, modernizing the forms of words only when, in our opinion, that did not damage the line. Words, fragments of words, or stage directions set within brackets have been supplied by us to facilitate reading or acting.

[2] *"The Castle of Perseverance: Redactions, Place and Date," Medieval Studies*, XXIV (1962), pp. 141–52.

THE CASTLE OF PERSEVERANCE

The Banns

FIRST FLAGBEARER: Glorious God! in all degrees lord most of
    might
  That heaven and earth made of nought, both sea and land,
The angels in heaven Him to serve bright,
  And mankind in middle-earth He made with His hand,
And our lovely Lady that lantern is of light,
  Save our liege lord, the King, the leader of this land,
And all royals of this realm, and rede them the right,   *counsel*
    And all the good commons of this town that before us stand
      In this place!
      We muster you with menschepe   *honor* 10
      And freyn you of frely friendship!   *ask/frank*
      Christ save you from all schenchepe   *harm*
      That knowen will our case!
SECOND FLAGBEARER: The case of our coming, you to declare,
  Every man in himself, forsooth he it may find:
When mankind into this world is born full bare—
  And bare shall buried be at the last end—
God him giveth two angels full yepe and full yare,   *bold/ready*
  The Good Angel and the Bad, to him for to lend.
The Good teacheth him goodness, the Bad sin and sare;   *grief* 20
  When the one hath the victory, the other goeth behind,
    By reason.
    The Good Angel coveteth evermore man's salvation,
    And the Bad besetteth him ever to his damnation;
    And God hath given man free arbitration
      Whether he will himself save or his soul peril.
FIRST FLAGBEARER: Spilt is man spetously when he   *destroyed/terribly*
  to sin assent.
  The Bad Angel then bringeth him three en'mies so stout:
The World, the Fiend, the foul Flesh so jolly and jent.   *courteous*
  They leadeth him full lustily with sins all about.   30
Pyth with Pride and Covetous, to the World is he went   *furnished*
  To maintain his manhood. All men to him lout.   *bow*

5

After Ire and Envy, the Fiend to him hath lent
  Backbiting and Indicting, with all men for to rout   *quarrel*
    Full even.
    But the foul Flesh, homliest of all,
    Sloth, Lust and Lechery 'gun to him call,
    Gluttony and other sins, both great and small:
      Thus man's soul is soiled with sins more than seven.
SECOND FLAGBEARER: When man's soul is soiled with
  sin and with sore,   *grief* 40
  Then the Good Angel maketh mickle mourning   *much*
That the lovely likeness of God should be lore   *lost*
  Through the Bad Angel's false enticing.
He sendeth to him conscience, pricked full poor,   *attired*
  And clear Confession with Penance doing.
They moven man to mendment that he misdid before;
  Thus they callen him to cleanness and to good living,
    Withouten distance.   *disagreement*
    Meekness, Patience and Charity,
    Soberness, Busyness and Chastity,   50
    And Largety, virtues of good degree,   *generosity*
      Man calleth to the Castle of Good Perseverance.
FIRST FLAGBEARER: The Castle of Perseverance, when
  mankind hath tan,   *entered*
  Well armed with virtues and overcome all vices,
There the Good Angel maketh full merry then
  That mankind hath overcome his ghostly en'mies.
The Bad Angel mourneth that he hath missed man;
  He calleth the World, the Fiend and the foul
  Flesh, iwis,   *certainly*
And all the seven sins to do that they can
  To bring Mankind again to bale out of bliss,   60
    With wrong.
    Pride assaileth Meekness with all his might;
    Ire against Patience full fast 'gan he fight;
    Envy against Charity striveth full right;
      But Covetous against Largety fighteth over   *generosity*
    long.

SECOND FLAGBEARER: Covetous, Mankind ever coveteth for to
    quell.
    He gathereth to him Gluttony against Soberness;
    Lechery with Chastity fighteth full fell,   *fiercely*
    And Sloth in God's service against Busyness.
    Thus Vices against Virtues fighten full snell.   *vigorously* 70
      Every busketh to bring man to distress;   *every[one] fights*
    But Penance and Confession with Mankind   *unless*
      will mell,   *speak*
      The Vices are full likely the Virtues to oppress
        Sans doubt;
        Thus in the Castle of Good Perseverance
        Mankind is maskered with   *bewildered with*
          mickle variance.   *much quarreling*
      The Good Angel and the Bad be ever at distance:
        The Good holdeth him in; the Bad would bring him
          out.
FIRST FLAGBEARER: Out of Good Perseverance when Mankind
    will not come,
      Yet the Bad Angel with Covetous him can assail,   80
    Finding him in poverty and penance so benome,   *destitute*
      And bringeth him in belief in default for to fail;   *poverty/fall*
    Then he proffer'th him good and gold, so great a sum,
      That if he will come again and with the World dayle.   *dally*
    The Bad Angel to the World tolleth him down,   *draws*
      The Castle of Perseverance to flee from the dayle   *security*
        And bliss.
        Then the World beginneth him to restore.
        Have he never so mickle, yet would he have more—
        Thus the Bad Angel learneth him his lore.   90
          The more a man ageth, the harder he is.
    Hard a man is in age and covetous by kind.   *nature*
      When all other sins man hath forsake,
    Ever the more that he hath, the more is in his mind
      To gather and to get good with woe and with
        wrake;   *persecution*
    Thus the Good Angel cast is behind,

And the Bad Angel Man to him taketh,
That wringeth him wrenches to his last end,   *deceives him with tricks*
Till Death cometh full dolefully and lodgeth him in a lake
    Full low.   100
      Then is Man on molde maskered in mind;   *earth/confused*
      He sendeth after his secutors,   *executors*
        full fickle to find,   *difficult*
    And his heir afterward cometh ever behind:
      I-wot-not-who is his name, for he him not know.   *know*
SECOND FLAGBEARER: Man knows not who shall be his heir
    and govern his good.
He cares more for his chattel than for his cursed sin.
To put his good in governance he mengeth his mod.[1]
He would that it were shifted amongst his nigh kin.
But there shall come a lither lad with a torn hood—   *evil*
    I-wot-never-who shall be his name, his clothes be full
      thin—   110
Shall herit the heritage that never was of his blood.
    When all his life is lighted upon a little pin
      At the last,
      On live when he may no longer lend,   *alive/stay*
      Mercy he calleth at his last end:
      "Mercy, God! Be now my friend!"
      With that, man's spirit is passed.
FIRST FLAGBEARER: When man's spirit is passed, the Bad Angel
    full fell   *quickly*
Claimeth that for Covetous man's soul should be his,
And for to bear it full boisterously with him into hell.   120
    The Good Angel sayeth, "Nay! the spirit shall to bliss,
For at his last end of mercy he gan spell,   *call*
    And therefore of mercy shall he not miss.
And our lovely Lady, if she will for him mell,   *speak*
    By mercy and by menys in purgatory he is,   *prayers*
      In full bitter place.
    Thus mouth's confession,
    And his heart's contrition,

[1] To put . . . his mod: To control his wealth he troubles his mind.

Shall save man from damnation,
   By God's mercy and grace.   130
SECOND FLAGBEARER: Grace if God will grant us of His mickle
   might,
   These parcels in properties we purpose us to play   *parts/costumes*
This day seven-night before you in sight
   At _____ on the green, in royal array.[2]
Ye haste you then hitherward, sirs, hendly in hyth;   *most courteous*
   All good neighbours, full specially we you pray,
And look that ye be there betime, lovely and light,   *early*
   For we shall be onward by underne of the day.   *morning (9–12 AM)*
      Dear friends,
      We thank you of all good dalliance   140
      And of your special sportance,
      And pray you of good countenance
         To our lives' ends.
FIRST FLAGBEARER: Deus, our lives we love you, thus taking
   our leave.
   Ye manly men of _____, thus Christ save you all.
He maintain your mirths and keep you from grieve,
   That born was of Mary mild in an ox stall.
Now mercy be all _____, and well might ye sheve!   *fare*
   All our faithfull friends, thus fair might ye fall!
Ya, and welcome be ye when ye come price   *[our] worth*
   for to preve,   *for to test*   150
   And worthy to be worshipped in bower and in hall
      And in every place.
   Farewell, fair friends
   That lovely will listen and lendes!   *remain*
   Christ keep you from fiends!
      Trump up, and let us pace!

The Play

[*Enter* MUNDUS *on his scaffold.*]
MUNDUS: Worthy wights, in all this world wide   *men*
   By wild wood wonys and every way-went,   *dwellings*

---

[2] A space left blank for the name of the town where the performance was to be given.

Precious in price, prickéd in pride,

Through this proper pleyn place in peace be ye bent! *playing?* 160

Busk ye, bold bachelors, under my banner to abide, *prepare*

Where bright basnets are battered and backs are shent. *helms / broken*

Yea, sirs seemly, all same sitteth on side,

For both by sea and by land my sondes I have sent: *messengers*

All the world mine name is ment, *[to] all the world / told*

All abouten my bane is blow, *proclamation*

In every coast I am know.

I do men ravin on rich row *carry away / in great numbers*

Till they be dight to death's dent. *put / blow*

Assyria, Achaia, and Al'many, 170

Canadoyse, Cappadoce, and Cananee,

Babylon, Brabon, Burgoyne and Britain,

Greece, Galice, and to the Greekish sea;

I move also Macedone in my mickle main, *great power*

France, Flaunders and Friesland, and also Normandy,

Pynceras, Paris, and long Pygmanne,

And every town in Trage, even to the dreye tree, *Thrace?*

Rhodes and rich Rome:

All these lands at mine avise *direction*

Are casten to my worldly wise; *manner* 180

My treasurer, Sir Covetise,

Hath seized them wholly to me.

Therefore my game and my glee grow full glad;

There is wight in this world, that my wit will me werne. *[not a] person / deny*

Every rich rengne rap'th him full rad *ruler hastens / full quickly*

In lusts and in likings my laws to learn.

With fair folk in a field, freshly I am fad; *fed*

I dance down as a doe by dales full derne. *dark or secret*

What boy biddeth battle or debateth with blade,

Him were better to been hangen high in hell herne, *corner* 190

Or burnt on light levene. *bright lightning*

Whose speaketh against the word, *world*

In a prison he shall be sperd;   *cast*
Mine hest is holden and heard   *command*
  Into the high heaven.
  [*Enter* BELIAL *upon his scaffold.*]
BELIAL: Now I sit, Satanas, in my sad sin,   *deep*
  As devil doughty, in draff as a drake;   *dregs/dragon*
I champ and I chase, I chock on my chin;   *thrust out*
  I am boistrous and bold as Belial the black.
What folk that I grope, they gapen and grin.   *tear/gape* 200
  Iwis, from Carlisle into Kent my carping they take.   *orders*
Both the back and the buttock bursteth all on brenne   *burning*
  With works of wreche. I work them   *vengeance*
    mickle wrake;   *harm*
      In woe is all my wenne.   *delight*
    In care I am cloyed,
    And foul I am annoyed,
    But Mankind be destroyed
      By dikes and by den.
Pride is my prince, in pearls i-pight;   *adorned*
  Wrath, this wretch, with me shall wawe;   *go* 210
Envy into war with me shall walken wyth.   *bravely*
  With these faytouris I am fed—in faith I am fawe.   *rascals/joyful*
As a dyngne devil in my den I am dight;   *worthy/set*
  Pride, Wrath and Envy, I say in my saw,
Kings, Kaisers, and Kempys and many a keen knight,   *soldiers*
  These lovely lords have learned them my law.
    To my den they will draw.
    All wholly, Mankind,
    To hell but I win,
    In bale is my bin,   *ruins/prison* 220
      And shent under schawe.   *destroyed/grove*
On Mankind is my trust, in contre I-knowe,   *widely known?*
  With my tyre and my tail tightly to tene.   *attire/quickly to harm*
Through Flanders and Friesland, fast I gan flow
  Fele folk on a flock to flappen and flene.   *many/flap and flay*
When I grasp on the ground,   *when I touch the ground*
  grim there shall grow.   *fury there, etc.*

Gather you together, ye boys, on this green!
In this broad bugle a blast when I blow,
   All this world shall be wood, iwis, as I ween,   *mad/think*
      And to my bidding bend.   *230*
      Wythly on side,   *quickly*
      On bench will I bide,
      To tene this tide   *harm*
         All wholly Mankind.
        [*Enter* FLESH *upon his scaffold.*]

FLESH: I bide as a broad bursten gut abouyn on these   *aloft*
     towers.
     Everybody is the better that to my bidding is bent.
I am Mankind's fair flesh florchyd in flowers.   *adorned*
    My life is with lusts and liking i-lent;   *fixed*
With tapytys of taffeta I timber my towers;   *hangings/decorate*
    In mirth and in melody my mind is i-ment.   *set* 240
Though I be clay and clad, clappéd under clowris,[3]
    Yet would I that my will in the world went,
       Full true I you behight.   *promise*
      I love well mine ease,
      In lusts me to please;
      Though sin my soul seize,
        I give not a mite.
In Gluttony gracious now am I grow;
    Therefore he sitteth seemly here be my side;
In Lechery and Liking lent am I low,   *sunk* 250
    And Sloth, my sweet son, is bent to abide.
These three are noble, truly I trow,   *believe*
    Mankind to tenyn and tricken a tide.   *deceive*
With many berdis in bower my blasts are blow   *maidens*
    By ways and by woods through this world wide,
       The sooth for to sayen;
      But if man's flesh fare well   *but-unless*
      Both at meat and at meal,
      Dight am I in great del,   *set/grief*
       And brought into pain.   260

[3] Though I be clay (flesh) and clad (in a winding sheet) and clapped under ground. . . .

And after good fare, in faith though I fell,
　　Though I drive to dust, in dross for to drepe,　　　　*turn/drip*
Though my sely soul were harried to hell—　　　　　　*blessed*
　　Who-so will do these works, iwis, he shall weep
　　　　Ever withouten end.
　　Behold the World, the Devil and me!
　　With all our mights, we kings three,
　　Night and day busy we be
　　　　For to destroy Mankind,
　　　　　　If that we may.　　　　　　　　　　　　270
　　Therefore on hill
　　Sitteth all still
　　And seeth with good will
　　　　Our rich array.

[*Enter* MANKIND *into the playing area, the* GOOD ANGEL *on his right, the* BAD ANGEL *on his left.*]

MANKIND:　After our form father's kende　　　　*first father's way*
　　This night I was of my mother born.
From my mother I walk, I wend;
　　Full faint and feeble I fare you beforn;　　　　*walk/before*
I am naked of limb and lend　　　　　　　　　　*loin*
　　As Mankind is shapen and shorn.　　　　　　280
I not whither to go nor to lend,　　　　　　*[know] not/stay*
　　To help myself, midday nor morn.
　　　　For shame I stand and schende.　　　　*am bewildered*
　　I was born this night in bloody ble;　　　　*color*
　　And naked I am, as ye can see.
　　Ah, Lord God in Trinity,
　　　　How Mankind is unthende!　　　　　　*miserable*
Whereto I was to this world brought
　　I ne wot; but to woe and weeping　　　　　*don't know*
I am born, and have right nought　　　　　　290
　　To help myself in no doing.
I stand and study, all full of thought;
　　Bare and poor is my clothing;
A sely chrisom mine head hath caught,　　　*blessed/baptismal cloth*
　　That I took at mine christening;

Certes, I have no more.
Of earth I came, I wot right well,   *know*
And as earth I stand this sele;   *time*
Of Mankind it is great dele,   *pity*
Lord God, I cry thine ore!   *mercy* 300
Two Angels been assigned to me.
The one teacheth me to good;
On my right side ye may him see;
He came from Christ that died on rood.   *cross*
Another is ordained here to be
That is my foe, by fen and flood;
He is about in every degree
To draw me to those devils wood,   *mad*
That in hell been thick.   *numerous*
Such two hath every man on live   *alive* 310
To rulen him and his wits five.
When man doth evil, the one would shrive,
The other draweth to wick.   *sin*
But since these angels been to me fall,
Lord Jesu, to you I bid a bone,   *ask a boon*
That I may follow, by street and stall,
The angel that came from heaven throne.
Now, Lord Jesu in heaven hall,
Hear when I make my moan!
Coryows Christ, to you I call!   *careful* 320
As a grisly ghost, I grucche and groan,   *complain*
I ween, right full of thought.   *suppose*
Ah, Lord Jesu, whither may I go?
A chrisom I have and no mo.   *more*
Alas, men may be wonder woe
When they be first forth brought.
GOOD ANGEL: Yea, forsooth, and that is well seen!
Of woefull woe man may sing,
For each creature helpeth himself bedene,   *quickly*
Save only man at his coming.   330
Nevertheless, turn thee from tene   *harm*
And serve Jesu, heaven king,

And thou shalt, by groves green,
  Fare well in all thing.
    That Lord thy life hath lent;
    Have him always in thy mind,
    That died on rood for mankind,   *cross*
    And serve him to thy life's end,
    And certes thou shalt not want.
BAD ANGEL: Peace, Angel! Thy words are not wise.   340
  Thou counsellest him not a-right.
He shall him drawen to the World's service
  To dwell with kaiser, king and knight,
    That in land be him none like.
    Come on with me, still as stone!
    Thou and I to the World shall gone,
    And then thou shalt see anon
    How soon thou shalt be rich.
GOOD ANGEL: Ah, peace, Angel! Thou speakest folly!
  Why should he covet World's good   350
Since Christ in earth and His many,
  All in povert here they stood?   *poverty*
World's weal, by street and stye,
  Faileth and fadeth, as fish in flood;
But heaven rich is good and trye,   *true*
  There Christ sitteth, bright as blood,
    Withouten any distress.
    To the World would He not flit,
    But forsook it every whit:
    Example I find in holy writ,   360
    He will bear me witness:
Divicias & Paupertates ne dederis mihi, Domine.[4]
BAD ANGEL: Ya, ya, Man! Leve him not,   *believe*
  But come with me, by stye and street.
Have thou a gobbet of the World caught,   *morsel*
  Thou shalt find it good and sweet.
A fair lady thee shall be tawth,   *given*
  That in bower thy bale shall bete;   *remedy*

---

[4] *Divicias . . . Domine:* Cp. Proverbs 30, 8: "Give me neither poverty nor riches."

With rich rents thou shalt be fraught,
  With silk sendal to sitten in seat.   *robe* 370
      I rede, let bedes be!   *prayers*
    If thou wilt have well thine hele,   *health*
    And faren well at meat and meal,
    With God's service may thou not deal,
      But come and follow me.
MANKIND: Whom to follow, witen I ne may;   *know*
  I stand and study, and gin to rave;
 I would be rich in great array,
    And fain I would my soul save—
      As wind in water I wave.   380
    Thou wouldest to the World I me took,
    And he would that I it forsook.
    Now, so God help me, and the holy book,
      I not which I may have.   *[know] not*
BAD ANGEL: Come on, Man! Whereof hast thou care?
  Go we to the World, I rede thee blyve,   *advise/quickly*
 For there thou shalt mow right well fare,   *be able*
    In case if thou think for to thrive;
      No lord shall be thee like.
    Take the World to thine entent,   *attention* 390
    And let thy love be thereon lent;   *fixed*
    With gold and silver and rich rent,
      Anon thou shalt be rich.
MANKIND: Now, since thou has beheten me so, *promised*
  I will go with thee and assay.   *try*
 I ne let for friend nor foe,   *will not stop*
    But with the World I will go play,
      Certes, a little throw.   *time*
      In this World is all my trust,
      To liven in liking and in lust;   400
    Have he and I once cust,   *kissed*
      We shall not part, I trow.
GOOD ANGEL: Ah, nay, Man! For Christ's blood,
  Come again, by street and stile!
  The World is wicked and full wood,   *mad*

And thou shalt liven but a while.
What covetest thou to win?
Man, think on thine ending day
When thou shal be closed under clay;
And if thou think of that array,   *state* 410
Certes, thou shalt not sin.
Homo memento finis! & in eternum non peccabis.[5]
BAD ANGEL: Ya, on thy soul thou shalt think
all be-time   *soon enough*
Come forth, Man, and take no heed!
Come on, and thou shalt holden him in.
Thy flesh thou shalt foster and feed
With lovely life's food.
With the World thou mayest be bold
Till thou be sixty winter old;
When thy nose waxit cold,   *grows* 420
Then mayest thou draw to good.
MANKIND: I vow to God, and so I may
Make merry a full great throw,   *long time*
I may liven many a day;
I am but young, as I trow,
For to do that I should.
Might I ride by swamp and syke,   *rill*
And be rich, and lord i-like,   *like a lord*
Certes then should I be fryke,   *joyful*
And a merry man on molde.   *earth* 430
BAD ANGEL: Yes, by my faith, thou shalt be a lord,
And else hang me by the hals!   *neck*
But thou must be at mine accord;
Other while thou must be false
Among kith and kin.
Now go we forth swythe anon!   *quickly*
To the World us must gone;
And bear thee manly ever among,
When thou comest out or in.
MANKIND: Yes, and else have thou my neck,   440

[5] *Homo ... peccabis:* Remember your end, man, and forever you will not sin.

But I be manly by down and dike.
And though I be false, I ne reck,   *care not*
  With so that I be lord i-like,
    I follow thee as I can.
      Thou shalt be my bote of bale;   *remedy*
      For, were I rich of holt and hale,   *woods/hall*
      Then would I give never tale,   *consideration*
        Of God ne of good man.

[MANKIND *and the* BAD ANGEL *begin to cross toward the scaffold
of the World. During the next eighty lines they weave their way slowly
around the playing area.*]

GOOD ANGEL: I wail and wring and make moan!
  This man with woe shall be pilt.   *tormented*   450
I sigh sore and grisly groan,
  For his folly shall make him spilt.   *destroyed*
    I not whither to gone;
    Mankind hath forsaken me!
    Alas, Man, for love of thee!
    Ya, for this game and this glee,
      Thou shalt grocchyn and groan.   *complain*

(*Trumpets blow.*) [*Enter the* WORLD, PLEASURE, LIKING *and*
VAINGLORY *upon the World's scaffold.*]

WORLD: Now I sit in my seemly sale;   *hall*
  I trotte and tremle in my true throne;   *strut and shake*
As a hawk, I hop in my hende hale;   *noble/hall*   460
  King, knight and kaiser to me maken moan.
Of God ne of good man give I never tale;   *consideration*
  As a liking lord, I leyke here alone: *pleasing/sport*
Who-so brawl and boast, by down or by dale,
  Through Gadlyngis shall be gastyd, and   *rascals/frightened*
    grislych groan,   *horribly*
    Iwis.
    Lust, Folly and Vainglory,
    All these are in my memory;
    There beginneth the noble story
      Of this World's bliss.   470
  Lust-liking and Folly,

Comely knights of renown,
Be-lyve this land do cry.   *at once*
All abouten in tower and town,
If any man be far or nigh
That to my service will buske him boun.   *make himself ready*
If he will be trost and trye,   *trusty and faithful*
He shall be king and wear the crown,
With richest robes in res.   *in use*
Who-so to the World will draw,   480
Of God ne of good man giveth he not a hawe,   *care*
Such a man, by land's law,
Shall sitten on my dees.   *dais*
LUST-LIKING: Lo, me, here! Ready, Lord, to faren and to flee,
To seeken thee a servant dinge and dear.   *worthy*
Who-so will with Folly ruled be,
He is worthy to be a servant here,
That draweth to sins seven.
Who-so will be false and covetous,
With this World he shall have a land and house;   490
This World's wisdom giveth not a louse
Of God nor of high heaven.
(*Here* LUST-LIKING *descends from the scaffold into the playing area.*)
Peace, people! of peace we you pray!
Sythe and sethe well to my saw!   *attend*
Who-so will be rich and in great array,
Toward the World he shall draw.
Who-so will be false all that he may,
Of God Himself he hath none awe,
And liven in lusts night and day,
The World of him will be right fawe,   *glad* 500
To dwell in his house.
Who-so will with the World have his dwelling,
And been a lord of his clothing,
He must needs, over all thing,
Evermore be covetous:
Non est in mundo dives qui dicit "habundo". [6]

---

[6] *Non . . . babundo:* There is not a rich man in the world who says "I have enough."

FOLLY: Ya, covetous he must be,
    And me, Folly, must have in mende;   *mind*
For who-so will always folly flee
    In this world will be unthende.   *unhappy* 510
Through World's wisdom of great degree,
    Shall never man in World moun wend   *be able to get on*
But he have help of me,
    That am Folly fair and hende;   *courteous*
        He must hangen on my hook.
    Worldly wit was never nought
    But with Folly it were fraught;
    Thus the wise man hath taught
        Abouten in his book:
Sapientia penes Domini.[7]   520

LUST-LIKING: Now, all the men that in this World would thrive,
    For to riden on horse full high,
Come speak with Lust and Liking belyve,   *quickly*
    And his fellow, young Folly.
        Let see who-so will us know.
    Who-so will draw to Liking and Lust,
    And as a fool in Folly rust?
    On us two he may trust,
        And liven lovely, I trow!

[*Here the* BAD ANGEL *and* MANKIND *arrive before the World's scaffold.*]

BAD ANGEL: How, Lust-Liking and Folly!   530
    Take to me good entent!   *attention*
I have brought, by downs drye,   *distant or dreary*
    To the World a great present.
I have guiled him full quaintly,   *beguiled*
    For, since he was born, I have him blent; *blinded*
He shall be servant good and try;   *true*
    Among you his will is lent.   *fixed*
        To the World he will him take,
    For, since he could wit, I understand,   *think*
    I have him tysyd in ever land.   *tempted* 540

---

[7] *Sapientia penes Domini:* Wisdom belongs with God.

His Good Angel, by street and strand,
  I have done him forsake.
Therefore, Lust, my true fere,   *companion*
  Thou art ready always iwis;
Of worldly laws thou him lere,   *teach*
  That he were brought in worldly bliss.
    Look he be rich, the sooth to tell,
    Help him fast he 'gin to thrive;   *begin to thrive quickly*
    And when he weeneth best to live,   *thinks*
    Then he shall die, and not be shrive,   550
    And go with us to hell.
LUST-LIKING: By Satan, thou art a noble knave
  To teachen men first from good!
Lust and liking he shall have;
  Lechery shall be his food;
    Meats and drinks he shall have trye.   *delightful*
    With a liking lady of lofte   *high estate*
    He shall sitten in sendal soft,   *robe*
    To catchen him to hell croft
    That day that he shall die.   560
FOLLY: With rich rents I shall him blind,
  With the World till he be pytte;   *buried*
And then shall I, long ere his end,
  Make that caitiff to be knit
    On the World when he is set sore.
    Come on, Man! Thou shalt not rue;
    For, thou wilt be to us true,   *[if] thou*
    Thou shalt be clad in clothes new,
    And be rich evermore.
MANKIND: Marry, fellow, grammercy!   570
  I would be rich and of great renown.
Of God I give no tale truely,   *consideration*
  So that I be lord of tower and town,
    By bushes and banks brown.
    Since that thou will make me
    Both rich of gold and fee,
    Go forth, for I will follow thee

By dale and every town.

(*Trumpets blow, and* PLEASURE, FOLLY, *the* BAD ANGEL *and* MANKIND *cross to the World's scaffold.*)

PLEASURE: How, Lord! Look out! For we have brought
  A servant of noble fame.   580
Of worldly good is all his thought;
  Of Lust and Folly he hath no shame;
    He would be of great name,
    He would be at great honor,
    For to rule town and tower;
    He would have to his paramour
      Some lovely dynge dame.   *well-born*
WORLD: Welcome, sir, seemly in sight!
  Thou art welcome to worthy wede,   *lady*
For thou wilt be my servant, day and night.   590
  With my service I shall thee foster and feed;
Thy back shall be beaten with bezants bright.[8]
  Thou shalt have byggyngys by banks   *buildings by banks broad*
    brede;
To thy corse shall kneel kaiser and knight,
    And ladies lovely on lere,   *of face*
    Where that thou walk, by stye or by street.
    But God's service thou must forsake,
    And wholly to the World thee take,
    And then a man I shall thee make,
      That none shall be thy peer.   600
MANKIND: Yes, World, and thereto mine hand
  To forsake God and His service,
To meeds thou give me house and land,   *[if] for reward*
  That I reign richly at mine enprise.   *will*
So that I fare well by street and strand
  While I dwell here in worldly wise,
I reck never of heaven wonde,   *consider/punishment*
  Nor of Jesu, that gentle justice;
    Of my soul I have none ruth.
    What should I reckon of doomsday,   610

[8][The robe for] thy back shall be embroidered with [gold.]

So that I be rich and of great array?
   I shall make merry while I may;
     And thereto, here my troth.
WORLD: Now certes, sir, thou sayest well!
   I hold thee true from top to the toe.
But thou were rich, it were great del,   *pity*
   And all men that will fare so.
Come up, my servant true as steel!
     (MANKIND *climbs up onto the World's scaffold.*)
   Thou shalt be rich where-so thou go;
Men shall serven thee at meal,   620
   With minstrelsy and bemys' blow   *trumpets'*
     With meats and drinks trye.   *delightful*
     Lust and Liking shall be thine ease;
     Lovely ladies thee shall please;
     Who-so do thee any dis-ease,
       He shall be hangen high.

Liking, belyve   *quickly*
Let clothe him swythe   *quickly*
In robes ryve   *abundant*
   With rich array.   630
Folly thou fond,   *fool*
By street and strond,
Serve him at hond
   Both night and day.
PLEASURE: Trustily,
Lord, ready!
Je vous prie.[9]
   Sir, I say,
In liking and Lust
He shall rust   640
Till Death's dust
   Do him to day.   *die*
FOLLY: And I, Folly,
Shall highen him high   *raise*
Till some enemy

[9] *Je vous prie:* "I pray you," said to usher Mankind off to receive his new clothes.

Him overgo.
In World's wit
That in Folly sit,
I think yet
His soul to slo.   *slay*   650
(*Trumpets blow.*) [PLEASURE *and* FOLLY *take* MANKIND *off to dress him. Enter* BACKBITER.]

BACKBITER: All things I cry against the peace
To knight and knave: this is my kend.   *nature*
Ya, dyngne dukes on their des,   *thrones*
In bitter bales I them bind.
Crying and care, chiding and ches   *strife*
And sad sorrow to them I send.
Ya, loud lesyngis lachyd in les,   *loud lyings tied with a leash*
Of tales untrue is all my mind;
Man's bane abouten I bear,
I will that ye witten, all those that been here;   *know*   660
For I am known far and near;
I am the World's messenger;
My name is Backbiter.
With every wight I walk and wend,
And every man now loveth me well;
With loud lesyngys under lende,   *lyings/linden* (lime trees)
To Death's dint I dress and deal.
To speak fair before and foul behind
Amongst men at meat and meal,
Truely, lords, this is my kind.   *nature* 670
There I run upon a wheel,
I am feller than a fox.   *more fierce*
Flittering and flattering is my lesson;
With lesyngis I tene both tower and town,   *harm*
With letters of defamation
I bear in my box.
I am light of lopys through every land;   *leaps*
Mine holy happys may not be hid.   *deeds?*
Two may not together stand,
But I, Backbiter, be the third.   680

I shape young boys to shame and schonde, *disgrace*
 All that will bowen when I them bid.
To law of land in faith I fonde; *pose a test*
 When tales untrue are betid, *told*
  Backbiter is wide sprung.
 Through the world, by down and dales,
 All about I brew bales:
 Every man telleth tales
  After my false tongue.
Therefore I am made messenger 690
 To leapen over lands leye, *untilled*
Through the world, far and near,
 Unsaid saws for to say. *sayings*
In this holt I hunt here
 For to spy a privy play; *trick*
For when Mankind is clothed clear,
 Then shall I teachen him the way
  To the deadly sins seven.
 Here I shall abiden with my peas,[10]
 The wrong to do him for to chese, *choose* 700
 For I think that he shall lese *lose*
  The light of high heaven.

[*Enter* PLEASURE *and* FOLLY *with* MANKIND, *now dressed in rich clothes.*]

PLEASURE: Worthy World, in wealth's wound, *in rich goods dressed*
 Here is Mankind full fair in folde. *dress*
In bright bezants he is bound *gold coins*
 And bon to bow to you so bold. *ready*
He liveth in lusts every stounde; *moment*
 Wholly to you he hath him yolde; *given*
For to maken him gay on ground,
 Worthy World, thou art behold. *beholden* 710
  This World is well at ease;
 For, to God I make a vow,
 Mankind had liever now *rather*
 Grieve God with sins row *numerous*

[10] Does Backbiter carry a bladder of dried peas?

Than the World to displease.

FOLLY: Displease thee, he will for no man;
On me, Folly, is all his thought.
Truly Mankind not ne can
Think on God that hath him bought.
Worthy World, white as swan,   720
In thy love lely is he lawth.   *loyally|caught*
Sithen he could and first began,   *since*
Thee forsaken would he not,
But give him to Folly;
And sithen he hath to thee be true,
I rede thee forsaken him for no new;   *advise*
Let us please him till that he rue,
In hell to hangen high.

WORLD: Now, Folly, fair thee befall!
And Lust, blessed be thou ay!   *ever*
Ye have brought Mankind to mine hall,   730
Certes in a noble array.
With World's wealths within these wall,
I shall him feoff of that I may.   *endow*
Welcome, Mankind! To thee I call,
Clenner clothed than any clay,   *finer*
By downe, dale and ditch.
Mankind, I rede that thou rest
With me, the World, as it is best;
Look thou hold my hand fest,   *fast* 740
And ever thou shalt be rich.

MANKIND: How shall I but thy hests helde?   *commands obey*
Thou workest with me wholly my will;
Thou feoffest me with fen and field,   *endowest*
And high hall, by holts and hill.
In worldly weal my wit I wield:
In joy I jette with jewels gentle;   *strut*
On blissfull bank my bower is build;
In vainglory I stand still;
I am keen as a knight.   *bold* 750
Who-so against the World will speak,

Mankind shall on him be wreke;
In strong prison I shall him stick,
Be it wrong or right.
WORLD: Ah, Mankind, well thee betide,
That thy love on me is set.
In my bowers thou shalt abide
And yet fare mickle the bet.   *much the better*
I feoff thee in all my wonys wide,   *dwellings*
In dale of dross till thou be deth.   *in the grave/put.* 760
I make thee lord of mickle pride,
Sir, at thine own mouth's mette.   *might*
I find in thee no treason.
In all this world, by sea and sand,
Parks, places, lawnde and land,   *linen*
Here I give thee with mine hand,
Sir, an open seisin.   *possession*
Go to my treasurer, Sir Covetous!
Look thou tell him as I say.
Bid him to make thee master in his house,   770
With pence and pounds for to play.
Look thou yeve not a louse   *care*
Of the day that thou shalt die.
Messenger, do now thine use!
Backbiter, teach him the way!
Thou art sweeter than mead.
Mankind, take with thee Backbiting!
Leave him for no manner thing!
Flepergebet, with his flattering,[11]
Standeth Mankind in stead.   780
BACKBITER: Backbiting and Detraction
Shall go with thee from town to town.
Have done, Mankind, and come down!
I am thine own page.
I shall bear thee witness with my might,
When my lord, the World, it behight   *commands*
[*He points to Covetous' scaffold.*]

[11] Flippertigibbet: One of the devils of folklore.

Lo, where Sir Covetous sit,
　　And biddeth us to his stage.
MANKIND:　Sir World, I wende,　　　　　　　　　　　*think*
　　In Covetous to chasen my kende.　　　*follow my nature?* 790
WORLD:　Have him in mende,
　　And iwis then shalt thou be right thende.　　　*prosperous*
　　　　[THE GOOD ANGEL *cries out from his place near the Castle.*]
GOOD ANGEL:　Alas, Jesu, gentle justice!
　　Whither may Man's Good Angel wend?
　　Now shall careful Covetise
　　　　Mankind truely all to-schende;　　　　　　*harm*
　　His sely ghost may sore a-gryse;　　*holy spirit/be disgusted*
　　　　Backbiting bringeth him in bitter bond.
　　Worldly wits, ye are not wise;
　　　　Your lovely life, amiss ye spend,　　　　　　　800
　　　　　　And that shall ye sore smart.
　　　　Parks, pounds and many pence,
　　　　They seemen to you sweeter than sense;
　　　　But God's service, ne his commandments,
　　　　　　Standeth you not at heart.
BAD ANGEL:　Ya! When the fox preacheth, keep well your geese!
　　He speaketh as it were a holy pope.
　　Go, fellow, and pick off the lice,
　　　　That creep there upon thy cope.　　　　　　*cloak*
　　Thy part is played all at the dice,　　　　　　810
　　　　That thou shalt have here, as I hope.
　　Till Mankind falleth to podys price,　　　*frog's worth*
　　　　Covetous shall him grip and grope　　　　*tear*
　　　　　　Till some shame him schende.
　　　　Till Man be dight in Death's dow,　　　*set/grip*
　　　　He sayeth never he hath enow;
　　　　Therefore, good boy, come blow
　　　　　　At my nether end!
　　　　[BACKBITER *and* MANKIND *approach the scaffold of Covetous.*]
BACKBITER:　Sir Covetous, God thee save,
　　Thy pence and pounds all!　　　　　　　　　820
　　I, Backbiter, thine own knave,

Have brought Mankind unto thine hall.
The World bade thou shouldst him have,
  And feoffen him, what-so befall.
In green grass till he be grave,   *buried*
  Put him in thy precious pall,   *robe*
    Covetous, it were all ruth.   *[else] it were*
    While he walketh in worldly wolde,   *power*
    I, Backbiter, am with him holde,   *friendly*
    Lust and Folly, those barons bold,   830
      To them he hath plight his truth.
COVETOUS: Oh, Mankind, blessed might thou be!
  I have loved thee dear-worthly many a day,
And so, I wot well, that thou dost me.   *know*
  Come up, and see my rich array!
It were a great point of pity
  But Covetous were to thy pay.   *liking*
Sit up right here in this see;   *seat*
  I shall thee lere of World's lay,   *teach/learning*
    That fadeth as a flood.   840
    With good enow I shall thee store;
    And yet our game is but lore   *lost*
    But thou covet mickle more   *much*
      Than ever shall do thee good.
Thou must give thee to simony,
  Extortion and false assize;
Help no man but thou have why;
  Pay not thy servants their service.
Thy neighbors, look thou destroy.
  Tithe not on none wise;   850
Hear no beggar though he cry;
  And then shalt thou full soon rise.
    And when thou useth merchandise,
    Look that thou be subtle of sleights,
    And also swear all be deceits;
    Buy and sell by false weights,
      For that is kind covetise.   *natural covetousness*
Be not aghast of the great curse;   *damnation*

This lovely life may long last.
Be the penny in thy purse,   860
    Let them cursen and do their best.
What, devil of hell, art thou worse
    Though thou breakest God's hest?   *command*
Do after me! I am thy nurse.
    Always gather, and have none rest;
        In winning be all thy work.
    To poor men take none entent,   *pay no attention*
    For that thou hast long time hent,   *accumulated*
    In little time it may be spent,
        Thus sayeth Cato, the great clerk: 870
Habitur exiguo quod partum tempore longo.[12]
MANKIND: Ah, Avarice! Well thou speed!
    Of worldly wit thou canst, iwis.   *knowest*
Thou wouldest not I had need,
    And shouldest be wroth if I fared amiss.
I shall never beggar bede   *offer*
    Meat nor drink, by heaven bliss;
Rather or I should him clothe or feed,
    He should starve and stink, iwis.
        Covetous, as thou wilt, I will do.   880
        Where-so that I fare, by fen or flood,
        I make a vow, by God's blood,
        Of Mankind, getteth no man good,
            But if he sing "*si dedero*".[13]
COVETOUS: Mankind, that was well sung!
    Certes now thou canst some skill;   *knowest*
Blessed be thy true tongue!
    In this bower thou shalt bide and bill.   *dwell*
More sins I would thou underfonge;   *receive* (get to know)
    With covetise thee feoff I will,   *endow* 890
And then some Pride I would sprung,
    High in thy heart to holden and hyll,   *cherish*
        And abiden in thy body.

---

[12] *Habitur ... longo:* That which was produced at length is possessed briefly.
[13] *Si dedero:* If I shall have given.

Here I feoff thee in mine heaven
With gold and silver, light as leaven.
The deadly sins, all seven,
    I shall do comen in hy.   *cause to come in haste*
Pride, Wrath and Envy,
    Come forth, the Devil's children three!
Lechery, Sloth and Gluttony,   900
    To man's flesh ye are fiends fre!   *excellent?*
Driveth down over dales drye;   *distant*
    Be-eth now blithe as any bee!
Over hill and holts ye you hie,
    To come to Mankind and to me,
        From your doughty dens!
      As Duke's doughty, ye you dress!
      When ye six be come, I guess,
      Then be we seven and no less,
        Of the deadly sins.   910
    [*Enter* PRIDE, WRATH *and* ENVY *on the scaffold of Belial.*]
PRIDE: Wonder high howtis on hill heard I   *shouts/shouted*
    houte!
    Covetous cryeth; his carping I ken.   *speech/recognize*
Some lord or some lordeyn lely shall loute   *lowly/bow*
    To be pight with pearls of my proud pen.   *loaded/stock*
Bon I am to bragging and busking about,   *apt/bustling*
    Rathely and readily on rowte for to ren.   *frolic*
By down, dales or dens, no dukes I dowt;   *fear*
    Also fast for to fogge, by floods and by fen,   *jog*
      I roar when I rise.
      Sir Belial, bright of ble,   *hue* 920
      To you I recommend me:
      Have good day, my father fre,   *noble*
        For I go to Covetise.
WRATH: When Covetise cried and carped of care,   *complained*
    Then must I, wood wretch, walken and wend   *mad*
High over holts, as hound after hare.
    If I let and were the last, he should me   *delayed*
    sore schende;   *punish*

I buske my bold baston, by banks full bare;   *prepare/staff*
   Some boy shall be beaten and brought under bond.
Wrath shall him wrecken and weyin his ware;[14]   930
   Forlorn shall all be, for lusty lakes and land,   *games*
      As a little page.   *boy*
    Sir Belial black and blo,   *blue*
    Have good day! Now I go
    For to fill thee fo   *full*
      With wicked wage.

ENVY: When Wrath ginneth walk in any wide wonys, *dwellings*
   Envy flet as a fox and followeth on fast.   *flits*
When thou stirrest or startest or stumble upon   *stir or start*
   stones,
   I leap as a lion. Me is loathe to be the last.   940
Ya, I breed bitter bales in body and bones;
   I fret mine heart, and in care I me cast.
Go we to Covetous, all three at onys   *once*
   With our grisly gear a groom for to gast.   *frighten*
      This day shall he die.
    Belzabub, now have good day!
    For we wenden in good array,
    All three in fere, as I thee say,   *together*
      Pride, Wrath and Envy.

BELIAL: Farewell now, children, fair to find!   950
   Do now well your old ouse   *use (deeds)*
When ye come to Mankind!
   Make him wroth and envious;
Liveth not lightly under linde;   *lime tree*
   To his soul breweth a bitter juice.
When he is dead, I shall him bind
   In hell, as cat doth the mouse.
      Now busk you forth on brede!   *haste/abroad*
    I may be blithe as any bee,
    For Mankind in every country   960
    Is ruled by my children three,
      Envy, Wrath and Pride.

[14] Wrath shall him beat and weigh (test?) his defense

[*Enter* GLUTTONY, LECHERY *and* SLOTH *on the scaffold of the Flesh.*]

GLUTTONY: A groom gan gredyn gaily on ground;   *boy/call out*
  Of me, gay Glutton, gan all his gale.   *song*
I stamp and I start and stint upon stounde;   *stop/moment*
  To a staunch death I stagger and stale.   *certain/wear out*
What boys with their bellies in my bonds be bound!
  Both their back and their blood I brew all to bale.
I fese folk to fight till their flesh fonde;   *incite/hurts*
  When some hath drunken a draught, they droppen in a
    dale;   970
      In me is their mind.
      Man's flourishing flesh,
      Fair, frail and fresh,
      I rape to rule in a rush,   *hurry/rush*
        To claw it in my kind.

LECHERY: In Man's kith I cast me a castle to keep.   *countryman*
  I, Lechery, with liking am loved in each a land.
With my sokelys of sweetness, I sit and I sleep;   *comfits*
  Many berdys I bring to my bitter bond.   *people*
In woe and in wrake, wicked wits shall weep   *harm* 980
  That in my wonys wild will not out wend.   *dwellings*
When Mankind is casten under clowris to creep,   *grasses*
  Then the ledrouns for their liking I shall all   *rogues*
    to-schende,   *tear apart*
      Truely to tell.
      Sir Flesh, now I wend
      With Lust in my lende   *loins*
      To catchen Mankind
        To the devil of hell.

SLOTH: Ya! What sayest thou of Sir Sloth, with my
    sour syth?   *sigh*
  Mankind loveth me well wise, as I ween;   *certainly/think* 990
Men of religion I rule in my right;
  I let God's service, the sooth may be seen.   *hinder*
In bed I breed brothel, with my berdis bright;   *maidens*
  Lords, ladies and lederounnys to my lore lean.   *rogues*

Mickle of Mankind in my cloaks shall be knit   *much*
 Till death driveth them down in dales bedene.   *quickly*
  We may none longer abide.
 Sir Flesh, comely king,
 In thee is all our breeding.
 Give us now thy blessing,   *1000*
 For Covetous hath cried.
FLESH: Gluttony and Sloth, farewell in fere!   *both*
 Lovely in land is now your lesse;   *prosperity*
And Lechery, my daughter so dear,
 Dapperly ye dress you so dyngne on desse.   *nobly/dais*
All three my blessings ye shall have here;
 Goeth now forth, and give ye no fors;   *thought*
It is no need you for to lere   *teach*
 To catchen Mankind to a care full close   *death*
  From the bright bliss of heaven.   *1010*
  The World, the Flesh and the Devil are know
  Great Lords, as we well owe,
  And through Mankind we setten and sow
   The deadly sins seven.
[GLUTTONY, SLOTH *and* LECHERY *leave the scaffold of the Flesh,
and* PRIDE, WRATH *and* ENVY *leave the scaffold of Belial; together
they cross the playing area to Covetous' scaffold.*]
PRIDE: What is thy will, Sir Covetise?
 Why hast thou after us sent?
When thou criedest, we gan a-gryse,   *shudder*
 And come to thee now par assent.   *willingly*
  Our love is on thee lent.   *fixed*
  I, Pride, Wrath and Envy,   *1020*
  Glutton, Sloth and Lechery,
  We are come all six for thy cry,
   To be at thy commandment.
COVETOUS: Welcome be ye, brethren all,
 And my sister, sweet Lechery!
Wit ye why I gan to call?   *know*
 For ye must help me, and that is hy.   *quickly*
Mankind is now come to mine hall,

With me to dwell, by downs drye;
Therefore ye must, what-so befall,　　　　　　　　　　　1030
　　Feoffen him with your folly,　　　　　　　　　　　　*endow*
　　　　And else ye do him wrong.
　　　For when Mankind is kendly covetous,　　　　　　*naturally*
　　　He is proved wrathful and envious;
　　　Glutton, Sloth and Lecherous,
　　　　They are other while among.
Thus every sin tilleth in other,　　　　　　　　　　　*draweth*
　　And maketh Mankind to be a fool.
We seven fallen on a fodyr　　　　　　　　　　　　　*heap*
　　Mankind to chase to pynyngis stole.　　　*pain's seat*　1040
Therefore Pride, good brother,
　　And brethren all, take ye your toll;
Let each of us take at other,
　　And set Mankind on a stumbling stool.
　　　　While he is here on live,
　　　Let us lullen him in our lust
　　　Till he be driven to damning dust;
　　　Cold care shall be his crust
　　　　To death when he shall drive.
PRIDE:　In glee and game I grow glad!　　　　　　　1050
　Mankind, take good heed,
And do as Covetous thee bade.
　Take me in thine heart, precious Pride!
Look thou be not over-lad;　　　　　　　　　　　*lorded over*
　Let no bachelor thee misbede;　　　*young man|mistreat*
Do thee to be doubted and drad.　　*feared and dreaded*
　　Beat boys till they bleed;
　　Cast them in care full kettis,　　　　　　　　*troubles*
　Friend, father and mother dear,
　Bow them not in no manner;　　　　　　　　　　1060
　And hold no manner man thy peer;
　　And use these new jettis.　　　　　　　　　　*fashions*
Look thou blow mickle boast,　　　　　　　　　　*great*
　With long crakows on thy shoes;　*curved and pointed toes*
Jagge thy clothes in every cost,　　　*prick-up|way*

And else men shall lete thee but a goose.   *think*
It is thus, man, well thou wost;   *knowest*
    Therefore do as no man does,
And every man set at a thost,   *piece of dung*
    And of thyself make great ros;   *esteem*   1070
        Now see thyself on every side.
    Every man thou shalt schende and   *injure and shove aside*
        schelfe,
    And hold no man better than thyself;
    Till Death's dint thy body delfe,   *stroke/pierce*
        Put wholly thine heart in Pride.
MANKIND: Pride! By Jesu, thou sayest well:
    Who-so suffer is over-lad all day.   *permits [it]*
While I rest on my running-wheel   *Fortune's wheel?*
    I shall not suffer, if that I may.   *endure [it]*
Much mirth, at meat and meal,   1080
    I love right well, and rich array.
Truly I think in every sel   *season*
    On ground to be graythyd gay,   *attired*
        And of myself to take good guard.
        Mickle mirth thou wilt me make,
        Lordly to live, by land and lake;
        Mine heart wholly to thee I take,
            Into thine own award.   *custody*
        [PRIDE *joins* MANKIND *on the scaffold.*]
PRIDE: In thy bower to abide,
    I come to dwell by thy side.   1090
MANKIND: Mankind and Pride
    Shall dwell together in every tide.
WRATH: Be also wroth, as thou were wood!   *mad*
    Make thee be dread, by dales derne!   *dark*
Who-so thee wrethe, by fen or flood,   *make angry*
    Look thou be avenged yerne!   *quickly*
Be ready to spill man's blood!
    Look thou him fear, by fields ferne!   *[make] fear/distant*
Always, man, be full of mod!   *temper*
    My loathly laws, look thou learn,   1100

I rede, for anything.
Anon take vengeance, Man, I rede;
And then shall no man thee over-lead,
But of thee they should have dread,
And bow to thy bidding.
MANKIND: Wrath, for thy counsel hende,   *courteous*
Have thou God's blessing and mine!
What caitiff of all my kende
Will not bow, he shall abyn;   *suffer*
With mine vengeance I shall him schende,   *injure* 1110
And wrekyn me, by God's eyen.   *avenge/eyes*
Rather or I should bow or bend,
I should be sticked as a swine
With a loathly lance.
Be it early or late,
Who-so make with me debate,
I shall him hitten on the pate,
And taken anon vengeance.
[WRATH *joins* MANKIND *on the scaffold.*]
WRATH: With my ruely rothyr   *sorrowful rudder (i.e. guidance)*
I come to thee, Mankind, my brother.   1120
MANKIND: And, Wrath, thy fair father
Maketh each man to be venged on other.
ENVY: Envy with Wrath must drive
To haunt Mankind also.
When any of thy neighbors will thrive,
Look thou have envy thereto;
On the high name I charge thee belyve,   *of Satan?*
Backbite him, how-so thou do;
Kill him anon, withouten knife,
And speak him some shame where thou go,   1130
By dale or downs drye.
Speak thy neighbor mickle shame;
Put on him some false fame;
Look thou undo his noble name,
With me, that am Envy.
MANKIND: Envy, thou art both good and hende,

And shalt be of my council chief.
Thy counsel is known through Mankind,
    For each man calleth other "whore and thief".
Envy, thou art root and rind,   1140
    Through this world, of mickle mischief.
In bitter bales I shall them bind,
    That to thee putteth any reprefe!   *reproof*
        Come up to me above!
    For more Envy than is now reigning,
    Was never since Christ was king.
    Come up, Envy, my dear darling,
        Thou hast Mankind's love.
[ENVY *joins* MANKIND *on the scaffold.*]
ENVY: I climb from this croft,
    With Mankind, O, to sitten on loft.   1150
MANKIND: Come, sit here soft,
    For in abbeys thou dwellest full oft.
GLUTTONY: In gay gluttony, a game thou begin;
    Ordain thee meat and drinks good;
Look that no treasure thee part a-twin
    But thee feoff and feed with all kynnys food.   *royal*
With fasting shall man never heaven win:
    These great fasters, I hold them wood.   *mad*
Though thou eat and drink, it is no sin.
    Fast no day! I rede by the rood   *advise/cross* 1160
        Thou chide these fasting churls.
      Look thou have spices of good odor,
      To feoff and feed thy fleshly flower;
      And then mayest thou boltyn in thy bower,   *bolt (gulp down)*
      And serdyn gay girls.   *copulate with*
MANKIND: Ah, Gluttony! Well I thee greet!
    Sooth and sad it is, thy saw;   *true and solemn*
I am no day well, by sty nor street,
    Till I have well filled my maw;
Fasting is felled under feet.   1170
    Though I never fast, I reck not a haw,   *care not a bit*
It serveth of nought, by the rood, I lete,   *cross/think*

But to do a man's jaws to gnaw:
  To fast, I will not fonde. *act foolishly*
I shall not spare, so have I rest,
To have a morsel of the best;
The longer shall my life mow last, *be able to*
  With great liking in londe. *on earth*
[GLUTTONY *joins* MANKIND.]
GLUTTONY: By banks on brede, *broad banks*
  Otherwhile to spew, thee speed! *sometimes* 1180
MANKIND: While I life lead,
With fair food my flesh shall I feed.
LECHERY: Ya! When thy flesh is fair fed,
Then shall I, lovely Lechery,
Be bobbed with thee in thy bed; *bounced up and down*
  Hereof serve meat and drinks trye. *therefore/rich*
In love thy life shall be led;
  Be a lecher till thou die;
Thy needs shall be the better sped,
If thou give thee to fleshly folly 1190
  Till Death thee down drepe. *drop*
Lechery, since the world began,
Hath advanced many a man.
Therefore, Mankind, my leve lemman, *dear lover*
  In my cunt thou shalt creep.
MANKIND: Ah, Lechery! Well thee be!
Man's seed in thee is sow;
Few men will forsake thee
In any country that I know.
Spouse-breech is a friend right fre; *adultery/common* 1200
Men use that more than enow.
Lechery, come sit by me!
Thy banns be full wide i-know; *edicts/widely known*
  Liking is in thy lende. *loins*
On none other, I see no wight, *on-for*
That will forsake thee day nor night;
Therefore, come up, my berd bright, *maid*
  And rest thee with Mankind.

[LECHERY *joins* MANKIND.]

LECHERY: I may sooth sing:
 "Mankind is caught in my sling."   1210

MANKIND: For any earthly thing,
 To bed thou must me bring.

SLOTH: Ya, when ye be in bed brought both,
 Wrapped well in worthy weed,   *covers*
Then I, Sloth, will be wroth
 But two brothelys I may breed.   *scoundrels*
When the mass-bell goeth,
 Lie still, Man, and take none heed!
Lap thine head then in a cloth
 And take a sweat, I thee rede;   1220
  Church-going thou forsake.
  Losengeris in land I lift,   *flatterers*
  And dight men to mickle unthrift.   *set*
  Penance enjoined men in shrift
   Is undone; and that I make.

MANKIND: Oh, Sloth, thou sayest me skill!   *speakest wisely*
 Men use thee mickle, God it wot.   *knows*
Men love well now to lie still,
 In bed to take a thorough swot;   *sweat*
To church-ward is not their will;   1230
 Their beds they thinken good and hot;
Harry, Jeffrey, Joan and Jill
 Are laid and lodged in a lot
  With thine unthende charms.   *unprofitable*
 All mankind, by the holy rood,
 Are now slow in works good.
 Come near, therefore, my fair food,
  And lull me in your arms.
 There is poor nor rich, by land ne lake,
 That all these seven will forsake,   1240
 But with one or other he shall be take
  And in their bitter bonds bound.

 [SLOTH *joins* MANKIND.]

SLOTH: I make men, I trow,

In God's service to be right slow.
MANKIND: Come up this throwe!   *at once*
  Such men thou shalt finden anow.
Mankind I am called by kind,
  With cursedness, in costis knet,   *circumstances knit*
In sour sweetness my syth I sende,   *lifetime spend*
  With seven sins sad beset.   1250
Mickle mirth I move in mind,
  With melody at my mouth's met.   *power*
My proud power shall I not pende,   *limit*
  Till I be put in pain's pit,
      To hell hent from hence.   *snatched*
    In dale of dole till we are down,
    We shall be clad in a gay gown;
    I see no man but they use some
      Of these seven deadly sins.

For commonly, it is seldom seen,   1260
  Who-so now be lecherous,
Of other men he shall have disdain,
  And been proud or covetous:
      In sin each man is found.
    Men are loath on thee to cry,
    Or do penance for their folly;
    Therefore have I now mastery
      Well nigh over all mankind.
GOOD ANGEL: So mickle the worse (wail a woe!)
  That ever Good Angel was ordained thee!   1270
Thou art ruled after the fiend that is thy foe,
  And nothing, certes, after me.
Weleaway! Whither may I go?
  Man doth me bleykyn bloody ble;   *bleach a bloody hue*
His sweet soul he will now slay;
  He shall weep all his game and glee
      At one day's time.
    Ye see well all soothly in sight,
    I am about both day and night
    To bring his soul into bliss bright;   1280

And himself will it bring to pyne.   *pain*

BAD ANGEL: No, Good Angel, thou art not in seisin!
    Few men in the faith they find;
For thou hast showed a balled reason.   *bald*
    Good sir, come blow mine hole behind!
Truely, man hath non chesun   *cause*
    On God to grede and grind,   *cry out and gnash his teeth*
For that should con Christ's lesson,   *learn*
    In penance his body he must bind
        And forsake the World's mind.   *mind (i.e. way)* 1290

GOOD ANGEL: Alas, Mankind
    Is bobbed and blent as the blind!   *tricked and misled*
In faith, I find,
To Christ he cannot be kind.
Alas, Mankin
Is soiled and sagged in sin!   *sunken*
He will not blynne   *cease*
Till body and soul part a-twin.
        Alas, he is blinded!
        Amiss, man's life is i-spended,   *1300*
        With fiends fended!   *hedged about*
        Mercy, God, that Man were amended!
    [*Enter* SHRIFT *and* PENANCE.]

SHRIFT.   What! Man's angel, good and true!
    Why sighest thou and sobbest sore?
Certes, sore it shall me rue
    If I see thee make mourning more.
May any bote thy bale brew,
    Or anything thy state a-store?
For all fellowships old and new,
    Why makest thou grochynge under   *complaining under clothing*
        gore,   *(i.e. Why do you complain?)*
        With pining points pale?   *painful state* 1310
    Why was all this greting 'gun,
    With sore sighing under sun?
    Tell me, and I shall, if I cun,   *can*
        Brew thee bote of bale.   *remedy*

GOOD ANGEL: Of bitter bales thou mayest me bete, *remedy*
  Sweet Shrift, if that thou wilt.
For Mankind, it is that I grete; *mourn*
  He is in point to be spilt; *on the verge of being destroyed*
He is set in seven sins' seat, 1320
  And will, certes, till he be kilt.
With me he thinketh never more to meet;
  He hath me forsake, and I have no guilt;
    No man will him amend.
  Therefore, Shrift, so God me speed,
  But if thou help at this need,
  Mankind getteth never other meed,
    But pain withouten end.
SHRIFT: What, Angel! Be of comfort strong
  For thy Lord's love that died on tree! 1330
On me, Shrift, it shall not be long,
  And that thou shalt the sooth see.
If he will be a-know his wrong, *make known*
  And nothing hele, but tell it me, *conceal*
And do penance soon among,
  I shall him steer to gamen and glee
    In every joy that ever shall last.
  Who-so shrive him of his sins all,
  I be-hete him heaven hall, *promise*
  Therefore go we hence, what-so befall, 1340
    To Mankind fast.
(SHRIFT *and* PENANCE *cross to* MANKIND *on Covetous' scaffold.*)
SHRIFT: What, Mankind! How goeth this?
  What dost thou with these devils seven?
Alas, alas, Man, all amiss!
  Bliss in the mane of God in heaven, *rejoice in the power*
    I rede, so have I rest.
  These lotly lordeynys, away thou lift, *loathsome scoundrels/cast*
  And come down and speak with Shrift,
  And draw thee yerne to some thrift. *quickly*
    Truely it is the best. 1350
MANKIND: Ah, Shrift, thou art well be-note *known*

Here to Sloth, that sitteth herein;
He sayeth thou mightest a come to man's cote   *dwelling*
On Palm Sunday all betime.   *early*
    Thou art come all too soon;
    Therefore, Shrift, by thy fay,   *faith*
    Go forth till Good Friday!
    Tend to thee then, well I may;
      I have now else to doon.   *do*

SHRIFT: Oh! That harlot is now bold!   1360
  In bale he bindeth Mankind belyve.   *quickly*
Say Sloth I prayed him that he would
  Find a charter of thy live.
Man, thou mayest been under mold   *earth*
  Long ere that time, killed with a knive,
With podys and froskis many fold;   *toads and frogs*
  Therefore shape thee now to shrive,
    If thou wilt come to bliss.
    Thou sinnest. Ere sorrow thee ensense,   *teach*
    Behold thine heart, thy preve spense,   *true steward* 1370
    And thine own conscience,
      Or, certes, thou dost amiss.

MANKIND: Ya, Peter! So do mo!   *more*
  We have eaten garlic everyone.
Though I should to hell go,
  I wot well I shall not go alone,
    Truely I tell thee.
    I did never so evil truely,
    That other have done as evil as I.
    Therefore, sir, let be thy cry,   1380
      And go hence from me.

PENANCE: With point of Penance I shall him preve,   *prove*
  Man's pride for to fell;
With this lance I shall him leve,   *secure*
  Iwis, a drop of mercy well.
Sorrow of heart is that I mean;
  Truely, there may no tongue tell
What washeth souls more clean

From the foul fiend of hell,
　　Than sweet sorrow of heart.   1390
　　God, that sitteth in heaven on high,
　　Asketh no more, ere that thou die,
　　But sorrow of heart, with weeping eye,
　　　For all thy sins smart.
They that sigh in sinning,
　In sad sorrow for their sin,
When they shall make their ending,
　All their joy is to begin.
Then medeleth no mourning,   *mixeth*
　But joy is joined with gentle gynne.   *contrivance* 1400
Therefore, Mankind, in this tokening,
　With spete of spear to thee I spin;   *point/thrust?*
　　God's laws to thee I learn.
　With my spud of sorrow swote,   *knife/sweet*
　I reach to thine heart root;
　All thy bale shall turn thee to bote:
　　Mankind, go shrive thee yerne!
[*He touches* MANKIND *with his lance.*]
MANKIND:　A seed of sorrow is in me set;
　Certes, for sin I sigh sore;
Moan of mercy in me is met;   *cry/come* 1410
　For World's mirth I mourn more;
In weeping woe my weal is wet.
　Mercy! Thou must mine fatte a-store;   *richest part*, i.e. soul
From our Lord's light thou hast me let,
　Sorry sin, thou grisly gore!
　　Out on thee, deadly sin!
　Sin, thou hast Mankind schent;   *injured*
　In deadly sin my life is spent.
　Mercy, God omnipotent!
　　In your grace I begin.   1420
For though Mankind have done amiss,
　And he will fall in repentance,   *and-if*
Christ shall him bringen to bower of bliss,
　If sorrow of heart lache him with lance.   *prick*

Lordings, ye see well all this:
  Mankind hath been in great bobance;   *vanity*
I now forsake my sin, iwis.
  And take me wholly to Penance;
    On Christ I cry and call.
    An mercy, Shrift! I will no more;   1430
    For deadly sin mine heart is sore;
    Stuff Mankind with thine store,
      And have him to thine hall!
SHRIFT: Shrift may no man forsake.
  When Mankind cryeth, I am ready.
When sorrow of heart thee hath take,
  Shrift profiteth verily.
Who-so for sin will sorrow make,
  Christ him heareth when he will cry.
Now, Man, let sorrow thine sin slake,   1440
  And turn not again to thy folly,
    For that maketh distance.
    And if it hap thee turn again to sin,
    For God's love lie not long therein!
    He that doth always evil and will not blynne,   *cease*
      That asketh great vengeance.
MANKIND: Nay, certes, that shall I not do!
  Shrift, thou shalt the sooth see;
For though Mankind be wont thereto,
  I will now all amend me.   1450
I come to thee, Shrift, all wholly. Lo!
    (*He descends from Covetous' scaffold.*)
  I forsake you sins, and from you flee!
Ye shapen to man a sorry show;
  When he is beguiled in this degree,
    Ye blekyn all his ble.   *bleach all his color*
    Sin, thou art a sorry store;
    Thou makest Man to sink sore;
    Therefore, of you I will no more.
      I ask, Shrift, for charity.
SHRIFT: If thou wilt be a-knowe here   *acknowledged* 1460

Only all thy trespass,
I shall thee sheild from hell fere, *fire*
  And put thee from pain, unto precious place.
If thou wilt not make thine soul clear,
  But keep them in thine heart case,
Another day they shall be rawe and rere, *crude and fresh?*
  And sink thy soul to Satanas
      In ghastful glowing glede. *coal*
    Therefore, Man, in mody monys, *proud sins*
    If thou wilt wend to worthy wonys, *dwelling* 1470
    Shrive thee now, all at onys, *once*
      Wholly of thy misdeed.
MANKIND: Ah, yes, Shrift! Truly I trow
  I shall not spare for odd nor even
That I shall reckon, all on a row,
  To lache me up to life's leaven. *bind*
To my Lord God I am a-knowe,
  That sitteth aboven in high heaven,
That I have sinned many a throwe *time*
  In the deadly sins seven, 1480
      Both in home and in hall.
    Pride, Wrath and Envy,
    Covetise and Lechery,
    Sloth and also Gluttony,
      I have used them all.
The ten commandments broken I have;
  And my five wits, spent then amiss.
I was then wood and gan to rave; *mad*
  Mercy, God, forgive me this!
When any poor man gan to me crave, 1490
  I gave him naught; and that forthinketh me iwis. *repenteth*
Now Saint Savior, ye me save,
  And bring me to your bower of bliss!
    I cannot all say;
    But to earth I kneel a-down,
    Both with bede and orison, *prayer*
    And ask my absolution!

   Sir Shrift, I you pray.
SHRIFT: Now Jesu Christ, God holy,
 And all the saints of heaven hende,   *loving* 1500
Peter and Paul, apostoly,
 To whom God gave power to loose and bind,
They forgive thee thy folly
 That thou hast sinned with heart and mind.
And I, of my power, thee asoly   *assoil*
 That thou hast been to God unkynde, *unnatural*
   Quantum peccasti.   *all that you have sinned*
  In Pride, Ire and Envy,
  Sloth, Gluttony and Lechery,
  And Covetise, continually,   1510
   Vitam male continuasti. *You have lived in sin continually*
I thee assoil with good intent
 Of all the sins that thou hast wrought
In breaking of God's commandment
 In word, work, will and thought.
I restore to thee the sacrament
 Of penance, which thou never rowt.   *practiced*
Thy five wits miss dispent   *used amiss*
 In sin, the which thou shouldest not,
   Quicquid gesisti. *whatever you have done* 1520
  With eye sense, ear's hearing,
  Nose smelled, mouth speaking,
  And all thy body's bad working,
   Vicium quodcunque fecisti. *whatever sin you have committed*
I thee assoil, with mild mood,
 Of all that thou hast been full mad,
In forsaking of thine Angel Good,
 And the foul Flesh that thou hast fad,   *fed*
The World, the Devil that is so wood,
 And followed thine Angel that is so Bad. 1530
To Jesu Christ that died on rood,
 I restore thee again full sad;   *truly*
   Noli peccare!   *do not sin*
  Of all the good deeds that thou hast done,

And all the tribulation,
Stand thee in remission:
Posius noli viciare.   *do not sin any more*
MANKIND: Now, Sir Shrift, where may I dwell
To keep me from sin and woe?
A comely counsel ye me spell,   1540
To fend me now from my foe.   *defend*
If these seven sins here tell
That I am thus from them go,
The World, the Flesh and the Devil of hell
Shall seeken my soul for to sloo   *slay*
Into bale's bower.
Therefore I pray you put me
Into some place of surety,
That they may not harmen me
With no sins sore.   1550
SHRIFT: To such a place I shall thee kenne,   *guide*
There thou mayest dwell withouten
distance;   *disagreement*
And always keep thee from sin
Into the Castle of Perseverance.
If thou wilt to heaven win
And keep thee from worldly distance,
Go yon castle, keep thee therein,
For it is stronger than any in France;
To yon castle I thee send.
That castle is a precious place,   1560
Full of virtue and of grace;
Who-so liveth there his life's space,
No sin shall him schende.   *harm*
MANKIND: Ah, Shrift! Blessed might thou be!
This castle is here but at hand;
Thither rathely will I tee,   *quickly/go*
Secure over this sad sand.
Good perseverance, God send me
While I live here in this land!
From foul filth now I flee;   1570

Forth to faren now I fonde   *go*
    To you precious port.
   Lord! What man is in merry live
   When he is of his sins shrive!
   All my dole a-down is drive;   *is overcome*
    Christ is my comfort.
BAD ANGEL: Eh! What devil, Man! Whither schat?   *do you rush?*
   Wouldest draw now to holiness?
 Go, fellow, thy good gat!   *get*
   Thou art forty winter old, as I guess;   1580
Go again, the Devil's mat,   *mate*
   And play thee awhile with Sara and Ciss!
She would not else, yon old trat,   *hag*
   But put thee to penance and to stress,
    Yon foul feterel fyle.   *rascally cheat*
    Let men that are on the pit's brink
    Forbearen both meat and drink,
    And do penance as them good think;
     And come and play thee awhile!
GOOD ANGEL: Ya, Mankind, wend forth thy way,   1590
   And do no thing after his rede!
He would thee lead over land's lay
   In dale of dross till thou were dead.
Of cursedness he keepeth the key,
   To baken thee a bitter bread;
In dale of dole till thou shouldst dey,   *die*
   He would draw thee to cursedhead,
    In sin to have mischance.
    Therefore, speed now thy pace
    Pertly to yon precious place   1600
    That is grown all full of grace,
     The Castle of Perseverance.
MANKIND: Good Angel, I will do as thou wilt
   In land while my life may last;
 For I find well in holy writ
   Thou counselest ever for the best.

[*There is a leaf missing in the manuscript at this point. Apparently it bore the end of Mankind's farewell to the Good Angel and the speeches of greeting and instruction by Meekness and Patience. The manuscript resumes with* MANKIND *standing before the Castle of Perseverance, being addressed by the seven* MORAL VIRTUES.]

CHARITY: To Charity, Man, have an eye
    In all things, Man, I rede.
  All thy doing as dross is drye   *dreary*
    But in Charity thou dight thy deed.   *set* 1610
  I destroy always Envy:
    So did thy God when He gan bleed;
  For sin He was hangen high,
    And yet sinned He never in deed,
        That mild mercy well.
        Paul in his 'pistle putteth the prefe,   *proof*
        "But Charity be with thee chief;"
        Therefore, Mankind, be now lief   *willing*
        In Charity for to dwell.
ABSTINENCE: In Abstinence lead thy life!   1620
    Take but skillful refection,   *refreshment*
  For Glutton killeth withouten knife,
  And destroyeth thy complection.
  Who-so eat or drink over blithe
  It gathereth to corruption.
  This sin brought us all in strife
    When Adam fell in sin down
        From precious paradise.
        Mankind, learn now of our lore!
        Who-so eat or drink more   1630
        Than skillfully his state a-store,   *restore*
        I hold him nothing wise.
CHASTITY: Mankind, take keep of Chastity,
    And move thee to maiden Mary,
  Fleshly folly look thou flee,
    At the reverence of our Lady.
  That courteous queen, what did she?

Kept her clean and steadfastly,
And in her was trussed the trinity;   *bound up*
Through ghostly grace she was worthy   1640
    And all for she was chaste.
    Who-so keepeth him chaste and will not sin,
    When he is buried in banks brynne,   *brown?*
    All his joy is to begin;
    Therefore to me take taste.   *heed*

INDUSTRY: In busyness, Man, look thou be,
With worthy works, good and thick!   *numerous*
To Sloth if thou cast thee,
    It shall thee draw to thoughts wick.   *wicked*
        Osiositas parit omne malum:[15]   1650
It putteth a man to poverty,
    And pulleth him to pain's prick.
Do somewhat alway for love of me,
    Though thou shouldest but thwyte a stick.   *whittle*
        With bedes sometime thee bless,   *prayers*
        Sometime read, and sometime write,
        And sometime play at thy delight;
        The devil thee waiteth with despite
        When thou art in idleness.

GENEROSITY: In Largety, Man, lay thy love.   *generosity* 1660
    Spend thy good, as God it sent;
In worship of Him that sit above,
    Look thy goods be dispent.
In dale of dross when thou shalt drove,
    Little love is on thee lent;   *fixed*
The sekatouris shall say it is here behove   *executors* (of his estate)
    To make us merry, for he is went
        That all this good gan owle.   *accumulate*
        Lay thy treasure and thy trust
        In place where no ruggynge rust   *corroding* 1670
        May it destoy to dross ne dust,
        But all to help of soul.

MANKIND: Ladies in land, lovely and light,   *gentle*

---

[15] *Osiositas . . . malum:* Idleness prepares all evil.

Liking lelys, ye be my leech!   *dear fair ones/physician*
I will bow to your bidding bright;
   True tokening to me ye teach.
Dame Meekness, in your might
   I will me wryen from wicked wretch;
All my purpose I have pight,   *fixed*
   Patience to do, as ye me preach;   1680
      From Wrath ye shall me keep.
    Charity, ye will to me attend,
    From foul Envy ye me defend;
    Man's mind ye may amend,
      Whether he wake or sleep.

Abstinence, to you I trist,   *trust*
   From Gluttony ye shall me draw;
In Chastity to liven me list,   *desire*
   That is our Lady's law.
Busyness, we shall be cyst;   *joined* 1690
   Sloth, I forsake the sleper saw.   *untrustworthy saying*
Largety, to you I trist,
   Covetous to don of dawe.
     This is a courteous company.
    What should I more monys make?   *say more*
    The seven sins I forsake,
    And to these seven virtues I me take,
    Maiden Meekness, now, mercy!
MEEKNESS: Mercy may mend all thy moan.
   Come in here at thine own will!   1700
We shall keep thee from thy fon   *foes*
   If thou keep thee in this castle still.
Stand herein as still as stone,
   Then shall no deadly sin thee spill;
Whether that sins come or gon,
   Thou shalt with us thy bouris bylle;   *dwelling build*
     With virtues we shall thee 'vance.
    This castle is of so quaint a gynne   *design*
    That whosoever hold him therein,
    He shall never fall in deadly sin: 1710

It is the Castle of Perseverance.
Qui perseveraverit usque in finem, hic saluus erit.[16]

     [MANKIND *enters the Castle while* THE VIRTUES *sing*
     "eterne rex altissime".]

MEEKNESS: Now, blessed be our Lady, of Heaven empress!
Now is Mankind from folly fallen,
And is in the Castle of Goodness.
  He haunteth now heaven hall
     That shall bringen him to heaven.
     Christ that died with dying dose,   *of vinegar and gall?*
     Keep Mankind in this castle close,
     And put alway in his purpose   1720
        To flee the sins seven.

BAD ANGEL: Nay, by Belial's bright bones,
There shall he no while dwell.
  He shall be won from these wonys
     With the World, the Flesh and the Devil of hell;
        They shall my will a-wreke.   *avenge*
        The sins seven, the kings three,
        To Mankind have enmity;
        Sharply they shall helpen me   *quickly*
           This castle for to break.   1730
How! Flepergebet! Backbiter!
     Yerne our message look you make!   *quickly*
Blithe about look you bear!
  Say Mankind his sins hath forsake;
With yon wretches he will him were.   *guard*
  All to holiness he hath him take;
In my heart it doth me dere;   *injure*
     The boast that those mothers crake,   *brag*
        My gall ginneth to grind.
     Flepergebet, run upon a rashe;   *rush* 1740
     Bid the World, the Fiend and the Flesh
     That they come to fighten fresh,
        To win again Mankind.

BACKBITER: I go, I go on ground glad,

---

[16] *Qui . . . erit:* Matthew 24, 13: But he that shall endure unto the end, the same shall be saved.

Swifter than ship with rudder!
I make men mazed and mad,
 And every man to killen other
  With a sorry cheer.
  I am glad, by saint James of Galys,
  Of shrewdness to tellen talës   *1750*
  Bothen in England and in Walës;
   And, faith, I have many a fere.   *companion*
(*He crosses to the scaffold of Belial.*)
  Hail, set in thy sell!
  Hail, digne devil in thy dell!   *throne*
  Hail, low in hell!
  I come to thee, tales to tell.
BELIAL: Backbiter, boy, always by holts and heath,
 Say now, I say, what tidings? Tell me the sooth.
BACKBITER: Teneful tales I may thee say, *painful*
  To thee no good, as I guess!   *1760*
 Mankind is gone now away
  Into the Castle of Goodness!
There he will both liven and die,
  In dale of dross till Death him dress. *the grave*
Hath thee forsaken, forsooth I say,
  And all thy works, more and less!
   To yon castle he gan to creep.
  Yon mother, Meekness, sooth to sayen,
  And all yene maidens on yon plain, *yon*
  For to fighten they be full fain,
   Mankind for to keep.   *1770*
(BELIAL *calls for* PRIDE, WRATH *and* ENVY.)
PRIDE: Sir King, what wit?   *do you want*
 We be ready throats to kytte.   *cut*
BELIAL: Say, gadelyngis, have ye hard grace! *rascals*
 And evil death might ye die!
 Why let ye Mankind from you pass
  Into yon castle, from us away?
   With tene I shall you tey! *pain/punish*
  Harlots! At onys   *once*

From this wonys!   *dwelling* 1780
By Belial's bonës,
    Ye shall a-beye!   *suffer for it*
(BELIAL *knocks them down and beats them.*)
BACKBITER: Ya! For God this was well go,   *done*
Thus to work with backbiting!
I work both wrack and woe,
    And make each man other to dynge.   *beat*
I shall go about and maken mo   *more*
    Raps for to route and ring.
        [*to the audience*]
Ye backbiters, look that ye do so!
    Make debate abouten to spring   1790
        Between sister and brother!
    If any backbiter here be left,
    He may learn of me his craft;
    Of God's grace he shall be reft,
        And every man to killen other.
(*He crosses to the scaffold of the Flesh.*)
    Hail, king I call!
    Hail, prince, proud pricked in pall!   *proudly dressed in rich clothes*
    Hail, hende in hall!   *courteous*
    Hail, sir king, fair thee befall!
FLESH: Roi Backbiting,   *king* 1800
Full ready in robes to rynge.   *reign*
Full glad tiding,
By Belial's bones, I trow thou bring.
BACKBITER: Ya, for God, out I cry
    On thy two sons and thy daughter yinge!   *young*
Glutton, Sloth and Lechery
    Hath put me in great mourning.
They let Mankind go up on high
    Into yon castle at his liking,
Therein for to live and die,   1810
    With those ladies to make ending,
        The flowers fair and fresh.
        He is in the Castle of Perseverance,

And put his body to penance.
Of hard hap is now thy chance,
    Sir king, Mankind's Flesh.
(FLESH *calls for* GLUTTONY, SLOTH *and* LECHERY.)
LECHERY: Say now thy will!
    Sir Flesh, why cryest thou so shrill?
FLESH: Ah, Lechery, thou skallyd mare!   *scabby*
    And thou, Glutton, God give thee woe!   *1820*
And vile Sloth, evil might thou fare!
Why let ye Mankind from ye go
    Into yon castle so high?
    Evil grace come on thy snout!
    Now am I dressed in great doubt.
    Why n'ad ye looked better about?   *had not*
        By Belial's bones, ye shall a-bye!   *suffer for it*
(*He beats* GLUTTONY, SLOTH *and* LECHERY.)
BACKBITER: Now, by God, this is good game!
    I, Backbiter, now bear me well.
If I had lost my name,   *1830*
    I vow to God it were great del.   *pity*
I shape these shrews to mickle shame:
    Each rappeth on other with routing reel;   *oaring*
I, Backbiter, with false fame
Do breaken and bursten hoods of steel.
    Through this country I am know.
    Now will I gin forth to go,
    And make Covetous have a knock or two;
    And then, iwis, I have do
        My deuer, as I trow.   *duty* *1840*
(*He crosses to the scaffold of the World.*)
Hail, stiff in stounde!   *valiant in battle?*
Hail, gaily girt upon ground!   *dressed*
Hail, fair flower i-found!
Hail, sir World, worthy in wodis wound!   *blue cloth*
WORLD: Backbiter in rout!
    Thou tellest tales of dought
    So stiff and so stout.

What tidings bringest thou about?

BACKBITER: Nothing good, that shalt thou wete.   *know*

Mankind, sir World, hath thee forsake;   1850

With Shrift and Penance he is smete,   *smitten*

And into yon castle he hath him take,

Among yon ladies, white as lake.

Lo, sir World, ye might a-gryse   *be disgusted*

That ye be served on this wise.

Go play you with sir Covetise

Till his crown crake.   *crack*

(WORLD *blows a horn to summon* COVETOUS.)

COVETOUS: Sir bolnynge bowde,   *swelling drunkard*

Tell me why blow ye so loud.

WORLD: Loud, Losel! The devil thee burn!   *good-for-nothing* 1860

I pray God give thee a foul hap!

Say, why lettest thou Mankind

Into yon castle for to 'scape?

I trow thou ginnest to rave.

Now, for Mankind is went,

All our game is schent;   *ruined*

Therefore a sore driving dent,   *blow*

Harlot, thou shalt have!

[*He beats Covetous.*]

COVETOUS: Mercy! Mercy! I will no more!

Thou hast rapped me with rewly rowtis!   *pitiful blows* 1870

I snowre, I sob, I sigh sore!   *sniffle*

Mine head is clattered all to clowtis!   *shaken all to pieces*

In all your state I shall you 'store,   *restore*

If ye abate your dyntis dowtis.   *fearful blows*

Mankind, that ye have forlore,

I shall do come out from yon skowtis   *rascals*

To your hende hall.

If ye will no more beaten me,

I shall do Mankind come out free;

He shall forsake, as ye shall see,   1880

The fair virtues all.

WORLD: Have do then! The devil thee tear!

Thou shalt hangen in hell herne.   *corner*
Belyve, my banner up thou bear,   *quickly*
  And besiege we the castle yerne,   *at once*
    Mankind for to steal.
    When Mankind groweth good,
    I, the World, am wild and wood;
    Those bitches shall bleryn in their blood   *be blinded*
      With flappys fell and fele.   *blows fierce and many* 1890
Yerne let flapyr up my fane,   *hoist/flag*
  And shape we schance and schonde!   *direct/chance/shame*
I shall bring with me those bitches' bane;
  There shall no virtues dwellen in my land.
Meekness is that mother that I mean:
  To her I brew a bitter bonde;
She shall die upon this green
  If that she come into mine hand—
    Yeve rappokis with their rumps!   *yon scoundrels*
    I am the World! It is my will,   1900
    The Castle of Virtue for to spill.   *destroy*
    Howteth high upon yon hill,   *shout*
    Ye traitors in your trumps.   *trumpets*
BELIAL: I hear trumpets trebelen all of tene: *blowing/battle*
  The worthy World walketh to war,
For to cleaven yon castle clean,
  The maidens' minds for to mar.
Spread my pennon upon a prene,   *pole*
  And strike we forth now under sterre!   *discipline*
Shapeth now your shields schene,   *prepare/splendid* 1910
  Yon skallyd skoutis for to scare   *scabby scamps*
    Upon yon green grass!
    Busk you now, boys, belyfe!
    For ever I stand in mickle strife;
    While Mankind is in clean life,
    I am never well at ease.
Make you ready, all three,
  Bold battle for to bede!   *offer*
To yon field let us flee,

And bear my banner forth on brede!   *abroad* 1920
To yon castle will I tee;   *go*
 Those mammerynge mothers shall have their meed.   *chattering*
But they yielden up to me,
 With bitter bales they shall bleed;
  Of their rest I shall them reave.
  In woeful waters I shall them wash.
  Have done, fellows! Take your trash,   *gear*
  And wend we thither on a rash,
   That castle for to cleave.
PRIDE: Now, now! Now, go now!   1930
 On high hills let us howte—   *shout*
For in pride is all my prow—   *prowess*
 Thy bold banner to bear about.
To Golyas I make a vow   *Goliath*
For to schetyn yon iche skowte.   *shoot/scoundrel*
On her ass, ragged and row,   *raw*
 I shall both clatter and clout,
  And give Meekness mischance.
 Belial bright, it is thine hest   *order*
 That I, Pride, go thee nest,   *next* 1940
 And bear thy banner before my breast
  With a comely countenance.
FLESH: I hear a hideous hooting on hight;
 Belyve bid my banner forth for to blaze!
When I sit in my saddle, it is a selkowth sight;   *strange*
 I gape as a Gogmagog when I gin to gaze.
This worthy, wild world I wag with a weight.   *move*
 You rappokis I ruble and all to-raze;   *scoundrels/crush*
Both with shot and with sling I cast with a sleight,
 With care to yon castle to cracken and to crase   *shatter* 1950
  In flood.
 I am Man's flesh: where I go
 I am Man's most foe;
 Iwis, I am ever woe
  When he draweth to good.
Therefore, ye bold boys, busk you about!

Sharply on shields, your shafts ye shiver!

And Lechery, ledron, shoot thou a skoute!   *rogue/rascal*

Help we, Mankind from yon castle to kevere!   *recover*

Help! We must him win.   1960

Shoot we all at a shot,

With gear that we can best note,

To chase Mankind from yon cote   *dwelling*

Into deadly sin.

GLUTTONY: Lo, sir Flesh, how I fare to the field

With a faggot on mine hand for to setten on a fire!

With a wreath of the wood well I can me wield;

With a long lance the loselys I shall lere.   *good-for-nothings/teach*

Go we with our gear!

The bitches shall blekyn and blodyr,   *blanch and blubber*   1970

I shall maken then such a powder,

Both with smoke and with somodyr,   *fumes*

They shall shitten for fear.

(THE VICES *come down from their respective scaffolds into the playing area, and cross to the Castle of Perseverance.*)

BAD ANGEL: "As Armes!" as an hayward,[17] high   *"To arms,"*

now I howte.   *shout*

Devil, dight thee as a duke to do the damsel's dote!   *fear*

Belial, as a bold boy, thy brodde I bear about: *escutcheon*

Help to catch Mankind from caitiff's cote!   *coward's dwelling*

Pride, put out thy pennon of rags and of rowte!

Do this mother Meekness melten to mote!   *earth*

Wrath, prove Patience, the skallyd skowte!   1980

Envy, to Charity shape thou a shot

Full yare!   *ready*

With Pride, Wrath and Envy,

These devils, by downs drye,   *dreary*

As comely king, I descry,

Mankind to catchen to care.

Flesh, frele and fresh, frely fed!   *beautiful/generously*

With Glutton, Sloth and Lechery, Man's souls thou slo!   *slay*

As a duke doughty, do thee to be dread;   *feared*

---

[17] Hayward: A minor official whose job was to keep cattle from breaking through hedges.

Gere thee with gears from top to the toe!   *arm thee with arms*   1990
Kyth this day thou art a king frely fed!   *show*
Glutton, slay thou Abstinence with wicked woe!
With Chastity, thou Lecher, be not over-led!
Sloth, beat thou Busyness, on buttocks bloo!   *blue*
   Do now thy craft, in coste to be know!   *everywhere*
(*Turns to the* WORLD.)
   Worthy, witty and wise, wounden in wede!   *dressed in clothes*
   Let Covetise carpen, cryen and grede!   *cry out*
   Here be bold bachelors, battle to bede,   *offer*
      Mankind to tene, as I trow.   *harm*
MANKIND: That dynge duke that died on rood,   *noble* 2000
   This day my soul keep safe!
When Mankind draweth to good,
   Behold what enemies he shall have.
The World, the Devil, the Flesh are wood;   *wild*
   To men been casten a care-full kave;   *fate*
Bitter bales they breaken on brode,   *cause*/*abroad* (on every side)
   Mankind in woe to welter and wave,
      Lordings, sooth to say.
   Therefore each man beware of this!
   For while Mankind clean is,   2010
   His enemies shall tempten him to do amiss,
      If they might, by any way.
Omne Gaudium existimate, cum variis temtacionibus insideritis.[18]
Therefore, lords, beeth now glad,
   With alms deed and orison
For to do as our Lord bade.
   Stiffly withstand your temptation!
With this foul fiend I am near mad;
   To battle they busken them bown.   *make them ready*
Certes, I should been over-lad—   *overcome*
   But that I am in this castle town—   2020
      With sins sore and smart.
      Who-so will liven out of distress
      And leaden his life in cleanness,

[18] *Omne . . . insideritis:* Think of all joy when you sink into various temptations.

In this castle of virtue and of goodness
   Him must have whole his heart.
Delectari in Domino dabit tibi peticiones cordis tui.[19]
GOOD ANGEL: Ah, Meekness, Charity and Patience—
   Primrose pleyeth parlasent—[20]
Chastity, Busyness and Abstinence,
   Mine hope, ladies, in you is lent!   *fixed*   2030
So come, paramours, sweeter than sense,
   Red as rose on rys i-rent!   *branch*
This day ye dight a good defense!
   While Mankind is in good intent,
      His thoughts are un-hende.   *disobedient*
      Mankind is brought into this wall   *well*
      In frailty to faden and fall;
      Therefore, ladies, I pray you all,
         Help this day Mankind!
MEEKNESS: God, that sitteth in heaven high,   2040
   Save all mankind by sea and sand,
Let him dwellen here, and be us by,
   And we shall putten to him helping hand.
Yet, forsooth, never I see
   That any fault in us he found,
But that we saved him from sins sly,
   If he would by us stiffly stand
      In this castle of stone.
      Therefore, dread thee not, Man's angel dear!
      If he will dwellen with us here,   2050
      From seven sins we shall him were,   *defend*
         And his enemies each one.
Now, my seven sisters sweet,
   This day falleth on us the lot,
Mankind to shield and schete   *guard*
   From deadly sin and shamely shot. *shame-bringing assault*
His enemies strayen in the street

[19] *Delectari ... tui:* Psalms 37, 4: "Delight thyself also in the Lord, and He shall give thee the desires of thine heart."
[20] Does this line mean that the exercise of these virtues is generally agreed (parlesent) to bring to man (pleyeth = direct) the benefits of Christ's passion (primrose)?

To spill man with spetows spot;   *spiteful*
Therefore our flowers let us now flete,   *let fly*
    And keep we him, as we have het,   *promised* 2060
        Among us in this hall.
    Therefore, seven sisters swote,   *sweet*
    Let our virtues reign on rote!   *in a troop*
    This day we will be Man's bote   *salvation*
        Against these devils all.
BELIAL: This day the vaward will I hold.   *vanguard*
    Avaunt my banner, precious Pride,   *advance*
Mankind to catch in cares cold!
Bold battle now will I bide.
        Busk you, boys, on brede!   *hurry/abroad* 2070
    All men that be with me withold
    Both the young and the old,
    Envy, Wrath, the boys bold,
        To round raps ye rape, I rede.   *hard/rush*
PRIDE: As arms, Meekness! I bring thy bane,   *to arms*
    All with pride painted and pight.
What sayest thou, faytour? By mine fair fane,   *rascal/flag*
    With robes round rayed full ryth,
Great gounse, I shall thee gane,[21]   *goose/beat*
    To mar thee, Meekness, with my might!   2080
No worldly wits here are wane;   *wanting*
    Lo, thy castle is all beset!
        Mothers, how shall ye do?
    Meekness, yield thee to me, I rede.
    My name in land is precious Pride;
    My bold banner to thee I bede.   *offer* (in battle)
        Mother, what sayest thereto?
MEEKNESS: Against thy banner of Pride and boast,
    A banner of Meekness and mercy;
I put against Pride, well thou wost,   *knowest* 2090
    That shall schende thy care-full cry.
This meek king is known in every coast,
    That was crossed on Calvary.

---

[21] By mine . . . gane: By my fair flag, with my robes fittingly adorned, great goose I shall thee beat.

When he came down from heaven host
  And lighted with meekness in Mary,
    This Lord thus lighted low.
  When he came from the Trinity,
  Into a maiden lighted He,
  And all was for to destroy thee:
    Pride, this shalt thou know.   2100
    Deposuit potentes de sede, et exaltavit humiles.[22]
For, when Lucifer to hell fell,
  Pride, thereof thou were chesun;   *cause*
And thou, devil, with wicked will,
  In paradise trapped us with treason,
So thou us bound in bales ill;   *wickedly*
  This may I prove by right reason.
Till this duke that died on hill,
  In heaven might man never have seisin,   *possession*
    The gospel thus declared.   2110
    For who-so love Him shall be high;   *exalted*
    Therefore thou shalt not comen us nigh;
    And though thou be never so sly,
      I shall fell all thy fare.   *fortune*
     Qui se exaltet, humiliabitur, et qui se humiliat exaltabitur.[23]
WRATH: Dame Patience, what sayest thou to Wrath and Ire?
  Put Mankind from thy castle clear,
Or I shall tappen at thy tyre   *headdress*
  With stiff stones that I have here.
I shall sling at thee many a vyre,   *bolt* (from a crossbow) 2120
  And be avenged hastily here:
Thus Belzabub, our great sire,
  Bade me burn thee with wild fire,
    Thou bitch black as coal.
    Therefore, fast, foul skowte,
    Put Mankind to us out,
    Or of me thou shalt have doubt,

[22] *Deposuit . . . humiles:* Luke 1, 52: "He hath put down the mighty from their seats, and exalted them of low degree."
[23] *Qui . . . exaltabitur:* Who exalts himself shall be humbled, and who humbles himself exalted.

Thou mother, thou motyhole!   *moth-hole?*

PATIENCE: From thy doubt, Christ me shield   *fear*

This iche day, and all mankind!   *very*   2130

Thou wicked wretch, wood and wild,

Patience shall thee schende!

Quia ira viri justicia Dei non operatur.[24]

For Mary's son, meek and mild,

Rent thee up, root and rind,   *tore*

When He stood meeker than a child

And let boys him beaten and bind.

Therefore, wretch, be still!

For those pelouris that gan him pose,   *rascals/beat*

He might have driven them to dross,   2140

And yet, to casten him on the cross,

He suffered all their will.

Thousands of angels he might have had

To a-wrokyn him full yerne;   *avenge/eagerly*

And yet, to dien he was glad,

Us, patience to teachen and learn.

Therefore, boy, with thy boistrous blade,

Fare away by fields ferne!   *distant*

For I will do as Jesu bade—

Wretches, from my wonys werne   *dwellings/keep away* 2150

With a dyngne defense.   *stout*

If thou fonde to comen aloft,   *try*

I shall thee cachë from this croft   *chase*

With these rolls sweet and soft

Painted with Patience.[25]

ENVY: Out! Mine heart ginneth to break

For Charity that standeth so stout.

Alas, mine heart ginneth to wreak.

Yield up this castle, thou whore clowte!

It is mine office, foul to speak,   2160

False slanders to bear about.

Charity, the devil might thee check,

---

[24] *Quia . . . operatur:* Because of the justice of God, the anger of man is powerless.
[25] Rolls: The sacramental wafers of communion.

But I thee rap with rewly rowte,   *pitiful blow*
   Thy targe for to tear.   *shield*
Let Mankind come to us down,
Or I shall shooten to this castle town
A full foul defamation.
   Therefore this bow I bear.
CHARITY: Though thou speak wick and false fame,
   The worse shall I never do my deed.   2170
Who-so paireth falsely another man's name,   *impairs*
   Christ's curse he shall have to meed:
      Ve homini illi quem scandalum venit.[26]
Who-so will not have his tongue tame—
   Take it sooth as mass creed—   *as true*
Woe, woe to him, and mickle shame!
   In holy writ this I read:
      Forever thou art a shrew.
     Though thou speak evil, I ne yeve a gres;   *care a blade of grass*
     I shall do never the worse;   2180
     At the last the sooth verse
      Certes Himself shall show.
Our lovely Lord, withouten lack,
   Gave example to Charity:
When He was beaten blue and black
   For trespass that never did He—
In sorry sin he had no tak,   *blenish*
   And yet for sin He bled bloody ble—   *color*
He took His cross upon His back,
   Sinful Man, and all for thee: 2190
      Thus He made defense.
     Envy, with thy slanders thick,
     I am put at my Lord's prick;   *command*
     I will do good against the wick,
      And keep in silence.
BELIAL: What, for Belial's bones,
   Whereabouten chide ye?
Have done, ye boys, all at onys!   *once*

[26] *Ve . . . venit:* Cp. Matthew 18, 7: "Woe unto that man by whom the offense cometh."

Lash down these mothers, all three!
Work wreck to this wonys!   2200
The vanward is granted me.
Do these mothers to maken moans!
Your doughty deeds now let see!
Dash then all to daggys!   *tatters*
Have do, boys, blue and black!
Work these wretches woe and wrack!
Clarions, cryeth up at a krake,   *loudly*
And blow your broad bags!   *bag-pipes*
(*They attack the castle*) [*but are driven back when* THE VIRTUES
throw roses, symbols of Christ's passion, down upon them.]

PRIDE: Out! My proud back is bent!
Meekness hath me all for-beat;   2210
Pride with Meekness is for-schent.   *overcome*
I wail and weep, with wounds wet;
I am beaten in the head.
My proud pride a-down is driven,
So sharply Meekness hath me shriven,   *punished*
That I may no longer liven;
My life is me bereft.

ENVY: All my enmity is not worth a fart;
I shit and shake all in my sheet;
Charity, that sour swart,   *shrew* 2220
With fair roses mine head gan break:
I breed the malaundyr.   *scab*
With worthy words and flowers sweet,
Charity maketh me so meek,
I dare neither cry nor creep,
Not a shot of slander.

WRATH: I, Wrath, may singen wele-a-woe!
Patience me gave a sorry dint;   *blow*
I am all beaten black and blue
With a rose that on rode was rent;   2230
My speech is almost spent.
Her roses fell on me so sharp
That mine head hangeth as an harp;

I dare neither cry nor carp;
She is so patient.
[*They flee to Belial's scaffold.*]

BAD ANGEL: Go hence! Ye do not worth a turd!
Foul fall you, all four!
Yerne, yerne, let fall on board!   *quickly*
Sir Flesh with thine eyen sour,   *eyes*
For care I cukke and cower.   *chatter* 2240
Sir Flesh with thine company,
Yerne, yerne, make a cry!
Help we have no felony,   *betrayal*
That this day may be our!

FLESH: War, war! Let Man's Flesh go to!
I come with a company.
Have do, my children, now have do,
Glutton, Sloth and Lechery!
Each of you winneth a scho,   *conquer/she* (one of the virtues)
Lete not Mankind with mastery.   *yield* 2250
Let sling him in a foul slo,   *slough*
And fonde to feoff him with folly!   *endeavor/endow*
Doeth now well your deed!
Yerne let see how ye shall 'gin   *begin*
Mankind to tempten to deadly sin.
If ye might this castle win,
Hell shall be your meed.

GLUTTONY: War! Sir Glutton shall maken a smeke   *smoke*
Against this castle, I vow.
Abstinence, though thou bleyke,   *blanch* 2260
I look on thee with bitter brow.
I have a faggot in mine neck
To setten Mankind on a lowe;   *flame*
My foul leye shalt thou not let,   *flame/prevent*
I vow to God, as I trow,
Therefore put him out here!
In meselynge Gluttony,   *diseaseful*
With good meats and drinks trye,   *delightful*
I nourish my sister Lechery

Till man runneth on fere.   *fire* 2270

ABSTINENCE: Thy meats and thy drinks are unthende: *unhealthy*
   When they are out of measure take,
They maken men mad and out of mende,   *mind*
   And worken them both woe and wrake.   *injury*
That, for thy fire though thou here kindle,
   Certes I shall thee well a-slake
With bread that brought us out of hell,
   And on the cross suffered wrake:
      I mean the sacrament.
    That iche blissful bread   *same* 2280
    That hung on hill till He was dead,
    Shall temper so mine maidenhead
      That thy purpose shall be spent.
In Abstinence this bread was bought,
   Certes, Mankind, and all for thee.
Of forty days eat He nought
   And then was nailed to a tree;
Example us was betaught;
   In soberness He bade us be.
Therefore Mankind shall not be caught,   2290
   Gluttony, with thy degree:
      The sothë thou shalt see.
    To nourish fair, though thou be fawe,   *fain* (to nourish improperly)
    Abstinence it shall withdraw[27]
    Till thou be schet under schawe,   *buried/grove*
    And fain for to flee.   *eager*

LECHERY: Lo, Chastity, thou foul skowte!
   This ilke day here thou shalt die.   *same*
I make a fire in Man's towte,   *ass*
   That lanceth up as any leye.   *flame* 2300
These cursed coals I bear about,
   Mankind in tene for to teye.   *pain/bind*
Men and women hath no doubt,
   With pissing pokes for to play;   *genitals*
      I bind them in my bonds.

[27] Withdraw: i.e. the bread of the sacrament so that it should not be eaten gluttonously.

I have no rest, so I rowe,   *run*
  With men and women, as I trow,
Till I, Lechery, be set on a lowe,   *flame*
  In all Mankind's londs.   *lands*
CHASTITY: I, Chastity, have power in this place,   2310
  Thee, Lechery, to bind and beat.
Maiden Mary, well of grace,
  Shall quench that foul heat.
     Mater et Virgo! extingue carnales concupiscentias![28]
Our Lord made thee no space
  When His blood strayed in the street.
From this castle He did thee chase
  When he was crowned with thorns great
    And green.
    To dreary death when He was dight,   2320
    And boys did him great despite,
    In Lechery had He no delight,
    And that was right well seen.
At our Lady I learn my lesson,
  To have chaste life till I be dead.
She is queen and beareth the crown;
  And all was for her maidenhead.
Therefore go from this castle town,
  Lechery, now I thee rede;
For Mankind gettest thou not down,   2330
  To soloyen him sinful seed: *sow*
    In care thou wouldest him cast.
    And if thou come up to me,
    Truely thou shalt beaten be
    With the yerde of Chastity   *rod*
    While my life may last.
SLOTH: War, war! I delve with a spade;
  Men call me "the lord sir Slowe."
Ghostly grace I spill and shed;
  From the water of grace, the ditch I fowe;   *clean* (dry up)   2340
Ye shallen come right enow

[28] *Mater . . . concupiscentias:* Mother and Maiden! Quench carnal desires.

By this ditch dry, by banks brede.   *broad*
Thirty thousand that I well know,
    In my lovely life I lead,
        That had liever sitten at the ale,
        Three-men's songs to singen loud,
        Than toward the church for to crowd.
        Thou Busyness, thou bolnyd bowde!   *swollen drunkard*
    I brew to thee thine bale.
INDUSTRY: Ah, good men, beware now all   2350
    Of Slug and Sloth, the foul thief!
To the soul he is bitterer than gall;
    Root he is of mickle mischief;
God's service, that leadeth us to heaven hall,
    This lordeyn, for to letten us is lief.   *rascal/prevent/eager*
Whoso will shriven him of his sins all,
    He putteth this brethel to mickle mischief,   *rogue*
        Mankind he that miscarried.
        Men might do no penance for him this,   *i.e. this one*
        N'ere shrive them when they do amiss,   2360
        But ever he would in sin, iwis,
            That Mankind were tarried.
Therefore he maketh this dike dry,
    To putten Mankind to distress;
He maketh deadly sin a ready way
    Into the Castle of Goodness;
But with tene I shall him teye,   *pain/bind*
    Through the help of heaven empress;
Within my bedys he shall a-beye;   *prayers/suffer for it*
    And other occupations more and less   2370
        I shall shape, him to schonde;   *shame*
    For who-so will Sloth put down
    With bedes and with orison
    Or some honest occupation,
        As book to have in hand.
        Nec lege, nec hora, nec disce, neque labora.[29]

---

[29] *Nec . . . labora*: Don't read, don't pray, don't learn, don't work. Industry seems to be ironically recapitulating the message of Sloth.

FLESH: Ey! For Belial's bones, the king,
    Whereabout stand ye all day?
  Caitiffs, let be your cackling,
    And rap at rowtis of array.   *groups of warriors*   2380
  Gluttony, thou foul gadlynge,   *rascal*
    Slay Abstinence, if thou may!
  Lechery, with thy working,
    To Chastity make a wicked array
      A little throwe.   *while*
    And while we fight
    For our right,
    In bemys bright   *trumpets*
      Let blasts blow!
  (*They attack the castle, and are driven back.*)
GLUTTONY: Out, Glutton! A-down I drive.   2390
  Abstinence hath lost my might.
  Sit Flesh, I shall never thrive;
    I do not worth the devil's dirt;
      I may not liven long.
    I am all beaten, top and tail;
    With Abstinence will I no more dayl;   *dally*
    I will go couch and quail   *hide*
      At home in your gonge.   *privy*
LECHERY: Out on Chastity, by the rood!
  She hath dayshyd and so drenched!   *beaten*   2400
  Yet have she the curse of God,
    For all my fire the quean hath quenched;   *whore*
      For fear I fall and faint.
    In hard raps might she ride!
    Here dare I not long abide;
    Somewhere my head I would hide,
      As an urchin that were schent.   *punished*
SLOTH: Out! I die! Lay on water!
  I swoon, I sweat, I faint, I drulle!   *drool ? or feel giddy?*
  Yon quean, with her pitter-patter,   2410
  Hath all to-dayshyd my skallyd skull! *broken/scabby*
    It is as soft as wool.

Ere I have here more skathe,   *injury*
I shall leap away, by lurking lathe,   *barn*
There I may my ballokys bathe   *testicles*
   And leykyn at the full.   *play* (i.e. rest)
[*They flee to Flesh's scaffold.*]
BAD ANGEL: Ya! The devil speed you, all the pack!
For sorrow I mourn on the mowle;   *earth*
I carp, I cry, I cower, I kacke,   *mutter*
I fret, I fart, I fizzle foul.   2420
   I look like an owl.
  Now, sir World, what-so it cost,
  Help now, or this we have lost;
  All our fare is not worth a thost;   *piece of dung*
   That maketh me to mowle.   *crumble?*
WORLD: How, Covetise! Banner avaunt!
  Here cometh a battle, noble and new;
For, since thou were a little faunt,   *child*
  Covetise, thou hast been true.
Have do that damsel; do her daunt;   2430
  Bitter bales thou her brew!
The meeds, boy, I thee grant,   *as reward*
  The gallows of Canwick to hangen on new—
   That would thee well befall.
   Have done, sir Covetise!
   Work on the best wise;
   Do Mankind come and arise
   From yon virtues all.
COVETOUS: Now, Mankind! I am a-tenyde   *vexed*
  For thou art there in that hold.   2440
Come and speak with thy best friend,
  Sir Covetise! Thou knowest me of old.
What devil! Shalt thou there longer lende   *remain*
  With great penance in that castle cold?
Into the world, if thou wilt, wend
  Among men to bear thee bold,
   I rede, by Saint Gile.
   How, Mankind! I thee say,

Come to Covetise, I thee pray.
We shall together play,   2450
  If thou wilt, a while.
GENEROSITY: Ah, God help! I am dismayed.
  I curse thee, Covetise, as I can;
For certes, traitor, thou hast betrayed
  Nearhand now each earthly man.
So much were men never a-frayed   *embattled*
  With Covetise since the world began.
God Almighty is not paid,
  Since thou, fiend, bore the World's ban;   *edict*
    Full wide thou ginnest wend.   *range* 2460
    Now are men waxen near wood: *mad*
      They would go to hell for World's good;
      That Lord that rested on the rood
        Is maker of an end.

      Maledicti sunt avariciosi huius temporis![30]

There is no dis-ease nor debate   *trouble*
  Through this wide world so round,
Tide nor time, early nor late,
  But that Covetise is the ground.   *source*
Thou nourishest Pride, Envy and Hate,   2470
  Thou Covetise, thou cursed hound!
Christ thee shield from our gate,   *keep*
  And keep us from thee safe and sound,
    That thou no good here win!
    Sweet Jesu, gentle justice,
    Keep Mankind from Covetise,
    For iwis, he is, in all wise,
      Root of sorrow and sin.
COVETOUS: What aileth thee, lady Largety,   *generosity*
  Damsel dyngne upon thy dais?   2480
And I spake right not to thee,
  Therefore I pray thee hold thy peace.
How, Mankind! Come speak with me!
  Come, lay thy love here in my les!   *leash*

[30] *Maledicti . . . temporis:* The avaricious are condemned from this moment.

Covetise is a friend right free,
   Thy sorrow, Man, to slake and cease.
      Covetise hath many a gift.
      Mankind, thine hand hither thou reach!
      Covetise shall be thy leech;   *physician*
      The right way I shall thee teach   2490
         To thedom and to thrift.   *prosperity*
MANKIND: Covetise, whither should I wend?
      What way wouldest that I should hold?
To what place wouldest thou me send?
      I gin to waxen hoary and cold;
My back ginneth to bow and bend;
      I crawl and creep, and wax all cold.
Age maketh man full unthende,   *miserable*
      Body and bones, and all unwolde.   *stiff*
         My bones are feeble and sore;   2500
         I am arrayed in a sloppe;   *loose gown*
         As a young man I may not hop;
         My nose is cold and ginneth to drop;
           Mine hair waxit all hoar.
COVETOUS: Peter! Thou hast the more need
      To have some good in thine age;
Marks and pounds, lands and lede,   *lead*
      Houses and homes, castle and cage;
Therefore do as I thee rede!
      To Covetise cast thy parage!   *alliance* 2510
Come, and I shall thine erdyn bede;   *cause plead*
      The worthy World shall give thee wage,
         Certes not a lyth.   *little*
      Come on, old man, it is no reprefe   *reproof*
      That Covetise be thee lief;   *dear*
      If thou die at any mischief,
         It is thyself to wyth.   *blame*
MANKIND: Nay, nay! These ladies of goodness
      Will not let me fare amiss;
And though I be a while in distress,   2520
      When I die, I shall to bliss.

It is but folly, as I guess.
 All this World's weal, iwis;
These lovely ladies, more and less,
 In wise words they tell me this.
  Thus sayeth the book of kendes.   *generations* (The Bible)
  I will not do these ladies despite,
  To forsaken them for so light;   *little*
  To dwellen here is my delight;
   Here are my best friends.   2530

COVETOUS: Ya! Up and down thou take the way,
 Through this world to walken and wend,
And thou shalt find, sooth to say,
 Thy purse shall be thy best friend.
Though thou sit all day and pray,
 No man shall come to thee, nor send;
But if thou have a penny to pay,
 Men shall to thee then listen and lende,   *remain*
  And kelyn all thy care.   *cool*
  Therefore to me thou hang and helde,   *hold* 2540
  And be covetous whilest thou may thee welde; *rule*
  If thou be poor and needy and eld,
   Thou shalt often evil fare.

MANKIND: Covetise, thou sayest a good skill.
 So great God will me advance,   *so-if*
All thy bidding do I will.
 I forsake the Castle of Perseverance;
In Covetise I will me hyle,   *hide*
 For to get some sustenance.
Afore meal, men meat shall till;   *cultivate* 2550
 It is good for all chance
  Some good owhere to hide,   *somewhere*
  Certes, this ye well know:
  It is good when-so the wind blow
  A man to have somewhat of his owe,   *own*
   What hap so-ever betide.

GOOD ANGEL: Ah, ladies! I pray you of grace,
 Helpeth to keep here Mankind!

He will forsake his precious place,
And draw again to deadly sin.   2560
Help, ladies, lovely in lace!
He goeth from this worthy wonnynge.   *dwelling*
Covetise away ye chase,
And shutteth Mankind somewhere herein,
In your worthy wise!   *manner*
Oh wretched Man! thou shalt be wroth!
That sin shall be thee full loath!
Ah, sweet ladies, help! He goeth
Away with Covetise.

(MANKIND *leaves the castle and joins* COVETOUS.)

MEEKNESS: Good Angel, what may I do thereto?   2570
Himself may his soul spill.   *destroy*
Mankind to do what he will do,
God hath given him a free will.
Though he drench and his soul slo,   *drown/slay*
Certes we may not do there-till.
Since he came this castle to,
We did to him that us befell,
And now he hath us refused.
As long as he was within this castle wall,
We kept him from sin, ye saw well all;   2580
And now he will again to sin fall,
I pray you hold us excused.

PATIENCE: Reason will excusen us all;
He held the axe by the helve.   *handle (i.e. it was deliberate)*
Though he will to folly fall,
It is to wytyn but himselve.   *blame*
While he held him in this hall,
From deadly sin we did him schelve: *shield*
He breweth himself a bitter gall;
In death's dynt when he shall delve   *stroke* 2590
This game he shall be-grete.   *lament*
He is endowed with wits five
For to rulen him in his live;
We virtues will not with him strive.

A-vyse him and his deed! *consider*

CHARITY: Of his deed have we not to doon;
He will no longer with us be led.
When he asked out, we heard his bone, *prayer*
And of his presence we were right glad;
But, as thou sayest, he hath forsaken us soon; 2600
He will not do as Christ him bade.
Mary! Thy son a-bouyn the moon, *above*
As make Mankind true and sad, *has*
  In grace for to gon. *go*
  For if he will to folly flit,
  We [ne] may him not with-sit; *resist*
  He is of age and can his wit, *knows his mind*
  Ye know well everyone.

ABSTINENCE: Each one, ye knowen he is a fool
In Covetise to dight his deed. 2610
World's weal is like a three-footed stool:
It faileth Man at his most need.
When he is dight in dedys dole, *set in Death's dale* (valley)
The right register I shall him read:
He shall be tore with teneful tole; *painful tool*
When he shall burn on gremys glede, *wrath's coals*
  He shall learn a new law.
  Be he never so rich of World's wone, *treasure*
  His seketouris shall maken their moan: *executors* (heirs)
  "Make us merry and let him gon! 2620
  He was a good fellow!"

CHASTITY: When he is dead, their sorrow is least:
The one seketour sayeth to the other,
"Make we merry, and a rich feast,
And let him lie in dead's fodyr." *heap*
So his part shall be the least:
The sister semyt thus the brother. *serves*
I lete a man no better than a beast, *consider*
For no man can beware by other
  Till he hath all full spun. 2630
  Thou shalt see that day, Man, that a bede *prayer*

      Shall thee stand more in stead
        Than all the good that thou mightest get,
          Certes, under sun.

INDUSTRY: Mankind, of one thing have I wonder,
      That thou takest not into thy mende.   *mind*
When body and soul shall parten asunder,
      No World's good shall with thee wend.
When thou art dead, and in the earth laid under,
      Misgotten good thee shall schende;   *harm* 2640
It shall thee weighen, as peys in punder,   *weights/scale*
      Thy sely soul to bringen in bende,   *bondage*
        And make it full unthende.
        And yet Mankind, as it is seen,
        With Covetise goeth on this green!
        The traitor doth us all this tene   *injury*
          After his life's end.

GENEROSITY: Out, I cry, and nothing low,
      On Covetise, as well I may!
Mankind sayeth he hath never enow   2650
      Till his mouth be full of clay.
        Avarus nunquam replebitur pecunia.[31]
When he is closed in Death's dow,   *grip*
      What helpeth riches or great array?
It flieth away as any snow
      Anon after thy ending day,
        To wild world's wise.
        Now, good men all that here be,
        Have my sisters excused, and me;
        Though Mankind from the castle flee: 2660
          Wit it Covetise!   *know that Covetise is responsible*

BAD ANGEL: Ya! Go forth and let the queans cackle!   *whores*
      There women are, are many words.
Let them go hopping with their hackle!   *mantles*
      There geese sitten, are many turds!
With Covetise thou run on rakle   *in haste*
      And hang thine heart upon his hoards.

---

[31] *Avarus ... pecunia:* The covetous is never satisfied with wealth, Cp. Ecclesiastes 5, 10.

Thou shalt be shaken in mine shackle.
  Unbind thy bags on his boards,
    On his benches above.   2670
      Parde! thou goest out of mankind, by God,   *differ from*
      But Covetise be in thy mind;   *unless*
      If ever thou think to be thende,   *prosperous*
        On him thou lay thy love.
MANKIND: Needs my love must on him lende,   *fix*
  With Covetise to walter and wave.
 I know none of all my kind,
  That he ne coveteth for to have;
Penny-man is mickle in mind:
  My love in him I lay and lave.   *leave* 2680
Where that ever I walk or wend,
  In weal or woe he will me have;
    He is great of grace.
    Where-so I walk in land or lede,   *nation*
    Penny-man best may he speed:
    He is a duke to do a deed
      Now in every place.
GOOD ANGEL: Alas, that ever Mankind was born!
  On Covetise is all his lust.
Night and day, midnight and morn,   2690
  In Penny-man is all his trust.
Covetise shall maken him lorn   *lost*
  When he is dolven all to dust;   *buried*
To mickle shame he shall be schorn,   *condemned*
  With foul fiends to rotten and rust.
    Alas, what shall I do?
    Alas, alas, so may I say!
    Man goeth with Covetise away.
    Have me excused, for I ne may
      Truely not do thereto.   2700
WORLD: Ah, ah! This game goeth as I would.
  Mankind will never the World forsake;
 Till he be dead and under mold,
  Wholly to me he will him take;

To Covetise he hath him yolde;   *given*
  With my weal he will awake;
For a thousand pound I nolde   *would not*
  But Covetise were man's make,   *mate*
    Certes, on every wise.
    All these games he shall bewail,   2710
    For I, the World, am of this entail,   *fashion*
    In his most need I shall him fail,
      And all for Covetise.

COVETOUS: Now, Mankind, beware of this:
  Thou art a party well in age;
I would not thou faredest amiss;
  Go we now to my castle cage!
In this bower I shall thee bless;
  Worldly weal shall be thy wage;
More muck than is thine, iwis.   *money* 2720
  Take thou this in trust terage,   *payment*
    And look that thou do wrong.
    Covetise, it is no sore,
    He will thee feoffen full of store,
    And always, always, say "more and more";
      And that shall be thy song.

MANKIND: Ah, Covetise, have thou good grace!
  Certes, thou bearest a true tongue:
"More and more," in many a place,
  Certes, that song is often sung.   2730
I wist never man, by banks base,   *low*
  So sayen, in clay till he were clonge: *buried*
"Enow, enow" had never space;
  That full song was never sung.
    Nor I will not begin.
    Good Covetise, I thee pray
    That I might with thee play!
    Give me good enow or that I die,
      To wonne in World's wynne.   *live/joy*

COVETOUS: Have here, Mankind, a thousand mark!   2740
  I, Covetise, have thee this got;

Thou mayest purchase therewith both pond and park,
    And do therewith mickle note.
Lend no man hereof, for no karke,   *distress*
    Though he should hang by the throat,
Monk nor friar, priest nor clerk,
    Nor help therewith church nor cote,   *cottage*
        Till Death thy body delve.
        Though he should starve in a cave,
        Let no poor man thereof have;   2750
        In green grass till thou be grave,
        Keep somewhat for thyself.
MANKIND: I vow to God, it is great husbandry.
    Of thee I take these nobles round.
I shall me rapen, and that in hye,   *hurry/haste*
    To hide this gold under the ground;
There shall it lie till that I die;
    It may be kept there safe and sound.
Though my neighbor should be hangen high,
    Thereof getteth he neither penny nor pound.   2760
        Yet am I not well ease: *contented*
        Now would I have castle walls,
        Strong steeds and stiff in stalls.   *valiant*
        With high holts and high halls,   *woods*
        Covetous, thou must me sese.   *endow*
COVETOUS: All shalt thou have already, lo,
    At thine own disposition.
All this good, take thee, too,
    Cliff and coast, tower and town:
Thus hast thou gotten, in sinful slo,   *cleverness* 2770
    Of thine neighbors, by extortion.
"More and more," say yet, have do;   *go on*
    Till thou be dead and droppen down,
        Work on with World's wrenches.   *tricks*
        "More and more," say yet, I rede;
        To more than enow thou hast need;
        All this World, both length and brede,   *breadth*
        Thy covetise may not quench.

MANKIND: Quench, never no man may:
 Me thinketh never I have enow;   *2780*
There ne is World's weal, night nor day,
 But that me thinketh it is too slow.
"More and more," yet I say,
 And shall ever, while I may blow;
On Covetise is all my lay,   *song*
 And shall till death me overthrow.
  "More and more," this is my stevene.   *dream*
  If I might always dwellen in prosperity,
  Lord God, then well were me!
  I would, the medys, forsake Thee,   *as reward*   *2790*
  And never to comen in heaven.
 [*Enter* DEATH.]
DEATH: Oh, now it is time high
 To casten Mankind to Death's dynt.   *blow*
In all his works he is unslye;   *foolish*
 Mickle of his life he hath misspent.
To Mankind I ney nigh;   *approach*
 With rewly raps he shall be rent.   *pitiful blows/torn*
When I come, each man dread forthi,   *on that account*
 But yet is there no gain i-went,   *no help hoped for*
  High hill, holt, nor heath.   *2800*
  Ye shall me dread, everyone;
  When I come, ye shall groan;
  My name in land is left alone:
  I hatte "dreary Death."   *am called*
Dreary is my death-draught;
 Against me may no man stand;
I durke, and down I bring to nought   *strike*
 Lords and ladies in every land.
Whom-so I have a lesson taught,
 Onethys sithen shall he   *scarcely a moment*
  mowe stand;   *be able to stand*   *2810*
In my care-full cloths he shall be caught,
 Rich, poor, free and bond:
  When I come, they go no more.

Where-so I wend in any lede,   *nation*
Every man of me has dread;
Lette I will for no meed,   *forbear*
    To smite sad and sore.   *heavily*
Dyngne dukes are a-dread
    When my blasts are on them blow;
Lords in land are over-led,   2820
    With this lance I lay them low.
Kings keen and knights kyd,   *brave/renowned*
    I do them delven in a throwe;   *bury/moment*
In bank I busk them a bed;   *prepare*
    Sad sorrow to them I sow;
      I tene them, as I trow.   *harm*
      As keen colts though they kynse,   *high-spirited/wince*
      Against me there is no defense.
      In the great pestilence,
        Then was I well know.   2830
But now almost I am foryete;   *forgotten*
    Men, of Death, hold no tale.   *have no care*
In Covetous their good they get;
    The great fishes eat the small.
But when I deal my derne dette,   *dark dart*
    Those proud men I shall a-vale: *humble*
Them shall helpen neither meal nor meat
    Till they be drawn to Death's dale:
      My law they shall learn.
      There ne is penny nor pound   2840
      That any of you shall save sound
      Till ye be graven under ground.
        There may no man me werne.   *keep away*
To Mankind now will I reach;
    He has whole his heart on Covetise.
A new lesson I will him teach,
    That he shall both grucchyn and gryse.   *complain and tremble*
No life in land shall be his leech;   *physician*
    I shall him prove of mine empryse;   *power*
With this point I shall him breach,   2850

And wappyn him in woeful wise;   *strike*
   Nobody shall be his bote.
[DEATH *crosses to* MANKIND.]
   I shall thee shapen a shameful shape;
   Now I kill thee with mine knappe!   *blow*
   I reche to thee, Mankind, a rap   *give*
     To thine heart root!
MANKIND: Ah, Death, Death! Dry is thy drift!   *dreary*
Dead is my destiny!
Mine head is cleaven all in a cleft!
   For clap of care now I cry;   2860
Mine eyelids may I not lift;
Mine brains waxen all empty;
I may not once mine hood up shift.   *raise my head*
   With Death's dynt now I die!
     Sir World, I am hent!   *overcome*
   World! World! have me in mind!
   Good sir World, help now Mankind!
   But thou help me, Death shall me schende;
     He has dight to me a dynt!   *given to me a blow*
World, my wit waxit wrong;   *grows* 2870
   I change, both hide and hue;
Mine eyelids waxen all outwrung;   *begin to flow with tears*
   But thou help me, sore it shall me rue!
Now hold that thou hast behete me long!   *promised*
   For all fellowships old and new,
Lesse me of my pains strong!   *relieve*
   Some bote of bale thou me brew,   *relief from harm*
     That I may of thee yelpe.   *speak praise*
   World, for old acquaintance,
   Help me from this sorry chance!   2880
   Death hath lacched me with his lance!   *struck*
     I die but thou me help.
WORLD: Oh, Mankind! Hath Death with thee spoke?
   Against him helpeth no wage.   *challenge*
I would thou were in earth be-loke,   *enclosed*
   And another had thine heritage.

Our bond of love shall soon be broke,
  In cold clay shall be thy cage.
Now shall the World on thee be wroke,   *avenged*
  For thou hast done so great outrage;   2890
    Thy good thou shalt forego.
    World's good thou hast foregone,
    And with tottys thou shalt be torn.   *teeth*
    Thus have I served here beforn
      A hundred thousand mo.   *more*
MANKIND: Oh, World! World! Ever worth woe!   *woe befall thee*
    And thou, sinful Covetise,
When that man shall from you go,
  Ye work with him on wonder wise!
The wit of this World is sorrow and woe.   2900
  Beware, good men, of this gyse!   *fate*
Thus hath he served many on mo.
  In sorrow slaketh all his assize;
    He beareth a tenynge tongue.   *lying*
    While I laid with him my lot,
    Ye seen how fair he me behete;
    And now he would I were a clot,
      In cold clay for to cling.   *be buried*
    [THE WORLD *calls for* GARCIO, *who enters.*]
WORLD: How, boy, arise! Now thou must wend
  On mine earthen, by step and stall;   2910
Go brew Mankind a bitter bende,   *captivity*
  And put him out of his hall!
Let him therein no longer lende!   *remain*
For-brostyn, I trow, by his gall!   *[he will] burst apart*
For thou art not of his kende,   *family*
  All his heritage will thee well befall:
    Thus fareth mine fair feres.   *companions*
    Often time I have you told,
    Those men that ye are to least behold,   *beholden to least*
    Commonly shall your wonnynge wold,   *dwelling/govern* 2920
      And be your next heirs.
GARCIO: World worthy, in weeds wound,   *in clothes dressed*

I thank thee for thy great gift.
I go glad upon this ground,
  To put Mankind out of his thrift.
I trow he stinketh this ilke stounde;   *very moment*
  Into a lake I shall him lift;
His parks, places and pennies round,
  With me shall driven in this drift,   *remain/life*
    In bags as they been bound.   2930
    For I think for to deal,
    I vow to God, neither corn nor meal.
    If he have a sheet, he beareth him well,
      Wherein he may be wound.
    [GARCIO *crosses to* MANKIND.]
How farest, Mankind? Art thou dead?
  By God's body, so I ween.   *think*
He is heavier than any lead.
I would he were graven under green.
MANKIND: Abide! I breyd up with mine head!   *wrench*
  What art thou? What wouldest thou mean?   2940
Whither comest thou for good or qwed?   *evil*
  With pain's prick thou dost me tene,   *hurt*
    The sooth for to say.
    Tell me now, so God thee save,
    For whom comest thou, good knave.
    What dost thou here? What wouldest thou have?
      Tell me ere I die.
GARCIO: I am come to have all that thou hast.
  Pounds, parks and every place;
All that thou hast gotten first and last,   2950
  The World hath granted it me of his grace,
    For I have been his page.
    He wot well thou shalt be dead,   *knows*
    Never more to eat bread;
    Therefore he hath for thee red   *determined*
      Who shall have thine heritage.
MANKIND: What devil! Thou art not of my kin;
  Thou didst me never no manner good;

I would liever some nyfte, or some cousin, *nephew*
 Or some man had it of my blood; 2960
  In some stead I would it stood,
 Now shall I in a dale be delve,
 And have no good thereof my selve.
 By God and by His apostles twelve,
  I trow the World be wood. *think/mad*
GARCIO: Ya, ya! Thy part shall be the least.
 Die on! For I am master here.
I shall thee maken a noble feast,
 And then have I done mine devere. *duty*
The World bade me this gold arrest, 2970
 Holt and halls and castle clear.
The World's joy and his gentle jest
 Is now thine, now mine, both far and near.
  Go hence, for this is mine!
 Since thou art dead, and brought of dawe, *deprived of day*
 Of thy death, sir, I am right fawe. *glad*
 Though thou know not the World's law,
  He hath yove me all that was thine. *given*
MANKIND: I pray thee now, since thou this good shall get,
 Tell thy name ere that I go. 2980
GARCIO: Look that thou it not forget:
 My name is "I wot never who."
MANKIND: "I wot never who?" So well say
 Now am I sorry of my life:
I have purchased, many a day,
 Lands and rents with mickle strife;
I have purchased holt and hay,
 Parks and ponds and bowers blithe,
Good gardens, with gryffys gay, *blossoms*
 To mine children and to mine wife, 2990
  In death when I were dight.
 Of my purchase I may be woe;
 For, as thought, it is not so;
 But a gedelynge, "I wot never who," *rascal*
  Hath all that the World me behight.

Now, alas, my life is lack!
    Bitter bales I gin to brew!
Certes, a verse that David spake
    In the Psalter, I find it true:
Tesaurizat, et ignorat cui congregabit ea.[32]   3000
Treasure, treasure, it hath no tak;   *endurance*
    It is other men's, old and new.
Oh, oh, my good goeth all to wrack!
    Sore may Mankind rue.
        God keep me from despair!
    All my good, withouten fail,
    I have gathered with great travail,
    The World hath ordained of his entail   *Fashion*
    I wot never who to be mine heir.
Now, good men, taketh example of me!   3010
    Do for yourself while ye have space!
For many men thus served be
    Through the World in divers place.
I bolne and bleyke in bloody ble,   *swell and blanch in bloody color*
    And as a flower fadeth my face.
To hell I shall both fare and flee
    But God me grant of His grace.
        I die certainly.
        Now my life I have lore.
        Mine heart breaketh. I sigh sore.   3020
        A word may I speak no more.
        I put me in God's mercy.

[MANKIND *dies. His soul comes out from under the bed in the Castle.*]
SOUL: "Mercy!" That was my last tale
    That ever my body was about.
But Mercy help me in this vale,
    Of damning drink sore I me doubt.   *fear*
Body, thou didst brew a bitter bale,
    To thy lusts when gannest loute!   *submit*
Thy sely soul shall been a-kale.   *poor/frozen* (with suffering)
    I pay thy deeds with rewly rowte;   *pitiful* 3030

---

[32] *Tesaurizat . . . ea:* Psalms 39, 6: "He heapeth up riches, and knoweth not who shall gather them."

And all it is for guile.
Ever thou hast been covetous,
Falsely to getten land and house;
To me thou hast brewen a bitter juice,
So weleway the while!
[THE SOUL *turns to the* GOOD ANGEL.]
Now, sweet Angel, what is thy rede?
The right rede thou me reche!   *give*
Now my body is dressed to dead,
Help me now, and be my leech,
Dight thou me from devils dread!   3040
Thy worthy way thou me teach!
I hope that God will helpen and be mine heed,
For "Mercy" was my last speech:
Thus made my body his end.

[*There is a page missing from the manuscript at this point. The text resumes in the middle of a speech by the* BAD ANGEL.]

BAD ANGEL: Witness of all that be about,
Sir Covetise he had him out;   *out* (of the Castle)
Therefore he shall, withouten doubt,
With me to hell pit.
GOOD ANGEL: Yea, alas! and Welawo!
Against Covetise can I not tell.   3050
Reason will I from thee go,   [*for a reason*]
For, wretched soul, thou must to hell!
Covetise, he was thy foe;
He hath thee shapen a shameful schelle.   *dwelling*
Thus hath served many one mo,
Till they be dight to Death's dell,
To bitter bale's bower.
Thou must to pain, by right reason.
With Covetise, for he is chesun,   *the cause*
Thou art trapped full of treason,   3060
But Mercy be thy succour.   *but-unless*
For right well this found he have:

Against Righteousness may I not hold.
Thou must with him to care-full cave,
   For great skills that he hath told.   *reasons*
From thee away I wander and wave;
   For thee I cling in cares cold;
Alone now I must thee leave,
   Whilst thou fallest in fiend's fold,
      In hell to hide and hylle.   *be shut away and buried* 3070
      Righteousness will that thou wend
      Forth away with the fiend;
      But Mercy will to thee send,   *unless*
        Of thee can I no skill.   *do nothing*

SOUL: Alas, Mercy, thou art too long!
   Of sad sorrow now may I sing!
Holy Writ it is full wrong,
   But Mercy pass all thing.   *but-unless*
I am ordained to pains strong;
   In woe is dressed my wonnynge;   *prepared my dwelling* 3080
In hell on hooks I shall hang.
   But Mercy from a well spring,
      This devil will have me away.
      Weleaway! I was full wood
      That I forsook mine Angel Good,
      And with Covetisë stood
        Till that day I should die.

BAD ANGEL: Ya! Why wouldest thou be covetous,
   And draw thee again to sin?
I shall brew thee a bitter juice!   3090
   In bolnynge bonds thou shalt brenne;   *swelling/burn*
In high hell shall be thy house;
   In pick and tear to groan and grin,
Thou shalt lie drenkelyd as a mouse.   *drowned*
   There may no man therefrom thee werne   *defend*
      For that ilke will.   *same*
      That day the ladies thou forsook
      And to my counsel thou thee took,
      Thou were better an-hangen on hook

   Upon a gibbet hill.   *gallows* 3100
Farter foul! Thou shalt be a-frayed   *beaten*
  Till thou be fretted and all for-bled;   *bloodied*
Foul might thou be dismayed
  That thou shalt thus be overled;   *overcome*
For Covetise thou hast assayed,
  In bitter bales thou shalt be bred;   *roasted*
All mankind may be well payed
  When Covetise maketh thee a-dread.
    With raps I thee ring.
   We shall to hell, both two,   3110
   And bide forever in inferno;
   Nulla est redempcio,[33]
    For no kynnys thing.   *natural*
Now dagge we hence a dog trot;   *jog*
  In my dungeon I shall thee dere;   *vex*
On thee is many a sinful spot;
  Therefore this shame I shall thee schere   *shear* (punish?)
    When thou comest to my nest.
   Why wouldest thou—schrewe shalt never thee—   *condemn*
   But in thy life do after me?   3120
   And thy Good Angel, he taught thee
    Always to the best.
Ya! But thou wouldest him not leve;   *believe*
  To Covetise always thou drew;
Therefore shalt thou evil preve;   *prove*
  That foul sin thy soul slew.
I shall fonde thee to grieve,
  And put thee in pain's plough.
Have this! and evil might thou scheve,   *prosper*
  For thou saidest never, "enow, enow":   3130
    Thus lache I thee thus low.   *strike*
   Though thou kewe as a cat,   *mew*
   For thy covetise have thou that!
   I shall thee bunche with my bat,   *beat*
    And ronge thee on a row.   *hit*

[33] *Nulla est redempcio:* None is redeemed.

Lo! Sinful tiding,
Boy, on thy back I bring.
Speedily thou spring;
Thy placebo I shall sing;   *placebo: I will make satisfaction*
   To devil's dell   3140
   I shall bear thee to hell.
   [*to the audience*]
   I will not dwell.
   Have a good day! I go to hell!
   [THE BAD ANGEL *carries* THE SOUL *on his back to Belial's scaffold.
   Enter the four daughters of God;* RIGHTEOUSNESS, MERCY, PEACE
   and JUSTICE.]
MERCY: A moan I heard of "Mercy" meve.   *beg*
   And to me, Mercy, can cry and call;
But if it have mercy, sore it shall me grieve,   *unless*
   For else it shall to hell fall.
Righteousness, my sister cheve,   *dear*
   This ye heard, so did we all:
For we were made friends leve   *dear* 3150
   When the Jews proffered Christ eysyl and gall   *vinegar*
      On the Good Friday.
      God granted that remission,
      Mercy and absolution,
      Through virtue of His passion,
         That no man should be said nay.
Therefore, my sisters, Righteousness,
   Peace and Truth, to you I tell,
When man cryeth Mercy and will not cease,
   Mercy shall be his washing well: 3160
      Witness of holy kirk.   *church*
      For the least drop of blood
      That God bled on the rood,
      It had been satisfaction good
         For all Mankind's work.
JUSTICE: Sister, ye say to me a good skill,
   That Mercy passeth Man's misdeed;
But take Mercy, who-so will,

He must it ask with love and dread;
And every man that will fulfill   3170
　The deadly sins and foul misdeed,
To grant him mercy, me thinketh no skill;   *unreasonable*
　And therefore, sister, you I rede,
　　Let him abide his misdeed;
　　For, though he lie in hell and stink,
　　It shall me never over-think: *trouble*
　　　As he hath brewen, let him drink;
　　　The devil shall quit him his meed.
　　　　Unus quisque suum honus portabit.[34]
Trow ye that when a man shall die,   3180
　Then, though that he Mercy crave,
That anon he shall have Mercy?
　Nay, nay, so Christ me save!
For, should no man do good
　All the days of his life,
But hope of Mercy by the rood,
　Should make both war and strife,
　　And turn to great grievance.
　　Who-so in hope doth any deadly sin
　　To his life's end, and will not blynne,   *cease* 3190
　　　Rightfully then shall he win
　　　Christ's great vengeance.
TRUTH:　Righteousness, my sister free,
　Your judgement is good and true;
In good faith, so thinketh me;
　Let him his own deeds rue.
I am Veritas, and true will be
　In word and work to old and new.
Was never man, in fault of me,
　Damned nor saved, but it were due: 3200
　　I am ever at man's end.
　　When body and soul parten a-twin,
　　Then weigh I his good deeds and his sin:
　　　And whether of him be more or mynne,   *less*

---

[34] *Unus . . . portabit:* Galatians 6, 5: "For every man shall bear his own burden."

He shall it right soon find.
For I am Truth, and Truth will bare,
As great God himself us bid.
There shall nothing the soul dere   *harm*
But sin that the body did.
Since that he died in that covetous sin,   3210
I, Truth, will that he go to pain.
Of that sin could he not blynne;   *cease*
Therefore he shall his soul tyne   *lose*
          To the pit of hell.
     Else should we, both Truth and Righteousness,
     Be put to our mickle distress,
     And every man shall be the worse
          That thereof might hear tell.

PEACE: Peace, my sister Verity!
     I pray you, Righteousness, be still!   3220
Let no man by you damned be,
     Nor deem ye no man to hell.
He is akin to us three,
     Though he have now not all his will;
For His love that died on tree,
     Let save Mankind from all peril
          And shield him from mischance.
     If ye twain put him to distress,
     It should make great heaviness
     Between us twain, Mercy and Peace;   3230
          And that were great grievance.
Righteousness and Truth, do by my rede!
     And, Mercy, go we to yon high place!
          [*She points to God's scaffold.*]
We shall inform the high Godhead,
     And pray Him to deem this case.
Ye shall tell Him your intent
     Of Truth and Righteousness;
And we shall pray that His judgement
     May pass by us, Mercy and Peace.
          All four, now go we hence   3240

Witly to the trinity;   *quickly*
And there shall we soon see
What His judgement shall be,
    Withouten any defence.   *hindrance, i.e. assuredly*
[*They cross to God's scaffold.*]
TRUTH: Hail, God Almight!
  We come, thy daughters, in sight,
  Truth, Mercy and Right,
  And Peace, peaceable in fight.
MERCY: We come to preve   *determine*
  If Man, that was Thee full leve,   *dear* 3250
  If he shall cheve   *go*
  To hell or heaven, by Thy leave.
JUSTICE: I, Righteousness,
  Thy daughter, as I guess,
  Let me, nevertheless,
  At Thy doom put me in pres.   *judgement/include me*
PEACE: Peaceable king!
  I, Peace, thy daughter yinge,   *young*
  Hear my praying
  When I pray Thee, Lord, of a thing.   3260
GOD: Welcome, in fere,   *all together*
  Brighter than blossoms on brere!   *briar*
  My daughters dear,
  Come forth and stand ye me near.
TRUTH: Lord, as Thou art king of kings, crowned with crown,
    As Thou lovest me, Truth, Thy daughter dear,
  Let never me, Truth, to fall a-down,
    My faithful Father, *sans* peer!
      Quia veritate dilexisti.[35]
For in all truth standeth Thy renown,   3270
  Thy faith, Thy hope, and Thy power.
Let it be seen, Lord, now at Thy doom,
  That I may have my true prayer
    To do truth to Mankind.
      For if Mankind be dempte by right,   *judged*

---

[35] *Quia . . . dilexisti:* Because you have esteemed the truth.

And not by Mercy, most of might,—
Hear my truth, Lord, I Thee plight—
   In prison Man shall be pynyde.   *tortured*
Lord, how should Mankind be saved
   Since he died in deadly sin,   3280
And all Thy commandments he depraved,
   And of false Covetous he would never blynne?
      Aurum sitisti; aurum bibisti.[36]
The more he had, the more he craved,
   While the life left him within.
But he be damned, I am a-bavyd,   *astonished*
   That Truth should come of righteous kin,
      And I am Thy daughter Truth.
         Though he cried "Mercy," *moriendo,*
         Nimis tarde penitendo;   3290
         Talem mortem reprehendo:[37]
            Let him drink as he breweth.
Late repentance, if Man save should,
   Whether he wrought well or wickedness,
Then every man would be bold
   To trespass, in trust of forgiveness.
For sin in hope is damned, I hold;
   Forgiven is never his trespass.
He sinneth in the Holy Ghost many fold;
   That sin, Lord, thou wilt not release,   3300
      In this world nor in the other,
         Quia veritas manet in eternum,
         Tendit homo ad infernum;
         Nunquam venit ad supernum,[38]
      Though he were my brother.
For man on molde has wealth and weal,   *earth*
   Lust and liking in all his life,
Teaching, preaching, in every sele;   *time*
   But he forgetteth the Lord belyve,   *quickly*

---

[36] *Aurum . . . bibisti:* He has thirsted for gold, he has drunk gold.
[37] *Moriendo . . . reprehendo:* in dying,/too late in repenting;/I censure such a death.
[38] *Quia . . . supernum:* Because truth remains in eternity,/man goes to hell;/He comes never to heaven.

High of heart, happe and hele,   *fortune and health* 3310
  Gold and silver, child and wife;
Dainty drink at meat and meal;
    Unnethe, Thee to thank, he can not kyth   *hardly/show*
      In any manner thing.
    When man's wealth ginneth awake,
    Full soon, Lord, thou art forsake.
    As he hath brewen and bake,
      Truth will that he drink.
For if Man have mercy and grace,
  Then I, thy daughter Sothfastness,   3320
At thy doom shall have no place,
  But be put a-back by wrong duress.
Lord, let me never flee Thy fair face,   *go from*
  To make my power any less.
I pray Thee, Lord, as I have space,
  Let Mankind have due distress,
    In hell fire to be brent.   *burned*
    In pain look he be still,
    Lord, if it be Thy will,
    Or else I have no skill   3330
      By Thy true judgement.
MERCY: *O pater maxime, et Deus tocius consolacionis,*
    Qui consolatur nos in omni tribulacione nostra![39]
Oh Thou Father, of mights most,
  Merciful God in Trinity!
I am Thy daughter, well Thou woste,   *knowest*
  And Mercy from heaven Thou broughtest free.
Show me Thy grace in every coast!
  In this case my comfort be!
Let me, Lord, never be lost   3340
  At Thy judgement, how-so it be,
    Of Mankind.
    Ne had Man's sin never come in case,
    I, Mercy, should never in earth had place;

[39] *O Pater . . . nostra:* Cp. II Corinthians 1, 3–4: O greatest father and "God of all comfort, who comforteth us in all our tribulation."

Therefore grant me, Lord, Thy grace,
   That Mankind may me find.
And Mercy, Lord, have on this Man
   After Thy mercy, that mickle is,
Unto Thy grace that he be ta'en,
   Of Thy mercy that he not miss!   3350
As Thou descended from Thy throne
   And lieth in a maiden's womb iwis,
Incarnate was in blood and bone,
   Let Mankind come to Thy bliss,
      As Thou art King of Heaven!
     For worldly vainglory
     He hath been full sorry
     Punished in purgatory
      For all the sins seven.
        Si pro Peccato vetus Adam non cecidisset,   3360
        Mater pro nato nunquam gravidata fuisset.[40]
Ne had Adam sinned here before,
   And Thy hests in paradise been offent,   *commands/broken*
Never of Thy mother Thou shouldest have been bore,
   From heaven to earth to have been sent.
But thirty winter here, and more,
   Bounden and beaten and all to-schent,   *battered*
Scorned and scourged, sad and sore,
   And on the rood newly rent,   *pitifully torn*
      Passus sub Pilato Poncio. [40]   3370
     As Thou hung on the cross,
     On high Thou madest a voice,
     Man's health, the gospel says,
      When Thou saidest "*scicio.*"   *I thirst*
Then the Jews that were unquert   *unkind*
   Dressed Thee drink, eysyl and gall;   *vinegar*
It to taste Thou might not styrt,   *avoid*
   But said, "*consummatum est*" was all.   *it is finished*

[40] *Si pro . . . fuisset:* If old Adam had not fallen through sin, your mother would never have been heavy with child.
[41] *Passus. . . Poncio:* "Suffered under Pontius Pilate."

A knight, with a spear so smert,   *smart*
  When Thou forgave thy foemen thrall,   3380
He stonge the Lord unto the heart.   *pierced*
  Then water and blood gan out wall,   *flow*
    Aqua baptisimatis et sanguis redempcionis.[42]
    The water of baptoum,   *baptism*
    The blood of redemption,
    That from Thine heart ran down
      Est causa salvacionis.   *is the cause of salvation*
Lord, Thou that Man hath done more miss than good,
  If he die in very contrition,
Lord, the least drop of Thy blood   3390
  For his sin maketh satisfaction.
As Thou diedest, Lord, on the rood,
  Grant me my petition!
Let me, Mercy, be his food,
  And grant him Thy salvation.
    Quia dixisti " misericordiam amabo."[43]
    Mercy shall I sing and say,
    And *misere* shall I pray
    For Mankind ever and ay;
      Misericordis domini in eternum cantabo.[44]   3400
JUSTICE: Righteous king, Lord God almighty!
I am Thy daughter Righteousness.
Thou hast loved me ever, day and night,
  As well as other, as I guess:
    Justicias Dominus justicia dilexit.[45]
If thou Man's kind from pain acquit,
  Thou dost against Thine own process.
Let him in prison be pight   *put*
  For his sin and wickedness,
    Of a boon I Thee pray.   3410
    Full often he hath Thee, Lord, forsake,
    And to the devil he hath him take;

[42] *Aqua . . . redempcionis:* The water of baptism and the blood of redemption.
[43] *Quia. . . amabo:* Because you have said "I will love mercy."
[44] *Misericordia . . . cantabo:* I will sing the mercy of God in eternity.
[45] *Justicias . . . dilexisti:* The just God has loved justice.

Let him lien in hell lake,
Damned forever and ay.
Quia Deum, qui se genuit, dereliquit.[46]
For when Man to the World was born,
He was brought to holy kirk,
Faithly followd in the fount stone,   *baptised*
And washed from original sin so dark;
Satanas he forsook as his fone,   *foe* 3420
All his pomp and all his work,
And hight to serve Thee alone;   *promised*
To keep Thy commandments he should not irk,   *be loath*
Sicut Iusti Tui.   *as your law requires*
But when he was come to man's estate,
All his behests he then forgot:
He is worthy be damned for that,
Quia oblitus est Deum creatoris sui.[47]
For he hath forgotten Thee that him wrought,
And formedest him like Thine own face,   3430
And with Thy precious blood him bought,
And in this world Thou gave him space.
All Thy benefits he set at nought,
But took him to the devil's trace;   *course*
The Flesh, the World, was most in his thought,
And purpose to please them in every place,
So grimly on ground.
I pray Thee, Lord lovely,
Of Man have no mercy!
But, dear Lord, let him lie!   3440
In hell let him be bound!
Man hath forsake the King of Heaven
And his Good Angel's governance,
And soiled his soul with sins seven
By his Bad Angel's cumbrance.
Virtues he hath put full evil away
When Covetise gan him advance;

[46] *Quia . . . dereliquit:* Because he forsook the God who begat Himself.
[47] *Quia . . . sui:* Because he has forgotten the God who created him.

He wende that he should a'lived ay,   *thought*
  Till Death tripped him on his dance;
    He lost his wits five.   3450
    Over late he called confession;
    Over light was his contrition;
    He made never satisfaction;
      Damn him to hell belyve!
For if Thou take Man's soul to Thee
  Against Thy Righteousness,
Thou dost wrong, Lord, to Truth and me,
  And puttest us from our devnesse.   *right*
Lord, let us never from Thee flee,
  Nor strain us never in stress,   *constrain* 3460
But let Thy doom be by us three,
  Mankind in hell to press,
    Lord, I Thee beseech.
    For Righteousness dwells ever sure,
    To deem Man after his deserviture;
    For to be damned, it is his ure;   *destiny*
      On Man I cry wreche.   *vengeance*
      Letabitur justus cum viderit vindictam.[48]
MERCY: Mercy, my sister Righteousness!
  Thou shape Mankind no schonde!   [let] *thou*/*harm* 3470
Leve sister, let be thy dress!   *dear*/*plea*
  To save Man, let us fonde!   *endeavor*
For if Man be damned to hell darkness,
  Then might I wringen mine honde,   *hand*
That ever my state should be less,
  My freedom to make bond;
    Mankind is of our kin.
    For I, Mercy, pass all thing
    That God made at the beginning,
    And I am His daughter yinge: *young* 3480
      Dear sister, let be thy din!
      Et misericordia eius super omnia opera eius.[49]

---

[48] *Letabitur . . . vindictam:* The just man will rejoice when he sees punishment.
[49] *Et misericordia . . . eius:* Psalm 145, 9: "And his tender mercies are over all his works."

Of Mankind ask thou never wreche   *vengeance*
  By day nor by night,
For God Himself hath been his leech,
  Of His merciful might;
To me He gan him betake,
  Beside all His right.
For him will I pray and preach,
  To get him free respite,   3490
      And my sister Peace.
    For His mercy is without beginning,
    And shall be withouten ending,
    As David sayeth, that worthy king,
      In scripture is no les.   *lying*
        Et misericordia eius a progenie in progenies, et cetera.[50]
TRUTH: Mercy is Mankind not worthy,
  David though thou record and read;
For he would never the hungry
  Neither cloth nor feed,   3500
Nor drink give to the thirsty,
  Nor poor men help at need;
For if he did none of these, forthy   *therefore*
  In heaven he getteth no meed;
      So sayeth the gospel.
    For he hath been unkind
    To lame and to blind,
    In hell he shall be pynde: *tortured*
      So is reason and skill.
PEACE: Peaceable King in majesty,   3510
  I, Peace, Thy daughter, ask Thee a boon
Of Man, how-so it be.
  Lord, grant me mine asking soon,
That I may evermore dwell with Thee,
  As I have ever yet done;
And let me never from Thee flee,
  Specially at Thy doom
      Of Man, Thy creature.

[50] *Et misericordia ... progenies:* And His mercy extends from generation to generations.

Though my sisters, Right and Truth,
　　Of Mankind have none ruth,　　　　　　　　　　3520
Mercy and I full sore moveth,
　　　To cacche him to our cure.　　　　　　　　*take/charge*
For when Thou madest earth and heaven,
　　Ten orders of angels to be in bliss,
Lucifer, lighter than the levyn,　　　　　　　　　*brighter/rest*
　　Till when he sinned, he fell iwis;
To restore that place full even,
　　Thou madest Mankind with this,
To fill that place that I did nevene;　　　　　　　　*mention*
　　If Thy will be reason it is,　　　　　　　　　　3530
　　　　In peace and rest,
　　　Among Thine angels bright,
　　　To worship Thee in sight.[51]
　　　Grant, Lord God almight,
　　　　And so I hold it best!
For though Truth, that is my sister dear,
　　Argueth that Man should dwell in woe,
And Righteousness, with her power,
　　Would fain and fast that it were so,
But Mercy and I, Peace, both in fere,　　　　　*together* 3540
　　Shall never in faith accord thereto;
Then should we ever discord here,
　　And stand at bate for friend or foe,　　　　　*discord*
　　　And ever at distance.　　　　　　　　　*disagreement*
　　　Therefore my counsel is,
　　　Let us four sisters kiss,
　　　And restore Man to bliss,
　　　　As was God's ordinance.
For if ye, Right and Truth, should have your will,
　　I, Peace, and Mercy should ever have travest;　　*injury* 3550
Then us between had been a great peril
　　That our joys in heaven should have been lest;　*lost or lessened*
Therefore, gentle sisters, consenteth me till,

[51] To restore . . . sight: To restore Lucifer's place you made Mankind; and if your will is to be accomplished Mankind must come to peace and rest, to worship before you among the bright angels.

Else between ourself should never be rest.
Where should be love and charity, let there come no ill!
Look our joys be perfect, and that I hold the best,
   In heavenly bliss.
   For there is peace withouten war;
   There is rest withouten fear;
   There is charity withouten dere: *difficulty* 3560
      Our Father's will so is:
         Hic pax, hic bonitas, hic laus, hic semper honestas.[52]
Therefore, gentle sisters, at one word,
   Truth, Right and Mercy hende,   *courteous*
Let us stand at one accord,
   At peace withouten end.
Let love and charity be at our board,
   All vengeance away wend,
To heaven that Man may be restored;
   Let us be all his friend   3570
      Before our Father's face!
   We shall devoutly pray,
   At dreadful doomsday,
   And I shall for us say
      That Mankind shall have grace.
         Et tuam, Deus, deposamus pietatem, ut ei tribuere digneris
         lucidas et qui[etas] mansiones.[53]
Lord, for Thy pity and that pes   *peace (i.e. death)*
   Thou sufferest in Thy passion—
Bounden and beaten without les,   *cease*
   From the foot to the crown,   3580
Tanquam ovis ductus es;[54]
   When *gutte sanguinis* ran a-down,   *drops of blood*
Yet the Jews would not cease,
   But on Thy head they thrust a crown,
      And on the cross Thee nailed—
      As piteously as Thou were pynyd,   *tormented*

[52] *Hic . . . bonestas:* Here peace, here goodness, here glory, here virtue forever.
[53] *Et tuam . . . mansiones:* We intreat your mercy, O God, so that you will consider it fitting to grant to him bright and peaceful mansions.
[54] *Tanquam . . . . es:* You were led like a sheep.

Have mercy of Mankind,
So that he may find
Our prayer may him avail.

GOD: *Ego cogito cogitaciones pacis, non afflicionis.*[55]   3590
Fair fall thee, Peace, my daughter dear!
On thee I think, and on Mercy.
Since ye accorded beeth all in fere,   *together*
My judgement I will give you by,
Not after deserving to do reddere,   *harshness*
To damn Mankind to tormentry,
But bring him to My bliss full clear,
In heaven to dwell endlessly,
At your prayer forthy.
To make My bliss perfyth,   *perfect* 3600
I menge with My most might,   *mix*
All peace, some truth and some right,
And most of My mercy.

Misericordia Domini plena est in terra. Amen![56]
My daughters hende,   *gentle*
Lovely and lusty to lende,   *remain*
Go you to yon fiend,
And from him take Mankind!
Bring him to Me!
And set him here by My knee,   3610
In heaven to be,
In bliss with gamen and glee.

TRUTH: We shall fulfill
Thine hests, as reason and skill,   *right and proper*
From yon ghost grylle,   *horrid*
Mankind to bring Thee till.

(*They cross to the* BAD ANGEL *on Belial's scaffold.*)

PEACE: Ah, thou foul wight!
Let go that soul so tyth!   *quickly*
In heaven light,   *bright*
Mankind soon shall be pight.   *set* 3620

---

[55] *Ego . . . afflicionis:* Cp. Jeremiah 29, 11: "I think thoughts of peace, not of evil."
[56] *Misericordia . . . terra:* The earth is filled with the mercy of God.

JUSTICE: Go thou to hell,
  Thou devil bold as a bell,
  Therein to dwell,
  In brass and brimstone to well.   *boil*
        (*Leading* THE SOUL *of* MANKIND, *they cross to God's scaffold
        and ascend to His throne.*)
MERCY: Lo, here Mankind,
  Lighter than leaf is on linde,   *lime tree*
  That hath been pynyd!   *tortured*
  Thy mercy, Lord, let him find!
GOD: *Sicut sintille in medio maris,*[57]
  My mercy, Mankind, give I thee.   3630
      Come, sit at My right hand!
  Full well have I loved thee,
      Unkind though I thee found.
  As a spark of fire in the sea,
      My mercy is sin-quenchand.   *quenching*
  Thou hast cause to love me
      Aboven all thing in land,
          And keep my commandment.
      If thou Me love and dread,
          Heaven shall be thy meed;   3640
      My face thee shall feed:
          This is Mine judgement.
*Ego occidam et vivificabo percuciam et sanabo; et nemo est qui de manu
mea possit eruere.*[58]
  King, kaiser, knight and champion,
      Pope, patriarch, priest and prelate in pes,   *peace*
  Duke doughtiest in deed by dale and by down,
      Little and mickle, the more and the less,
  All the states of the world, is at mine renown;   *control*
      To me shall they give accompt at my dygne des.   *worthy throne*
  When Michael his horn bloweth at my dread doom,   3650

---

[57] *Sicut . . . maris:* Like a spark in the middle of the sea.
[58] *Ego . . . eruere:* Deuteronomy 32, 39: "I kill and I make alive; I wound and I heal; neither is there any that
can deliver out of my hand."

The count of their conscience shall putten them in press,
    And yield a reckoning
   Of their space how they have spent;
   And of their true talent
   At my great judgement,
    An answer shall me bring.

Ecce! requiram gregem meum de manu pastorum.[59]

And I shall inquire of my flock and of their pasture,   *pastor*
   How they have lived, and led their people subject.
The good on the right side shall stand full sure;   3660
   The bad on the left side, there shall I set.
The seven deeds of mercy, who-so had ure   *custom*
   To fill—the hungry for to give meat,
Or drink to thirsty; the naked, vesture;
   The poor or the pilgrim, home for to fette,   *fetch*
    Thy neighbor that hath need;
    Who-so doth mercy to his might
    To the sick, or in prison pight,
    He doth to me—I shall him quit: *reward*
     Heaven bliss shall be his meed.   3670

Et qui bona egerunt, ibunt in vitam eternum; qui vero mala, in ignem
eternum.[50]

And they that well do in this world here, wealth shall
     a-wake;   *reward*
   In heaven they shall heynd be in bounty and in bliss.   *exalted*
And they that evil do, they shall to hell lake,
   In bitter balës to be burnt: my judgement it is.
My vertus in heaven then shall they quake: *power/fear*
   There is no wight in this world that may 'scape this.
All men example here-at may take,
   To maintain the good and menden their miss.
[*He turns to the audience.*]
     Thus endeth our games.   *play* 3680

---

[59] *Ecce . . . pastorum:* Behold! I inquire of my flock at the hand of the shepherds.
[60] *Et qui . . . eternum:* And whosoever does good will go to eternal life; whosoever does evil, assuredly to
eternal fire.

To save you from sinning,
Ever at the beginning
Think on your last ending!
   Te, Deum, laudamus!

✳ *EVERYMAN*

(*c. 1485*)

Even if the teachers and editors who were responsible for the great popularity of *Everyman* had read the other moralities with the sympathetic eye possessed by some of their successors, it is difficult to imagine them having selected any other play to enjoy the privileged position that this one maintains. The reader of *Everyman*, Christian or not, is immediately touched by two things: the dignity and clarity of the langauge and the naked terror experienced by the central figure.

The play seems to have come along at an especially propitious moment in the history of the language. It is free of the fundamental difficulty of its predecessors, which are written in what is, for all practical purposes, Middle English. And it is equally free of the crabbed quirky sort of speech that the Elizabethan morality writers loved to wallow in; not to mention its freedom from the prosodic excesses of both. It is so singularly free from decoration of all kinds that one can apply to it the high compliment of the middle twentieth century—it "tells it like it is."

What "it is" is loneliness (our word is "alienation") and death, and the joyful knowledge of a soul safe in heaven. The playwright contrives to bring us much closer in feeling to his hero than any other playwright by shaping his play as a single, sustained race against death. This is a thriller, and we are to understand that

Everyman wins, that is, attains his release, by a hair. To add to the poignancy of his plight, the writer has forced him to undergo the desertion of his supporters not once, but twice. First his false friends beg off, then, when he, and we too, have built a sense of real confidence (during the penitential sequence), we are shocked back to reality by the sudden desertion of Everyman by his personal attributes.

This is a Catholic Humanist play, akin in spirit as well as in time and in clarity of language, to Medwall's *Nature*. It is Catholic (perhaps even polemic) in its insistence on the sole efficacy of Good Deeds. It is Humanist in its crucial placement of Knowledge (that is, reason) as the pivot that turns Everyman toward salvation, and in its attack upon the corrupt clergy.

Everyman is also unique in several respects: alone among the moralities it is without the ribald humor of the Vice characters (if a few lines of Fellowship's be excepted); it is the only play in which the central figure enacts a sacramental penance on stage (11.611–618); and it has a way all its own of dramatizing Everyman's whole life while seeming to give us only its last hours. The *order* of those he petitions for help—Fellowship to Goods to Knowledge—is in fact a review of the condition of the human individual in each of the traditional Three Ages of Man. Fellowship represents the sins of the flesh, Goods those of the world, and knowledge brings in the last Age, that of repentance and death.

The play has of course been printed in innumerable editions. Our text is substantially the modernized spelling text of R. Heilman, *An Anthology of English Drama Before Shakespeare,* New York, 1955, checked with John Skot's edition of 1530. In a few instances the readings of Richard Pynson's edition are preferred to Skot's and are so noted.

EVERYMAN

Here beginneth a treatise how the High Father of Heaven sendeth Death to summon every creature to come and give account of their lives in this world, and is in manner of a moral play.

MESSENGER: I pray you all give your audience,
　　And hear this matter with reverence,
　　By figure a moral play—
　　The *Summoning of Everyman* called it is,
　　That of our lives and ending shows
　　How transitory we be all day.
　　This matter is wondrous precious,
　　But the intent of it is more gracious,
　　And sweet to bear away.
　　The story saith:—Man, in the beginning,　　　　10
　　Look well, and take good heed to the ending,
　　Be you never so gay!
　　Ye think sin in the beginning full sweet,
　　Which in the end causeth the soul to weep,
　　When the body lieth in clay.
　　Here shall you see how Fellowship and Jollity,
　　Both Strength, Pleasure, and Beauty,
　　Will fade from thee as flower in May.
　　For ye shall hear how our Heaven King
　　Calleth Everyman to a general reckoning.　　　　20
　　Give audience, and hear what he doth say.
　　　　(GOD *speaketh*.)
GOD: I perceive, here in my majesty,
　　How that all creatures be to me unkind,
　　Living without dread in worldly prosperity.
　　Of ghostly sight the people be so blind,　　　　*spiritual*
　　Drowned in sin, they know me not for their God.
　　In worldly riches is all their mind,
　　They fear not my rightwiseness, the sharp rod;
　　My love that I showed when I for them died
　　They forget clean, and shedding of my blood red;　　30

113

I hanged between two, it cannot be denied;
To get them life I suffered to be dead;
I healed their feet, with thorns hurt was my head.[1]
I could do no more than I did, truly;
And now I see the people do clean forsake me.
They use the seven deadly sins damnable;
As pride, covetise, wrath and lechery,
Now in the world be made commendable;
And thus they leave of angels the heavenly company.
Every man liveth so after his own pleasure,   40
And yet of their life they be nothing sure.
I see the more that I them forbear
The worse they be from year to year;
All that liveth appaireth fast.   *worsens*
Therefore I will, in all the haste,
Have a reckoning of every man's person;
For, and I leave the people thus alone   *and = if*
In their life and wicked tempests,
Verily they will become much worse than beasts;
For now one would by envy another up eat;   50
Charity they all do clean forget.
I hoped well that every man
In my glory should make his mansion,
And thereto I had them all elect;
But now I see, like traitors deject,
They thank me not for the pleasure that I to them meant,
Nor yet for their being that I them have lent.
I proffered the people great multitude of mercy,
And few there be that asketh it heartily;
They be so cumbered with worldly riches,   60
That needs on them I must do justice,
On every man living, without fear.
Where art thou, Death, thou mighty messenger?[2]
            [*Enter* DEATH.]

---

[1] Here we have a graphic assertion of Trinitarianism—God is being both God the Father and God the Son
[2] God's language in this passage recalls the *Genesis* accounts of both the Fall of Man and the episode of Noah and the Flood, but when Death arrives on earth he is quite clearly in 15th century England. It is characteristic of the morality thus to force the audience to live in different planes of time simultaneously.

DEATH: Almighty God, I am here at your will,
  Your commandment to fulfil.
GOD: Go thou to Everyman,
  And show him, in my name,
  A pilgrimage he must on him take.[3]
  Which he in no wise may escape;
  And that he bring with him a sure reckoning   70
  Without delay or any tarrying.
DEATH: Lord, I will in the world go run over all,
  And cruelly out search both great and small.
        [*Exit* GOD.][4]
  Every man will I beset that liveth beastly
  Out of God's laws, and dreadeth not folly.
  He that loveth riches I will strike with my dart,
  His sight to blind, and from heaven to depart,
  Except that alms be his good friend,
  In hell for to dwell, world without end.
  Lo, yonder I see Everyman walking;   80
  Full little he thinketh on my coming;
  His mind is on fleshly lusts and his treasure;
  And great pain it shall cause him to endure
  Before the Lord, Heaven King.
  Everyman, stand still! Whither art thou going
  Thus gaily? Hast thou thy Maker forgot?
EVERYMAN: Why askest thou?
  Wouldst thou wete?   *know*
DEATH: Yea, sir, I will show you;
  In great haste I am sent to thee   90
  From God out of his Majesty.
EVERYMAN: What, sent to me?[5]
DEATH: Yea, certainly.

[3] The Pilgrimage is perhaps the richest of all metaphors for human life. The ultimate Judaeo-Christian source is probably *Hebrews* 11, 13. See also *The Pilgrimage of Life* by S. C. Chew (New Haven, 1962), and an unpublished dissertation of E. T. Schell, *The Pilgrim of Life in English Renaissance Drama*, University of California, 1966.
[4] It is conceivable that instead of leaving God takes up a position at the back of the playing space and oversees the rest of the play.
[5] The following passages sets Everyman for us as a concrete individual character, as he tries every known "dodge" to escape the inescapable.

Though thou have forgot him here,
He thinketh on thee in the heavenly sphere,
As, ere we depart, thou shalt know.
EVERYMAN: What desireth God of me?
DEATH: That shall I show thee;
A reckoning he will needs have
Without any longer respite.   100
EVERYMAN: To give a reckoning longer leisure I crave;
This blind matter troubleth my wit.
DEATH: On thee thou must take a long journey;
Therefore thy book of count with thee thou bring;
For turn again thou can not by no way.
And look thou be sure to thy reckoning,
For before God thou shalt answer and show
Thy many bad deeds, and good but a few,
How thou hast spent thy life, and in what wise,
Before the Chief Lord of paradise.   110
Have ado [that] we were in that way,   *bestir yourself*
For, wete thou well, thou shalt make none attorney.
EVERYMAN: Full unready I am such reckoning to give.
I know thee not. What messenger art thou?
DEATH: I am Death, that no man dreadeth.
For every man I 'rest, and no man spareth;   *arrest*
For it is God's commandment
That all to me should be obedient.
EVERYMAN: O Death! thou comest when I had thee least in
mind!
In thy power it lieth me to save,   120
Yet of my goods will I give thee, if thou will be kind;
Yea, a thousand pound shalt thou have,
If thou defer this matter till another day.
DEATH: Everyman, it may not be, by no way!
I set not by gold, silver, nor riches,
Nor by pope, emperor, king, duke, nor princes.
For, and I would receive gifts great,
All the world I might get;
But my custom is clean contrary.

I give thee no respite. Come hence, and not tarry. 130
EVERYMAN: Alas! shall I have no longer respite!
I may say Death giveth no warning.
To think on thee, it maketh my heart sick,
For all unready is my book of reckoning.
But twelve year and I might have abiding,
My counting-book I would make so clear,
That my reckoning I should not need to fear.
Wherefore, Death, I pray thee, for God's mercy,
Spare me till I be provided of remedy.
DEATH: Thee availeth not to cry, weep, and pray; 140
But haste thee lightly that thou were gone that journey,
And prove thy friends if thou can.   *test*
For wete thou well the tide abideth no man;
And in the world each living creature
For Adam's sin must die of nature.
EVERYMAN: Death, if I should this pilgrimage take,
And my reckoning surely make,
Show me, for saint charity,   *saint = holy*
Should I not come again shortly?
DEATH: No, Everymen; and thou be once there, 150
Thou mayst never more come here,
Trust me verily.
EVERYMAN: O gracious God, in the high seat celestial,
Have mercy on me in this most need!
Shall I have no company from this vale terrestrial
Of mine acquaintance that way me to lead?
DEATH: Yea, if any be so hardy,
That would go with thee and bear thee company.
Hie thee that thou were gone to God's magnificence,
Thy reckoning to give before his presence. 160
What! weenest thou thy life is given thee,   *do you think*
And thy worldly goods also?
EVERYMAN: I had weened so, verily.
DEATH: Nay, nay; it was but lent thee;
For, as soon as thou art gone,
Another a while shall have it, and then go therefrom

Even as thou hast done.
Everyman, thou art mad! Thou hast thy wits five,   *five senses*
And here on earth will not amend thy life;
For suddenly I do come.   170
EVERYMAN: O wretched caitiff! whither shall I flee,
That I might 'scape endless sorrow?
Now, gentle Death, spare me till tomorrow,
That I may amend me
With good advisement.
DEATH: Nay, thereto I will not consent,
Nor no man will I respite,
But to the heart suddenly I shall smite
Without any advisement.
And now out of thy sight I will me hie;
See thou make thee ready shortly,
For thou mayst say this is the day
That no man living may 'scape away.
            [*Exit* DEATH.]
EVERYMAN: Alas! I may well weep with sighs deep.
Now have I no manner of company
To help me in my journey and me to keep;
And also my writing is full unready.
How shall I do now for to excuse me?
I would to God I had never been gete![6]
To my soul a full great profit it had be;   190
For now I fear pains huge and great.
The time passeth; Lord, help, that all wrought.
For though I mourn it availeth naught.
The day passeth, and is almost a-go;
I wot not well what for to do.
To whom were I best my complaint to make?
What if I to Fellowship thereof spake,
And showed him of this sudden chance?
For in him is all mine affiance,
We have in the world so many a day   200

---

[6] In the popular tradition of religious literature, the wish to repudiate one's existence is a "tag," identifying the onset of the state of despair, in a sense the deadliest of all sins.

Been good friends in sport and play.
I see him yonder, certainly;
I trust that he will bear me company;
Therefore to him will I speak to ease my sorrow.
Well met, good Fellowship, and good morrow!
     (FELLOWSHIP *speaketh*.)

FELLOWSHIP. Everyman, good morrow, by this day!
  Sir, why lookest thou so piteously?
  If any thing be amiss, I pray thee me say,
  That I may help to remedy.

EVERYMAN: Yea, good Fellowship, yea,   210
  I am in great jeopardy.

FELLOWSHIP: My true friend, show to me your mind;
  I will not forsake thee to my life's end
  In the way of good company.

EVERYMAN: That was well spoken, and lovingly.

FELLOWSHIP: Sir, I must needs know your heaviness;
  I have pity to see you in any distress;
  If any have you wronged, ye shall revenged be,
  Though I on the ground be slain for thee,
  Though that I know before that I should die.   220

EVERYMAN: Verily, Fellowship, gramercy.

FELLOWSHIP: Tush! by thy thanks I set not a straw!
  Show me your grief, and say no more.

EVERYMAN: If I my heart should to you break,
  And then you to turn your mind from me,
  And would not me comfort when you hear me speak,
  Then should I ten times sorrier be.

FELLOWSHIP: Sir, I say as I will do, indeed.

EVERYMAN: Then be you a good friend at need;
  I have found you true here before.   230

FELLOWSHIP: And so ye shall evermore;
  For, in faith, and thou go to hell,
  I will not forsake thee by the way!

EVERYMAN: Ye speak like a good friend. I believe you well:
  I shall deserve it, and I may.

FELLOWSHIP: I speak of no deserving, by this day!

For he that will say and nothing do
Is not worthy with good company to go;
Therefore show me the grief of your mind,
As to your friend most loving and kind.   240

EVERYMAN: I shall show you how it is:
Commanded I am to go a journey,
A long way, hard and dangerous,
And give a strict count without delay
Before the high judge, Adonai.[7]   *God*
Wherefore, I pray you, bear me company,
As ye have promised, in this journey.

FELLOWSHIP: That is matter indeed! Promise is duty;
But, and I should take such a voyage on me,
I know it well, it should be to my pain.   250
Also it maketh me afeared, certain.
But let is take counsel here as well as we can,
For your words would fright a strong man.

EVERYMAN: Why, ye said if I had need,
Ye would me never forsake, quick nor dead,
Though it were to hell, truly.

FELLOWSHIP: So I said, certainly,
But such pleasures be set aside, the sooth to say.
And also, if we took such a journey,
When should we come again?   260

EVERYMAN: Nay, never again till the day of doom.

FELLOWSHIP: In faith, then will not I come there!
Who hath you these tidings brought?

EVERYMAN: Indeed, Death was with me here.

FELLOWSHIP: Now, by God that all hath bought,
If Death were the messenger,
For no man that is living today
I will not go that loath journey—
Not for the father that begat me!

EVERYMAN: Ye promised otherwise, pardie.   *indeed* 270

---

[7] "Adonai" is the Hebrew substitute for the unsayable *tetragrammaton* (which non-Jews called "Jahweh" of "Jehovah"). It is not clear why the playwright should have used it, but perhaps it is only for literary effect, like the description of God as "the highest Jupiter of all" at 1.407 of Pynson's edition.

FELLOWSHIP: I wot well I said so, truly;
   And yet if thou wilt eat, and drink, and make good cheer,
   Or haunt to women the lusty company,
   I would not forsake you while the day is clear,
   Trust me verily!
EVERYMAN: Yea, thereto ye would be ready;
   To go to mirth, solace, and play,
   Your mind will sooner apply,
   Than to bear me company in my long journey.
FELLOWSHIP: Now, in good faith, I will not that way.   280
   But and thou wilt murder, or any man kill,
   In that I will help thee with a good will!
EVERYMAN: O, that is a simple advice indeed!
   Gentle fellow, help me in my necessity;
   We have loved long, and now I need,
   And now, gentle Fellowship, remember me!
FELLOWSHIP: Whether ye have loved me or no,
   By Saint John, I will not with thee go.
EVERYMAN: Yet, I pray thee, take the labor, and do so much
      for me
   To bring me forward, for saint charity,   290
   And comfort me till I come without the town.
FELLOWSHIP: Nay, and thou would give me a new gown,
   I will not a foot with thee go;
   But, and thou had tarried, I would not have left thee so.
   And as now God speed thee in thy journey,
   For from thee I will depart as fast as I may.
EVERYMAN: Whither away, Fellowship! Will you forsake me?
FELLOWSHIP: Yea, by my fay, to God I betake thee.   *hand over*
EVERYMAN: Farewell, good Fellowship! For thee my heart
   is sore;
   Adieu for ever! I shall see thee no more.   300
FELLOWSHIP: In faith, Everyman, farewell now at the end!
   For you I will remember that parting is mourning.
      [*Exit* FELLOWSHIP.]
EVERYMAN: Alack! shall we thus depart indeed
   (Ah, Lady, help!) without any more comfort?

Lo, Fellowship forsaketh me in my most need.
For help in this world whither shall I resort?
Fellowship here before with me would merry make.
And now little sorrow for me doth he take.
It is said, "In prosperity men friends may find,
Which in adversity be full unkind."   310
Now whither for succor shall I flee,
Sith that Fellowship hath forsaken me?
To my kinsmen I will, truly,
Praying them to help me in my necessity;
I believe that they will do so,
For "kind will creep where it may not go."[8]
I will go say, for yonder I see them go.   *speak*
Where be ye now, my friends and kinsmen?

[*Enter* KINDRED *and* COUSIN.]

KINDRED: Here be we now, at your commandment.
  Cousin, I pray you show us your intent   320
  In any wise, and do not spare.
COUSIN: Yea, Everyman, and to us declare
  If ye be disposed to go any whither,
  For, wete you well, we will live and die together.
KINDRED: In wealth and woe we will with you hold,
  For over his kin a man may be bold.
EVERYMAN: Gramercy, my friends and kinsmen kind.
  Now shall I show you the grief of my mind.
  I was commanded by a messenger
  That is a high king's chief officer;   330
  He bade me go a pilgrimage, to my pain,
  And I know well I shall never come again;
  Also I must give a reckoning straight,
  For I have a great enemy that hath me in wait,   *lies in wait*
  Which intendeth me for to hinder.
KINDRED: What account is that which ye must render?
  That would I know.

[8] The writer has given us three *sententiae* in the space of 14 lines. This one means, roughly, "Relatives will stick up for you no matter how much it puts them out," or "blood is thicker than water." The writer gets a nice irony by giving a rather pompous *sententia* to Fellowship at l.302.

EVERYMAN: Of all my works I must show
　　How I have lived, and my days spent;
　　Also of ill deeds that I have used   340
　　In my time, sith life was me lent;
　　And of all virtues that I have refused.
　　Therefore I pray you go thither with me,
　　To help to make mine account, for saint charity.
COUSIN: What, to go thither? Is that the matter?
　　Nay, Everyman, I had liefer fast bread and water
　　All this five year and more.
EVERYMAN: Alas, that ever I was bore!
　　For now shall I never be merry
　　If that you forsake me.   350
KINDRED: Ah, sir, what! Ye be a merry man!
　　Take good heart to you, and make no moan.
　　But one thing I warn you, by Saint Anne,
　　As for me, ye shall go alone.
EVERYMAN: My Cousin, will you not with me go?
COUSIN: No, by our Lady! I have the cramp in my toe.
　　Trust not to me; for, so God me speed,
　　I will deceive you in your most need.
KINDRED: It availeth not us to tice.   *entice*
　　Ye shall have my maid with all my heart;   360
　　She loveth to go to feasts, there to be nice,   *affectedly sociable*
　　And to dance, and abroad to start;
　　I will give her leave to help you in that journey,
　　If that you and she may agree.
EVERYMAN: Now show me the very effect of your mind.
　　Will you go with me, or abide behind?
KINDRED: Abide behind? Yea, that will I, and I may!
　　Therefore farewell till another day.
　　　　　　[*Exit* KINDRED.]
EVERYMAN: How should I be merry or glad?
　　For fair promises men to me make,   370
　　But when I have most need, they me forsake.
　　I am deceived; that maketh me sad.
COUSIN: Cousin Everyman, farewell now,

For verily I will not go with you;
Also of mine own life an unready reckoning
I have to account; therefore I make tarrying.
Now, God keep thee, for now I go.
    [*Exit* Cousin.]

EVERYMAN   Ah, Jesus! is all come hereto?
Lo, fair words maketh fools fain;
They promise and nothing will do certain.   380
My kinsmen promised me faithfully
For to abide with me steadfastly,
And now fast away do they flee.
Even so Fellowship promised me.
What friend were best me of to provide?
I lose my time here longer to abide.
Yet in my mind a thing there is:
All my life I have loved riches;
If that my Goods now help me might,
He would make my heart full light.   390
I will speak to him in this distress.
Where art thou, my Goods and riches?
    [Goods *is discovered.*]

GOODS: Who calleth me? Everyman? What, hast thou haste?
I lie here in corners, trussed and piled so high,
And in chests I am locked so fast,
Also sacked in bags—thou mayst see with thine eye—
I cannot stir; in packs low I lie.
What would ye have? Lightly me say.

EVERYMAN: Come hither, Goods, in all the haste thou may.
For of counsel I must desire thee.   400

GOODS: Sir, and ye in the world have sorrow or adversity,
That can I help you to remedy shortly.

EVERYMAN: It is another disease that grieveth me;
In this world it is not, I tell thee so.
I am sent for another way to go,
To give a strict count general
Before the highest Jupiter of all;
And all my life I have had joy and pleasure in thee;

Therefore I pray thee go with me,
For, peradventure, thou mayst before God Almighty   410
My reckoning help to clean and purify;
For it is said ever among,
That "money maketh all right that is wrong."
GOODS: Nay, Everyman; I sing another song,
I follow no man in such voyages;
For, and I went with thee,
Thou shouldst fare much the worse for me;
For because on me thou did set thy mind,
Thy reckoning I have made blotted and blind,
That thine account thou cannot make truly;   420
And that hast thou for the love of me.
EVERYMAN: That would grieve me full sore,
When I should come to that fearful answer.
Up, let us go thither together.
GOODS: Nay, not so! I am too brittle, I may not endure;
I will follow no man one foot, be ye sure.
EVERYMAN: Alas! I have thee loved, and had great pleasure
All my life-days on goods and treasure.
GOODS: That is to thy damnation, without lesing!   *lying*
For my love is contrary to the love everlasting.   430
But if thou had me loved moderately during,
As to the poor to give part of me,
Then shouldst thou not in this dolor be,
Nor in this great sorrow and care.
EVERYMAN: Lo, now was I deceived ere I was ware,
And all I may wyte my spending of time.   *suffer for*
GOODS: What, weenest thou that I am thine?
EVERYMAN: I had weened so.
GOODS: Nay, Everyman, I say no;
As for a while I was lent thee,   440
A season thou hast had me in prosperity.
My condition is man's soul to kill;
If I save one, a thousand I do spill;
Weenest thou that I will follow thee
From this world? Nay, verily.

EVERYMAN: I had weened otherwise.

GOODS: Therefore to thy soul Goods is a thief;
  For when thou art dead, this is my guise—   *trick*
  Another to deceive in the same wise
  As I have done thee, and all to his soul's reprief.   *harm* 450

EVERYMAN: O false Goods, curséd thou be!
  Thou traitor to God, that hast deceived me
  And caught me in thy snare.

GOODS: Marry! thou brought thyself in care,
  Whereof I am right glad.
  I must needs laugh, I cannot be sad.

EVERYMAN: Ah, Goods, thou hast had long by heartly love;
  I gave thee that which should be the Lord's above.
  But wilt thou not go with me indeed?
  I pray thee truth to say.   460

GOODS: No, so God me speed!
  Therefore farewell, and have good day.

      [*Exit* GOODS.]   *(see note 21)*

EVERYMAN: O, to whom shall I make my moan
  For to go with me in that heavy journey?
  First Fellowship said he would with me gone;
  His words were very pleasant and gay,
  But afterwards he left me alone.
  Then spake I to my kinsmen, all in despair,
  An[d] also they gave me words fair,
  They lacked no fair speaking,   470
  But all forsook me in the ending.
  Then went I to my Goods, that I loved best,
  In hope to have comfort, but there had I least;
  For my Goods sharply did tell me
  That he bringeth many into hell.
  Then of myself I was ashamed,
  And so I am worthy to be blamed;
  Thus may I well myself hate.
  Of whom shall I now counsel take?
  I think that I shall never speed   480
  Till that I go to my Good Deeds.

But alas! she is so weak
That she can neither go nor speak.
Yet will I venture on her now.
My Good Deeds, where be you?

    [GOOD DEEDS *speaks from the ground.*]

GOOD DEEDS: Here I lie, cold in the ground.
Thy sins have me sore bound,
That I cannot stir.

EVERYMAN: O Good Deeds! I stand in fear;
I must you pray of counsel,   490
For help now should come right well.

GOOD DEEDS: Everyman, I have understanding
That ye be summoned account to make
Before Messias, of Jerusalem King;
And you do by me, that journey with you will   *follow my advice*
    I take.

EVERYMAN: Therefore I come to you my moan to make;
I pray you that ye will go with me.

GOOD DEEDS: I would full fain, but I cannot stand, verily.

EVERYMAN: Why, is there anything on you fall?

GOOD DEEDS: Yea, sir, I may thank you of all;   500
If ye had perfectly cheered me,   *kept in good condition*
Your book of count full ready had be.
Look, the books of your works and deeds eke;
Ah, see how they lie under the feet,
To your soul's heaviness.

EVERYMAN: Our Lord Jesus help me!
For one letter here I can not see.

GOOD DEEDS: There is a blind reckoning in time of distress!

EVERYMAN: Good Deeds, I pray you, help me in this need,
Or else I am for ever damned indeed;   510
Therefore help me to make my reckoning
Before the Redeemer of all thing,
That King is, and was, and ever shall.

GOOD DEEDS: Everyman, I am sorry of your fall,
And fain would I help you, and I were able.

EVERYMAN: Good Deeds. your counsel I pray you give me.

GOOD DEEDS: That shall I do verily;
  Though that on my feet I may not go,
  I have a sister that shall with you also,
  Called Knowledge, which shall with you abide,   520
  To help you to make that dreadful reckoning.
     [*Enter* KNOWLEDGE.]
KNOWLEDGE: Everyman, I will go with thee, and be thy guide
  In thy most need to go by thy side.[9]
EVERYMAN: In good condition I am now in every thing,
  And am wholly content with this good thing;
  Thanked be God my Creator.[10]
GOOD DEEDS: And when he hath brought thee there,
  Where thou shalt heal thee of thy smart,
  Then go you with your reckoning and your Good Deeds
     together
  For to make you joyful at heart   530
  Before the blesséd Trinity.
EVERYMAN: My Good Deeds, gramercy!
  I am well content, certainly,
  With your words sweet.
KNOWLEDGE: Now go we together lovingly
  To Confession, that cleansing river.
EVERYMAN: For joy I weep; I would we were there!
  But, I pray you, give me cognition
  Where dwelleth that holy man, Confession.
KNOWLEDGE: In the house of salvation;   540
  We shall find him in that place,
  That shall us comfort, by God's grace.
  Lo, this is Confession. Kneel down and ask mercy,
  For he is in good conceit with God almighty.   *good standing*
EVERYMAN: [*Kneeling*]. O glorious fountain, that all uncleanness
    doth clarify,
  Wash from me the spots of vice unclean,
  That on me no sin may be seen.

---

[9] Here is the pivot point of the play. It introduces what might be called "Act II". the penitential sequence which runs to l.794.
[10] Skot's edition reads "by".

I come, with Knowledge, for my redemption,
Redempt with hearty and full contrition;
For I am commanded a pilgrimage to take,   550
And great accounts before God to make.
Now I pray you, Shrift, mother of salvation.
Help my Good Deeds for my piteous exclamation.
CONFESSION: I know your sorrow well, Everyman.
  Because with Knowledge ye come to me,
  I will you comfort as well as I can,
  And precious jewel I will give thee,
  Called penance, voider of adversity;
  Therewith shall your body chastised be,
  With abstinence, and perseverance in God's service.   560
  Here shall you receive that scourge of me.
  Which is penance strong, that ye must endure
  To remember thy Savior was scourged for thee
  With sharp scourges, and suffered it patiently;
  So must thou ere thou 'scape that painful pilgrimage.
  Knowledge, keep him in this voyage,
  And by that time Good Deeds will be with thee.
  But in any wise be seeker of mercy,
  For your time draweth fast, and ye will saved be;
  Ask God mercy, and He will grant truly;   570
  When with the scourge of penance man doth him bind,
  The oil forgiveness then shall he find.
          [*Exit* CONFESSION.]
EVERYMAN: Thanked be God for his gracious work!
  For now I will my penance begin;
  This hath rejoiced and lighted my heart,
  Though the knots be painful and hard within.
KNOWLEDGE: Everyman, look your penance that ye fulfil,
  What pain that ever it to you be,
  And Knowledge shall give you counsel at will
  How your account ye shall make clearly.   580
          [EVERYMAN *kneels*.]
EVERYMAN: O eternal God! O heavenly figure!
  O way of rightwiseness! O goodly vision!

Which descended down in a virgin pure
Because he would Everyman redeem,
Which Adam forfeited by his disobedience.
O blessed Godhead! elect and high divine,
Forgive me my grievous offence;
Here I cry thee mercy in this presence.
O ghostly treasure! O ransomer and redeemer!
Of all the world hope and conductor,   590
Mirror of joy, and founder of mercy,
Which illumineth heaven and earth thereby,
Hear my clamorous complaint, though it late be.
Receive my prayers; unworthy in this heavy life.
Though I be a sinner most abominable,
Yet let my name be written in Moses' table.
O Mary! pray to the Maker of all thing,
Me for to help at my ending,
And save me from the power of my enemy,
For Death assaileth me strongly.   600
And, Lady, that I may by means of thy prayer
Of your Son's glory to be partner,
By the means of his passion I it crave;
I beseech you, help my soul to save.
> [*He rises*]
Knowledge, give me the scourge of penance.
My flesh therewith shall give a quittance.
I will now begin, if God give me grace.
KNOWLEDGE: Everyman, God give you time and space.
Thus I bequeath you in the hands of our Savior,
Now may you make your reckoning sure.   610
EVERYMAN: In the name of the Holy Trinity,
My body sore punished shall be.
Take this, body, for the sin of the flesh;
Also thou delightest to go gay and fresh,
And in that way of damnation thou did me bring;
Therefore suffer now strokes of punishing.
Now of penance I will wade the water clear,
To save me from purgatory, that sharp fire.

[GOOD DEEDS *rises from floor.*]

GOOD DEEDS: I thank God, now I can walk and go,
  And am delivered of my sickness and woe.   620
  Therefore with Everyman I will go, and not spare;
  His good works I will help him to declare.
KNOWLEDGE: Now, Everyman, be merry and glad!
  Your Good Deeds cometh now, ye may not be sad;
  Now is your Good Deeds whole and sound,
  Going upright upon the ground.
EVERYMAN: My heart is light, and shall be evermore.
  Now will I smite faster than I did before.
GOOD DEEDS: Everyman, pilgrim, my special friend,
  Blesséd be thou without end.   630
  For thee is prepared the eternal glory.
  Ye have me made whole and sound,
  Therefore I will bide by thee in every stound.   *occasion*
EVERYMAN: Welcome, my Good Deeds; now I hear thy voice,
  I weep for very sweetness of love.
KNOWLEDGE: Be no more sad, but ever rejoice;
  God seeth thy living in his throne above.
  Put on this garment to thy behoof,
  Which is wet with your tears,
  Or else before God you may it miss,   640
    When you to your journey's end come shall.
EVERYMAN: Gentle Knowledge, what do ye it call?
KNOWLEDGE: It is the garment of sorrow;
  From pain it will you borrow;
  Contrition it is
  That getteth forgiveness;
  It pleaseth God passing well.
GOOD DEEDS: Everyman, will you wear it for your heal?
      [EVERYMAN *puts on the garment of contrition.*][11]
EVERYMAN: Now blessed be Jesu, Mary's Son,
  For now have I on true contrition.   650
  And let us go now without tarrying;
  Good Deeds, have we clear our reckoning?

[11] This would be a version of the mourner's sack cloth.

GOOD DEEDS: Yea, indeed I have it here.

EVERYMAN: Then I trust we need not fear.

Now, friends, let is not part in twain.

KNOWLEDGE: Nay, Everyman, that will we not, certain.[12]

GOOD DEEDS: Yet must thou lead with thee[13]

Three persons of great might.

EVERYMAN: Who should they be?

GOOD DEEDS: Discretion and Strength they hight,   *are called* 660

And thy Beauty may not abide behind.

KNOWLEDGE: Also ye must call to mind

Your Five Wits as for your counselors.

GOOD DEEDS: You must have them ready at all hours.

EVERYMAN: How shall I get them hither?

KNOWLEDGE: You must call them all together.

And they will hear you incontinent.

EVERYMAN: My friends, come hither and be present;

Discretion, Strength, my Five Wits, and Beauty.

[*Enter* DISCRETION, STRENGTH, FIVE WITS *and* BEAUTY.]

BEAUTY: Here at your will we be all ready.   670

What will ye that we should do?

GOOD DEEDS: That ye would with Everyman go,

And help him in his pilgrimage.

Advise you, will ye with him or not in that voyage?

STRENGTH: We will bring him all thither,

To his help and comfort, ye may believe me.

DISCRETION: So will we go with him all together.

EVERYMAN: Almighty God, lovéd may thou be!

I give thee laud that I have hither brought

Strength, Discretion, Beauty, and Five Wits. Lack I naught;   680

And my Good Deeds, with Knowledge clear,

All be in company at my will here.

I desire no more to my business.

STRENGTH: And I, Strength, will by you stand in distress,

Though thou would in battle fight on the ground.

---

[12] All the early editions give this line and line 666 to Kindred, which is not possible. Perhaps the error arose because the same actor played both parts.

[13] Skot reads "led."

FIVE WITS: And though it were through the world around,
  We will not depart for sweet nor sour.
BEAUTY: No more will I, unto death's hour,
  Whatsoever thereof befall.
DISCRETION: Everyman, advise you first of all;   690
  Go with a good advisement and deliberation.
  We all give you virtuous monition
  That all shall be well.
EVERYMAN: My friends, hearken what I will tell:
  I pray God reward you in his heavenly sphere.
  How hearken, all that be here.
  For I will make my testament
  Here before you all present:
  In alms half my goods I will give with my hands twain
  In the way of charity, with good intent,   700
  And the other half still shall remain;
  I it bequeath to be returned there it ought to be.
  This I do in despite of the fiend of hell,
  To go quite out of his peril
  Ever after and this day.
KNOWLEDGE: Everyman, hearken what I say;
  Go to Priesthood, I you advise,
  And receive of him in any wise
  The holy sacrament and ointment together;
  Then shortly see ye turn again hither;   710
  We will all abide you here.
FIVE WITS: Yea, Everyman, hie you that ye ready were.
  There is no emperor, king, duke, nor baron,
  That of God hath commission
  As hath the least priest in the world being;
  For of the blessèd sacraments pure and benign
  He beareth the keys, and thereof hath the cure
  For man's redemption—it is ever sure—
  Which God for our soul's medicine
  Gave us out of his heart with great pain,   720
  Here in this transitory life, for thee and me.
  The blessèd sacraments seven there be:

Baptism, confirmation, with priesthood good,
And the sacrament of God's precious flesh and blood,
Marriage, the holy extreme unction, and penance.
These seven be good to have in remembrance,
Gracious sacraments of high divinity.

EVERYMAN: Fain would I receive that holy body
And meekly to my ghostly father I will go.

FIVE WITS: Everyman, that is the best that ye can do.   730
God will you to salvation bring,
For priesthood exceedeth all other thing;
To us Holy Scripture they do teach,
And converteth man from sin, heaven to reach;
God hath to them more power given,
Than to any angel that is in heaven.
With five words he may consecrate
God's body in flesh and blood to make,
And handleth his Maker between his hands.
The priest bindeth and unbindeth all bands,   740
Both in earth and in heaven;
Thou ministers all the sacraments seven;
Though we kissed thy feet, thou wert worthy;
Thou art the surgeon that cureth sin deadly:
No remedy we find under God
But all only priesthood.
Everyman, God gave priests that dignity,
And setteth them in his stead among us to be;
Thus be they above angels, in degree.

> [*Exit* EVERYMAN.]

KNOWLEDGE: If priests be good, it is so, surely.   750
But when Jesus hanged on the cross with great smart,
There he gave out of his blessèd heart
The same sacrament in great torment.
He sold them not to us, that Lord omnipotent.
Therefore Saint Peter the Apostle doth say
That Jesus' curse hath all they
Which God their Savior do buy or sell,
Or they for any money do take or tell.

Sinful priests giveth the sinners example bad;
Their children sitteth by other men's fires, I have heard;   760
And some haunteth women's company
With unclean life, as lusts of lechery.
These be with sin made blind.

FIVE WITS: I trust to God no such may we find.
Therefore let us priesthood honor,
And follow their doctrine for our souls' succor.
We be their sheep, and they shepherds be
By whom we all be kept in surety.
Peace! for yonder I see Everyman come,
Which hath made true satisfaction.   770

GOOD DEEDS: Methinketh it is he indeed.

[*Re-enter* EVERYMAN.]

EVERYMAN: Now Jesu be our alder speed.[14]   *of all of us*
I have received the sacrament for my redemption,
And then mine extreme unction.
Blesséd be all they that counseled me to take it!
And now, friends, let is go without longer respite.
I thank God that ye have tarried so long.
Now set each of you on this rood your hand,[15]   *cross*
And shortly follow me.
I go before, there I would be. God be our guide.[16]   780

STRENGTH: Everyman, we will not from you go,
Till ye have done this voyage long.

DISCRETION: I, Discretion, will bide by you also.

KNOWLEDGE: And though this pilgrimage be never so strong,
I will never part you fro.
Everyman, I will be as sure by thee
As ever I was by Judas Maccabee.[17]

EVERYMAN: Alas! I am so faint I may not stand,
My limbs under me do fold.

---

[14] Skot reads "your," but since Everyman has now taken the sacrament, Pynson's reading of "our" seems preferable.

[15] All the early editions read "rod," which, though it is an allowable spelling, we amend to "rood" for clarity's sake. This is the cross placed in the hands of the dying.

[16] Again it is Skot who reads "your," but, since they are going together, Pynson's "our" is preferable.

[17] Skot reads "did," but "will be" seems to demand "was."

Friends, let is not turn again to this land,   790
Not for all the world's gold;
For into this cave must I creep
And turn to earth, and there to sleep.

BEAUTY: What, into this grave? Alas!

EVERYMAN: Yea, there shall you consume, more and less.

BEAUTY: And what, should I smother here?

EVERYMAN: Yea, by my faith, and never more appear.
In this world live no more we shall,
But in heaven before the highest Lord of all.

BEAUTY: I cross out all this; adieu, by Saint John!   800
I take my cap in my lap and am gone.

EVERYMAN: What, Beauty, whither will ye?

BEAUTY: Peace! I am deaf. I look not behind me,
Not and thou would give me all the gold in thy chest.
    [*Exit* BEAUTY.]

EVERYMAN: Alas, whereto may I trust?
Beauty goeth fast away from me;
She promised with me to live and die.

STRENGTH: Everyman, I will thee also forsake and deny.
Thy game liketh me not at all.

EVERYMAN: Why, then ye will forsake me all?   810
Sweet Strength, tarry a little space.

STRENGTH: Nay, sir, by the rood of grace,
I will hie me from thee fast,
Though thou weep till thy heart to-brast.[18]   **break**

EVERYMAN: Ye would ever bide by me, ye said.

STRENGTH: Yea, I have you far enough conveyed.
Ye be old enough, I understand,
Your pilgrimage to take on hand.
I repent me that I hither came.

EVERYMAN: Strength, you to displease I am to blame;   820
Yet promise is debt, this ye well wot.[19]

STRENGTH: In faith, I care not!
Thou art a but fool to complain.

---

[18] Skot reads "to thy heart."
[19] Skot's line reads "will ye break promise that is debt," which kills the rhyme with "not."

You spend your speech and waste your brain;
Go, thrust thee into the ground.
　　　　[*Exit* STRENGTH.]
EVERYMAN:　I had weened surer I should you have found.
He that trusteth in his Strength[20]
She him deceiveth at the length.
Both Strength and Beauty forsaketh me,
Yet they promised me fair and lovingly.　　　　　　　　830
DISCRETION:　Everyman, I will after Strength be gone;
As for me I will leave you alone.
EVERYMAN:　Why, Discretion, will ye forsake me?
DISCRETION:　Yea, in faith, I will go from thee;
For when Strength goeth before
I follow after evermore.
EVERYMAN:　Yet, I pray thee, for the love of the Trinity,
Look in my grave once piteously.
DISCRETION:　Nay, so nigh will I not come.
Now farewell, every one!　　　　　　　　　　　　　840
　　　　[*Exit* DISCRETION.]
EVERYMAN:　O all thing faileth, save God alone—
Beauty, Strength, and Discretion;
For when Death bloweth his blast,
They all run from me full fast.
FIVE WITS:　Everyman, my leave now of thee I take;
I will follow the other, for here I thee forsake.
EVERYMAN:　Alas! then may I wail and weep,
For I took you for my best friend.
FIVE WITS:　I will no longer thee keep;
Now farewell, and there an end.　　　　　　　　　　850
　　　　[*Exit* FIVE WITS.]
EVERYMAN:　O Jesu, help! All hath forsaken me!
GOOD DEEDS:　Nay, Everyman; I will bide with thee,
I will not forsake thee indeed;
Thou shalt find me a good friend in need.

---

[20] In Pynson the next four lines read, "But I see well he that trusteth in his strength/Is greatly deceived at length,/For strength and Beauty forsaketh me,/Yet they promised me steadfast to be."

EVERYMAN: Gramercy, Good Deeds! Now may I true friends
>   see.
>   They have forsaken me, every one;
>   I loved them better than my Good Deeds alone.
>   Knowledge, will ye forsake me also?

KNOWLEDGE: Yea, Everyman, when ye to death shall go;
>   But not yet, for no manner of danger.   860

EVERYMAN: Gramercy, Knowledge, with all my heart.

KNOWLEDGE: Nay, yet I will not from hence depart
>   Till I see where ye shall be come.

EVERYMAN: Methink, alas, that I must be gone
>   To make my reckoning and my debts pay,
>   For I see my time is nigh spent away.
>   Take example, all ye that this do hear or see,
>   How they that I loved best do forsake me,
>   Except my Good Deeds, that bideth truly.

GOOD DEEDS: All earthly things is but vanity.   870
>   Beauty, Strength, and Discretion do man forsake,
>   Foolish friends and kinsmen, that fair spake,
>   All fleeth save Good Deeds, and that am I.

EVERYMAN: Have mercy on me, God most mighty;
>   And stand by me, thou Mother and Maid, holy Mary!

GOOD DEEDS: Fear not, I will speak for thee.

EVERYMAN: Here I cry God mercy!

GOOD DEEDS: Short our end, and 'minish our pain.
>   Let us go and never come again.

EVERYMAN: Into thy hands, Lord, my soul I commend.   880
>   Receive it, Lord, that it be not lost.
>   As thou me boughtest, so me defend,
>   And save me from the fiend's boast,
>   That I may appear with that blessèd host
>   That I shall be saved at the day of doom.
>   *In manus tuas*—of might's most
>   For ever—*commendo spiritum meum.*[21]

>   [EVERYMAN *and* GOOD DEEDS *descend into the grave.*]

[21] Into Thy hands (O Lord) I commend my spirit. The next stage direction is a modern addition, but Everyman does now go *somewhere*. Earlier, Good Deeds was said to have risen from the ground, and earlier still, Goods told Everyman that he could not move. Hypothesis: this may be a rudimentary three-area, stage; a main stage, a lowered area, and a curtained-off area where a character like Goods may be "discovered" and then "covered."

KNOWLEDGE: Now hath he suffered that we all shall endure;
   The Good Deeds shall make all sure.
   Now hath he made ending.   890
   Methinketh that I hear angels sing
   And make great joy and melody
   Where Everyman's soul received shall be.
ANGEL: Come, excellent elect spouse to Jesu!
   Here above thou shalt go
   Because of thy singular virtue.
   Now the soul is taken the body fro,
   Thy reckoning is crystal clear.
   Now shalt thou into the heavenly sphere,
   Unto the which all ye shall come   900
   That liveth well before the day of doom.
          [*Exit* KNOWLEDGE. *Enter* DOCTOR.[22]]
DOCTOR: This moral men have in mind;
   Ye hearers, take it of worth, old and young,
   And forsake Pride, for he deceiveth you in the end,
   And remember Beauty, Five Wits, Strength, and Discretion,
   They all at the last do Everyman forsake,
   Save his Good Deeds there doth he take.
   But beware, and they be small
   Before God he hath no help at all.
   None excuse may be there for Everyman.   910
   Alas, how shall he do then?
   For, after death, amends may no man make,
   For then mercy and pity doth him forsake.
   If his reckoning be not clear when he doth come,
   God will say, "*Ite, maledicti, in ignem aeternum.*"[23]
   And he that hath his account whole and sound,
   High in heaven he shall be crowned.
   Unto which place God bring us all thither,
   That we my live body and soul together.
   Thereto help the Trinity!   920
   Amen, say ye, for saint charity.

Thus endeth this Moral Play of Everyman

---

[22] Not a doctor of medicine; perhaps of Philosophy or Theology.
[23] Go, cursed ones, into everlasting fire.

Thenterlude of youth.

Iesu that his armes dyd sprede
And on a tree was done to dead
From all perils he you defende
I desyre audyence tyl I haue made an ende:
For am come from God aboue
To occuppe his lawes to your behoue
And am named Charytye
There maye no man saued be
wythout the helpe of me
For he that Charytye doth refuse
Other vertues thought he do vse

                                        J. t.

Plate 3. The title page of John Waley's edition of *The Interlude of Youth* (c. 1557).

✳ THE INTERLUDE OF YOUTH

(c. 1513)

The Interlude of Youth may be the earliest (see below) and is certainly the finest of the "youth" moralities, those plays which engage the vices and the patterns of behavior characteristic of young people. Like Everyman, Youth narrows down the full-scope structural pattern of The Castle of Perseverance to focus upon the life-in-sin and the repentance of its hero, neglecting his temptation and his eventual salvation. But where Everyman prepares for death, Youth prepares for life. If the action of Everyman may be said to be informed by the totentanz, the action of Youth is informed by the parable of the Prodigal Son. And in presenting the education of the Prodigal, the play opens out on the one hand toward humanistic experiments in Christianizing Terentian comedy, and on the other toward more formal educational moralities, The Nature of the Four Elements (1517–1518), the "wit" plays, and the Parnassus trilogy. More important, through the mediation of historical and political moralities like Magnificence (1513–1516) and Respublica (1553), the pattern of Youth adumbrates the pattern of such Elizabethan moral histories as Woodstock (c. 1592), and Shakespeare's Richard II (1595–1596), and Henry IV (1597–1598), in each of which the career of a royal prodigal is traced through life in sin to repentance.[1]

[1] For a discussion of the influence of Youth and plays like it upon Henry IV, see J. Dover Wilson, The Fortunes of Falstaff (New York, 1943).

Of the five editions of *The Interlude of Youth* which were almost certainly printed during the sixteenth century, three have survived: the so-called Lambeth Palace fragment (1528–1535), the Waley edition (c. 1557), and the Copland edition (c. 1560). After a suggestion by R. B. McKerrow, we have constructed an ecclectic text, following the Lambeth Palace fragment through l. 246 (where it breaks off), then the Copland text, correcting from Waley when Copland makes changes in the direction of Protestant readings.[2] Significant variants are given in the notes.

The date of the play is an open question. Conjectures about it have ranged from before 1500 to after 1550. The Lambeth Palace fragment fixes the latest possible date at about 1528, but comparison with *Hickscorner*, which seems to have been based upon *Youth*, suggests that *Youth* was probably written before 1513.[3]

[2] Introduction to *Youth*, *Materialien zur Kunde des alteren englischen Dramas*, Band XII (1905), pp. 15–24.

[3] E. T. Schell, "*Youth* and *Hyckescorner*: Which Came First?" *PQ*, XLV (1966), pp. 468–74.

Plate 4. Title page of the Lambeth Palace
fragment (c. 1528).

THE INTERLUDE OF YOUTH

CHARITY: Jesu that his arms did spread
And on a tree was done to dead,
From all perils He you defend.
I desire audience till I have made an end,
For I am come from God above
To occupy His laws to your behove,   *To teach His laws for your benefit*
And am named Charity.
There may no man saved be
Without the help of me,
For he that Charity doth refuse,   10
Other virtues though he do use,
Without Charity it will not be;
For it is written in the faith:
Qui manet in charitate, in Deo manet.[1]
I am the gate, I tell thee,
Of heaven, that joyful city.
There may no man thither come
But of charity he must have some,
Or he may not come, iwis,   *indeed*
Unto heaven, the city of bliss.   20
Therefore charity, who will him take,
A pure soul it will him make
Before the face of God.
In the A B C, of books the least,[2]
It is written *Deus charitas est.*[3]
Lo, charity is a great thing,
Of all virtues it is the king.
When God in earth was here living,
Of charity He found none ending.
I was planted in His heart,   30
We two might not depart.   *be separated*
Out of His heart I did spring,

---

[1] *Qui . . . manet:* "He that dwelleth in love dwelleth in God," I John 4, 16.
[2] *ABC Book:* A child's prayer book used to teach reading; thus "least" in the sense of most elementary and also of containing fundamental doctrine.
[3] *Deus . . . est:* "God is love," I John 4, 8 and 16.

Through the might of the Heaven King.
And all priests that be
May sing no mass without charity.[4]
And charity to them they do not take,   *and = if*
They may not receive Him that did them make
And all this world of   *...that made them and all this world out of nothing.*
    nought.

YOUTH: Aback, fellows, and give me room,
    Or I shall make you to avoid soon!   40
    I am goodly of person,
    I am peerless wherever I come.
    My name is Youth, I tell thee,
    I flourish as the vine tree.
    Who may be likened unto me,
    In my youth and jollity?
    My hair is royal and bushed thick,
    My body pliant as a hazel stick,
    Mine arms be both big and strong,
    My fingers be both fair and long,   50
    My chest big as a tun,   *beer barrel*
    My legs be full light for to run,
    To hop and dance and make merry:
    By the mass, I reck not a cherry   *care*
    Whatsoever I do!
    I am the heir of my father's land,
    And it is come into my hand—
    I care for no more.

CHARITY: Are you so disposed to do,
    To follow vice and let virtue go?   60

YOUTH: Yea, sir, even so:
    For now a days he is not set by,   *esteemed*
    Without he be unthrifty.   *unless*

CHARITY: You had need to ask God mercy.
    Why did you so praise your body?

YOUTH: Why, knave, what is that to thee?
    Wilt thou let me to praise my body?   *forbid*

---

[4] C. reads "may not live without charity."

Why should I not praise it, and it be goodly?
I will not let for thee.   *stop*

CHARITY: What shall it be when thou shalt flit   70
   From thy wealth into the pit?[5]
   Therefore of it be not too bold,
   Lest thou forthink it when thou art old.   *repent*
   Ye may be likened to a tree,
   In youth flourishing with royalty,
   And in age it is cut down
   And to the fire is thrown.
   So shalt thou, but thou amend,
   Be burned in hell without end.

YOUTH: Yea whoreson! Trowest thou so?   *thinkest* 80
   Beware, lest thou thither go!
   Hence, caitiff, go thy way,   *wretch*
   Or with my dagger I shall thee slay!
   Hence, knave, out of this place,
   Or I shall lay thee on the face!
   Sayest thou that I shall go to hell,
   For evermore there to dwell?
   I had liever thou had evil fare.   *rather*

CHARITY: Ah yet, sir, do by my rede   *advice*
   And ask mercy for thy misdeed;   90
   And thou shalt be an heritor of bliss,
   Where all joy and mirth is,
   Where thou shalt see a glorious sight
   Of angels singing with saints bright
   Before the face of God.

YOUTH: What, sirs, above the sky?
   I had need of a ladder to climb so high.
   But what and the ladder slip?
   Then I am deceived yet,
   And if I fall I catch a queck;   *get a knock* 100
   I may fortune to break my neck,
   And that joint is ill to set.   *difficult*
   Nay, nay, not so.

[5] Thus L.; W. and C. read "*for* thy wealth. . . ."

CHARITY: Oh, yet remember and call to thy mind
  The mercy of God passeth all thing.
  For it is written by noble clerks,
  The mercy of God passeth all works;
  That witnesseth holy scripture, saying thus:
  Miserationes domini super omnia opera eius;[6]
  Therefore doubt not God's grace: 110
  Thereof is plenty in every place.

YOUTH: What! Methink ye be clerkish,
  For ye speak good gibb'rish!
  Sir, I pray you, and you have any store,
  Soil me a question, ere ye cast out any more,   *answer*
  Lest when your cunning is all done
  My question have no solution.
  Sir, and it please you, this:
  Why do men eat mustard with salt fish?
  Sir, I pray you soil me this question   120
  That I have put to your discretion.

CHARITY: This question is but a vanity.
  It longeth not to me
  Such questions to assoil.

YOUTH: Sir, by God that me dear bought,
  I see your cunning is little or nought.
  And I should follow your school,
  Soon you would make me a fool.
  Therefore crake no longer here,   *talk*
  Lest I take you on the ear   130
  And make your head ache.

CHARITY: Sir, it falleth not for me to fight,
  Neither by day nor by night;
  Therefore do by my counsel, I say,
  Then to heaven thou shalt have the way.

YOUTH: No, sir, I think ye will not fight;
  But to take a man's purse in the night
  Ye will not say nay.
  For such holy caitiffs   *wretches*

[6] *Miserationes . . . eius:* "His tender mercies are over all his works," Psalms 145, 9.

Were wont to be thieves,   140
And such would be hanged as high
As a man may see with his eye.
In faith, this same is true.
CHARITY: God save every Christian body
From such evil destiny,
And send us of His grace
In heaven to have a place.
YOUTH: Nay, nay, I warrant thee,
He hath no place for thee.
Weenest thou He will have such fools   *do you think*   150
To sit on His gay stools?
Nay, I warrant thee, nay!
CHARITY: Well, sir, I put me in God's will[7]
Whether He will me save or spill.   *destroy*
And, sir, I pray you do so,
And trust in God, whatsoever you do.
YOUTH: Sir, I pray thee hold thy peace,
And talk to me of no goodness;
And soon look thou go thy way,
Lest with my dagger I thee slay!   160
In faith, and thou move my heart,
Thou shalt be weary of thy part,
Ere thou and I have done.
CHARITY: Think what God suffered for thee:
His arms to be spread upon a tree,
A knight with a spear opened His side,
In His heart appeared a wound wide,
That bought both thee and me!
YOUTH: God's fast, what is that to me?
Thou daw, wilt thou rede me   *advise*   170
In my youth to lose my jollity?
Hence, knave, and go thy way,
Or with my dagger I shall thee slay!
CHARITY: Oh sir, hear what I will you tell,

---

[7] All texts agree in assigning this speech to Humility, but that seems to be an obvious error: there is no other reference to Humility in this scene, and Charity decides to go off and counsel with Humility at line 184.

And be ruled after my counsel,
That ye might sit in heaven on high
With God and His company.

YOUTH: And yet of God wilt thou not cease
Till I fight in good earnest!
On my faith I tell thee true,   180
If I fight thou wilt it rue
All the days of thy life.

CHARITY: Sir, I see it will none otherwise be.
I will go to my brother Humility,
And take counsel of him
How it is best to do therein.

YOUTH: Yea, marry, sir, I pray you of that.
Methink it were a good sight of your back.
I would see your heels hither,
And your brother and you together   190
Fettered fine fast.
Iwis, and I had the kay,   *truly/key*
You should sing well-away8
Ere I let you loose.

CHARITY: Farewell, my masters everyone!
I will come again anon,
And tell you how I have done.
          [*Exit* CHARITY]

YOUTH: And thou come hither again,
I shall send thee hence in the devil's name.
What, now I may have my space   200
To jet here in this place.   *strut*
Before I might not stir,
When that churl Charity was here;
But now among all this cheer,
I would I had some company here.
Iwis, my brother Riot would help me
For to beat Charity
And his brother, too.
          [*Enter* RIOT]

8 *Well-away:* A conventional exclamation of grief, from the Anglo-Saxon *Wa La Wa.*

RIOT: Huffa, huffa! Who calleth after me?
    I am Riot, full of jollity.   *210*
    My heart is light as the wind,
    And all on riot is my mind
    Wheresoever I go.
    But wot ye whet I do here?   *know*
    To seek Youth my compeer.
    Fain of him I would have a sight,
    But my lips hang in my light.
    God speed, master Youth, by my fay.
YOUTH: Welcome, Riot, in the devil way!
    Who brought thee hither today?   *220*
RIOT: That did my legs, I tell thee.
    Methought thou did call me,
    And I am come now here
    To make royal cheer,
    And tell thee how I have done.
YOUTH: What! I weened thou hadst been hanged,   *thought*
    But I see thou art escaped;
    For it was told me here
    You took a man on the ear   *struck a man*
    That his purse in your bosom did fly,   *230*
    And so in Newgate ye did lie.
RIOT: So it was, I beshrew your pate!   *curse your head*
    I come lately from Newgate,
    But I am as ready to make good cheer
    As he that never came there.
    For and I have spending,
    I will make as merry as a king,
    And care not what I do.
    For I will not lie long in prison,
    But I will get forth soon;   *240*
    For I have learned policy,
    That will loose me lightly
    And soon let me go.
YOUTH: I love well thy discretion,
    For thou art all of one condition;

Thou art stable and steadfast of mind,
And not changeable as the wind.
But, sir, I pray you at the least,
Tell me more of that jest
That thou told me right now.   250
RIOT: Moreover, I shall tell thee:
The Mayor of London sent for me
Forth of Newgate for to come,
For to preach at Tyburn.
YOUTH: By our Lady, he did promote thee,
To make thee preach at the gallow-tree!
But, sir, how didst thou 'scape?
RIOT: Verily, sir, the rope brake,
And so I fell to the ground,
And ran away, safe and sound.   260
By the way I met a courtier's lad,
And twenty nobles of gold in his purse he had;
I took the lad on the ear,
Beside his horse I felled him there;
I took his purse in my hand,
And twenty nobles therein I fand.   *found*
Lord, how I was merry!
YOUTH: God's foot! Thou didst enough there
For to be made knight of the collar.
RIOT: Yea, sir, I trust to God Almight   270
At the next sessions to be dubbed a knight.
YOUTH: Now, sir, by this light,
That would I fain see!
And I plight thee, so God me save,   *promise*
That a surer collar thou shalt have;
And because gold collars be so good cheap,
Unto the roper I shall speak
To make thee one of a good price,
And that shall be of warrantise.   *guaranteed*
RIOT: Youth, I pray thee, have ado,   *have done* 280
And to the tavern let us go,
And we will drink divers wine,

And the cost shall be mine.
Thou shalt not pay one penny, iwis,   *truly*
Yet thou shalt have a wench to kiss,
Whensoever thou wilt.
YOUTH: Marry, Riot, I thank thee
That thou wilt bestow it on me,
And for thy pleasure so be it.
I would not Charity should us meet   *290*
And turn us again;
For right now he was with me,
And said he would go to Humility,
And come to me again.
RIOT: Let him come, if he will!
He were better to bide still.
And he give thee crooked language,
I will lay him on the visage;
And that thou shalt see soon,
How lightly it shall be done.   *300*
And he will not be ruled with knocks,
We shall set him in the stocks
To heal his sore shins.
YOUTH: I shall help thee if I can,
To drive away that hangman.
Hark, Riot, thou shalt understand
I am the heir of my father's land;
Methink it were best, therefore,
That I had one man more
To wait me upon.   *310*
RIOT: I can speed thee of a servant of price,   *find quickly*
That will do thee good service.
I see him go here beside.
Some men call him Master Pride.
I swear by God in Trinity
I will go fetch him unto thee,
And that even anon.
YOUTH: Hie thee apace and come again,   *hasten*
And bring with thee that noble swain.

[*Exit* RIOT *and return with* PRIDE]

RIOT: Lo, Master Youth, here he is,   320
  A pretty man and a wise;
  He will be glad to do you service
  In all that ever he may.
YOUTH: Welcome to me, good fellow.
  I pray thee, whence comest thou?
  And thou wilt my servant be,
  I shall give thee gold and fee.
PRIDE: Sir, I am content, iwis,
  To do you any service
  That ever I can do.   330
YOUTH: By likelihood thou should do well enow:
  Thou art a likely fellow.
PRIDE: Yes, sir, I warrant you,
  If ye will be ruled by me,
  I shall bring you to high degree.
YOUTH: What shall I do? Tell me,
  And I will be ruled by thee.
PRIDE: Marry, I shall tell you:
  Consider ye have good enow
  And think ye come of noble kind;   340
  Above all men exalt thy mind;
  Put down the poor, and set nought by them;
  Be in company with gentlemen;
  Jet up and down in the way;   *strut*
  And your clothes—Look they be gay.
  The pretty wenches will say then,
  Yonder goeth a gentleman,
  And every poor fellow that goeth by
  Will do off his cap and make you courtesy.
  In faith, this is true.   350
YOUTH: Sir, I thank thee, by the rood,   *cross*
  For thy counsel that is so good,
  And I commit me even now
  Under the teaching of Riot and you.
RIOT: Lo, Youth, I told you

That he was a lusty fellow.

YOUTH: Marry, sir, I thank thee
That you would bring him unto me.

PRIDE: Sir, it were expedient that ye had a wife
To live with her all your life.   360

RIOT: A wife? Nay, nay, for God avow,
He shall have flesh enow,
For, by God that me dear bought,
Over much of one thing is nought.
The devil said he had liever burn all his life   *rather*
Than once for to take a wife;
Therefore I say, so God me save,
He shall no wife have.
Thou hast a sister, fair and free,
I know well his leman she will be;   *mistress*   370
Therefore I would she were here,
That we might go and make good cheer
At the wine somewhere.

YOUTH: I pray you thither thou do her bring,
For she is to my liking.

PRIDE: Sir, I shall do my diligence
To bring her to your presence.

YOUTH: Hie thee apace and come again;   *hasten*
To have a sight I would be fain
Of that lady free.   380
          [*Exit* PRIDE]

RIOT: Sir, in faith I shall tell you true,
She is afresh and fair of hue,
And very proper of body.
Men call her Lady Lechery.

YOUTH: My heart burneth, by God of might,
Till of that lady I have a sight.
          [*Enter* PRIDE *and* LECHERY]

PRIDE: Sir, I have fulfilled your intent,
And have brought you in this present
That you have sent me for.

YOUTH: Thou art a ready messenger.   390

Come hither to me, my heart so dear;
Ye be welcome to me as the heart in my body.

LECHERY: Sir, I thank you, and at your pleasure I am;
Ye be the same unto me.

YOUTH: Masters, will ye to tavern walk?
A word with you there will I talk,
And give you the wine.

LECHERY: Gentleman, I thank you verily,
And I am all ready
To wait you upon.   400

RIOT: What, sister Lechery,
Ye be welcome to our company.

LECHERY: Well, wanton, well, fie for shame!
So soon ye do express my name!
What if no man should have known!
Iwis, I shall you beat. Well, wanton, well!

RIOT: A little pretty niset!   *wanton*
Ye be well nice, God wot!
Ye be a pretty little pye, iwis! Ye go full gingery!   *magpie*

LECHERY: Well, I see your false eye   410
Winketh on me full wantonly.
Ye be full wanton, iwis.

YOUTH: Pride, I thank you of your labor
That you had to fetch this fair flower.

PRIDE: Lo, Youth, I told thee
That I would bring her with me.
Sir, I pray you tell me now,
How doth she like you?

YOUTH: Verily, well she pleased me,
For she is courteous, gentle and free.   420
How do you, fair Lady?
How fare you, tell me?

LECHERY: Sir, if it please you, I do well enow,
And the better that you will wit.   *know*

YOUTH: Riot, I would be at the tavern fain,
Lest Charity us meet and turn us again;
Then would I be sorry because of this fair lady.

RIOT: Let us go again betime   *quickly*
    That we may be at the wine
    Or ever that he come.   430
PRIDE: Hie thee apace and go we hence;   *hasten*
    We will let for none expense.   *stop*
YOUTH: Now we will fill the cup and make good cheer.
    I trust I have a noble here.   *gold coin*
    Hark, sirs, for God almight,
    Hearest thou not how they fight?[9]
    In faith we shall them part.
    If there be any wine to sell,
    They shall no longer together dwell.
    No, then I beshrew my heart.   *curse* 440
RIOT: No sir, so mote I thee,   *may I thrive*
    Let not thy servants fight within thee,
    For it is a careful life
    Evermore to live in strife.
    Therefore, if ye will be ruled by my tale,
    We will go to the ale,
    And see how we can do.
    I trust God that sitteth on high,
    To lose that little company
    Within an hour or two.   450
PRIDE: Now let us go, for God's sake,
    And see how merry we can make.
RIOT: Now let us go apace.
    And I be last there, I beshrew my face.   *curse*
YOUTH: Now let us go that we were there
    To make this lady some cheer.
LECHERY: Verily, sir, I thank thee
    That thou will bestow it on me;
    And when it please you on me to call,
    My heart is yours, body and all.   460
YOUTH: Fair Lady, I thank thee,
    On the same wise ye shall have me,

[9] Youth apparently has more than one noble, and he seems to be jingling his coins together, thus making them "fight."

Whensoever ye please.

PRIDE: Riot, we tarry very long!

RIOT: We will go even now, with a lusty song.

PRIDE: In faith, I will be rector chori.[10]   *choir master*

YOUTH: Go to it then hardily, and let us be agate.   *on the way*

      [*Enter* CHARITY]

CHARITY: Abide, fellow; a word with thee:

  Whither go ye, tell me?

  Abide and hear what I shall you tell,   470

  And be ruled by my counsel.

PRIDE: Nay, no fellow, nor yet mate;

  I trow thy fellow be in Newgate.

  Shall we tell thee whither we go?

  Nay, iwis, good John-a-Peepo!

  Who learned thee, thou mistaught man,

  To speak so to a gentleman?

  Though his clothes be never so thin,

  Yet he is come of noble kin.

  Though thou give him such a mock,   480

  Yet he is come of a noble stock.

  I let thee well to wit.

RIOT: What! Sir John, what say ye!

  Would you be fettered now?

  Think not too long, I pray you;

  It may fortune come soon enow,

  Ye shall think it a little soon.

CHARITY: Yet, sirs, let this cease,

  And let us talk of goodness.

YOUTH: He turned his tail; he is afeard;   490

  But, faith, he shall be skeared.   *scared*

  He weeneth by flattering to please us again,   *thinks*

  But he laboreth all in vain.

CHARITY: Sir, I pray you me not spare,

  For nothing I do care

  That ye can do to me.

---

[10] Thomas Dekker uses the expression "rector chori" in *The Belman of London* to refer to the leader of a gang of beggars and thieves. Cp. *Materialien*, p. 91.

RIOT: No, whoreson? Sayest thou so?
  Hold him, Pride, and let me go;
  I shall fetch a pair of rings
  That shall sit to his shins,   *500*
  And that even anon.
PRIDE: Hie thee apace and come again,
  And bring with thee a good chain
  To hold him here still.
CHARITY: Jesu that was born of Mary mild,
  From all evil he us shield,
  And send you grace to amend,
  Ere our life be at an end;
  For I tell you truly
  That ye live full wickedly.   *510*
  I pray God it amend.
RIOT: Lo, sirs, look what I bring.
  Is this not a jolly ringing?
  By my troth, I trow it be.   *think it is*
  I will go wit of Charity: *ask*
  How sayest thou, Master Charity,
  Doth this gear please thee?
CHARITY: They please me well indeed.
  The more sorrow, the more meed.
  For God said while he was man,   *520*
  Beati qui persecutionem patiuntur propter justitiam;[11]
  Unto his apostles he said so,
  To teach them how they should do.
PRIDE: We shall see how they can please.
  Sit down, sir, and take your ease.
  Methink these same were full meet   *proper*
  To go about your fair feet.
YOUTH: By my truth, I you tell
  They would become him very well;
  Therefore hie that they were on,   *hasten* 530
  Unto the tavern that we were gone.
RIOT: That shall ye see anon,

---

[11] *Beati . . . justitiam:* "Blessed are they which are persecuted for righteousness' sake," Matthew 5, 10.

How soon they shall be on;
And after we will not tarry long,
But go hence with a merry song.

PRIDE: Let us begin all at once.

YOUTH: Now have at it, by Cock's bones,   *God's bones*
  And soon let us go.

  [*Exit* PRIDE, YOUTH, RIOT *and* LECHERY]

CHARITY: Lo, Masters, here you may see beforne,
  That the weed overgroweth the corn.   540
  Now may ye see all in this tide
  How vice is taken, and virtue set aside.
  Yonder ye may see youth is not stable,
  But evermore changeable;
  And the nature of men is frail,
  That he wotteth not what may avail   *knows*
  Virtue for to make.
  Oh good Lord, it is a pitiful case,
  Sith God hath lent man wit and grace   *since*
  To choose of good and evil,   550
  That man should voluntarily
  To such things himself apply,
  That his soul should spill.   *destroy*

  [*Enter* HUMILITY]

HUMILITY: Christ that was crucified and crowned with thorn,
  And of a virgin for man was born,
  Some knowledge send to me
  Of my brother Charity.

CHARITY: Dear brother Humility,
  Ye be welcome unto me.
  Where have ye been so long?   650

HUMILITY: I shall do you to understand
  That I have said mine evensong.
  But, sir, I pray you tell me now,
  How this case happened to you.

CHARITY: I shall tell you anon.
  The fellows that I told you on
  Have me thus arrayed.

HUMILITY: Sir, I shall undo the bands
From your feet and your hands.
Sir, I pray you tell me anon   570
Whither they be gone,
And when they come again.
CHARITY: Sir, to the tavern they be gone,
And they will come again anon,
And that you shall see.
HUMILITY: Then will we them exhort
Unto virtue to resort, and so forsake sin.
CHARITY: I will help you that I can
To convert that wicked man.
                    [*Enter* YOUTH, RIOT *and* PRIDE]
YOUTH: Aback, gallants, and look unto me,   580
And take me for your special,   *companion*
For I am promoted to high degree.
By right I am king eternal.
Neither duke nor **lord**, baron **nor** knight,
That may be likened unto me;
They be subdued to me by right,
As servants to their masters should be.
HUMILITY: Ye be welcome to this place here.
We think ye labor all in vain;
Wherefore your brains we will stir,   590
And kele you a little again.   *cool*
YOUTH: Sayest thou my brains thou wilt stir?
I shall lay thee on the ear.
Were thou born in Trumpington,
And brought up at Hogsnorton?[12]
By my faith, it seemeth so.
Well, go, knave, go!
CHARITY: Do by our counsel and our rede,   *advice*
And ask mercy for thy misdeed;
And endeavor thee, for God's sake,   600
For thy sins amends to make

[12] *Trumpington* is near Cambridge; *Hogsnorton* (or Hoch Norton) is a village in Oxfordshire whose inhabitants were supposed to be crude and boorish.

Ere ever that thou die.

RIOT: Hark, Youth, for God avow,   *before God I swear*
    He would have thee a saint now.
    But, Youth, I shall you tell,
    A young saint, an old devil.
    Therefore I hold thee a fool,
    And thou follow his school.

YOUTH: I warrant thee, I will not do so;
    I will be ruled by you two.   610

PRIDE: Then shall ye do well;
    If ye be ruled by our counsel,
    We will bring you to high degree,
    And promote you to dignity.

HUMILITY: Sir, it is a pitiful case,
    That ye would forsake grace
    And to vice apply.

YOUTH: Why, knave, doth it grieve thee?
    Thou shalt not answer for me.
    When my soul hangeth on the hedge once,   620
    Then take thou and cast stones
    As fast as thou wilt.

CHARITY: Sir, if it please you to do thus,
    Forsake them and do after us,
    The better shall you do.

RIOT: Sir, he shall do well enow,
    Though he be ruled by neither of you;
    Therefore crake no longer here   *talk*
    Lest you have on the ear,
    And that a good knock.   630

PRIDE: Lightly see thou avoid the place,   *quickly*
    Or I shall give thee on the face.
    Youth, I trow that he would   *believe*
    Make you holy ere ye be old;
    And I swear by the rood,
    It is time enough to be good
    When that ye be old.

YOUTH: Sir, by my truth, I thee say,

I will make merry whiles I may;
I cannot tell you how long.   640

RIOT: Yea, sir, mote I thrive,   *may*
Thou art not certain of thy life;
Therefore thou wert a stark fool
To leave mirth and follow their school.

HUMILITY: Sir, I shall him exhort
Unto us to resort,
And you to forsake.

PRIDE: Ask him if he will do so,
To forsake us and follow you two.
Nay, I warrant you, nay!   650

HUMILITY: That you shall see even anon.
I will unto him gone,
And see what he will say.

RIOT: Hardily go on thy way;
I know well he will say nay.

YOUTH: Yea, sir, by God that me dear bought,
Methink ye labor all for nought.
Weenest thou that I will for thee,   *think*
Or thy brother Charity,
Forsake this good company?   660
Nay, I warrant thee.

PRIDE: No, master, I pray you of that,
For anything forsake us not;
And all our counsel rule you by,
Ye may be emperor ere ye die.

YOUTH: While I have life in my body
Shall I be ruled by Riot and thee.

RIOT: Sir, then shall ye do well,
For we be as true as steel.
Sir I can teach you to play at the dice,   670
At the queen's game and at the Irish,
The treygobet and the hazard also,
And many other games mo;[13]   *more*

---

[13] These are all dice games: The *Queen's Game* and the *Irish* were like backgammon; *Treygobet* is obscure, but it may have been a game played with three dies (trey = three, gobet = piece).

Also at the cards I can teach you to play,
At the triump, and one and thirty,
Post, pinion, and also aums-ace,
And at another they call deuce-ace;[14]
Yet I can tell you more, and ye shall con me thank,   *thank me*
Pink and drink, and also at the blank,
And many sports more.[15]   680

YOUTH: I thank thee, Riot, so mote I thee,   *may I thrive*
For the counsel thou hast given me.
I will follow thy mind in everything,
And guide me after thy learning.

CHARITY: Youth, leave that counsel, for it is nought,
And amend that thou hast miswrought,
That thou mayest save that God hath bought.

YOUTH: What say ye, Master Charity?
What hath God bought?
By my troth, I know not   690
Whether He goeth in black or white.
He came never in at the stews,
Nor in any place where I do use.
Iwis, He bought not my cap,
Nor yet my jolly hat.
I wot not what He hath bought for me;   *know*
And He bought anything of mine,
I will give Him a quart of wine
The next time I Him meet.

CHARITY: Sir, this He did for thee: 700
When thou wast bond, He made thee free,
And bought thee with His blood.

YOUTH: Sir, I pray you tell me,
How may this be;
That I know I was never bond

[14] These are all card games: *Triump* resembled whist; *One and Thirty* was like twenty-one; *Post* was played with three cards and seems to have been an early version of poker; *Pinion* is obscure, and the only reference in the *OED* is to this passage from *Youth*; *Aums-Ace* = Ace-Ace, or two single points, *Deuce-Ace* = two and one: they would seem to be dicing games, but the context suggests that they may have been card games.
[15] *Pink and drink*: McKerrow suggests that this is a reduplicated phrase for drinking. Pink may refer to a lost card game, since the word was sometimes used to indicate the suit of diamonds; or it may mean to prick or pierce, and thus it may refer to drunken brawling.

Unto none in England.
CHARITY: Sir, I shall tell you:
When Adam had done great trespass,
And out of paradise exiled was,
Then all the souls, as I can you tell,
Were in the bondage of the devil of hell,   710
Till that the Father of heaven, of his great mercy,
Sent the Second Person in Trinity
Us for to redeem;
And so with His precious blood
He bought us on the rood,   *cross*
And our souls did save.
YOUTH: How should I save it? Tell me now,
And I will be ruled after you my soul to save.
RIOT: What, Youth, will you forsake me?   720
I will not forsake thee.
HUMILITY: I shall tell you shortly:
Kneel down and ask God mercy
For that you have offended.
PRIDE: Youth, wilt thou do so—
Follow them and let us go?
Marry, I trow nay.
YOUTH: Here all sin I forsake,
And to God I me betake.
Good Lord, I pray Thee have no indignation,   730
That I, a sinner, should ask salvation.
CHARITY: Now thou must forsake Pride,
And all Riot set aside.
PRIDE: I will not him forsake,
Neither early nor late;
I wende he would not forsake me,   *thought*
But if it will none otherwise be,
I will go my way.
YOUTH: Sir, I pray God be your speed
And help you at your need.   740
RIOT: I am sure thou wilt not forsake me,
Nor I will not forsake thee.

YOUTH: I forsake you also,
  And will not have with you to do.
RIOT: And I forsake thee utterly.
  Fie on thee, caitiff, fie!
  Once a promise thou did me make,
  That thou would me never forsake;
  But now I see it is hard
  For to trust the wretched world.   750
  Farewell, masters, everyone.
HUMILITY: For your sins, look ye mourn;
  And evil creatures, look ye turn.
  For your name, who maketh inquisition,
  Say it is Good Contrition
  That for sin doth mourn.
CHARITY: Here is a new array
  For you to walk by the way,
  Your prayer for to say.
HUMILITY: Here be beads for your devotion,[16]   760
  And keep you from all temptation;
  Let not vice devour.
  When ye see misdoing men,
  Good counsel give them,
  And teach them to amend.
YOUTH: For my sin I will mourn;
  All creatures I will turn;
  And when I see misdoing men,
  Good counsel I shall give them,
  And exhort them to amend.   770
CHARITY: Then shall ye be an heritor of bliss,
  Where all joy and mirth is.
YOUTH: To the which eternal
  God bring the persons all
  Here being. Amen.
HUMILITY: Thus have we brought our matter to an end
  Before the persons here present.
  Would every man be content,

[16] Thus W; C reads "Here be *books* for your devotion."

Lest another day we be shent. *shamed*
CHARITY: We thank all this present 780
Of their meek audience.
HUMILITY: Jesu that sitteth in heaven so high,
Save all this fair company,
Men and women that here be.
Amen, amen, for Charity.

Plate 5. Characters from the
title page of William Copland's
edition (c. 1562).

✳ *THE WORLD AND THE CHILD*

(Mundus et Infans, c. 1508–1522)

In a historical view of the development of the morality play *Mundus et Infans*, as it is usually called, is of considerable importance, for it reaffirms, after more than a hundred years, the basic interpretation of the course of man's life set down in *The Castle of Perseverance*, and then points the way toward the shorter moral interludes by crystallizing the spiritual biography very clearly into three phases, the Three Ages of Man.

There are at least three aspects of the play worth noting. The first is the handling of time. We note that the central figure is supposed to be newborn when he first enters, and that he grows to majority without leaving the stage and within the scope of a few score of lines. This very self-conscious telescoping of time is to become such a commonplace in Elizabethan dramaturgy that we scarcely notice it, and we wonder how the neoclassical critics could ever have taken the Elizabethans to task for it. In the second place there is the use of language to indicate character. The author of this play seems to have been the first to have sufficient verbal facility to make his hero's diction change as he lives through the ages of his life. He speaks flat narrative verse as an infant—perhaps the equivalent of no speech at all. As a child he babbles in fluent Childish. As a young man he utters love lyrics, as an adult the alliterative bombastic vaunting of the King of Life and of the Herods and Pilates in the mystery plays. As an old man he whines out his complaint.

The third thing to notice is that as soon as the hero becomes Manhood Mighty what we get is a history play in miniature. Like Magnificence, Manhood takes Folly as his servant, and he is going out to break the laws of chivalry and moderation when he is restrained by Conscience.

At last he appears as Age, and is put through a fairly complete version of the whole penitential cycle—contrition, confession, penance, and absolution. As a sign of his regeneration he is given a new name, Repentance (the equivalent of Youth's new robe in the Interlude, and ultimately deriving from the Prodigal Son's new robe). It is interesting to note that at the end of the play the other characters call him "Repentance" while his own speech-tags continue to insist on "Age." This is another small instance of the fact that for all its experimental vitality the morality play is basically conservative and never forgets its key formulations.

The only surviving edition of the play is that of 1522, by one of the great early Tudor printers, Wynkyn de Worde. Our text is a modernized-spelling version of the Tudor Facsimile Text Society's facsimile, London, 1907.

THE WORLD AND THE CHILD

The Interlude of the World and the Child, otherwise called Mundus et
Infans, *and it showeth of the estate of Childhood and Manhood.*

[*Enter* MUNDUS]

MUNDUS: Sirs, peace of your saws, what so befall,   *be quiet*
  And look ye bow bonerly to my bidding,   *politely*
  For I am ruler of realms, I warn you all,
  And over all fodes I am king;   *dwellings*
  For I am king and well known in these realms round.
  I have also palace ypight;   *built*
  I have steeds in stable stalwart and strong,
  Also streets and strands full strongly ydight.   *decorated*
  For All-the-World-Wide I wot is my name;
  All richess redely it runneth in me,   *wealth truly* 10
  All pleasure worldly, both mirth and game.
  Myself, seemly in sale, I send with you to be,   *hall (Fr. salle)*
  For I am the world I warn you all.
  Prince of power and of plenty,
  He that cometh not when I do him call,
  I shall him smite with poverty,
  For poverty I part in many a place   *allot*
  To them that will not obedient be.
  I am a king in every case,
  Methinketh I am a god of grace.   20
  The flower of virtue followeth me,
  Lo, here I sit seemly in see,   *enthroned*
  I command you all obedient be
  And with free will ye follow me.
    [*Enter* INFANS]

INFANS: Christ our King grant you clearly to know ye case,
  To move of this matter that is in my mind.   *give judgment*
  Clearly [to] declare it Christ grant me grace.
  Now seemly sirs, behold on me
  How Mankind doth begin.
  I am a child, as you may see,   30

Gotten in game and in great sin.   *begotten*
Forty weeks my mother me found,   *held*
Flesh and blood my fode.   *dwelling*
When I was ripe from her to found   *fall*
In peril of death we stood both two.
Now to seek death I must begin[1]
For to pass that strait passage,
For body and soul that shall then twin   *part*
And make a parting of that marriage.
Forty weeks I was freely fed   40
Within my mother's possession,
Full oft of death she was adread
When that I should part her from;
Now into the world she hath me sent,
Poor and naked as ye may see.
I am not worthily wrapt nor went,   *decked out*
But poorly pricked in poverty.
Now into the world will I wend,
Some comfort of him for to crave.
All hail, comely crowned King!   50
God that all made you see and save!   *may God protect you*
MUNDUS: Welcome fair child, what is thy name?
INFANS: I wot not, sir, withouten blame.
   But ofttime my mother in her game
   Called me Dalliance.
MUNDUS: Dalliance, my sweet child,
   It is a name that is right wild,
   For when thou waxest old
   It is a name of no substance.
   But my fair child what wouldst thou have?   60
INFANS: Sir, of some comfort I you crave,
   Meat and clothes my life to save,
   And I your true servant shall be.
MUNDUS: Now fair child, I grant thee thine asking.
   I will thee find, while thou art young,   *support*

---

[1] There is no punctuation at all in the only surviving early version. This passage illustrates the difficulties attendant upon this fact. The punctuation offered here is perhaps not the only one that makes sense.

So thou wilt be obedient to my bidding.
These garments gay I give to thee
And also I give to thee a name,
And clep thee Wanton, in every game,   *call*
Till fourteen year be come and gone,   70
And then come again to me.
WANTON: Gramercy World, for mine array,
  For now I purpose me to play.
MUNDUS: Farewell fair child, and have good day,
  All recklessness is kind for thee.   *natural*
    [*Exit*]²
WANTON: Ah ha! Wanton is my name
  I can many a quaint game.   *know*
  Lo, my top I drive in same,³   *also*
  See, it turneth round.
  I can with my scourge-stick   80
  My fellow upon the head hit,
  And wightly from him make a skip,   *spryly*
  And bleer on him my tongue.   *insult him*
  If brother or sister do me chide
  I will scratch and also bite,
  I can cry and also kick,
  And mock them all berew.   *confound them*
  If father or mother will me smite
  I will wring with my lip
  And lightly from him make a skip   90
  And call my dame shrew.   *mother*
  Ah ha! A new game have I found.
  See this gin, it runneth round;   *toy*
  And here another have I found
  And yet mo can I find.

---

² There are no stage directions in the original. The title page, however, shows Mundus enthroned in what appears to be a small booth. This could be his "mansion," or his "scaffold," as in *The Castle of Perseverance*. Thus perhaps rather than exiting he simply withdraws to this area and watches the Child's antics. See also the implied "stage direction" at l.130.

³ "In same" is simply a line filler and an arbitrary rhyme word. The extent to which this speech is simply a verbal *tour de force* should be noted. The whole play has something of the air of a jaunty musical piece about it, rather like the Elizabethan jig, an effect that is reinforced by the short-lined mocking multiple rhymes, reminiscent of Skelton.

I can mow on a man   *make a face at*
And tell a lesing well I can   *lie*
And maintain it right well then.
This cunning came me of kind.
Yea sirs, I can well geld a snail   100
And catch a cow by the tail,
This is a fair cunning,
I can dance and also skip,
I can play at the cherry pit
And I can whistle you a fit   *stanza of a tune*
Sirs, in a willow rind,   *piece of bark*
Yea sirs, and every day
When I to school shall take the way,
Some good man's garden I will assay,
Pears and plums to pluck.   110
I can spy a sparrow's nest,
I will not go to school but when me lest,   *when I feel like it*
For there beginneth a sorry fest
When the master should lift my dock.   *buttocks*
But sirs, when I was seven year of age
I was sent to the World to take wage,
And this seven year I have been his page
And kept his commandment.
Now I will wend to the World, that worthy Emperor.
Hail, Lord of great honor!   120
This seven year I have served you in hall and in bower
With all my true intent.
MUNDUS: Now welcome, Wanton, my darling dear,
    A new name I shall give thee here,
    Love-Lust-Liking in fere   *all together*
    These they names they shall be.
    All game and glee and gladness
    All love-longing in lewdness,
    This seven year forsake all sadness
    And then come again to me.   130
LUST-AND-LIKING: Ah ha! Now Lust-and-Liking is my name,
    I am fresh as flowers in May,

I am seemly shapen in same
And proudly apparelled in garments gay.
My locks been full lovely to a lady's eye
And in love-longing my heart is sore set.   *beset*
Might I find a fode that were fair and free
To lie in hell till doomsday for love I would not let.   *hesitate*
My love for to win
All game and glee   140
All mirth and melody
All revel and riot
And of boast will I never blin.   *cease*
But sirs, now I am nineteen winter old,
Iwis, I wax wonder bold.
Now I will go to the World
A higher science to assay,
For the World will me advance,
I will keep his governance,
His pleasing will I pray,   150
For he is a king in all substance.
All hail, master full of might!
Now I comen as I you behight.
One and twenty winter is comen and gone.
MUNDUS: Now welcome, Love-Lust-and-Liking,
For thou hast been obedient to my bidding.
I increase thee in all thing
And mightily I make thee a man.
Manhood Mighty shall be thy name
Bear thee prest in every game   *eagerly* 160
And wait well that thou suffer no shame,   *take care*
Neither for land nor for rent.
If any man would weight thee with blame
Withstand him with thy whole intent,
Full sharply thou beat him to shame
With doughtiness of deed,
For of one thing, Manhood, I warn thee,
I am most of bounty
For seven kings suen me   *follow*

Both by day and night.   170
One of them is the King of Pride,
The King of Envy, doughty in deed,
The King of Wrath, that boldly will abide,
For mickle is his might,   *much* (great)
The King of Covetous is the fourth,
The fifth King he hight Sloth.   *is called*
The King of Gluttony hath no jollity
There poverty is pight.   *where/in power*
Lechery is the seventh King,
All men in him have great delighting,   180
Therefore worship him above all thing
Manhood, with all thy might.
MANHOOD: Yes, Sir King, without lesing
  It shall be wrought.
  Had I knowing of the first King, without lesing,
  Well joyen I mought.   *I might well have had a good time*
MUNDUS: The first King hight Pride.
MANHOOD: Ah Lord, with him fain would I bide.
MUNDUS: Yea, but wouldst thou serve him truly in every
    tide?
MANHOOD: Yea sir, and thereto my truth I plight   190
  That I shall truly Pride present.   *represent*
  I swear by Saint Thomas of Kent,
  To serve him truly is mine intent,
  With main and all my might.
MUNDUS: Now Manhood I will array thee new
  In robes royal right of good hue,
  And I pray thee principally be true
  And here I dub thee a knight,
  And haunt alway to chivalry.   *follow*
  I give thee grace and also beauty,   200
  Gold and silver great plenty,
  Of the wrong to make the right.
MANHOOD: Gramercy World, and Emperor,
  Gramercy World, and Governor,
  Gramercy comfort in all color,   *in every respect*

And now I take my leave. Farewell.

MUNDUS: Farewell Manhood, my gentle knight,
Farewell my son, seemly in sight,
I give thee a sword and also strength and might
In battle boldly to bear thee well.[4]   210

MANHOOD: Now I am dubbed a knight hende   *gracious*
Wonder wide shall wax my fame,
To seek adventures now will I wend,
To please the World in glee and game.

MUNDUS: Lo sirs, I am a Prince perilous yprobèd,   *proven*
I proved full perilous and pithily ypight;
As a lord in each land I am beloved,
Mine eyen do shine as lantern bright,
I am a creature comely, out of care,
Emperors and Kings they kneel to my knee,   220
Every man is afeard when I do on him stare,
For all merry middle-earth maketh mention of me,
Yet all is at my handwork, both by down and by dale,
Both the sea and land and fowls that fly,
And I were once moved, I tell you in tale,   *If*
There durst no star steer that standeth in the sky,
For I am lord and leader so that in land
All boweth to my bidding bonerly about.
Who that stirreth with any strife or weighteth me with
            wrong
I shall mightily make him to stammer and stoop   230
For I am rich in mine array,
I have knights and towers,
I have ladies, brightest in bowers,
Now will I fare on these flowers,
Lordings, have good day.
            (*Exit.*)

MANHOOD: Peace now, peace ye fellows all about,
Peace now, and hearken to my saws,
For I am lord both stalworthy and stout.   *stalwart and strong*

---

[4] Since the dressing and knighting of Manhood are carried out while Mundus speaks, it is possible that he might have some unmentioned attendants on stage.

All lands are led by my laws,
Baron was there never born that so well him bore,   240
A better ne a bolde nor a brighter of ble,   *nor/bolder/complexion*
For I have might and main over countries far,
And Manhood Mighty am I named in every country,
For Salerne and Samers and Ynetheloys,[5]
Calais, Kent and Cornwall I have conquered clean,
Picardy and Punt and gentle Artois,
Florence, Flanders and France, also Gascoyne,
All I have conquered as a knight.
There is no emperor so keen
That dare me lightly teen   250
For lives and limbs I lean   *make lean*
So mickle is my right.
For I have boldly blood full piteously de-spilled
There many hath left fingers and feet, both head and face.
I have done harm on heads and knights have I killed
And many a lady for my love hath said "Alas,"
Brigand Ernys[6] I have beaten to back and to bones
And beaten also many a groom to ground.
Breastplates I have beaten as
    Stephen was with stones   *(St. Stephen martyr)*
So fell a fighter in field was there never yfound.   *terrible* 260
To me no man is nakèd,   *comparable*
For Manhood Mighty that is my name
Many a lord have I do lame   *made*
Wonder wide walketh my fame

[5] One item in this very traditional list remains mysterious. The convention abounds in medieval literaturet perhaps the best known lists being those of Chaucer's Knight and Squire in the General Prologue. Most of the place names are associated with the Crusades or the wars with France: "Salerne" is Salerno, "Samers" is Samaria, "Punt" is East Africa, and the rest are obvious, except for "Yndetheloys," which we print exactly as it appears in the original. There are three interpretations of it that seem to have merit. Since Inde is the usual contemporary spelling of India, perhaps we have an accidentally run together descriptive phrase, "India the ——." The other solutions are related to the heavy incidence of French names in the rest of the passage. One is that we should read "Inde. Toulouse" (suggested by Professor D. C. Baker of the University of Colorado). Another is that we should forget about India and read "Andelys," the site in northern France of a famous siege by the English Richard the Lion-hearted. While the passage asserts Manhood's ubiquity, one may be tempted to consider the ironic use of highly restricted geography, in view of the fact that there were towns in France called Salerne, Florennes, and Samer.

[6] Brigand Ernys has not been tracked down. He is probably a character out of folklore or romance, perhaps of the same family that gives us Giant Tediousness in *Wit and Science*.

And many a King's crown have I cracked.
I am worthy and wight, witty and wise,   *sharp*
I am royal arrayed to reven under the rise,[7]
I am proudly apparelled in purpure and bice,   *dark blue*
As gold I glister in gear,   *array*
I am stiff, strong, stalworthy and stout,   270
I am royalest, redely, that runneth in this rout.   *truly*
There is no knight so grisly that I dread nor doubt   *gear*
For I am so doughtily dight there may no dint me dere,   *hurt*
And the King of Pride full prest with all his proud presence,
And the King of Lechery lovely his letters hath me sent,
And the King of Wrath full worldly with all his intent,[8]
They will me maintain with main and all their might.
The King of Covetous and the King of Gluttony,
The King of Sloth and the King of Ervy,   280
All those send me their livery.
Where is now so worthy a wight?
A wight?
Yea, as a wight witty
Here in this seat sit I
For no loves let I[9]
Here for to sit,
                    [*Enter* CONSCIENCE]
CONSCIENCE: Christ, as he is crowned king,
Save all this comely company
And grant you all his dear blessing,
That bonerly bought you on the rood tree.   290
Now pray you prestly on every side
To God omnipotent
To set our enemy sharply on side,
That is the devil and his convent,   *community of adherents*
And all men to have a clear knowing

[7] As it stands, "reven under the rise" seems to mean "to rob under the hill," which makes some kind of sense. *OED*, however, cites this passage and suggests that it should be amended to "rennen under the rice," which would mean, roughly, to "run along in the bushes," which also makes a certain kind of sense. The difference is that the original is a boast, while the emendation is self-mockery.
[8] Original reads "wordly."
[9] These three lines were probably perfect rhymes, in contemporary pronunciation.

Of heaven bliss, that high tower.
Methinketh it is a necessary thing
For young and old, both rich and poor,
Poor Conscience for to know,
For Conscience Clear it is my name,   300
Conscience counseleth both high and low,
And Conscience commonly beareth great blame—
Blame?—
Yea, and oftentimes set in shame,
Wherefore I rede you men, both in earnest and in game,   *advise*
Conscience that ye know,   *become acquainted with*
For I know all the mysteries of man,
They be as simple as they can,
And in every company where I come
Conscience is outcast.   310
All the world doth conscience hate
Mankind and Conscience been at debate
For if Mankind might Conscience take   *capture*
My body would they brast.   *break*
Brast, yea, and work me much woe.

MANHOOD:　Say how, fellow, who gave thee leave this way to go?
　　What, wenest thou I dare not come thee to?
　　Say, thou harlot, whither in haste?   (generalized term of abuse)

CONSCIENCE:　What, let me go sir. I know you not.

MANHOOD:　No, bitched brothel, thou shalt be taught,   320
　　For I am a knight, an I were sought.   *if*
　　The World hath advanced me.

CONSCIENCE:　Why, good sir knight what is your name?

MANHOOD:　Manhood Mighty, in mirth and in game,
　　All power of Pride have I ta'en,
　　I am as gentle as jay on tree.

CONSCIENCE:　Sir, though the World have you to manhood
　　　　brought,
　　To maintain manner[s] ye were never taught;
　　No conscience clear ye know, right nought,
　　And this longeth to a knight.   *is part of* 330

MANHOOD:　Conscience! What the devil man is he?

CONSCIENCE: Sir, a teacher of spirituality.

MANHOOD: Spirituality? What the devil may that be?

CONSCIENCE: Sir, all that be leaders into light—

MANHOOD: Light, yea but hark fellow, yet light fain would I
   see!

CONSCIENCE: Will ye so, sir? Then do after me.

MANHOOD: Yea, an it to Pride's pleasing be,
  I will take thy teaching.

CONSCIENCE: Nay, sir, beware of Pride and you do well,
  For Pride, Lucifer fell into hell,   340
  Till doomsday there shall he dwell
  Without any outcoming,
  For Pride, sir, is but a vainglory.

MANHOOD: Peace, thou brothel, and let those words be!
  For the World and Pride hath advanced me.
  To me men lout full low.   *bow down*

CONSCIENCE: And to beware of Pride, sir, I would counsel you,
  And think on King Robert of Sicily[10]
  How he, for pride, in great poverty fell
  For he would not Conscience know.   350

MANHOOD: Yea, Conscience, go forth thy way,
  For I love Pride, and will go gay.
  All thy teaching is not worth a straw[11]
  For Pride I clep my king.

CONSCIENCE: Sir, there is no king but God above,
  That bodily bought us with pain and passion,
  Because of man's soul['s] redemption,
  In Scripture thus we find.

MANHOOD: Say, Conscience, sith ye wouldst have Pride fro
     me,   *since*
  What sayest thou by the King of Lechery?   360
  With all mankind he must be
  And with him I love to ling.   *linger*

CONSCIENCE: Nay Manhood, that may not be.

---

[10] An often-mentioned medieval figure who underwent a strikingly moralitylike career of sin, suffering and penitence.

[11] Original reads "stray," rhyming with "gay." We modernize for clarity of the colloquial expression.

From lechery fast you flee,
For encumbrance it will bring thee
And all that to him will lind.   *lean, incline*
MANHOOD: Say, Conscience, of the King of Sloth.
  He hath behight me mickle troth,
  And I may not forsake him, for ruth,
  For with him I think to rest.   370
CONSCIENCE: Manhood, in Scripture thus we find,
  That Sloth is a traitor to heaven king.
  Sir knight, if you will keep your kind   *support*
  From Sloth clean you cast.
MANHOOD: Say, Conscience, the King of Gluttony,
  He saith he will not forsake me
  And I purpose his servant to be
  With main and all my might.
CONSCIENCE: Think, Manhood, on substance,
  And put out gluttony, for 'cumbrance,   380
  And keep with you good governance
  For this longeth to a knight.
MANHOOD: What, Conscience, from all my masters ye wouldst
              have me,
  But I will never forsake Envy
  For he is king of company
  Both with more and less.
CONSCIENCE: Nay Manhood, that may not be.
  An ye will cherish Envy
  God will not well pleased be
  To comfort you in that case.   390
MANHOOD: Aye, aye! from five kings thou has counselled me,
  But from the King of Wrath I will never flee,
  For he is in every deed doughty,
  For him dare no man rout.[12]
CONSCIENCE: Nay Manhood, beware of Wrath,
  For it is but superfluity that cometh and goeth,
  Yea, and all men his company hateth,

[12] "Rout" is susceptible of at least two meanings in *OED* that might apply here. The likelier is "make trouble," "for him" meaning "in his presence."

For oft they stand in doubt.   *fear*
MANHOOD: Fie one thee, false flattering friar!
  Thou shalt rue the time that thou came here.   400
  The devil mote set thee on a fire   *may the devil*
  That ever I with thee meet,
  For thou counsellest me from all gladness,
  And would me set unto all sadness,
  But, or thou bring me in this madness,   *ere*
  The devil break thy neck!
  But sir friar, (evil mote thou thee),   *may you fare badly*
  From six kings thou hast counselled me,
  But that day shall thou never see
  To counsel me from Covetous.   410
CONSCIENCE: No sir, I will not you from Covetous bring,
  For Covetous I clep a king
  Sir, Covetous, in good doing
  Is good in all wise;
  But, sir knight, will ye do after me,
  And Covetous your king shall be.
MANHOOD: Yea sir, my truth I plight to thee,
  That I will work at thy will.
CONSCIENCE: Manhood, will ye by this word stand?
MANHOOD: Yea Conscience, here is my hand.   420
  I will never from it fong,   *take away*
  Neither loud ne still.
CONSCIENCE: Manhood, ye must love God above all thing;
  His name in idleness ye may not ming;   *use (mix)*
  Keep your holyday from worldly doing;
  Your father and mother worship aye;
  Covet ye to slay no man
  Ne do no lechery with no woman;
  Your neighbor's good take not by no way,
  And all false witness ye must deny;   430
  Neither ye must not covet no man's wife
  Nor no good that him belieth.   *belongs to*
  This covetise shall keep you out of strife.
  These been the commandments ten

Mankind, and ye these commandments keep
Heaven bliss I you beheet.   *promise*
For Christ's commandments are full sweet[13]
And full necessary to all men.
MANHOOD: What, Conscience, is this thy Covetous?
CONSCIENCE: Yea Manhood, in all wise,   440
 And covet to Christ's service,
 Both to matins and to mass.
 Ye must, Manhood, with all your might
 Maintain Holy Church's right,
 For this longeth to a knight
 Plainly in every place.
MANHOOD: What, Conscience, should I leave all game and
  glee?
CONSCIENCE: Nay Manhood, so mote I thee.   *so may I prosper*
 All mirth in measure is good for thee,
 But sir, measure is in all thing.   450
MANHOOD: Measure, Conscience? What thing may measure be?
CONSCIENCE: Sir, keep you in charity
 And from all evil company
 For doubt of folly doing.   *fear*
MANHOOD: Folly? What thing callest thou folly?
CONSCIENCE: Sir, it is Pride, Wrath and Envy,
 Sloth, Covetous and Gluttony,
 Lechery the seventh is,
 These seven sins I call folly.
MANHOOD: What, thou liest! To this[14]   460
 Seven the World delivered me
 And said they were kings of great beauty
 And most of main and mights.
 But yet I pray thee sir, tell me
 My I not go arrayed honestly?
CONSCIENCE: Yes Manhood, hardily   *certainly*
 In all manner of degree.
MANHOOD: But I must have sporting of play.

[13] Original reads "all full sweet." We emend because the next line seems to demand an understood "are."
[14] Here again we have chosen *a* punctuation that makes sense of the passage.

CONSCIENCE: Sikerly, Manhood, I say not nay,   *surely*
  But good governance keep both night and day   470
  And maintain meekness and all mercy.
MANHOOD: All mercy, Conscience? What may that be?
CONSCIENCE: Sir, all discretion that God gave thee.
MANHOOD: Discretion I know not, so mote I thee.
CONSCIENCE: Sir, it is all the wits that God hath you sent.
MANHOOD: Ah, Conscience, now I know and see,
  Thy cunning is much more than mine,   *knowledge*
  But yet I pray thee sir, tell me
  What is most necessary for man in every time.
CONSCIENCE: Sir, in every time beware of folly;   480
  Folly is full of false flattering.
  In what occupation that ever ye be,
  Always, or ye begin to think on the ending,
  For blame [   ]¹⁵
  Now farewell Manhood, I must wend.
MANHOOD: Now farewell Conscience, mine own friend.
CONSCIENCE: I pray you, Manhood, have God in mind
  And beware of folly and shame.
          [*Exit.*]
MANHOOD: Yes, yes! Ye come wind and rain,
  God let him never come here again!   490
  Now he is forward I am right fain,
  For in faith, sir, he had near counselled me all amiss.¹⁶
  Ah, ah, now I have bethought me if I shall heaven win
  Conscience's teachings I must begin
  And clean forsake the kings of sin
  That the World me taught,
  And Conscience's servant will I be
  And believe, as he hath taught me,
  Upon one God and Persons three
  That made all thing of nought;   500

¹⁵ This is neither a blotted nor a worm-eaten passage; there is simply nothing there at all. A guess would be that the compositor stopped setting type in order to query the MS reading, and then somehow went on setting and forgot about this half-line.
¹⁶ The "sir" here, as elsewhere in the moralities, is apparently addressed to the ranking member of the audience.

For Conscience Clear I clep my king
And [I] his knight in good doing
For right of reason, as I find,
Conscience's teaching is true.
The world is full of boast
And saith he is of mights most,
All his teaching is not worth a cost,   *the price*
For Conscience he doth refuse.
But yet will I him not forsake,
For Mankind he doth merry make   510
Though the World and Conscience be at debate,
Yet the World will I not despise.
For both in church and in cheaping   *business*
And in other places being
The World findeth me all thing
And doth me great service.
Now here full prest
I think so to rest,   *(i.e. I will remain in this opinion)*
Now mirth is best.

      [*Enter* FOLLY]

FOLLY: What, hey ho! now care, away!   520
  My name is Folly, am I not gay?
  Is here any man that will say nay,
  That runneth in this rout?   *crowd*
  Ah sir, God give you good eve.

MANHOOD: Stand, utter fellow, where dost thou thy courtesy
      prove?[17]

FOLLY: What, I do but claw mine arse sir, by your leave.
  I pray you, sir, rive me this clout.   *tear out/lump*

MANHOOD: What, stand out, thou feigned shrew!   *wretch*

FOLLY: By my faith, sir, there the cock crew,[18]
  For I take record of this row   *swear by this crowd (i.e. the audience)*   530
  My theedom is near past.   *prosperity*

MANHOOD: Now truly, it may well be so.

---

[17] The original reads "you thy," which is dialectical, but Manhood is not a dialect character, therefore we substitute the above.
[18] Original reads "By by faith." "There the cock crew" means "my time has come."

FOLLY: By God, sir, yet have I fellows mo,
  For in every country where I go
  Some man his thrift hath lost.
MANHOOD: But hark, fellow, art thou any craftsman?
FOLLY: Yea sir, I can bind a sieve and tink a pan,   *repair*
  And thereto a curious buckler player I am.   *clever/shield*
  Arise, fellow! Wilt thou assay?
MANHOOD: Now truly sir, I trow thou canst but little skill   540
    play.
FOLLY: Yes, by Cock's bones, that I can!   *by God's bones*
  I will never flee for no man
  That walketh by the way.
MANHOOD: Fellow, though thou have cunning
  I counsel thee, leave thy boasting,
  For here thou may thy fellow find.
  Whether thou wilt at long or short.   *(i.e. with sword or dagger)*
FOLLY: Come look an thou darest: arise and assay!
MANHOOD: Yea sir, but yet Conscience biddeth me
    nay.
FOLLY: No sir, thou darest not, in good fay,   *faith*   550
  For truly thou failest now, false heart.[19]
MANHOOD: What, sayest thou I have a false heart?
FOLLY: Yea sir, in good fay.
MANHOOD: Manhood will not that, I say nay!
  Defend thee, Folly, if that you may,[20]
  For, in faith, I purpose to wete what thou art.
      [*They fight*]
  Now, faith, how now Folly, hast thou not a touch?
FOLLY: No, ywis, but a little on my pouch.
  On all this meinie I will me vouch
  That standeth here about.   560
MANHOOD: And I take record on all this row
  Thou hast two touches, though I say but few.
FOLLY: Yea, this place is not without a shrew
  I do you all out of due.   *I'll bet*

[19] Original reads "failest no false heart."
[20] Original reads "if t you may."

MANHOOD: But hark fellow, by thy faith, where was thou
    bore?   *born*

FOLLY: By my faith, in England have I dwelled yore, *long*
 And all mine ancestors me before;
 But sir, in London is my chief dwelling.

MANHOOD: In London! Where, if a man thee sought?

FOLLY: Sir, in Holborn I was forth brought   570
 And with the Courtiers I am betaught.
 To Westminster I used to wend.[21]

MANHOOD: Hark fellow why dost thou to Westminster
    draw?

FOLLY: For I am a servant of the law.
 Covetous is mine own fellow,
 We twain plead for the king,   *before*
 And poor men that come from upland *the countryside*
 We will take their matter in hand
 Be it right or be it wrong
 Their thrift with us shall wend.   580

MANHOOD: Now hear, fellow, I pray, whither wendest thou
    then?

FOLLY: By my faith sir, into London I ran,
 To the taverns to drink the wine,
 And then to the [   ] I took the way *(illegible-name of an Inn)*
 And there I was not welcome to the hosteler
 But I was welcome to the fair tapster
 And to all the household I was right dear,
 For I have dwelled with her many a day.

MANHOOD: Now I pray ye, whither took ye then the way?

FOLLY: In faith sir, over London Bridge I ran 590
 And the straight way to the stews I came, *brothels*
 And took lodging for a night,
 And there I found my brother Lechery
 There men and women did folly
 And every man made of me as worthy
 As though I had been a knight.

MANHOOD: I pray thee, yet tell me mo of thine adventures.

[21] The centre of governmental activities in England.

FOLLY: In faith, even straight to all the friars,
   And with them I dwelled many years
   And they crowned Folly a king   600
MANHOOD: I pray thee fellow, whither wendest thou then?
FOLLY: Sir, all England to and fro,
   Into abbeys and into nunneries also,
   And always Folly doth fellows find.
MANHOOD: Now hark fellow, I pray thee, tell me thy name.
FOLLY: Iwis, I hight Folly and Shame.
MANHOOD: Ah ha! Thou art he that Conscience did blame
   When he me taught.
   I pray thee Folly, go hence and follow me not.
FOLLY: Yes good sir, let me your servant be.   610
MANHOOD: Nay, so mote I thee,
   For then a shrew had I caught.
FOLLY: Why good sir, what is your name?
MANHOOD: Manhood Mighty, that beareth no blame.
FOLLY: By the rood, and Manhood mistereth in   *finds it necessary*
     every game
   Somedeal to cherish Folly.   *somewhat*
   For Folly is fellow with the World
   And greatly beloved with many a lord,
   And if ye put me out of your ward
   The World right wroth will be.   620
MANHOOD: Yea sir, yet had I lever the World be wroth
   Than lose the cunning that Conscience me gave.
FOLLY: A cuckoo for Conscience, he is but a daw   *fool*
   He can not else but preach.
MANHOOD: Yea, I pray thee leave thy lewd clattering,
   For Conscience is a counsellor for a king.
FOLLY: I would not give a straw for his teaching;
   He doth but make men wroth.
   But wotest thou what I say man?
   By that ilk truth that God me gave,   *same* 630
   Had I that bitched Conscience in this place
   I should so beat him with my staff
   That all his stones should stink.   *testicles*

MANHOOD:　I pray thee Folly, go hence and follow me not.

FOLLY:　Yes sir, so mote I thee
　Your servant will I be,
　I ask but meat and drink.

MANHOOD:　Peace man, I may not have thee for thy　　*because of*
　　　name,
　For thou sayest thy name is both Folly and Shame.

FOLLY:　Sir, here in this clout I knit Shame,　　*cloth/bind up* 640
　And clep me but proper Folly.　　　　　　　　*Folly itself*

MANHOOD:　Yea Folly, will thou be my true servant?

FOLLY:　Yea Sir Manhood, here is my bond.　　　*(of indenture)*

MANHOOD:　Now let us drink at this covenant[22]
　For that is courtesy.

FOLLY:　Marry master, ye shall have in haste.
　Ah ha, sirs, let the cat wink,
　For all ye wot not what I think.
　I shall draw him such a draft of drink
　That Conscience he shall away cast.　　　　　　　650
　Have, master, and drink well,
　And let us make revel, revel,
　For I swear by the Church of Saint Michael
　I would we were at stews,
　For there is nothing but revel rout.　　　　*a wild gang*
　An we were there I have no doubt[23]
　I should be known all about,
　Where Conscience they would refuse.

MANHOOD:　Peace, Folly my fair friend
　For, by Christ, I would not that Conscience should me here
　　　find.　　　　　　　　　　　　　　　　　　　660

FOLLY:　Tush master, thereof speak nothing,
　For Conscience cometh no time here.

MANHOOD:　Peace, Folly, there is no man that knoweth me.

FOLLY:　Sir, here my truth I plight to thee
　An thou wilt go thither with me
　For knowledge have thou no care.　　*(Don't worry about being recognized)*

---

[22] Original reads "comnaunt."
[23] Original reads "had no doubt."

MANHOOD: Peace, but it is hence a great way.
FOLLY: Pardee sir, we may be there on a day,
   Yea, and we shall be right welcome, I dare well say,
   In Eastcheap for to dine,   670
   And then we will with Lombards at Passage play,
   And at the Pope's Head sweet wine assay.[24]
   We shall be lodged well, *à fin*.   *finally*
MANHOOD: What sayest thou, Folly? Is this the best?
FOLLY: Sir, all this is manhood, well thou knowest.
MANHOOD: Now Folly, go we hence in haste,
   But fain would I change my name,
   For well I wot if Conscience meet me in this tide
   Right well I wot he would me chide.
FOLLY: Sir, for fear of you his face he shall hide.   680
   I shall clep *you* Shame.
MANHOOD: Now gramercy Folly, my fellow in fere, *companionship*
   Go we hence, tarry no longer here,
   Till we be gone me think it seven year.
   I have gold and good to spend.
FOLLY: Ah ha! master, that is good cheer,
   And or it be past half a year
   I shall shear thee right a lewd friar[25]
   And hither again thee send.
MANHOOD: Folly, go before and teach me the way.   690
FOLLY: Come after, Shame, I thee pray,
   And Conscience Clear ye cast away.
   Lo, sirs, this Folly teacheth aye,   *always*
   For where Conscience cometh with his cunning
   Yet Folly full featly shall make him blind; *cleverly*
   Folly before and Shame behind,
   Lo, sirs, thus fareth the world alway.
     [*Exit.*]
MANHOOD: Now I will follow Folly, for Folly is my man,
   Yea, Folly is my fellow and hath given me a name.

[24] Name of an Inn.
[25] To shear is to give someone a tonsure; hence, "I'll make you a member of quite a wild brotherhood" ("friar" is the French word *frere*, "brother" in both the literal and the religious senses.)

Conscience called me Manhood, Folly calleth me Shame,   700
Folly will me lead to London to learn revel,
Yea, and Conscience is but a flattering brothel,
Forever he is carping of "care."
The World and Folly counselleth me to all gladness,
Yea, and Conscience counselleth me to all sadness,
Yea, too much sadness might bring me into a madness.
And now, have good day sirs, to London to seek Folly will I
    fare.
       [*Enter* CONSCIENCE]
CONSCIENCE: Say, Manhood friend, whither will ye go?
MANHOOD: Nay sir, in faith, my name is not so.
  Why frere, what the devil hast thou to do[26]   *brother(?)* 710
  Whether I go or abide?
CONSCIENCE: Yes sir, I will counsel you for the best.
MANHOOD: I will none of thy counsel, so have I rest.
  I will go whither me list
  For thou canst nought else but chide.
      [*Exit*]
CONSCIENCE: Lo, sirs, a great example you may see,
  The frailness of mankind
  How oft he falleth in folly
  Through temptation of the Fiend,
  For when the Fiend and the flesh be at one assent   720
  Then Conscience Clear is clean outcast.
  Men think not on the great Judgement
  That the silly soul shall have at the last,
  But would God all men would have in mind
  Of the great Day of Doom
  How he shall give a great reckoning
  Of evil deeds that he hath done.
  But natheless, sith it is so[27]   *nevertheless*
  That Manhood is forth with Folly wend,   *gone* (old form of past tense)
  To seek Perseverance now will I go.   730

---

[26] Here "frere" probably does just mean brother and not friar. It is conventional for the Vices to use a little French, a bit of nationalistic byplay which Shakespeare uses quite often.
[27] Original reads "nedeless."

With the grace of God omnipotent
His counsels been in fere.   *in touch*
Perseverance's counsel is most clear,
Next to him is Conscience Clear
From sinning.
Now into his presence to Christ I pray
To speed me well in my journey.
Farewell lordings, and have good day,
To seek Perseverance will I wend.
>   [*Exit.*]
>   [*Enter* PERSEVERANCE.[28]]

PERSEVER: Now Christ our comely creatur clearer than
>   crystal clean   740
That craftily made every creature by   *artfully*
>   good recreation,   *creative power*
Save all this company that is gathered here bedene,   *by your worthiness*
And set all your souls into good salvation.
Now good God, that is most wisest and wieldy of wits,
This company counsel, comfort and glad,   *gladden*
And save all this similtude that seemly here sits,   *group* (of equals)
Now good God for His mercy that all men made.
Now Mary, mother meekest that I mean,
Shield all this company from evil inversation   *backsliding*
And save you from our enemy, as She is bright and clean   750
And at the last Day of Doom deliver you from everlasting
>   damnation.
Sirs, Perseverance is my name,
Conscience's born brother is;
He sent me hither mankind to indoctrinate
That they should to no vices incline,
For oft mankind is governed amiss
And through folly mankind is set in shame.
Therefore in this presence to Christ I pray
Or that I hence wend away
Some good word that I may say   760

---

[28] For lack of sure knowledge we give "Exit" and "Enter," but again it seems that what Conscience does is to to go the "mansion" of Perseverance and "discover" him there.

To borrow man's soul from blame.   *ransom*
          [*Enter* MANHOOD *as* AGE]
AGE: Alas, alas, that me is woe!
    My life, my liking I have forlorn,   *lost*
    My rents, my riches, it is all ygo,   *gone*
    Alas the day that I was born,
    For I was born Manhood most of might
    Stiff, strong, both stalworthy and stout.
    The World full worthily hath made me a knight,
    All bowed to my bidding bonerly about
    Then Conscience Clear comely and kind   770
    Meekly he met me in seat there I sat,   *where*
    He learned me a lesson of his teaching,
    And the seven deadly sins full loathly he did hate,
    Pride, Wrath and Envy, and Covetous in kind.
    The World all these sins delivered me until,   *unto*
    Sloth, Covetous and Lechery that is full of false flattering,
    All these Conscience reproved both loud and still.
    To Conscience I held up my hand   *swore*
    To keep Christ's commandments
    He warned me of Folly, that traitor, and bade me beware,   780
    And thus he went his way.
    But I have falsely me foresworn,
    Alas the day that I was born,
    For body and soul I have forlorn!
    I clung as a clod in clay
    In London many a day
    At the Passage I would play;
    I thought to borrow and never pay.
    Then was I sought and set in stocks,
    In Newgate I lay under locks,   (a prison) 790
    If I said aught I caught many knocks.
    Alas, where was Manhood tho?   *then*
    Alas, my lewdness hath me lost.
    Where is my body, so proud and prest?[29]

—————
[29] This recalls two medieval poetic traditions, the Debate of the Body and the Soul, and the *ubi sunt*, or
"where are they now" lament.

I cough and rough, my body will brast,   *clear the throat*
Age doth follow me so
I stare and stagger as I stand,
I groan grisly upon the ground,
Alas, death, why lettest thou me live so long?
I wander as a wight in wo   800
And care
For I have done ill
Now wend I will
Myself to spill,   *kil*
I care not whither or where.
PERSEVER: Well ymet sir, well ymet, and whither away?
AGE: Why, good sir, whereby do ye say?
PERSEVER: Tell me sir, I you pray
  And I with you will wend.
AGE: Why good sir, what is your name?   810
PERSEVER: Forsooth sir, Perseverance, the same.
AGE: Sir, ye are Conscience's brother that did me blame,
  I may not with you ling.
PERSEVER: Yes, yes Manhood, my friend in fere.
AGE: Nay sir, my name is in another manner,
  For Folly his own self was here
  And hath cleped me Shame.
PERSEVER: Shame?
  Nay Manhood, let him go,
  Folly and his fellows also,   820
  For they would thee bring into care and woe,
  And all that will follow his game.
AGE: Yea, game whoso game
  Folly hath given me a name
  So wherever I go
  He clepeth me Shame.
  Now Manhood is gone
  Folly hath followed me so.
  When I first from my mother came
  The World made me a man   830
  And fast in riches I ran

Till I was dubbed a knight,
And then I met with Conscience Clear,
And he me set in such manner[30]
Methought his teaching was full dear
Both by day and night.
And then Folly met me
And sharply he beset me
And from Conscience he fet me,   *etched*
He would not fro me go.   840
Many a day he kept me
And to all folks he cleped me
Shame,[31]
And unto all sins he set me
Alas, that me is woe!
For I have falsely me forsworn,
Alas that I was born,
Body and soul I am but lorn,   *lost*
Me liketh neither glee not game.

PERSEVER: Nay, nay Manhood, say not so,   850
Beware of wanhope, for he is a foe.   *despair*
A new name I shall give you to,
I clep you Repentance,
For, an you here repent your sin
Ye are possible heaven to win,
But with great contrition ye must begin,
And take you to abstinence,
For though a man had do alone
The deadly sins everychone,   *every one*
An he with contrition make his moan   860
To Christ our heaven king,
God is also glad of him   *as glad*
As of the creature that never did sin.

AGE: Now good sir, how should I contrition begin?

PERSEVER: Sir, in shrift of mouth, without varying,   *confession/always*
And another example I shall you show to:

[30] In the original a fragment of a letter stands between "such" and "manner," but it was not "a."
[31] Original reads "Fro shame," which does not make sense.

Think on Peter and Paul, and other mo,
Thomas, James and John also
And also Mary Magdalen,
For Paul did Christ's people great villainy,   870
And Peter at the Passion forsook Christ thrice,
And Magdalen lived long in lechery
And Saint Thomas believed not in the resurrection,
And yet these to Christ are darlings dear,
And now be saints in heaven clear,
And therefore, though ye have trespassed here
I hope ye be sorry for your sin.

AGE: Yea Perseverance, I you plight,
I am sorry for my sin both day and night,
I would fain learn with all my might   880
How I should heaven win.

PERSEVER: So to win heaven five necessary things there
        been
That must be known to all mankind.
The five wits doth begin
Sir, bodily and spiritually.

AGE: Of the five wits I would have knowing.

PERSEVER: Forsooth sir, hearing, seeing, and smelling,
The remnant tasting and feeling,
These been the five wits bodily,
And sir, other five wits there been.   890

AGE: Sir Perseverance I know not them.

PERSEVER: Now Repentance I shall you ken.
They are the powers of the soul:
Clear-in-mind there is one,
Imagination, and all reason,
Understanding and compassion,
These belong unto Perseverance.

AGE: Gramercy Perseverance, for your true teaching,
But good sir, is there any more behind   *to follow*
That is necessary to all mankind   900
Freely for to know?

PERSEVER: Yea Repentance, more there be

That every man must on believe.
The twelve Articles of the Faith
That Mankind must on trow:
The first that God is one substance,
And also that God is in three persons,
Beginning and ending without variance,
And all this world made, of nought;
The second that the Son of God sikerly   910
Took flesh and blood of the Virgin Mary
Without touching of men's flesh company,
This must be in every man's thought;
The third, that that same God's Son
Born of that holy Virgin
And after she His birth maiden as She was beforn
And clearer in all kind;   *purer*
Also the fourth, that same Christ, God and Man,
He suffered pain and passion
Because of man's soul's redemption,   920
And on a Cross did hang;
The fifth Article I shall you tell—
Then the spirit of Godhead went to hell
And brought out the souls that there did dwell[32]
By the power of his own might;
The sixth Article I shall you say,
Christ rose upon the third day,
Very God and Man, withouten nay,   *true/undeniably*
That all shall deem and dight.   *judge and dispose*
He sent man's soul into heaven   930
Aloft all the angels everychone
There is the Father, the Son and that sothfast Holy   *true*
     Ghost.
The eighth Article we must believe on:
That same God shall come down
And deem men's souls at the Day of Doom,
And on mercy then must we trust.
The ninth Article, withouten strife,

---

[32] Original reads "bought out."

Every man, maiden and wife
And all the bodies that ever bore life
At the Day of Doom body and soul shall pare.[33]   *part* 940
Truly the tenth Article is:
All they that hath kept God's service
They shall be crowned in heaven bliss
As Christ's servants, to Him full dear.
The eleventh Article, the soth to sayen:
All that hath falsely to God gaded them,   (dialect past tense of *go*)
They shall be put into hell pain
There shall be no sin covering.
Sir, after the twelfth we must work,
And believe in all the sacraments of Holy Church,   950
That they been necessary to both last and first,
To all manner of mankind.
Sir, ye must also hear and know the commandments ten.
Lo, sir, this is your belief and all men's,[34]
Do after it, and ye shall heaven win
Without doubt I know.

AGE: Gramercy Perseverance, for your true teaching,
For in the spirit of my soul well I find[35]
That it is necessary to all mankind
Truly for to know.   960
Now sirs, take all example by me, [*to the audience*]
How I was born in simple degree,
The World royal received me
And dubbed me knight,
Then Conscience met me,
So after him came Folly;
Folly falsely deceived me,
Then Shame my name hight.

PERSEVER: Yea, and now is your name Repentance
Through the grace of God almight,   970
And therefore without any distance   *further ado*

---

[33] In the original an "and," apparently picked up from the preceding line, is printed at the start of this line.
[34] Original reads "all men."
[35] Original reads "will I find."

I take my leave of king and knight
And I pray to Jesu which as made us all
Cover you with his mantle perpetual. Amen.

Here endeth the Interlude of Mundus et Infans,/Imprinted at
London in Fleet Street at the sign of the/Sun, by me Wynkyn de
Worde. The year of our Lord/MCCCCC and xxii, The xvii day
of July.

✳ *WIT AND SCIENCE*

(John Redford, c. 1531–1547)

In *Wit and Science* the morality pattern is cast in the form of a romance and set to make an educational rather than a theological point: if natural wit is to achieve knowledge (Science-*scientia*), it must overcome the tediousness involved in the pursuit of knowledge by having confidence in its goal and by having the aid of instruction, study and diligence. That point must have been of some practical moment to John Redford, the play's author, for he was Master of the Choristers at St. Paul's Cathedral and charged with their education. And while that point may seem to promise a rather dull and labored exercise, what the play delivers is graceful, charming, and at times very funny. It seems reasonable to assume that the play was performed by the boys under Redford's charge, perhaps at court; but we have no record of its performance there or elsewhere.

Wit and Science offers a clear example of the deflection of the morality form from religious to secular themes during the early part of the sixteenth century; but it offers, as well, an example of a subtler and perhaps ultimately more important process. That is the development of a plot which is not strictly bound in action or in interest to the ethical thesis it imitates. In the main the plot of *Wit and Science* is controlled by its thesis, but at times the logical relationship between thesis and plot, a relationship which accounts for all of the incidents in a play like *The Castle of Perseverance* or *The Interlude of Youth,* is loosened a bit, and incidents grow out of the plot rather than the thesis. The love songs in the play, for example, are merely love songs, and Science's anger at Wit is the anger of a woman who thinks she has been scorned, and not merely the reaction of knowledge to the failure of natural wit. And thus *Wit and Science* points toward the transfer of the logical center of action from the thesis to the plot, and toward those plays of the Elizabethan period that refer loosely to the morality form as a general shaping principle while allowing particular plots to work out their own specific ends.

There is some indication that *Wit and Science* may have been published during the sixteenth century but, if it was, all copies have been lost. The play has survived only in a commonplace book along with a few fragments of interludes and some songs. The present text is based on a transcription of the manuscript which was published in 1951 by the Malone Society. As for the date of the play, we can guess only that it was written sometime during Redford's tenure at St. Paul's, which would place it between c. 1531 and 1547.

WIT AND SCIENCE

[*The manuscript is defective at the beginning. Wit has apparently asked Reason for the hand of his daughter, Science, and Reason has been telling him that to win her he must overcome the giant Tediousness and climb Mount Parnassus. Instruction, Study and Diligence are to help Wit on his journey.*]

REASON: Then in remembrance of Reason, hold ye
   A glass of Reason, wherein behold ye
   Yourself to yourself. Namely when ye
   Come near my daughter, Science, then see
   That all things be clean and trick about ye,
   Lest of some sluggishness she might doubt ye.   *suspect*
   This glass of Reason shall show ye all;
   While ye have that, ye have me, and shall.
   Get ye forth now. Instruction, fare well.
INSTRUCTION: Sir, God keep ye!
REASON: And ye all from peril!   10
                 (*Here all go out save* REASON)

   If any man now marvel that I
   Would bestow my daughter thus basely,
   Of truth I, Reason, am of this mind:
   Where parties together be inclined
   By gifts of graces to love each other,
   There let them join the one with the other.
   This Wit such gifts of graces hath in him
   That maketh my daughter to wish to win him:
   Young, painful, tractable and capax,   *painstaking capable*
   These be Wit's gifts which Science doth axe.   *ask* 20
   And as for her, as soon as Wit sees her,
   For all the world he would not then lese her.   *lose*
   Wherefore, since they be so meet matches   *proper* or *suited*
   To love each other, straw for the patches
   Of Worldly muck. Science hath enough
   For them both to live. If Wit be thorough
   Stricken in love, as he since hath showed,
   I doubt not my daughter well bestowed.

The end of his journey will approve all.   *show*
If Wit hold out, no more proof can fall;   30
And that the better hold out he may,
To refresh my son, Wit, now by the way,
Some solace for him I will provide.
An honest woman dwelleth here beside,
Whose name is called Honest Recreation.
As men report, for Wit's consolation
She hath no peer. If Wit were half dead,
She would revive him—thus it is said.
Wherefore, if money or love can hire her
To hie after Wit, I will desire her.   *hasten* 40
    (*Exit* REASON)
    (CONFIDENCE *cometh in with a picture of* WIT)
CONFIDENCE: Ah, sir, what time of day ist, who can tell?   *is it*
The day is not far past, I wot well,   *know*
For I have gone fast, and yet I see
I am far from where as I would be.
Well I have day enough yet, I spy;
Wherefore, ere I pass hence, now must I
See this same token here, a plain case,
What Wit hath sent to my lady's grace.
Now will ye see a goodly picture
Of Wit himself? His own image sure.   50
Face, body, arms, legs, both limb and joint
As like him as can be in every point.
It lacketh but life. Well I can him thank,
This token indeed shall make some crank;   *merry*
For, what with this picture so well favored,
And what with those sweet words so well savored
Distilling from the mouth of Confidence,—
Shall not this appease the heart of Science?
Yes, I thank God I am of that nature,
Able to compass this matter sure;   60
As ye shall see now, who list to mark it,
How neatly and featly I shall wark it.   *finely/work*
    [*Exit* CONFIDENCE]

(WIT *cometh in without* INSTRUCTION, *with* STUDY, *et al.*)

WIT: Now, sirs, come on! Which is the way now?
  This way, or that way? Study, how say you?
  Speak, Diligence, while he hath bethought him.

DILIGENCE: That way, belike; most usage hath wrought him.   *it*

STUDY: Yea, hold your peace! Best we here now stay
  For Instruction. I like not that way.

WIT: Instruction, Study? I ween we have lost him.   *think*
      (INSTRUCTION *cometh in*)

INSTRUCTION: Indeed, full gently about ye have tossed him!   70
  What mean you, Wit, still to delight
  Running before thus, still out of sight,
  And thereby out of your way now quite?
  What do ye here, except ye would fight?
  Come back again, Wit, for I must choose ye
  An easier way than this, or else lose ye.

WIT: What aileth this way? Peril here is none.

INSTRUCTION: But as much as your life standeth upon!
  Your enemy, man, here lieth before ye,—
  Tediousness, to brain or to gore ye.   80

WIT: Tediousness! Doth that tyrant rest
  In my way now? Lord, how am I blest
  That occasion so near me stirs
  For my dear heart's sake to win my spurs!
  Sir, would ye fear me with that foul thief,
  With whom to meet my desire is chief?

INSTRUCTION: And what would ye do, you having nought
  For your defence? For though ye have caught   *got*
  Garments of Science upon your back,
  Yet weapons of Science ye do lack.   90

WIT: What weapons of Science should I have?

INSTRUCTION: Such as all lovers of their loves crave:
  A token from Lady Science, whereby
  Hope of her favor may spring, and thereby
  Comfort, which is the weapon doubtless
  That must serve you against Tediousness.

WIT: If hope or comfort may be my weapon,

Then never with Tediousness me threaten;
For as for hope of my dear heart's favor—
And thereby comfort—enough I gather.   100
INSTRUCTION: Wit, hear me! Till I see Confidence
Have brought some token from Lady Science
That I may feel she favoreth you,
Ye pass not this way, I tell you true.
WIT: Which way then?
INSTRUCTION: A plainer way, I told ye,
Out of danger from your foe to hold ye.
WIT: Instruction, hear me! Ere my sweetheart
Shall hear that Wit from that wretch shall start
One foot, this body and all shall crack.
Forth I will, sure, whatever I lack.   110
DILIGENCE: If ye lack weapon, sir, here is one.
WIT: Well said, Diligence, thou art alone!
How say ye, sir; is not here weapon?
INSTRUCTION: With that weapon your enemy never threaten,
For without the return of Confidence,
Ye may be slain, sure, for all Diligence.
DILIGENCE: Good sir! and Diligence, I tell you plain,
Will play the man ere my master be slain.
INSTRUCTION: Yea, but what sayeth Study? No word to this?
WIT: No, sir, ye know Study's office is   120
Meet for the chamber, not for the field.   *suited*
But tell me, Study, wilt thou now yield?
STUDY: My head acheth sore; I would we returned.
WIT: Thy head ache now? I would it were burned.
Come on, walking may hap to ease thee.
INSTRUCTION: And will ye be gone, then, without me?
WIT: Yea, by my faith. Except ye hie ye after   *hasten*
Reason ye shall know are but an hafter.   *laggard*
            (*Exit* WIT, STUDY *and* DILIGENCE)
INSTRUCTION: Well, go your way! When your father Reason
Heareth how ye obey me at this season,   130
I think he will think his daughter now
May marry another man for you.   *in your place*

When wits stand so in their own conceit,
Best let them go, till pride in his height
Turn and cast them down headlong again,
As ye shall see proved by this Wit plain.
If Reason hap not to come, the rather
His own destruction he will sure gather;
Wherefore to Reason will I now get me,
Leaving that charge whereabout he set me.   140
    (*Exit* INSTRUCTION. TEDIOUSNESS *cometh in with a visor over
    his head.*)
TEDIOUSNESS: Oh the body of me!
  What caitiffs be those
  That will not once flee
  From Tediousness' nose,
  But thus disease me   *disturb*
  Out of my nest,
  When I should ease me
  This body to rest?
  That Wit! That villain!
  That wretch! A shame take him!   150
  It is he plain
  That thus bold doth make him,
  Without my license
  To stalk by my door
  To that drab, Science,
  To wed that whore!
  But I defy her,
  And for that drab's sake,
  Ere Wit come near her,
  The knave's head shall ache.   160
  These bones, this mall   *club*
  Shall beat him to dust,
  Ere that drab shall
  Once quench that knave's lust.
  But, hah! Methinks
  I am not half lusty;
  These joints, these links   *links of the body*

Be rough and half rusty.
I must go shake them,
Supple to make them.   170
Stand back, ye wretches!
Beware the fetches   *tricks*
Of Tediousness,
These caitiffs to bless.
Make room, I say!
Round every way—
This way, that way!
What care I what way?
Before me, behind me,
Round about wind me!   180
Now I begin
To sweat in my skin;
Now am I nemble   *nimble*
To make them tremble.
Pash head! Pash brain!
The knaves are slain,
All that I hit.
Where art thou, Wit?
Thou art but dead!
Off goeth thy head   190
At the first blow!
Ho, ho! Ho, ho!

      (WIT *speaketh at the door*)

WIT: Study!
STUDY: Here, sir!
WIT: How, doth thy head ache?
STUDY: Yea, God wot, sir, much pain I do take.   *knows*
WIT: Diligence!
DILIGENCE: Here, sir, here!
WIT: How dost thou?
  Doth thy stomach serve thee to fight now?
DILIGENCE: Yea, sir, with yonder wretch—a vengeance on him—
  That threateneth you thus! Set even upon him!
STUDY: Upon him, Diligence? Better, nay!

DILIGENCE: Better nay Study? Why should we fray?   *fear* 200
STUDY: For I am weary; my head acheth sore.
DILIGENCE: Why, foolish Study, thou shalt do no more
   But aid my master with thy presence.
WIT: No more shalt thou neither, Diligence.
   Aid me with your presence, both you twain;
   And for my love, myself shall take pain.
STUDY: Sir, we be ready to aid you so.
WIT: I ask no more, Study. Come then, go!
     (TEDIOUSNESS *riseth up*)
TEDIOUSNESS: Why, art thou come?
WIT: Yea, wretch, to thy pain!
TEDIOUSNESS: Then have at thee!
WIT: Have at thee, again!   210
     (*Here* WIT *falleth down and dieth*)
TEDIOUSNESS: Lie thou there. Now have at ye, caitiffs!   *wretches*
   Do ye flee, i' faith? Ah, whoreson thieves!
   By Mahownd's bones, had the wretches tarried,   *Mohammed's*
   Their neck without head they should have carried.
   Yea, by Mahownd's nose, might I have patted them,   *hit*
   In twenty gobbets I should have squatted them,   *pieces/squashed*
   To teach the knaves to come near the snout
   Of Tediousness. Walk further about
   I trow, now they will! And as for thee,   *think*
   Thou wilt no more now trouble me.   220
   Yet, lest the knave be not safe enough,
   The whoreson shall bear me another cuff.
   Now, lie still, Caitiff, and take thy rest,
   While I take mine in mine own nest.
     [*Exit* TEDIOUSNESS]
(*Here cometh in* HONEST RECREATION, COMFORT, QUICKNESS *and*
STRENGTH, *and go and kneel about* WIT; *and at the last verse raiseth
him upon his feet, and so make an end.*[1])
   Give place, give place to Honest Recreation;
   Give place, we say now, for thy consolation.

[1] The three songs in the play are contained in the same manuscript volume, but separated from the play itself. We have restored them to what seem to be their proper places.

When travail great in matters thick
Have dulled your wits and made them thick,
What medicine then your wits to quick?
If ye will know, the best physic   230
   Is to give place to Honest Recreation.
   Give place, we say now, for thy consolation!
Where is that Wit that we seek than?   *hen*
Alas, he lieth here pale and wan.
Help him at once now, if we can.
Oh, Wit, how dost thou? Look up, man!
   Oh, Wit, give place to Honest Recreation;
   Give place, we say now, for thy consolation.
After place given, let ear obey.
Give an ear, Oh Wit, now we thee pray;   240
Give ear to that we sing and say;
Give an ear and help will come straightaway;
   Give an ear to Honest Recreation,
   Give an ear now for thy consolation.
After ear given, now give an eye.
Behold thy friends about thee lie:
Recreation I, and Comfort I,
Quickness am I, and Strength hereby.
   Give an eye to Honest Recreation;
   Give an eye now for thy consolation.   250
After an eye given, an hand give ye.
Give an hand, Oh Wit, feel that ye see;
Recreation feel, feel Comfort free,
Feel Quickness here, feel Strength to thee.
   Give an hand to Honest Recreation,
   Give an hand now for thy consolation.
Upon his feet, would God he were!
To raise him now we need not fear.
Stay you his hand, while we here bear.
Now all at once upright him rear.   260
   Oh Wit, give place to Honest Recreation;
   Give place, we say now, for thy consolation.
      (*And then* HONEST RECREATION *sayeth as followeth:*)

HONEST RECREATION: Now, Wit, how do ye? Will ye be lusty?

WIT: The lustier for you needs be must I.

HONEST RECREATION: Be ye whole after your fall?

WIT: As ever I was, thanks to you all.

(REASON *cometh in and sayeth as followeth:*)

REASON: Ye might thank Reason that sent them to ye.
  But since they have done that they should do ye,
  Send them home soon and get ye forward.

WIT: Oh father Reason, I have had an hard   270
  Chance since ye saw me.

REASON: I wot well that.   *know*
  The more to blame ye, when ye would not
  Obey Instruction, as Reason willed ye.
  What marvel though Tediousness had killed ye?
  But let pass now, since ye are well again.
  Set forward again, Science to attain.

WIT: Good father Reason, be not too hasty.
  In honest company, no time waste I.
  I shall to your daughter all at leisure.

REASON: Yea, Wit, is that the great love ye raise her?   *bear* 280
  I say, if ye love my daughter, Science,
  Get ye forth at once, and get ye hence.

  (*Here* COMFORT, QUICKNESS *and* STRENGTH *go out.*)

WIT: Nay, by Saint George, they go not all yet!

REASON: No? Will ye disobey Reason, Wit?

WIT: Father Reason, I pray ye, content ye,
  For we part not yet.

REASON: Well, Wit, I went ye   *thought*
  Had been no such man as now I see.
  Fare well!

      (*Exit* REASON.)

HONEST RECREATION: He is angry.

WIT: Yea, let him be;
  I do not pass.   *care* 290
  Come now, a basse!   *kiss*

HONEST RECREATION: Nay, sir, as for basses
  From hence none passes

But as in gage   *token*
  Of marriage.
WIT: Marry, even so!
  A bargain, lo!
HONEST RECREATION: What, without license
  Of Lady Science?
WIT: Shall I tell you truth?   300
  I never loved her.
HONEST RECREATION: The common voice goeth
  That marriage ye moved her.
WIT: Promise hath she none.
  If we shall be one,
  Without more words grant!
HONEST RECREATION: What! upon this sudden?
  Then might ye plain
  Bid me avaunt.   *begone*
  Nay, let me see   310
  In Honesty
  What ye can do
  To win Recreation.
  Upon that probation
  I grant thereto.
WIT: Small be my doing,
  But apt to all things
  I am, I trust.
HONEST RECREATION: Can ye dance than?   *then*
WIT: Even as I can,   320
  Prove me ye must.
HONEST RECREATION: Then for awhile
  Ye must exile   *put off*
  This garment cumbering.
WIT: Indeed, as you say,
  This cumbrous array
  Would make Wit slumbering.
HONEST RECREATION: It is gay gear
  Of Science clear.
  It seemeth her array.   330

WIT: Whosoever it were,
  It lieth now there.
HONEST RECREATION: Go to, my men, play!
  (*Here they dance. And in the meanwhile* IDLENESS *cometh in and sitteth down. And when the galliard is done,* WIT *sayeth as followeth, and so falleth down in* IDLENESS' *lap!*)
WIT: Sweetheart, gramercys!   *thanks*
HONEST RECREATION: Why, whither now? Have ye done,
  since?   *already*
WIT: Yea, in faith! With weary bones ye have possessed me;
  Among these damsels now will I rest me.
HONEST RECREATION: What, there?
WIT: Yea, here; I will be so bold.
IDLENESS: Yea, and welcome, by him that God sold.   *i.e. Judas*
HONEST RECREATION: It is an harlot! May ye not see?   340
IDLENESS: As honest a woman as ye be!
HONEST RECREATION: Her name is Idleness. Wit, what mean ye?
IDLENESS: Nay, what mean you to scold, you quean, you?   *whore*
WIT: There, go to! Lo, now for the best game:
  While I take my ease, your tongues now frame!   *use*
HONEST RECREATION: Yea, Wit, by your faith, is that your
  fashion?
  Will ye leave me, Honest Recreation,
  For that common strumpet Idleness,
  The very root of all viciousness?
WIT: She sayeth she is as honest as ye.   350
  Declare yourselves both now as ye be.
HONEST RECREATION: What would ye more for my declaration
  Than even my name, Honest Recreation?
  And what would ye more her to express
  Than even her name, too, Idleness—
  Destruction of all that with her tarry?
  Wherefore, come away, Wit; she will mar ye.
IDLENESS: Will I mar him, drab? Thou calat, thou!   *whore*
  When thou has marred him already now?
  Callest thou thyself Honest Recreation,   360
  Ordering a poor man after this fashion,

To lame him thus, and make his limbs fail,
Even with the swinging there of thy tail?
The devil set fire on thee! For now must I,
Idleness, heal him again, I spy.
I must now lull him, rock him, and frame him
To his lust again, where thou didst lame him.   *desires*
Am I the root, sayest thou, of viciousness?
Nay, thou art root of all vice, doubtless.
Thou art occasion, lo, of more evil,   370
Than I, poor girl—nay, more than the devil.
The devil and his dam cannot devise
More devilishness than by thee doth rise.
Under the name of Honest Recreation,
She, lo, bringeth in her abomination.
Mark her dancing, her masking and mumming—
Where more concupiscence than there coming?
Her carding, her dicing daily and nightly—
Where find ye more falsehood than there? Not lightly!   *easily*
With lying and swearing by no poppets,   *idols* 380
But tearing God in a thousand gobbets.   *pieces*
As for her singing, piping and fiddling—
What unthrift therein is twiddling!   *trifling*
Search the taverns and ye shall hear
Such bawdry as beasts would spew to hear.
And yet this is called Honest Recreation,
And I, poor Idleness, an abomination!
But which is worst of us twain, now judge, Wit.
WIT: By 'r lady, not thou, wench, I judge yet.
HONEST RECREATION: No? Is your judgement such then
          that ye   390
Can neither perceive that beast, how she
Goeth about to deceive you, nor yet
Remember how I saved your life, Wit?
Think you her meet with me to compare,   *proper*
By whom so many wits cured are?
When will she do such an act as I did,
Saving your life when I you revived?

And as I saved you, so save I all
That in like jeopardy chance to fall.
When Tediousness to ground hath smitten them,   400
Honest Recreation up doth quicken them
With such honest pastimes, sports or games
As unto my honest nature frames,
And not as she sayeth, with pastimes such
As be abused little or much.
For where Honest Reaction be abused,
Honest Recreation is refused.
Honest Recreation is present never
But where honest pastimes be well used ever.   410
But indeed Idleness, she is cause
Of all such abuses. She, lo, draws
Her sort to abuse mine honest games,
And thereby full falsely my name defames.
Under the name of Honest Recreation,
She bringeth in all her abomination,
Destroying all wits that her embrace,
As yourself shall see within short space.
She will bring you to shameful end, Wit,
Except the sooner from her you flit;
Wherefore, come away, Wit, out of her paws.   420
Hence, drab, let him go out of thy claws!

IDLENESS: Will ye get ye hence? or, by the mace,   *mass*
These claws shall claw you by your drab's face!

HONEST RECREATION: Ye shall not need. Since Wit lieth as one
That neither heareth nor seeth, I am gone.

       (*Exit* HONEST RECREATION.)

IDLENESS: Yea, so? Farewell! And well fare thou, tongue!
Of a short peal, this peal was well wrung—
To ring her hence, and him fast asleep,
As full of sloth as the knave can creep!
How, Wit! Awake! How doth my baby?   430
Neque vox neque sensus, by'r lady.[2]
A meet man for Idleness, no doubt.   *fit*

---

[2] *Neque . . . sensus:* Neither voice nor feeling.

Hark, my pig! how the knave doth rout.　　　　　　*snore*
Well, while he sleepeth in Idleness' lap,
Idleness' mark on him shall I clap.[3]
Some say that Idleness cannot wark,　　　　　　　　*work*
But those that say so, now let them mark!
I trow they shall see that Idleness　　　　　　　　*think*
Can set herself about some business;
Or at the least, ye shall see her tried,　　　　　　440
Neither idle nor well occupied.
Lo, sir, yet ye lack another toy!
Where is my whistle to call my boy?
　　(*Here she whistleth and* INGNORANCY *cometh in.*)

INGNORANCY:　I come, I come!
IDLENESS:　　　　　　　Come on, ye fool!
　All this day ere ye can come to school?
INGNORANCY:　Um! Mother will not let me come.
IDLENESS:　I would thy mother had kissed thy bum.
　She will never let thee thrive, I trow.　　　　　*think*
　Come on, goose! Now, lo, men shall know
　That Idleness can do somewhat; yea,　　　　　　450
　And play the schoolmistress, too, if need be.
　Mark what doctrine by Idleness comes:
　Say thy lesson, fool.
INGNORANCY:　　　　Upon my thumbs?
IDLENESS:　Yea, upon thy thumbs. Is not there thy name?
INGNORANCY:　Yees.
IDLENESS:　　　　　Go to, then; spell me that same.
　Where was thou born?[4]
INGNORANCY:　Chwas i-bore in Ingland, mother said.[5]　*I was born*
IDLENESS:　In Ingland?
INGNORANCY:　Yea.
IDLENESS:　And what's half "Ingland"? Here's "ing" and　460
　　here's "land." What's this?
INGNORANCY:　What's this?

---

[3] Here Idleness blackens his face.
[4] We have followed J. Q. Adams in treating what follows as prose.
[5] Ingnorancy speaks in a Southern dialect: ch = Ich = I.

IDLENESS: What's this, whoreson? What's this? Here's "ing"
and here's "land." What's this?
INGNORANCY: 'Tis my thumb.
IDLENESS: Thy thumb! "Ing," whoreson, "ing," "ing"!
INGNORANCY: Ing, ing, ing, ing.
IDLENESS: Forth! Shall I not beat thy narse now?
INGNORANCY: Ummm—
IDLENESS: Shall I not beat thy narse now?
INGNORANCY: Ummm—
IDLENESS: Say "no," fool, say "no." 470
INGNORANCY: Noo, noo, noo, noo, noo.
IDLENESS: Go to, put together: "Ing."
INGNORANCY: "Ing."
IDLENESS: "No."
INGNORANCY: "Noo."
IDLENESS: Forth now: What sayeth the dog?
INGNORANCY: Dog bark.
IDLENESS: Dog bark? Dog ran, whoreson, dog ran!
INGNORANCY: Dog ran, whoreson, dog ran, dog ran.
IDLENESS: Put together: "Ing." 480
INGNORANCY: "Ing."
IDLENESS: "No."
INGNORANCY: "Noo."
IDLENESS: "Ran."
INGNORANCY: "Ran."
IDLENESS: Forth now: what sayeth the goose?
INGNORANCY: Lag! Lag!
IDLENESS: "Hiss," whoreson, "hiss!"
INGNORANCY: Hiss, His-s-s-s.
IDLENESS: Go to, put together: "Ing." 490
INGNORANCY: "Ing."
IDLENESS: "No."
INGNORANCY: "Noo."
IDLENESS: "Ran."
INGNORANCY: "Ran."
IDLENESS: "Hiss."
INGNORANCY: "His-s-s-s-s-s-s."

IDLENESS: Now, who is a good boy?

INGNORANCY: I, I, I, I, I, I.[6]

IDLENESS: Go to, put together: "Ing."   500

INGNORANCY: "Ing."

IDLENESS: "No."

INGNORANCY: "Noo."

IDLENESS: "Ran."

INGNORANCY: "Ran."

IDLENESS: "Hiss."

INGNORANCY: "His-s-s-s-s."

IDLENESS: "I."

INGNORANCY: "I."

IDLENESS: "Ing-no-ran-hiss-I."   510

INGNORANCY: "Ing-no-ran-his-s-s."

IDLENESS: "I."

INGNORANCY: "I."

IDLENESS: "Ing."

INGNORANCY: "Ing."

IDLENESS: Forth!

INGNORANCY: "His-s-s-s?"

IDLENESS: Yea! "No," whoreson, "no!"

INGNORANCY: "Noo, noo, noo, noo."

IDLENESS: "Ing-no."   520

INGNORANCY: "Ing-noo."

IDLENESS: Forth now!

INGNORANCY: "His-s-s-s-s-s"?

IDLENESS: Yet again! "Ran," whoreson, "ran"!

INGNORANCY: "Ran, whoreson, ran, ran."

IDLENESS: "Ran," say!

INGNORANCY: "Ran say."

IDLENESS: "Ran," whoreson!

INGNORANCY: "Ran whoreson."

IDLENESS: "Ran"!   530

INGNORANCY: "Ran."

IDLENESS: "Ing-no-ran."

INGNORANCY: "Ing-no-ran."

[6] Pronounced as *E*, thus making the final vowel of Ingnorancy.

IDLENESS: Forth now: what said the goose?

INGNORANCY: Dog bark.

IDLENESS: Dog bark? "Hiss," whoreson, "hiss-s-s-s"!

INGNORANCY: "His-s-s-s-s-s."

IDLENESS: "I."

INGNORANCY: "I."

IDLENESS: "Ing-no-ran-hiss-I."   540

INGNORANCY: "Ing-no-ran-his-s-s-s."

IDLENESS: "I."

INGNORANCY: "I."

IDLENESS: How sayest now, fool? Is not there thy name?

INGNORANCY: Yea.

IDLENESS: Well then, con me that same.   *study by repeating*
    What hast thou learned.

INGNORANCY: Ich can not tell.

IDLENESS: "Ich can not tell"? Thou sayest even very well;
    For if thou couldst tell, then had I not well   550
    Taught thee thy lesson which must be taught—
    To tell all when thou canst tell right nought.

INGNORANCY: Ich can my lesson.

IDLENESS: Yea; and therefore
    Shalt have a new coat, by God I swore.

INGNORANCY: A new coat?

IDLENESS: Yea, a new coat, by-and-by.   *at once*
    Off with this old coat. "A new coat," cry!

INGNORANCY: A new coat! A new coat! A new coat!

IDLENESS: Peace, whoreson fool! Wilt thou wake him now?   560
    Unbutton thy coat, fool. Canst thou do nothing?

INGNORANCY: I not how choold be.   *know not how it should be*

IDLENESS: "I not how choold be"! A fool betide thee!
    So wisely it speaketh! Come on, now. When?
    Put back thine arm, fool!

INGNORANCY: Put back?

IDLENESS: So, lo! Now let me see how this gear
    Will trim this gentleman that lieth here.[7]
    Ah, God save it, so sweetly it doth sleep,

[7] Here Idleness puts Ingnorancy's coat on Wit.

While on your back this gay coat can creep,   570
As feat as can be for this one arm.   *fine*

INGNORANCY: Oh, cham a-cold.   *I am*

IDLENESS: Hold, fool, and keep thee warm.
And come hither; hold this head here. Soft now, for waking!
Ye shall see one here brought in such taking
That he shall soon scantily know himself.
Here is a coat as fit for this elf
As it had been made even for this body.
So! It beginneth to look like a noddy.   *fool*

INGNORANCY: Um-m-m-m.   580

IDLENESS: What ailest now, fool?

INGNORANCY: Now coat is gone.

IDLENESS: And why is it gone?

INGNORANCY: 'Twool not bide on.

IDLENESS: "Twool not bide on"? 'Twould if it could.
But marvel it were that bide it should—
Science's garment on Ingnorancy's back!
But now, let's see, sir—what do ye lack?
Nothing but even to buckle here this throat.
So! Well this Wit becometh a fool's coat!   590

INGNORANCY: He is I now.

IDLENESS: Yea. How likest him now?
Is he not a fool as well as thou?

INGNORANCY: Yeas.

IDLENESS: Well then, one fool keep another!
Give me this, and take thou that brother.[8]

INGNORANCY: Um-m.

IDLENESS: Pike thee home, go!   *go*

INGNORANCY: Chill go tell my mother.   *I will*

IDLENESS: Yea do!   600
(*Exit* INGNORANCY.)
But yet to take my leave of my dear, lo![9]
With a skip or twain, here lo, and here lo,
And here again; and now this heel

---

[8] This: apparently Ingnorancy's cap fitted with ass' ears, which she exchanges for Wit's cap.
[9] She dances around the sleeping Wit.

To bless this weak brain. Now are ye weel,   *well*
By virtue of Idleness' blessing tool,
Conjured from Wit into a stark fool.

>   (*Exit* IDLENESS.)

>   (CONFIDENCE *cometh in with a sword by his side, and sayeth as
>   followeth:*)

CONFIDENCE: I seek and seek, as one on no ground
   Can rest, but like a masterless hound
   Wandering all about seeking his master.
   Alas, gentle Wit, I fear the faster   610
   That my true service cleaveth unto thee,
   The slacker thy mind cleaveth unto me.
   I have done thy message in such sort
   That I not only for thy comfort,
   To vanquish thine enemy, have brought here
   A sword of comfort from thy love dear,
   But also, further, I have so inclined her
   That upon my words she assigned her
   In her own person halfway to meet thee,
   And hitherward she came for to greet thee.   620
   And sure, except she be turned again,
   Hither will she come ere be long, plain,
   To seek to meet thee here in this coast.   *place*
   But now, alas, thy self thou hast lost.
   Or, at the least, thou wilt not be found.
   Alas gentle Wit, how dost thou wound
   Thy trusty and true servant, Confidence,
   To lose my credence to Lady Science!
   Thou losest me, too; for if I cannot
   Find thee shortly, longer live I may not,   630
   But shortly get me even into a corner
   And die for sorrow through such a scorner.

>   (*Here* [FAME, FAVOR, RICHES, *and* WORSHIP] *come in with viols.*)

FAME: Come, sirs, let us not disdain to do
   That the World hath appointed us to.
FAVOR: Since to serve Science the World hath sent us,
   As the World willeth us, let us content us.

RICHES: Content us we may, since we be assigned
  To the fairest lady that liveth, in my mind.
WORSHIP: Then let us not stay here mute and mum,
  But taste we these instruments till she come.   640
     (*Here they sing "Exceeding Measure."*)
Exceeding measure, with pains continual,
  Languishing in absence, alas! what shall I do?
Unfortunate wretch, devoid of joys all,
  Sighs upon sighs redoubling my woe,
  And tears down falling from mine eyes too.
Beauty with truth so doth me constrain
Ever to serve where I may not attain!
Truth binding me ever to be true,
  How so that fortune favoreth my chance.
During my life none other but you   650
  Of my true heart shall have the governance.
  Oh Good sweetheart, have you remembrance
Now of your own, which for no smart   *pain*
Exile shall you from my true heart.
    [*Enter* EXPERIENCE *and* SCIENCE.]
EXPERIENCE: Daughter, what meaneth that ye did not sing?
SCIENCE: Oh mother, for here remaineth a thing.
  Friends, we thank you for these your pleasures,
  Taken on us as chance to us measures.
WORSHIP: Lady, these our pleasures and persons, too,
  Are sent to you, you service to do.   660
FAME: Lady Science, to set forth your name,
  The World to wait on you hath sent me, Fame.
FAVOR: Lady Science, for your virtues most plenty,
  The World, to cherish you, Favor hath sent me.
RICHES: Lady Science, for your benefits known,
  The World, to maintain you, Riches hath thrown.
WORSHIP: And as the World hath sent you these three,
  So he sendeth me, Worship, to advance your degree.
SCIENCE: I thank the World. But chiefly God be praised
  That in the World such love to Science hath raised.   670
  But yet to tell you plain, ye three are such

As Science looketh for little nor much;
For, being as I am, a lone woman,
Need of your service I neither have nor can.
But, thanking the World and you for your pain,
I send ye to the World even now again.

WORSHIP: Why, lady, set ye no more store by me,
Worship? Ye set nought by yourself, I see.

FAME: She setteth nought by Fame; whereby I spy her—
She careth not what the World sayeth by her. 680

FAVOR: She setteth nought by Favor; whereby I try her—
She careth not what the World sayeth or doeth by her.

SCIENCE: Indeed, small cause given to care for the World's
favoring,
Seeing the wits of the World be so wavering.

EXPERIENCE: What is the matter, daughter, that ye
Be so sad? Open your mind to me.

SCIENCE: My marvel is no less, my good mother,
Than my grief is great, to see, of all other,
The proud scorn of Wit, son to Dame Nature, 690
Who sent me a picture of his stature
With all the shape of himself there opening,
His amorous love thereby betokening,
Borne towards me in abundant fashion;
And also, further, to make right relation
Of his love he put in commission
Such a messenger as no suspicion
Could grow in me of him—Confidence.

EXPERIENCE: Um!

SCIENCE: Who, I assure ye, with such vehemence
And faithful behavior in his moving 700
Set forth the pith of his master's loving
That no living creature could conject   *suspect*
But that pure love did Wit direct.

EXPERIENCE: So!

SCIENCE: Now, this being since the space
Of three times sending from place to place
Between Wit and his man, I hear no more,

Neither of Wit nor his love so sore.
How think you of this, my own dear mother?
EXPERIENCE: Daughter, in this I can think none other
But that it is true, this proverb old: 710
"Hasty love is soon hot and soon cold."
Take heed, daughter, how you put your trust
To light lovers too hot at the first.
For had this love of Wit been grounded,
And on a sure foundation founded,
Little void time would have been between ye
But that this Wit would have sent or seen ye.
SCIENCE: I think so.
EXPERIENCE: Yea, think ye so or no,
Your mother, Experience, proof shall show
That Wit hath set his love—I dare say,   720
And make ye warrantise—another way.   *guarantee*
          (WIT *cometh before*.)
WIT: But your warrantise warrant no truth!
Fair lady, I pray you be not wroth
Till you hear more; for, dear Lady Science,
Had your lover, Wit, or Confidence,
His man, been in health all this time spent,
Long ere this time Wit had either come or sent.
But the truth is they have been both sick,
Wit and his man; yea, and with pains thick
Both stayed by the way, so that your lover   730
Could neither come nor send by none other.
Wherefore blame not him, but chance of sickness.
SCIENCE: Who is this?
EXPERIENCE: Ingnorancy, or his likeness.
SCIENCE: What, the common fool?
EXPERIENCE: It is much like him.
SCIENCE: By my sooth, his tongue serveth him now trim.
What sayest thou, Ingnorancy? Speak again!
WIT: Nay, lady, I am not Ingnorancy, plain,
But I am your own dear lover, Wit,
That hath long loved you, and loveth you yet.

Wherefore I pray thee now, my own sweeting,   740
Let me have a kiss at this our meeting.
SCIENCE: Yea, so shall ye anon, but not yet.
Ah sir, this fool hath got some wit.
Fall you to kissing, sir, nowadays?
Your mother shall charm you. Go your ways!
WIT: What needeth this, my love of long grown?
Will ye be strange to me, your own?
Your acquaintance to me was thought easy,   *pleasurable*
But now your words make my heart all queasy,
Your darts at me so strangely be shot.   750
SCIENCE: Hear what terms this fool here hath got!
WIT: Well, I perceive my foolishness now;
Indeed, ladies no dastards allow.   *dullard or coward*
I will be bold with my own darling:
Come now, a basse, my own proper sparling!   *kiss*
SCIENCE: What wilt thou, arrant fool?
WIT: Nay, by the mass,
I will have a basse ere I hence pass.
SCIENCE: What wilt thou, arrant fool? Hence, fool, I say!
WIT: What, nothing but "fool" and "fool" all this day?
By the mass, madam, ye can do no good!   760
SCIENCE: Art a swearing, too? Now, by my hood,
Your foolish knave's breech seven stripes shall bear.
WIT: Yea, God's bones! "Fool" and "knave," too?
Be ye there?   *are you up to that?*
By the mass, madam, call me "fool" once again,
And thou shalt sure call a blow or twain.
EXPERIENCE: Come away, daughter, the fool is mad.
WIT: Nay, nor yet neither hence ye shall gad;   *go*
We will 'gree better ere ye pass hence.
I pray thee now, good sweet Lady Science,
All this strange manner now hide and cover,   770
And play the goodfellow with thy lover.
SCIENCE: What good fellowship would ye of me,
Whom ye know not, neither yet I know ye?
WIT: Know ye not me?

SCIENCE: No. How should I know ye?

WIT: Doth not my picture my person show ye?

SCIENCE: Your picture?

WIT: Yea, my picture, lady,
   That ye spake of. Who sent it but I?

SCIENCE: If that be your picture, then shall we
   Soon see how you and your picture agree.
   Lo, here the picture that I named is this.   780

WIT: Yea, marry, mine own likeness this is.
   You having this, Lady! And so loath
   To know me, which this so plain showeth!

SCIENCE: Why, you are nothing like, in mine eye.

WIT: No? How say ye?

EXPERIENCE: As she sayeth, so say I.

WIT: By the mass, then are ye both stark blind!
   What difference between this and this can ye find?

EXPERIENCE: Marry, this is fair, pleasant and goodly,
   And ye are foul, displeasant and ugly.

WIT: Marry, avaunt, thou foul ugly whore!   *go away* 790

SCIENCE: So, lo! Now I perceive ye more and more.

WIT: What, perceive you me as ye would make me,
   A natural fool?

SCIENCE: Nay, ye mistake me;
   I take ye for no fool natural,
   But I take ye thus—shall I tell all?

WIT: Yea, marry! Tell me your mind, I pray ye,
   Whereto I shall trust. No more delay ye!

SCIENCE: I take ye for no natural fool
   Brought up among the innocents' school,
   But for a naughty, vicious fool,   800
   Brought up with Idleness, in her school.
   Of all arrogant fools, thou art one!

WIT: Yea, Gog's body!   *God's body*

EXPERIENCE: Come, let us be gone.

WIT: My sword, is it gone? A vengeance on them!
   Be thy gone, too, and their heads upon them?
   But, proud queans, the devil go with ye both!   *whores*

Not one point of courtesy in them goeth!
A man is well at ease by suit to pain him
For such a drab, that so doth disdain him!
So mocked, so louted, so made a sot,   *flouted* 810
Never was I erst since I was begot.   *before*
Am I so foul as those drabs would make me?
Now shall this glass of Reason soon try me   *show*
As fair as those drabs that so doth belie me.
Ha! Gog's soul! What have we here, a devil?
This glass, I see well, hath been kept evil.
Gog's soul! A fool! A fool, by the mass!
What a very vengeance aileth this glass?
Other this glass is shamefully spotted,   *either*
Or else I am too shamefully blotted.   820
Nay, by Gog's arms, I am so, no doubt.
How look their faces here round about?[10]
All fair and clear they, everyone;
And I, by the mass, a fool alone,
Decked, by God's bones, like a very ass!
Ingnorancy's coat, hood, ears—yea, by the mass,
Cockscomb and all. I lack but a bauble!   *fool's baton*
And as for this face, [it] is abominable,
As black as the devil. God for his passion!
Where have I been rayed after this fashion?   *arrayed* 830
This same is Idleness—a shame take her!
This same is her work—the devil in hell rake her!
The whore hath shamed me forever, I trow.   *think*
I trow? Nay verily, I know.
Now it is so—the stark fool I play
Before all people. Now see it I may.
Every man I see laugh me to scorn.
Alas, alas, that ever I was born!
It was not for nought, now well I see,
That those two ladies disdained me.   840
Alas, Lady Science, of all other—
How have I railed on her and her mother!

[10] Wit holds the glass up to the audience.

Alas, that lady I have now lost
Whom all the world loveth and honoreth most!
Alas, from Reason had I not varied,
Lady Science ere this I had married!
And those four gifts which the World gave her
I had won, too, had I kept her favor;
Where now, instead of that lady bright,
With all those gallants seen in my sight—   850
Favor, Riches, yea Worship and Fame—
I have won Hatred, Beggary and Open Shame.
   (SHAME *cometh in with a whip*.) [REASON *follows*.]
WIT: Out upon thee, Shame! What dost thou here?
REASON: Marry, I, Reason, bade him here appear.
Upon him, Shame, with stripes enow smitten,   *presently*
While I rehearse his faults herein written:
First, he hath broken his promise formerly
Made to me, Reason, my daughter to marry;
Next, he hath broken his promise promised
To obey Instruction, and him despised;   860
Thirdly, my daughter Science to reprove,   *reject*
Upon Idleness he hath set his love;
Fourthly, he hath followed Idleness' school
Till she hath made him a very stark fool;
Lastly, offending both God and man,
Swearing great oaths as any man can,
He hath abused himself, to the great shame
Of all his kindred and loss of his good name.
Wherefore, spare him not, Shame! Beat him well there!
He hath deserved more than he can bear.   870
   (WIT *kneeleth down*.)
WIT: Oh father Reason, be good unto me!
Alas, these stripes of Shame will undo me!
REASON: Be still a while, Shame! Wit, what sayest thou?
WIT: Oh, sir, forgive me, I beseech you!
REASON: If I forgive thee thy punishment,
 Wilt thou then follow thy first intent
 And promise made, my daughter to marry?

WIT: Oh sir, I am not worthy to carry
The dust out where your daughter should sit!
REASON: I wot well that; but if I admit   *know* 880
Thee, unworthy, again to her wooer,
Wilt thou then follow thy suit unto her?
WIT: Yea, sir, I promise you, while life endureth.
REASON: Come near, masters, here is one insureth   *promises*
In words to become an honest man.
    (*Here cometh* INSTRUCTION, STUDY *and* DILIGENCE *in.*)
Take him, Instruction, do what ye can.
INSTRUCTION: What! to the purpose he went before?
REASON: Yea, to my daughter prove him once more.
Take him and trim him in new apparel,
And give that to Shame there to his farewell.[11]   890
INSTRUCTION: Come, on your way, Wit. Be of good cheer!
After stormy clouds cometh down weather clear.
    (INSTRUCTION, STUDY, WIT *and* DILIGENCE *go out.*)
REASON: Who list to mark now this chance here done,
May see what Wit is without Reason.
What, was this Wit better than an ass,
Being strayed from Reason as he was?
But let that pass now, since he is well punished,
And thereby, I trust, meetly well 'monished.   *properly admonished*
Yea, and I like him never the worse, I,
Though Shame hath handled him shamefully;   900
For like as if Wit had proudly bent him
To resist Shame, to make Shame absent him,
I would have thought then that Wit had been—
As the saying is, and daily seen—
"Past Shame once and past all amendment":
So contrary, since he did relent
To Shame when Shame punished him even ill,   *harshly*
I have, I say, good hope in him still;
And think as I thought—if join they can—
My daughter well bestowed on this man.   910

[11] To his farewell: apparently Shame receives Ingnorancy's clothes as his payment. That was one of the prerogatives of an executioner.

But all the doubt now is to think how
My daughter taketh this; for I may tell you,
I think she knew this Wit even as well
As she seemed here to know him no deal;   *not at all*
For lack of knowledge in Science there is none;
Wherefore, she knew him, and thereupon
His misbehavior perchance even striking
Her heart against him, she now misliking—
As women oftimes will be hard hearted—
Will be the stranger to be reverted.   920
This must I help. Reason now must walk,
On Wit's part with my Science to talk.
A near way to her, know I, whereby
My son's coming prevent now must I.
Perchance I may bring my daughter hither;
If so, I doubt not to join them together.
>   (*Exit* REASON. CONFIDENCE *cometh in*.)

CONFIDENCE: I thank God yet at the last I have found him.
I was afraid some mischance had drowned him,
My master, Wit, with whom I have spoken—
Yea, and delivered token for token,   930
And have another to Science again,
A heart of gold, signifying plain
That Science hath won Wit's heart forever;
Whereby I trust by my good endeavor
To that good lady, so sweetly and so sortly,   *properly*
A marriage between them ye shall see shortly.
>   (*Exit* CONFIDENCE. INSTRUCTION *cometh in with* WIT,
>   STUDY *and* DILIGENCE.)

INSTRUCTION: Lo, sir, now ye be entered again
Toward that passage where doth remain
Tediousness, your mortal enemy.
Now may ye choose whether ye will try   940
Your hands again on that tyrant stout,
Or else walk a little about.

WIT: Nay, for God's passion! Sir, let me meet him.
Ye see I am able now for to greet him.

This sword of comfort sent from my love,
Upon her enemy needs must I prove.
INSTRUCTION: Then forth there, and turn on your right hand
Up that mount before ye shall see stand.
But hear ye, if your enemy chance to rise,
Follow my counsel in any wise: 950
Let Study and Diligence flee their touch—   *blow*
The stroke of Tediousness—and then couch
Themselves as I told ye, ye wot how.   *know*
WIT: Yea, sir, for that how, mark the proof now!
INSTRUCTION: To mark it indeed, here will I abide,
To see what chance of them will betide;
For here cometh the pith, lo, of this journey:
That mountain, before which they must assay,
Is called in Latin *Mons Pernassus:*   *Mount Parnassus*
Which mountain, as old authors discuss,   960
Who attaineth once to sleep on that mount,
Lady Science his own he may count.
But ere he come there, ye shall see fought
A fight with no less policy wrought
Than strength, I trow—if that may be praised.   *think*
TEDIOUSNESS: Oh! Ho, Ho!
INSTRUCTION: Hark!
TEDIOUSNESS: Out, ye caitiffs!   *wretches*
INSTRUCTION: The fiend is raised.
TEDIOUSNESS: Out, ye villains! Be ye come again?
Have at ye, wretches!
WIT: Flee, sirs, ye twain!
TEDIOUSNESS: They flee not far hence!
DILIGENCE: Turn again, Study!
STUDY: Now, Diligence!   970
INSTRUCTION: Well said. Hold fast now!
STUDY: He fleeth.
DILIGENCE: Then follow!
INSTRUCTION: With his own weapon, now work him
        sorrow!
 Wit lieth at receipt.   *in ambush*

TEDIOUSNESS: Oh! Ho, Ho!
    (*Dieth*)
INSTRUCTION: Hark, he dieth!
  Where strength lacketh, policy supplieth.
    (*Here* WIT *cometh in and bringeth in the head upon his sword, and sayeth as followeth*)
WIT: I can thank you sirs; this was well done.
STUDY: Nay, yours is the deed.
DILIGENCE: To you is the thank.
INSTRUCTION: I can ye thank all; this was well done.
WIT: How say ye, man, is this field well won?
    (CONFIDENCE *cometh running in.*)
CONFIDENCE: Yea, by my faith, so sayeth your dear heart.
WIT: Why, where is she, that here now thou art?   980
CONFIDENCE: Upon yonder mountain on high,
  She saw ye strike that head from the body;
  Whereby ye have won her, body and all;
  In token whereof receive here ye shall
  A gown of Knowledge, wherein you must
  Receive her here straight.
WIT: But sayest thou just?   *true*
CONFIDENCE: So just I say, that, except ye hie ye,
  Ere ye be ready she will be by ye.
WIT: Hold! Present unto her this head here,
  And give me warning when she cometh near.   990
  Instruction, will ye help to devise,
  To trim this gear now in the best wise?   *put on this gown*
INSTRUCTION: Give me that gown and come with me all.
DILIGENCE: Oh, how this gear to the purpose doth fall.
    (CONFIDENCE *cometh running in.*)
CONFIDENCE: How, master, master! Where be ye now?
WIT: Here, Confidence; what tidings bringest thou?
CONFIDENCE: My lady at hand here doth abide ye.
  Bid her welcome! What, do ye hide ye?
      (*Here* WIT, INSTRUCTION, STUDY *and* DILIGENCE *sing* "*Welcome, My Own,*" *and* SCIENCE, EXPERIENCE, REASON *and* CONFIDENCE *cometh in at left and answer every second verse.*)

WIT and his COMPANY:
 Oh lady dear   1000
 Be ye so near
  To be known?
 My heart you cheer
 Your voice to hear.
  Welcome, mine own!
SCIENCE and her COMPANY:
 As ye rejoice
 To hear my voice
  From me thus blown,
 So in my choice   1010
 I show my voice
  To be your own.
WIT and his COMPANY:
 Then draw we near
 To see and hear
  My love long grown.
 Where is my dear?
 Here I appear
  To see mine own.
SCIENCE and her COMPANY: 1020
 To see and try
 You love truly
  Till death be flown,
 Lo, here am I,
 That ye may spy
  I am your own.
WIT and his COMPANY:
 Then let us meet,
 My love so sweet,
  Halfway here thrown!   1030
SCIENCE and her COMPANY:
 I will not fleet
 My love to greet.
  Welcome, mine own!
WIT and his COMPANY;

Welcome, mine own!

All sing:

Welcome, mine own!

(*And when the song is done,* REASON *sendeth* INSTRUCTION, STUDY
and DILIGENCE *and* CONFIDENCE *out; and then, standing in the
middle of the place,* WIT *sayeth as followeth*:)

WIT: Welcome, mine own, with all my whole heart,

Which shall be your own, till death us depart.   *separate* 1040

I trust, lady, this knot even since knit.

SCIENCE: I trust the same; for since ye have smit   *struck*

Down my great enemy, Tediousness,

Ye have won me forever, doubtless,

Although ye have won a clog withal.   *encumbrance*

WIT: A clog, sweetheart? What?

SCIENCE: Such as doth fall

To all men that join themselves in marriage:

In keeping their wives, a careful carriage.   *conduct*

WIT: Careful? Nay, lady, that care shall employ

No clog, but a key of my most joy.   1050

To keep you, sweetheart, as shall be fit,

Shall be no care, but most joy to Wit.

SCIENCE: Well, yet I say—mark well what I say—

My presence bringeth you a clog, no nay,

Not in the keeping of me only,

But in the use of Science chiefly.

For I, Science, am in this degree

As all, or most part, of woman be:

If ye use me well, in a good sort,

Then shall I be your joy and comfort;   1060

But if ye use me not well, then doubt me,

For, sure, ye were better without me.

WIT: Why lady, think you me such a Wit,

As being advanced by you and yet

Would misuse ye? Nay, if ye doubt that,

Here is one loveth ye more than somewhat!

If Wit misuse ye at any season,

Correct me then your own father, Reason.

REASON: Lo, daughter, can ye desire any more?
      What needs these doubts? Avoid them, therefore!   1070
EXPERIENCE: By 'rlakyn, sir, but under your favor,   *by our Ladykin*
      This doubt our daughter doth well to gather   *bring out*
      For a good warning now at beginning
      What Wit in the end shall look for in winning;
      Which shall be this, sir: If Science here,
      Which is God's gift, will be used mere
      Unto God's honor, and profit both
      Of you and your neighbor—which
      Goeth of her kind to do good to all—   *is her nature*
      This seen to, Experience, I, shall   1080
      Set you forth, Wit, by her to employ   *get*
      Double increase to your double joy;
      But if you use her contrary wise
      To her good nature, and so devise
      To evil effect to wrest and to wry her,
      Yea, and cast her off and set nought by her,
      Be sure I, Experience, shall than   *then*
      Declare you so before God and man
      That this talent from you shall be taken,   *thing of value*
      And you punished, and your gain forsaken.   1090
WIT: "Once warned, half armed," folk say; namely when
      Experience shall warn a man, then
      Time to take heed. Mother Experience,
      Touching your daughter, my dear heart, Science,
      As I am certain that to abuse her
      I breed mine own sorrow, and well to use her
      I increase my joy (and so to make it   *bring it about*
      God's grace is ready if I will take it),
      Then, but ye count me no wit at all,   *unless*
      Let never these doubts into your head fall;   1100
      But, as yourself, Experience, clearing
      All doubt at length, so, till time appearing,
      Trust ye with me in God.[12] And, sweetheart,

[12] But as yourself . . . with me in God: Since only you, Experience, can show whether I may be trusted to use Science properly, trust with me in God until that time has come.

While your father, Reason, taketh with part
To receive God's grace as God shall send it,
Doubt ye not our joy till lives end it.
SCIENCE: Well, then, for the end of all doubts past,
And to that end which ye spake of last,
Among our wedding matters here rendering,
Th'end of our lives would be in remembering;   1110
Which remembrance, Wit, shall sure defend ye
From the misuse of Science, and send you
The gain my mother to mind did call;
Joy without end—that wish I to all!
REASON: Well said! And as ye, daughter, wish it,
That joy, To folks in general,
So wish I the same. But yet
First in this life wish I here to fall
To our noble king and queen in especial,
To their honorable Council, and then to all the rest,   1120
Such joy as long may rejoice them all best.
        (*Here cometh in four with viols and sing* "Remember me," *and
        at the last choir all make curtsey, and so go forth singing.*)

**Thus endeth the play of Wit and Science,
made by Master John Redford**

✳ *RESPUBLICA*

(1553, attributed to N. Udall)

It is probably misleading to think of *Respublica* as having contributed to the development in dramatic form, for it was played, as far as we know, only at Court and only in the special occasion mentioned in the Prologue, and it was never printed. The play does gain some standing by being almost certainly the work of Nicholas Udall, noted Latinist, anthologist, and the author of *Ralph Roister Doister*, a comedy in the Roman manner, and, like *Respublica*, one meant for performance by children.

But perhaps more importantly, *Respublica* presents an example of the adaptation of the versatile morality formula to two ulterior purposes—the presentation of a courtly entertainment by children, and the grinding of a specific religious and political axe by the author. These two motives taken together probably account for the unusual, one might say the disproportionate, emphasis on the comic byplay of the Vice characters. Horseplay being the natural mode of children, one can well imagine the pleasure, especially for an aristocratic audience, of seeing children cavorting through what the Prologue calls "high" matters of state. Their very presence is a kind of dramatic strategy for the neutralizing of evil. One also senses in the handling of the rustic character People, the good shrewd English peasant, a mixture of affection and condescension that might be expected of an aristocratic audience.

On the other hand, the play has to be largely about the Vices because it is primarily a history play and it is about the Reformation, which, for Udall, was a period of unbridled vice. Chronicle history and allegory interpenetrate each other in a remarkable way in this play. It preserves the unity of its own allegorical "plot," and yet it is explicitly stated, for instance, that Oppression is concerning himself with the dissolving of the monastic properties, and it is no less clear that Nemesis, who restores order at the end, *is* Queen Mary.

In addition to these characteristics, and to the appearance of the nation and the people as central figure, in place of the single Mankind character, we may note what is perhaps an unusual interest in language for its own sake. The play is full of verbal pyrotechnics, from Avarice's catalogue of loot, to Respublica's rhetorical lamentations, to the thunder of Nemesis. What is impressive is the broad range of verbal resources available to the author and his willingness to use them.

All these features suggest a moment when the moral play is groping for a shape and a tongue to speak in.

The Play has been edited from the manuscript three times; by Brandl (see Bibliography), and twice for the Early English Text Society, by L. Magnus in 1905 and by W. W. Greg in 1952. Our text is a modernized-spelling version of Greg's. In the difficult spots, if we have preferred a reading of Brandl's or Magnus' to Greg's, we have so noted.

RESPUBLICA

A merry interlude entitled Respublica *made in the year of our Lord 1553 and the first year of the most prosperous reign of our most gracious sovereign Queen Mary the first.*

THE PARTS AND NAMES OF THE PLAYERS

THE PROLOGUE, a poet

AVARICE, alias Policy, the Vice of the play

INSOLENCE, alias Authority, the chief gallant

OPPRESSION, alias Reformation, another gallant

ADULATION, alias Honesty, the third gallant

PEOPLE, representing the poor commonalty

RESPUBLICA, a widow

MISERICORDIA

VERITAS

JUSTITIA

PAX

} four Ladies

NEMESIS, the goddess of redress and correction, a goddess

The Prologue

First, health and success, with many a good new year,
Wished unto all this most noble presence here.
I have more to entreat you of gentle sufferance,[1]
That this our matter may have quiet utterance.
We that are the actors have ourselves dedicate,
With some Christmas device your spirits to recreate,
And our poet trusteth the thing we shall recite
May without offence the hearer's minds delight.
Indeed, no man speaketh words so well fore pondered
But the same by some may be misconstrued,[2]   10
Nor nothing so well meant but that by some pretence
It may be wrong interpreted from the author's sense.

[1] Original reads "tentreate." Throughout the play, to preserve the meter, " to" and "the" when followed by a word beginning with a vowel, elide with that word.
[2] The MS reads "misconstrued." Greg emends to "misconstred," a common Elizabethan form, to rhyme with "pondered."

But let this be taken no worse than it is meant,
And I hope nor we nor our poet shall be shent.   *shamed*
But now of the argument to touch a word or twain,
The name of our play is *Respublica*, certain;
Our meaning is (I say not as by plain story,
But, as it were, in figure, by an allegory)
To show that all commonweals' ruin and decay
From time to time hath been, is, and shall be alway   20
When insolence, flattery, oppression
And avarice have the rule in their possession.
But though these vices, by cloakèd colusion
And by counterfeit names hidden their abusion,[3]
Do reign for a while, to commonweals' prejudice,
Perverting all right and all order of true justice,
Yet time trieth all, and time bringeth truth to light,
That wrong may not ever still reign in place of right.
For when pleaseth God such commonweals to restore
To their wealth and honor wherein they were afore,   30
He sendeth down his most tender compassion
To cause truth go about in visitation;[4]
Verity, the daughter of sage old Father Time,
Showeth all as it is, be it virtue or crime,
Then doth Justice all such as commonweal oppress,
Tempered with Mercy, attempt to suppress,
With whom anon is linked tranquillity and Peace,
To commonweal's joy and perpetual increase.
But shall boys (saith some now) of such high matters play?
No, not as discussers; but yet the Book doth say;   40
Ex ore infantium perfecisti laudem;[5]
For when Christ came riding into Jerusalem
The young babes with the old folk cried out all and some,
"Blessed be the man that in the Lord's name doth come!"
So, for good England['s] sake this present hour and day,
In hope of her restoring from her late decay,

[3] This is evidently an ablative absolute construction—"their abusion having been hidden . . ."
[4] Visitation is technically the periodical inspection, by Bishop or his delegate, of parish priests and their churches.
[5] Matthew 21, 16—Out of the mouths of babes and sucklings thou hast brought perfect praise.

We children to you old folk, both with heart and voice,
May join altogether to thank God and rejoice
That he hath sent Mary our sovereign and Queen
To reform the abuses which hitherto hath been,   50
And that ills which long time have reigned uncorrect
Shall now forever be redressed with effect.
She is our most wise and most worthy Nemesis,
Of whom our play meaneth to amend that is amiss,
Which, to bring to pass that she may have time and space,
Let us both young and old to God commend Her Grace.
Now, if you so please, I will go, and hither send
That shall make you laugh well if ye abide the end.   *stay until*

Finis.

Actus primi, scena prima[6]

[*Enter*] AVARICE

AVARICE: Now Godigood everychone, both great and small,[7]
From highest to lowest, Godigood to you all!
Godigood—what should I say?—even or morrow?
If I mark how the day goeth God give me sorrow![8]
But Godigood each one, twenty and twenty score,
Of that ye most long for what would ye have more?
Ye must pardon my wits, for I tell you plain
I have a hive of humble bees swarming in my brain
And he that hath the compass to fetch that   *reach/that which*
    I must fetch,
I may say in Council, had need his wits to stretch.   10
But now what my name is and what is my purpose,
Taking you all for friends I fear not to disclose.
My very true unchristian name is Avarice,
Which I may not have openly known in no wise,

---

[6] The rather pretentious Latin Act and Scene numbering marks the play as a courtly production. Each entrance of a new character is designated a new scene.

[7] "Godigood" is "God give you good," and then he can't decide whether it is good evening or good morning. "Everychone" is an archaic form of "everyone," which carries with it a suggestion of a lower-class dialect.

[8] This is one of those rather long-winded Elizabethan expressions that should not be read literally word for word. It is equivalent to "I'll be damned if I know what time of day it is!"

For though to most men I am found commodious,
Yet to those that use me my name is Odious,
For who is so foolish that the evil he hath wrought
For his own behoof he would to light should be brought,
Or who had not rather his ill doings to hide
Than to have the same bruited on every side?   20
Therefore to work my feat I will my name disguise,
And call my name Policy instead of Covetise.
The name of Policy is praised of each one
But to rake gromwell seed Avarice is alone.   (rake in money)
The name of Policy is of none suspected,
Policy is ne'er of any crime detected,
So that under the name and cloak of Policy
Avarice may work facts and 'scape all jealousy.   *deeds/suspicion*
And now is the time come that, except I be a beast,   *if I'm not a fool*
E'en to make up my mouth and feather my nest[9]   30
A time that I have waited for a great long space.
And now may I speed my purpose, if I have grace,
For, hear ye sirra, our great grand lady mother,
Noble Dame Respublica, she and none other,
Of the offals, the refuse, the rags, the parings,
The baggage, the trash, the fragments, the sharings,
The odd ends, the crumbs, the driblets, the chippings,
The patches, the pieces, the brooklets, the drippings,[10]
The fleetance, the scrapings, the wide waifs and strays,[11]   *flotsam*
The skimmings, the gubbins of booties and preys,   *gobbets* 40
The gleanings, the casualties, the blind escheats,   *secret*
The forging of forfeits, the 'scape of extracts,   *fines*
The excess, the waste, the spoil, the superfluities,
The windfalls, the shreddings, the fleecings, the petty fees,
With a thousand things mo which she may right well lack,
Would fill all these same purses that hang at my back,
Yea, and ten times as many mo bags as these
Which should be but a flea biting for her to lese,   *lose*

[9] Greg glosses "make up my mouth" as "furnish my meal with a special dainty."
[10] Original reads "broklets" which might be another word.
[11] Original reads "waives."

That if I may have the grace and hap to blind her,   *luck*

I doubt not a sweet lady I shall find her.   50

To her it were nothing, yet many a small maketh a great,

And all things would help me, whatever I may get.

Full little know men the great need that I am in,

Do I not spend daily of that that I do win?

Then age cometh on, and what is a little gold

To keep a man by dread that is feeble and old?[12]

No man therefore blame me though I would have more,

The world waxeth hard, and store (they say) is no sore.

Now the chance of thieves in good hour be it spoken—

Out, alas, I fear I left my coffer open!   60

I am surely undone! Alas, where be my keys?

It is gone that I have sweat for all my   *sweat* = past tense

    live days!   *life's*

Woe worth all whoreson thieves and such covetous knaves,

That for their winding sheet would scrape men out of their

    graves!

    [*Exit*]

Actus primi, scena secunda

(ADULATION, INSOLENCE, OPPRESSION *intrant cantantes*)   *enter singing*

ADULATION: Oh noble Insolence, if I could sing as well

I would look in heaven among Angels to dwell.

INSOLENCE: Sing? How do I sing but as other many do?

ADULATION: Yes, an Angel's voice ye have to hearken unto.

INSOLENCE: Yea, but what availeth that to high dignity?

OPPRESSION: By His arms, not a whit, as far as I can see.   70

INSOLENCE: Or what helpeth that thing to set a man aloft?

OPPRESSION: By His wounds, not a straw, so have I told you

    oft.

ADULATION: No, but ye are one of such goodly personage,

  Of such wit and beauty and of sage parentage,

  So excellent in all points of every art—

INSOLENCE: Indeed, God and nature in me have done their part.

ADULATION: That if ye will put yourself forward to the most,

---

[12] Apparently " by" means "from" here.

Ye may throughout the whole land rule the roost.
How say you, Oppression? Is it not even so?

OPPRESSION: Thou sayest sooth Adulation,
    so mote I go!   *that's for sure* 80
If he were disposed to take the charge in hand
I warrant him achieve to rule the whole land.[13]

ADULATION: Lo, Master Insolence, ye hear Oppression?

INSOLENCE: I thank both him and thee, good Adulation,
And long have I dreamed of such an enterprise,
But how or where to begin I cannot devise.

OPPRESSION: Wherefore serve friends, but your enterprise to
    allow?

ADULATION: And then must you support them, as they must
    maintain you.

OPPRESSION: And wherefore do friends serve, but to set you in?

ADULATION: And ye shall have all my help, whenever ye
    begin.   90

INSOLENCE: But we may herein nothing attempt in no wise
Without the counsel of our founder Avarice.

ADULATION: He must direct all this gear by his holy ghost.

OPPRESSION: For he knoweth what is to be done
    in each coast.   *on all sides*
He knoweth where and how that money is to be had,
And yonder he cometh methinketh, more than half mad.
    (*Intrat* AVARITIA)   *enter*

Actus primi, scena tertia

AVARICE, INSOLENCE, OPPRESSION, ADULATION

AVARICE: It was a fair grace that I was not undone clean,
Yet my key was safe locked under nine locks, I ween,
But e'en as against such a thing my heart will throb,
I found knaves about my house ready me to rob.   100
There was such tooting, such looking and such prying,   *peeping*
Such hearkening, such stalking, such watching, such spying,
"What would ye, my masters?" "We look after a cat."

---

[13] I promise he would achieve the rule of . . .

"What make ye hereabout?" "We have smelled a rat."

Now, a wheal on such noses, I thought by and by,   *a pox on*

That so quickly can scent where hidden gold doth lie!

But had I not come when I did, without all fails

I think they had digged up my walls with their nails!

INSOLENCE: Let us speak to him and break his chafing talk.

AVARICE: Such greediness of money among men doth walk   110

That have it they will, either by hook or by crook—

OPPRESSION: Let us call to him that he may this way look.

AVARICE: Whether by right or by wrong, in faith, some care
    not.

Therefore catch that catch may, hardily, and spare not—

ADULATION: All hail, our founder and chief master Avarice!

AVARICE: The devil is a knave an I catch not a
    fleece—   *if/some booty*

ADULATION: When ye see your time, look this way your
    friends upon.

AVARICE: I doubt not to scramble and rake as well as one—

ADULATION: Here be that would fain be disciples of your art.

AVARICE: I will not be behind to get a child's part.   120

ADULATION: Now if ye have done I pray you look this way back.

AVARICE: Who buzzeth in mine ear so? What, ye saucy jack?

ADULATION: Are ye yet at leisure, with your good friends to
    talk?

AVARICE: What, clawest thou mine elbow, prattling merchant?
    Walk!

Ye flaterabundus, you! You fleering claw-back[14] you!   *mocking*

You "the crow is white," you! You "the swan is black," you!

You "John hold my staff," you! You "what is the clock," you!

You "*ait . . . aio*," you! You "*negat . . . nego*," you!

ADULATION: I marvel you speak to me in such fashion.

AVARICE: Why troublest thou me, then, in my contemplation.   130

ADULATION: I came of right good love,
    not minding you to let.   *thinking to stop you*

AVARICE: Thou ne'er camest to any man of good love yet!

---

[14] "Merchant" means "fellow;" "flaterabundus" is a mock Latin coinage meaning full of flattery; "*ait . . .*
aio . . . negat . . . nego" means "He says . . . I say . . . he denies . . . I deny," in other words, a "yes-man."

ADULATION: And these men's minds it was I should so do.

AVARICE: As false wretches as thyself, and falser too!

INSOL. and OPPRESS.:   We have been loving to you, and faithful alway.

AVARICE: For your own profits then, and not mine, I dare say,
And e'en very you three it was and others none,
That would have robbed me not yet half an hour gone!

INSOL., OPPR., ADULA: We never robbed any man later or rather!

AVARICE: Yes, many a time and oft—your own very father!   140

OPPRESSION: And to you have we born hearty favors alway.

AVARICE: And I warrant you hanged for your labors one day.

OPPR., ADUL: Even as our god we have alway honored you.

AVARICE: And e'en as your god I have aye succored you.

OPPRESSION: We call you our founder, by All Holy Hallows!

AVARICE: Founder me no foundering, but beware of the gallows!

INSOLENCE: I pray you leave these words and talk friendly at last!

AVARICE: Content at your request, my fume is now well past,
And in faith, what saith our friend Adulation?

ADULATION: I wonder at your rough communication,   150
That ye would to me use words of such vehemence.

AVARICE: Faith man, I spoke but even to prove your
patience,   *try*
That is thou hadst grunted or stormed thereat—

ADULATION: Nay, few times do I use such lewd manner as that.

AVARICE: Come, shake hands, and forever we two be at one.

ADULATION: As for grudge in me, there shall never remain none.

AVARICE: Now, Master Insolence, to your ghostly purpose.

INSOLENCE: We accorded a matter to you to disclose.

AVARICE: I understand all your agreement and accord,
For I lay in your bosoms when ye spoke the word,   160
And I like well the advice of Oppression
And eke of Flattery, for your progression.   *getting ahead*

INSOLENCE: If there were matter whereon to work, I care not.

AVARICE: Ye shall have matter enough. Be doing, spare not!

INSOLENCE: What, to come to honor and wealth for us all three?

AVARICE: Ah, then ye could be well content to leave out me?

INSOLENCE: No, for I know ye can for yourself well provide.

AVARICE: Yea, that I can, and for twenty hundred beside!

ADULATION: Oh, would Christ, good founder, ye would that
thing open!

AVARICE: Bones, knave! Wilt thou have it ere it can be   170
spoken?

OPPRESSION: For the passion of God, tell it us with all speed!

AVARICE: By the Cross, not a word here in haste made, indeed!

INSOLENCE: Yes, good sweet Avarice, dispatch and tell at once!

AVARICE: Nay then, cut my throat; ye are fellows for the nonce.
Will ye have a matter before it can be told?
If ye will have me tell it ye shall your tongues hold.
Whist! Silence! Not a word! Mum! Let your clatter cease.
Are ye with child to hear, and cannot hold your peace?
So sir, now; Respublica, the lady of estate,
Ye know now lately is left almost desolate.   180
Her wealth is decayed, her comfort clean a-go,
And she at her wits ends for what to say or do.
Fain would she have succor and easement of her grief,
And highly advance them that would promise relief.
Such as would warrant her spirits to revive
Mote mount to high estate and be most sure to thrive.   *must*

INSOLENCE: So.

ADULATION: Well said.

OPPRESSION: Ha.

AVARICE: What is this hum, ha, hum?   190

INSOLENCE: On forth.

ADULATION: Go to.

OPPRESSION: Tell on.

AVARICE: Body of me!

ADULATION: Mum.

AVARICE: What say ye?

INSOLENCE: Hake.   *(representing a cough, perhaps)*

ADULATION: Tuff.

OPPRESSION: Hem.

AVARICE: Who haken tuffa hum?   200
  What say ye?

OPPRESSION: Nothing.

INSOLENCE: Not a word.

AVARICE: Nor you neither?

ADULATION: Mum.

AVARICE: Did ye speak or not?

INSOLENCE: No.

OPPRESSION: No.

ADULATION: No.

AVARICE: Nor yet do not?   210

INSOLENCE: No.

OPPRESSION: No.

ADULATION: No.

OPPRESSION: No.

INSOLENCE: No.

ADULATION: No.

AVARICE: That that that that that that?[15]
  Sir, I intend Dame Respublica to assail
  And so to creep in to be of her counsel
  I hope well to bring her in such a paradise   220
  That herself shall sue me to have my service.
  Then shall I have time and power to bring in you three.

OPPRESSION: Do this out of hand, founder, and first speak for
    me.
  Bring me in credit, that my hand be in the pie;
  An I get not elbow room among them, let me lie.[16]

AVARICE: Nay, see an Oppression, this eager elf,
  Be not since more covetous than Covetous' self!   *already*
  Soft, be not so hasty! I pray you sir, soft awhile!
  You will over the hedge ere ye come at the stile!   *gate*

OPPRESSION: I would fain be shouldering and rumbling among
    them!   230

AVARICE: Nay, I will help javels as shall wrong them.   *rascals*

ADULATION: I pray you good founder, let not me be the last.

---

[15] This is probably intended as a sound, not a word; perhaps "tut, tut."
[16] Original is unpunctuated. This is perhaps not the only possible pointing.

AVARICE: Thou shalt be well placed where to thrive very fast.

ADULATION: I thank you Master Avarice, with all my heart.

AVARICE: And when thou art in place see thou play well thy
part.

When ye claw her elbow remember your best friend

And let my recommendations be ever at one end.   *always be a part*

ADULATION: I warrant you.

INSOLENCE: And what, shall I be left clean out?

AVARICE: No sir, ye shall be chief to bring all things about.   240

Ye shall amongst us have the chief preeminence,

And we to you, as it were, owe obedience.

Ye shall be our leader, our captain and our guide,

Then must ye look aloft, with the hands under the side.   (?)

I shall tell Respublica ye can best govern.

Be not ye then squeamish to take in hand the stern,

Then shall we assist you as friends of perfect trust,

To do and to undo, and command what ye lust,

And when you have all at your own will and pleasure,

Part of your livings to your friends ye may measure,   250

And punish the proudest of them that will resist.

OPPRESSION: He that once winceth shall feel the weight of my
fist.

ADULATION: Yea, we must all hold and cleave together like
burrs.

AVARICE: Yea, see ye three hang and draw together like furs!

OPPRESSION: And so shall we be sure to get store of money

Sweeter than sugar

AVARICE: Sweeter than any honey.

INSOLENCE: Very well spoken! This gear will right well accord.

ADULATION: Did not I say ye were worthy to be a lord?

AVARICE: I will make Insolence a lord of high estate.   260

INSOLENCE: And I will take upon me well, both early and late.

OPPRESSION: But Insolence, when ye come to the encroaching
of lands,[17]

Ye may not take all alone into your hands.

[17] This line seems to refer to the "enclosing" of farm lands for sheep pasture, but the next line suggests that what is being talked about is the dissolution of the monasteries under Henry VIII.

I will look to have part of goods, lands and plate.

INSOLENCE: Ye shall have enough, each body after his rate.

ADULATION: I must have part too, ye must not have all alone!

INSOLENCE: Thou shalt be laden till thy shoulders shall crack
  and groan.

ADULATION: I pray you, let me have a good lordship or two.

INSOLENCE: Respublica shall feed thee till thou wilt say "Hoo!"

ADULATION: And I must have good manor places two or
  three.   270

INSOLENCE: But the chief and best lordship must remain to me.

OPPRESSION: Mass! and I will look to be served of
  the best,   *By the Mass!*
  Or else some folk somewhere shall sit but in small rest!

INSOLENCE: I must have castles and towns in every shire.

ADULATION: And I change of houses, one here, and another
  there.

INSOLENCE: And I must have pastures and townships and
  woods.

OPPRESSION: And I must needs have store of gold and other
  goods.

INSOLENCE: And I must have change of farms and pastures for
  sheep,
  With daily revenues my lusty port for to keep.   *deportment*

AVARICE: I would have a bone here, rather than a groat,   280
  To make these snarling curs gnaw out each other's throat.
  Here be eager whelps, lo! To it, Boy! Box him, Ball!
  Poor I may pick straws, these hungry dogs will snatch all!

OPPRESSION;   Each man snatch for himself. By God's, I will be
  sped!

AVARICE: Lack who lack shall, Oppression will be corn fed.
  Is not Dame Respublica sure of good handling
  When these whelps, ere they have it, fall thus to scrambling?
  And me, their chief founder, they have e'en since forgot.

INSOLENCE: Thou shalt have gold and silver enough to thy lot,
  Respublica hath enough to fill all our laps.   290

ADULATION: Then I pray you sir, let our founder have some
  scraps.

AVARICE: Scraps, ye doltish lout! Feed you your founder
    with scraps?

  If you were well served your head would have some raps!

ADULATION: I spoke of good will.   *in*

INSOLENCE: Nay, fight not, good Avarice.

OPPRESSION: What any of us get, thou hast the chief price.

AVARICE: Then whatever ye do ye will remember me?

[All]:   Yea.

AVARICE: Well, so do then, and I forgive you all three.

INSOLENCE: But when do we enter every man his charge?   300

AVARICE: As soon as I can spy Respublica at large
  I will board her, and I trow so win her favor
  That she shall hire me and pay well for my labor.
  Then will I commend the virtues of you three,
  That she shall pray and wish under our rule to be.
  Therefore from this hour be ye all in readiness.

OPPRESSION: Doubt not of us, thou seest all our   *fear not*
    greediness.

INSOLENCE: If it be at midnight, I come at the first call.
    (*they go forward one after other.*)

ADULATION: Do but whistle for me, and I come forth withal.

  That is well spoken. I love such a toward twig.   *eager youngster*   310
    (*he whistleth.*)

ADULATION: I come, founder.

AVARICE: That is mine own good spaniel Rigg.

  And come on back again all three, come back again.

INSOLENCE: Our founder calleth us back.

OPPRESSION: Return then amain.

Actus primi, scena quarta [The Same]

AVARICE: Come on, sirs, all three. And first to you, best
    betrust,[18]   *trusted*

  What is your brainpan stuffed withal, wool or sawdust?

ADULATION: Why so?

AVARICE: What is your name?

---

[18] Original reads "best be trust."

ADULATION: Flattery.   320

AVARICE: E'en so, just?

ADULATION: Yea, or else Adulation, if you so lust.   *prefer*

Either name is well known to many a body.

AVARICE: An honest mome! Ah ye dolt, ye lout, ye noddy!

Shall Respublica hear your commendation

By the name of Flattery or Adulation?

Or when ye command me to her will ye say this,

"Forsooth, his name is Avarice or Covetise"?

And you that should have wit, is't your discretion

Bluntly to go forth and be called Oppression?   330

And you, Insolence, do ye think it would well frame

If ye were presented to her under that name?

INSOLENCE: I thought nothing thereupon, by my holydom!

OPPRESSION: My mind was another way, by my christendom.

ADULATION: That thing was least part of my thought, by

    St. Denis   **(pronounced *Denny*)**

AVARICE: No, marry, your minds were all on your half-penny.

But, my masters, I must on mine honesty pass,

And not run on head, like a brute beast or an ass,

For is not oppression each where sore hated?

And is not flattery openly rated?   *berated* 340

And am not I, Avarice, still cried out upon?

ADULATION: Yes, I could have told you that a great while

    agon

But I would not displease you.

AVARICE: And you, Insolence, I have heard you ill-spoken of a

    great way hence.

ADULATION [*aside*]: In my conscience, the devil himself doth

    love you!

AVARICE: But changing your ill name fewer shall reprove you,

As I mine own self, where my name is known

Am right sore assailed to be overthrown.

But doing as I will now counterfeit my name,

I speed all my purposes and yet escape blame.   350

INSOLENCE: Let us then have new names, each man without

    delay.

AVARICE: Else will some of you make good hanging stuff one
    day.

OPPRESSION: Thou must new christen us.

INSOLENCE: First, what shall my name be?

AVARICE: Faith sir, your name shall be—Monsieur Authority![19]

OPPRESSION: And for me what is your determination.

AVARICE: Marry sir, ye shall be called Reformation.

ADULATION: Now I pray you devise for me an honest name.

AVARICE: Thou art such a beast, I cannot, for very shame.

ADULATION: If ye think good, let me be called Policy.   360

AVARICE: Policy! A rope ye shall! Nay—*Hypocrisy!*

ADULATION: Fie! That were as slanderous a name as Flattery

AVARICE: And I keep for myself the name of Policy.
  But if I devise for thee, wilt thou not shame me?

ADULATION: Nay, I will make thee proud of me, or else blame
    me.

AVARICE: Well then, for this time thy name shall be Honesty.

ADULATION: I thank you, Avarice. *Honesty, Honesty.*

AVARICE: Avarice, ye whoreson? Policy, I tell thee!

ADULATION: I thank you, Policy. Honesty, Honesty.
  How say you, Insolence? I am now *Honesty.*   370

AVARICE: We shall at length have a knave of you, Honesty.
  Said I not he should be called Monsieur Authority?

ADULATION: Oh friend Oppression, *Honesty, Honesty!*

AVARICE: Oppression? Ha, Is the devil in thy brain?
  Take heed, or in faith ye are Flattery again.
  Policy, Reformation, *Authority.*

ADULATION: Hypocrisy, Diffamation, *Authority!*

AVARICE: Hypocrisy, hah? Hypocrisy, ye dull ass?

ADULATION: Thou namedst Hypocrisy even now, by the Mass!

AVARICE: Policy I said, Policy, knave, Policy!   380
  Now say as I said.

ADULATION: "Policy knave Policy."

AVARICE: And what callest thou him here?

ADULATION: Diffamation.

---

[19] Standard Tudor chauvinism required that the Vices be given French designation or names, or speak
some French.

AVARICE: I told thee he should be called Reformation.

ADULATION: Very well.

AVARICE: What is he now?

ADULATION: Deformation.

AVARICE: Was there ever like ass born in all nations?

ADULATION: A pestel on him, he comes of the   *plague* 390
    Asians.[20]

AVARICE: Come on, ye shall learn to *sol fa*: Reformation.
  Sing on now: Re.

ADULATION: Re.

AVARICE: Refor.

ADULATION: Reformation!

AVARICE: Policy, Reformation, Authority.

ADULATION: Policy, Reformation, Honesty.

AVARICE: In faith, ye ass, if your tongue make any mo
    trips
  Ye shall both be Flattery and have on the lips.   *have a blow*
  And now, Monsieur Authority, against I you call   *by the time I* 400
  Ye must have other garments, and so must ye all.
  Ye must for the season counterfeit gravity.

INSOL., OPPR.: Yes, what else?

ADULATION: And I must counterfeit Honesty.

AVARICE: And I must turn my gown in and out, I ween,
  For these gaping purses may in no wise be seen.
  I will turn it e' en here. Come help me Honesty.

ADULATION: Here at hand.

AVARICE: Why how now? Play the knave, Honesty?
  Help, what dost thou now?[21]   410

ADULATION: I counterfeit Honesty.

AVARICE: Why then come thou help me, my friend
    Oppression.
  What help call you that?

OPPRESSION: Fit for your discretion.

AVARICE: Oh, I should have said help Sir Reformation.

OPPRESSION: Yea marry sir, that is my nomination.   *name*

---

[20] Original reads "Acyons." "Asians" is Greg's conjecture.

[21] Apparently some slapstick comedy having to do with the gowns gets going here.

AVARICE: And when you are in your robe, keep it afore
    closed.
OPPRESSION: I pray you Master Policy, for what purpose?
AVARICE: All folk will take you, if they peep under your gown,
    For the veriest caitiff in town.   420
    Now go, and when I call, see that ye ready be.
INSOLENCE: I will.
OPPRESSION: And I will
ADULATION: And so will I, Honesty.
      (*exeant.*)   ("let them go out")
    Well, now will I depart hence also for a space,
    And to board Respublica wait a time of grace.
    Wherever I find her a time convenient
    I shall say and do that may be expedient.
      (*exeat Avar.*)

Actus secundi, scena prima

    [*Enter*] RESPUBLICA.
RESPUBLICA: Lord, what earthly thing is permanent or stable,
    Or what is all this world but a lump mutable?   430
    Who would have thought that I, from so florent estate   *flourishing*
    Could have been brought so base as I am of late?
    But as the waving seas do flow and ebb by course,
    So all things else do change to better and to worse:
    Great cities and their fame in time go fade and pass,
    Now is a champion field where noble Troy was;   *open*
    Where is the great empire of the Medes and Persians?
    Where be the old conquests of the puissant Grecians?
    Where Babylon? Where Athens? Where Corinth so wide?
    Are they not consumed, with all their pomp and pride?[22]   440
    What is the cause hereof, man's wit cannot discuss,
    But of long continuance the thing is found thus.
    Yet by all experience thus much is well seen,
    That is commonweals while good governors have been
    All thing hath prospered, and where such men do lack,

---

[22] This is called an *ubi sunt* lament, i.e. "where are they now?"

Commonweals decay and all things do go back.
What marvel then if I, wanting a perfect stay,   *support*
From most flourishing wealth be fallen in decay?
But like as by default quick ruin doth befall,
So may good government at once recover all.   450
   (*Intrat* AVAR. *cogitabundus et ludibundus*)   *musing playfully*

Actus secundi, scena secunda

AVARICIA, RESPUBLICA

AVARICE: Alas, my sweet bags, how lank and empty ye be!
But in faith and truth, sirs, the fault is not in me.

RESPUBLICA: Well, my help and comfort, oh Lord, must come
from thee.

AVARICE: And my sweet purses here I pray you all see, see,
How the little fools gasp and gape for gromwell seed.

RESPUBLICA: If it be thy will, Lord, send some redress with
speed.

AVARICE: But in faith good sweet fools, it shall cost me a fall
But I shortly will fill you and stop your mouths all.

RESPUBLICA: Oh that it were my hap on friendly friends to
light—

AVARICE: Ha he? Who is that same that speaketh yonder in
sight?   460
Who is't? Respublica! Yea, by the Mary Mass!

RESPUBLICA: Then might I be again as well as ere I was.

AVARICE: Hide up these pipes—now I pray God she be   *bags?*
blind!
I am half afraid lest she have an eye behind.
We must now change our copy—oh Lord, how I   *behavior*
fray   *am afraid*
Lest she saw my toys and heard what I did say!

RESPUBLICA: Is there no good man that on me will have mercy?

AVARICE: Remember now, my name is Master Policy;
All thing, I tell you, must now go by policy.   *be according to*

RESPUBLICA: Hark! Methink I hear the name of Policy.   470

AVARICE: Who calleth Conscience? Here am I, Policy.

RESPUBLICA: I pray you come to me if you be Policy.

AVARICE: Yea forsooth, yea forsooth, my name is Policy.

RESPUBLICA: I am sore decayed through default of policy.

AVARICE: Yea most noble Respublica, I know that well
And do more lament it than any tongue can tell,
For an if good policy had had you in hand
Ye had now been the wealthiest in any land,
But good policy hath long been put in exile.

RESPUBLICA: Yea, God wot, ye have been barred from me a
great while.   480

AVARICE: Yea, I have been put back, as one clean off shaken,
And what can a man do, till he be forth taken?

RESPUBLICA: Well, I feel the lack of your helping hand, by the
Rood.

AVARICE: Alack, noble lady, I would I could do you good.

RESPUBLICA: Yes Policy, ye might amend all if you lust.

AVARICE: Yea faith, I durst put myself to you of trust,
But there be enough that for you could shift make.

RESPUBLICA: Yet none like to you, if you would it undertake.
And I will put myself wholly into your hands,
Metal, grain, cattle, treasure, goods and lands.   490

AVARICE: Well, I will take some pain, but this to you be known,
I will do it not for your sake but for mine own.

RESPUBLICA: How say ye that, Policy?

AVARICE: This to you be known,
I will do all for your sake, and not for mine own.[23]

RESPUBLICA: I thank you, Policy.

AVARICE: Nay, I thank you, lady,
And I trust ere long to ease all your malady.
Will ye put yourself now wholly in my hands?

RESPUBLICA: Order me as you will.   500

AVARICE: Treasure, goods and lands?

RESPUBLICA: Yea, every whit.

AVARICE: Well, I thank you once again,
But now, that you may think my dealing true and plain,
And because one cannot do so well as many,

[23] This joke is an early instance of the literary "Freudian slip."

Ye must associate me with mo company,
And first, by my will, ye shall set up Honesty.

RESPUBLICA: Marry, with all my very heart; but where is he?

AVARICE: Very hard to find, but I think I could fet him.   *fetch*

RESPUBLICA: Call him straightways hither; see that nothing
    let him.   510

AVARICE: It were best if I shall go fet men for the nones,
To make but one voyage and bring them all at once.

RESPUBLICA: Whom more than him?

AVARICE: Ye must 'stablish Authority.

RESPUBLICA: That must needs be done.

AVARICE: And eke Reformation.
We four will rule things of another fashion.   *in*

RESPUBLICA: Policy, I pray you go fet all these straightway.

AVARICE: Yes, for this your present case may bide no delay.
I will go, and come with all festination.   *speed* 520
    (*exeat.*)

RESPUBLICA: I like well this trade of Administration!
Policy for to devise for my commodity,   *advantage*
No person to be advanced but Honesty,
Then Reformation good wholesome laws to make
And Authority see the same effect may take,
What commonweal shall then be so happy as I?
For this (I perceive) is the drift of Policy.
    (*Intrat* AVARICE *ad ducens* INSOL., OPPR., *et* ADULAC.)   *leading*
And behold, where he is returned again since!
He showeth himself a man of much diligence.

Actus secundi, scena tertia

ADULATION, AVARICE, RESPUBLICA, INSOLENCE, OPPRESSION.

ADULATION: I will do her double service to another.   530

AVARICE: Ye double knave you, will ye never be other?

ADULATION: She shall have triple service of me, Honesty.

AVARICE: Ye quadruple knave, will you ne'er use modesty?
Thou drunken whoreson dost thou not see nor perceive
Where Respublica stands ready us to receive?

RESPUBLICA: What talk have they yonder among themselves
together?

ADULATION: I have spied her now. Shall I first to her thither?

AVARICE: Soft, let me present you.

RESPUBLICA: I ween they be in fear.

Policy, approach, and bring my good friends near.   540

AVARICE: Come on, my dear friends, and execute with good
will

Such offices as each of you shall be put until.   *into*

Dame Respublica it is that for you hath sent.

Come on, friends, I will you unto Her Grace present.

INSOL., OPPR.: To serve her we are prest, with heart and whole
intent.

AVARICE: Madame, I have brought you these men for whom
I went.

RESPUBLICA: Policy, I thank you. Ye have made speedy speed,

Therefore, be double welcome, and welcome friends indeed.

AVARICE: Madame, Your Grace to serve we are all fully bent.

ADULATION: And Madame, ye shall find me double diligent.   550

RESPUBLICA: That is spoken of a good heart, but who be ye?

ADULATION: Forsooth, Madame, my name is Master Honesty.

RESPUBLICA: Honesty? Well said.

AVARICE: Madame, this is Honesty.

ADULATION: Yea, forsooth, an please Your Grace, I am Honesty.

AVARICE: Madame, he is for you; on my word, regard him.

RESPUBLICA: Yes, and with large preferment I will reward him.

ADULATION: I thank Your Grace, and I will for you take such
pain

That ere I deserve one ye shall give me twain.

AVARICE: Honesty, your tongue trippeth.   560

RESPUBLICA: How said ye? "Take such pain—"

ADULATION: That ere ye give me one I will deserve twain!

By your license, madame, to take away this mote.   *spot*

AVARICE: Nay, Honesty will not see a wem on   *allow blemish*
your coat.

Now unto you I commend Reformation.

RESPUBLICA: Of him is no small need now in this nation.

OPPRESSION: Well, now that ye bid me abuses to redress,
  I doubt not all enormities so to repress
  As shall redound to your wealth and honor at length.

RESPUBLICA: Thereto shall Authority aid you with his
      strength.   570

AVARICE: Yea, for Authority to govern is most fit.

INSOLENCE: If ye, Dame Respublica, do me so admit,
  I doubt not to hamper the proudest of them all.

RESPUBLICA: And among you destroy Avarice—

ADULATION: Hem.

INSOL., OPPR.:   We shall.

RESPUBLICA: Vanquish Oppression and Adulation,
  For these three have nigh wrought my desolation.

AVARICE: Hem sirs, hem there, keep your gowns close afore,
      I say,
  Have ye forgotten now what I told you one day?   580
  There is another two that would be chased hence.

RESPUBLICA: Who is that?

AVARICE: Lucifer's son, called Insolence.

RESPUBLICA: Ye say truth, and many naughty ones mo than he.

INSOL., OPPR.:   If ye dare trust us—

INSOL.:   All—

OPPR.:   All shall reformed be.

RESPUBLICA: I thank you, and I trust you for my maintenance
  To be administer for your good governance.   *administrator*

INSOLENCE: Then without fear or care ye may yourself
      repose.   590

OPPRESSION: And let us alone with all such matters as those.

RESPUBLICA: Then I leave you here on our affairs to consult.
      (*exeat* RESP.)

INSOLENCE: When you please, in God's name.

OPPRESSION: We must both sift and bolt.   *examine things*

ADULATION: She is gone.

AVARICE: Well then, sirs, let us make no delay.
  But about our market depart each man his way.

ADULATION: Nay, first let us sing a song to lighten our
      hearts.

AVARICE: Then are ye like, for me, to sing   *as far as I'm concerned*
   but of three parts.
 Can Avarice's heart be set on a merry pin,   *note (?)* 600
 And see no gain, no profit at all, coming in?
INSOLENCE: We shall have enough to drive away all sorrow.
AVARICE: Then sing we on, *bon voyage* and St. George
   the borrow!   *save us*
  (*Cantent "Bring ye to me and I to ye" etc., et sic exeant.*)

Actus tercii, scena prima

  [*Enter*] RESPUBLICA

RESPUBLICA: The good hope that my misters have   *administrators (?)*
   put me in
 To recover ruin that in me doth begin,
 Hath so recomforted my spirits and mine heart
 That I feel much easement of my great grief and smart.
 Now I do less wonder that lost men life to save,
 Far from land do labor against the roaring wave,
 For hope, I see, hath mighty operation   610
 Against the mortal sting of drooping desperation.
 Now if I might but hear what Policy hath wrought,
 Or some one good thing that my friends to pass had brought
 I would put no doubts but all thing should soon be well.
 Lo, where cometh Honesty—he will the truth tell.

Actus tercii, scena secunda

  ADULATION, RESPUBLICA

ADULATION: Three hundred pound by year, and a good manor
   place.
 Well, it is meetly well in so short time and space.
 More will come right shortly; this gear doth gaily walk.   *affair*
 Bones, here is Respublica! What use I such talk?
 I seek Lady Respublica.   620
RESPUBLICA: Lo, I am here.
 And welcome, Honesty. What do my friends most dear?

ADULATION: Certes, madame, we rest nor day nor night nor
      hour
   To practice and travail for your wealth and honor.
   But O Lord, what a prudent man is Policy,
   What a deep head he hath to devise and to spy.
RESPUBLICA: He is fine indeed.
ADULATION: Also Reformation.
   How earnest he is in his operation.
RESPUBLICA: I think of him no less.   630
ADULATION: Now then, Authority,
   The stoutest in his office that ever I did see.
   I will no farther praise them madame, for doubtless
   They far surmount all praise that my tongue can express.
   Ye may bless the time ye met with such as they be.
   And I do my poor part.
RESPUBLICA: I doubt not, Honesty.
   And condign reward shall ye all have for your pain.
ADULATION: I have scarce a house wherein myself to maintain.
RESPUBLICA: Honesty shall not lack.   640
ADULATION: I do not crave nor care,
   We shall take but scraps and refuse, that ye may spare.
   We will not encroach the people's commodity,
   We shall take only that may come with honesty.
RESPUBLICA: Christ's blessing have ye. But lo, yonder cometh
      People.
ADULATION [*aside*]: I had thought as soon to have met here
      Paul's steeple!

Actus tercii, scena tertia

PEOPLE, ADULATION, RESPUBLICA

PEOPLE: Where's Rice Puddingcake? I pray God she be in
      heal.   *health*
ADULATION: Who? Rice Puddingcake?
PEOPLE: Yea, *alese dicts* Commonweal.   *alias dicta* (otherwise called)
ADULATION: I know her not.   650

PEOPLE: Mass! You liest valsely in your heart![24]

    She is this way. Che war't a false harlot you art! *I warrant*

ADULATION: I know Respublica.

PEOPLE: Yea marry, where is she?

ADULATION: She is busy now.

PEOPLE: Mass! Ere ich go 'ch'll her zee, for this way she came.

RESPUBLICA: Let my people come to me.

ADULATION: God forbid else! Come on People, is this same she?

PEOPLE: Yea, malkin is't. *that's my girl*

RESPUBLICA: People, what would you with me now? 660

PEOPLE: Marry, mistress madame my lady, how do you?

RESPUBLICA: Even so-so, People, I thank you with all my
    heart

  And I hope for better.

PEOPLE: Then let poor volk ha' zome part.

  Vor we ignoram people whom ich do perzent

  Were ne'er zo y-polled, zo wrong[ed], and zo y-torment. *sheared*

  Lord Jesu Christ, when he was y-pounced and y-pilate[25]

  Was ne'er zo y-trounced as we have been of years late.

ADULATION: How so? Who hath wrought to you such
    extremity?

PEOPLE: Nay, to tell how zo passeth our captivity. 670

RESPUBLICA: It passeth any man's imagination.

PEOPLE: You zay zooth, it passeth any man's Madge Mason,

  Vor we think ye love us as well as ere ye did.

RESPUBLICA: My love towards you, my People, cannot be hid.

PEOPLE: And we think ye would fain we poor volk did well.

RESPUBLICA: And better than ere ye did, if how I could tell.

PEOPLE: And we think ye would we zilly poor volk should
    thrive.

RESPUBLICA: Yea, doubtless, as any like creature alive.

ADULATION: What need ye of her good will towards you to
    doubt?

---

[24] People is a dramatic stock figure, the stage rustic. His dialect is of Southwestern England, and its chief characteristics, besides the colloquial expressions which are glossed, are "ich" for "I," "v" for "f" and "z" for "s".

[25] This is probably the best pun in the whole morality drama, fusing the description of Christ's torments with the name of his Roman persecutor.

PEOPLE: Peace thou, with sorrow, and let me tell my
   tale out!   680

RESPUBLICA: Say on, my good People, let me hear all your
   mind.

PEOPLE: Bum vay, we ignoram people beeth not zo *by my faith*
   blind,
 But we p'ceive there falleth of corn and cattle, *perceive*
 Wool, sheep, wood, lead, tin, iron and other metal,
 And of all things, enough vor good and bad,
 And as comedians for us as ere we had. *commodious* (enough)
 And yet the price of everything is zo dear
 As though the ground did bring vorth no such thing nowhere.

RESPUBLICA: Indeed, I have enough if it be well ordered,
 But few folk the better if I be misordered.   690

PEOPLE: Nay, now you zay zooth, even thik same way goeth *this*
   the hare.
 Ill ordering 'tis hath made both you and we threadbare.

ADULATION: What naughty folks were they? Can you their
   names read?   *tell*

PEOPLE: Yea, that I's can, a whole mess of 'em, for a need.
 There is virst and vormost Flattery, ill's thee, *ill may he fare*
 A slipper, sugar-mouthed horecop as can be. *bastard*
 He fleereth on you, and beareth us fair in hand, *sneers/cheats us*
 And therewith robbeth both you and we of our land.
 Then cometh the sour, rough, crabbed child, Oppression,
 He tumbleth whom 'a lust out of possession.   700
 Then is there the third, I's cannot 'member his name—
 What call ye thik same fellows, God give them shame!—
 That beeth still climbing up aloft for premidence *pre-eminence*
 And cannot be content with their state?

ADULATION: Insolence?

PEOPLE: Yea, thik same is he, Zoryless.

ADULATION: Nay, Insolence.

PEOPLE: Well, he'll rule all the roost alone, cha heard it zaid,
 Or else make the best of them aghast and afraid,
 And zuch good men as could and would order you well 710
 He is so copped he nil not suffer to mell. *proud/be involved*

If they nil not be ruled, then hence, out of favor,
Yea, and perhaps corrupt 'em zore for their labor. *punish (?)*
Yet he and the other twain work all after the Vice,
Of—cha forget the one name, t'other is Covetise.
This hungry horecop hath such a policate wit[26] *politic (?)*
That he teacheth them to rake and scrape up each whit.
And zo these vour (but it shall never come out
    for me) *I'll never tell*
Volk think will never cease to spoil both you and we.
Vor sometime they face us and call us peason *peasant*
    knaves, 720
And zweareth God's Bones they will make us all slaves.
Therevore 'chwas besirance your ladydom to zee, *desirous*
And to give you warning.
RESPUBLICA: Hear ye this, Honesty?
PEOPLE: Well, and God mend all, an 'a be zo good a *amend*
    clerk—
RESPUBLICA: Hear ye this, Honesty?
PEOPLE: Though tinkers should lack work.
RESPUBLICA: I am put in comfort all shall shortly amend.
ADULATION: It is in good way already, else God defend!
RESPUBLICA: Lo, People, hearest thou this? Be of good
    cheer! 730
PEOPLE: Yea, ich hear his vair words, but what beeth we
    the nearer?
RESPUBLICA: People, understand ye that this is Honesty.
PEOPLE: Whether 'a be, trow? 'Cha zeen zome as zmooth as he
    Have by trial be vound valse flatterers to be.
RESPUBLICA: I take this man for no such; this is Honesty.
PEOPLE: When I's find it, 'ch'ill believe it.
RESPUBLICA: 'Tis Honesty.
PEOPLE: I's cry him mercy then.
RESPUBLICA: He and Authority, joining with Policy and
    Reformation
    Travail to restore the old wealth to this nation. 740

---

[26] In the MS this line is written in the margin as a replacement for the line "This he teacheth them to rake and scrape up each whit."

PEOPLE: Whough! Then 'ch'll war't all within two years as
    plenty   *Wow!*
  As 'twas any time within these years twice twenty.
  But how may we know and see that this thing is true?
ADULATION: Ye shall prove at length by the effect that shall
    ensue.
PEOPLE: Nay, an we shall alway be served but with shales,   *husks*
  Then 'ch'ill believe still that vair words beeth but tales.
ADULATION: The thing already to such forwardness is brought,
  That much to your benefit is already wrought.
PEOPLE: Yea? What any good act have ye already done?
ADULATION: It is but young days yet, things are but now
    begun.   750
  The fruit of our doings cannot so soon appear,
  But, People, ye shall feel it within seven year.
  Ye know it is no small work from so great delay—
RESPUBLICA: People, he saith truth.
ADULATION: To set all in good stay
  Therefore be ye quiet and hope for a good end.
PEOPLE: Yes, 'ch'ill tarry leisure and take what God shall send.
RESPUBLICA: Then People, let us twain depart in quietness,
  For this talking here may hinder their business.
PEOPLE: Come on, I chil wait avore you, and be your man.   760
    (*exeant.*)
ADULATION: And I will to my fellows as fast as I can.
  Be they gone? Farewell they! God send them both
    the pippe!   *poultry disease*
  But in faith People, I will have you on the hip,   *injure you*
  I will be even with you for your broad carping.
  Ah ye peasant wretch, on us four to be harping!
  And yet must we our matters handle discreetly,
  Or else I fear it will end not very sweetly.
  But now I would Avarice or else Insolence
  Or Oppression were here, rather than six pence.
  And lo, where Avarice cometh,
    a wolf in the tale,   *"speak of the devil"* 770
  (As the proverb saith) what doth he after him hale?

Actus tercii, scena quarta

AVARICE, ADULATION

AVARICE: Come on, sweet bags of gold, come on with a
   good will,

I on you so tender and ye so froward still?   *reluctant*

Come forward I pray you, sweet bags. Ah, will ye so?

Come or I must draw you whether ye will or no.

I know your desire; ye would fain be in my chest;

When the belly is full the bones would be at rest.

Be content a while, I will couch you all up soon

Where ye shall not be spied neither of sun nor moon.   780

What now, brother Honesty? What pry ye this way?

Is there anything here that is yours, can ye say?

Look off from my bags! It is a pretty matter;

Ye can see no green cheese but your teeth will water.

ADULATION: *In nomine patris*, hast thou got all this since?

AVARICE: Why, thinkest thou I have sat idle since I went hence?

Nay, I have filled my little purses too, each one.

ADULATION: Hast thou so indeed? Thou art a fellow alone.

AVARICE: With old Angelets and Edwards I   *(denomination of coins)*
   think I have.

Come forth. How say ye, sir? Peep out, ye little knave.

How think you by this bunting? Is he full   *little bird* (?)
   or no?   790

And his fellows all, doth not their skin stretch for woe?

Now these little buttons no bigger than two nuts,

Have they not played gluttons, and filled well their guts?

ADULATION: But look who cometh yonder, puffing and tuffing.

AVARICE: Come the devil if him lust, staring and snuffing.

Actus tercii, scena quinta

OPPRESSION, AVARICE, ADULATION

OPPRESSION: In all my whole life was I never wearier!

AVARICE: Come near, on God's 'half, the mo knaves   *behalf*
   the merrier.

Where have ye lost your breath, in some coffer diving?

OPPRESSION: Shouldering amonst them for a piece of a living.

ADULATION: And what, are you now in any good hope to
    thrive?   800

OPPRESSION: Faith, if I lust I may wear mitres four or five,
 I have so many half bishoprics at the least.

ADULATION: By the arms of Calais, then am I a very beast.

AVARICE: Why, what hast thou gotten to thy share in this
    space?

ADULATION: Three hundred pound by the year, and one
    manor place.

AVARICE: Ah, the Passion of God! Three hundred pound and
    no more?

ADULATION: Is not that fair for him that had nothing before?

AVARICE: What? Three hundred pound by years? Call thee
    Honesty?
 Call thee a knave, thou shamest our fraternity.
 Three hundred pound? If some man had been in thy room   810
 A thousand pound a year ere this time might have come!
 Three hundred pound a year? Against our next meeting
 Get more, or I shall give thee a homely greeting!

ADULATION: He here hath flitched the bishoprics   *sliced off*
    already!

AVARICE: Yea, I can him thank, he hath been somewhat
    speedy.

OPPRESSION: But yet have I left many a good gobbet loose.
 Change thou for the rest, give a feather for a goose.

ADULATION: Didst thou with any one of them make such
    exchange?

OPPRESSION: Yea, I almost left them neither a farm nor grange.
 I told them Respublica at their wealth did grutch,   820
 And the fifth penny they had was for them too much.
 So Authority and I did with them so chop
 That we left the best of them a threadbare bishop.
 To some we left one house, to some we left none,
 The best had but his see place that he might keep home.
 We enformed them and we deformed them   *shaped*
 We conformed them and we reformed them.

ADULATION: And what gave ye them in your
    permutations?   *exchange*

OPPRESSION: Bare parsonages of appropriations,
  Bought from Respublica and first
    emprowed,   *improved* (i.e. enclosed) 830
  Then, at the highest extent, to bishops allowed,
  Let out to their hands for fourscore and nineteen year.

AVARICE: Lo Cousin Honesty, lo, do you hear this gear?
  Faith, your ma'ship will thrive at the latter   *mastership*
    Lammas!   (i.e. never)

ADULATION: I now grant myself to have been a very ass,
  But all is not yet gone, in case I have good luck.

OPPRESSION: No, there is yet enough left for a better pluck,
  For some of them were aged and yet would not die,
  And some would in no wise to our desires apply.
  But we have rods in piss for them   840
    everychone   *punishments in store*
  That they shall be fleeced if we reign, one by one.

AVARICE: And how did all frame with our Monsieur
    Authority?

OPPRESSION: At length he won the full superiority.

ADULATION: But the rude gross People at him repineth sore,
  And against us all four with a wide throat doth he roar.
  But soft, peace, methinketh I hear him hem and hake.
  If we meet here all four we shall some order take.

Actus tercii, scena sexta

INSOLENCE, ADULATION, OPPRESSION, AVARICE

INSOLENCE: What, mine old friends all three? By my truth sirs,
    well found!

ADUL., OPPR.: Faith sir, most heartily welcome into this
    ground!

INSOLENCE: Bones, what have we here?   850

AVARICE: A! hah!

INSOLENCE: Bags of money, I trow?

AVARICE: Have we? Nay, I have, but none of you that I know.

Lo sir, thus might an honest man come to his harms.
I will lie down on them and keep them in mine arms.
INSOLENCE: Hast thou got all this? I myself have not so much.
AVARICE: Then have ye whole towns and castles; I have none
   such.
Yet will ye not deny, I judge in my fancy,
That ye got them by the drift of me, Policy.
INSOLENCE: I confess that.   860
OPPRESSION: All my lands are scarce so much worth.
AVARICE: They were less when I, Policy, first set you forth.
ADULATION: He hath purses with gold; would I had so many!
AVARICE: It were pity that such a goose should have any!
Your good ma'ship appointed me to crumbs and scraps,
But Policy will live by his neighbors, perhaps.
But thus I see you would poll me an ye wist how;
Therefore I will go hoard it, I make God a vow,
I will make it sure under nine doors and nine locks,
And who but looketh that way shall sit in nine stocks.   870
INSOLENCE: Nay, first declare to us how thou didst all this get.
AVARICE: For your learning I will you a spectacle set,
But first get ye from me and stand a good way hence.
This shall not lie within your reach, by your license.
Nay, yet farther, lest ye take my bags for bluddings,   *blood puddings*
For such hungry dogs will slab up sluttish puddings.   *gobble/dirty*
ADULATION: Is it well now?
AVARICE: Yea, now hardly stand there still,
And the names of my bags to you declare I will.
First and foremost, this bag is my very clean gain   880
Of leases encroached and forthwith sold again.
This bag is mine interest, of this year's usury,
And this of matters bolstered up with perjury.
This is bribes above my stipend in offices,
This fifth I have by selling of benefices.
This is my rents that my clerks yearly render me,
To be and continue in office under me.
This same I got by a 'secutorship of my Mother,   *executorship*
A vengeance on her, old witch, for such another!

This bag have I kept of other 'secutorships whole, *890*
Which the mad knaves would have scattered by
    penny dole. *in bits*
This is of Church goods scraped up without a law,
For which was as quick scrambling as ever I saw.
Of their plate, their jewels, and copes we made them louts,
Stopping people's barking with linen rags and clouts.
They had the altar cloths, the albs and amices *surplices/scarves*
With the sindons in which were wrapped the chalices. *fine cloths*
This ninth hath beguiled the king of his custom,
This tenth of selling counterfeit wares hath come.
Now this eleventh is of tallow, butter, cheese, *900*
Corn, raw cloths, leather by stealth sent beyond seas.
This twelfth is of grain, bell metal, tin and lead,
Conveyed out by creeks when Respublica was in bed. *tricks*
This thirteenth I fill through facing out of daws *fools*
Both from lands and goods, by pretence of laws.
Thus these thirteen small jobs are mine by policy.
All men must shift for a poor living honestly.
If ere I bestow them, it shall be the next Lent,
To the Prior of Prickingham and his convent!
ADULATION: Well, now we may come near, may we not, if
    we lust? *910*
AVARICE: Ye are near enough. Out of my reach I dare you trust.
ADULATION: Well, now let us sing, if it please Authority,
    To refresh our spirits it is restority.
INSOLENCE: I reck not, for company's sake, to sing *I don't object*
    once more.
AVARICE: I have less mind to sing now than I had before.
    Then I had no lust to sing because I was bare,
    And now, how to keep that I have got I do care. *worry*
OPPRESSION: Solace we must needs have, when that we are
    weary.
ADULATION: It prolongeth the life of man to be merry.
AVARICE: An if ye sing so much, Honesty, without fail *920*
    Thirst and you at length, I fear, will make a battle.
    But go to, sing on, if there be no remedy.

An ye look at my bags ye mar my melody!
  (*Cantent "Hey nonny nonny, hough for money" etc.*)
OPPRESSION: Now, about profit divide we ourselves abroad.
AVARICE: Yea, and hear ye, masters—while time is, lay on load.
  Consider ye have but a time of hay making,
  And harvest is not mued without pains taking.   ? *mewed* (brought in)
  Now time will not tarry, and therefore take good heed,
  Dispatch while time serveth, and all your matters speed.
  Time hath no rein nor bridle, but runneth apace.   930
INSOLENCE: Mark Policy's words, sirs, excellent in our case.
AVARICE: And time hath this one ungracious property,
  To blab at length, and open all that he doth see.
  Then a daughter, eke, he hath, called Verity,
  As unhappy a long-tongued girl as she can be.   *unlucky*
  She bringeth all to light, some she bringeth to shame;
  She careth not a groat what man hath thank or blame.
  If men be praiseworthy she doth so declare them,
  And if otherwise, in faith she doth not spare them!
OPPRESSION: We will feather our nests ere time may us espy,   940
  Or Verity have power our doings to descry.
AVARICE: Remember this verse: *Ut sint omnia salva*
  Fronte capillata, post h[a]ec occasio calva.
OPPRESSION: Make me understand that fine rag of rhetoric.
AVARICE: Lo, here a fine fellow to have a bishopric!
  A verse of Latin he cannot understand,
  Yet dareth he presume boldly to take in hand,
  Into a Deanery or Archdeaconry to chop
  And to have the livelihood away from a bishop.
OPPRESSION: To me show thy verse, and leave this
        persuasion.   950
AVARICE: Forsooth sir, it was of the goddess Occasion.
  She weareth a great long tuffet of hair before,
  And behind hath not one hair, neither less nor more;
  Whereby is taught you that when Occasion is
  Ye must take it betime, or of your purpose miss.   *at once*
ADULATION: Then while Occasion doth now serve so well
  I pray you give ear to one thing that I must tell.

INSOL., OPPR.: What is that?

ADULATION: Monsieur, if ye hear People mumbling
 Ye must storm, and sharply take him up for stumbling. 960
 Ye would not think what he said a little while since
 Of us to Respublica, in mine own presence!

INSOLENCE: When I meet them next I shall tell them both my
   mind.

AVARICE: And Policy to help you will not be behind.

ADULATION: Gentle Respublica was soon pacified,
 But People was sturdy and would not be qualified.

AVARICE: Alas, good poor silly soul, bear her fair in hand
 And ye may win her as you lust, to use her land.

OPPRESSION: But of goddess Occasion one little more.

AVARICE: Marry sir, even as I would have said before, 970
 She standeth with winged feet on a rolling wheel,
 To take flight or any grass may grow on her heel, *ere* (before)
 And even while we stand jangling in this presence,
 I dare say she is flown twice twenty score mile hence!

OPPRESSION: Yea? Cock's Bones then, adieu!

INSOLENCE: Farewell!

ADULATION: And I am gone!
  (*exeant currentes*) *running*

AVARICE: Faith, and have after, as fast as I can, anon.
 Now, my God-Almighties, as I did hither tug you,
 So will I on my back to your lodging lug you, 980
 And sure if ye can be quiet there, and lie still,
 I will shortly bring you mo fellows, so I will.
 I have a good benefice of an hundred marks;
 It is small policy to give such to great clerks;
 They will take no benefice but they must have all;
 A bare clerk can be content with a living small. *mere*
 Therefore Sir John Lack-Latin, my friend, shall have mine,
 And of him may I farm it for eight pounds or nine.
 The rest may I reserve to myself for mine own share,
 For we are good feeders of the poor, so we are, 990
 And we patrons are bound to see (I do you tell)
 The Church patrimony to be bestowed well.

Other odd corners besides these I have many,
Which, with all good speed shall increase your company.
Come on now, therefore, in faith I do great wrong
To promise you lodging and keep you thence so long.
    (*exeat*.)

Actus quarti, scena prima

RESPUBLICA

RESPUBLICA: O Lord, what may it mean to be thus
    born in hand   *cheated*
And yet none amendment to feel nor understand?
People doth daily and hourly to me resort,
Challenging my promise of relief and comfort.   1000
I report to him, as my rulers do to me;
People still affirmeth that they devourers be.
The more I do him cheer, the more he doth despair,
I say his wealth doth mend, he saith it doth appair.   *dwindle*
What should I judge of this? May it be credible
Or by any reason may it be possible
That such four as those in whom I have put my trust,
Showing such face of friendship, should be men unjust?
I will know if People feel yet any redress
Of his former sores and of his rueful distress.   1010
We shall meet soon, I doubt not, and talk together.
    (*Intrat* PEOPLE)
And lo, as I would wish, he approacheth hither.

Actus quarti, scena secunda

RESPUBLICA, PEOPLE

RESPUBLICA: Well met, People! What place go ye now unto?
PEOPLE: Ich am at the farthest to zee how you do.
  We twain must eftwhiles come physic either other,   *often/heal/each*
  For we beeth your children and you beeth our mother.
RESPUBLICA: And how do you mend now in your thrift and
    your purse?
PEOPLE: As zour ale in zummer, that is still worse and worse.

RESPUBLICA: People, what should I say?

PEOPLE: Nay, Mass, I's cannot tell,   1020
 But we ignorams all would fain ye should do well.
 And how feel you yourself? Better than ye did, trow?

RESPUBLICA: Till God send better hap, rather decay than grow.
 This bringeth me in a conceit of zelousy.   *gives me an idea of mistrust*
 Rather than much good would I speak with Policy.

PEOPLE: Was not he drowned, trow, last year, when Conscience
  was?

RESPUBLICA: I see him yonder appear; this cometh well to pass.

PEOPLE: Is this same he?

RESPUBLICA: Yea.

PEOPLE: An ich heard not you zo zay,   1030
 'Ch'ould zwear 'a had be dead, or else clean run away.

Actus quarti, scena tertia

AVARICE, RESPUBLICA, PEOPLE

AVARICE: O most noble lady, that I have not of late
 Made to you relation how ye stand in state,
 Hath not been of negligence nor to work by stealth,
 But of my deep studies, devising for your wealth.

RESPUBLICA: To hear the truth thereof, I wished you to see.

PEOPLE: Doth you stud' your brains, Mas' Gent'man, pray you
  tell me,
 For our lady Rice Puddingcake's commodity?

AVARICE: I devise what I can for the properity
 Of this lady, Respublica, and her people.   1040

PEOPLE [*aside*]: That lie, ere this, is flown as far hence   *by now*
  as Paul's steeple.
 [*to him*]: I's pray ye stud' not as cha heard of zome elves,
 That study for the common profit of their own selves!

AVARICE: To study for both your wealths I am a debtor.

PEOPLE: Vay then, as good ne'er a whit as ne'er the better.

AVARICE: I do nothing but compass therefore,   *arrange for that*
  without doubt.

PEOPLE: I' vay, then, thee vet too far a compass about,   *fet (fetched)*

Vor zome good might ha' be done in all this season.

AVARICE: So there is, if to perceive it ye had reason.

RESPUBLICA: Truly I feel myself hitherto worse and worse.   1050

PEOPLE: And I's veel the same both in my ground and my purse.

Vive or zix year ago 'ch'ad your kine to my pail,   *cows*
And at this present hour 'cham scarce worth a good cow tail.

And that time 'ch'ad a widge, and her voal, and ten sheep,   *mare*
Now I's can get nothing myzelf and my wife to keep.

Then, an chad I be with the King's Mas' Constable,
'Ch'ould zet myself vorth pertly, and zo 'chwas   *dress up properly*
able.

Now, vor lack of a sallet when my liege hath need   *helmet*
'Cham vain to take an hat of godsgood on my head.   *fain/worthless hat*

And 'vor God, my dame, this is but small   *before God, madame*
amendment!   1060

I's comport me to you—how thinketh your   *I appeal to you*
judgment?

"Compassing" k'a? Gent'man, call ye this same   *quoth he*
"compassing?"

AVARICE: No sir.

PEOPLE: Now, by the compass that God compassed—

RESPUBLICA: Blame have they, of God and man, that this hath
compassed.

PEOPLE: A small compass more now, may zoon, by the Rood,
To make forty thousand volks' hair grow through their hood.[27]

AVARICE: That is their own fault, not the fault of Policy.

RESPUBLICA: God above, He knoweth whose fault it is, and
not I.

PEOPLE: But did not ich daily give you warning?   1070

RESPUBLICA: Doubtless.

PEOPLE: And did not ich plain me to you   *complain*

RESPUBLICA: I grant, no less.

PEOPLE: And when ich made my moan, what would ye to me
tell?

RESPUBLICA: As my hope was, that at length all thing should
be well.

---

[27] Greg takes this to mean that their clothing is so threadbare that their hair grows through it.

PEOPLE: "Compassing," k'a?

RESPUBLICA: People, I put trust in other.

PEOPLE: Valse bezeivers, of zeemlity, by God's   *deceivers/seemingly*
    mother!

AVARICE: Well, suffer me then for my declaration
  To fet Authority and Reformation   1080
  That ye may both hear and charge them as well as me.

RESPUBLICA: With all my heart, good Policy, let it so be.
  I pray you call them thither, if they may be got.

PEOPLE: An 'che hear 'em, I's can tell whe'er they say true or
    not!

    [Exit AVAR. and immediately return with INSOL. and OPPR.,
  talking aside to them]

Actus quarti, scena quarta

    AVARICE, INSOLENCE, RESPUBLICA, OPPRESSION, PEOPLE

AVARICE: The foulest open-mouthed wretch that ere ye heard!

INSOLENCE: Couldst thou by no means make the peasant
    afeared?

AVARICE: No, but anon I trow we shall his ma'ship trim.
  Convey her away, and then all we three chide him.
  But whist, and come apace.   *be quiet*

RESPUBLICA: I hear Policy's voice.   1090

AVARICE: That I met you so well I do much rejoice.
  Lady Respublica would you come her before.

INSOLENCE: Madame, God ye save.

OPPRESSION: And preserve forevermore.

RESPUBLICA: This is happy hap, ye come so soon together.

AVARICE: As I went I met them both twain hasting hither.

RESPUBLICA: Never in better time.

INSOLENCE: Madame, what is your will?

OPPRESSION: Is there anything that you would say us until?

RESPUBLICA: People crieth out, and I am much aggrieved   1100
    That we feel ourselves in nothing yet relieved.

OPPRESSION: No? That is not true. Many declare I can—

RESPUBLICA: Even in brief words I pray you do it, then.

PEOPLE: Pray you, let me spose with this same new come
    gent'man.   *dispute* (?)

INSOLENCE: No sir.

PEOPLE: Mass, but 'ch'll speak an 'che can spy my time when.

OPPRESSION: First, your priests and bishops have not as they
    have had.

RESPUBLICA: When they had their livings men were both fed
    and clad.

OPPRESSION: Yea, but they ought not, by Scripture, to be
    called lords.

RESPUBLICA: That they rule the Church with Scripture well
    accords.   1110

OPPRESSION: They were proud and covetous and took much
    upon them.

PEOPLE: But they were not covetous that took all from them!

OPPRESSION: The coin also is changed.

PEOPLE: Yea, from zilver to dross,
  ('Twas told us) for the best, but poor we bore the loss.
  When 'ch'ad with zweat of brows got up a few small crumbs,
  At paying of my debts ich could not make my sums!
  My landlord for my corn paid me zuch sums and zuch;
  When he should ha' it for rent, it was but half zo much.
  Zix pence in each shilling as y-struck quite away,   1120
  Zo vor one piece ich took, 'chwas vain to pay him   *obliged*
    twai.   *two*
  One would think 'twere brass, and zorrow have I else
  But ich ween most part on't was made of our old bells!   *of it*

INSOLENCE: Yet if ye mark it well, for one piece ye have three,
  Which for your people is no small commodity.

PEOPLE: Well, I nill meddle in this same matter no more,
  But I's reck not an 'twere zilver as 'twas avore.   *reckon/before*

OPPRESSION: People, ye shall at length find it all for the best.

PEOPLE: 'Ch'a heard our parish clerk say *Divum este, Juslum*
    weste.[28]

RESPUBLICA: Undoubtedly, I feel many things are amiss.   1130

---

[28] Brandl takes this to be a corruption of *divites estis juste fuistes*, i.e. "you rich ones are as you were," or "the rich get richer and the poor get poorer."

PEOPLE: Yea, I's can tell mo things yet an me lust, by Jiss!
 They have all the woods throughout the realm destroyed,
 Which might have served long years, being well employed.
 And then the great cobs have zo take the rest to   *lords*
     hire,   *rented out*
 That poor volk cannot get a stick to make a fire.
 Then their great grazing hath made flesh so dear, I   *meat so costly*
     wote,
 That poor volk at shambles cannot bestow their groat.   *butcher*
RESPUBLICA: I lament it, People. Alack, what may I do?
 I myself, I fear, shall come to ruin too.
 Policy, what comfort? When will you ease my smart?   1140
AVARICE: Ye are as safe even now, but for your false heart
 As any lady of your name in christendom.
PEOPLE: If ich had zo zaid, 'ch'ad lied, by my halidom!   *I swear it*
RESPUBLICA: Ye hear what People saith, which feeleth as I do.
AVARICE: But rude people's words will ye give credit unto?
 Will ye judge yourself after his foolish jangling?
 Ye were well enough till he begun his wrangling.
INSOLENCE: Will ye believe people that hath no manner of skill
 To judge or to discern what thing is good or ill?
 He is so headstrong he must be bridled with laws.   1150
PEOPLE: Though zome be stark bedlams, yet wise volk   *madmen*
     beeth no daws.
INSOLENCE: We have oft found People most disobedient,
 To orders most requisite and expedient.
 Who such a maintainer of wrong opinions
 As People in all countries and dominions?
 Ye ought therefore to rebuke him at all hours,
 For discouraging any ministers of yours.
OPPRESSION: Ye must tarry time ere we can your purpose
     serve.
PEOPLE: Yea, and then while the grass shall grow the horse
     shall starve.
INSOLENCE: Do ye not see this, by all experience plain,   1160
 That men from diseases recovered again
 Do after sickness past remain a long time weak?

RESPUBLICA: People, hark. Authority doth good reason speak

INSOLENCE: So ye, though oppressed with long adversity,
  Yet, doubt not, are toward wealth and prosperity.

RESPUBLICA: Lo, People, to hope a while longer shall be best.

PEOPLE: Well then, 'cham persuaded to do at your enquest.

INSOLENCE: Madame, mistrust not us, your painfull   *painstaking*
  ministers.

AVARICE: Never had lady more watchful officers.

OPPRESSION: For my part, I will swear the Gospel book
  upon,   1170
  That if the laws I have made should every one
  Redound to mine own singular commodity
  They should not be friendlier framed than they be!

INSOLENCE: Therefore, repose yourself madame a while,
  and wink;   *take a nap*
  Ye are in better case toward, than you can think.

AVARICE: We shall here remain and give People good counsel
  Quiet for to be till Policy may prevail.

RESPUBLICA: He will do well with your good informations.

PEOPLE: Yea, vay, 'ch'ill vollow their good exaltations.

RESPUBLICA: Then I leave you all here to God. I will depart.   1180
  (*exeat* RESP.)

PEOPLE: Now how, destructions to 'member in my heart.   *instructions*

AVARICE: Destructions? Ye miser!

INSOLENCE: Ye peasant!

OPPRESSION: Ye lout!

INSOLENCE: Can ye naught else do but rage and rave and cry
  out?

OPPRESSION: And cannot tell on whom?

AVARICE: No more than can a daw.

OPPRESSION: Crow against your betters

INSOLENCE: And murmur against the law.
  Let me hear thee prate as thou hast done heretofore,   1190

AVARICE: Or trouble lady Respublica any more.

OPPRESSION: Thou canst not see, thou wretch, canst thou, when
  thou art well?

AVARICE: Is't part of thy play, with such high matters to mell?

INSOLENCE: Doth it become thee to bark with such a wide throat?

AVARICE: And to have an oar in everybody's boat?

INSOLENCE: If thou do so again, it shall with thee be worse.

AVARICE: We shall wring and pinch thee both by belly and purse.

INSOLENCE: I would advise you, friend, to grunt and groan no more.

AVARICE: Do the like again and thou shalt rue it full sore.

INSOLENCE: It were best for you, friend, all murmuring to cease.   1200

PEOPLE: Bum vay, then 'ch'ill e'en go home, and vair hold my peace.

INSOLENCE: Do so, by my rede, and fall to honest labor   *advice*

AVARICE: Hence home and be quiet, and thou shalt find favor.

PEOPLE: Then 'ch'ill bid you varewell.

OPPRESSION: No words, but hence, apace!

PEOPLE: But how, one word ere 'che go—ye'll give volks leave to think?

OPPRESSION: No, marry, will we not, nor to look, but wink.

PEOPLE: Yes, by Jiss, but 'ch'ill lo; nay, ho there! thought   *look*
is free,[29]

And a cat, they zaith, may look on a king, pardee!   *indeed*
   (*exeat.*)

INSOLENCE: Now where do we be come? I home.   1210
   (*exeat.*)

OPPRESSION: And I abroad.
   (*exeat.*)

AVARICE: And I must see what feet about my door have trod.
   (*exeat.*)

Actus quinti, scena prima

[Enter] MISERICORDIA

MISERICORDIA: Wherein appeareth the graciousness of God

---

[29] The character People, the canny peasant, is worth analyzing, particularly at such moments of duress as this one.

More than infinitely to exceed man's goodness,
But that He keepeth back the sharp stroke of His rod
When man would rage in most furious woodness?   *madness*
Scarce any amends may man's eagerness appease,
Yea, and though He forgive, He will not soon forget,
Toward true penitence God's wrath forthwith doth cease,
And He their past sins behind His back doth set.   1220
Of long sufferance He is with weakness to bear,
While any hope of amendment doth remain,
And though He plague sinners, to call them home by fear,
Yet his mercy and grace are aye ready again.
His grievous displeasure dureth not forever.
And why? *quia miserationes eius,*
Which to show He delighteth ever,
Manent super omnia opera eius.[30]
It grieveth Him sore when He must needs take vengeance;
His delight and glory is mercy to practice;   1230
His tender compassion on true repentance
He hath still from the beginning sought to exercise.
The mass of this world in His mercy did He frame,
The sky, earth and sea His mercy replenished;
In His mercy did He after redeem the same,
When else remedyless it must have perished.
In His Mercy was Israel delivered
From the Egyptian thralldom and captivity;
In His mercy the same through the Red Sea was led
And through wildness to a land of liberty.   1240
Sith that time all commonweals He hath protected,   *since*
And to such as with earnest prayer have made moan,
Me, Compassion, He hath quickly directed,
To revive and recover them every one.
Now lastly hath He heard the most doleful lament
Of woeful Respublica, His darling most dear.
Therefore me, Compassion, with speed He hath sent,
Her most sorrowful heart to recomfort and cheer.
I tarry her coming that I may her salute,

[30] For His mercies endure over all His works. Psalms 145, 9.

And lo, methinketh I see her appear in place,   1250
Of friendship devoid and of succor destitute.
I will hear her, and then give words of solace.

Actus quinti, scena secunda

RESPUBLICA, MISERICORDIA, [*then*] AVARICE, ADULATION

RESPUBLICA: O Lord, hast thou forever closed up thine ear?
Wilt thou nevermore the desolate's prayer hear?
Wilt thou still turn away thy face from my distress?
Wilt thou clean forsake me and leave me comfortless?
The secret sighs and sobs and prayers of mine heart,
Shall they not forever thine eyes to me convert?   *turn*
I grant that mine offences have so much deserved,
But for whom save sinners is thy mercy reserved?   1260
Thou promised so, which hitherto hast been just.
Despair, Lord, I will not, nor thy goodness mistrust.
Lo down on my distress and for thy glory's sake,
Though I be ill worthy, yet mercy on me take.

MISERICORDIA: Now will I speak to her.

RESPUBLICA: Who maketh me afeared?

MISERICORDIA: No, I will thee comfort; God hath thy prayer
heard.
And now, Respublica, be of good hope and trust.

RESPUBLICA: O Lord, now do I see that thou art ever just.

MISERICORDIA: I am sent to recomfort thee, Respublica.   1270

RESPUBLICA: O Lady Compassion, Misericordia!

MISERICORDIA: What say ye to me? What, woman, can ye not
speak?
I am come down all your sorrows at once to break.
Speak, woman—

RESPUBLICA: Misericordia.

MISERICORDIA: Out comfortably.
Ye shall have now no more cause to speak desperably.

RESPUBLICA: My heart in God's mercy is so delated   *uplifted*
That my very spirit to heaven is elated.   *raised*
O Lady Compassion welcome, verament!   *truly* 1280

Ever be God praised that you to me hath sent!

MISERICORDIA: Now that I have put you in sure hope of
   relief,

I must go fet Verity, to try out all your grief.   *examine*

Verity shall open how your decay hath grown

And then the causers thereof shall be overthrown.

RESPUBLICA: Who be the causers thereof I cannot discern.

But yond cometh one of them that do me govern.

MISERICORDIA: What is his name?

RESPUBLICA: Policy.

MISERICORDIA: Policy is good,   1290

He doth work you many good things, of likelihood.

AVARICE: A vengeance upon him, and God give him His
   curse!

I am besieged now of every cutpurse.

I can go nowhere now, in city neither town

But Piers Pickpurse playeth at organs, under my gown.   *fingers*

MISERICORDIA: What talketh he?

AVARICE: Who speaketh yond? Respublica?

RESPUBLICA: What of the pickpurse?

AVARICE: For sooth, Dame Respublica,

I said "An we had two pillories mo, 'twere ne'er the worse,   1300

For it is a light thing now to meet Piers   *common occurrence*
   Pickpurse."

God preserve you, right fair lady, and Christ you save!

Who are you, and what would you in this country have?

RESPUBLICA: This same is the Lady Misericordia,

Sent from God purposely.

AVARICE: Unto you, Respublica?

MISERICORDIA: Yea.

AVARICE: Then must ye needs be most heartily welcome,

We had ne'er more need of you, by my halidom.

There be in this country, which, but ye comfort   *be those/unless*
   send,   1310

Are full like to make both a mad and a short end.

MISERICORDIA: I will go to do that I said, Respublica, and
   return with speed.

RESPUBLICA: Sweet Misericordia.

    (*exeat* MISERICORDIA.)

AVARICE: Good Misericordia now, and lady most dear,

  Christ blister on your heart, what make you here?

RESPUBLICA: Come back, Policy.

AVARICE: I come.

RESPUBLICA: Whither would ye now?

AVARICE [*aside*]: Convey myself hence honestly, if I wist how!

RESPUBLICA: When come ye, Policy? What look ye? Something

    lost?   1320

AVARICE: Anon. [*Aside*]. If I tarry it will turn to my cost.

RESPUBLICA: Ah, friend Policy.

AVARICE: Yea.

RESPUBLICA: Now shall I be in bliss, thanks to God.

AVARICE [*Aside*]: We must find provision for this.

RESPUBLICA: Hah?

AVARICE: Did not I ere tell you that God would you save?

  Ye may see now what it is, good rulers to have.

RESPUBLICA: Ye say truth. But look, yonder cometh Honesty.

AVARICE: Pray God amen!   1330

RESPUBLICA: Yes, look else.

AVARICE: What news bringeth he?

ADULATION: I should speak a word in the ear of Policy;

  If I may not so, I will speak it openly.

RESPUBLICA: I have not seen you a great while, Honesty.

ADULATION: O noble Lady Respublica, well you be!

RESPUBLICA: All shall be now, such news I have to me brought.

ADULATION: I hear it told for truth. Policy, all will be nought!

RESPUBLICA: Hearest thou any joyful news abroad, or not?

ADULATION: Yea, I hear certain news which are both breme   *loud*

    and hot.   1340

  There is a new start-up, a lady called Verity.

RESPUBLICA: Then I am all safe, and sure of prosperity!

  How was it spoken?

ADULATION: Thus in Latin gross and blunt:

  Misericordia et veritas sibi obviaverunt;[31]

---

[31] Mercy and Truth are met together—Psalms 85, 10.

That is, mercy and truth are both met together.

RESPUBLICA: Then will it not be long ere they both come
   hither.

AVARICE: Hither? How so?

RESPUBLICA: Yea, both Mercy and Verity.

AVARICE: A pestel on them both, saving my charity!   1350
   But soft, brother Honesty. Ye might mistake it.
   Of which Verity was't, trow you, that they spake it?

ADULATION: Of the general Verity, old Time's daughter.

AVARICE: Faith, they were not our friends that first hither
      brought her!
   Old Time's daughter? That shuttle-brained, tall long man
   That ne'er standeth still but flyeth as fast as he can,
   Much like as he swimmed or glided upon ice?

ADULATION: Yea.

RESPUBLICA: For all that, of wise men he is thought most wise.

AVARICE: I know him; he carrieth a clock on his head,   1360
   A sand glass in his hand, a dial in his forehead.

RESPUBLICA: Ye say truth, Policy, the same is very he.

AVARICE: Old Time the eavesdropper? I know him, pardee!
   An ancient turner of houses upside down
   And a common consumer of city and town.
   Old Time's daughter, quoth he? I shrew his naked heart!
   Many of my friends hath he brought to pain and smart.
   Compassion and that Truth come hither to you?

RESPUBLICA: Mercy, before ye came, promised so right now.

AVARICE: It is no time now, Honesty, to be idle.   1370

ADULATION: Something breweth?

AVARICE: It is time for us to bridle.
   Well, go your ways afore, in all haste, Honesty,
   And tell Reformation and Authority
   That both these ladies, in all goodly fashion
   Must be entertained here in this nation.
   Madame Respublica, is't not your pleasure so?

RESPUBLICA: What else? In all the haste, Honesty, see ye go.

AVARICE: Say further that I would we four anon might meet
   Here, or where they will, save in the open street.   1380

And hear you, Honesty—
ADULATION: What now?
AVARICE: A little nearer.
Provide in any wise that Verity come not here.
Let Insolence and Oppression keep her hence.
ADULATION: We shall all three therein do our best diligence.
Bid them well remember, the world will wax queasy;
Some of us erelong may hap leap at a daisy,
Or put out the "i" of Misericordia,
And without an "i" play e'en plain   1390
    trussing *corda*.   *miser corda* (hangmans's rope)
        (*exeat* ADULA.)
RESPUBLICA: Policy, what is it that ye talk there so long?
AVARICE: I send instructions that they may not do wrong.
RESPUBLICA: Said ye aught to him that may not be told to me?
AVARICE: Should we with every trifling trifle trouble ye?
Well then, ye look for these two ladies, I am sure.
RESPUBLICA: I trust they will not fail on me to do their cure.
AVARICE: I told you ever, did I not, that your wealth would
    frame.
RESPUBLICA: I shall regard your pains, or else I were to blame.
AVARICE: Then best I go now straight to my fellows and see—
RESPUBLICA: That things needful for us may not
    unready be.   1400
Do so, I pray you.
AVARICE: Fare ye well, Respublica, till I see you next.
        (*exeat.*)
RESPUBLICA: Now, Misericordia, when shall be thy pleasure,
    bring hither Verity.
        (*Intrant* MISERICORDIA *et* VERITAS.)
Behold, e'en with the word speaking, where they both be!

Actus quinti, scena tertia

MISERICORDIA, VERITAS, RESPUBLICA
MISERICORDIA: I dare say Respublica thinketh the time long.
VERITY: Who can blame her, having endured so much wrong?

But as meat and drink and other bodily food
Is never found to be so pleasant nor so good
As when fretting hunger and thirst hath pinched afore,
And as health after sickness is sweeter evermore,   1410
So after decay and adversity overcome
Wealth and prosperity shall be double welcome.

MISERICORDIA: How now, Respublica? Have I not been long
hence?

RESPUBLICA: Come ye first or last ye bless me with your
presence.

MISERICORDIA: As I was commanded, I bring you Verity,
To help you, your people, and their posterity.

VERITY: Dear jewel Respublica, I do you embrace.

RESPUBLICA: I thank your goodness, and submit me to your
grace.

MISERICORDIA: Embrace Verity forever, Respublica, and cleave
fast to her.

RESPUBLICA: Yes, Misericordia.   1420

MISERICORDIA: Now please it you to declare, sister Verity,
How she may recover her old prosperity.
Her honor, her wealth, her riches, her substance,
Her commons, her people, her strength, and her puissance [?]

VERITY: All this will be recovered incontinent   *at once*
And to better state also, by good government.

RESPUBLICA: No lady of my name upon earth, I esteem,
Hath had better administers than mine have been;
Policy, Reformation and Authority.

MISERICORDIA: These three be very good.   1430

RESPUBLICA: And the fourth, Honesty.

VERITAS: But what if these which have had you and yours to
keep,
Have been ravening wolves in the clothing of sheep?

RESPUBLICA: If I heard not you, Verity, such sentence give,
By no man's persuasion I could it believe.

VERITY:[32]   Ah good Respublica, thou hast been abused!

---

[32] With Truth, Justice and Peace, the author uses the Latin and English forms of the names in the speech
tags quite interchangeably.

Whom thou chosest are vices to be refused;
Whom thou callest Honesty is Adulation,
And he that in pretence was Reformation,
Is indeed Oppression and huge violence;   1440
Whom thou callest Authority is proud Insolence;
Then he that was Policy, the chief man of price,
Indeed is most stinking and filthy Avarice.
He first inveigled thee, and his purpose to frame,
Cloaked each of these vices with a virtuous name.

RESPUBLICA: *Benedicité!* Is this a possible case?   *Bless me!*

VERITY: Ye shall see it proved true before your own face.
They shall be convinced before you one by one.   *convicted*

RESPUBLICA: O Lord, what marvel if my thirst were well nigh
gone?
But what redress shall I have hereof, and when?   1450

MISERICORDIA:,   Such as may be most fit, and as soon as
we can.
Justice and Mercy are appointed to descend,
The one to keep you quiet, the other you to defend.
As soon as we four sisters together shall be met,
An order for your establishment shall be set.
By the eternal Providence it is decreed so.

RESPUBLICA: O most merciful Lord, all praise be thee
unto.

MISERICORDIA: I will leave you here with my sister
Verity,
And learn of their coming with all celerity.

VERITY: Ye need not, for I know they be now very near,   1460
And behold, they begin already to appear.

Actus quinti, scena quarta

PAX, JUSTITIA, VERITAS, MISERICORDIA, RESPUBLICA

PEACE: Now once again in God let us two sisters kiss.[33]
In token of our joining to make a perfect bliss.

[33] The allegory of the Four Daughters of God, from Psalms 85 has quite a literary history. See Hope
Traver, *The Four Daughters of God*, Philadelphia, 1907.

JUSTITIA: And now let is never be sundered any more,
  Till we may Respublica perfectly restore.
VERITY: Let us meet them, sister Misericordia.
MISERICORDIA: And unto their sight present Respublica.
JUSTITIA, PAX: All hail, most dear sisters Mercy and Verity!
  And all hail Respublica, with sincerity!
RESPUBLICA: O ye ladies celestial, how much am I bound   1470
  With thanks to fall flat before you on the ground,
  That ye thus vouchsafe a forlorn creature
  By your heavenly protection to recure.
JUSTITIA: I, Justice, from heaven am come, you to visit.
PAX: And I, Peace, forever with you to inhabit.
MISERICORDIA: And all we four sisters to the utmost of our
        power
  Shall restore, establish and defend your honor.
JUSTITIA: We shall first restore your most happy estate
  And suppress all them that had made you desolate.
VERITY: Verity shall all truth open as it is.   1480
JUSTITIA: I, Justice, shall redress what e'er is found amiss.
MISERICORDIA: I, Mercy, where the member may recured be
  Shall temper the rigor, and slake extremity.   *mitigate*
PAX: I, Peace, when the uncurable is clean cut away
  And the ill made good, shall flourish for ever and aye.
RESPUBLICA: And I, which cannot otherwise your goodness
        deserve,
  Shall your wholesome directions duly observe.
  And what if Insolence shall come, or Avarice?
VERITY: Detest them, abhor them, and refuse their service.
  I doubt not but they will be still haunting hither,   1490
  Till we four shall them four take here altogether.
MISERICORDIA: Now sisters, go we, and Respublica with us,
  To be new apparelled otherwise than thus.
JUSTITIA: Come on Respublica, with us from wealth to woe;
  God hath given us in charge that it must be so.
  The blissful renovation ye shall reign in
  Must from henceforth now immediately begin.
    (*Cantent "The mercy of God" etc., et exeant.*)

Actus quinti, scena quinta

[*Enter*] AVARICE, ADULATION

AVARICE: Such greedy covetous folk as now of days been,
  I trow before these present days were never seen!
  An honest man can go in no place of the street   1500
  But he shall, I think, with an hundred beggars meet.
  "Give, for God's sake!" "Give, for St. Charity!"
  "Give, for Our Lady's sake!" "Give, for the Trinity!"
  "Give, in the way of your good speed!" "Give, give, give,
       give!"
  Find we our money in the street, do they believe?
  If I had not a special grace to say nay
  I were but undone amongst them in one day!
  But who cometh yond? Honesty? He cometh in haste.

ADULATION: I seek Policy.

AVARICE: Here, boy!   1510

ADULATION: All is in waste!

AVARICE: How so?

ADULATION: We strive against the stream, all that we do.

AVARICE: Wherein?

ADULATION: That Verity come not this place unto.
  For, wot ye what?

AVARICE: I shall when ye have spake the word.

ADULATION: Justice, and Peace too, with full consent and
       accord,
  Are come down from heaven and have kissed together.

AVARICE: God give grace that they twain also come not
       hither!   1520

ADULATION: As Mercy and Truth *sibi obviaverunt,*
  So *Justitia et Pax osculatae sunt.*   *have kissed*

AVARICE: Is it true? Are they come?

ADULATION: And have kissed together.

AVARICE: Then carry in, apace, for fear of foul   *take cover, quickly*
       weather!
  Have they kissed together?

ADULATION: Yea,

AVARICE: What needeth that? Men should kiss women.
 And what point be they at?

ADULATION: All the four sisters, I do you to understand,   1530
 Have already taken Respublica in hand.
 They four progress with her in every border,
 And mar all that ever we have set in order.
 And what doth Insolence, or what saith he to that?

ADULATION: He stampeth, he stareth, and huffeth sore thereat.

AVARICE: I advise him to storm and to show himself stout;
 They be women and perchance may be faced out,
 And Peace is an honest lady and a quiet.

ADULATION: Verity and Justitia are not for our diet.

AVARICE: Then Mercy is a good one. I like her well.   1540

ADULATION: Yet oft turneth she her face away, and will not
  mell.

AVARICE: Well, fall back, fall edge, I am once at a   *I am ready*
  point,[34]
 If Respublica come, to adventure a joint.   *risk a limb*

ADULATION: She is fresh and gay, and flourisheth, who but she?

AVARICE: Who brought it to such pass will I tell her, but we?
 Or else, making these new ladies of her weary,
 We should triumph and reign.

ADULATION: Oh never so merry!

AVARICE: Well, go to our company. I will remain here.
 I may perhaps see Dame Respublica appear.   1550
 I will be in hand with her, and make a good face.

ADULATION: And what shall I do?

AVARICE: Give warning in the mean space,
 That Insolence shrink not, but play the stout man.

ADULATION: That I know he will do; for once I know he can.

AVARICE: And that you all three be prest to come hither
 When need shall require we lay our heads together.
 Why art thou here yet?

ADULATION: I am gone, with all my might.
    (*exeat.*)

---

[34] "Fall back, fall edge" obviously means "whatever happens," but one can only guess what the falling object is that originated the expression. Perhaps a knife in some kind of game.

(*Intrat* RESPUBLICA)

AVARICE: And lo, where Respublica appeareth in sight.   1560
  She is now at her nymphs bearing up her train.   *at* (with ?)
  I will stand aside and listen a word or twain.

Actus quinti, scena sexta

RESPUBLICA, AVARICE

RESPUBLICA: O Lord, thy mercies shall I sing evermore,
  Which dost so tenderly thy handmaid restore.
  But what creature would suspicion have had
  That my late administers had been men so bad?
  Or who would have thought them counterfeits to have been,
  That had heard their words, and their countenance seen?
  And chiefly Avarice, which did the matter break.

AVARICE: That word toucheth me; now is time for me to
    speak.   1570

RESPUBLICA: I thought him Policy, as just and true as steel.

AVARICE: I am glad that by me ye do such goodness feel.

RESPUBLICA: And that my wealth did grow, as it hath grown
    of late!

AVARICE: I ever told ye you should grow to this estate!

RESPUBLICA: Thou told me?

AVARICE: Yea, I told you so in very deed
  And highly I rejoice it doth so well succeed.
  And *salve festa dies* upon you, Madame,   ("Welcome, festive day")
  I am glad ye have got a new robe, so I am!
  What saint in the calendar do we serve today,   1580
  That ye be so gorgeously decked, and so gay?

RESPUBLICA: In rejoicing that I shall be clean rid of thee!

AVARICE: Nay, by this cross, ye shall never be rid for me.

RESPUBLICA: And of thy compeers.

AVARICE: Well, let them do as they lust;
  I will ride upon Jill, mine own mare, that is just.   *look out for myself*
  Other ways I shall do you service of the best.

RESPUBLICA: Thou wicked wretch, darest thou with me
    to jest?

AVARICE: What? Now I see
  honores mutant mores,   ("honors alter manners")
 But, as seemeth here, *raro in meliores.* [but] rarely for the better")   1590

RESPUBLICA: Thee and all thy service I do from me exile.

AVARICE: Is that the high reward ye promised me erewhile?
 Is not this a wise woman, and minded to thrive,
 That would me, Policy, out of the country drive?

RESPUBLICA: Thee and thy 'complices from me I shall out cast.

AVARICE: Then I pray you, pay us for our pains that are past.

RESPUBLICA: Ye shall be paid,

AVARICE: Once I have done the best I can.
 Authority also, he hath played the man;
 Reformation hath done his part, I can tell;   1600
 If ye mistrust Honesty, faith, ye do not well.
 And as for Avarice, he is conveyed quite.
 I bade him get him hence or I would him indict.
 I, Policy, have made him to pluck in his horns;
 I swore I would else lay him on prickles and thorns,
 Where he should take not rest neither day nor night,
 So he had as lief be hanged as come in sight.

RESPUBLICA: I may say with Job: how vainly do ye cheer me,
 When all the words ye give from truth doth disagree;
 And with the wise man I may most justly say this: 1610
 Justitia tamen non luxit in nobis. ("justice does not yet begin to shine on us")
 Or else with the Prophet in most sorrowful mood,
 "The fruit of our justice is turned into wormwood."[35]
 Well, the best of you is a detestable vice,
 And thou, for thy part, art most stinking Avarice.

AVARICE: Jesu, when were you wont so foul mouthed to be,
 To give such nicknames? Ah, in faith, Dame Verity
 Hath had you in schooling of late. Well, in God's name,
 I am sorry for you, e'en sorry, that I am.
 Iwis I have wrought to set you in good state,   1620
 And watched for that purpose both early and late,
 And Iwis if you would abide by my framing
 And not thus to have fall to checking and blaming,

---

[35] Amos 5, 7.

An ich did, they zwore I's should be corrupt   *destroyed*
    therefore.   1680
Zo thik proud horecop—what call ye him?

RESPUBLICA: Insolence?

PEOPLE: Yea, even thik same, he vair popped me to silence.

RESPUBLICA: And how is it with you now? Better than it was?

PEOPLE: All beginneth now to come gaily to pass.
We hear of your good vortune that goeth about,
How ye beeth permounted, which maketh all us proud.   *promoted?*
And ich am able since to buy me a new coat,
And I's thank God 'ch'ave in my purse a zilver groat.
Iwis ich could not zo zay these zix years afore.   1690
Whoever caused it, ill thank have they therefore!

RESPUBLICA: They will be here soon. Bide you them here
    for a train.   *as a trap*

PEOPLE: Mass, but I ni'not. Would ye have 'em squat out   *smash*
    one's brain?[37]

RESPUBLICA: They shall not do thee harm the value of a point.

PEOPLE: Then, an you zay the word ich'll jeopard a joint.

RESPUBLICA: If they but offer thee wrong they shall smart
    therefore.

PEOPLE: Nay, will ye be zo good to tie 'em up avore?
And what shall che zay to 'em?

RESPUBLICA: Nothing, but be a bait.
Till take them all here suddenly I may await.   1700
    (*exeat.*)

PEOPLE: Well, it shall be do. 'Ch'ould laugh and both my hands
    clap
To zee Rice Puddingcake's envies take in a trap.   *enemies*
And a-zee, pray, if zome of 'em come not yonder.
'Ch'ould my lady had bode ne'er zo little longer.

Actus quinti, scena octava

INSOLENCE, ADULATION, OPPRESSION, PEOPLE, AVARICE

INSOLENCE: Where is Avarice, ho? He doth not now appear.

---

[37] "Nill not" is a double negative from "will not"—cf. willy nilly, i.e. will he, nill he.

ADULATION: He bade me monish you that we might all meet
    here.

OPPRESSION: But see where People standeth.

ADULATION: What doth he here now?

OPPRESSION: About little goodness, I dare my word avow!

INSOLENCE: Let us speak unto him. People, wherefore and
    why,   1710

  Like a loitering losel standest thou here idly?   *bum*

OPPRESSION: Thou comest to Respublica to make some
    moan.

ADULATION: Or else some complaint.

PEOPLE: You all see 'cham here alone.

INSOLENCE: Ye must have silver money, must ye, gentleman?
  You cannot be content with such coin as we can.

OPPRESSION: Ye must burn wood and coal, must ye, all of
    pleasance?

  Burn turfs, or some of thy bedstraw, with a vengeance!

ADULATION: Ye must eat fresh meat bought from the shambles,
    must ye?

  Eat garlick and onions and roots, or grass, an lust ye!   1720

INSOLENCE: In faith, I will whip you for this, ye peasant lout!

ADULATION: And twig you.

INSOLENCE: Ere another year come about.

ADULATION: But see where Avarice cometh running very fast.
      (*Intrat* AVARICE.)

AVARICE: I have trod and scudded till my wind is almost past,
  Yet my mates are not where.

INSOL., ADUL.:   We be here come of late.

AVARICE: Be there not, trow ye, honester men in Newgate?

INSOLENCE: No words of reproach, brother mine, I rede you.

AVARICE: None but Godigood eve and Godigood speed
    you.   1730

  Fare ye well again, an ye be falling out now.

INSOL., ADUL.:   We mind it not.

AVARICE: 'Twere more need to look about you.

INSOLENCE: How goeth all, tell us?

AVARICE: My lady is waxed froward.

Our names be all known, so there is array toward.   *trouble coming*

INSOL., OPPR.:   God speed us well.

AVARICE: Once I am thrust out of service.   *already*

ADULATION: Alas, what may I do?

INSOL., OPPR.;   Tell us thy best advice.   1740

AVARICE: Nay, I cannot have you when I would, none of you
all;

Therefore shift for yourselves each one,
for me you shall.   *for all I care*

ADULATION: Nay, for the pash of God, tell us what best to
do!   *passion*

Ye know I was ne'er slack to resort you unto.

AVARICE: These ladies that are come for Commonweal's
relief

Prepare to work us woe end do us all mischief.

INSOLENCE: Nay, by His precious populorum, I swear,[38]

Not the proudest of them all can hurt me a hair!

OPPRESSION: If they offer of us to make their gauds or toys

They shall find, I trow, we are no babes nor boys![39]   1750

AVARICE: To prevail against them with force I do despair.

INSOLENCE: Be that as be may.

ADULATION: I will fall to speaking fair.   *resort to flattering*

But of all this trouble we may thank People, this wretch!

OPPRESSION: Faith, villain, if we 'scape, thou shalt an halter
stretch.   *noose*

ADULATION: But what remedy, therewhile?

AVARICE: Faith, all will be naught.

ADULATION: Tell us what to do.

AVARICE: I will. They come! We are caught!

ADULATION: Whither shall I run.   1760

AVARICE: Now sing a song, Honesty.

ADULATION: I am past singing now.

AVARICE: Yes, one song, Honesty.

Hey, hey, hey, hey,
I will be merry while I may.

---

[38] Simply a meaningless expletive, made to alliterate with "precious."

[39] A joke for the contemporary audience; they *are*, of course, boys.

Actus quinti, scena nona

VERITY, JUSTICE, AVARICE, RESPUBLICA, ADULATION,
MISERICORDIA, PEACE, PEOPLE, INSOLENCE, OPPRESSION.[40]

VERITY: Here they be, all four. This is a happy chance.

AVARICE: Take each man a lady sirs, and let us go dance!

RESPUBLICA: I left People here for a train, to hold them talk.

AVARICE: Alas, that I could tell which way best hence to walk!
   What be these fair ladies? And whither will they, trow?   1770

JUSTICE: We arrest you sirs, all four as ye stand in a row,
   Not so hardy in your hearts our arrest to gainsay.

AVARICE: Nay, we are content if ye let us go our way.

JUSTICE: No, not a foot. We must first your reckoning take.

AVARICE: I ne'er bought nor sold with you, reckoning to make,
   Nor I know not who you be.

JUSTICE: Justice is my name.

AVARICE: Where is your dwelling?

JUSTICE: In heaven, and thence I came.

AVARICE: Dwell ye in heaven, and so mad to come hither?   1780
   All our hucking here is how we may get thither!   *activity*

JUSTICE: I bring heaven with me, and make it where I am.

AVARICE: Then I pray you, let me be your prentice, madame.
   I will be at your beck.

JUSTICE: Ye shall, ere ye depart.

AVARICE: I would learn how to make heaven, with all my heart.
   Well, as for Lady Misericordia
   I remember I saw you with Respublica.

ADULATION: You, if you so please, may do much good in this
       land;
   Many at this hour do need your good helping hand.   1790

AVARICE: And ye came down from heaven too, I judge.

MISERICORDIA: Yea, sure.

AVARICE: Why, what folk are ye, that cannot heaven endure?
   And what may I call you, Lady?

PAX: My name is Peace.

---

[40] The presence of ten on stage at a time tells us in still another way that this is not a play of the popular theatre, with its company severely limited in size.

AVARICE: Ye have long dwelt with us. We have been long in
    peace.
PEACE: Call ye it peace sirra, when brother and brother
    Cannot be content to live one by another?
    When one for his house, for his land, yea, for his groat,
    Is ready to strive, and pluck out another's throat?   1800
    I will in all such things make perfect union.
AVARICE: Then good-night the lawyers' gain, by   (Holy Trinity)
    St. Trunnion!
    Westminster Hall might go play, if that came to pass!
    Faith, we must serve you with a *supersedeas*!   *writ of injunction*
VERITY: Well, leave vain prattling and now come answer to me.
AVARICE: I must hear first what ye say and who ye be.
VERITY: I am Dame Verity.
AVARICE: What? The daughter of Time?
VERITY: Yea.
AVARICE: I know my master your father well, à fin.   *indeed* 1810
    Welcome fair lady, sweet lady, little lady,
    Plain lady, smooth lady, sometime 'Spital   *hospital* (leper colony)
    lady,
    Lady Long-tongue, Lady Tell-all, Lady Make-bate.   *discord*
    And I beseech you, from whence are ye come of late?
VERITY: I am sprung out of the earth.
AVARICE: What? Ye do but jest.
VERITY: The Book saith, *Veritas de terra orta est*.[41]
AVARICE: Happy is he which hath that garden plat, I trow,
    Out of which such fair blossoms do spring and grow.
    Yet this one thing I say.   1820
VERITY: What?
AVARICE: Ye are friend to few,
  Prest to open all things, and men's manners to show.
VERITY: If ye be true and just, that is your benefit.
AVARICE: True or untrue, just or unjust, it is your spite,
    And glad ye are to take other folks in a trip   *catch an error*
    [   ] and then your own self on the whip.[42]

---

[41] Truth is risen from the earth. Psalms 85, 11.
[42] A worm hole that runs through the whole MS makes this phrase undecipherable.

Well ye might be honest of your tongue, if you would.

VERITY: If your acts were honest, ye did but as ye should.

AVARICE: Who chargeth me with the crime of any vice? 1830

VERITY: Thou callest thyself Policy and art Avarice.

AVARICE: Nay, I defy your malice! I am Policy.
   Ask of my fellows here. Am not I Policy?

VERITY: Ladies, will ye all see him openly tried?

JUSTICE: If he be an ill one, let him be descried.

VERITY: What hast thou in thy bosom?

AVARICE: Nothing I, truly.

VERITY: Nothing truly got, say. Show it forth
   openly.   *honestly obtained*

AVARICE: What should I show forth?

VERITY: That bag in thy bosom hid.   1840

AVARICE: It lieth well, I thank you, as much as though I did.

VERITY: Nay, come on, out with it.

AVARICE: Lo, here 'tis, for your fancy.

VERITY: Give it me.

AVARICE: Yea, nay, I defy that policy.

VERITY: Open it.

AVARICE: Yea, that each body might be catching!
   Some's teeth, I think, water e'en since, to be snatching.

VERITY: We must needs see what it is.

AVARICE: 'Tis a bag of rye.   1850

VERITY: Rye? What rye?

AVARICE: A bag of rye.

VERITY: Such as men do eat?

AVARICE: A bag of rye flour a great deal better than wheat.

VERITY: Let us see what rye it is. Pour it out in haste.

AVARICE: Yea, shall? I trow not. Indeed so might we make
   waste.

VERITY: There is no remedy; pour it out in my lap.

AVARICE: Nay, if there be no choice I will use mine own cap.

VERITY: So! A bag of rye, quoth thou?

AVARICE: Yea, so God me speed.   1860

VERITY: Thou sayest even truth. 'Tis a bag of "rye" indeed:
   Usu*rye*, perju*rye*, pitche*rye* patche*rye*,

Pilferye, briberye, snatcherye, catcherye,
Flatterye, robberye, clouterye, botcherye,
Trumperye, harlotrye, miserye, treacherye.

AVARICE: There is too, an please you, a little sorcerye,
Witcherye, bawderye, and such other grosserye.

VERITY: And how gottest thou all this in thy possession?

AVARICE: Pardon me, and I will make my confession.
The world is hard and the bag is but very small.   1870
I got it where I could, to go on begging withal.
A plain true-dealing man that loveth not to steal,
And I durst not be bold to crave of Commonweal.

VERITY: Now do off thy gown, and turn the inside outward.

AVARICE: Let me alone, and an Angel for a reward.

VERITY: Come, off at once! When? Come, off! No more
gawdies nor japes.   *tricks*

AVARICE: Must I needs whip over the chain, like   *skip rope*
Jackanapes?

RESPUBLICA: Out! In the virtue of God, what do ye here see?

AVARICE: All this had been lost, Respublica, but for me.

RESPUBLICA: O Lord! Where hast thou dragged up all these
purses?   1880

VERITY: Where he hath had for them many thousand curses.

RESPUBLICA: Where hast thou gotten them? Tell truth and do
not lie.

AVARICE: Where no honest man could have gotten them but I.
In blind corners where some would have hoarded them,
Had not I take [n] them, with the manor, and burdened   *accused*
them.

RESPUBLICA: And whither was it thine intent to convey them
now?

AVARICE: I hid them that I might bring them safely to you.
I durst not bear them openly, to God I vow,
Iwis ye have heard me blame pickpurses or now.   *before now*
And this is all yours.   1890

VERITY: It is hers in very deed.

AVARICE: With sufferance I could get mo to help her need.

VERITY: How say ye, Respublica, now, to Policy?

RESPUBLICA: I ne'er suspecte[d] him nor had him in zelousy.
VERITY: E'en suchlike counterfeits shall all the rest appear.
  Sirs, do off your utmost robes each one, even here.   *outer*
  Now what these are ye see plain demonstration.
RESPUBLICA: Insolence! Oppression! Adulation!
  O Lord, how have I be used, these five years past?   *been*
PEOPLE: Nay, I's ne'er thought better of 'em, ich, by God's
      vast!   1900
  Vay, madame my lady, such 'structioners as these[43]
  Have oft made you believe the moon was a green cheese.
VERITY: Now ye see what they are, the punishment of this
  Must be referred to the goddess Nemesis.
  She is the most high goddess of correction,
  Clear of conscience and void of affection,
  She hath power from above, and is newly sent down
  To redress all outrages in city and in town.
  She hath power from God all practice to repeal
  Which might bring annoyance to Lady Commonweal.   1910
  To her office belongeth the proud to overthrow,
  And such to restore as injury hath brought low.
  'Tis her power to forbid and punish in all estates
  All presumptuous immoderate attemptates.   *attempts*
  Her cognizance therefore is a wheel and wings to fly,   *emblem*
  In token her rule extendeth far and nigh.
  A rudder eke she beareth in her other hand,
  As directory of all things in every land.   *guide*
  Then pranketh she her elbows out under her side,   *struts (?)*
  To keep back the heady, and to temper their pride.   1920
  To her, therefore, dear sisters, we must now resort,
  That she may give sentence upon this naughty sort.   *group*
  She knoweth what is fittest for their correction;
  Nemesis must therefore herein give direction.
JUSTICE: Then People, while we Lady Nemesis do fet,
  All these offenders in thy custody we set,
  Them to apprehend and keep till we come again.

---

[43] Both "destructioners" and "constructioners" have been suggested here, the latter meaning people who put false constructions upon things.

[Exeunt four ladies and RESPUBLICA].

PEOPLE: An ye give me 'thority, 'ch'ill keep 'em, that is plain!

INSOL., OPPR.:   Shall People keep us, of whom we have been
     lords?

PEOPLE: Stand still, or by Jiss, 'ch'ill bind you vast with
     cords!   1930

Nay, sirs, ich ha' you now in my custody.

AVARICE: Mass, I will be gone, for mine own commodity.

PEOPLE: Zoft! Whither wilt thou? Nilt thou not be
     roiled?   *ruled*

Stand still, skit-brained thief, or thy bones shall be   *harebrained*
     coiled.   *beaten*

Yond be they coming now, che war't, that will tame ye.

A zee, art thou gone too? Come back, and evil 'a thee![44]

Actus quinti, scena decima

NEMESIS, RESPUBLICA, MISERICORDIA, VERITAS, JUSTITIA,
PAX, PEOPLE, INSOLENCE, OPPRESSION, ADULATION,
     AVARICE.

NEMESIS: Come forth, Respublica, our darling most dear.

RESPUBLICA: At your word, most gracious lady, I am here.

NEMESIS: Are these your trusty men that had you in
     government?

PEOPLE: The skitbrains n'ould not be roiled, ne'er since
     ye went.   1940

NEMESIS: People, why art thou bashful, and standest so far?
     Be of good cheer now, and I warrant thee come near.

PEOPLE: I nill come no nearer; cha not be
     haled up with 'states,   *high born*

But I's cannot be fitchant enough with my mates.   *nimble (?)*

NEMESIS: Come near when I bid thee.

PEOPLE: Marry, but I ninot
     I nam not worthy to perk with you, no I nam not.   *advance myself*

NEMESIS: Well Respublica, are these your late governors,

---

[44] Evidently what happens here is that the Vices try to run out but run right into Nemesis and the others
who are just coming in at that moment.

Whom ye took for faithful and trusty counsellors?

RESPUBLICA: Yea, forsooth madame.   1950

AVARICE: These three be, but I am none,

For I was discharged nigh half an hour agone.

NEMESIS: Come, first stand forth here, thou Adulation.

ADULATION: Speak a good word for me, Lady Compassion.

PEOPLE: Nay, she shall not need. I chill speak for thee myself.

Madame, take good heed, for this is a naughty elf!

ADULATION: Nay madame, the cause of all this was Avarice.

He forged us new names, and did us all entice.

OPPRESSION: We neither did nor could work but by his advice!

ADULATION: Because I got no more, he chid me once or

twice!   1960

INSOLENCE: Madame, only Avarice made us all to fall.

AVARICE: Yea? Fall to peaching? Nay, then will I tell all.   *tattling*

Madame, ere I had taught these merchants any while,   *fellows*

They were cunninger than I, all men to beguile.

And Verity saw mine were small purses and bags,

Tottering loose about me like windshaken rags,

But he that should have bagged that Insolence did win,   *that which*

Must have made a poke to put five or six shires in.   *sack*

He must have made wide sacks for castles, towns and woods;

The canvas to make them of were worth ten times my

goods.   1970

Then Oppression here, to feather well his nest,

Cared not of their livelihood whom he dispossessed:

Bishops, deans, provosts, ye poor folk from the 'spital,

Lands with church and chapel, all was for him too little.

Poor I did not so—I scraped but little crumbs,

And here and there with odd ends patched up my sums.

Flattery got his thrift by counterfeit honesty,

Yet by these ten bones, I bid him use modesty.

Therefore spare not him; he will ne'er come to good pass,

But I may well be mended, by the Mary Mass!   1980

MISERICORDIA: Lady Nemesis, now have ye occasion

And matter to show your commiseration.

It is much more glory, and standeth with more skill

Lost sheep to recover, than the scabby to spill.   *kill*

JUSTICE: But how shall this redress be well prosecuted
  If justice with mercy shall be executed?
  Straight justice must such enormities redress;
  Severity must put men in fear to transgress;
  Justice must give each man that he doth deserve.

MISERICORDIA: If offenders were not, wherefore might mercy
      serve?   1990

AVARICE: Stick hard to it, good sweet Lady Compassion!
  We are else undone, by Cock's bitter passion!

MISERICORDIA: Verity, how say you? Have I not spoken well?

VERITY: Mercy in one place with justice sometime may dwell,
  And right well agree together. How say you, Peace?

PAX: Where all thing is well amended, I do increase.

NEMESIS: Ladies, we have heard all your discrete advices,
  And each one shall have some part of your devices.
  Neither all nor none shall taste of severity,
  But as they are now known, through Lady Verity,   2000
  So shall they receive our mercy or our ire,
  As the wealth of Respublica shall best require.
  Now, Adulation, what saith you in this case?

ADULATION: Nought in mine excuse, but submit me to your
      grace.
  Only this: I promise, if I may mercy find,
  Utterly forever to change my wicked mind.
  I ne'er sought afore mine own private gain so much
  But I will further Commonweal's ten times so much.

NEMESIS: Well, thou mayest become a worthy subject, it is
      plain.

ADULATION: Else, ye know at all times how to reach me
      again.   2010

NEMESIS: Thou mightest swerve of frailty, thou mightest do
      to please,
  Thou mightest do for fear, thou mightest do to live in
      ease.
  Well, upon thy promise for once we pardon thee.
  Go, and see that from henceforth thou be perfect honesty.

ADULATION: So long as shall please God to give me life and
heal
  I shall most duly serve God and the commonweal.
        [*Exit.*]
AVARICE [*aside*]:   Now to thee, Avarice. Have at thy   *be stripped*
petticoat.
NEMESIS: Now the plague of commonweals, as all men do note,
  Come forth, Avarice! To spare thee will be no boot.   *to no avail*
  Thou must be plucked up e'en by the very root,   2020
  Because thou scrapest up whatever thou mightest get.
AVARICE: Indeed I thank God there is no man in my debt.
NEMESIS: And because thou caughtst it by wrong contribution,
  Thou shalt first and foremost make restitution.
AVARICE: Let me then with pardon go
        hence about it, lightly.   *at once*
NEMESIS: No, ye shall have help, to see it done rightly.
  People, take this fellow—
AVARICE: God save me from this plunge!
NEMESIS: That he may be pressed, as men do press a sponge,
  That he may drop ought to every man his lot,   2030
  To the utmost farthing that he hath falsely got.
PEOPLE: An ye bid me, 'ch'ill squeeze him as
        dry as a kex.   *dry stalk*
AVARICE: Nay, the pash of God, I shall then die of the
        flux!   *dysentery*
NEMESIS: Nay, thou shalt deliver him to the head officer
  Which hath authority justice to minister.
PEOPLE: 'Ch'ill 'liver him to the Constable and come again.
NEMESIS: Now, justice for these two that do here remain.
  Because the fault of Insolence is heinous and great,
  Lucifer's own fault, to aspire to the highest seat,
  And because Oppression hath wronged men so sore,   2040
  That he 'spoiled innocents of all they had, and more,   *despoiled*
  People shall deliver them unto safe custody,
  Where they may no farther annoy anybody.
  When the time may serve to examine and try their cause,   *case*
  Call them both before you and judge them by the laws.

PEOPLE: And shall che carry away these same two men also?

NEMESIS: Yea, go deliver them to an officer, go.

[*Exeunt* PEOPLE, AVARICE, INSOLENCE, OPPRESSION.]

Now darling Respublica, ye are in the old good estate,
And they taken away that 'spoiled you of late.
Now cleave to these ladies, from heaven to you
    direct;   *directed* 2050
They from all corruption will you safe protect.
Well, I must go hence to another country now,
That hath of redress the like case that was in you.
I leave you for this time, immortal thanks to give
To God and your sovereign, which do you thus relieve.

RESPUBLICA: Thanks be to thee, O Lord, which hast this world
    wrought,
And hast me to this state from utter ruin brought.

PAX: Now let us altogether, both with heart and voice,
In God and Queen Mary most joyfully rejoice.

VERITY: Praying that her reign, most graciously begun,   2060
May long years endure, as hitherto it hath done.

MISERICORDIA: Pray we for her Council to have long life and
    health.

JUSTICE: Their sovereign to serve.

PAX: And to maintain Commonwealth.

Omnes: Amen.
    (*Cantent et exeant*)

Finis

※ *THE TIDE TARRIETH NO MAN*

(G. Wapull, 1576)

In this play, as in several others of the 1560s and '70s, the moral
comedy finds a dramatic form for the barbs it wishes to launch at
the excesses and evils of the day. The central figure of redemptive
comedy, the Youth character, is depressed to a minor role, and the
Vice takes over, setting in motion a series of intrigues by giving a
series of petitioners the pep-talk they need in order to achieve their
desires. The Vice's name, Courage, is best modernized as "nerve."

The Youth figure we recognize in Willing-to-Win-Worship, the
young courtier making his first appearance in society. He is drawn
between the court and his home in the provinces (an antagonism
which brings us close to the pastoral), and he wants very much to
do the right thing.

What follows suggests as strongly as anything can that we are
in the presence of a transitional and experimental drama, one that is
quite conscious of the conventional expectations of its audience. The
innocent courtier of course falls into the hands of Courage and his
henchmen. He disappears from the play, but the mandatory redemption sequence does not. It is simply given to another character, who
comes into the play after the courtier has gone and is almost certainly to be played by the same actor. This is Wastfulness, the
husband of one of Courage's victims. His lament "I know it is folly

unto God to call/For God I know my petition will shun" is a para-
phrase of the Prodigal Son and is the language that identifies the
grievous sin of despair. The redemption of Wastfulness is accomplished, in the language of St. Paul, with the injunction "To be a
new man."

The reader should note the way in which Courage becomes a
real individual crook at the end (for the writer recognizes that the
concept of Courage cannot be captured and eliminated from the
world), as the play finally gives in to the pressure of its own intense
London realism.

Of the author and the external circumstances of the play nothing is known. Our text is a modernized-spelling reproduction of the
1576 edition, from the Tudor Facsimile Text Society's facsimile,
London, 1907.

THE TIDE TARRIETH NO MAN

The Prologue

As the worm which in the timber is bred
The self same timber doth consume and eat,
And as the moth which is commonly fed
In the cloth with her breed and the same doth fret,   *devour*
So many persons are a damage great
To their own country, which hath them relieved,
And by them their own country oft times is grieved.
So many cities and towns are defamed
By reason that some inhabitant is ill,   *evil*
So that for one's fact the whole town is blamed   *deed* 10
Although the residue to good do their will.
Yet the fact of this one the others' good name doth spill,   *kill*
And thus a reproach to his own town engendereth
And the good name of the whole town he hindereth.
To what end these words we have spoken
In our matter shall be more plainly expressed,
Which *The Tide Tarrieth No Man* to name hath taken,
For that it is most agreeable and best
Because that no man from his pleasure will rest
But each man doth take the time of his gain   20
Although the same be to others great pain.
For so greedy is the person avaricious,
Whom Saint Austen doth well liken to hell,   *St. Augustine*
For that they both are so much insatious,   *insatiable*
That neither of them know when they are well.
And Ambrosius doth verify and tell   *St. Ambrose*
How that covetous persons do lack that they have
And therefore not satisfied till they are in grave.
But where such people are, small love there doth rest
But greedy desire supplieth the place.   *replaces it* 30
The simple ones commonly by such are oppressed,
For they nothing weigh any man's case,
But with greedy grip their gain they embrace;
No kind of degree that they will forbear

Neither any time they will let slip or spare.
And although that here a Courtier is named,
Yet thereby is not meant the Courtier alone
But all kinds of persons who their suits have framed
Or to any such greedy-guts have made their moan,
Being driven to their shifts to have aught by loan;   *schemes* 40
How greediness at such times doth get what he can
And therefore still crieth, "Tide tarrieth no man!"
Which proverb right well might be applied
To a better sense than it is used:
There is time to ask grace, this may not be denied,
Of thy sinful life so greatly abused.
Let not that time, then, be refused
For *that* tide most certain will tarry no man.
Thus taking the proverb, we rightly do scan.[1]   *interpret*
Thus, worshipfull Audience, our Author desireth   50
That this history you will not deprave,   *dislike*
But if any fault be, he humbly requireth
That due intelligence thereof he may have,
Committing himself to your discretions grave.
And thus his Prologue he rudely doth end,
For at hand to approach the Players intend.

Finis

(COURAGE the Vice entereth.)
To the Barge to![2]
Come they that will go.
Why sirs, I say "When?"
It is high tide,
We may not abide,
Tide tarrieth no man.
If ye will not go,

---

[1] Emphasis added. This is the keystone of repentance doctrine—it is too late to repent when you are dead.
[2] An allusion to the Ship of Fools. The second "to" is an emphatic. It is conceivable that the author wrote
"To the bargetto," or "To the bargette, O!" since *bargette* was an extant word meaning little barge, but
neither conjecture seems preferable to the reading offered here.

Why then tell me so,
Or else come away straight.
If you come not soon
You shall have no room,   10
For we have almost our freight.
There are usurers great,
Who their brains do beat
In devising of guiles,
False dealers also
A thousand and mo,   *more*
Which know store of wiles.
Crafty cutpurses,
Maidens, milknurses,
Wives of the stamp,[3]   20
Who love more than one,
For lying alone
Is ill for the cramp.
Husbands as good
As wigs made of wood
We have there also,
With servants so sure
As packthread most pure
Which men away throw.   30
There are such a sight   *great number*
I cannot recite
The half that we have.
And I of this Barge
Have the greatest charge
Their lives for to save.
Courage Contagious
Or Courage Contrarious
That is my name.[4]
To that which I will   40
My mind to fulfill

[3] Those who have the mark of being good wives—ironic.
[4] "Courage" of course does not mean bravery here, but rather simply brazenness, "nerve." In the next line the original reads "which that."

My manners I frame.
Courage Contagious
When I am outrageous
In working of ill,
And Courage Contrary
When that I do vary
To compass my will.   *achieve*
For as in the bee
For certain we see   50
Sweet honey and sting,
So in my mind,
The better to blind,
Two courages bring.
And as with the sour,
Each day and hour,
The physician inventeth
To mingle as meet
Something that is sweet,
Which his patient contenteth,   60
Even so some while
To color my guile   *disguise*
[I] do give courage to good,
For I, by that mean
Will convey very clean[5]
And not be understood.
Now sir, to show
Whither we do go
Will do very well.
We mean to prevail   70
And therefore we sail
To the Devil of hell.
And though it be far
Yet welcome we are,
When thither we come.
No cheer there is
Whereof we shall miss,

[5] "Conveyance" is crooked brokerage, that is the illegal transfering of goods or property.

But be sure of some.
I Courage do call
Both great and small   80
To the Barge of Sin
Wherein they do wallow
Till hell do them swallow,
That is all they do win.
"When come ye away?"
Thus still I do say,
As loud as I can.
Take time while time is,
Lest that you do miss,
Tide tarrieth no man.   90
With catching and snatching,
Waking and watching,
Running and riding
Let no time escape
That for you doth make.   *is to your advantage*
For tide hath no biding,
But ebbing and flowing,
Coming and going,
It never doth rest.
Therefore when you may,   100
Make no delay
For that is the best.

      ([Enter] HURTING HELP, PAINTED PROFIT, FEIGNED
      FURTHERANCE.)

HELP: By the mass sirs, see where he is.
PROFIT: I told thee that here we should him not miss.
HELP: Good master Courage, most heartily good even.
      (*Salute* COURAGE)
COURAGE: In faith my friends, welcome, all three, by Saint
    Steven.
Jesus good Lord, how do ye fare?
Cover your heads, why are you bare?
And how sirs, now sirs, lead you your lives?
Which of all you three now the best thrives?   110

HELP: Tush man, none of us can do amiss,
  For we do always take time while time is.
  And wherever we go, like counsel we give,
  Telling all men that here they shall not still live.   *forever*
COURAGE: Therein, Hurtful Help, thou dost very well.
  The tide tarrieth no man, thou must always tell.
HELP: Indeed, Hurtful Help, that is my name,
  But I would not that all men should know the same.
  For I am a broker, the truth is so,   *an arranger of crooked deals*
  Wherefore if men in me hurtfulness should know   120
  There are few or none that with me would deal.
  Therefore this word hurtful I never reveal.
  My name I say plain Help to be,
  Wherefore each man for help doth come unto me.
  "Good master Help, help to that or this,
  And of good reward you shall not miss."
PROFIT: And as thou from Help Hurtful dost throw,
  So Painted from Profit I must forgo,
  For if any man know me for profit but painted,   *false*
  Men will but little with me be acquainted.   130
  My master, who a good gentleman is,
  Thinketh me as profitable as he can wish.
  So that plain Profit he thinketh my name,
  And before his face my deeds show the same.
FURTHER: Farewell my masters, for I may hence walk,
  For I see you two will have all the talk.
        (*Feign a going out.*)
COURAGE: What, Feigned Furtherance, are you so coy?
  Will you never leave the tricks of a boy?
  Come again I say, lest I do you fet,   *fetch*
  And say what thou wilt, here shall no man let.   *hinder*   140
FURTHER: Fet me?
COURAGE: Yea, fet thee.
FURTHER: Marry, do what thou dare.
COURAGE: That will I not spare.
        (*Out quickly with his dagger.*)
HELP: Good sir, hold your hand, and bear with his rudeness.

COURAGE: Nay, I cannot nor will not suffer his lewdness.
FURTHER: Tush, a fig for him, let him do what he can.
COURAGE: Alas sir, who are you but a merchant's man?
  Good sir, what you are we know right well,
  Who is your master and where you do dwell.   150
  You profess that your master you do greatly further
  And yet for his goods you would him gladly murther.
FURTHER: If so I do wish, it is long of thee,   *because of*
  For thou thereunto hast encouraged me.
PROFIT: What, husht I say, no more of these words,
  For preaching oft, the preacher disturbs.
  Be friends again as you were at the first,
  Let each man say the best and leave out the worst.
FURTHER: I for my part do thereunto consent.
     (*And shake hands.*)
COURAGE: Then give me thy hand if thou be content.   160
  Now are we friends, as at first we were,
  Therefore thy mind straightway let us hear.
FURTHER: Truly, I mean to do even as do the rets,
  For in mine opinion that is the best,
  And as Hurting Help hath Hurting forgone,
  And Painted Profit is Profit alone,
  So I, Feigned Furtherance, henceforth do mind
  To be Furtherance plain, leaving Feigned behind.
  Other men's furtherance to seek, I will say,
  Yet will I seek my own as much as I may.   170
COURAGE: Else wert thou unwise, yea and a very fool.
  Thou learnedst none otherwise, I trow, in my school.
  I am a schoolmaster for you three most fit,
  Who indued you with courage, instead of great wit.
HELP: To be our master wilt thou take in hand?
  Why, we are as good as thou, thou shalt understand.
COURAGE: Alas, poor knaves, what could you three do,
  If you have not courage belonging thereto?
HELP: And what can courage do without help,
  As much as a kitling or a suckling whelp?   180
COURAGE: And by Hurtful Help what am I the better?

Being holp to a hurt, I am no greater getter.   *helped*
HELP: It is folly with thee thus to contend.
We are as good as thou and so I do end.
COURAGE: Since that by words I can no mastery have,
I will prove what my manhood will do, Sir Knave.
PROFIT: Why, art thou blind, mayest thou not see
That against thee one we are here three?
COURAGE: And what can three do against one,
I having courage and they having none?   190
Therefore Courage will claw you or you go hence.   *ere* (before)
Now defend youselves—I will see your fence.   *fencing, swordsmanship.*
HELP: What, Courage, I say, thy hand now stay.
COURAGE: Will you then consent to that which I say?
HELP: There is no remedy but we must be content,
Therefore I am content to be thine inferior,
And I will from henceforth take thee for superior.[6]
COURAGE: And so will the residue, I trow, also?
PROFIT: If you say aye, sir, we will not say no.
COURAGE: Well, sirs, then I will show you my mind,   200
But first I will describe you, each in his kind.
Thou, Help, art a broker between man and man,
Whereby much deceit thou usest now and then.
Profit is one who by service in sight[6]
Doth cause his master to think him most right.
A profitable servant he thinketh him to be,
Because he is profitable while he doth him see.
And Feigned Furtherance doth feign him to further
His master and others, whom fain he would murther.
Thus in seeking wealth you all do agree,   210
And yet you profess others' friends for to be.
PROFIT: *Ne quisque sapit, qui sibi non sapit.*
This saying I read when as I went to school,
One not wise for himself is but a very fool.[8]
HELP: By my troth, and of that opinion am I,

[6] This is a good and quite pointed demonstration of how *not* to establish a social order.
[7] Original reads "in fight." The Elizabethan long "s" is so close in appearance to "f" that the compositor probably misread the MS. Also there has just been a "fight."
[8] The Latin literally says "Who knows not himself, knows not anything."

And in that opinion I mean for to die.

FURTHER: Tush, why spend you time in speaking of that?

While thereon you talk in vain is your chat,

For who helps not himself before any other,

I count him a fool, if he were my brother, *even if* 220

And as I count him, all people do so.

Therefore cease this talk, and hence let us go,

For some of us may chance to meet with a chiding,

Because that so long from home we are biding.

PROFIT: By St. Anne, I think therein thou say well,

For I know thereof I am like to hear tell.

COURAGE: Why man, a little while breaketh no square.[9]

HELP: Tush, Help hath excuse to color that care.

FURTHER: Yea, but already we have tarried too long.

HELP: Why then, we were best go without a song. 230

FURTHER: Nay, I will tarry to sing though therefore I should die.

PROFIT: My help to singing I did never deny.

COURAGE: Why then, sirs, have at it courageously.

The Song

First Courage causeth minds of men to wish for good or ill,

And some by Courage now and then at Tyburn make their will.[10]

   Help, Profit and Furtherance do feign

     Where Courage doth catch in any man's brain.

Then Help, in hope to have his prey full secretly doth wait,

And as the time doth serve always, he throweth forth his bait.

   Help, Profit etc.

Profit prolongeth not the time to please his painted mind,

He passeth not though master pine, so he his *does not care*

     pleasure find

   Help, Profit etc. 240

And Furtherance, though[11] last of all he came into the rout,

He waiteth not his master's thrall, nor seeks to help him out.

   Help, Profit etc.

Finis

[9] Several instances of this proverb, meaning "it is a trivial matter" are recorded, but not its origin. To "color a care" is to get out of a bad spot by the use of one's wits.

[10] Tyburn is the place in London where criminals were executed.

[11] Original reads "thou last of all."

PROFIT & FURTHER: Now Courage farewell, for we must be
    gone.
HELP: Nay sirs, you two shall not go alone
  For I do mean to bear you company,
  And so shall we be even a whole trinity.   250
  Therefore Courage, adieu.
    (*They three go out.*)
COURAGE: Sir, here was a trinity in a witness.   *indeed*
  A man might have shaped three knaves by their likeness.
  A trinity much like to the trinity of late
  Where goodwife Gull broke her goodman's pate.   *husband's*
  In came her man to make up the number,
  Who had his nose shod with the
      steal of a scummer[12]   *handle of a ladle*
  But in fine these three began to agree,   *finally*
  And knit themselves up in one trinity.
  And after, they loved like brother and brother,   260
  For very love they did kill one another.
  And then they were buried, I do well remember
  In Stawtons-straw-hat, 7 mile from December,[13]
  Where they had not lain the space of a day
  But four of those three were thence run away.
  The Constable came, with a back on his bill,
  And because they were gone he did them kill.
  I, Courage, so cleft their cushions asunder   *buttocks?*
  To see how they bled it made me to wonder.
  I myself was smitten twice to the ground,   270
  I was very sore hurt, but I had not a wound.
  I busked myself as though fight I would[14]   *prepared*
  And took me to my legs as fast as I could.
  And so with much pain hither I did come,
  But husht sirs, I say, no mo words, but mum.

---

[12] The original reads "scumber," which rhymes with "number." "Scumber" is not a recorded variant of "scummer," but it happens to mean "dung," so perhaps the scatological pun and the forced rhyme were intended.

[13] The morality Vices are given to breaking out into outright nonsense occasionally. This nice instance includes the parody of English place-names, a joke also found in *Piers Plowman*.

[14] Original reads "buskeled." Perhaps a combined word with "buckled" was intended.

(GREEDINESS *enter*.)

GREED: Tush, talk not of that, for in vain you do prate,
For there are none but fools that wealthiness do hate.

COURAGE: What, Greediness I say, why what is the matter?
"Master Wealthiness" I would say, whereon do you clatter?

GREED: What, old friend Courage, art thou so near hand?   280
Marry, I will show thee how the matter doth stand.
As I walked along, through by the street,
By such ways as mine assays did lie,
It was my chance with a preacher to meet,
Whose company to have I did not deny.
And as we two together did walk,
Amongst other communication we had
The Preacher broke out with reproachable talk,
Saying that we citizens were all too bad;
Some of us, he sayeth, are greedy-guts all   290
And evil members of a commonwealth.
He sayeth we care not whom we bring to thrall,
Neither have we regard unto our souls' health.
His talk, I confess, my conscience did nip,
Wherefore no longer I would him abide,
But suddenly I gave him the slip
And crossed the way to the other side.
So alone I let Master Preacher walk
And here by chance I stumbled in.

COURAGE: And art thou so foolish for any such talk   300
To cease or stay thy wealth for to win?

GREED: Sirra, he cried out of excessive gain,[15]
Saying when any of our wares have need
Then do we hoist them up, to their pain,
And commonly make them pay for their speed.

COURAGE: I perceive that fellow was hot of the spirit,
He would not have you take time while time is;
If ye follow his counsel he will beggar you quite.
But what answer didst thou give him to this?

---

[15] Note that the attack here is not on usurers, but on the new entrepreneurial business men. See also the last scene of the play on this problem.

GREED: Why thou knowest my quality is such   310
  That by contrary talk I use no man to blame,
  For although often my doings they touch,
  Yet my talk always to the time I frame.
  When he said excessive gainers were ill,
  I said for them it was a shame,
  And in all things else I pleased his will,
  And so I feigned myself without blame.

COURAGE: Thou dost wisely therein, I commend thee
     therefore,
  For whatever thou think, yet say as they do,
  So shalt thou have their favors evermore   320
  And that way no blame thou shalt come unto.

GREED: Yea, but surely his words did my conscience prick,
  Of me he did so unhappily guess,   *unluckily*
  I promise thee he touched me unto the quick
  For that in gaining I used excess.
  My conscience doth tell me I have done amiss
  And of long time I have gone astray,
  And a thousand witnesses the conscience is,
  As Salust in most plain words doth say.[16]

COURAGE: Why, doltish patch, art thou so unwise   330
  To quail for the saying of such a knave?
  Thou knowest all the world will thee despise,
  And a-begging thou mayest go if that nought thou have.
  And how shalt thou have aught
  If thy gain be not great?
  Consider this well in thy mind,
  Remember thy house, and thy wife, that pet,   *pet, pretty girl*
  Must still be kept in their costly kind;
  Therefore take the time while the time doth serve.
  Tide tarrieth no man, this thou dost know,   340
  If thy goods decay then mayest thou starve—   *die*
  So doing thou seekest thine own overthrow.

GREED: Indeed, as thou sayest, it does me behoove

---

[16] Here as everywhere in the moralities (see *All for Money*, for instance) ideas that are common enough to be cliches are attributed to the ancient authorities perhaps as much out of convenience as out of accuracy.

Not so rashly to lay my gaining aside,
Lest to myself a fool I do prove
By shooting from my profit too wide.   *departing too far*
I consider my wealth is now at good stay,
Which I would be loath should be impaired,
For once rich and after in decay
Is a miserable thing, as Hyemes hath declared.[17]   350
Therefore I mean thy counsel to take,
Lest of that misery I know the smart.
Then is it too late any moan to make,
Or from such foolishness to revert.
Therefore Courage, adieu unto thee,
For it behooveth me hence to depart.

COURAGE: Adieu, Wealthiness till again we see,
Adieu, great Greediness, with all my heart.

> [Exit GREEDINESS]

Hath not Courage contagious now showed his kind,   *nature*
By encouraging Greediness unto evil,   360
Which late was drawing to a better mind
And now again doth follow the Devil.

> (*Enter* HELP *and* NO GOOD NEIGHBORHOOD)

HELP: Lo thee Neighborhood, where Courage doth stand.

COURAGE: What, No Good Neighborhood, give me thy hand.

NEIGHBOR: Those two first syllables might be put out
And then thou hittest my name without doubt.

COURAGE: Why, is not No Good Neighborhood thy name?

NEIGHBOR: Put away No Good and see how it will frame,
For if thou do put away No Good,
There resteth no more by Neighborhood.   370

COURAGE: Then is it Neighborhood, neither good nor bad.
Nay, though we leave the first, it is good the next we had.
For leaving out No, put Good to the rest,
Then is it Good Neighborhood, thus I think is best.

NEIGHBOR: Nay, I will have them both two left out,

---

[17] "Hyemes" is something of a mystery. We are indebted to Professor J. L. Murphy of the University of Colorado for the suggestion that it is "James," that is, the author of the New Testament letter. In fact, James 5, 1–6 says the same thing that "Hyemes" says, but not in the same words.

Because of my name men should stand in doubt.
For if No Good Neighborhood I be named,
Then of all men I shall be blamed.
And if that Good to Neighborhood I have,
Men will say I do it praise to crave.   380
So I will leave out both No and Good,
And will be indifferent sole Neighborhood.

COURAGE: Then Neighborhood be it, if so it shall be,
And Neighborhood, what is thy errand to me?

NEIGHBOR: Sir, my coming is for occasions two:
The first is for your counsel, what were best to do
In a matter which I have lately begun,
If I shall proceed or else leave it undone;
The second is, if I shall proceed
That you will stand my friend if I need.   390

COURAGE: Assure thyself thereof without doubt.
Therefore show me the matter thou goest about.

NEIGHBOR: I thank you sir, even with all my heart,
And I trust also that Help will do his part.

HELP: Doubt not but that I to thee will be cleaving,
Therefore proceed and show him thy meaning.

NEIGHBOR: Then sir, this is the matter, if it shall please you
      give ear:
I have a neighbor who dwelleth to me somewhat near,
Who hath a tenement commodious and feat,   *elegant*
To which tenement I bear a love very great.[18]   400
This man, my neighbor, as far as I can learn,
Hath in his tenement but a short term,
Four or five years or thereabout,
Which term, you know, will soon be worn out.
Now sir, might I in reversion a lease thereof have,
I would give the Landlord even what he would crave.

COURAGE: And who is the Landlord, thereof can you tell?

NEIGHBOR: Master Greediness, a man whom you know right
      well.

---

[18] Tenement does not have the modern meaning here. As the Latin origin of the word suggests, it simply
means a "holding" of property.

He is one which never did money hate.

COURAGE: Why then, speak in time, lest thou be too late. 410
The tide tarrieth no man, the proverb hath said;
Therefore see no time herein be delayed.
Master Help here shall be to thee a stay,
For with Master Greediness he beareth great sway.

HELP: I will do for him what lieth in me.

NEIGHBOR: And then to your pains I will gladly see.

COURAGE: Doubt not then but thou shalt have thy mind.

NEIGHBOR: As you say, I wish that I may it find,
But I doubt that of my purpose I shall miss, *fear*
By reason of one thing, and that is this: 420
My foresaid neighbor which now holdeth the same
Hath been there a long dweller of good name and fame,
And well he is beloved both of young and old,
Wherefore not only the neighbors with him will hold
But also the Landlord, I am in great doubt,
Will be therefore unwilling to put him out,
And I but a stranger among them, God wote. *knows*

HELP: Marry sir, it is much the better for that,
For if thou wert more strange and born out of land
Thou shouldst sooner have it, I dare take in hand, *I'd swear it* 430
For among us now such is our country zeal
That we love best with strangers to deal. *foreigners*
To sell a lease dear, whosoever that will,
At the French or Dutch Church let him set up his
bill *advertisement*
And he shall have chapmen, I warrant you, good
store. *bargainers/many*
Look what an Englishman bids, they will give as much more.
We brokers of strangers well know the gain,
By them we have good reward of our pain.
Therefore though thou be strange the matter is not great,
For thy money is English, which must work the feat. 440

NEIGHBOR: Indeed my money as a neighbor will agree
With any man wheresoever it be.
And I myself would be a neighbor too,

And therefore the rather I do that I do,   *that which*
For if it were not to be a neighbor by them
I wisse I would not take a house so neigh them.
HELP: I dare say each man would be glad at his heart
To have all his neighbors such as thou art.
What matter is it if thou thyself be sped   *advanced*
Though thou take thy neighbors house over his head?   450
COURAGE: Tush, that is no harm, but rather it is good,
For he doth it only for pure neighborhood.
See, yonder cometh one, if thou canst make him thy friend,
Then mayest thou shortly bring thy purpose to end.
          (FURTHERANCE *entereth.*)
FURTHER: Now Master Courage, how do you fare?[19]
COURAGE: ----glad---that you so merry are.
Furtherance-----pleasure a friend of mine.
FURTHER: ------I am ready at each tide and time
To do for him what in me doth lie.
Therefore let me know your mind by and by.   460
COURAGE: Sirra, of thy master a lease he would have,
And therein thy friendship it is he doth crave.
NEIGHBOR: Sir, if that herein my friend you will stand
I will give you therefore even what you will demand.
FURTHER: .Then Neighborhood thou shalt shortly see
That I can do somewhat between my master and thee.
Thou couldst never speak better to speed,
For of money now he standeth in need.
To pay for a purchase of certain land
Which needs he must discharge out of hand.   *at once* 470
Therefore this time for thee well doth fall
If that thou have money to tempt him withal.
NEIGHBOR: Tush man, for money I will not spare.
FURTHER: Then needest thou no whit for to care,
And if thou take pain now to walk home
There shalt thou find him sitting alone.
COURAGE: Cock's passion man, hie thee away,   *By God's passion*

---

[19] The following passage is smeared in the original. The sense is clear enough so that there is no real need to supply conjectural readings.

Thou knowest the tide for no man will stay.

NEIGHBOR: Why sir, but will you not walk with us thither?

FURTHER: No, do Help and you go before together,   480
  And I warrant you I will not long be behind you,
  For though I be absent, yet will I mind you.

NEIGHBOR: Then sir, adieu till we meet again,
  Doubt not but I will consider your pain.
  Come Help, shall we go.

HELP: It is time, I trow.
    (*Exeunt.*)

FURTHER: Ah sir, this gear doth trimly fall out.   *business*
  I know this lease which he goeth about;
  Wherefore I will work so on both the sides
  That of both parties I will obtain bribes.   490
  I will show the old tenant how one goeth about
  To take his land and to thrust him out,
  Wherefore he will largely grease me in the hand
  Because his friend therein I shall stand.
  The other here did promise me plain
  That he would reward me for my pain.
  Therefore Courage, farewell unto thee.   [*Exit*]

COURAGE: Farewell Furtherance, my gentle friend,
  A man may seek Hell and such two not find.   *search through*
  I mean a friend so worthy to trust   500
  And a neighbor that is so honest and just.
  Of honesty, I trow, he is meetly well sped
  Who will take his neighbor's house over his head.
  I think there is no man within this place
  But he would gladly such neighbors embrace.
  Where two such neighbors die out of one town
  The Devil shall be sure to have one black gown.
  As well he is worthy, if I might be judge,
  For in their affairs he daily doth trudge.
  Good counsel he gives them, both morning and evening,   510
  What means they shall work to their neighbor's grieving.
  He teacheth them how to pill and to poll,   *pluck and shave* (i.e. cheat)
  In hope, after death, to have body and soul.

Tush, what mean I thus of soul for to speak?
In vain with such talk my brains I do break.
For soul there is none when the body is dead—
In such kind of doctrine my scholars I lead.
Therefore, say I, take time while time is,
For after this life there is nothing but bliss.
There is no soul any pain to abide,   520
The teachers contrary from truth are   *those who teach the contrary*
    far wide.[20]
      (WILLING-TO-WIN-WORSHIP *enter* COURTIER-LIKE.)
COURTIER: Oh, so my heart is filled with doubt
    Which way I may work, my worship to win.
    Shall I leave of Courtiers so jolly a rout,   *group, crowd*
    And eke of Ladies a company so trim,   *also*
    And shall I home to my cottage rude
    There to live like a country clown?
    Truly I know not which way to conclude
    To get myself worship and renown.
    To win worship I would be right glad,   530
    Therefore Willing-to-Win-Worship is my name.
    In the country there is none such to be had,
    And the Court doth ask great cost for the same,
    So that what I shall do I know not yet.
    I consider it is toward a good time,
    Wherein triumphing is used, as is most fit,[21]   *parading*
    And where Courtiers must show themselves,   *all dressed up*
      brave and fine,
    But this I conclude, as forced I am
    The Court for to leave and homeward to pack.
    For where is money? Here is the man   540
    If man he may be, that money doth lack.
COURAGE: Sir, are you so foolish the court for to leave
    When the time is that worship you should win?

---

[20] This seems to be an expression either of materialism or else of the heresy of "mortalism," which holds that the soul dies with the body.

[21] The records collected in the Harbage-Schoenbaum *Annals of the English Drama* (London, 1964) abound in all kinds of court entertainments. The "triumph" is actually a sort of elaborate, often allegorical, procession; sometimes a *tableau vivant* that moves on a "float."

For in times of triumphing we always perceive
The Courtier's worship doth first begin.
Therefore do you from such foolishness stray,
And Fortune may chance give you as you wish.

COURTIER: But the wheels of Fortune, as Socrates doth say,
Are like the snares wherewith men take fish.
And in another place Plautus doth shew   550
A saying in Latin, and that is this:
Festo die si quid prodigeris,
Profesto egere liceat nisi peperceris.
If on the holiday wasting thou do use
On the work day thou mayest beg unless well thou get.[22]
So in triumphing like effect ensues
That next after waste indigence is set.

COURAGE: Then Periander's words you account least
Who unto honor an encourager is.
Honor (sayeth he) *Immortalis est.*   560
Now sir, I pray you, how like you this?

COURTIER: Those words to be true I must need confess,
For honor indeed is an immortal fame
And now is the time the same to possess,
But I have not wherewith to achieve the same.
For money is he that the man must deck
And though I have attire both costly and gay,
Yet unless it be new I shall have but a geck.   *be scorned*
Therefore much better for me [to] be away.

COURAGE: Tush man, for money be thou not sad.   570
You Courtiers I know have jewels good store,
And money for jewels will always be had.
Therefore for that matter care thou no more.

COURTIER: Yea, but how it is had I partly do know,
And what excessive interest is paid.
Therefore you may say the more is my woe.
Would God that I had it never assayed.

COURAGE: Well, whatever it cost it must needs be had.
Therefore withstand not thy fortunate chance,

[22] The original has *pepereris*. The source of the quote is *Aulularia*, II, viii, 10.

For I will count thee fool, worse than mad,   580
If thou wilt not spend money thyself to advance.
Now is the time of hap, good or ill—   *luck*
Venture it therefore, while it is hot,
For the tide will not tarry for any man's will.
Never shalt thou speed if now thou speed not.

COURTIER: Truly this talk doth encourage me so much
That to see the Court again I do pretend.   *aspire*
But I pray thee, dost thou know any such
As use, upon gages, money to lend?   *pledges*

COURAGE: Why man, for that matter you need not to doubt;   590
Of such men there are enough everywhere.
But see how luckily it doth fall out!
See yonder two friends of mine do appear.
There is a broker between man and man,
Whenas any bargains they have in hand.
The other a merchant's man now and then
In borrowing money thy friends they may stand.

    (HELP *and* FURTHERANCE *enter.*)

HELP: So are we indeed, and what of that?
Who is it that with us anything would have?

COURTIER: Even I, a gentleman whom money do lack,   600
And therein your friendship would gladly crave.

HELP: Therein we can help you if your pleasure it be,
And will do, or else we were greatly to blame,
Provided always that to our pains you do see
And also put in a good pawn for the same.

COURTIER: A pawn sufficient I will therefore lay,
And also your pains I will recompence well,
But I must needs have it out of the way   *quickly*
Although my lands therefore I do sell.

HELP: You shall have it, sir, as soon as you will,   610
And therein you shall be friendly used,
For in friendly using this fellow hath skill.

    (*pointing to* FURTHERANCE.)

Therefore his counsel must not be refused.
He is servant unto a merchant man

Who is partly ruled after his mind.

COURTIER: Indeed, as you say, help me he can.
  I doubt not but his friendship I shall find.
  Doubt you not sir but in pleasuring me
  I will recompense your pains with the most.

FURTHER: What I can do for you soon you shall see; 620
  It is but folly thereof to boast.

COURTIER: Well then, it is time that hence we were packing,
  For fain an end thereof I would know.

HELP: Why sir, no diligence in us shall be lacking.
  For we are ready, if that you be so.

COURTIER: Why then, that we go I think it were best.
  Think you your master is now at home?

FURTHER: Yea, I know well at home he doth rest,
  And I guess that now he is sitting alone;
  Therefore no longer here let us stay. 630

COURTIER: Then sir, adieu, and I will lead the way.
      (*Speaking to* COURAGE *& goeth out with* FURTHERANCE *&*
      HELP.)

COURAGE: Now may you see how Courage can work,
  And how he can encourage both to good and bad.
  The merchant is encouraged in greediness to lurk,
  And the Courtier to win worship by Courage is glad.
  The one is good, no man will deny,
  I mean courage to win worship and fame;
  So that the other is ill, all men will say.
  That is courage to greediness which getteth ill name.
  Thus may you see Courage contagious 640
  And eke contrarious—both in me do rest,
  For I, of kind, am always various *by nature*
  And change as to my mind seemeth best.
  Between man and wife sometimes I do show
  Both my kindness, when my pleasure it is.
  The goodwife giveth her husband a blow
  And he for reward doth give her a kiss.
  The goodwife, by Courage, is hardy and stout, *strong*
  The goodman, contrary, is patient and meek,

And suffreth himself to be called lout,   650
Yea, and worse misused, thrice in a week.
How say you, good wives, is it not so?
I warrant you, not one that can say nay,
Whereby all men here may right well know
That all this is true which I do say.
But yet Courage tells you not all that he knows,
For then he must tell of each wife the name,
Which is no great matter, the best are but shrews,
But I will not say so, for fear I have blame.
     (GREEDINESS *enter*.)

GREEDINESS: Now Courage, I say, what news
     in the coast?   *from your side* 660
What good tidings abroad dost thou hear?

COURAGE: Why, what dost thou here? hie thee home
     in post,   *quickly*
For I sent home a Gentleman to seek for thee there.

GREEDINESS: And what is the matter that with me he would
     have?

COURAGE: He must borrow some money his worship to save.

GREEDINESS: Tush then, to tarry he will be glad
If that he come any money to borrow.

COURAGE: Yea, but take the time while it is to be had,
And defer not thy profit until tomorrow.
This Gentleman is a Courtier brave,   670
And now in need of money doth stand;
Therefore thine own asking of him thou mayest have,
So that thou wilt pleasure him out of hand.   *at once*

GREEDINESS: And is he a Courtier and standeth in need?
This to my purpose doth rightly fall,
For the needy Courtiers my coffers do feed,
And I warrant thee that pinch him I shall.
For since I know his need to be such
That money he must needs occupy,   *procure*
I know I cannot ask him too much   680
If I his mind will satisfy.
Therefore now Courage, to thee adieu.

(*Feign a going out.*)

COURAGE: Nay soft, yet one word with you.
You told me not yet how you did agree
With No Good Neighborhood, that goodman growt.   *blockhead*
GREEDINESS: Marry, sir, he hath gone thorough
        with me   *closed the deal*
And the old tenant he will thrust out.
But I with that matter have nought to do;
Let them two now for that agree—.
If known I should never have come unto   690
So much as therefore he hath paid to me.
Therefore I might be counted mad
If I to his proffer would not have tended.
This profitable lesson which of thee I had,
The tide tarrieth no man, was not unremembered.
        (PROFIT *entereth.*)
PROFIT: God speed sir, I pray you show me if you can,
Did you not Master Wealthiness hereabout see?
COURAGE: Cock's passion, this is the Gentleman's man   *servant*
        (*Speaking to* GREEDINESS)
Which at home doth tarry for thee.
        (*Turning to* PROFIT.)
Sir, Wealthiness is not hence far away.   700
GREEDINESS: I am he, sir. What would you of me require?
PROFIT: My Master at home for your worship doth stay,
And to speak with you he doth greatly desire,
If it be your pleasure home to repair;
Or it ye will, he shall hither come.
Your masterhip's pleasure therefore declare
And I know incontinent it shall be done.   *immediately*
GREEDINESS: Nay, I mean homeward to hie,
For that I suppose to be the best,
And by all the means that in me doth lie   710
I will fulfill your master's request.
PROFIT: I trust also you will consider my pain.
Thereby I trust you shall not lose,
For perchance I may prefer your gain

By means which with my master I do use.

GREEDINESS: As I find thee ready in furthering of me,
So doubt thou not but thou shalt find
Me even as ready in pleasuring of thee.
A word is enough, thou knowest my mind.
Therefore hence let is now take the way.   720

PROFIT: My master thinketh us long, I dare say.
    (*Exeunt.*)

COURAGE: I warrant you I will not be long behind.
I know no cause why here I should stay.
A company of my scholars I know where to find,
Therefore toward them I will take the way.
    (*Exit.*)[23]

  (*The* TENANT TORMENTED *entereth.*)

TENANT: Whither shall I go, or which way shall I take
To find a Christian, constant and just?
Each man himself a Christian would make,   *call himself*
Yet few or none that a man may trust,
But for the most part feigned, inclined to lust,   730
As to insatiable covetousness most abhominable,[24]
Or some other vice most vile and detestable.
It is well known what rigor doth reign
In that cruel tiger, my landlord Greediness,
Who in my house would not let me remain
But hath thrust me out, with spiteful speediness,
Having no respect to my naked neediness,
But altogether regarding his gain
Hath bereaved my living from me, to my pain.   *snatched*
What neighborhood is, may also be seen;   740
My neighbour supposed, is my deadly foe.
What cruel chance like to mine hath been?
Both my house and living I must now forgo.
What neighbor is he that hath served me so?
Thus cruelly to take my house over my head,

---

[23] Original reads "Exiunt." This repeated error and the garbled state of some of the quotes suggests that, in contrast to *All for Money*, the author is unsure of his Latin.

[24] The spelling of the original is retained because the author, like other Elizabethans, thought the etymology was *ab homine*, i.e. that which is away from, or foreign to man.

Wherein these forty years I have been harbored and fed,
And now being aged must thus be thrust out
With mine impotent wife, charge and family.   *servants*
Now how I shall live I stand in great doubt,
Leading and ending my life in misery.   750
But better do so, than as they live, by thievery,
Catching and snatching all that ever they can,
Because that (say they) [the] tide tarrieth no man.
But God grant that they, in following that tide
Lose not the tide of God's mercy and grace.[25]
I doubt that from them alway it will slide   *I fear*
If they still pursue the contrary race,
As daily they do, God's laws to deface
To their own soul's hurt and to the neighbor's damage,
Still following the instructions of cursed Courage.   760
I see whom I seek is not here to be found,
I mean Christianity, constant and just.
I doubt that in bondage he lieth fast bound,[26]
Or else he is dead and lieth buried in dust.
But if he be living to find him I trust,
Therefore till I find him I will nowhere stay,
Neither in seeking of him will I make delay.
          [*Exit*]
     (*The maid* WILLFUL WANTON *enter.*)
WANTON: Of all misfortunes mine is the worst,
     Truly I think I was accursed
     When I was an infant not fully nursed.   770
     Alas, for grief my heart it will burst!
     I daily see women as young as I
     Which in white caps our door do go by.   [sign of wifehood]
     I am as able as they with a man to lie,
     Yet my mother doth still my wedding deny.
     She saith for wedding that I am unfit,
     Maids of fourteen years, she saith, hath no wit,

---

[25] He is not suggesting that God's mercy ebbs and flows. "Tide" also means "time."
[26] There may be in this a reminiscence of an earlier piece of dramatized moral allegory—the stocks scene in *Youth*.

And so every day she saith I shall tarry yet,
That would God I were put quick in the pit.   *buried alive*
God wot, we maids abide such misery,   780
And always kept in from having liberty.
Of evil tongues we walk in jeopardy,
Most people are now so full of jealousy
If a young man a maid do but kiss
Now, (say the people) you may see what she is.
Where, if I were a wife, nothing I should miss,
But live like a Lady, in all joyful bliss.
I right well do know the peoples' spite
Because that to be pleasant I have delight.
Therefore grace they say I am, quite,   790
And a Willfull Wanton my name they do write.[27]
Yet I trust in God once to see the day
That to recompense their spite I may;
For if ever I be married and bear any sway,
Then I know what I have to say.
Therefore good God, make me shortly a wife,
Or else shortly take away my life.
               [*Enter* COURAGE.]
COURAGE: Alas, pretty Pernel,[28] you may soon end this strife;
   Young men fit for husbands in this town are rife,
   And your mother's ill will you may soon prevent   800
   If you follow my counsel and intent.
WANTON: Oh, but if my mother would thereto consent,
   To be married this night I would be content.
COURAGE: But consent she or not, yet it is for thee
   Unto thine own preferment to see.
   Dost thou with any young man so agree
   That he would consent thy husband to be.
WANTON: Diverse there are who gladly would have me,
   And being their wife would trimly bebrave me;   *dress me up*
   From all wrong they would defend and save me.   810
   Tush, enough there are which to wife do crave me.

[27] Original reads "do wright."
[28] Pernel is a stock name for a wanton woman.

COURAGE: Then defer no time, if that thou be wise,
For now to preferment thou art like to arise.
The tide tarrieth no man, else the proverb lies.
In delaying comes harms, thou seest with thine eyes.
But by marriage all thy grief shall be eased
And thy joys shall manifold ways be increased.

WANTON: But alas, my mother will so be displeased
That I know her wrath will never be appeased.

COURAGE: And wilt thou, for displeasing of her,   820
Thine own preferment and fortune defer?
Now art thou youthful, thyself to prefer,
And thy youthful beauty men's hearts may stir;[29]
But youthful beauty will not always last;
The tide tarrieth no man, but soon it is past.
Therefore to wedding see thou make haste,
For now much time thou dost lose in waste.

WANTON: Oh what comfortable words are these!
Truly your talk doth me greatly please.
I will not stint but speak out always,   830
Until that I have found some ease.
I care not what my mother do say,
This matter I will no longer delay,
But a husband I will have, out of the way,
And then may I boldly dally and play.
No man dare me then once to control,
Lest my husband chance for to scowl.
If any man use to entreat me foul,
My husband will lay him over the nowl.   *hit him on the head*
It doth me good to think of the bliss   840
Which between newly married couples is.
To see their dalliance, sometimes iwis,
It setteth my teeth on edge, by Gisse.
Truly I would gladly give my best frock
And all things else, unto my smock,
To be married in the morning by 6 of the clock.
I beshrew my heart if that I do mock.

[29] Note that the part is being played by a boy or young man.

Sir you will not believe how I long
To be one of the wedded throng.
Methinks it lieth in no tongue   850
To show the joys that is them among.
COURAGE: It passeth joy which they embrace,
They take their pleasure in every place,
Like angels they do run their race
In passing bliss and great solace.
WANTON;   Well sir, I will no longer tarry,
But some man, out of hand, will marry.
Although from my mother's mind I vary,
Yet your words in mind I carry.
Therefore good sir, to you adieu,   860
Until again I meet with you.
If I speed well, a good coat new
To your part may chance ensue.
          (*Exit.*)[30]
COURAGE: Alas Willful Wanton, my pretty pet,
My words have set her in such a heat,
Now toward wedding her love is so great
That scarce she can either drink or eat.[31]
Now I, Courage, in her do begin,
So that for her mother she cares not a pin.
Now all her mind is a husband to win,   870
To be unwedded she thinketh a sin.
How say you, my virgins every one,
Is it not a sin to lie alone?
When 12 years of age is gone
I dare say you think so every one.
          (HELP *entereth.*)
HELP: Nay now, let him shift for himself if he will,
Since I am paid the thing I did seek.
Alas, good Gentleman, he is served but ill,
In faith, he is in now by the week.   *making weekly payments*

---

[30] Original reads "Exiunt."
[31] Original reads "neither ... nor," another typical Elizabethan double negative, which we emend for clarity.

He hath naught but that for which he hath paid. 880
The loan of his money he hath dearly bought.
I warrant you it might be boldly said,
His cards being told, he hath won right nought.

COURAGE: And how so, Help? Is he so pinched, I say?
By my troth, that is a sport for to hear.

HELP: Sirra, he stands bound forty pounds to pay,
But little more than thirty away he did bear;
For what with the merchant's duty for loan,
Item: for writing, unto the scribe—
The third part into my pouch is gone, *one third* 890
And the merchant's man hath not lost his bribe.
So that, amongst us four almost ten pounds
Is clearly dispersed and spent.
The Gentleman sweareth, "Heart, blood and wounds!"
Repenting that after thy counsel he went.

COURAGE: Yea, but sirs, my part is the least,
Who am the Captain of all this rout. *gang*

HELP: Tush man, for that matter set thy heart at rest,
For that which we have, thou shalt not be without
But sirra, seest thou not who doth yonder appear? 900
By my troth, methinks two knaves they are.

(PROFIT *and* FURTHERANCE, *enter together.*)

[FURTHER:][32] Indeed, whosoever unto thee is near,
For a knave he needeth not to seek far.

COURAGE: Sirs, I will tell troth to make you agree—
By Gisse, I think you are knaves all three.

[HELP:]? Indeed, three we are, we are no less,
And you are the fourth to make up the mess.[33]

[COURAGE:]? Well, for that matter we will not greatly strive,
But sirs, what wind now did you hither drive?

[FURTHER:]? In faith, to show thee what luck we have had 910
By Willing-to-Win-Worship, that lusty lad.
To make talk thereof is now no time,

---

[32] The speech tags on this leaf of the original are cropped. From line 902 to l. 910 we assign the speeches on the basis of the only letter showing, the final "r" of Furtherance at l. 902.

[33] With four participants a meal becomes a "mess" in the sense in which the military still uses the term.

But if thou wilt go with us we will give thee the wine.

PROFIT: And as my Master pleased you two, and the scribe,
So of Greediness the merchant I had a bribe,
So that none of us went vacant away
But of one of the parties had honestly our pay.

HELP: Yea, but of them both I had my bribes!
My masters, the broker can play of both sides.
He is almost paid as well for his trotting   920
As is the scribe for his writing or blotting.
Yea, and yet both parties are not content,
For I dare say the gentleman his bargain doth repent.

FURTHER: Marry sir, can you blame him that so hath been
         wrung?
He may say he hath paid to hear a fair tongue,[34]
And now without his man he is gone;
His man gives him leave for to walk alone.

PROFIT: Let me alone, I warrant thee some   *leave it to me*
         excuse I will have,
And the worst fall I know I shall be called knave.
And yet sirs, after him I will hie,   930
And by the way I will invent some lie.

COURAGE: Nay soft, Profit, you must not go so.
You must help to sing a part or you go.   *ere* (before)

PROFIT: So it be short, I am well content.

COURAGE: And all the residue thereto do consent.

The Song

We have great gain, with little pain,
And lightly spend it too:[35]
We do not toil, nor yet we moil   *strive*
As other poor folks do.
We are winners all three   940
And so will we be
Wherever that we come, O![36]
For we know how

---

[34] This apparently is a colloquialism meaning "cheated."
[35] Original reads "spend it to."
[36] Original reads "come, a."

To bend and bow
And what is to be done, O!
To kneel and to crouch, to fill the pouch,
We are full glad and fain:
We ever still, even at our will,
Are getters of great gain.
  We are winners, etc.   950
  It is our will to poll and pill
All such as do us trust:
We bear in hand, good friends to stand,   *cheat*
Though we be most unjust.
  We be winners, etc.
  Full far abouts we know the routes
Of them that riches had;
Whom through deceit, as fish to bait
We made their thrift forth gad   *their wealth rush away*
  We are winners, etc.   960

Finis

COURAGE: Now, Cole Profit, in faith   [nickname for crooked dice player]
    gramercy for thy song.
PROFIT: Much good do it thee, but I am afeared I tarry too long.
    Therefore friends, adieu, for I will be gone.
HELP: Nay, soft, Profit, leave us not behind,
    For hence to depart we also do mind.
COURAGE: Then three knaves on a cluster get you together.
    Needs knaves you must go, for so you came together.
PROFIT: But here we found thee, a knave most of all,
    And so we leave thee, as thou dost us call.
    [*Exeunt*]
COURAGE: Now so is the purpose, and this is the case,   970
    Good cousin Cutpurse, if you be in place   *in the audience*
    I beseech you now your business to ply.
    I warrant thee, I, no man shall thee espy.
    If they do, it is but an hour's hanging,
    But such a purse thou mayst catch, worth a year's spending.
    I warrant thee, encouraging thou shalt not lack.
    Come hither, let me clap thee in the back,

And if thou wilt now follow my request,
At Tyburn I may chance clap thee on the breast,
So that of clapping thou shalt have store;[37]   980
Here clapping behind and at Tyburn before.
But cousin Cutpurse, if aught thou do get,
I pray thee let me have part of thy cheat.
I mean not of thy hanging fare
But of thy purse, and filched share.
Well sirs, it is time that hence I do pack me,
For I am afraid that some men do lack me,
For some are perhaps about some good deed
And for lack of courage they dare not proceed.

> (*Exit.*)[38]
> (*The* Courtier *entereth.*)

Courtier: As with the poison which is most delectable   990
The heart of man is soonest infected,
So the foe most hurteth who seemeth most amiable,
And of all wise men is to be detected.
At this time this saying I have elected,
For that they which friendship to me professed
Instead thereof, my hurt have addressed.
They promised me my friends for to stand,
And to help me to that which I did crave,
Until that I had obligated my land,
And then was I subject to every knave;   1000
The merchant for loan, the broker for his pain,
And the scribe for writing, each man had a gain.
Nimbula pluvia imbrem parit,
A mizzling shower engendreth great wet,
Which saying *officium proverbiae non terit,*[39]
Many a little maketh a great.

---

[37] The reference to clapping on the breast at Tyburn remains obscure.
[38] Original reads "Exiunt."
[39] Original reads *officium proverbia non tarit. Tarit* is nonexistent. Professor Ogilvy (see note 55) suggests *terit,* which, with the correction of *proverbia* to the genitive, makes the phrase mean that the preceding proverb about rain "does not serve the office, or role, of a proverb." If this is correct, we must then suppose that the Courtier mis-speaks and it is up to the audience to enjoy his error. Another possibility is that *non tarit* is a misreading from the MS for *nuntiaret,* "announces." *Nimbula* is emended from the original *ninubula.*

So every of them by me wrought his feat,
And every of these bribes, being cast to account,
To a good portion I feel do amount.
But what villainy is there in such,   1010
Who, knowing a man of their help to have need,
Will encroach upon him so unreasonable much,
Their own greedy desires to feed?
Juvenal, I remember, doth teach them indeed,
Whose words are these, both open and plain:
The vicious man only seeketh his own gain.
Yea, twice vicious may they be named
Who do avarice so much embrace.
But what is their answer, when they are blamed?
Say they, we have here but a little space,   1020
Therefore we have need to be getting, apace;
Wherefore should we gaining lay away?
The tide tarrieth no man, this is all they can say.
     (COURAGE *entereth.*)
COURAGE: And as soon as she had supped up the broth,
The ladle she laid upon his face,
Woman, quoth she, get thee out of this place.
     (*And smiteth the gentleman.*)
COURTIER: Why, friend, art thou not well in thy wit?
Wherefore smitest thou me in such sort?
COURAGE: Jesus, gentleman, are you here yet?
I thought long or this you had been at the Court,   1030
Therefore you must pardon mine offence
For I little thought it had been you.
COURTIER: Thy company is so good I will get me hence,
Therefore, cursed Courage, adieu.
COURAGE: And, if faith, will you needs be gone?
What, man, you might tarry awhile.
COURTIER: In thy company I have tarried too long,
For I perceive thou art full of guile.
COURAGE: Farewell frost, will you needs be gone?
Adieu, since that you will needs away   1040
In faith, this sport is trimsy done,
                             pleasant

That I can thus a gentleman fray.

      (GREEDINESS *and* HELP *enter together.*)

GREED: Oh Help, might I once see that day

  Tush, I would not care who I did wrong.

HELP: Doubt not, you need not that for to fray.   *be afraid of that*

  You shall see that day, or that it be long.

COURAGE: What day is that whereof you do speak?

  May not a body your counsel know?

HELP: Marry sir, this day whereof we do entreat   *converse*

  Is a day of notable show   1050

  When the Courtiers in their bravery shall be   *fine clothes*

  Before their Prince, some show to make.

  If such a day Wealthiness might see

  He hopeth then some money to take,

  For without cost they may not be brave,

  And many lack money, as he doth suppose,

  Wherefore at some a good hand he would have.

  I warrant thee, by none he hopeth to lose.

COURAGE: Tush man, doubt not such days there will come.

  That matter, thou need it not to fear.   1060

GREED: To hear of such days I would ride and run,

  So glad I would be of such days to hear.

  Oh, with these Courtiers I love to deal well,

  Or with other young gentlemen who have pounds or lands;

  For whether I do lend them, or my wares to them sell

  I am sure to win largely at their hands.

  And specially where in need they do stand,

  Then in faith I do pinch them home,

  When I see they must needs have money out of hand

  And that other shift to work they have none.   *other ways* 1070

HELP: Why, that is the way, sir, to come aloft.

  Great wealth thereby I know you do get.

GREED: I warrant thee, no time do I drive off,

  Neither for any man's saying, the same, will I let.   *cease*

  Well sirs, I must now leave off this talk

  And I must bid you both twain adieu.

      (*Feign a going out.*)

COURAGE: Soft Master Greediness, whither do you walk?
  What, sir, I pray you, one word with you.
GREED: Towards Paul's Cross from hence I do go,
  Perchance some profit there I may meet.   1080
COURAGE: To Paul's Cross! What there will you do?
  Do you the preachers' words so well like?[40]
GREED: Tush, for the preaching I pass not a pin
  It is not the matter wherefore I do go,
  For that goeth out whereas it it comes in;
  But herein my meaning to thee I will show:
  You know that many thither do come,
  Wherefore, perchance such may be my hap
  Of my ill debtors there to spy some
  Whom without delay by the heels I will slap.[41]   1090
HELP: Why sir, and will you arrest them there
  While they at sermon preaching be?
GREED: Will I, quoth you, wherefore should I fear?
  It is best taking them while I may them see.
COURAGE: Yea, by Our Lady sir, full wisely you say,
  Take them while you may them get
  Or else perchance it will be many a day
  Or on them again your eye you shall set.
GREED: I remember what you have said,
  Tide tarrieth no man, mark you that.   1100
  Wherefore no time herein shall be delayed,
  Therefore sirs, adieu! Too long I do chat.
       (Exit.)[42]
COURAGE: Now that here is none but you and I
  I pray thee deliver to me my part.
  Dispatch, and give me it by and by,   *immediately*
  And that I say with a willing heart.
HELP: I know no part I have of thine
  Therefore of me thou gettest no part.
COURAGE: I will make thee confess a part of mine

[40] St. Paul's Cross was an outdoor pulpit which came to be used increasingly by Puritan preachers to attack, among other things, the drama. Note that it is the Vices who malign Paul's Cross preaching.
[41] Creditors could have debtors arrested on sight the minute the debt was overdue.
[42] Original reads "Exiunt."

Or else I will make thy bones to smart.   1110

HELP: When the residue do thereto agree
Then will I also give thee a part.
But if they no part give unto thee
If I give thee any, beshrew my heart.

COURAGE: Yea friend Help, are you at that point?
I will make you otherwise to say
Or else I will heat you in every joint.
Now, Master Help, how like you this play?

> (*And fighteth to prolong the time while* WANTONNESS *maketh her ready.*)[43]

HELP: What, hold thy hand, man, art thou so mad?

COURAGE: To confess me a part I will make thee glad.   1120

HELP: A part thou shalt have when home we do come.

COURAGE: Upon that condition mine anger is done.
Ah, sirra. think you to make me your knave,
And yet all the profit yourselves you would have?

> (*Enter* WASTEFULNESS, *the husband of* WANTONNESS.)

WASTEFUL: What joy is like the linked life?
What hope might hold me from my wife?
Can man his tongue so frame
Or eke dispose me from my dame?
What doth my substance good to me?
I will therefore be frank and free.   1130
Where couples young do meet
That pliant piece so sweet
My joy for to declare
Whose beauty is so rare.
In coffers lockt to lie,
To serve my wife and I.[44]

COURAGE: Then do you wisely, I swear by St. Anne.
Take time while time is, for time will away;

---

[43] This is the actor who played Greediness. He thus has 49 lines and a fight in which to change costume.

[44] The passage is badly garbled. A suggested alternative reading of the passage would be: "What joy is like the linked life?/ What hope might hold me from my wife?/ Can man his tongue so frame/ Or eke dispose me from my dame/ Whose beauty is so rare/ My joy for to declare/ That pliant piece so sweet/ Where couples young do meet./ What doth my substance good to me/ In coffers for to lie/ To serve my wife and I?/ I will therefore be frank and free."

The niggard is never counted a man.
Therefore remember to do as you say.   1140
WASTEFUL: I warrant thee, what I have said
  Nothing I mean shall be delayed.
  I will the same fulfill
  To ease and please my will.
HELP: Truly sir, you do wisely therein,
  For what good of hoarding ensues?
  Undoubtedly I think it a sin,
  And beasts they are which the same do use.
WASTEFUL: Use it who list, for me he shall; I mean to hoard
        no store.⁴⁵
  I mean to serve my time withal, and then I seek no more.   1150
        (WANTONNESS *enter*.)
WANTON: Jesus, husband, what do you mean,
  To run abroad and leave me at home?
  You are such a man as I have not seen.
  I see well hereafter you will leave me alone,
  That so soon begin from me to be straying.
  What, man, it is yet but honeymoon!
WASTEFUL: What, woman, would you have me always playing?
  So may we shortly both be undone.
  As for pleasure there is a time
  So for profit there is the like.   1160
  Therefore I pray thee, gentle wife mine,
  Be contented that my profit I seek.
WANTON: Yea, but husband I say consider in your mind
  That now we are young, and pliant to play,
  But age, approaching, makes us lame and blind,
  And lusty courage doth then draw away.
  Then what may substance us avail,
  For age no pleasure doth regard?
  Therefore, good sweetheart, do not quail.
  Think never that the world is hard.   1170
COURAGE: Undoubtedly, most true it is,
  The woman herein doth truly say.

⁴⁵ "For me he shall" means "let him, as far as I'm concerned."

Sir, have not you heard before this,
Tide tarrieth no man, but will away?

WASTEFUL: But better it is hardly to begin,   *in poverty*
And after in better estate to be,
Than first to be aloft full trim
And after to fall to lower degree.

WANTON: Truly, that is but a foolish toy,
At the first to live hardly and bare.   1180
Many we see miss that hoped joy,
And then it proveth for others they spare.   *save money*
Have not many had full sorrowful hearts
By losing of that which they did spare?
Had they not better have taken their parts
Than so for others themselves to make bare?
And what know we if we shall live
To take our parts of that we scrape?
Would it not then your heart grieve
To leave your substance in such rate?   1190

WASTEFUL: Yea, but sweetheart, if naught we shall have,
When hereafter we shall aged wax
Then needy poverty should us vex.

WANTON: Doubt you that such chance shall befall?   *Do you fear*
Truly you are greatly unwise;
We are able to keep us from such thrall.

WASTEFUL: "Spend, and God will send," else the proverb
      lies.
This sending, woman, we daily do see,
Is a staff and a wallet into such
Who such excessive spenders be.   1200
Experience thereof we have too much.

WANTON: Well husband, this talk is in vain,
Therefore cease so sharply to speak,
For unless such talk you do refrain
I fear for unkindness my heart will break.
I little thought that you would thus
Have now restrained me of my will,
But now right well I may discuss

That you do love some other Jill.
　　(*She weepeth.*)
WASTEFUL: Why, woman, dost thou think that I   1210
　　Have thought all this while as I have said?
　　I did it only thy mind to try,
　　For pleasure in me shall not be delayed.
　　While the time is, the time I will take.
　　Whatsoever I list to say
　　Of my goods no god I will make;
　　Therefore good wife, do thy sorrow away.
WANTON: Ah, faith, are you such a one indeed?
　　By Gisse, you made me almost afeared.
　　My heart in my belly was ready to bleed   1220
　　When such foolish words in you I heard.
HELP: I would have counted him greatly unwise
　　If he were so foolish as himself he made.   *pretended*
　　Fools they are, which such pleasures despise,
　　But I knew that therein he would not wade,
　　And truly I am right glad to see
　　That so good and agreement between you is;
　　For, truly, where couples do so well agree
　　It may not be chosen but there is great bliss.
　　I am sorry that thus we must part you fro.   1230
WANTON: But yet, my friends, before that you go,
　　Of a song help us to sing a part.
　　By my troth husband, we must need have a song!
　　Will you not help to further the same?
WASTEFUL: Yes, by my troth, so it be not long,
　　Or else you might count me greatly to blame
COURAGE: And I am content a part for to bear.
HELP: Then be sure I will help in with a share.
　　　　　　　　　The Song
　　Though Wastefulness and Wantonness
　　Some men have us two named,   1240
　　Yet Pleasantness and Pliantness
　　Our names we have now framed.
　　For as ye one is pleasant, to kiss and to cully,   *cheat*

The other is pliant as ever was holly.[46]
   As youth would it have
   So will we be brave.
To live in bliss we will not miss,
What care we for men's sayings?
What joy is this, to sport and kiss,
But hurt comes in delayings.   1250
The one is full ready to the other's becking,
Between us there is neither chiding nor checking.
   As youth would it have, etc.
Full brave and full fine we pass the time,
Take time while time is biding,
What joy is thine the same is mine,
My mind shall not be sliding.
Our goods are our own, why should we spare,
Or for time to come why should we care?
   As youth would it have, etc.   1260

COURAGE: Now friends, adieu, for we must depart.
WASTEFUL: Farewell my gentle friends, with all my heart.
WANTON: Well, husband, now I will home repair,
   To see that your dinner dresséd be.
      (*Exeunt.*)
WASTEFUL: Do so, wife, and see we have good fare;
   I mean not long to tarry after thee.
      (*Pause.*)
   Whose joy may be compared to mine?
   I have a wife beautiful and gay,
   She is young, pleasant, proper and fine,
   And pliant to please me both night and day.   1270
   For whom should I pinch, for whom should I spare,
   Why should I not be liberal and free?
   However the world go I do not care.
   I have enough for my wife and me,
   And if my substance chance to decay
   I know my credit is not so ill
   But that I can borrow twenty pound alway,
   To serve me at my pleasure and will.

[46] Holly is, of course, stiff and prickly.

For repayment thereof, no care I will take;
No matter it is, if the same I may get.   1280
While it lasteth, therewith I will merry make,
What skills it, though that I come in debt?   *what does it matter*
While young I am, youthful I will be,
And pass my time in youthful sort,
For, as my wife here said unto me,
Age doth delight in no pleasant sport;
Wherefore, since pleasure I do love,
In youth it behooves to take the same.
Nothing therefore my heart shall move,
But I thereto my heart will frame.   1290
I fear me that I tarry too long,
My wife do look for me before this;
Therefore homeward I will be gone,
For there is joy and heavenly bliss.
     (*Exit.*)[47]
     (*The* Sergeant *and the* Debtor *arrested entereth.*)
Debtor: What infidelity in him doth rest
Who no time forbeareth to take his prey,
Most like the greedy or savage beast
Who in cruelty rageth both night and day?
Might he not the space of one Sermon stay?
What care of mind gave he to God's word,   1300
Who at preaching thereof did me so disturb?
Is the Sabbath day, and Paul's Cross
A time and place to vex thy debtor?
Or hast thou, Greediness, by me had any loss?
Nay, by me thou art a hundred pound the better,
I speak of the least and not of the greater.
Yet I never denied my debt for to pay,
But indeed, I required a longer day.
Sergeant: Tush sir, this talk is all but in vain;
Mean you thus the time to delay?   1310
Dispatch, therefore, and please me for my pain,
And toward the Counter let us away.[48]

---

[47] Original reads "Exiunt."
[48] The Counter is a debtor's prison. The sergeant seems to be asking for a bribe.

DEBTOR: No hast, but good, stay yet awhile,
  Or else take the pain with me for to walk
  About the quantity of half a mile,
  With a friend of mine that I might talk.

SERGEANT: For a royal I will not so far go,   (a coin of high value)
  Therefore set your heart at quiet.

DEBTOR: I mean to please no Sergeant so,
  I am no customer for your diet.   1320
  But since to go you do not intend,
  You must take pain here to tarry with me,
  Until for a friend of mine I do send,
  Which I trust shortly my bail will be.

SERGEANT: Neither will I with thee here remain,
  Therefore, dispatch, and let us away.
  Thinkest thou that I, having naught for my pain,
  Will either go with thee or here for thee stay?

DEBTOR: And what wilt thou ask, here with me to stay?
  At one word let me that understand.   1330

SERGEANT: At one word, ten groats thou shalt pay,
  Or else to the Counter we must out of hand.

DEBTOR: That will I do with a right good will
  Rather than so much thou shalt get.
  I will not so much thy mind fulfill,
  If that my heart my hand may let.   *stop*

SERGEANT: Why then, with speed let us away.
  This deed thou wilt repent, I trow.

DEBTOR: Well, wherefore now do we stay?
  I am ready hence to go.   1340

SERGEANT: Come on, then.
        (*They two* [*go out.*])

(Christianity must enter with a sword, with a title of "Policy,"
but on the other side of the title must be written "God's Word";
also a shield, whereon be written "Riches," but on the other
side of the shield must be "Faith.") [49]

[49] Here the play takes a marked turn into topical allegory. There is a force within the Church of England using religion as an instrument of statecraft, and the businessmen of the City of London are having their reputations impugned. It seems very likely that the first problem refers to the machinations toward a marriage of Queen Elizabeth to the Duc d'Alencon, which would have implied toleration of Catholicism. Putting this together with the defense of the City men, who were by and large Puritans, we may have here an extremely unusual instance of a Puritan morality play. It is worthwhile, in light of this suggestion, to contrast this play with the social and theological doctrines of *All for Money*.

CHRISTIAN: Christianity I do represent.
    Muse not, though the sword of Policy I bear;
    Neither marvel not what is mine intent.
    That this fallible shield of riches I wear
    Greedy great will have it so everywhere.
    Greedy great for this cause I have named,
    For that the greater part use greediness, which is to be blamed.
    As the greater part will, thereto must I yield;
    Their cruel force I may not withstand.   1350
    Therefore I bear this deformed sword and shield
    Which I may be ashamed to hold in my hand,
    But the Lord deliver me from their thralldom and band,
    For if the enemy assail me, then am I in thrall,
    Because I lack such Armour as is taught in St. Paul,[50]
    For instead of God's word and the shield of faith
    I am deformed with Policy, and riches vain,
    And still I say, as the greater part saith,
    I am still a Christian, and so shall remain.
    My Christianity, say they, no damage doth sustain,   1360
    But alas, they are deceived, their armour is not sure,
    For neither Policy nor riches may long time endure,
    Yet upon those two we greatly depend.
    We say by Policy ourselves we can save,
    Riches as a shield we say will defend,
    And by riches we possess whatever we crave,
    So that for riches we sell all that we have,
    Not only the body and all things terrestrial
    But also the soul, which ought to be celestial.
        (FAITHFUL FEW *enter*.)
FAITHFUL: Alas, I lament to hear the report   1370
    Which of us citizens in every place is spread.
    It is not long since I came from the Court
    Where I would have been glad to have hid my head,
    With the spoil of the simple there they say we are fed,[51]
    So that, for the covetous greediness which some citizens use,
    A shameful ill to the whole ensues.

---

[50] The reference is to St. Paul's description of the Christian soldier, Ephesians 6, 11.
[51] Original reads "say were fed."

But I must needs confess, some among us there be,
For whose sakes the whole number beareth great blame.
They abuse themselves so, towards every degree,   *social class*
As men without reason and past worldly shame.[52]   1380
Neither regard they their own nor their ill name,
So they may have the chaffy treasure of the world,
They pass not both with God and man to be abhorred.
There is no time nor place that they will forbear,
When any of their help hath most need;
Then shall he pay treble for his money or ware,
Or else of them he is not like to speed.
They nothing regard his poverty or need.
But who is it which yonder doth stand,
            (*he goeth toward him.*)
Holding the sword of policy in his hand?   1390
Most certain I am that face I should know.
Sir, is not your name Christianity?
CHRISTIAN: Yes, undoubtedly my name is so,
As you are Faithful Few, embracer of verity.
FAITHFUL: And shall the sword of Policy by Christianity be
        borne?
Truly that is contrary to your nature and kind;
Now are you deformed like a thing forlorn,
Which maketh me suspect of thee in my mind.[53]
CHRISTIAN: Oh Faithful Few, of me have no doubt;
I am Christianity, though thus deformed,   1400
And though thus abused by the great rout,
Yet by God I trust my title shall be turned.
FAITHFUL: By the power of God, I will not delay
            (*he turneth the titles.*)
To turn this title most untrue and feigned,
And I will endue thee, and that straightway,
With such weapons as Saint Paul hath ordained.
CHRISTIAN: Alas, in vain this pain you do take,
For as you, faithful in number, are few,

---

[52] Original reads "As man . . . past wordly shame."
[53] Original reads "suspect of me." "Forlorn" here has the theological meaning "damned."

So the power is but small that you can make
To resist the greedy great ones who are against you.   1410
FAITHFUL: *Si deus nobiscum, quis contra nos,*[54]
If God be with us, who may us resist?
Weigh not then the number, but weigh His purpose
Who ruleth all things as Himself doth list.
I know how greediness with the great part is used,
Their pilling, polling, pinching and spoiling,
How both the simple and others with them are abused;   *by them*
They live by the fruits of other men's toiling,
But God is not dead, neither is He asleep,
Although for a time His hand He doth hold,   1420
Yet doth He remember His little sheep,
And will revenge the wrong done to His fold.
    (COURAGE *and* GREEDINESS *enter as though they saw not*
    CHRISTIANITY.)
COURAGE: Let them say what they will, do thou as I told thee;
Trust thou not to any knave of them all,
Not a Preacher of them all in thy need will uphold thee;
Try them who will, their devotion is small.
GREED: Thou wilt not believe how the knave did prate,
"Ye citizens, repent!" thus he did cry.
"Look about in time," quoth he, "or it be too late,
For the vengeance of God at hand is full nigh,"   1430
As though he knew what were in God's mind!
Surely it is a shame they are so suffered to lie.
COURAGE: But in my talk great profit thou dost find.
They are all liars, as their talk doth try.
By my doctrine thou hast great profit and gain;
Great riches and substance thereby thou dost win.
To instruct thee daily I take great pain
Which way thou shalt thy riches bring in.
GREED: Thou dost so, indeed, and thanks I thee give,
But sirra, now I remember a thing   1440
Which made me not long since to laugh in my sleeve.
To me a young gentleman the broker did bring,

[54] Romans 8, 31.

Whose father was dead of late, as it seemed,
And his lands in mortgage to a merchant was laid,
Wherefore it behooved the same were redeemed,
For the day was at hand when the same should be paid.
And I, perceiving his need to be such,
I thought I would pinch him or that I went.
To give mine own asking he did not greatly grudge,
And when I had girded him, thence I him sent.   1450

FAITHFUL: More shame for thee and such as thou art,
That with life thou art permitted it is great pity.
Thou art a Christian with a cankered heart
And the cause of reproach to a whole city.
Christianity by thee is greatly abused;
Of his righteous armor thou dost him bereave,
And instead thereof, by him to be used,
The armor of Satan with him thou dost leave.

GREED: Why, would you not have me how to invent
Which way were best to bring in my gain?   1460

FAITHFUL: But not in such sort to set thine intent
That all the world of thee should complain.

GREED: I cry you mercy! I know where you are now!
In a Courtier's behalf this oration you make.
Of late there was one complained how
Excessive gain of him I did take.
It is the cast of them all so to say,
When prodigally their money is spent,
Or if the Prince will them not pay,
Then on the merchant some lies they invent.   1470

FAITHFUL: Art thou not ashamed of thy Prince to speak ill,
Thine own abused doing to excuse?
No marvel though the city have all men's ill will,
When both in word and deed thyself thou dost misuse.
Sed Reginum est male audiri cum bene fecerint;[55]

---

[55] For this conjectural reading we are indebted to Professor J. D. A. Ogilvy of the University of Colorado. The original reads "*Sed Reginum est male audire cum besecerint.*" The key word is of course the verb. Professor Ogilvy suggests that MS "f" has been misread as long "s" and the common abbreviation "be" for *bene* has been used, producing "*besecerint.*" This emendation, together with that of *audire* to the passive infinitive produces something like what the author then proceeds to give as his translation.

Antisthenes doth truly this saying recite:
It is given to Princes (saith he), though they be benevolent,
To be evil spoken of, which is against all right.
GREED: Sir, you are best say no more than you are able to
    prove,
Lest I make you to repent your boldness,   1480
For if my patience you too much do move
I may chance turn your heat into a coldness.
Why, I lend my money like a friend, for good will,
And thereby do help men at their need.
FAITHFUL: A friend thou art indeed, though a friend but ill.
Pythagoras thy friendship hath plainly decreed:
There be many, saith he, who no friends do lack,
And yet of friendship they have but scant.
So thou art a friend for their money's sake,
And yet thy friendship they always shall want.   1490
CHRISTIAN: Assuredly thou highly offendest,
For that so double in dealing thou art.
Aristotle saith by the same thou pretendest,
And not so to bear a dissembling heart.
A Christian ought not unto riches to yield,
For it is a thing but fallible and vain.
Riches is no perpetual shield,
But the shield of faith shall ever remain.
Take therefore Faith, and God's Word for thy sword,
And arm Christianity in this wise.   1500
GREED: Shall Policy and riches then be abhorred?
Sir, they are fools that them will despise.
I put case poverty should me assail,   *let's suppose*
Can God's Word and Faith me anything avail?
I am sure, sir, this may not be denied.
FAITHFUL: We deny not but in this world riches bear the
    sway,
Yet is not riches to be callèd sure,[56]
For in God's power it is to make riches decay,
Whereas God's Word and Faith shall ever endure.

[56] Original reads "it not riches."

GREED: But give me riches, take you God's Word and
    Faith,   1510
And see which of us shall have the better gain.

CHRISTIAN: Now Faithful Few, you hear what he saith,
    Therefore to turn the titles I must be fain.

FAITHFUL: Well, since it will no better be,
    To God let us the cause betake,
    Who, I trust, whenas time He doth see,
    He will for us a deliverance make.[57]

COURAGE: Come Master Wealthiness, let us away.
    What should we here any longer do?

GREED: Indeed, I hold it best as you say,   1520
    Therefore your saying I agree unto.
        (*They two go out.*)

FAITHFUL: Sorry I am to see his estate;
    Now near he is to the fount of perdition;
    God grant him repentance or it be too late,
    That of his sins he may have remission.

CHRISTIAN: But alas, he goeth the contrary way,
    For of his covetousness he taketh no ruth,
    And Aristotle I remember doth say
    The covetous man cannot learn the truth,
    Wherefore he cannot, or will not know   1530
    The way to reform me, Christianity.
    Therefore from this place now I will go,
    To pray unto God to show him the verity.
    Now Faithful Few, adieu unto thee;
    I will pray unto God for thy comfort and aid;
    I beseech thee make the like intercession for me,
    And that my reformation be not long delayed.
        (*Exit.*)[58]

FAITHFUL: Doubt not thereof, good Christianity;
    My endeavor herein shall not be delayed.
    Alas, what is man, not knowing the verity?   1540

---

[57] Original reads "Whom." This is permissible Elizabethan grammar, the emendation being offered only to make it slightly less offensive to the modern ear.
[58] Original reads "*Exiunt.*"

No man, but a beast, he may be said.
Yet many there are which in the world doth live,
Who for Christians will needs accounted be,
Though to all abhominations their selves they do give,
And from no kind of vice be clear or free.
Covetousness is accounted no sin,
Usury is science and art,
All ways are good whereby we may win,
Although it be to our neighbor's smart.
Whereby it appeareth from love we are free;   1550
The words of the wise we nothing regard,
For without love no virtue can perfect be,
As Plato the wise hath plainly declared.
No good thing without love it is possible to do;
Seneca of that opinion hath been;
Then how many good things do they now, think you,
In whom no love at all there is seen?
They watch their times, the simple to snare;
No time they forbear their pleasures to work.
God grant we therefore of them may beware,   1560
For privily to snare us they daily do lurk.
        (*Enter* WASTEFULNESS, *poorly.*)
WASTEFUL: Oh more than wretch, which so foolishly hast spent
    Not only thine own goods but also other men's!
    What account shall I make for the goods to me lent,
    Which never I am able for to recompense?
    Now wastefully have I, with Wantonness my wife,
    Consumed our goods, substance and treasure,
    That would to God I were out of my life,
    For the remembrance thereof is grief without measure.
    My wife and I now are asunder dispersed,   1570
    Each of us to seek our living alone.
    Alas, our woe may not be rehearsed!
    Unto whom now should we make our moan?
    In taking the time too toward we were;   *eager*
    We were afeared too long to abide.
    Courage's counsel in mind we did bear;

He said that for no man would tarry the tide.
But well-away now, which way shall I run?
I know it is folly unto God to call,
For God I know my petition will shun,   1580
And into perdition I am now like to fall.
Despair, despair!
   (DESPAIR *enter in some ugly shape, and stand behind him.*)
Why should I despair, since God doth behold
The sinner with mercy, as the Scripture doth say?
DESPAIR: But thy prodigal sins are so manifold
 That God of mercy doth utterly deny.
 Therefore to end thy life it is best;
 Thy calling for mercy is all in vain.
 By ending thy life thou shalt be at rest,
 But if longer thou live, great shall be thy pain.   1590
WASTEFUL: Well then, will I seek some place where I may
 Finish my life with cord or with knife,
 The dispatch whereof I will not delay.
 Farewell now all the world, but chiefly my wife.
   (*Feign a going out.*)
  (FAITHFUL FEW *plucketh him again.*)
FAITHFUL: Soft, stay awhile, and be not so rash.
 Thinkest thou God unmerciful to be?
 Wilt thou trust despair, even at the first dash?
 Hast thou no faith in God's mercy so free?
 Call upon God with repentance and faith,
 By such ways and means as I will instruct thee.   1600
WASTEFUL: I believe God is merciful, as the Scripture saith.
   (*They both kneel, and* WASTEFUL *saith after* FAITHFUL)
FAITHFUL: Well, follow me and I will conduct thee.
 Oh heavenly Father, pardon my offence
WASTEFUL: Oh heavenly Father, pardon mine offence
FAITHFUL: And grant that thy mercy may to me repair.
WASTEFUL: And grant that thy mercy may to me repair.
FAITHFUL: Also, O Father, banish thou hence
WASTEFUL: Also, O Father, banish thou hence
FAITHFUL: That wicked monster of Despair.

WASTEFUL: That wicked monster of Despair.   1610
      (DESPAIR *flyeth, and they arise.*)[59]
FAITHFUL: How feelest thou now, thy conscience and mind;
  Hopest thou not of God's mercy and grace?
WASTEFUL: Well, God is praised that here I thee find.
  How happy I was to approach this place.   *fortunate*
  Despair is now fled, I perfectly know,
  And in God's mercy I firmly do trust.
  Therefore, O Lord, deliver me from thrall,
  And pardon me, a sinner most vile and unjust.
FAITHFUL: That is very well said, if so thou do think;
  And now, frame thyself thy life to amend.   1620
  Let despair no more into thy mind sink,
  But to be a new man do thou now pretend,
  And as heretofore thy mind for to please
  Thou hast learned the tide will tarry no man,
  So now it behooveth for thy greater ease
  That saying after God's will for to scan.
  Take time while time is. Thus I do mean:
  Amend thy life whilst here thou hast space;
  To God's merciful promises see that thou lean,
  So shalt thou enjoy the tide of His grace.   1630
WASTEFUL: To follow your counsel I will do my endeavor;
  I will seek the same in all points to perform.
  The effect of your words I will forget never,
  And now I will hence, my wife to reform,
  That she and I, in manner new,
  May amend our lives, to God's glory and praise,
  Wherefore good sir, unto you adieu;
  I beseech the Lord to send thee good days.
      (*Exit.*)[60]
FAITHFUL: See how the time-takers their fact doth repent,   *deed*
  Who no time will spare in pleasing their will?   1640
  And although the beginning have a pleasant scent,
  Yet of the ending the taste is as ill,

---

[59] What we have here is an *exorcism*, perhaps the only instance of it in the moralities.
[60] Original reads "*Exiunt.*"

For whoever it be that without measure
Doth consume his substance in prodigal sort,
Although he had abundance of treasure
Yet he will be a beggar, and that in time short.
I marvel where Authority is,
Who should be a help for the simple oppressed.[61]
Many things there are greatly amiss
Which by his means must needs be redressed.   1650
His absence greatly disquieteth my mind;
I will not cease seeking until him I do find.
     (Exit.)[62]
   (*Enter* COURAGE, *weeping.*)

COURAGE: Out, alas, these tidings are ill![63]
My friend Master Greediness hath ended his days!
Despair upon him hath wrought his will,
And desperately now he is gone his ways,
As one enraged and out of his wit,
No remembrance of God he would have.
Alas poor man, he had a great fit
Before that well he was laid in his grave.   1660
     (*reasoning with himself*)
Why, but is Greediness dead, in good sadness?   *really*
Methinks these news are not true which you tell.
Yes, truly, he died in a great madness,
And went with the tide-boat straight into hell.
Why fool, Greediness will never die
So long as covetous people do live!
Then you belike do think that I do lie?
I am as honest a man as any in your sleeve.
I am sure he is dead, or one in his likeness,
For when he was buried I stood by,   1670
And some said he died of the new sickness.   *plague*
Therefore sir, think not that I do lie,
For I am as sorry for the death of the man

---

[61] Original reads "see a help."
[62] Original reads "*Exiunt.*"
[63] Original reads "this tidings."

As any man that liveth this day.
Wherefore I must needs weep if I can.
But husht, somebody is coming this way.
    (*Enter Authority and Faithful Few*)

FAITHFUL: Surely, Authority, the same is even he;
I warrant you sir, you need not to doubt.

AUTHORITY: Then will we handle him kindly,   *according to his kind*
   thou shalt see.
Therefore see that from us he escape not out.   1680

COURAGE: God save Your Honor, and prosper your estate!
I am glad to see you approach this place.
Those which say ill of you I bitterly do hate;
I answer for Your Honor in every case.

AUTHORITY: Ah crafty caitiff, why dissemblest thou so?
Dost thou think that us thou mayest so blind?
Thy contagious doings we right well do know,
And eke thy property, nature and kind.
Thou art an encourager to all kinds of vice,
The aged to avarice and greedy desire,   1690
The younger sort lack none of thine advice,
To all such acts as the devil doth require.

COURAGE: Lo sir, I thought you did me mistake!
I know right well the man whom you mean.
To fetch him hither good speed I will make.
I warrant you I will shortly be here again.
    (*Feign a going out.*)

FAITHFUL: Nay, soft. He is here whom that we would have;
Therefore you need not him for to fetch.

COURAGE: Yes, I will fetch him, for he is a very knave,
And alms it is that a rope he should stretch.   1700
    (*Still feign to go out.*)

AUTHORITY: Upon thyself just judgement thou dost give.
Juvenal saith cities are well governed
Whereas such rebels as are now suffered to live
But after their deserts are justly punished.

COURAGE: They which are rebels it behooveth indeed
That they be corrected and punished so,

For they do much harm in every stead;   *place*
But I am none such, I would you should know.
AUTHORITY: Thou shalt know what thou art or hence we
    depart.
Faithful Few, upon him lay hold.   1710
COURAGE: By Giss sir, then I will cause him to smart.
Therefore to touch me be not so bold.
FAITHFUL: Sir, see where cometh Correction also.
        (CORRECTION *enter*.)
AUTHORITY: Draw near, Correction, and thine office do.
Take here this caitiff unto the Jail.
CORRECTION: Sir, to do your commandment I will not fail.
Come on sirra, and let us away.
COURAGE: Nay, soft awhile Your Wisdom, stay.
Hold me when you have me, but you have me not yet,
And perchance ere you have me your nose I will slit.   1720
CORRECTION: Thinkest thou with brags to make me afeared?
        (*And beginneth to lay hands on him*)
COURAGE: You are best stand further, lest I shave your beard.
        (*They strive, he draweth his dagger and fighteth*.)
CORRECTION: In faith sir, now I will give you the check.
        (*and catcheth him*.)
COURAGE: Ah, God's passion, wilt thou break my neck?
Is there no man here that has a curst wife?   *shrewish*
If he will in my stead he shall lose his life.
CORRECTION: Tush, let us hence. Thy talk is in vain.
COURAGE: Since there is no remedy, best is a short pain.
        (*Exeunt*.)[64]
FAITHFUL: When all malefactors are duly thus punished
According to the good and godly laws,   1730
Then shall Christianity duly be burnished,[65]
And to praise God we shall have cause.
AUTHORITY: O Faithful Few, doubt not but as we
Are able Christianity's estate to reform,
So his reformation in short time thou shalt see,

[64] Here the original reads "*Exit*."
[65] Original reads "burnished," that is, shined, but "furnished" was probably intended.

For we for his estate do lament and mourn.
Of ourselves we are not able to compass this thing,
But by the sword of God's power, which to us is lent;
Wherefore Faithful Few, have thou no doubting
But we thereunto do gladly consent,   1740
For to Socrates' saying some respect we have,
Who saith a city is not to be praised
For the greatness of buildings, gorgeous and brave,[65]
But for the good inhabitants which therein are placed.
So we account those countries but ill
Which vicious persons doth maintain and nourish,
Although they have all things at their will,
And although in treasure they abundantly flourish.

FAITHFUL: Oh noble Authority, by this your occasion
Great tranquillity to us shall befall;   1750
We shall be joy to each godly nation
When Christianity is delivered from thrall,
For better it were unchristened to be
Than our Christianity for to abuse.
The Jewish infidel to God doth more agree
Than such as Christianity do so misuse.
But see yonder, where he doth appear,
Whom abusèd armor doth greatly oppress.

(CHRISTIANITY *enter in as at the first*.)

AUTHORITY: O Christianity, unto us draw near,
That we thy abused estate may redress,   1760
And as freely as this power unto us is lent,
Here we now by force of the same
To thee, Faithful Few, do here condescend   *defer*
That thou Christianity's estate shall frame
In such good form, fashion and shape
As the same shall not be turned again
But shall continue in a godly rate
From henceforth evermore to remain.

FAITHFUL: God grant that so it may be kept
As all Christians it may become,   *be suitable to* 1770

[66] Original reads "or buildings."

And as for my part, it shall not be slipped,[67]
But my duty shall straightway be done.
　　　(*he turneth the titles.*)
CHRISTIAN: Now God be praised, who thus again
　Hath restored me to my former estate
　And hath extinguished from me all pain.
　God grant that now I be not found ungrate,
　And God grant that all Christians may me duly embrace
　In such sort as God's will it is.
　So shall they be sure of a resting place
　In heaven, where reigneth all joy and bliss.　　　　　1780

Finis

[67] Original reads "slept."

✳ *ENOUGH IS AS GOOD AS A FEAST*

(William Wager, c. 1560–1570)

Enough Is as Good as a Feast was written by W. Wager, whose
first name is generally given as William. Three other plays have been
ascribed to him: one, *The Longer Thou Livest* (1569) is certainly his;
the other two, *The Cruel Debtor* (c. 1565) and *The Trial of Treasure*
(1567) are doubtful. *Enough* shares a number of lines with the *Trial*,[1]
but whether it or the *Trial* is the debtor is open to question. *Enough*
appeared without a date, and at best we can place it sometime
between 1560 and 1570. Beyond his authorship of these two plays,
we know nothing about Wager.

It is unfortunate that we do not know anything about him,
because on the evidence of *Enough* he was a very skillful dramatist in
the mode of moral tragedy. The death of Worldly Man is one of the
best scenes in mid-century drama. But like many dramatists with a
passionate moral vision, Wager is not a very skillful poet, and his
sure sense of action is often cast in rather clumsy language. The
reader would do well, then, to restrain his impatience with Wager's
language until he has gotten some distance into the play and allowed
the action to develop.

---

[1] Louis B. Wright, "Social Aspects of Some Belated Morality Plays." *Anglia*, LIV (1930), 116. See also
Leslie Oliver, "William Wager and *The Trial of Treasure*," *Huntington Library Quarterly*, IX (1946), pp.
419–29.

Enough has survived in a single copy of a sixteenth-century quarto edition, now owned by the Huntington Library. A facsimile of that copy was prepared by S. de Rici and published in 1920. The present text is based upon that facsimile.

ENOUGH IS AS GOOD AS A FEAST

Seven may easily play this interlude

The Players

Worldly Man: *for one*		Inconsideration ⎫
Prologue ⎫		Servant
Heavenly Man ⎬ *for one*		Rest ⎬ *for one*
Contentation ⎫		Prophet ⎭
Temerity		Precipitation ⎫
Ignorance ⎬ *for one*		Tenant
Satan ⎭		God's Plague ⎬ *for one*
Enough ⎫		Physician ⎭
Hireling ⎬ *for one*		Covetousness the Vice: *for another*

PROLOGUE:

I know that this worshipful audience
Is at this time together congregate,
Of our practice to have intelligence,
And with the same themselves to recreate.
God grant us grace the same well to publicate;   *make public*
  But for them that have slept at Parnassus—
  This faculty is more meet for them than for us.   *tuitable*
Pandite pierides vestro sacra ostia vita![1]
Open up your holy doors, Oh pleasant muses!
Direct our tongues to speak eloquently,   10
Virtues to praise and to touch abuses,
Dividing either of them plain and directly,
That it may appear to all our audience evidently
  That this matter which we now go about
  By your inspiration was first found out.
Oh, that with some grace you would us inspire,
And deal with us as with Orpheus you dealt!
Then should all affections have their desire,
For through his music he made stones to melt;
No kind of pain in hell then the souls felt,   20

---

[1] *Pandit . . . vita*: "Open, O Muses, your holy doors of life"

For he played so pleasantly with his harp
That they forgot their pains grievous and sharp:
Tantalus forgot his hunger and thirst,
Sisiphus left off rolling his stone,
Ixion, tormented among the worst,
Forgot his wheel that he was hanged on,
The woman Belides left work, anon,
    Whose labor was continually to fill a tun,
    Whereout by clefts the liquor still doth run.[2]
These fables wherefore do I call to mind?   30
Truly, because I desire with all my heart
That our English meter may be of such kind,
Both to leave all grievousness and smart
And also to be pleasant in every part,
    That those which come for recreation
    May not be void of their expectation.
Poets feigned Mercurius to have wings,
Both on his head and on his heels also,
For lively and swift he was in all things,
Appearing rather to flee than to go.   40
Of him they feigned many goodly things mo,   *more*
    But for our purpose this shall serve this season;
    And why I speak, you shall know the reason.
Mercurius is the god of eloquence,
By whom I understand the ministers of[t] talk.
Such must have the wings of intelligence
In their heads, before their tongues too far do walk:
The danger of rash speech they must wisely calk;   *reckon*
    When, where and to whom they speak they must note,
    Before that anything pass out of their throat.   50
As Mercurius hath wings upon his head,
So hath he wings on his heels, ready to fly.
When affections standeth in reason's stead,

---

[2] Tantalus, Sisiphus, Ixion and Belides: all malefactors punished by Zeus with eternal torment; Tantalus because he killed his son Pelops and served him in a stew at a banquet of the gods, Sisiphus because he betrayed the secrets of the gods, and Ixion because he attempted to seduce Hera; the Belides are better known as the Danaides, fifty daughters of Danaus who slew their husbands on their wedding night.

Reporters of tales use eftsoons to lie: *at times*
The heels, affections do also signify;
   The wings do always reason comprehend,   *encompass*
   Which unto virtue ought to condescend.
Few words to wise men are sufficient.
Without a cause I give not this monition:
Unto good men it is plain and evident   60
That many men have that lewd condition,
By their evil words to bring men into suspicion.
   By their indiscreet talk they do much harm,
   Because they want reason their tongues to charm.
Let this pass, and go we to the Argument,
Which we will declare in words general.
Now, such as have a learned judgement
Know that among the poets comical
In brief sentence it was usual
   To show the whole contents of the comedy   70
   In the Argument, which did well, verily;
But our tongues hath not so comely a grace
In that point, as hath the Latin and Greek.
We cannot, like them, our sentences eloquently place,
That our poets to their orators may be like—
As they know well which for such masters do seek.
   But to do our best, indeed we will not neglect,
   Trusting that wise men the same will accept.
Our title is Enough is as Good as a Feast,
Which rhetorically we shall amplify   80
So that it shall appear both to most and least
That our meaning is but honesty;
Yet now and then we will dally merrily
   So we shall please them that of mirth be desirous,
   For we play not to please them that be curious.   *overly precise*
For a Preface, I fear I am too long;
But I have said that I will say now.
The Worldly Man is frolic, lusty and strong   *merry*
Who will show his qualities before you;
Stout, he is, and in any wise will not bow.   *proud* 90

Behold, yonder he cometh into this place;
Therefore, thus I finish our simple Preface.

Finis

(*Enter* WORLDLY MAN, *stout and frolic.*)

WORLDLY MAN: Because I am a man endued with
    treasure,   *endowed*
Therefore a Worldly Man men do me call.
Indeed I have riches and money at my pleasure—
Yea, and I will have more, in spite of them all.
    A common saying, "Better is envy than ruth."
I should rather they should spite than pity me,
For the old saying nowadays proveth truth:
"Nought have nought set by," as daily we see.   100
    Iwis, I am not of the mind as some men are   *indeed*
Which look for no more than will serve necessity;
No, against a day to come I do prepare,
That when age cometh I may live merrily.
    "Oh," sayeth one, "Enough is as Good as a Feast!"
Yea, but who can tell what his end shall be?
Therefore I count him worse than a beast
That will not have that in respect and see.   *consideration*
    As by mine own father an example I may make:
He was beloved by all men and kept a good house   110
While riches lasted; but when that did slake
There was no man that did set by him a louse.   *care for him at all*
    And so at such time as he from the world went—
I mean when he died—he was not worth a groat;
And they that all his substance had spent,
For the value of twelve pence would have cut his throat.
    But, I trow, I will take heed of such!
They shall go ere they drink when they come to me.
It doth me good to tell the chinks in my hutch   *coins in my chest*
More than at the tavern or ale house to be.   120
    [*Enter* HEAVENLY MAN]

HEAVENLY MAN: God careth for His, as the prophet David
  doth say,
 And preserveth them under His merciful wing:
 The heavenly, I mean, that His will do obey,
 And observe His holy commandments in all thing—
 Yet not for our sakes, nor for our deserving,
 But for His own name sake openly to declare
 That all men here on earth ought to live in His fear.

WORLDLY MAN: This same is one of our jolly talkers
 That prattleth so much of Heaven and Hell!
 Oh, I tell you, these are godly walkers!   130
 Of many strange things they can tell.
 They pass men—yea, angels they excel!
 Sir, are you not called the Heavenly Man?
 I have been in your company ere now, but I cannot tell
  whan.   *when*

HEAVENLY MAN: Yes certainly, sir, that is my name.
 Unworthy of any such title, I do confess.
 God grant that I may deserve the same,
 And that my faults I may amend and redress!
 Therefore enow the truth do you here express: *now*
 Is not the Worldly Man your name?   140

WORLDLY MAN: Yea indeed, sir, I am the very same.
  [*Enter* CONTENTATION]

CONTENTATION: From the Heavenly Man I cannot be long
  absent,
 Which in God's promises hath his consolation,
 Considering that he always is content
 Patiently to suffer God's visitation;
 For, understand you, my name is Contentation,   *contentment*
 Whom the Worldly Man doth mock and deride,
 And will not suffer him once in his mind to abide.

WORLDLY MAN: This same is the grandsire of them all!
 This is he that will through water and fire!   150
 Good reasoning betwixt us now hear you shall,
 For to follow him he will me earnestly require;
 But he shall be hanged ere he have his desire.

You are welcome, sir, saving my quarrel indeed.
You have reported of me much more than you need.

CONTENTATION: Nothing but truth, sir, certainly I have said.
Oftimes I have counselled you your covetousness to leave,
But my words as feathers in the wind you have weighed,
And stuck to them as glue to the water doth cleave.
But take heed the reward thereof you shall receive!   160
Once again I advertise thee to be content,   *advise*
And give thanks to God for that He hath thee sent.

WORLDLY MAN: I pray you, be content, for I am pleased;
And meddle you no more with me than I do with you.

HEAVENLY MAN: To be angry without a cause, without mends
    must be eased.
We will be more earnest than ever we were, now.
"Woe," sayeth our Saviour, "to those that are rich,
Which therein only have their consolation."
He curseth them not because they have too much,
But because they receive it not with contentation,   170
Building therewith to themselves a good foundation—
That is, to lay here on earth treasure great store,
To purchase a kingdom that lasteth evermore.

WORLDLY MAN: Passion of me, masters, what would ye have
    me to do?
You are fond fellows indeed, as ever I knew!
If I should not take pains, ride, run and go
For my living, what thereof would ensue?
A beggar should I die, masters, this is true!
Then my wife and my children that I leave behind,
I fear me at your hands small relief should find.   180

HEAVENLY MAN: "I have been young," sayeth David, "and
    now am old;
Yet the righteous forsaken I never did see,
Nor their seed begging bread I did not behold."
Therefore your mind to the Prophets doth not agree.
"Cast all thy burden and care," sayeth Christ, "on me,
And I will provide to keep thee from danger and strife;
Only seek thou to live a godly and good life."

CONTENTATION: When Solon was asked of Croesus the King
  What man was most happy in this vale terrestrial,
  To the end he seemed to attribute that thing,   190
  When men be associate with treasures celestial.
WORLDLY MAN: By the beginning no man can judge the
      same. Solon doth say
  That any man is happy that beareth breath.
  But yet by the end partly judge, we may,
  For true happiness, sayeth he, consisteth after death.
HEAVENLY MAN: If this be true, as undoubtedly it is,
  What men are more wicked, wretched and miserable
  Than those that in riches account their bliss,
  Being infected with ambition, that sickness uncurable?
CONTENTATION: The treasure of this world we may well
      compare   200
  To Circes the witch with her crafty cautility,[3]   *deceitfulness*
  Wherewith many men's minds so poisoned are,
  That quite they are carried to all infidelity.
    They are conjured so indeed, and bewitched so sore
  That treasure is their trust, yea, hope and delight.
  Enough serveth them not til that they have more;
  So against Contentation they still strive and fight.
HEAVENLY MAN: Though the worldly men do follow their lust,
  Crying, "On earth is our felicity and pleasure,"
  Yet God doth so rule the hearts of the just   210
  That their study is chiefly to get heavenly treasure.
WORLDLY MAN: Friends, I take you both for honest men.
  I promise you, I would be glad to do for the best.
  Marry, then, I take care which way and when
  I may get treasure, therewith to live in rest.
    Oh, methinks it is a very pleasant thing
  To see a great heap of old angels and crowns!   *coins*
  When I have store of money, I can be merry and sing!
  For money, as men say, winneth both cities and towns.
HEAVENLY MAN: Alas, why should you not have that in
      estimation   220

[3] Circe: in the Odyssey a goddess living on the island of Aeaea who turns Odysseus' men into swine.

Which God hath prepared for his dear elect?
Should not our minds rest in full contentation,
Having trust in that treasure most high in respect?
Saint Paul, whom the Lord so high doth erect,
   Sayeth it passeth the sense, our memories and mind;
   Much less can our outward eyes the same find.
As for the treasure that you possess here,
Through the fickleness of fortune soon fadeth away.
The greatest of renown and most worthy peer
Sometime in the end falleth to misery and decay.   230
   Record of Dionysius, a king of much fame,
Of the valiant Alexander, and Caesar the strong;
Record of Tarquinus, which had Superbus to name,
And of Heliogabalus that ministered with wrong—[4]
To recite them all it would be very long!
But these be sufficient plainly to prove
How soon and uncertainly riches doth remove.
CONTENTATION: It is true; and therefore a mind well content
Is great riches, as wise King Solomon doth say.   240
For we have seen of late this canker pestilent
Corrupting our realm to our utter decay:
   Ambition, I mean, which chiefly doth reign
Amongst those who should have been example to other.
Yea, we see how the Brethren they did disdain,
And burned with fire the child with the mother.[5]
   It is often seen that such monstrous ambition
As spareth not to spill the blood of the innocent
Will not greatly stick to fall to sedition,
The determinations of God thereby to prevent.   250
But God, I trust, shall disappoint their intent,
And overthrow the power of fading treasure,

---

[4] Dionysius: Tyrant of Syracuse (fourth century B.C.), he died at the height of his power; Tarquinus Superbus: the last king of Rome (sixth century B.C.), he was driven from the city and died a fugitive; Heliogabalus, Roman emperor (third century B.C.), he took the name of a Syrian sun god but was murdered during an uprising of the praetorians.

[5] Brethren: a reference to the persecution of Protestants under the Catholic Queen Mary. This play is roughly contemporary with the most extended and bitter account of the persecutions, John Foxe's *Acts and Monuments of the Church* (1563).

And cause us all to wish for the heavenly pleasure.
HEAVENLY MAN: Oh you ancient men whom God hath
    furnished with fame,
Be ye always mindful to walk in the ways of the just,
And add evermore virtue to your honest name,
And at no hand be overcome with covetous or lust,
But in God's holy promise put confidence and trust.
    And then double felicity at the last we shall possess;
    And then in all earthly doings God shall give good
      success.   260
Ye poor men and commons, walk in your vocation;
Banish fond fantasies which are not convenient;   *proper*
Settle your minds with enough to have contentation,
Considering that that leadeth to treasures most excellent,
For these are uncertain, but they are most permanent.
    Your necessity apply with treasure, faith and trust,
    And you shall have enough always among the just.
WORLDLY MAN: And indeed enough is as good as a feast!
Good Lord, how your words have altered my mind!
A new heart, me thinks, is entered in my breast,   270
For no thought of mine old in me I can find.
    I would to God you would take me in your company,
And learn me how I may be an Heavenly Man,
For now I perceive this world is but vanity,
Let a man therefore make of it as much as he can.
CONTENTATION: Do you speak as you think, and as you mind
    do you say?
Could you be content to lead the rules of a godly life?
WORLDLY MAN: I do mean it truly; and I will study them night
    and day,
For I regard neither treasure, children, nor wife.
HEAVENLY MAN: Give me your hand, then. Together let us
    depart.
WORLDLY MAN.   And I will wait on you, sir, with all my
    heart.   280
      [*Exit* WORLDLY MAN, HEAVENLY MAN *and* CONTENTA-
      TION.]

(*Enter* TEMERITY, INCONSIDERATION *and* PRECIPITATION, *singing this song.*)

When Covetous is busy,
Then we three be all merry,
   For he doth trimly invent,   *merry*
To make us fine frolic cheer,
Be vittles never so dear
   And all our money clean spent.
Therefore we spare for no cost;
We can be trusted of our host
   For shillings twenty and one.   290
Covetous hath a good wit;
He findeth a mean to pay it,
   When all our money is gone.
Therefore troll the bowl to me,   *pass*
With huf child and have to thee,   *bottoms up*
   The longest liver pay all!
Our trust is in Covetise,
For he is prudent and wise;
   Therefore money cannot fall.   *fail*
Oh Covetous, prudent prince,   300
All strong walls thou dost convince   *overcome*
   And rulest them, every one!
Thou dost drive many a drift,   *scheme*
And makest for us much shift   *trickery*
   When all our money is gone.
       (*Enter* COVETOUS, *the Vice, alone.*)
COVETOUS: At Blackheath field, where great Goliath was slain,
   The Moon lying in childbed of her last son,
   The Tyburn at Warwick was then King of Spain,
   By whom the Land of Canaan then was won.
     It happened between Peterborough and Pentecost,   310
   About such time as Ivy was made of Wormwood,
   That Child's work in Basil wood of fire was lost,
   And all through the treason of false Robin Hood.
     That saw Sir Guy of Warwick and Colebrand,
   Which fought against the sun and stopped his light.

"Yea," quoth Hobgoblin, "let me take them in hand—
Children, children not able to resist my might!"
  A wonderful bloodshed was in those days,
For Saint Stephen fought against the Golden Knight;
In so much that Peter was fain to give his keys   320
To those, God knows, that had to them no right.
  With the grief of that, all the saints in heaven
Proclaimed open wars at Barnard-in-the-field.
They fought from six of the clock to eleven,
Ere ever the traitors would give over and yield.
  But to say there was triumph—in faith, there was!
Saint Stephen the younger was made Captain of the Guard.
Wonderful it was to see such things he brought to pass,
As I am sure the like of them ye never heard.
  "By giss!" quoth Saint Stephen. It was time to   *by Jesus* 330
      trudge.
Friar Francis took his flight to Paul's steeple;
In faith he was even with them for an old grudge,
For he carried away the weathercock in spite of the people.
  Then was I dubbed a knight at Kiniston,
And made officer of all courts and laws;
I gave offices and livings, many a one,
Marry indeed, you may say it was for a cause.
  In faith, the same day that Midsummer was married,
I never laughed better in my life,
For even suddenly away Saint Uncumber carried   340
Both the Bridgegroom and the Bride, his wife.
  No remedy, on God's name, but I must bear them company.
Cheer, in faith there was, cheer in bowls!
And who was minstrel but Saint Anthony!
He made melody for all Christian souls.[6]

---

[6] This is pure comic fustian, but Wager contrives to associate Covetous with Roman Catholicism through his references to saints who appealed to Protestants as peculiarly characteristic of the Roman Catholic mentality. Saint Stephen the Younger was known for his defense of the veneration of images against the iconoclasm of the Emperor Constantine Copronymous; Uncumber is the English name for Wilgefortis, daughter of the King of Portugal, whose vow of chastity was kept when she grew a beard on the eve of her wedding—hence an example of the "superstitious" piety to which the reformers objected; Saint Anthony of the Desert, who of all of the saints named Anthony seems to be intended here was the father of monasticism.

    A quarter of a year we tarried there in the tent,
Wherein we had Capricorn baked like red deer.
I tarried so long til I was shent: *disgraced*
Jesu, how they cried out of me there.   *complained*
    Well, I must abroad among my friends;   350
Every hour til I come they think a day;
I will go among them to fulfill their minds.
Fare ye well, gossip! I must needs away!

TEMERITY: What! Brother Covetous! Whither away so fast?
    I saw you not, by the mass, til I was almost past.

COVETOUS: What, mine own brother Temerity!
    I rejoice to see you, I swear by the Trinity.

INCONSIDERATION: For thee we three have taken great thought.

PRECIPITATION: Lord, how far about for you we have sought!

COVETOUS: And I pray you, where have you three sought for
    me?   360

PRECIPITATION: In the King's Bench and in the Marshalsea;
    Yea, and in all the Counters, and at Newgate;
    For these are places meet for thine estate.[7]   *fit*

COVETOUS: I perceive well it must be my chance
    Above all your kinfolk you to enhance.
    Your place is at Saint Thomas à Watrings
    Or else at Wapping beyond Saint Katherine's.[8]
    There will I dub you knights of the halter,
    Among your mates there strongly to talter.   *hang (?)*

INCONSIDERATION: You are to blame, in faith, Precipitation,   370
    For you began this fond communication.   *foolish*

COVETOUS: You are knaves to use such salutation!

TEMERITY: Why, brother, we speak for your consolation!

COVETOUS: Speak what you will! Even with you I can make!
    Speak you in mirth, and in mirth I do it take;
    But, by the mass, if you go about me to flout,
    I will make the better of you all three a lout.

PRECIPITATION: No, sir, no! We come not hither you to molest;

---

[7] King's Bench, Marshalsea, Counters, and Newgate: the King's Bench was a court which sat where the sovereign resided, the others are prisons.
[8] Saint Thomas a Watrings, Wapping Beyond Saint Katherine's: these were both places of execution.

Our business, I tell you, is very earnest.

INCONSIDERATION: By God's ares, true! If now we make   *arse (?)*
   not shift,   380
We are all four like to have a great lift.

TEMERITY: If ever Covetous were in danger of punishment,
He standeth now at the point of banishment.

COVETOUS: *Sancte Blaci!* You make me much to muse.   *Holy Satan (?)*
Passion of me, sirs, why what news?

PRECIPITATION: I think the day of judgement be now at hand,
For it was never thus since the world did stand.
The Worldly Man hath forsaken Covetous clean,
And unto Contentation and Enough he doth lean.

COVETOUS: What, doth he? *Benedicite!* is this true?   *bless you* 390

INCONSIDERATION: Yea faith, he is quite becomen anew;
Moreover, with the Heavenly Man he is associate,
Where he studieth the rules of godly life early and late.

COVETOUS: Body of me! Precipitation, fetch me my gown,
My cap and my chain; I will to the town.
Marry, sir, indeed it is time to stir coals.
I will go near to fetch some of them out of their holes.

TEMERITY: Haste maketh waste, brother Covetous, ye wot;   *know*
No love so soon cold as that is most hot!
I warrant you the Worldly Man will soon be weary,   400
For they will not suffer him once to be merry,
And verily he is inclined to be naught;
Therefore think not that by them he will long be taught.

COVETOUS: Now, by the mass, of one that should have sapience,
I never heard none utter such a foolish sentence!
Know you not that whensoever a sinner doth repent,
That God forgiveth him his wickedness incontinent?   *immediately*

INCONSIDERATION: True indeed, as heretofore hath been seen;
Many have been made heavenly that worldly have been.

PRECIPITATION: Here is your gown, your chain and your cap.   410

COVETOUS: Body of me, but for shame thou shouldst bear me
   a rap!
Whoreson thief—the devil in hell thee choke
What meanest thou, foolish knave, to bring my cloak?

TEMERITY: Why, my brother is blind, I hold you a crown!   *bet*
  Body of me, he knoweth not a cloak from a gown.

INCONSIDERATION: Tush, Masters! He was stirring in the
      morning betime.   *early*
  At four of the clock in a cellar he was saying of prime.[9]

PRECIPITATION: I blame him not, though betimes he steer   *stare*
  For he is made ale-cunner in our parish this year.   *taster*
  His pains is so great in tasting of drink   420
  That many times his eyes into his head do sink,
  And then he looketh prettily as narrow as a crow—   *nearly*
  I tell you he can scarce read the letters of his crossrow.   *alphabet*

COVETOUS: Body of me, ye are knaves all three!
  Take gown, chain, cap and all, for me!
  I will be even with you all, I swear by God's mother!
  Choose you, shift how you can one for another.
          (*He starts out.*)
  I warrant you, I shall be able to shift for myself,
  Or else you may say I were a foolish elf.

TEMERITY: (*Holding him*) Why brother, you said you would all
      things well take!   430

COVETOUS: Yea, but I would not have you your fool me to
      make;
  For you know well enough that of you all three
  I am worthy the governor and ruler to be.
  "Covetous," sayeth the wise man, "is the root of all evil";
  Therefore Covetous is the chiefest that cometh from the devil.
  But this is that knave—I mean Precipitation—
  But I will be even with him, I swear by the Passion!

PRECIPITATION: (*Coming toward him*)   I am sorry, by my truth,
      that you are so sore offended.
  What, sir! If a fault be made, it shall be amended.

COVETOUS: Nay, faith! I am an ale-cunner, or some drunken
      fool!   440
  I am no better, but your courage I will cool!
          (*He fighteth with them both with his dagger.*)
  That witless knave, too, Inconsideration,

Prime: a canonical service celebrated at sunrise.

He was beginner of this disputation;
But it is no matter, once ere Christmas day
I will be even with you, be as ye may.

INCONSIDERATION (*Laying hold on him*): What, worshipful
    M. Covetous, are you angry with me?
I am sorry for it, man! What can I more be?
Hang me up by the neck like a strong thief   *flagrantly guilty*
If ever I speak any word that shall put you to grief.

COVETOUS: I would do for you, sirs, for I love you all three.   450
Marry, then, I look that as I am you should accept me.

TEMERITY: By my troth, brother, I dare say none of us all
But that to do as you bid us, ready find you shall.

COVETOUS: Marry, then, on good fellowship let us like friends
    agree.

ALL: Why above all things, that desire we!

COVETOUS: Will you help, then, to make me gay?

TEMERITY: As you will wish it, so we will you array.

COVETOUS: Will you consent to show unto me reverence?

PRECIPITATION: Yea, at all times we will show to you our
    obedience.

COVETOUS: Will you take me for your master and head?   460

INCONSIDERATION: Yea marry, sir, for so it standeth us in stead.

COVETOUS: And do you say as you think, in very deed?

TEMERITY: Yea, that shall you prove in all time of need.

COVETOUS: First, to help on my gown some pains do you take,
    And then I will see what court'sy you can make.

INCONSIDERATION: It is trim indeed! By the mass, in that gown
Me thinks you be worthy to be mayor of a town.

COVETOUS: Say you so? Then how like you this countenance?

PRECIPITATION: Very comely, and like a person of great
    governance.

COVETOUS: Then all is well. Come, come, do your duty.   470

ALL THREE: Oh worthy Prince Covetous, we humbly salute ye!

COVETOUS: Body of me! That same will mar all,
When in company I come if Covetous you do me call.

TEMERITY: Therefore it is best for us all to change our names

PRECIPITATION: Or else, peradventure, we shall come to shames.

COVETOUS: Well hold your peace, then; let me alone,
  And I will devise names for you, every one.
  (*He thinks.*)
  Sirra, nay you gape at me!
TEMERITY: What shall my name be?
COVETOUS: You will have it ere I have it, will ye?
  Sirra, thy name shall be—
PRECIPITATION: What, I pray you?   480
COVETOUS: A shame take thee, unmannerly lout,
  Thou camest so hastily thou hast put me out.
     [*indicating someone in the audience*]
  Nay, that maid looks on me!
     (*He thinks.*)
  Come hither, Inconsideration; I have a name for thee.
INCONSIDERATION: Have you, sir? I pray you, what shall it be?
COVETOUS: Nay, by the mass, it is gone again!
INCONSIDERATION: And I would know it, I tell you, very fain.
COVETOUS: Yea, but you must tarry till I have it.
TEMERITY: I tell you, my brother hath a brave wit!
COVETOUS: A shame take them! I have them now, all three.   490
     (*to Inconsideration*)
  Come hither, brother, I will tell you what your name shall be.
  You know that men nowadays to reason do trust;
  Therefore Reason, yourself from henceforth name you must.
  Temerity, I know well thy quality;
  Thou art heady, thou shalt be called Agility.
  I study a name for Precipitation, if it may hit.
  Let me see—by my truth, ye shall be called Ready Wit.
PRECIPITATION: An excellent name indeed, for I am ready and
     quick with a pen;
  For before I see one I can condemn ten;
  I pass not for any man's matters or cause;   *care* 500
  Money and wit shall govern the laws.
COVETOUS: Well masters, I have chosen names for each one
     of you,
  But mine own name I know not, I make God a vow.
  How if I call my name Wit, or Policy?

TEMERITY: Marry sir, that agreeth to your nature exceedingly.

COVETOUS: Truth, for what shall the worldly man do with
   you three,

 Except to maintain you he take in me;

 Little worth is Reason, Ready Wit and Agility,

 Except to maintain them there be a Policy.

 Sirs, you tell me the Worldly Man is converted?   510

PRECIPITATION: Yea, faith, that forever from us he is departed.

COVETOUS: Forever, quoth he. Ha, ha, ha! No, no, I warrant
   thee.

 What this gear meaneth, full well I do espy.   *whim*

 Tush, he purposeth to go both to heaven and to hell

 And fetch news from thence to the people to tell.

 He will be a prophet that was wont to be a devil.

TEMERITY: But his prophecy, I think, will prove but evil.

INCONSIDERATION: Well, no more words! Enough is as good as
   a feast.

 They say it is perilous with edge tools to jest.

COVETOUS: Now, sirs, I will tell you, this is all my drift,   520

 To get the Worldly Man hither by some shift.

 Temerity, thou shalt with him thyself acquaint,

 And what thou canst do to him, forth ye shall paint.   *show*

 Virtue is made an error by Temerity,

 For stoutly he standeth against the verity;

 For Temerity, learned men do say,

 Is a quality to do all things without delay;

 So that if thou mayest get into his habitation,

 He will soon be weary of Enough and Contentation.

 Then with him shall work Precipitation,   530

 Who is of this property and inclination—

 To see and to do all without forecast,

 Not thinking of things to come, or of things past;

 Therefore, after that Temerity doth once enter,

 Thou shalt put thy service in adventer.   *adventure*

 Then Inconsideration shall get into his mind,

 Who is a quality much of the same kind;

 He weigheth neither the time, person, nor place,

Neither, as they say, the tail nor the face.
Thus, if you three within him once be placed,　540
You shall see that Enough, of him shall soon be disgraced.
Under the name of Policy, to enter I do not doubt,
And I being entered, Enough shall be cast out;
For where Covetous in any place doth remain,
There Content with Enough cannot abide certain;
So that he shall run headlong into the pit,
Doing all things headlong, without modesty or wit.
Lo, here to you my mind I have disclosed;
All have I said, that I have now purposed.

TEMERITY:　By the faith of my body, it is worthily devised!　550

COVETOUS:　In all the haste go thou, and be thou disguised.
Marry, now there cometh another thing to my remembrance.
Are none of you acquainted with Ghostly Ignorance?　*spiritual*

INCONSIDERATION:　What, he pardy! He is my ghostly father.

COVETOUS:　I would speak with him, so much the rather.
For divers causes that I do consider,
My brother and thou shall depart hence together.
Look you make you trim as fast as you can,
And then in haste seek to speak with the Worldly Man.
Inconsideration, to Ghostly Ignorance thou shalt resort,　560
And this message from me to him thou shalt report:
First, that he name himself Devotion,
And we will help him to dignity and promotion;
Charge him not to be out of the way,
For we purpose to send for him this present day.

TEMERITY:　Forasmuch as you put your trust and confidence in
　　me,
What I can do for you, ere it be long you shall see.

INCONSIDERATION:　Where to find Ghostly Ignorance I am sure—
Seldom or never at home at his own cure.　*parish*

PRECIPITATION:　No, the sermons that Ghostly Ignorance hath
　　made　570
Hath almost brought all the parishes in England out of
　　trade.

COVETOUS:　Well, hie you apace, that you were gone;　*hasten*

Precipitation and I will tarry here alone.

TEMERITY: Farewell, Covetous, til we meet again!

INCONSIDERATION: That shall not be long, if our purpose we
    obtain.

COVETOUS: Nay! Here, you! God be with you, will you begone!
    Body of me, you are no better than knaves, every one!
    "Farewell, Covetous"? Nay, farewell, good Lob!
        (*He starts out, and then comes back.*)
    Ye have even as much manners as hath a dog!
    Plain Covetous! This is according to promise, is it not?   580
    Well what I intend to do for it, I wot what I wot!   *know*

TEMERITY: I cry you mercy, right worshipful Master Covetise,
    Most prudent, politic, sapient and wise!

INCONSIDERATION: Pardon us! By my truth, it was but
    forgotten.

COVETOUS: Nay, I take it even thus: soon ripe, soon rotten.
    I am nobody with you. But by Him I swear,
    I look the greatest stroke amongst you to bear.

TEMERITY: Enough is as good as a feast! We are warned, I
    trow.
    From henceforth our duties, I warrant ye, we will show.
    We take our leave of you, noble Prince Covetise,   590
    The King, the Emperor, yea, the God of all Vice.

INCONSIDERATION: Oh worthy visage and body well compact,
    Oh goodly man in wit, work and fact,
    We simple creatures do show to you obedience,
    Being minded to depart under your patience.

COVETOUS: Yea marry, this is somewhat like the matter.

PRECIPITATION: Crafty knaves, how they can a fool flatter!

COVETOUS: Fare ye well, both. Give me your hands, one after
    another;
    I love ye as dearly as the children of my mother.
        (*Exit* INCONSIDERATION *and* TEMERITY.)
    How sayest thou, Precipitation? How likest thou this
    matter?   600

PRECIPITATION: By my truth, I will tell the truth—yea, and
    not flatter.

I perceive well enough what here you do mean;
You will not leave til you have marred him clean.   *wholly*
Not only riches singular and private,
But also public weals you will spoliate;
For I perceive by your former monition
That through Ghostly Ignorance you will destroy devotion—
I mean true faith in God's love, and hope—
And cause him in clear sunshine for light to grope.   610

COVETOUS: Thou thinkest as truth is, in very deed.
I intend no less, if my device may likely speed.
There will I begin, and if error once rage in religion,
I warrant thee, in public weal will soon be division.

PRECIPITATION: Well, what you intend, to me doth not
          appertain;
My nature is to rage where haste doth reign.
And what causeth haste, but only Temerity.
That maketh fools hardy with security.
Precipitation forth doth this Worldly Man lead,
So that all his affairs be done rudely on head;   *rashly*
Then Inconsideration both night and day   620
Shall prompt him forward, nothing at all to weigh,
Neither to consider his beginning,
Neither at the end, what shall be the winning;
So that if all we do our proper nature and kind,
He shall not regard who shall the profit find.

COVETOUS: *Lupus est in fabula*, no more words![10]

PRECIPITATION: I never fear any such kind of burdes.   *games*
This is the Worldly Man, I suppose, indeed.

          (*Enter the* WORLDLY MAN *and* ENOUGH. *Let the* WORLDLY
          MAN *stand afar off in a strange attire.*)

COVETOUS: To work wisely with him, I see we had need.

WORLDLY MAN: I find it true, as the wise King Solomon
          doth say,   630
It is better to have a little with the fear of the Lord
Than to have much treasure and yet go astray—[11]

---

[10] *Lupus . . . fabula:* "It is the wolf in the story," that is, speak of the devil.
[11] See Proverbs 15, 16: "Better is little with fear of the Lord, than great treasure and trouble therewith."

I mean to decline from God's holy word.
 The proverb sayeth Enough is as Good as a Feast;
He that hath enough and cannot be content,
In my judgement is worse than a beast,
For he wanteth a good conscience, mind and intent.
ENOUGH (*poorly arrayed*):   The Chariot of Covetous, as Bernard
     doth write,
On four wheels of vices is carried away;
And these be the four vices that he doth recite: 640
Contempt of God, forgetfulness of death each day,
Faint courage, and ungentleness, he doth say.
These be the wheels that to adversity's cart doth belong.
These have persuasions to beguile men many and strong.
 The same chariot hath two horses which doth it draw,
The one named Raveny and the other   *robbery*
     Niggardship;   *stinginess*
Their carter is Desire-to-Have, who always doth claw,
By fraud or guile, one another to nip.
This carter hath two cords to his whip,
     The one is appetite-and-felicity-for-to-get,   650
     The other is called dread-and-fear-to-forlet.   *lose*
WORLDLY MAN: When this chariot goes in the ground of man's
     mind,
He is not once able to think a good thought;
For Covetous doth the heart so much to lucre bind,
That he judgeth all things to be vain and nought
Except some gain or profit thereby be brought.
 I myself am able to say it, for I do it know,
To have gotten money I studied to deceive high and low.
But thanks be to God, the Father of all might,
Which will not the death of sinners, as Scripture doth say!   660
It hath pleased Him to open unto me the true light,
Whereby I perceive the right path from the broad way.
Therefore I am content myself for to stay
With Enough, which bringeth me to quiet in body and mind—
Yea, and all other commodities therewith I do find.
ENOUGH: Godliness is great riches, if a man can be content

When God hath sent him plenty and Enough.
Let us praise Him for our food and raiment,
And live godly all our lives through;
For we must tread the paths of death so sharp and rough,   670
    And then we shall be sure to carry as little away
    As we brought with us, thus Saint Paul doth say.

COVETOUS: Body of me! He is marvelous foregone!
We will have somewhat to do with him, anon.

PRECIPITATION: It was ill luck that he came not alone.
I would that beggarly knave in hell were.

COVETOUS: Well, let me alone. I will go near
To cause him of his company to be weary.
I have done as great acts thrice this year;
I am not to learn to row in Illiran's ferry.   *(?)* 680
    I will go to him, and thou shalt wait upon me.
Thou shalt hear what a tale to him I will tell.

PRECIPITATION: If thou speed well now, I dare promise thee,
The devil will give thee the crown of hell.

        [COVETOUS *approaches* ENOUGH.]

COVETOUS: God speed you, sir. I pray you, might I be so bold
As to have a word or two with you in your ear?

ENOUGH: Yea hardily, my friend, say what you would.
Your mind unto me you may boldly declare.

COVETOUS: I pray you, are you not acquainted with this
      gentleman?
I would fain speak with him a word or twain alone.   690
I beseech you, help me to my request, if you can,
For I have haste; on my way I must needs begone.

ENOUGH: If you had required a greater thing of me,
I would have done it for you, I tell you certain.
    [*To Worldly Man*]
Sir, one of yonder men which you do see
Would speak with you alone, very fain.

WORLDLY MAN: I will go to him and know his mind.
Is it you that would speak with me, my friend?

COVETOUS: Yea, forsooth, sir.

WORLDLY MAN: What say you to me?

COVETOUS: Oh sir, Oh good sir! Oh, oh, oh, my heart will
    break!   700
  Oh, oh, for sorrow, God wot, I cannot speak!   *knows*
  (*He weeps.*)
WORLDLY MAN: What is the matter? Wherefore weep you thus?
  (*He weeps.*)
PRECIPITATION: Pure love causeth him, sir, I wus.   *think*
  I am sure that he loves you at the heart.
WORLDLY MAN: I thank him truely, it is undeserved on my part.
  Gentle friend, I pray you cease your lamentation.
  Sure, it is a strange thing to see a man weep on this fashion.
      (*Let the Vice weep and howl and make great lamentation to the
      Worldly Man.*)
COVETOUS: I cannot choose; Oh, oh, I cannot choose!
  Woe! I cannot choose, if my life I should lose!
  To hear that I hear! oh well, it is no matter.   710
  Oh, oh, oh, I am not he that any man will flatter.
WORLDLY MAN: To hear what you hear? Why, what hear you
    of me?
PRECIPITATION: Marry sir, he heareth that wonderfully changed
    you be.
WORLDLY MAN: I am so indeed, for that I give God the glory;
  And if you be my friend, for my change you are not sorry.
  I trust I have chosen all for the best,
  For my former wickedness I hate and detest.
COVETOUS: Woe! Nay, I would to God that were the worst!
  But I shall have ill will. I think I am accurst!
WORLDLY MAN: I judge him not to be of a discreet mind   720
  That for the truth will be angry with his friend.
  The talk of talkers' tongues I do not much weigh,
  Yet, I pray you heartily, tell me what they say.
COVETOUS: Covetous, covetous every man sayeth you be—
  A shame take them all, prattling knaves for me!
  I am of such a nature as no man is but I:
  To hear my friend ill spoken of, I had rather die.
  Yea, wise man you are called, even so.
  All the country of you speak both shame and woe.

"He was wont," sayeth one, "to keep a good house." 730
"But now," sayeth another, "there is no living for a mouse."
WORLDLY MAN: If this be the worst, for their talk I do not care;
Let them say so still hardily, and do not spare.
I trust I have chosen, with Mary, the better part.[12]
PRECIPITATION: Oh yet, good sir, this grieveth him to the heart.
COVETOUS: Yea, God wot! It is none other, it is none other!
I love you as well as mine own born brother.
Think you it grieveth me not to hear each boy and girl
To say that the Worldly Man is become a churl?
WORLDLY MAN: He had need to live very circumspectly 740
That would take upon him to please all men directly.
Behold Enough!
       (*He goes toward him.*)
COVETOUS (*plucking him back*):   Nay, hear you! This grieveth me
       worst, so God me save.
They say you keep company with every beggarly knave.
WORLDLY MAN: Where I keep company, they have nought to
       do.
As near as I can, into none but honest company I go.
See you, I pray you, Enough?
COVETOUS: Nay, but hear you, is Enough his name?
WORLDLY MAN: Yea indeed, it is even the very self same.
COVETOUS: Saint Dunstan! A man would not judge it by his
       coat. 750
Now truly, I would not take him to be worth a groat.
Hark you, hark you! In faith, know you not me?
WORLDLY MAN: No, truly. That I wot of, I did you never   *know*
       see.
PRECIPITATION: That is marvel indeed, the truth for to tell.
I dare say your father knew us both very well.
COVETOUS: Did you never hear him speak of one Policy?
WORLDLY MAN: Yes, that I have sure, an hundred times verily.
COVETOUS: I am he, verily, and this your friend Ready Wit,
With whom to be acquainted for you it is fit.

---

[12] Chosen, with Mary, the better part: Mary chose to follow Jesus, while her sister Martha remained at home. (See Luke 10: 38–41.)

PRECIPITATION: Truth, indeed! As Seneca sayeth wittily,   760
  The wise man and not the rich is void of misery.
WORLDLY MAN: Policy and Ready Wit! Now the truth is so,
  There is no man living that can spare you two.
  I trust God worketh for me happily indeed,
  To send me all such things whereof I have need.
  For, without a Ready Wit who can answer make;
  Without a Policy all commodities will slake.
  A Ready Wit will soon gather and conceive
  What he shall forsake and what he shall receive.
  Truely, now I remember a saying of Tully, the divine,   770
  Where he doth both wisdom and learning define:
  "Learning maketh young men sober," sayeth he,
  "And causeth old men of good comfort to be."
  Policy is the riches and possession of the poor—
  Yea, it garnisheth the rich with goodly adore—
  So that there is no state, calling or degree
  That may conveniently without you be.
  Give me your hands, for you are welcome heartily;
  I am exceeding joyful of your good company.
  Enough, I beseech you, bid my friends welcome hither,   780
  For from henceforth we must dwell all together.
ENOUGH: Be not rash in taking of a friend, Aristotle doth say,
  Nor when thou hast taken him, cast him not away.
  Admit not thy friend either high or low,
  Except his behavior to others thou dost know;
  For look how before he hath served his other friend,
  Even so he will serve thee, also, in the end.
WORLDLY MAN: Your parable, truly, I do not well understand,
  Except you mean I should have no other friend but you by
      me to stand.
ENOUGH: Enough is as good as a feast, well you wot;   790
  More than enough a man needeth not.
  Whether it be lands, money, friends or store,
  If he have enough, what needeth he any more?
COVETOUS: I perceive that against us two you do grutch.   *complain*
  Can a man of Policy and Ready Wit have too much?

The noble King Solomon was rich and had wisdom great
  store,
Yet he ceased not daily to pray to God for more.
PRECIPITATION: Get thee store of friends, sayeth Cicero, for
  it is deemed,
A true friend more than kinfolk is to be esteemed.
ENOUGH: It is an old proverb and of an ancient time   800
Which sayeth it is not all gold that like gold doth shine;
No more are all friends that friendship pretend,
As is approved with many in the end.
WORLDLY MAN: Yea, Enough, but I am sure that this Policy
And this Ready Wit are my friends verily.
COVETOUS: Are we? Ye faith, thereof you may be sure.
We are they which your wealth shall procure.
Enough is not enough without us two,
For, having not us, what can Enough do?
Enough is maintained by wisdom and Policy,   810
Which is contained of a Ready Wit naturally.
PRECIPITATION: Having a Ready Wit, and of Policy the skill,
You need not to care for this Enough, except you will.
There is another Enough which is invisible,
Which Enough to want is impossible.
As for this Enough is enough, I cannot deny;
But this Enough serveth but even competently.
You have no more now than doth yourself serve,
So that your poor brethren for all you may sterve.   *starve*
But Enough that cometh by us twain.   820
Is able yourself and many other to sustain.
WORLDLY MAN: Your words are even as true as the Gospel,
As one named Reason of late to me did tell.
"You may be more heavenly," sayeth he, "having riches,
Than if you had nothing, the truth to express."
And I find his words true, for when alms I would give,
I have not wherewith the needy to relieve.
Enough I have for myself, I cannot say nay,
But I would I had more to succor the needy alway.
ENOUGH: These words proceed from a covetous mind,   830

And from a worldly lust which doth you blind.
Was not the poor widow for her offering praised more
Than all they that offered from their superfluity and store?
The sacrifice of God, as the prophet David doth say,
Is a broken heart and a good mind alway.

COVETOUS: He says well, by Lady—yea, and like an honest man.
But yet, sir, riches to be good, well prove I can.
For every man is not called after one sort,
But some are called to prophecy, some to preach and exhort;
And he by that means heaven joys to win.   840
But every man knoweth not that way to walk in;
Therefore every man as his vocation is must walk.
I am sure that against this you will not talk.

ENOUGH: The greatest boasters are not the best givers,
Nor the earnest preachers are the best livers.
As lucre increaseth riches and honor,
So covetous enlarges daily more and more.
I know some in this realm which once were content
With poorly enough, which God to them had sent,
Wishing of a good conscience, as they said verily,   850
That God would once again restore the verity.
If it please thee, good Lord, said they, thy word to us again
      send,
And then truly our covetous lives we will amend.
But since it hath pleased God them to wealth to restore,
They are ten times more covetous than they were before.
Yea, headlong, without all consideration,
They for Covetous make some laws in that nation.
Such buying and selling of leases and benefices,
Such doubling of wares to extreme prices!
So shamefully God's ministers they poll and shave   *crop* 860
That not half enough to live upon they have.
But it is an old saying and a true, certainly,
It will not out of the flesh that is bred in the bone, verily.
The Worldly Man will needs be a worldly man still.
Well, choose you! I will let you alone. Do what you will.
I cannot think but those that of me who hold scorn.

Will be glad of me ere ever the year be half worn.
>   (*Exit* ENOUGH.)

WORLDLY MAN: Marry, farewell! Adieu to the devil!

Body of me, he would make me his drivel.   *drudge*

COVETOUS: You may see what a trusty friend he is!   870

WORLDLY MAN: A beggarly knave, I warrant you by the bliss!

And even so he and they went about me to make,

Within a while I should have gone to the hedge for a stake.[13]

PRECIPITATION: I warrant you, that you should have proved
>   shortly,

They would not have left you one groat nor penny.

I marvel you would tarry with them at any time or season;

You are old enough, I trow, to be ruled by reason.

WORLDLY MAN: A shame take them all! I have spent on them
>   twenty pound

That I had of money and of mine own good ground.

I am ashamed of myself, so God me save,   880

Because I have sold almost all that ever I have.

My friends and companions, when I go in the street—

So God help me—I am ashamed them to meet.

COVETOUS: Passion of me, it was time to look about!

They would quite have undone you, or else without doubt.

But I trow, I trow, if you will be ruled by me,

What I will do for you or ere it be long you shall see.

A thousand, thousand, thousand ways I can invent

To fetch in double as much as you have spent.

WORLDLY MAN: Be ruled by you? Yes! Here I do you both
>   embrace,   890

As mine own mind to follow all my life's space.

For I tell you plain, I am weary of their school.

PRECIPITATION: It is time for you, else they would have made
>   you a fool.

WORLDLY MAN; I perceived no less indeed by the talk of Reason,

But so it should have come to pass in season.

COVETOUS: And do you my brother Reason perfectly know?

---

[13] "Gone to the hedge for a stake": obviously the phrase means to have done something foolish. Perhaps its meaning turns on the hedge or bush which was the sign of a tavern.

WORLDLY MAN: Yea, and with him one called Agility, I trow.
  Reason came to me and *mihi flectere mentem,* he said,
  Sola solet ratio dux fida sophorn est,[14] it cannot be denied.
    To Nature and Reason he doth open injury   900
  Which of other men counsel doth seek;
  God hath given men reason, and their wits Policy
  To forsake that is ill and to take that he doth like.
PRECIPITATION: And believe you not these words to be very
      true?
WORLDLY MAN: Yes, and I have thought on them twenty
      times since, I tell you.
  Oh sirs, methinks if I had money and treasure again,
  In faith I would be a lively lad, I tell you plain!
  "Heavenly Man," quoth he! Let them be heavenly, for me.
  The best heaven, methinks, is rich for to be.
COVETOUS: In faith, it shall cost me and my friends a fall,   910
  But you shall be twice as rich as you were before.
  We will do it to spite them even withal,
  Though we do hundreds wrong therefore.
    I have set some aloft in high place
  Which had rather die, I dare well say,
  Than one inch of their state should fall or abase,
  But rather to climb up higher if they may.
    Whow! Of this world I rule the whole state.
  Yea faith, I govern all laws, rites and orders.
  I at my pleasure raise war, strife and debate,   920
  And again I make peace in all coasts and borders.
    Nay, yet a much more marvel than that:
  Behold! See you this little pretty hand?
  This is an arm of steel, for it overthroweth flat
  The strongest walls and towers in the whole land.
    Power I have, laws to alter and make,
  And all laws made are guided by me;
  All that is done is done wholly for my sake.
  What strength I have, by this you may see.
    Moreover, I have in this little hand   930

[14] *Mihi electere mentem:* turn your mind to me; *sola . . . est:* reason alone ought to be the true guide of the wise.

The hearts of all men and women upon earth;
I rule them both by sea and by land.
Plenty I make, and I make also dearth.
 Whow! It is wonderful that is done by Policy!
While you live, take heed—strive not against Policy!
The best of them all are glad of Policy.
Yea, in Westminster Hall they use much Policy.

WORLDLY MAN: *Prudentia noscit omnia*,[15] sayeth the noble man
 Tully;
Policy knoweth all things, both good and ill truly.
Oh Policy, what meant I from Reason and thee to stray?   940
Never will I forsake you nor yours after this day.
O help me, Policy, help me to some money,
Whose taste I love better than the taste of honey!

PRECIPITATION: Since worthy Policy you have entertained,
Now none of his instruments must be disdained.

WORLDLY MAN: Disdained? No, faith, let him teach me what he
 will,
And I will do it if it were mine own father to kill.

COVETOUS: Say you so? By the mass, give me your hand.
 Come, go with me, let us no longer idle stand.
 (*Exit all three together, and make you ready straightaway.*[16] *Enter*
 HEAVENLY MAN.)

HEAVENLY MAN: Oh how hard a thing and difficult it is   950
For them that in their riches do trust
To enter into the kingdom of heaven or bliss!
The words of our Savior to be true, grant we must:
It is as easy for a camel through a needle's eye to thrust,
 As for him that on riches hath fixed his mind
 The way to eternal salvation to find.
Example hereof you see with your eyes,
Of the Worldly Man given to vain pleasures.
He promised, you heard, from sin to arise,
And said he would not love neither money nor treasure   960

---

[15] *Prudentia . . . omnia:* prudence examines everything.
[16] Worldly Man at least will have to change costume for his entrance at line 1113, for he enters there as a
very wealthy and worldly man; Covetous may simply put on a steward's chain, or some article symbolic of
his office; but Precipitation will have to change, for he doubles in the role of tenant. See the list of players.

But as he ought to love it,—that is, in due measure.
  But behold how quickly his promise he hath broke;
Whereby he kindleth God's wrath against him to smoke.
  For now hath he entertained to him Temerity,
Precipitation and heady Inconsideration.
These cause him to work all things headily,
And covet to be had in reputation.
Then Covetous disguiseth him in such a fashion
  That, as Seneca sayeth, he doth good to no man,
But hurt, and most to himself, as time shall prove
    whan.   970
     (*Exit* HEAVENLY MAN.   *Enter an old man,* TENANT, *and
     speak in Cotswold speech.*)[17]

TENANT: Alas, alas! To whom should I make my moan?
Forever and a day cham quite undone.   *I am*
My landlord is so covetous as the devil of hell.
Except chill give him such a shameful rent,   *I will*
As cham not able, away ich must, incontinent.   *at once*
Chave dwelt there this six and thirty year—
Yea, these vorty, ich may tell you, well near—
And ich never paid above yearly vive pound,
And by our Lady, that to be enough chave vound.
Well, now I must give him even as much more,   980
Or else ich must void the next quarter or bevore. *depart*
Oh masters, is not this even a lamentable thing?
To zee how landlords their poor tenants do wring?
And they are not zo covetous to ask nother, ich believe,
But a sort of vools are as ready to give.
And especially strangers—yea, a shameful sort,
Are placed now in England, and that in every port,
That we, our wives and children no houses can get
Wherein we may live, such price on them is zet.
Chad thought a while ago my landlord would not have done
    thus,   990
For he said he would be a Heavenly Man, I wus. *thought*

---

[17] *Cotswold speech:* the speech of the area around Gloucester; it became a conventional dialect to indicate the rustic: ich *or* ch = I, v = *f*, z = *s*.

But zoul, the devil is as heavenly as he!
Three times worse than he was bevore, as var as I can zee!
> (*Enter poorly* [*dressed*] SERVANT.)

SERVANT: Body of me, this would make a man to swear!
A shame take them, marry, that ever they came there!
Nay, by giss, I thought he would not be heavenly long,   *Jesus*
For that to his nature were clean contrary and wrong.
Yonder are such a sort of rutterkins, lively and jolly,   *bullies*
That all that can be gotten is little enough for their belly.
Soul! We work, we labor—and that night and day—   1000
Yet can we scant have meat and drink, the truth to say.
And that which we have is ill enough for dogs,
And we are served withal like a many of hogs.

TENANT: What, servant? I pray thee, what news with thee?

SERVANT: By my truth, father Tenant, even as you see!
Kept like no man's servant, but rather like a slave!
That I am weary of my life, I tell you, so God me save.
My master taketh on like the devil of hell.
There was never one so hasty, cruel and fell.   *ruthless*
But so covetous, Lord, Lord, you will not believe!   1010
I think all his mind and study to bribery he doth give.
> (*Enter* HIRELING.)

HIRELING: Now a pestilence take him, vile, cankered churl!
He is neither good to man, woman, boy, nor girl.
Is this the Heavenly Man? A shame take him else!
Body of me, in all wickedness he now excels,
And if a thing come in his head, be it good or ill,
Without all wit or reason do it he will.
But so covetous,—Lord, I think if he might choose
The dropping of his nose he would not lose.
Every week, truly—nay, then, every day—   1020
He must have account how many eggs his hens lay.
Why, there was never seen such a miser as he—
That the plague cut the throat of him for me!
I have wrought for him this half year by the week;
And now my work is done, my money is to seek.
If I and all mine should starve for money,

Of him, I dare say, I should not get one penny.
A shame take him! How well the scripture of him is weighed,
Which sayeth, "Sleep not til the Hireling thou hast paid."

TENANT: I see well that I complain not of him alone,   1030
But others as well as I have good cause to moan.
Well, servant, weeping will not help this gear,   *situation*
But God will plague him for it, I do not fear.

SERVANT: I told you, Hireling, how you should be served.

HIRELING: What servant! Thou lookest as though thou were
     starved.

TENANT: He looketh as lustily, freshly and as well
As all the servants that with his master do dwell.

HIRELING: His master? Why, he is no better than a thief(!)
For so that he may have it, he cares not who suffer grief.

TENANT: Nay, by the mass, that words is but too true.   1040
So that his riches increaseth, he careth not who rue.

SERVANT: I know the occasion of all this gear,
But I would not for twenty pound it should come to his ear.
He sayeth that he will never leave his extortion
Til of riches he have gotten an innumerable portion.
He will build, plant, set and sow
Til such a fame of him abroad there grow
That there is none like to him in all the country;
And so by that means he shall come to authority.

HIRELING: But lightly those that come to authority after   *often*
     that rate   1050
Do end their lives in some miserable and unhappy state.

TENANT: Thou fool, saith Christ, this night will I fetch thy
     soul from thee,
And then who shall have the things that thine be?
Well, let him alone. I hope all will prove for the best.
Even as he leadeth his life, so shall he find rest.

SERVANT: Peace, peace, for God's sake! Look where the Steward
     comes.
Body of me, sirs, which way shall I run?
          (*He runs out.*
          Enter COVETOUS.)

COVETOUS: God speed you! What mean you? Would you speak
  with me?

TENANT: Yea, sir, even to desire your worship my vriend vor to
  be.

 Ich have a zertain petition to your ma'ship to move,   1060

 And Ich desire you to be my vriend in it, vor God's love.

COVETOUS: What is the matter? Let me know it at once.

 I have somewhat else to do than here to tread the stones.

TENANT: By my truth, sir, I beseech you vor me to speak a
  good word

 To your good master and my landlord.

 Ich have dwelt in his house this vorty years almost,

 And thereupon chave bestowed much money and cost;

 And now ich hear zay ich must double my rent

 Or else void out of it, and that incontinent.   *depart/at once*

 I beseech you, for God's sake on me take some pity and

  bone;   *kindness* 1070

 If I be put out, forever Ich am undone.

 Oh, good sir, I know that you may do much.

COVETOUS: By my truth, I can do nothing herein.

 And, so God help me, I esteem no such matters worth a
  pin.

 By'r Lady, sir, you have had it a fair season,

 And that a man should make what he can of his own, it is
  reason.

 I warrant you, there be enough that that rent will pay.

TENANT: But they shall never thrive on it then, I believe.

 Ich know what he may do with the house and ground;

 He may chance to vind rent enough of vive pound.   1080

COVETOUS: Well care not you for that, if you be a wise man.

 You were best to get one better cheap where you can,

 For I know that so much for it have he may—

 Yea, if it stood empty even this present day.

TENANT: Well, sir, yet methinks there should be a conscience;

 I think God hateth such covetous, sir, by your patience.

COVETOUS: Thou art a foolish fellow here of me to complain,

 For I meddle with no such matters, I tell you plain.

HIRELING (*with excessive courtesy*): Good gentleman—God save
    your life, I pray to our Lord—
May I be so bold to speak with you, gentleman, one word? 1090
COVETOUS: Whither the devil wilt thou? Into mouth, me
    think!
For God's ames, how he smells all of drink!   *arms*
HIRELING: Nay, by my truth, sir, I drink none other drink
    today
But a little fleet milk mingled with whey.   *skimmed milk*
For, so God help me, if for drink or meat I should die,
I have not one farthing any therewith to buy.
And, by my truth, sir, this is my suit at this time:
I served your master in making brick and lime
Half a year together, not missing one day;
And, by my truth, all my wages is yet for to pay.   1100
And if it please you herein to show me some pleasure,
The same to my power with like I will measure.
COVETOUS: Body of me, what a beggarly knave is here!
Why, canst thou not forbear thy money one year?
HIRELING: No, by my truth, sir, for I have no lands,
Nor nothing to live upon but only my hands.
I beseech you, be good to me!
COVETOUS: Why, I meddle not with such things, thou dost know.
HIRELING: Yes, sir; you are master Steward, I trow.
COVETOUS: No, faith, I am but master Receiver;   1110
I take in all, but, by giss, I am no payer.
HIRELING: Your master hath a great sort of receivers indeed,
But not one to pay the Hireling his true meed.   *salary*
      (*Enter* WORLDLY MAN.)
WORLDLY MAN: What, worthy Policy? What make you here
    today?
COVETOUS: About your affairs, I have business this way;
And behold, sir, as I travelled the street,
With these two fellows I chanced for to meet,
Who told me that they had an earnest suit to you!
One for his house that he dwelleth in now,
Wherein, he sayeth, you go about to do him much wrong,   1120

For he sayeth that he hath dwelt in it very long;
The other said you owe him a piece of money,
He wrought with you half a year and had never a penny.
And thus they took on with me before you did come,
And now have I showed you the whole circumstance and sum.

WORLDLY MAN: Marry, hang them! Villians! Have I nought to
    do
But to stand and reason matters with them two?
Hear you, Tenant, in few words you know my mind:
According as I have told you so you shall me find.
Other provide money your lease to renew,   1130
Or else you shall out incontinent, this is true.

TENANT: Oh, landlord, me thinks this is too much extremity.
Alas, upon mine age take you some pity;
Cham elde and have many children and much charge.
I trust, Landlord, ich shall find you better at large.

WORLDLY MAN: I cannot tell what I should do more, believe
    me;
Many landlords would not do as I do by thee;
For I am content for money thou shouldst have it before
    another.
I can do no more for thee if thou wert my brother.

COVETOUS: Thou must be answered, father, there is no remedy.
By Saint Anne, me think he speaketh very reasonably.   1140

TENANT: This reasonable speaking cometh from an unreasonable
    mind.
Woe be to him that to such inconveniences shall a man bind!

HIRELING: If it please you, sir, help me to my money, if you
    may.

WORLDLY MAN: No, by my faith, sir, you get it not today.
You shall tarry my leisure; I will pay you when I see cause.

HIRELING: You are happy, sir, in your hands you have the laws.
But, by giss, if I had anything that would do you pleasure,
You should have it when you would, and not tarry my leisure.
Well, I believe verily that the prayers of the poor and his cry
Shall ascend into the ears of the Lord God on high,   1150
And he will plague all those that righteousness withstand,

And, as the Prophet sayeth, root their posterity out of the land.

TENANT: Well, Hireling, let us depart this place.
It prevaileth not us of him to crave any grace.

HIRELING: No more shall it prevail him, the Scripture sayeth
   indeed,
To ask mercy of the Lord when he standeth in need.
      (*Exit* HIRELING *and* TENANT.)

WORLDLY MAN: Ha, ha, ha! I must laugh, so God me save,
To see what a lot of suitors nowadays we have.

COVETOUS: I warrant you, if you will be ruled by Reason and
   Policy,
You shall have all the world to sue to you shortly.   1160

WORLDLY MAN: A common saying, "The fox fareth the better
   and not the worse
When that the good wife doth him ban and curse."
So what care I though to curse me the people do not cease,
As long as by them my riches doth increase?
Oh Policy, how glorious my buildings do shine!
No gentleman's in this country like unto mine!
Sirra, what shall I do? I must make my barns more great,
For I have not room enough to lay in my rye and wheat.

COVETOUS: Set men a'work with it as soon as ye can.
If you lack room, make more you may than.   *then* 1170

WORLDLY MAN: By giss, I will. They shall in hand tomorrow.
I thank you, Policy, I need nothing to borrow.
Sirra, the little tenament that by my house doth stand—
I would I could get that, too, even out of hand.
I want a little buttery to lay in my drink,
And that would serve the turn handsomely, I think.
And to say the truth, it is not meet that such a beggar as he
Should dwell so near under the nose of me.

COVETOUS: Who the devil put that into your mind?

WORLDLY MAN: Marry, even that did Reason, my trusty
   friend.   1180

COVETOUS: I have been about it myself all this week.
Ready Wit all the laws for to delay doth seek.
We will have it, I warrant you, by hook or by crook.

Tush! I warrant you, for such odd ends daily we look.

PROPHET (*from offstage*): Oh thou earth, earth, earth, hear the
     word of the Lord;

Know thyself to be no better than clay or dust.
    (*Let the* WORLDLY MAN *look suddenly about him.*)

See that thy life to God's truth do always accord,

For from earth thou camest, and to earth thou must.

COVETOUS: What is the matter? Why, what ail ye? Why look
     you so about?

WORLDLY MAN: I heard a terrible noise, surely without
     doubt,   1190

Which pronounced the words of the Prophet Jeremy,

Saying, "Earth, Earth, turn thee speedily!"

COVETOUS: Why, and are you afraid and amazed at that?

I see well you have a heart like a gnat.

PROPHET: That servant that diligently doth fulfill,

And watcheth at all times for the coming of his master,

And doth in the mean season apply his will

Of his master's goods there be no spoil nor waster,

That servant shall be sure to be a taster

  Of God's blessings and joys everlasting,   1200

    Whereas is all consolation, and nothing wanting.

But that servant that liveth jollily without care,

And looketh not diligently unto his office—

His master shall come suddenly, ere he be aware,

And shall minister to him according to justice.

The portion of hypocrites shall be his;

    Into utter darkness cast him out will He,

    Whereas weeping and gnashing of teeth shall be.

      (*Exit* PROPHET.)

COVETOUS: Oh sirra, marry! God's blessing on his heart,

Full honestly he teacheth you, sir, their part.   1210

WORLDLY MAN: These be the words of the Holy Scripture,

Declaring the difference between the just and unpure.

Good Lord, I would know what these words do mean.

COVETOUS: Your Chaplain can tell you, for he is very
     well seen.   *versed*

WORLDLY MAN: I pray you, Policy, call him to me hither.
But look that you come again both together.
COVETOUS: Yes, that we will, I warrant. You need not to fear,
We will be here again ere a horse can lick his ear.
> [*Exit* COVETOUS.]
WORLDLY MAN: By my truth, me thinks I begin to war sick.   *be*
In sending away my counsellor I was somewhat too quick.   1220
Well, I will sit me down and say to sleep here,   *try*
Til they into this place again do appear. Oh, my head!
> (*Enter* GOD'S PLAGUE, *and stand behind him a while before*
> *he speaks.*)
GOD'S PLAGUE: It is even I that upon thee doth blow,
Filling thee with plagues and sundry disease.
What I am, indeed I will learn thee to know,
For I am not afraid thee to displease.
  Thou shalt depart from thy house and land;
Thy wife and children, beggars thou shalt leave;
Thy life thou shalt lose, even out of hand,
And after death thy just reward receive.   1230
  Thy ill-gotten goods shall not thee deliver;
Thine costly buildings shall nothing prevail;
Thy odors, thy sweet smells and thou shalt perish together;
Thy rings, thy bracelets and gold chains shall fall.
  Strangers and those whom thou didst never know
Shall possess that which by fraud thou hast got;
Thy seed from off thy ground God will overthrow,
Because at His Prophet's preaching thou amendest not.
  Thou sleepest in death, as the prophet David doth say,
Out of which sleep when thou shalt awake,   1240
Thou shalt perceive thou must needs away,
And that on thee God will no mercy take.
  I am the Plague of God, properly called,
Which cometh on the wicked suddenly;
I go through all towns and cities strongly walled,
Striking to death, and that without all mercy.
  Here thou wicked, covetous person I do strike,
Which once on the plow hadst taken hold;

But willingly again thou rannest in the dike,   *pit*

Therfore thy plague shall be doubled seven fold.   1250

      (*He goes out and stands at the door.*)[18]

   [*Enter* COVETOUS *and* GHOSTLY IGNORANCE, *who is drunk*]

COVETOUS: Come, Sir Nicholas! Come, Sir Nicholas! Come, Sir
    Nicholas, come!

IGNORANCE: Cham faint, by giss; would ich had a little more
    bum.   *drink*

COVETOUS: A pestilence take thee! Hast thou not enough yet?

IGNORANCE: No, I can drink a gallon and eat never a bit.

COVETOUS: Come, in the knave's name, you must expound a
    matter.

IGNORANCE: I can expound good ale from fair water.

COVETOUS: Tush, fellow, thou must expound a piece of Scripture.

IGNORANCE: I can do it as well as any bishop, I am sure.

I have spouted with the Genevians twenty on a row.[19]

COVETOUS: And thou wert too good for them all, I trow.   1260

IGNORANCE: Was I? Yea faith, that I was, you shall under-
    stand.

With a piece of Latin I set them all on dry land.

COVETOUS: And, I pray thee heartily, what was it? Let me hear.

IGNORANCE: Thou shalt if ye wilt promise to give me a pot of
    beer.

Magistrorum clericum inkepe miorum

Totus perus altus youngus et oldus

Multus knavoribus et quoque fasorum

Pickpursus omnius argentus shavus & polus.[20]

Let me see what they are all able to say to this.

COVETOUS: For out of doubt a worthy piece of learning it is. 1270

IGNORANCE: A man may as much edifying out of my Latin take

As ye may out of expositions that many ministers make.

COVETOUS: Even as thou sayest! In faith, much of a kind,

For they place the Scriptures as feathers in the wind.

Peace! Body of me, our master is asleep.

---

[18] So as to be ready to enter as the Physician.

[19] Genevians: the followers of John Calvin who had established a theocracy in Geneva and made of it a center of Protestant disputation.

[20] *Magistrorum . . . polus:* a passage of dog Latin.

IGNORANCE: Marry, it was time indeed for us silence to keep.

WORLDLY MAN: [*speaking in his sleep*]   Oh, I would if I could,
   but now it is too late!

   Hold thy peace, I pray thee, and do me no more rate!

COVETOUS: To whom speak you, sir, to him or to me?

WORLDLY MAN: There is no remedy now, man, and that thou
   dost see.   1280

IGNORANCE: Passion of me, sirra, he dreameth, me think.

WORLDLY MAN: Is there no remedy, but to hell I must needs
   sink?

COVETOUS: For my life, Devotion, he is haunted with the
   mare.   *nightmare*

IGNORANCE: Nay, it is some worser thing truly, I fear.

COVETOUS: I hold a crown he is not very well.

IGNORANCE: So me thinks, for he dreameth of going to hell.

COVETOUS: We will wake him out of that troublesome sleep.

IGNORANCE: Good Lord, seest thou not? Behold how he doth
   weep.

COVETOUS: How do you, good master? Is he asleep or awake?

WORLDLY MAN: Oh Good Lord, how my heart doth ache!   1290

   Oh sick, sick, never so sick before!

   Good Lord, Policy, I think I shall never go home more.

IGNORANCE: Marry, God forbid! Why, where is your grief?

WORLDLY MAN: All the parts of my body wanteth relief.

   Oh, Devotion, I have such pains in my head

   That truly, truly, I wish myself even dead.

COVETOUS: Me thought you dreamed, for to yourself you did
   talk.

WORLDLY MAN: Indeed, sir, I dreamed I had a great journey to
   walk.

   Oh what great pains and torments I thought myself in,

   Lying in fire, which to burn did never lin.   *cease* 1300

   And methought before me the Plague of God did stand

   Ready to strike me, with a sword in his hand;

   And ever I asked him what was the cause,

   He answered that I was a transgressor of God's laws.

   But Lord, how sick I am, and how terrible is my pain!

No place in my body but sickness therein doth reign.
I like not these foolish dreams, Policy my friend.

COVETOUS: Tush, a straw! Upon them never set your mind.
He that to dreams giveth any confidence or trust,
Without doubt very unquietly live he must. 1310

WORLDLY MAN: Oh, sick, sick, sick! Oh, my head! Oh, my
back!

COVETOUS: What would you have, sir? Tell us what you
lack.

IGNORANCE: Is it not best that I call hither a physician,
That he may of your sickness declare the disposition?

WORLDLY MAN: Oh yea, yea, do so, good Devotion! I pray
thee, Devotion,
God's blessing on thy heart for thy witty motion.
Depart, I pray thee, with as much haste as may be.

IGNORANCE: It shall not be long ere he be here, you shall see.
(*Exit* IGNORANCE.)

WORLDLY MAN: Oh Policy, sick, never so sick! Oh, hold my
head!
Oh, sirra, what shall become of all my goods when I am 1320
dead?

COVETOUS: Dead? Body of me, do you reckon to die this year?
Hold your peace. I warrant you, ye need not fear.
[*To the audience.*]
Lo, see you not how the Worldly Man showeth his kind?
As sick as he is, on his goods is all his mind.

WORLDLY MAN: Oh, Policy, if I might not die, what a fellow
would I be!
In all this country should be none like unto me.
Sirra, what a goodly turret have I made in my hall!
But yet my banqueting house pleaseth me best of all.
Oh, oh! Alas, what a pang is this at my heart!

COVETOUS: Body of me! Aqua vitae! Vinegar! Needs help 1330
he will depart!
Saint Uncumber be with us, and the blessings of Saint Anthony!
Help, help, our Lady of Walsingham and all her holy company!
(*Enter* IGNORANCE *and* PHYSICIAN.)

IGNORANCE: Why, how now? What is the matter? How doth he,
 Policy?

COVETOUS: Body of me,—help—he is gone else, and that verily!

IGNORANCE: Stand away, foolish knave, and let master Physician
 come.

COVETOUS: Master Flebishiten, should I say! M. Physician, I
 pray you look in his bum.

PHYSICIAN: By your leave, my masters, me thinks it is no time
 to jest.

 Stand back, I pray you, and do not me molest.

 Passion of me, masters, count you this a play?

 One of you, quickly bring me hither a key.   1340

 Some drink, Aqua vitae, that may be got!

 With speed let us have some drink that is hot!

COVETOUS: Nay, I told you before he was past remedy.

PHYSICIAN: No, there is life in him yet, I see verily.

 Run, I pray you, and fetch such things as we lack—

 Some drink and a pillow to lay at his back.

IGNORANCE: Here is drink and all things ready at hand.

PHYSICIAN: Give me room, I pray you! Out of my light stand!

 (*Be busy and daw him as though he were at dying.*)   *rouse*

COVETOUS: Jesu mercy! Lo, how busy master Physician is!

 Hear you sir? Is it not best you look on his piss?   1350

PHYSICIAN: Good fellow, be content, I pray you heartily;

 Thou art disposed to jest, me think verily.

COVETOUS: Good fellow? Goodman Whoball, I will make you
 change your note,

 Before that, for your labor, you get the value of a groat.

PHYSICIAN: What ho! Worldly Man! In God's name I say,

 Look up, for the love of God! Do not like a beast decay!

WORLDLY MAN: Who is there? What art thou that callest me?

COVETOUS: Marry, sir, Master Flebishiten Physician is come,
 and it was he.

WORLDLY MAN: Oh sirs, sirs, I fear me all this labor is in
 vain.

 You might have let me go; I was well out of my pain.   1360

 Oh master Physician, how think you? What say you to me?

PHYSICIAN: By my truth, there is no remedy but one that I can
see:

You must put your will to God's will. I can say no more.

COVETOUS: Why, foolish Physician, he knew that well enough
before.

WORLDLY MAN: What sayest thou? Is there no remedy but I
must die?

PHYSICIAN: No, sir, by my truth, as far as I can see or espy.

God may do much, for He is omnipotent;

But you are past help in this world, in man's judgement.

COVETOUS: What the devil dost thou here then? Get thee
away!

WORLDLY MAN: Depart, Physician, and thou hast no   *if* 1370
more to say.

PHYSICIAN: I trust, then, sir, you will content me for my
painstaking.

COVETOUS: You shall have a new loaf at the maid's next baking.

WORLDLY MAN: Go thy ways, I pray thee, and trouble not my
mind;

For these news to give thee anything, in my heart I cannot
find.

PHYSICIAN: Good Lord have mercy on thee! Belike it is too
late to amend.

In wickedness thou hast lived, even so thou wilt end.

Gentlemen, I trust you will not see me lose my labor.

COVETOUS: Gentleman, go as you came; you are not so much in
my favor.

PHYSICIAN: A common saying indeed—that is "Like unto like."

A wicked M[aster] for wicked servants God must needs   1380
strike.

(*Exit* PHYSICIAN.)

WORLDLY MAN: Oh sirs, is there no remedy? What shall I say?

Is it not best I set all things at a stay?   *in order*

COVETOUS: Yes, make sure work of that while as you be here.

IGNORANCE: It is time indeed, for death in you doth appear.

WORLDLY MAN: Once you know that I am greatly in debt,

And now every one will strive, their own for to get.

Bid my wife, therefore, get a letter of administration as soon
    as she may,
And then as she listeth, my creditors she may pay.
Indeed, I have enough to pay every man his,
But, by Lady, I cannot tell what mine own shall miss.   1390
Commend me to her, and bid her take no thought,
But in any wise let her, as near as she can, forego nought.
COVETOUS: By my truth, this is wonderfully well invented.
As you have said, I warrant you, it shall be frequented.   *done*
IGNORANCE: Your mind in this thing undoubted is not ill.
Now, as for other things, it is best you make a will.
WORLDLY MAN: It shall be, Devotion, even as thou hast said.
Write quickly, or of my life I am afraid.
Oh, must I needs die? Oh, must I needs away?
IGNORANCE: Here is ink and paper. What shall I write?   1400
WORLDLY MAN: "In the name," first of all do thou indite.
IGNORANCE: "In the name—In— In— In— In the name."
    What more?
WORLDLY MAN: "Of—of—of—of—" What more?
    (*He falls down and dies.*)
COVETOUS: Body of me! Down with the paper, away with the
    ink.
IGNORANCE: Passion of me, Covetous, he is gone, me think!
Hold him, hold him, let us see if any life in him be.
COVETOUS: Nay, hold him that will! The devil hold him, for me!
IGNORANCE: Passion of me, he is dead! How shall we do now?
COVETOUS: Canst thou not tell? No more can I, I make God a
    vow.
Sirra, here was a trim end that he did make;   *proper* 1410
Thou never heardst him the name of God in his mouth take.
IGNORANCE: Tush! God? A straw! His mind was other ways
    occupied;
All his study was who should have his goods when he died.
Indeed, all men may perceive his mind to be corrupt and ill,
For God would not suffer him to name Him in his will.
A strange matter—when men have given over God,
They may be sure to be scourged with His sharp rod.

COVETOUS: This is the end always where I begin,
For I am the root of all wickedness and sin.
I never rest to teach and instruct men to evil,   1420
Til I bring them, both body and soul, to the Devil,
As we have done this Worldly Man here, as you see.
Come therefore, Ignorance, wait thou upon me.
The Devil and I, thou shalt see, will not leave
Til we have made the greatest part to us to cleave.
Come, let us go hence, here is no more to be said.
Farewell, my masters, our parts we have played.
      [*Exit* COVETOUS *and* IGNORANCE.]
      (*Enter here* SATAN.)
SATAN: Oh, oh, oh, oh! All is mine, all is mine!
My kingdom increaseth every hour and day.
Oh, how they seek my majesty divine!   1430
To come to me, they labor all that they may.
   "The Worldly Man," quoth he? Nay, the devilish man
     than,
For more wickedness and mischief than he did use
I myself, indeed, never devise can.
Oh, at his jolly wisdom I must needs muse!
   How cunningly put he his money to usury—
Yea, and that without offense of any law!
He was not to learn any kind of bribery
Whereby wicked gains to him he might draw.
   An abominable drunkard, a stinking lecherer,   1440
A filthy sodomite, a corrupt conscience within,
A privy slanderer and a subtle murderer—
To be short, a very dunghill and sink of sin!
Oh my boy Covetous, I may thank thee of all this;
Thou nousledest him in all mischief and vice;   *trained*
Therefore shalt thou be sure to have my bliss,
For above all other thou indeed art most wise.
   Thou teachest the Worldly Man a leasemonger to be,
To oppress the poor and of his riches him to defraud,
Wickedly to use the laws he learned of thee;   1450
Therefore indeed thou art worthy of much laud.   *praise*

All you worldly men, that in your riches do trust,
Be merry and jocund, build palaces and make lusty cheer;
Put your money to usury, let it not lie and rust;
Occupy yourselves in my laws while ye be here.

Spare not nor care not what mischief you frequent;
Use drunkenness, deceit, take other men's wives;
Pass of nothing—one hour is enough to repent   *care for*
Of all the wickedness you have done in your lives.

Oh, if you will thus after my laws behave,   1460
You shall have all things, as this Worldly Man had.
Be bold of me what you will to crave,
And doubt you not but with you I will play the loving lad.

Yea, and after death I will provide a place
For you in my kingdom forever to reign.
You shall fare no worse than doth mine own grace—
That is, to lie burning forever in pain.

Come on, mine own boy, go thou with me.
Thou hast served me duely and hatest me never;
Therefore, now for thy pains rewarded shalt thou be   1470
In everlasting fire that burneth forever.

(SATAN *carries him out upon his back*.)
[*Enter* CONTENTATION, HEAVENLY MAN *and* ENOUGH.]

CONTENTATION: He that toucheth pitch shall be defiled with the
    same,
And he that keepeth company with those that be vicious
Shall at the length grow like unto the same,
Working things wicked and pernicious.
Even so it is also to be associate with the righteous,
For he that haunteth and keepeth honest company
Cannot choose but live according to the same actually.

Example: the Jews, being conversant with the heathen,
Drank of their superstition and idolatry.   1480
And by that means fell from the true God of heaven,
To worshipping of blocks, which was mere blasphemy.
Likewise it is at this day, verily.
Christian men are seduced by keeping of ill company,
And brought from the very truth to hypocrisy.

> And who are those that are thus deceived?
> Even such as are not content when [they] are well;
> They be not thankful for that they have received,
> But ever they think still more and more to excel;
> Contentation from their minds they do expell,   1490
> And, under the pretence of Reason, Wit and Policy,
> They covet to run to mischief and sin headily.

HEAVENLY MAN: Like as gold and silver is tried in the fire,
> So faithful men in the furnace of adversity be proved.
> The heavenly must not live as flesh and lust doth desire,
> But heavenly things of heavenly men be loved.
> With no kind of temptation he must be moved,
> Be it sickness, or poverty, or whatsoever of God is sent;
> The heavenly must take it patiently, and be therewith content.

ENOUGH: Enough is as good as a feast where Contentation   1500
>   doth dwell,
> For where he remaineth is the spirit of God with rest.
> The unquiet mind of the covetous doth grutch and   *complain*
>   swell,
> And to live with Enough he doth abhor and detest.
> The greedy gasping of Covetous doth him so molest
> That to be rich he all his whole mind doth set,
> Nothing regarding how the same he doth get.

CONTENTATION: Pythagoras sayeth that a man of covetous desire
> Cannot be contented neither with abundance,
> For the more he hath, the more still he doth require;
> Wherefore such persons provoke God to vengeance.   1510
> Example of the Worldly Man, late of remembrance,
> Whose wicked life offended the Lord so exceedingly
> That His heavy plagues came upon him suddenly.

HEAVENLY MAN: God grant his end example may be
> To all men, how their riches they shall use.
> Make not that thy god which should be servant unto thee,
> For in so doing, thou dost it greatly abuse.
> I pray God, I say, that our covetous we may refuse,
> And one of us to love another, for that pleaseth God best.
> So shall we be sure to inherit the good land of rest.   1520

(*Enter* REST.)

REST: By God's great goodness, I am sent unto thee.
Rest is my name, wherein the heavenly shall abide.
Happy are those persons that come unto me,
For, I being present, all troubles I do divide.   *take away*
With joys I am adorned—yea, on every side—
Which are prepared for the heavenly from the beginning,
And given unto them for a reward of their godly living.

HEAVENLY MAN: Thanks be given to thee, Oh Father Omnipo-
        tent!
Thy mercies, Lord, and not my deserts, truly,
Have caused those joys to me to be sent.   1530
Grant me grace, therefore, to praise Thy name duely.
Thy goodness appeareth to me every day newly.
Whilst breath and life prolong my days,
My mouth shall not cease Thy Holy Name to praise.

ENOUGH: Enough is as good as a feast. Here let us stay.
We have troubled our audience, that let us remember.
Let us conclude, therefore; but first let us pray
That it will please God in mercy our good mistress to tender
Our faith to establish, wherein we be slender,
That at the last day when the trump shall blow,   1540
For to be heavenly men the Lord may us all know.

CONTENTATION: First let us call to God for Jesu Christ's sake
Long to preserve Elizabeth, our most noble Queen.
Good Lord, grant her highness the heavenly path to take,
And that all byways of her highness may be seen.
Increase her wealth, prolong her health, preserve her life,
That long she may rule this realm without debate or strife.

Finis

✳ ALL FOR MONEY

(T. Lupton, 1577)

This rather extravagantly theatrical piece is characteristic of of the later years of the moral interlude. It takes the final step of eliminating the redemptive central figure, the Mankind character, altogether, and placing the Vices at the center. This produces the pure form of the satiric comedy, whose intention is solely to expose, laugh at, and deplore the way of the world. The elimination of the Mankind character should perhaps be read as one of the portents of the end of the moral interlude as a dramatic form, but a careful reading of the play should also make it clear that the critics of an earlier age erred in referring to plays like this as the "decadence" of the morality form. Rather, the author is groping for modes of expression and of dramatic form that are not yet in being. In other words, this is a theatre of experiment.

Like *The Tide Tarrieth No Man*, this play illustrates an aphoristic text, one which describes the genesis and consequences of sin. But the play is very unlike *The Tide* in several respects. First there is the obvious learnedness and relatively respectable Latinity of the author. Second, there is the very Anglican and almost feudal orientation of the Virtue characters, which is not the case in *The Tide*. And third, and perhaps most importantly, there is the dramatic form. The author has made an early attempt at the "multiple plot" play, echoing the same moral point four times in four very different kinds of dramatic scene. The first version is pure allegory, with Pleasure, Sin and Damnation successively vomited forth upon the stage, by what the writer tantalizingly calls a "fine conveyance" (perhaps a trap door?). Then we have a debate, very reminiscent of John Heywood's Interludes,[1] on the effects of money upon the life of the mind. Next we have a "realistic" scene, showing the activities of a fixer, who, for a price, will take care of whatever you want done, especially if it is illegal. Finally, there is a dramatization from the Bible, of the effects of money-loving upon Judas and Dives. The author has shown no clear preference for any one of these styles, unless it lies in the fact that he has framed the two relatively realistic scenes between an allegory and a Scriptural scene.

All that is known of Lupton is his bibliography, a curious miscellany of tracts and poems, all clustering around 1580. One piece, "A Dreame of the Devil and Dives" (1583), might have some relationship to the last scene of *All for Money*.[2]

Only one edition of the play is known. Our text is a modernized-spelling version of this one, from the Tudor Facsimile Text Society's photographic reproduction, London, 1907.

---

[1] See, especially, Heywood's *Play of Love*.

[2] It certainly seems likely that Lupton was a clergyman, especially since his four explications of his text look as though they might be based on the old fourfold interpretation of Scripture.

A MORAL AND PITIFUL COMEDY ENTITLED ALL FOR MONEY

The Prologue

What good gift of God but may be misused?
Nay, what good thing now but to evil is applied?
Now is the Scripture with many abused,
With mouth it is talked, but with living denied.
What jewel it is the just have well tried,
For if that be a jewel that comforts in care
Then this is a jewel of other most rare.
It is the consolation of the repentant sinner,
It is the chief comfort of Christ's persecuted,
The faithful and wronged person have therein pleasure,   10
The penitent which are with poverty oppressed
Thereby are made richer than the covetous and wicked,
For it is our guidance of all our joy and salvation
Whereby we are certified that Christ hath paid our ransom.
There be many godly sciences needful [to] be studied,
Whereof the body only hath the fruition:[1]
As the physical art whereby the sick are cured;   *medical art*
Music, through whose harmony the mind hath consolation;
Cosmography, which describes the country, city, nation;
Geometry, through whose subtle art and measuring   20
At this day there is much costly and sumptuous building;
The pleasant science of Astrology, whereby God's wonderful
    works
Are rather to be marked than mused on or marvelled,
Which art is not hidden from the Saracens, Pagans and Turks,
Whereby such stars and heavens they may know were not
    created

---

[1] Original reads "thereby many godly sciences needful be studied/Where of the body only hath fruition." If we take "thereby" as "in addition," which is possible, this is acceptable, the sense being "In addition, many godly needful sciences are studied, of which etc." But if, as seems likely, the "thereby" was picked up from the "Whereby" directly above it, the emendation offered here makes better sense. What follows is the *quadrivium*, the four studies leading to the Oxford and Cambridge M.A. degree. They follow the *trivium*, grammar, rhetoric and logic. "Astrology" includes what we call "astronomy."

But by a mighty God, whose name forever be honorèd;
And the moving of the planets to be learned very strange,
With the swift course of the Moon who monthly keeps her
    change.
Yet all other sciences with these before delated   *set forth*
Shall vanish as the smoke and be nothing at length,   30
Yet heavenly Theology, God's Word before declared,
Hath been, is now and ever of such force and strength,
That though heaven and earth perish, as Christ's words
    meaneth,
Yet His Word shall abide and remain forever,
The following whereof, God grant we endeavor,
Notwithstanding epicures and belly-gods so swarm,
Farced and flowing with all kind of evil   *stuffed*
That they fear not to do any kind of harm,
So much they favor their father, the devil.
The Scripture is taken with them as no jewel;   40
Their minds are so much on their riches and goods
That the learned they esteem less than fools that wear hoods.
But if the learned be rich, then be they esteemed,
Not for their learning but for their goods' sake.
Such power have riches and money obtained
That the rich are held up, the poor fools in the lake.
God give them grace not so much on goods to make.
Dives, methinks, might be to them a   *"the rich man", Luke, 16, 19-31*
    warning,
For pleasure therein, lieth now in hell burning.
What metal is this money that makes men so mad?   50
What mischief is it thereby is not wrought?
What earthly thing is not therefore to be had?   *therefore=for that*
What hath been so loved but money hath bought?
What virtue or goodness of us so much sought?
Who doth not wish for money, and that every day?
"I would I had thus much money," each one doth say.
How many for money have been robbed and murdered?
How many false witness, and for money perjured?
How many wives from their husbands have been enticed?

How many maidens to folly for money allured?   60
How many for money have spirits and devils conjured?
How many friends for money have been mortal foes?
Mo mischiefs for money than I can disclose.
How many kings and princes for money have been
    poisoned?
How many betrayers of their country for money every day?
How many with money from true judgment are led?
Did not the prophet *Baalam* curse God's people for money?
Did not *Judas* for money his master Christ betray?
Whereof he had no joy when he the same had done,
But like a damned wretch hung [sic] himself full soon.   70
One asked *Diogenes* why gold did look so wan.
"No marvel," said he, "it is though he so pale do look,
For everyone lays wait to catch him if they can."
Few will take the pains to catch hold on God's Book.
Money ill-used is the devil's snare and hook
Whereby many are brought to endless damnation,
But the godly do bestow it to their salvation.
Fire is the good gift and creature of God,
Whereby we may do good and also wickedly;
We may warm the poor therewith, as charity hath us bade,   80
And also seeth the meat wherewith to feed the hungry;   *cook*
We may keep houses therewith, as many have done truly,
And we may cut our necessaries and meat with our knife,
Wherewith many have cut their own throats and bereaved
    them of their life.
Thus the creature of God is not evil of himself,
But through our misuse from good to evil converted.
Even so, money ill-used is a most wicked pelf
And also as good where well it is bestowed.
Let all people take heed lest it of them be hoarded,
For at the last day against them it will witness,   90
And then that they had not done it, too late for to wish.
And because that every man of money is so greedy,
Our author a pleasant Tragedy with pains hath now made,
Whereby you may perceive All thing is for money,

For *omnia pecunia effici possunt*, as in Tully's sentence is   *Cicero'*
    said.[2]
In hearing us attentively we crave but your aid,
Beseeching God, the hearers that thereby shall be touched
May rather amend their lives than therewith be grieved.

The end of the Prologue

(THEOLOGY cometh in a long ancient garment, like a Prophet,
    and speaketh as doth follow.)
THEOLOGY: What felicity can man have more than in me?
    Wherein ought he to have more joy and consolation?
    What thing will make his conscience more quiet to be
    Than to study that thing which is his salvation?
    I pass all the Sciences, it needeth final probation,   *proof*
    And if you be desirous my name for to know,
    Theology I am called, the knowledge of God's law.
    But who doth not study me chiefly for lucre and gain
    And also thereby to have rich and easy living?
    But who to preach poorly in studying me is fain,   10
    And thereby to salvation the sinful wretch to bring?
    Nay, they had rather to be paid here than to abide God's
        rewarding;
    But such do not remember or believe Daniel,
    Saying, "The converting of a soul shall shine above the
        Angels."[3]
    So many would not study me but for money
    And thereby to live lordly and in wealth,
    The Bishop, the Priest and the Doctor of Divinity
    Would give over their study, not regarding their souls'
        health,
    And use some other thing, for, as it appeareth,   *practice/work*
    The artificer doth leave his art and occupying   *occupation*   20
    And becomes a minister, for money and easy living.[4]

---

[2] This does resemble a passage in Cicero *De Finibus*, II, 17, but the sentiment "Money makes everything possible" is so common that the attribution to Cicero may be more for prestige than for accuracy.
[3] Daniel 12, 3.
[4] This is an attack on the lay preachers of the numerous dissenting protestant sects that had begun to appear after mid-century.

Such as do study, having living by me,
Ought to be a lantern and a spectacle to other,
Whereby they may be allured all sinfullness to fly.
But many of them do use an unchristianly order,
For money they will handle full cruelly their neighbor.
Is not this an hindrance to the knowledge of God's word?
Without they amend, God will strike them with his sword   *unless*

[*Here cometh in* SCIENCE, *clothed like a Philosopher*]

SCIENCE: Many do embrace and study me daily,
But will you know why, and also to what end?   30
Forsooth, for great living, and also for money.
Not to help the needy therewith they do intend,
But vainly on their carcases to consume and spend,
And the rest to revenge malice wickedly they do spare,   *abstain*
Thus to live at pleasure is their delight and care.
But the most part care not for me, neither me regard,
So much they are led with the blind love of money.
Vile money before science and knowledge is preferred.
All good science and knowledge I represent, truly,
Which doth heal the mind, as medicines do the body.   40
Quemadmodum corpus medicina, sic animum curat Philosophia,
Et vita sine litteris mors est, et hominis sepultura.[5]
What, worthy Theology, I am glad to see you here.
I must needs confess you are my head and peer,
For as man through me hath necessary living,
Even so, both body and soul to heavenly joys you bring.

THEOLOGY: O, your argument from mine doth not much
        disagree,
For almost nothing is done unless it be for money,[6]
For the wicked rich man and the lover of money
Regard, but for gain, neither you nor me.   50
Terence the unlearned briefly describeth:
Homine imperito nunquam iniustius
Qui nisi quod ipse fecit, nihil rectum putat.

---

[5] The first line is translated by the preceding English line. The second line means "And life without letters is death, and the sepulcher of man."
[6] Original reads "For nothing is almost done."

So they have money, they care not for us a gnat.[7]
>   (ART *cometh in with certain tools about him of diverse*
>   *occupations.*)[8]

ART: *Artes bonae ubique sunt in praetio, nec possunt a fortuna eripi*—
Good arts are everywhere esteemed and had in price,
And cannot be taken away by Fortune, truly.
My name is called Art, wherein is used much vice;
All occupations and arts which daily now are wrought
By me are represented, throughout the whole earth.   60
Everyone for money me daily have sought,
And all for private gain, as plainly appeareth,
Who doth embrace me thereby to suppress death.
For a commonwealth few use me indeed,
And to bring up their household godly, and the poor to feed.
What husbandman is he that abates the price of corn?
Nay, he rather buys and keeps his own in store.
Many a merchantman that is right simple born,   *lower classes*
With insatiable gains increaseth more and more.
He will not abate his price for helping of the poor.   70
Who will not prevent his neighbor, with buying things over
>   his head?
All this is for money, so that love and charity are dead.
But do I notice here the most worthy Theology,
And also Science-and-Knowledge, next him in degree?
SCIENCE: To us you are welcome, Art most necessary,
No good order in the land can be without us three.
THEOLOGY: Even as I at the first lamented the inordinate love
Of money, which now of everyone is esteemed,
The same to be too true you both I have heard prove.
O Judas, Judas, thereby thyself thou hast damned;   80
Thou hadst been better money never [to] have handled,
And also such as have had in money their consolation
Without the mercy of God shall have everlasting damnation.
Dives vix bonus, a pretty saying, and true:
The rich man is scant good, this is the meaning,

---

[7] "Nothing is worse than the ignorant man who thinks nothing is right except what he himself does."
[8] "Arts" here means something very close to what we would call "crafts."

And money makes pleasure, this sentence doth show:
Pecunia effectrix multarum et magnarum voluptatum.
ART: And again it is written, the second *De Finibus*[9]
Pecunia voluptatis perimitur maximae
The meaning whereof I may thus discuss: 90
Most great pleasures be brought forth for money.
Then if money bring pleasure, pleasure brings forth sin,
And sin brings damnation unless God's grace we win.
THEOLOGY: Well, seeing everyone is so far out of frame
And gives themselves so much to the love of money,
Let us walk, as we ought, in praising God's name,
Beseeching God to send us his favor and mercy:
O Lord, bless thy people from everlasting misery.
Christ had but twelve Apostles and one betrayed his master,
Even Judas, the bag carrier, for money he played the
        traitor.   100
SCIENCE: According to your godly will I am content likewise,
Let us not with money commit (O Lord) any vice.
ART: And as you both have said, I am pleased therewith,
O Lord, keep thy people in thy faith, love and truth.
    (*These three going out,* MONEY *cometh in, having the one half of his*
    gown yellow and the other white, having the coin of silver and gold painted
    upon it, and there must be a chair for him to sit in, and under it or near
    the same there must be some hollow place for one to come up in.)
MONEY speaketh: Hoyghe, hoyghe for money, more sweeter
        than honey!
Who will not for me take a pain?
Each lord and knight for me will fight,
And hazard to be slain.
I wax of such force that no earthly corse
But embraceth me out of measure.   *no ... but=everybody*   110
The doctor, the draper, the plowman, the carter,
In me have their joy and pleasure.
Money is my name, all over is my fame,
I dwell with every degree.
Though great be their living, yet can they do nothing

[9] That is, the second book of Cicero's *De Finibus.*

Without the presence of me.
Many for my sake work while their heart ache
Yet never think themselves weary.
The smith and the shoemaker, the minstrel, the dancer,
With me will drink and be merry.   120
But the churl and the covetous of me are so jealous
That I cannot get out of their sight.
But the servingman, the spender, the usurer and the lender
Do send me abroad day and night.
I am worshipped and honored, and as a god am esteemed,
Yea, many loves me better than God.
No sooner come I to town but many bow down
And come if I hold up the rod.
What need I further show, that everyone doth know?
I do but waste my wind.   130
For servants and prentices will privily rob their masters,
To me they have such a mind.

> (*Here* MONEY *sitteth in a chair and* ADULATION *cometh in and speaketh.*)

ADULATION: O worthy Money, thine absence hath been
      long!
My sorrow in thine absence cannot be spoken with tongue,
For you, Money, is only the pain I do take.
Would I flatter or dissemble unless it were for your sake?

MONEY: What, Adulation, or Flattery, more welcome to me
Than any man this month that I did hear or see.
A true saying, no doubt: *Blandiloquio nihil nocentim;*
Than fair-speaking, or flattery, nothing is more pernicious.   140
Nemo suam turpitudinem perspicit, sed sibi quisque adulator est:
No man to see his filthiness is prest,
But everyone to himself is a very flatterer.
And thou wilt flatter also, to have money for thy labor.

ADULATION: Do you think I will flatter or feign any man
Unless for your sake? Nay, beshrew me then!
Such as love themselves and love their own ways best
Must needs be flattered therein, and then they be at rest.
They must be holden up, and flattered in their evil,

And for you I care not how many I send to the devil.　　150
　　(*Here* MONEY *feigneth himself to be sick.*)
MONEY:　Oh, what pain is this that I feel at my heart?
　My pain is as great as though I were smitten with a dart.
　What ails me, what ails me thus suddenly to be sick?
　I think I shall die without remedy of physic!
ADULATION:　Be of good cheer sir, of this I am sure,
　You cannot die so long as the world doth endure.
　Come hither, Mischievous Help, Money is almost dead,
　Come quickly in, thou Mischief, and help to hold his head.
　　(MISCHIEVOUS HELP *cometh in.*)
MISCHIEVOUS:　What need you call thus hastily, unless you had
　　more need?
　Money may be sick, but he will never be dead.　　160
　But to help at a mischief I am as quick as the best.
　O Lord and master, to help you I am prest.
MONEY:　Welcome, Mischievous Help, I was never so sick
　　before.
　Help to hold my stomach, I swell now more and more.
　I must either vomit or else I shall burst in two,
　What wicked disease is this that troubleth me so?
MISCHIEVOUS:　None can make me believe it is anything else
　But Pleasure, the occasion that thus your belly swells.
　You are so fraught with pleasures that I do perfectly know
　You will never be in quiet till he be rid from your maw,　　170
　Therefore provoke yourself to vomit him quickly,
　And then you will be at quiet, even by and by.
MONEY:　Now I believe truly that Pleasure is the occasion
　Of all my great sickness, malady and passion.
　Therefore, as thou hast said, certain and true it is,
　For money brings all pleasures that any can wish.
　Now I will assay to vomit if I can,
　Therefore either of you play now the pretty man.　　*both*
ADULATION:　Let him hold your head and I will hold your
　　stomach,
　And I hope with speed you shall have very good luck.　　180
　　(*Here* MONEY *shall make as though he would vomit, and with some*

fine conveyance PLEASURE *shall appear from beneath and lie there apparelled.*)

MONEY SPEAKETH: I hope he is coming, for I feel him at my
　　　throat,

Great sorrow pain and grief it is to me, God wot,

I would not for all the world be in such pains again.

As many as loves me, of him will be glad and fain.

PLEASURE: I must needs take Money for the father of me,
　　　Pleasure.

The most part, I am sure, will love me out of measure.

MONEY: Well, my son, well, forget not to do thy feat,

I must needs get me hence, my pains do make me sweat.
　　　[*Exit.*]

ADULATION: Money is to me such a sure friend

That, seeing he is gone, I will not tarry behind.　　　　　　190

PLEASURE: In what case were the world, were it not for
　　　money?

Without joy and pleasure better be dead than alive,

To live like dumb gods who would not be weary?　　　(statues)

To satisfy man's nature with pleasures I can contrive,

But I contain them at this time and hour:

Hawking and hunting, shooting and fishing,[10]

Eating and drinking, dicing and carding,

Riding and running, swimming and singing,

Dancing and leaping, with all kind of playing,

Banqueting with fine meats and wine of all sorts,　　　　200

Dallying with fair women, with other kind of sports,

All fine apparel that makes the heart joy,

With musical instruments, both with man and boy,

Thus no sport or joy wherein man hath solace

But I do contain them, though money bring them to pass.

MISCHIEVOUS: You say true, Pleasure, no tongue can express

What comfort and joy contained in you is.

　　　(PLEASURE *feigns himself sick and speaketh.*)

PLEASURE: What thing is this, that makes me thus to swell?

I promise you, even now I was perfectly well!

---

[10] Original reads "shouting."

I am in a strange case, whatever the matter be,   210
There is no way but shortly I must die.
ADULATION: There will none believe, I dare jeopard my hand,
That Pleasure shall die so long as the world doth stand.
Therefore take no care, nor yet lament or moan,
For suddenly it came and suddenly it will be gone.
PLEASURE: I am never able to abide it if it last long,
I fry in my fits, the pains be so strong.
ADULATION: Even as you were the occasion of the sickness of
     your father,
So is your son Sin to you, I answer;
So that you would, I think, be soon eased of your pains   220
If you could avoid same from you by any means.   *empty out*
PLEASURE: None in the world I think could guess better,
For as Money is to me, even so am I Sin's father,
Therefore to be at ease and to be rid of that lubber
Help now, all my friends, for love of Money and Pleasure.
          (*Here cometh in* PREST-FOR-PLEASURE.)
PREST: I cannot choose but help, you have so conjured us now,
For Money and Pleasure none but will take pains, I trow;
He is not worthy to live, I make God a vow,
That will not work his heart out for both you.
PLEASURE: Oh help, help quickly, I never stood in more need, 230
I am so full of sin I shall burst without quick speed!   *assistance*
     (*Here he shall make as though he would vomit, and* SIN, *being the*
     [   ]¹¹ *shall be conveyed finely from beneath as* PLEASURE *was*
     before.)
SIN: I was afraid of nothing but only of my dagger,
Lest in the time of my birth it would have sticked my father,
And then for my grandfather few would have cared,
If you my father Pleasure had been slain or killed.
Yea marry sir, now methinks I am more at liberty,
I could not once turn me, in my father's belly.
My father need not care in what company he doth eat,
I have made his throat so wide he cannot be choked with
     meat.

¹¹ The ink in the original is blotted here. What is visible is a final "e" of what seems to be a four-letter word,
probably "Vice."

PLEASURE: Although my pains were great, yet now I may be
  glad   240
 That I have to my son such a pretty fine lad.
SIN: If I be now a lad, what be you then?
 A boy of my age will never make man,
 And although I be young, yet am I well grown,
 No child of six year old is so big in all this town.
PLEASURE: Well, my son Sin, according to thy nature and name,
 All that loves Money and me see you do frame
 To all sinful living and all other wickedness.
 I need not bid thee, for I know well thy goodness.
ADULATION: I have ever to you, Pleasure, born such love 250
 That to depart with you my heart doth me move.
   (HELP, PLEASURE *and* ADULATION *goeth forth*.)
SIN: He hath as much need to bid me do this
 As to make a dog hold up his leg when he doth piss,
 And as Sin is the child of Pleasure in every nation
 Even so my son and heir is endless Damnation.
PREST: By the mass, I care not what sin I commit
 So that thereby I may purchase pleasure and profit.
 It is a hard thing that I would not do for money;
 I would cut my father's throat if I might get money thereby.
SIN: That is my boy, that I need not teach thee more, 260
 Or ever that he have money he committeth sin before!
 Out, alas masters, what thing is in my belly?
 Such pains as these will quickly make me weary.
 Who, who is able to abide this grief or pains?
 Even now in my belly, but now in my reins,
 Now in my buttocks and now in my heart,
 The pains are so great that I suffer grievous smart.
 I hold twenty pound it will turn to the gout.   *bet*
 Ever now at my heart and now at the sole of my foot,
 Out, alas, my neck, my sides and my back!   270
 Out, alas, my head asunder begins to crack!
PREST: I pray you, Sin, be quiet and be content a while,
 For I do think verily yourself you do beguile;
 Your pains are none other, I dare be bold to say,

But only Damnation, whereof you are so full.
Therefore to avoid him you must take pains to assay,
And to help you therein with all my power I will.
Do not make overmuch moan, Sin, for your child Damnation
Is the only occasion of all your grief and passion.

SIN: The whoreson's head is so great and he so ill-favored
    made   280
    That I must needs be ripped, I am greatly afraid!

PREST: Be content, Sin, I will call for more aid.
    Ho, Swift-to-Sin, come away in all haste!
    Sin is so sick I am afraid he will burst.
          [Enter SWIFT-TO-SIN]

SWIFT: Even as your grandfather did, and your father by you
    also,
    We will have with speed your son Damnation, I trow.

SIN: That ill-favored knave is like none of us,
    No more than a sow to a cow or a sheep to a goose!
    Now for a midwife I would give twenty pound!
    Hold me, sirs, for now I begin to sound.   *swoon*   290
    (*Here shall* DAMNATION *be finely conveyed, as the other was before,*
    who shall have a terrible vizard on his face, and his garment shall be
    painted with flames of fire.)

SIN: It is the heaviest lubber that ever man did bear!
    They say Sin is heavy, but he is heavier I swear.
    How say you, masters, is not this a well-favored baby
    That I, Sin, have brought forth so painfully?
    He is the worst-favored knave that ever was born;   *knave* also=boy
    It must needs be good ground that brings forth such good
        corn.
    When I look on him methinks him to be too evil-favored,
    Yet the crow thinks her blackbirds of all other the fairest.
    But I cannot love him if I should be hanged;
    Thou art never like, son, of me to be kissed.   300

DAMNATION: I am fearful Damnation, through Sin procreated.
    To such as in sin have all their felicity
    And dies without repentance, I shall be annexed;
    But the repentant sinner that obtains God's mercy

Shall enjoy the heavens, far separate from me.
Therefore father Sin, to thee be due honor,
That in bringing forth of me thou tookest such pains and labor.

SIN: In faith, much good do it you, and then to whom you
shall be married.
Iwis, they were better marry a sow that her pigs hath new
farried!

SWIFT: Now farewell Sin, of me you stand no more in need;   310
Do but beck when you lack me, and I will come with all
speed.[12]

PREST: In your necessity I am glad that we were here;
I cannot be long out of your company, I swear.
[*Exeunt.*]

DAMNATION: Farewell most sweet father. I am loath to depart;
So soon to be trudging it grieves me at the heart.
(*Here they three go forth.*)

SIN: Now farewell most sour son; to be sorry I cannot choose;[13]
Your going grieves me so much that the snot drops out of my
nose!
Had I not seen and felt the bearing of him myself
I would have thought surely he had been some changeling, or
elf.
Happy be they that are matched with my son Damnation,   320
They were better lie all their life in a dungeon or prison.
He is so sure a companion as I know but a few,
Who happeneth once in his company shall it never eschew.
My grandfather Money hath hatched a goodly litter,
An honester kindred can nowhere be found.
Pleasure, Sin and Damnation, of all other most bitter,
Who doth not love us that with the love of money is blind?
None but is my servant, that lives and treads on ground,
The greater power that is, the lowest state of all,
To be my servants cannot choose, and also still   *can't help it/always*
shall.   330

---

[12] Note that these exits are unmotivated by the plot, but are simply necessary because the actors have to get recostumed to play the parts in the next scene.
[13] Original reads "sour soon."

And is it any marvel why I so many servants have?
None with fine qualities with me can compare,[14]
Therefore in my sight everyone is but a slave.
What, off with your caps sirs! It becomes you to stand bare.
None can forswear themselves in trading for ware,
No picking of purses can be at market or fair,
No theft or robbery, no murder or killing
Can be without me, ne yet whoredom or swearing.
No pride, no sloth no gluttony can be used,
No perjury without me, neither envy nor hatred.   340
As my qualities be good, so my person is proper,
I am neither too high nor too low, too great nor too small,
No thicker nor thinner, no shorter no longer,
They decently appertain, as you may see all.
If I were higher I were the worse to fall.
If I were lower they would take me for a boy;
Therefore to behold my person you cannot choose but joy.
> (*Here cometh in* SATAN *the great devil, as deformedly dressed as
> may be.*)

SATAN: Oh, oh, oh, oh, my friend Sin I was never so merry!
In hearing thy qualities I cannot be weary,
In thy genealogy, Sin, I do more rejoice   350
Than can be thought with heart, or spoke with tongue or
    voice,
But my chiefest comfort is thy son, Man's Damnation,
Whereby they are excluded from eternal salvation.

SIN: Why you evil-faced knave, how came Your Friendship in?[15]
They be well-favored babes that be of your kin.

SATAN: Oh Sin, oh to see thee it doth me good!
Thy words, Sin, oh thy words do comfort my heart blood;
Through money and pleasure my kingdom doth increase,
Therefore to be merry why should I cease?

SIN: Then I and my son Damnation be nobody with you?   360
Sin and Damnation belike bring a man to heaven!

---

[14] That is, "no one can compare with me when it comes to fine qualities."
[15] Though the original gives lower-case letters, this is certainly intended to be a mock title. We print what is there, but it seems a safe bet that the writer intended "Your *Fiend*ship."

Is thy kingdom diminished through us, thinkest thou?
You bottle-nosed knave, I will see your nose caven!   *bashed in*
Iwis, you had been as good to have set me in the number,
I did not so much pleasure you, but I will work you as much
  cumber,
For I did never increase thy kingdom so much before,
But now I will diminish it twenty times more!
How can Money and Pleasure bring men into hell,
Without Sin and Damnation, Sir Good-face, me tell?
Nay, I will be gone, I will tarry no longer here,   370
I will turn all your mirth into sorrowful cheer.
   (*Here* SATAN *shall cry and roar.*)
SIN: I knew I would make him soon change his note;
  I will make him sing the black *sanctus*, I hold him a groat.
SATAN: Oh, my friend Sin, do not leave me thus,
  For without thee and thine own son Damnation
  My kingdom will decay, through my ancient enemy Jesus,
  For without man's company I can have no consolation;
  All had been mine own but for Christ's death and passion.
  Therefore without thy help and thy son Damnation
  Without company in hell I shall forever make my moan.   380
   (*Here he roareth and crieth.*)
SIN: You may laugh well enough that Sin and the devil be
  fallen out,
  But we will fall in again, or ever it be long.
  Stand back, in the mischief, or I will hit you on the snout!
  It is high time that you had ended your song.
SATAN: Come hither my sons Gluttony and Pride,
  Persuade my friend Sin with me to stick and abide.
   (*Here cometh in* GLUTTONY *and* PRIDE, *dressed in devils apparel,
  and stays* SIN *that is going out.*)
PRIDE: Our Lord and master I pray you, turn back again;
  Our father cannot be merry if you his company refrain.
[SIN]:   Thou canst thy liripoop, to call me lord and   *knowest/role*
  master,
  For I am thy chief head and thou art of me a member.   390
PRIDE: I pray thee for our sakes, once back again to turn,

For thy departing will cause him still to mourn.
SIN: Thou! Thy dogs and cats, thou evil-favored knave,
  Use me thus again and your nose from your face I will have!
PRIDE: We pray you most heartily to forgive that is past,
  And we never hereafter will misuse you again;
  If you forsake our father for sorrow he will brast,
  Therefore from your fury we hope ye will abstain.
SIN: Of all the three devils thou hast the most manner[s]
  For thy sake once again I will comfort thy father.   400
  Snottynose Sathanas, disable me no more,
  Lest you have more ado than you had before.
  Well, Satan's kingdom by me shall be increased
  And through my son Damnation, that it ne'er shall be empty.
PRIDE: I would not have you take all the pains alone,
  I myself will entice many to pride,
  That in hell, our habitation, they continually may groan.
  To help you at all times I will be at your side.
GLUTTONY: And I will allure them to fine fare and gluttony,
  That their delight may be filling the belly,   410
  Early up at drinking and late up at banqueting,
  So that all their joy shall be in drunkenness and surfeiting.
  They shall spend on their own bellies more than shall suffice,
  But the poor hungry from their doors shall arise.
SATAN: Oh, oh, oh my babes, my chickens, and my friend Sin,
  Many one through thee the kingdom of hell shall win!
  Oh for joy and gladness I cannot stand or sit,
  Upon these cheerful words I must needs dance a fit.   *measure, step*
SIN: Yea, but one thing, Snottynose, will be very hard—
  Where shall we get a pipe to play the devil a galliard?   420
SATAN: Before you turned back I did both cry and weep,
  But now through thy comfort I can dance without a pipe.
  I do now perceive Money is so beloved
  That of many above God he is esteemed and honored,
  And the world is given so much to delicacy and pleasure
  That Sin and Damnation increase out of measure.
GLUTTONY: We give you most hearty thanks, O Sin our master,
  Whose return again hath comforted our father.

PRIDE: If you had not returned, for aught we could have done
  Our father without doubt would have fallen in a swoon.   430
SIN: If the devil had died, who should have been his heir?
SATAN: No my friend, no, none can profess my chair,
  For as God is without end and his joys endless,
  Even so am I king of everlasting darkness.
SIN: Now if they be wise they will care for no such a friend,
  To procure them to pains that never shall have end.
SATAN: Even as the joys of heaven do pass all other pleasure
  Even so the pains of hell exceed all other, be sure.
  The greatest torments and pains that be on earth
  Is joy and pleasure in respect of pains of hell.[16]   *compared to* 440
  The Scripture maketh mention thereof, as plainly appeareth,
  There is gnawing and gnashing of teeth, as the damned shall
    tell.
SIN: Much good do it you, Snottynose, I long not for your
    cheer!
  I beshrew you and your babes, if thereof you spare,
  It is better be poor and after in heaven to dwell.
  Than to be rich on the earth and after live in hell.
PRIDE: Well, let us talk no more of the pains and sorrow,
  But seeing we are prepared in that place to dwell,
  Let is take pains both even and morrow
  To enlarge our dominion, the kingdom of hell.   450
  I am so esteemed throughout the world wide
  That they had rather dwell in hell than lay me aside.
GLUTTONY: And I begin with many to be in such favor
  That the preacher cannot allure them, whatso he doth say.
  In their throat and belly is all their joy and pleasure,
  No whit regarding the last fearful day.
SIN: As either of you contain one sin particularly,
  Even so I contain sins generally:
  Therefore, goodman Snottynose, if you reward me well,
  I and my son Damnation shall send enough to hell.   460
SATAN: Whatsoever thou wilt have I will not thee deny.

[16] With this passage compare, for instance, John Donne's *Sermon LXXVI*, "On Falling Out of God's Hand."

SIN: Then give me a piece of thy tail, to make a slap for a fly,
   For if I had a piece thereof, I do verily believe
   The humblebees stinging should never me grieve.

SATAN: No my friend, my tail I cannot spare,
   But ask what thou wilt besides and I will it prepare.

SIN: Then your nose I would have, to stop my tail behind,
   For I am cumbered with colic, and letting out of wind,
   And if it be too little to make thereof a case,
   Then I would be bold to borrow your face.   470

SATAN: Now I perceive well you are disposed to be merry,
   But ask me anything that is meet for to give,   *fitting*
   And in satisfying you thereof I will not tarry;
   To make you my chief officer it would not me grieve;
   Sure you are thereof, you may me believe.
   Besides, if any friend of yours of me do stand in stead   *need*
   The best thing in hell shall be his in his need.

SIN: Woe be to my friends if they stand need of you
   Or anything you have in that most pleasant place;
   I would not wish that friendship to either horse or cow,   480
   For they should be sure of small favor or grace.
   Is not here masters, think you, an amiable face?
   Happy may they be which with him shall dwell always,
   But thrice happier, then, which godly end their days.[17]

SATAN: Now my friend Sin, seeing I have seen you,
   Take here my blessing and so I bid you adieu.

   (*Here all the devils depart.*)

SIN: Are they not, think you, of all other most happy,
   Which shall forever and ever be in the devil's company?
   It were better be a post horse that rests night nor day,
   Or else to be a galley slave, than with the devils to play.   490
   Well, I am sure I have yet much to do,
   For if my father Pleasure have much work in hand
   I must needs travail through every land.
   I cannot tell what thing to do first,
   My head is so full of toys wherewith I think it will burst.   *tricks*

---

[17] The placing of pious sentiments in the mouths of Vices is frequent in the moralities. It makes not only a nice general irony, but also the specific point that "The Devil can quote Scripture."

If I go to my grandfather first, then my father will be angry,
And if I see my father before I see my son
Then he will take the matter, I tell you, sorrowfully;
Therefore, give me counsel what is best to be done:
If I should go to my grandfather where should I find him? 500
In the poor man's purse he doth seldom abide,
But in the beggar's cloak I might chance to have him.
I shall not find where he is unless I have a guide.
I am a wise young man that fears to find Money.
In the covetous churl's coffer I shall have him by and by;
I am sure to find him at the goldsmith's stall;
If there I miss him I shall never find him at all.

> (*Here* SIN *goeth out and* LEARNING-WITH-MONEY *cometh in, richly apparelled.*)

LEARNING-WITH: Who may be compared to me in degree?
Who is more happy than Learning-with-Money?
Learning at the first to riches me preferred, 510
And money is the cause that I am now honored.
Learning-with-Money I am of all men called.
Who is not desirous my favor to win?
For my money and riches my learning is esteemed.
Very few or none but at my table have been.
The learning Seneca these words hath expressed:
Iners malorum remedium ignorantia est.
Then if you counterpease me, Learning-with-Money,
Of all evils and mischief I am the best remedy.[18]

> [*Here cometh* LEARNING-WITHOUT-MONEY, *apparelled like a scholar.*]

LEARNING-WITHOUT: Learning may as well counsel, where
    money doth want, *be lacking* 520
But riches causeth the common sort to esteem counsel best,
For if a rich man well apparelled have a fine tongue to descant,

---

[18] "Ignorance is a poor remedy for one's ills." "Counterpease" means "to weigh in the balance." This scene turns into a quoting match, and we shall translate only the Latin that the characters themselves do not translate. The presence of translations suggests an educationally mixed audience. These Latin tags do not come from the works of the ancient authors themselves, but from phrase-books or *florilegia*, collections of choice Latin phrases. Scores of these "chap-books", as they were called, were in circulation, intended as aids in the teaching of Latin.

He shall be taken for learned though he know never a letter.
My learning as good as yours, I dare be bold to compare,
Yet there is great difference between our estimations;
But if your attire, as mine is, were coarse and as bare,
Then he should be best esteemed that had best
      conditions.   *behavior*
My name is Learning-without-Money, in poor degree, God wot,
I have not to help my need either penny or groat,
And though I have no money at this time present,   530
Yet I thank God, through my knowledge and learning
I ever have enough wherewith I am content,
So that contentation makes me as rich as a king.   *contentment*
The difference between our two livings is this only;
You live idly in pleasure and I in study take pain,
Which you cannot away with but think it a misery.   *do without*
But if with labor I have sufficient, I am right glad and fain;
Who will not be content with poverty to have sufficient gain?
Surely to live godly with poverty I had rather,
Than be damned in sin with continual pleasure.   540
LEARNING-WITH: I will not say but that riches be a great
      occasion
That we do live wantonly and out of God's fear,
But learning doth cause us to bridle our affection,
Therefore learning rules by riches everywhere.
LEARNING-WITHOUT: Whoso is rich doth fall into many a
      noisome lust.   *nagging*
But the godly poor alway in God doth put his trust.
If you do rule your goods and bestow them as you ought,
Few fellows you have, as I by proof have tried.   *others like you*
Of many learned rich I craved but could get nought,
But the poor sort, unlearned, have given me to feed.   550
Many that be learned and riches have withal
Are more out of frame than some who nothing have at all.
Their learning makes them think with their riches to be so
      strong
That they will oppress their neighbor, be it never so wrong.
LEARNING-WITH: Well, if you lack living be bold to come to me,

For I can be content to bestow where is need,
And especially upon such as godly learned be,
I thank God I have wherewith the poor to feed.

> (*Here cometh in* Money-without-Learning, *apparelled like
> a rich churl, with bags of money by his sides, and speaketh.*)

Money-without: What, Learning-with-Money, I am right glad
      to see you here!

I stand need of your counsel in diverse cases,   560
Wherefore, if you will help me I will recompense you, I swear.
I have many forward matters in hand in sundry places,
I have money enough to defend me in maugre   *in spite of*
      their faces.
Many beggarly knaves have good matters against me,   *legal cases*
But here is one will do well enough, mine old friend Money.

Learning-without: *Quique sua ducitur natura,* as here it may
      appear,

For the evil is wrought by the instrument according to nature.
This man is given naturally to oppress the poor
And money is the instrument that maketh him so bold
Many are given naturally to consume in keeping a whore,   570
Some naturally in drinking to spend their gold.
Nihil est tam munitum quod auro non expugnetur.[19]
Thou thinks thou lacks nothing, seeing thou art full of
      treasure.
Who, marrying their children, have any respect
To learning and honesty, but only to riches?
Nay, the one they do embrace, the other they neglect.
Well hereof a pretty answer was made by Themistocles.
One asked him whether it was better his daughter to marry
To a rich man not honest or to an honest poor man,
And he answered again both quickly and wisely   580
Ego, inquit, malim virum qui pecunia quam quae egeat viro pecunia.
I had rather, saith he, to have if I can,
A man that lacks money than money that lacks a man

Money-without: What prating fellow is this that is so talkative?
It seems he is learned, but yet he cannot thrive.

---

[19] "Nothing is so safe that gold cannot capture it."

LEARNING-WITH: Yea, surely he is learned, of whom it is great
    pity
He hath no certain living nor yet any money.

MONEY-WITHOUT: In faith then, he may dance among beggars
    well enough,
Thou wert best give up thy learning and help to hold the
    plough.

LEARNING-WITHOUT: Do you set so little by my knowledge and
    learning?   590

MONEY-WITHOUT: Who will esteem thee unless thou have
    living?

LEARNING-WITHOUT: The example of the philosopher may well
    be applied,
That kissed his gown for coming into the Emperor's chamber.
This gentleman of thee should not be esteemed
Unless he had riches, if thy words may be believed,
For even now thou saidest, (I am not deaf of hearing)
Who would esteem me unless I had a living.
There is none other difference between this gentleman and me
But that he doth abound in riches and I in poverty.

MONEY-WITHOUT: Believe him not sir, for you were ever a good
    gentleman.   600
If you stood need of me you should find me your friend.
There is nothing but I will do it for you if I can,
Nay, try me when ye list, ye shall me faithful find.

LEARNING-WITHOUT: As long as he needeth not, thou wilt help
    him at an inch,
But if in poverty he fall, then friendship will quench,
For it is the nature of the churlish rich man
To be friend to such as of him stands no need,
But if his riches fail, farewell friendship then!
He will not then bid him with him once to feed.
If I had your estate sir, by proof you should see,   610
All the crouching you have had should then be done   *bowing*
    to me.

LEARNING-WITH: Your wise words have brought this sentence
    to mind,

Written in *Tertio Tusculanorum,* where you may it find:[20]

Omnes, cum secundae, tum maxime secum meditari oportet, quo pacto
adversam aerumnam ferant.

It is meet for all men when they be in prosperity
To meditate how to suffer trouble in adversity.

LEARNING-WITHOUT: If you mark it as well as here you have it
placed
They will be the less grievous to you, come they never so
fast.
I promise you I would not change my estate with this man's
living,
To have his riches and money for my knowledge and
learning.   620

MONEY-WITHOUT: Marry, I am agreed! I intend not to change it.
To make such a bargain I were out of my wit.

LEARNING-WITHOUT: I have in my learning more perfect
consolation
Than thou hast or canst have in all thy gold and riches,
For I may carry it with me in any country or nation
And the more I spend thereof the more it will increase,
But the more thou spendest the more it doth diminish,
Thus no man that heareth us but may perceive well
That my learning thy riches and treasure doth excell.

MONEY-WITHOUT: I may carry money enough with me wherever
I go,   630
Which will me help and succor, both in well and woe.

LEARNING-WITHOUT: You cannot carry your money but it must
needs consume,
And perhaps be stolen or lost before ir be half done.
Many one of their money as they have travelled
Have been spoiled, some hurt therefore, and some also mudered.

MONEY-WITHOUT: I can have meat and drink in every place, for
money,
But if I had none at all I should go to bed hungry.

LEARNING-WITH: For that I am partaker with either of you
both,

[20] That is, the third of Cicero's *Tusculanae Disputationes.*

To disallow any of you I would be very loath,
But learning before riches ought to be preferred   640
Although the most part money more regard.   *most people*

MONEY-WITHOUT: I am the better esteemed, as everyone doth
        know.
I am taken for an honest man wherever I go,
And he shall be for an abject rascal and slave,
To whom each will say, "Pack hence, thou beggarly knave."

LEARNING-WITHOUT: Some that doth not know me perhaps will
        say so,
But where I am known, I trust, my usage is such
That they are very sorry when thus I do go.   650
And when I come again, of me they make much,
But thou amongst thy neighbors art so beloved
That though they flatter thee for fear to thy face,[21]
They will curse thee as soon as thy back from them is turned,
And call thee cankered churl in every place.

MONEY-WITHOUT: I would I knew them which speak such words
        of me,
They are but beggarly knaves I durst lay a wager.
I would hoise then at the next term, they should not know
        why,[22]
Then should you see the villains begin to crouch and flatter!
But yet, for all that, my money and my riches
Get me all the pleasures I can desire or wish.

LEARNING-WITHOUT: These words, of pleasures, are written by
        Cato: 660
Malorum esca voluptas qua homines capiuntar ut pisces hamo.
Pleasure is the meat of evil men, thus means the text and book,
Wherewith men be catched as fishes with the hook.
And again he hath written, read the same who list,
*Nulla capitalior pestis quam corporis voluptas, hominibus a natura
        data est.*
There is no greater plague given to man by nature
Than is of the body the desire of pleasure.

---

[21] Original reads "And though."
[22] Either "hoist" in a noose, or call up ("hoyse") before a judge.

LEARNING-WITH: And Sallust in few words thereof writeth
> thus:
>
> *In regno voluptatis, virtuti non est locus.*
> In the kingdom of pleasure there is no place for virtue,   670
> For pleasure bringeth loathsomeness, as Pliny doth show:
> *Nulla est adeo quae non assiduitate sui fastidium patiat voluptas,*
> No pleasure but with much use brings loathsomeness.

MONEY-WITHOUT: Nay, that is not true, for the more I have
> The more I desire, so God me help and save!

LEARNING-WITHOUT: Juvenal's words herein doth thee rightly
> hit:
>
> *Crescit amor nummi quantum ipsa pecunia crescit.*
> The love of money increaseth as much as money itself.
> To what mischief bringeth us this vile and wicked pelf!
> Money makes no man rich unless there be contentation,   680
> But the poor man contented is richer, I say,
> As in *Ultimo Paradoxo* I find a good probation:[23]   *proof*
> *Contentum suis rebus esse maximae sunt certissimae atque divitiae.*
> The most great and certain riches that is
> Hath he that is content with that which is his.
> Therefore thou are most poor, as I may well define,
> For thou art not content with that which is thine.
> *Egens est qui non satis habet et is cui nihil satis poteste esse:*
> He is poor that hath not enough or whom nothing will satisfy.
> And in *Primo Paradoxo* thou art trimly painted   690
> And such as thou art as be never satisfied.
> *Numquam expletur nec satiatur cupiditatis sitis*
> *Neque solum ea que habent libidine augendi cruciantur, sed etiam*
> > *amittendi metu.*
> The thirst of desire is never satisfied or filled
> And these goods they have to increase their desire
> Whereby they are not only grievously tormented
> But also to lose them they have as great a fear.

LEARNING-WITH: Horace doth verify you saying, I am sure,
> Saying *crescentem pecuniam cura sequitur,*[24]

---

[23] That is, the last of Cicero's *Paradoxa Stoicorum.* See also below, l. 690.
[24] "Worries follow, as one's money increases."

And eloquent Cicero saith in this phrase,   700
Virtuti qui praediti sunt soli sunt divites:
They are only rich that are with virtue adorned,
So that without virtue a man cannot be enriched.
Were it not for my learning I should be more covetous,
Therefore learning is to be preferred before anything,
Literae pulcherrimae sunt divitiae hominis:
The most fair riches of man is knowledge and learning.

LEARNING-WITHOUT: *Opes eius modi parandae quae navi fracta simul*
    cum domino quaeane enarare:
These riches of men are chiefly to be gotten
Which may swim to land with his master when the ship is
    broken.   710

MONEY-WITHOUT: Well, I have no learning to defend my cause
    withal,
So here is a friend will plead my matter in Westminster Hall.
        (*Here he shall clap his hands on his bags.*)
    (*Here cometh in* NEITHER-MONEY-NOR-LEARNING, *clothed like a*
    beggar, and speaketh.)

NEITHER: By the old proverb, every man may not wear a
    furred hood,
But if my coat were furred it would do me more good.
When I was able I labored, but now I wax old,
If I had sufficient meat to feed my body,
And also necessary clothes to keep away the cold
There is none of you would be so merry as I.
I have neither learning nor money myself to maintain
Therefore to beg for my living I am both glad and fain.   720

LEARNING-WITHOUT: Godliness is great riches, if a man be
    therewith content.
God for the godly will prepare that he shall have sufficient.

MONEY-WITHOUT: Thou art unhappy and born in an   *unlucky*
    evil hour
That hast no money nor for any canst labor.

LEARNING-WITHOUT: Do you see how he esteems this poor and
    simple wight?
Perhaps he is more accepted than thou in God's light.

He thinks none is happy but such as have money;
I will prove this man richer than thou by and by,
For he would be content with sufficient clothes and food
And thou are not satisfied with twenty men's good.   730
Inopiae pauca desunt avaritiae omnia, saith Horatius:
Few things to the needy but all wanting to the covetous.
Thou represents Dives, who had all his pleasures here,
But he represents Lazarus, who now hath heavenly cheer.
Beware, lest through thy riches thou have endless pain;[25]
The faithful and contented wight in the end shall heaven attain.

NEITHER: For Christ's sake I suffer this poverty meekly,
The cross of Christ I embrace most willingly.
The rich for the most part be so hardhearted
That nothing I can get wherewith to be relieved,   740
Yet God doth open the hearts of the poor sort
That I have always sufficient myself to support.
It is a world to see how greedy they be of money,   *it is amazing*
For having an hundred pound they will not part with a penny,
But they will not stick vainly to consume and spend   *not hesitate*
A noble at a shot upon a feignèd friend.
God's grace, I fear me, from such hard hearts is past,
That will not give the four-score part of that they spend in
        waste.   *one-eightieth*

Neither-Money-nor-Learning I am called wherever I go,
Whereby I do suffer much pain, hunger and woe;   750
Therefore good gentlemen, I beseech you of your goodness,
Give me your charity my body to refresh,
And though I be not able, God will pay it certain
At the last day, with treble-fold again.

LEARNING-WITH: God forbid I should from the poor withdraw
        my hand,
For then I should not be able before the Lord to stand.
What we give to the poor, that we give to Christ,
To give to the needy poor God grant us always prest.
        (*Here he shall give him something.*)

---

[25] Original reads "Beware lest through thy riches thou have not endless pain." The double negative is
standard Elizabethan practice, but we modernize for clarity's sake.

LEARNING-WITHOUT: You take yourself, I perceive in this case,
     to be afterward;
  Therefore you shall be to higher office preferred.   760
          (*Here he* [i.e. NEITHER] *shall ask his alms of* MONEY-
          WITHOUT-LEARNING.)
NEITHER: Good honest man, relieve me, I ask it for Christ's
     sake.
  If you knew my need you would than some pity take;
  Give me of your abundance but one groat or penny
  And you shall receive it with gain, at the last, truly.
MONEY-WITHOUT: God help thee, God help thee, mine own
     neighbors be very poor;
  Never a day but one or other is ever at my door.
  I had never so much to do with money in my life,
  God help thee good man, I have a household and a wife.
LEARNING-WITHOUT: *Duae res sunt quae maxime homines ad*
     maleficium impellunt, luxuries et avaritia:
  Two things chiefly doth man to mischief bring,   770
  Lechery and covetousness, O vile and sinful sting!
  Thou hadst even now enough thy neighbor to   *a moment ago*
     oppress,
  But thou hast not one penny on this poor man to spare!
  If thou shouldst give him twelve pence, what hadst thou the
     less?
  God hath hardened thy heart and cast thee by, I fear.[26]
MONEY-WITHOUT: If I should diminish my money but one groat
  I should not be quiet these two days, I wote.
  Well, come to my house tonight or tomorn,
  And I will see if I can spare thee a dish full of corn.
          (*Here* MONEY-WITHOUT-LEARNING *goeth out.*)
LEARNING-WITHOUT: Of money, pleasure and sin he is now
     enticed;   780
  I pray God with Damnation he be not infected.
  Well, walk thou in thy vocation, whatever thou hast,
  Praise thy God so long as life doth last.
NEITHER: What pains and troubles soever we bide here,   *endure*

[26] Original reads "cast thy by."

I pray God we be patient and the living God fear.
No pains we do suffer, of heaven can be worthy,   *make us worthy*
The joys be so great no tongue can express;
Therefore I care not for living never so painfully,
For, repenting in Christ, I shall have joys endless.
God reward you good gentlemen for your good alms deed;   790
I have sufficient three days my hungry corpse to   *living body*
    feed.
        (*Here he goeth out.*)

LEARNING-WITHOUT: For that I know God hath sent you riches,
Great knowledge, wisdom and learning withal,
Beware of pleasures, the mother of sin doubtless,
For if she once catch you, to sin you shall be thrall.
It is written in the Second *De Finibus*,
Nemo est dignus nomine hominis qui unum totum diem velit esse in
    voluptate.
He is not worthy the name of a man, be sure,
Which spends the whole day in voluptuousness and pleasure.

LEARNING-WITH: I thank God of such riches as I have,   800
But so long as I live it shall be my servile slave,
To lend to the needy, and give to the poor,
To suffer none go empty that comes to my door,
To bring up my household in God's fear and faith,
And to be an example to such as like hath.
And if you will be content home with me to come,
You shall not want living as long as I have some.

LEARNING-WITHOUT: I thank you heartily of your large
    promise;
I will wait upon you as my bounden duty is.
        (*Here they go forth, and* MONEY *cometh in puffing.*)[27]

MONEY: I was never so weary since the hour I was born!   810
There is none at all but do crave me, even and morn.
I never rest, night nor day.
I am ever busy when everyone doth play.
Few blind matters but I must be at their daying;   *hidden/exposing*
If I speak the word, it is done without praying.

[27] Original reads "Here he goeth forth."

Since I was here last, I swear by this light,
I have made many a crooked matter straight;
The thief that all night was robbing and stealing,
If I bear him witness, was all night in his bed sleeping;
A man's wife that was taken in bed with another,   820
Could have no harm when I did excuse her;
When I spake she was taken to be of good behavior
And they that found her were set by the heels for their   *punished*
    labor;
There was a man killed and twenty witnesses by,
But I said he killed himself with his own dagger, truly,
And when I had spoken everyone held his peace,
And then the officers the murderer did release.
So that I have been to many so friendly
That well is he can get me on his side to be;
I have many suits and matters in hand   830
That I would fain have an helper, by me fast to stand.
       (*Here cometh in* Sin *the Vice.*)[28]

Sin: I have been since I was here in many a nation,
So that I could not come to any town nor city
But I and my kindred are in good estimation.
If I hold up my finger, you may trust me,
It is a great matter that makes me to lie,
And as I came homeward I told these news to the devil,
Who was very glad to see us bear such rule.

Money: May I be so bold as to know of what kindred
Or else from what stock you are proceeded.   840

Sin: The last stocks I was in was even at Bambury,
They be worm-eaten, which shows them ancient to be;
If they were mine, because they are so old
I would burn them in winter to keep me from the cold.

Money: I meant of what degree you were descended.

Sin: I promise you, I am come of a high and mighty kindred;
I know not my grandfather, for I never yet saw him,

---

[28] It is perhaps odd that Sin is described as the Vice of the play, when All-for-Money is clearly the operative central Vice. Perhaps, like Merry Report in John Heywood's *Play of the Weather*, it is Sin's role as door-opener, banns-crier, setter-on of gulls, maker of scurrilous asides, and general *factotum*, that earns him the designation.

But Pleasure is my father sir, do you not know him?

MONEY: What, my son Sin, I never saw thee before!

I am thy grandfather Money, which sets by thee great   850
    store.

SIN: Marry sir, it is time on my marybones to kneel,   *marrowbones*

Blessing, blessing grandfather, of you I do ask!—

But take heed that none of it hit my left heel,

For I promise you I have a great and fervent lask!   *diarrhea*

MONEY: I am glad to see thee so merry, my child Sin,

It doth rejoice me to see such one of my kin.

SIN: Nay then, the fairest bird of all the generation

Is mine own son and heir, my fair son Damnation.

Such a one as he is you have seen but a few,

Never trust me again if I tell you not true.   860

His face doth shine as bright as the buttocks of a bear,

He hath a beautiful face, in the night when the moon shines
    not clear.

MONEY: I pray thee, when didst thou see my son Pleasure, thy
    father?

SIN: I did not see him of late, but I heard from him by the
    carrier.

In faith father Money, to put you out of doubt,

There is no place in the world but he bears a great rout;   *crowd*

But methinks I heard you complain very lately

That through great pains and travail you were very weary.

MONEY: I would I had a special friend that for me would take
    pain;

He should for his pains be sure of much to gain.[29]   870

SIN: Marry sir, I have a special friend in store,

That will not for any man than for you do more,

For he hath such a mind and great love to money

That he will do anything for you by and by.

MONEY: What is his name, and then I shall know

Whether he be able to do for me or no.

SIN: A man he is to whom nothing can come amiss,

In every kind of living he hath experience doubtless.

---

[29] Original reads "sure of to much gain."

All-for-Money is his name, you know him full well,
For [in] this your business all other he doth excell. 880
MONEY: Marry, that is he that I wish for only,
There is nothing at all but he will do it for me.
I pray you, call him, for he will not long tarry
If he wist I were here, so to me is he friendly.
SIN: What, All-for-Money! Come hither with all speed!
My grandfather Money tarries for you to help him at need.
> (*Here cometh in* ALL-FOR-MONEY *in haste, apparelled like a
> ruler or magistrate.*)
ALL-FOR-MONEY: Marry, that is well, should Money tarry
for me?
Nay, it is meet I wait on him both with cap and knee.
What would you with me, my lord and master Money?
Command what you will and I will do it speedily. 890
MONEY: I have taken such pain as sure hath made me
weary,
Wherefore I have sent for you my room to supply. *to take my place*
What suitors soever come to crave your aid,
If they come from me, let them not be delayed.
Whatever their matter be, have thereto no regard,
For if they come from me they will you well reward.
ALL-FOR-MONEY: Whatever I do for you I take it for no pain,
At midnight I would ride for you, in hail, snow or rain.
SIN: Let there come a thousand, if they do bring gain!
There cannot come so many but he'll them entertain. 900
MONEY: Farewell All-for-Money, in thee is all my trust.
You may both make and mar; you may do what you lust.
> (*Here* MONEY *goeth out, and* ALL-FOR-MONEY, *sitting in a
> chair, speaketh.*)
ALL-FOR-MONEY: Now my friend Sin, a proclamation make—
None but shall be heard, that comes for money's sake.
SIN: What be the words that I shall now proclaim?
ALL-FOR-MONEY: I have them written here, I will recite them by
name,
Say after me, and then you cannot miss;
You must speak aloud that they may know what it is.

*(Here the Vice shall turn the proclamation to some contrary
sense every time* ALL-FOR-MONEY *hath read it, and here
followeth the proclamation:)*[30]

All manner of men that have either matter or suit,

*Let them come hither between nine and ten and none against them
shall dispute;*   910

So they come from Money, then they shall be heard quickly.

Be their matter never so wrong, they shall speed and not tarry,

And that they make speed he hastily them prays,

For he cannot tarry past two or three days.

ALL-FOR-MONEY: Do you think I shall have any suitors at all?

I think any market will be very small.

SIN: If you have no suitors on you for to call,

I am sure shortly the heavens will fall.

They will not stand, I think, all in this hall,

Which will come right shortly, and
     still hereafter shall.   *continuously* 920

ALL-FOR-MONEY: Marry sir, the more the better for me,

If they be ten thousand they shall speed, for money.

          (Here shall one knock at the door.)[31]

SIN: What good fellow is it which knocks so boldly?

GREGORY GRACELESS: Marry, I am a suitor that comes from
     Money,

My name, if you list to know, is Gregory Graceless,

That can cut a man's purse and look in his face.

SIN: If your personage be as handsome as your qualities be
     good,

The hemp for your hanging begins for to bud.

ALL-FOR-MONEY: Let him in, I pray thee, let me see what he is.

If he come from Money he shall not speed amiss.   930

          (Here cometh in GREGORY GRACELESS, *like a ruffian, and
          speaketh.)*

GREGORY: God save you my lord, I am come from Money,

Who wills you to help me out of my troubles quickly.

---

[30] This is one of the opportunities for *ad lib* comic performance that abound in the moralities.

[31] One seizes on this sort of scrap of information in trying to recreate the original milieu of these plays. We have a "hall" at l. 919, and here a "door." This suggests true interlude conditions, perhaps a banquet hall.

ALL-FOR-MONEY: What is the matter? Rehearse it in brief.

GREGORY: Mine neighbors say they will hang me, because I am
    a thief.

The last night I chanced to take a budget with two   *purse*
    hundred pound,

And maimed also the party, that they think he will die.

The budget with money I did hide in the ground

So that they missed it although they took me.

Therefore, for your aid to you now I fly,

And the one half shall you have, for saving my life,   940

And the other must keep my house, my children and my wife.

ALL-FOR-MONEY: Deliver the money to this my friend Sin,

And take this token to show that with me thou hast been.

    (*Here he shall deliver him a paper, and* SIN *and he goeth out.*)

This is good luck at the first beginning, —

To have so much money it is an honest living!

Methinks suitors in coming are very slack;

Such as this first was, I think I shall lack.

I could sit in the cold a good while, I swear,

Or I would be weary such suitors to hear.

    (SIN *cometh in and saith:*)

SIN: My lord All-for-Money, here is another cheat!   950

It is better than the first, yea, or else as great.

ALL-FOR-MONEY: Let them come, whoever they be,

If your grandfather sent them, mine old friend Money.

SIN: Nay, the party doth lie now sore sick in her bed,

But her father doth will you that she may be helped,

And she hath given me for you an hundred pound and more;

Shall her neighbors be able to hurt her therefore?

ALL-FOR-MONEY: Nay, let them do to her the worst that they
    can;

Tell me her matter and I will release her then.

SIN: She is a fair young woman and very full of favor;   960

She began to be coltish, so that one must ride her,

And the thing she played for did after so prosper

That her belly was full, as lately did appear;

And she, fearing lest thereby she should be slandered,

Killed her child after she was delivered,
But as she conveyed it by some it was spied
And so it was found, whereby the truth was tried.

ALL-FOR-MONEY: What, this matter is not so great. Well, for
    money's sake
That she have no harm myself will undertake.
They that should give evidence shall be all tongue-tied   970
And the twelve men shall find her guiltless, let her not be
    afraid.

SIN: For a whore to have a child it is but a small matter,
And after it is born the same to kill and murder.
Is not my grandfather Money of great power and might,
That such a crooked matter so quickly can make straight?
    (*Now* MONEYLESS-AND-FRIENDLESS *knocketh at the door.*)

SIN: Who is that that knocks in such a great post haste?

MONEYLESS: One that without my lord's help away is like to be
    cast.

ALL-FOR-MONEY: Let him come in, let me hear his matter,
If he come from Money he shall not lose his labor.

MONEYLESS: O my lord, as I came by an hedge the last   980
    night,
Of a few rags and clothes I chanced to have a sight,
Which when I had viewed, with me I them took,
Which were not worth a crown, I dare swear on a book.
And I have a rich neighbor that threats me very sore
That I shall be hanged right shortly therefore.[32]

ALL-FOR-MONEY: Be merry, good fellow, and be not afraid!
It were pity thou were hanged for such a trifle.
Who will do thee hurt if I be on thy side?
They were as good, nay, as once thy goods
    to rifle.   *They might as well try*

SIN: His goods be soon rifled; I think he hath none at all!   990
It appears he is simple, the robbery was so small.
To come hither for help who put it in thy mind?

MONEYLESS: By my troth, myself, for I have none other friend.

SIN: Did not my grandfather Money in haste send thee hither?

[32] Instead of clotheslines, laundry was hung over hedges to dry. Petty theft was a hanging offence.

MONEYLESS: I am not acquainted with him; I will not be found
a liar.

SIN: What art thou called, whereabouts thou dost dwell?   *where*

MONEYLESS: I am Moneyless-and-Friendless, as many one can
tell.

SIN: Alas, poor soul, what didst thou coming hither?
I think for all thy comfort thou art never the better.[33]

ALL-FOR-MONEY: I can do thee no good; I did mistake thy
matter.   1000

Thou art come hither in vain, thou hast lost thy labor.

MONEYLESS: You promised me that I should not be troubled!

ALL-FOR-MONEY: By my troth, for all that, you are   *in spite of that*
like to be hanged.

If the law should not be executed of thieves and robbers,

Men should not live in quiet, for loitering lubbers.   *on account of*

SIN: Shall I tell thee one thing in thine ear, sirra?
Thou art sure shortly to play *sursum corda*.[34]

MONEYLESS: I trust, sir, you will not go against your word?

ALL-FOR-MONEY: Get thee hence, prating knave, I can do thee
no good.

MONEYLESS: God have mercy on us! Without a man have
money   1010

He shall be cast away for a trifle, we see.

But the thieves and robbers with money be stored

Escape well enough, but the poor thieves be hanged.
        (*Here he goeth forth.*)

ALL-FOR-MONEY: Ah sirra, here was a suitor that was not for
my profit.

None such were appointed to come, by the proclamation.

We should make a wise market if for such we should sit!

They shall starve and hang before on such I have compassion!

SIN: Through him you shall see that none after will come,
Unless they have money, either more or some.

Is not my grandfather Money, think ye, of great power,   1020

[33] The sense is "As regards your comfort, you're in no better shape now for having come here."
[34] "Lift up your hearts," a passage in the Preface to the Mass, with, of course, a pun on *corda*, "string," the hangman's rope.

That could save from hanging such abominable whore
That against all nature her own child did kill?
Thus you may do for money what mischief you will.
And yonder poor knave that did steal for his need
A few sort of rags and not all worth a crown,   (a coin)
Because he lacks money shall be hanged for that deed.
You may see my grandsire is a man of renown;
It were meet when I named him that you all kneeled down.
Nay, make it not so strange, for the best of you all
Do love him so well you will come at his call.   1030
     (*One other shall knock now at the door.*)

ALL-FOR-MONEY: Methinks I do hear one knock at the door.
He shall find me is good master if he be not too poor.
SIN: Knock softly, in the mischief, who made you so bold?
WILLIAM: I am William-with-the-Two-Wives. I have brought
    my lord gold.
ALL-FOR-MONEY: Let him in, let him in, I will his matter hear.
I will dispatch him quickly, he need not to fear.
     (*Here cometh in* WILLIAM-WITH-THE-TWO-WIVES, *dressed
     like a country man, a speaketh.*)
WILLIAM: My lord, from Money I have brought you such a
    token
That I trust from my trouble I shall soon be holpen.
Forty old angels I trust will you please,   (coin of very high value)
Beseeching you therefore my matter to ease.   1040
     (*Here he shall reach him a purse.*)
ALL-FOR-MONEY: I have felt thee already, now let me hear thee,
Whatever thy matter be I will soon speed thee.
SIN: Marry, he hath two wives, and I think he would have
    another!
ALL-FOR-MONEY: He shall have two mo, if it be his pleasure.
WILLIAM: I have two wives, I must needs confess.
I have too many by one; I had rather have less.
To say truth, to my first wife I have most right,
But I cannot love her, I swear by this light.
I married her only for her goods and riches;
She is an old crust, none would marry her for love.   1050

Her mouth would slaver ever when I did her kiss,
Therefore to take another my mind did me move,
Who is both young and honest as her deeds do well prove,
But the Bishop doth trouble me, whereby I know well
He will have me again with that old jade to dwell.

SIN: A tired jade by thee I think she hath not been,
For she is properly a jade that hath been over-ridden,
And because thou hast spared her, now she is fresh and
lusty;
Therefore hire her out for an hackney, and she will bring
thee money!

WILLIAM: The devil shall ride her if I set her out to hire,   1060
I would she were with him in the midst of hell-fire!

SIN: Hadst thou any riches by her, any lands or woods?

WILLIAM: I had three hundred pounds by her, besides her
other goods.

SIN: She may be very glad that on thee her goods did spare,
That would let her forth to be the devil's hackney mare!

WILLIAM: So I were rid on her, I care not where she were!   *rid of*

ALL-FOR-MONEY: Thou shalt be sped herein, even as thou
dost require;
I will find means with witness to be proved
That she before her marriage to another was betrothed,
Whereby with thy young wife thou shalt live at ease.   1070
Thou mayest thank Money, my old friend, Iwis,
Or else, thou mayst trust me, I would not have done this.

WILLIAM: I thank you sir, heartily, for the pains you have
taken.
I will remember you every year with a Christmas capon.
(*Here he goeth forth.*)

SIN: These be goodly old angels, take heed you do not lose
them,
Have not they pretty wings, that could fly into your bosom?

ALL-FOR-MONEY: I will keep them safe enough, I must needs
love them.
It is a crooked matter that I will not make straight for
them.

(NICHOL-NEVER-OUT-OF-LAW *knocks at the door*.)

SIN: There is some jolly suitor, do not you hear him knock?
Softer sir, softer, lest you break the lock!   1080

ALL-FOR-MONEY: Let him in quickly, whatsoever he be.
If Money have sent him he is welcome to me.

(*Here cometh in* NICHOL-NEVER-OUT-OF-LAW, *like a rich Franklin, with a long bag of books by his side*.)   country squire

SIN: Come near to my lord and tell him your matter.
Did my grandfather Money will you come hither?

NICHOL: I think I had come in vain unless he had sent me.
Sir, here is a dozen mortgages if you will help me.

(*Here he reacheth him something in a bag*.)

ALL-FOR-MONEY: Now I am ready to hear thee tell it out along.
I will help thee without doubt, be it right or wrong.

SIN: Either right or wrong thy matter must need be,
Therefore thou mayst speak. Thou speedst, I warrant thee.[35]   1090

NICHOL: There is a poor knave by me hath a piece of ground
Not worth by year past three or four pound,
And I have at the villain such hate and spite
That I would have it from him, although it be his right.
The land lieth so handsomely at the back side of my house
That I am as greedy thereof as [a] cat of a mouse.

ALL-FOR-MONEY: By what right and title do you the same claim?

NICHOL: His name is Nicholas, we are both of one name,
But no kin at all I am sure he is to me.
Yet though my title be nought I will weary him with
     money;   1100
The law is open, I am sure, for every man.
Marry, let him make his plea as well as he can!
Do not many give over their titles in a year,
Some for want of money and some for very fear?

ALL-FOR-MONEY: Is here all the title you have, goodman
     Nichol?
Thou carest not, so thou hast it, what becomes of thy fall?

NICHOL: So that I have it I care not for hereafter;

---

[35] In the original there is another "I" after the "thee." Such a doubling is a standard Elizabethan emphatic, but we emend to omit because its presence kills the rhyme of "thee" with "be."

When I am dead and rotten it will be good for my
    children.

SIN: It is a good wind that blows no man to evil,
But happy are those children whose father goes to the
    devil!   1110
No good plea herein I think thou canst invent.

NICHOL: Do you not think that I have feigned a dissent
And thereby claim a right that never was before?
The rich may soon overcome the moneyless and the poor,
And yet that I shall lose it I surely am afraid,
Unless you cause judgment the next term to be stayed.

ALL-FOR-MONEY: I will get it stayed, I have thee now promised,
But in the mean space see that you have writings forged
And also false witnesses two or three at the least,
Who may swear, if need be, thou hast bought his interest,   1120
And this way thou art sure to have thy desire.
Go about thy business—dry wood soon catcheth fire.

NICHOL: Marry sir, this is the way that must needs prevail.
I thank you sir, heartily, for telling me this tale.
    (*Here he goeth out.*)

ALL-FOR-MONEY: Iwis, Sin, my purse begins to fill.

SIN: Nay, it will be fuller if you may have your will.
    (*Here another knocketh.*)
Another suitor there is, I hear him knock amain.
Shall he come in sir, to tell his grief and pain?

ALL-FOR-MONEY: To come to me quickly see that he do not spare.
If he comes from Money, well falls out his share.   1130
    (*Here cometh in* SIR LAWRENCE LIVINGLESS, *like a foolish
    priest, and speaketh.*)[36]

SIR L: Sir, I have a petition to Your Lordship to make,
Trusting you will be good to me for Master Money's sake.

ALL-FOR-MONEY: Thou canst not come for anything to me
But I will do it gladly for the love of money.

SIR L: I have a present here not worthy for you to receive,
But I give you with all my heart even such as I have.

---

[36] The foolish priest is a stock figure in both medieval satire and in the moral drama—cf. Caconos, in *The Conflict of Conscience.*

An hundred *Dirige* groats, they be good silver   (refers to inscription)
    and old;
I have kept them so long they begin for to mould.
    (*Here he reacheth him something.*)

SIN: It is very near day when such birds fly.
You were wont to say Mass for a groat, but now they are
    dearer to buy.   1140
I pray thee, what is thy name? Art thou either vicar or parson?

SIR L: Sir Lawrence Livingless, without either living or
    mansion.

SIN: By the Mass, I thought thou wast even such another.
I knew by thy countenance thou wast never Doctor,
But thou hast been a Doctor at the ducking of women.   *baptism*
He hath ever had a good zeal to kerchiefs and linen.
I promise you he is very well learned, if you list to
    appose him,   *test*
But it must not be in Greek, Hebrew or Latin.
A cure he is able sufficiently to discharge,   *curateship*
He can read very well upon a pair of cards.   1150

SIR L: I am none of the best learned—it is but a folly to flatter.

SIN: In faith Sir Lawrence, I think you must play the carter,
Or else you must be a hedge priest, beggars to
    marry,   *traveling priest*[37]
Which is an easy living but you must fare hardly.
How didst thou with the Bishop when he did appose thee?

SIR L: Marry, I did so answer him that he did depose me,
From all my benefices and livings, with his power and might.
He would not once suffer me to serve a cure, by this light;
Therefore good my lord, I heartily you require
To help me to some living, according to my desire.   1160

ALL-FOR-MONEY: Do not fear, my priest, for wanting of any
    living,
I have devised already which way it shall come in.
My Chaplain thou shalt be, for here I do thee make,
A benefice thou shalt have none shall from thee it take.

---

[37] Rampant sexuality seems to have been the chief accusation against the disreputable itinerant preacher. To "play the carter" is to act like an ignorant boob (*OED*).

Sir L: Now God reward Your Lordship! In heaven may you
it find!
But one thing I had forgotten which now comes to my mind.
At every visitation when I shall be apposed,
For want of sufficient learning I shall be then discharged.

All-for-Money: Before every visitation be sure to come for
my letter,
Which when the Chancellor sees, straightways thou shalt have
favor.   1170

Sir L: The proudest of them all shall not make me now to
shrink!
The pots shall walk anon, I will full merrily   *drinking mugs*
drink!

Sin: How many planets, Sir Lawrence, is there in the third
heaven?

Sir L: Nay, I know how many cards I have when I have
played all seven.

Sin: How say you by Sir Lawrence? Is he not well skilled,
In the science of arithmetic when the cup is new filled?
How many chapters in the Gospel did St. Matthew write?

Sir L: Marry, one and all his fellows, that I can quickly recite.

Sin: I pray thee tell me truly, how many did he write in all?

Sir L: Would you fain know the truth you were best ask the
wall.   1180

Sin: Thou hast not very much studied that Gospel
Because the number of the chapters thou canst not tell.

Sir L: No, nor the other Gospels but a little I have studied;
In other things much more I have been occupied.

Sin: How many Epistles did St. Paul write after he was
converted?

Sir L: By the Mass, he writ too many! I would they were all
burned!
For had not they been, and the New Testament in English
I had not lacked living at this time, Iwis.
Before the people knew so much of the Scripture
Then they did obey us and loved us out of measure,   1190
And now we cannot go in the streets without a mock.

The little boys will say, "Yonder goes Sir John Smell-smock."
A boy called me so once amongst twenty people and more,
And indeed I smelled his mother's, not two hours before!
Another boy called a priest so, and the priest spake again
    quickly,
"I never smelled thy mother's smock but when I begat thee!"

SIN: Of a truth, Sir Lawrence, in thy time thou hast been
    good;
For lack of winter liveries thou hast given many a
    Christmas hood.[38]

ALL-FOR-MONEY: Well my friend Sin, carry Sir Lawrence home,
He shall be also my steward, which is an honest man's
    room.   *position* 1200

SIN: Indeed, the honesty of the man may make the room better
But the room cannot make Sir Lawrence honester.
    (*Here the priest and the Vice goeth out.*)

ALL-FOR-MONEY: I have filled my purse meetly well this day;
I do not intend much longer for suitors to stay.
One other good cheat would make me pack up and be gone.
It is marvel without suitors I am so long alone;
Methink [s] it is no trouble for all my long sitting,
As long as money thereby I may be fingering.
    (SIN *cometh in and speaketh.*)

SIN: It is marvel that no suitors have been here all this while.
There is coming to seek you that dwells many a mile.[39]   1210
    (*Here one other doth knock.*)

ALL-FOR-MONEY: There is one other doth knock. Whatever he
    be
If he come from Money he shall be welcome to me.
To me they do come, therefore let him in,
Open the door quickly, I pray thee good Sin.
    (*Here cometh in* MOTHER CROOTE, *dressed evil-favored like an
    old woman. She shall be muffled and have a staff in her hand and
    go stooping, and she speaketh.*)

---

[38] Though the sense is mocking and probably obscene, we have not been able to find the meaning of giving a Christmas hood.

[39] The sense is "There is one coming to see you who dwells many miles away."

MOTHER C: God save all, God save all, and our blessed Lady.
Who is this gentleman that will do all things for money?
SIN: Come hither, Mother Mabel, your terms you do misuse;
To see you come so far methinks it is strange news.
But what is your name Mother? My lord would have you tell.
MOTHER C: Marry, 'ch'ill my life, son, but ich do not   *ich=I*
hear you well.[40]   1220
Everyone that knows me do call me Mother Croote;
'Cham an hundred years old, cha can skantly go on foot.
ALL-FOR-MONEY: What is your matter, Mother, tell me and do
not spare.
If Money sent you hither the better shall you fare.
MOTHER C: He did send me to you, and I may say to you
'Ch'ave brought you hither the price of a good vat cow.   *v=f*
Have here is four old royals, ich would they were
a score.
Before yesterday cha did not see them this twenty year and
more.
(Here she giveth him the money.)
ALL-FOR-MONEY: Yea marry, Mother Croote, they be four good
royals of gold.
If you knew them not this twenty year it is marvel they did
not mould.   1230
MOTHER C: When ich put my hand in my coffer ich might then
feel them,
But 'ch'as been blind this thirty year, so that ich could not
see them.
Therefore 'ch'ill conclare the cause of my coming hither.
SIN: "Declare" you should say, Mother, for that is the right
speaking.
MOTHER C: You can conclout the matter much better than I.
SIN: You should say "conclude," Mother, but it is not much
away.
MOTHER C: 'Ch'ave, you may see, be brought up
amongst swine and kie,   *kine*

---

[40] The rustic is another dramatic stock figure—cf. People in *Respublica*. The dialect here is that of south-western England.

'Ch'ill now declare the cause of my coming.

ALL-FOR-MONEY: Go to then, Mother Croote, and I will give
    you the hearing.

MOTHER C: Because 'ch'am rich and have
    something to take, too,   *dowry* 1240

There came of late a young springal me to woo.   *stripling*

Nay, he is a wholesome young man of twenty year old
    and three;

It does me good to think on him, by Our Blest Lady.

He made full much on me, and loved me, God woot,

And cha love him again, even at the heart-root;

So that we plight our troths, each to other,

And so at pervenient time to marry together.

SIN: It is "convenient," Mother Croote, but it makes no
    great matter.

MOTHER C: You may see sir, old women have much clitter
    clatter.

But I pray you, good sir, bear with my budeness.   1250

SIN: I know, Mother Croote, your meaning is "rudeness."

MOTHER C: Whatsoever ich say, my meaning is no less—

But my husband, my husband was so well-favored,

That a young drab of him was enamoured,   *slut*

Who said unto him that it was a great shame

For him to marry such an old beldame,

And thus this young drab my husband enticed,

To whom she doth hope right shortly to be married.

But 'ch'ad rather the young whore were quick at the devil

Than she should have my husband, my sweetheart and
    jewel.   1260

My love in my youth was never so fervent

As it is on my sweetheart, now at this present.

Shall I never buss my sweetheart again?

Nothing in the world would make me so fain.

SIN: Goop-with-a-galled-back come up to supper,

Gill, my old mare, must have a new crupper!

A meeter marriage than this did I never see,

For she is not past four-score years older than he!

MOTHER C: I wish but one night with him for to lie,
  Oh, he would make me look young by and by.[41]   1270
SIN: When I was a boy it was an old saying
  That an old sack would lack much clouting and patching.
  Oh, it doth Mother Croote much good to have her bones
    rattled,
  And especially by her lover, and then her mind were settled.
  When you be with your husband you will be as good as a
    charm;
  If my wife were your age, he would do her little harm.
MOTHER C: Yea, but he is good in my bed to keep my back
    warm,
  And now and then 'ch'ill kiss him and clip him in my   *embrace*
    arm.
  Therefore my lord, for you friend Money's sake,
  That I may have my husband I pray you undertake.   1280
SIN: He is more meet your son than your husband to be.
MOTHER C: Yea, but the younger he is, the better he is
    for me.
SIN: Yea, but you are the worse for him the elder you are;
  Therefore he will labor other, and you for the holidays spare.
  I pray you, my lord, Mother Croote help to speed,
  For of this young man she standeth very great need.
ALL-FOR-MONEY: A couple of false witnesses must therefore
    be hired,
  Which must say they heard when you were betrothed,
  And then, willy nilly, he must be compelled
  To forsake the other and to you to be married.   1290
MOTHER C: There will no such be got, my dear heart-root!
ALL-FOR-MONEY: Enough for money I warrant you, Mother
    Croote.
MOTHER C: Now God's dear blessing light on that soot   *sweet*
    face of yours!
  'Ch'ave tarried too long by two or three hours.
  Now 'ch'ill desire from hence to depart.
    (*Here* MOTHER CROOTE *goeth forth.*)

[41] This perhaps recalls certain fairytale and folk motifs, like the "loathly lady."

ALL-FOR-MONEY: Now farewell Mother Croote, even with all
    my heart!

SIN: Do you not see yonder old Mother Croote,
  Would as fain be trod as a younger pullet.
  How will her husband do when he should kiss her?
  Her nose and her chin meets almost together.   1300
  Oh, she will be a trim bride, that day she is wed!
  One would think she smiled, if her teeth were in her head.

ALL-FOR-MONEY: I have had this day a trim sort of   *collection*
    suitors.
  How many sent I away with money in their purses?
  My purse is now full even unto the brink,
  Now it is high time for me to eat and drink.
  Have not I been friendly to your grandfather Money?
  All such as he sent they were dispatched quickly.

SIN: Many such days you may have when you will,
  Whereby all your bags and coffers may be full still.   1310

ALL-FOR-MONEY: I intend again shortly to sit in commission;
  I pray God I speed no worse then than now I have done.
    (*Here* ALL-FOR-MONEY *goeth out.*)

SIN: Do you not see how all is for money, masters?
  He helps to make good all wrong and crooked matters;
  He cares not though at length he go to the devil,
  So that with money he may his bags fill.
  His money brings him to pleasure, and pleasure sends him to
    me,
  And I send him to Damnation, and he sends him to hell
    quickly,
  And when he is there he hath got a proper place.
  Let him cry till his heart aches, he shall have no grace.   1320
  Oh, it is a goodly house; it is bigger than a grange;   *farmhouse*
  It passeth fee simple, for the title doth never change.[42]
  Therefore if any will be married to my fair son Damnation
  They shall be sure straightways thereof to have possession.
  Therefore, if any chance to marry my son hereafter,

---

[42] Fee simple is straight renting, but without the guarantee that the lease would stay in the family upon the demise of any given holder.

Let them not blame me, for I have told his behavior.
Before you proceed therefore in this marriage,
Weigh well with yourself the danger and charge.
It is now high time, methinks, to depart.
Will none of you speak to comfort my heart?   1330
I would have sworn that you had been more mannerly;
To match my son with such I pass not a fly!
My throat, for want of drink, begins to be dry.
Who is it that calls me to drink some good ale?
Forsooth, I will be with you by and by!
It is Sir Lawrence Livingless,
      twenty pound to a nail!   "dollars to donuts"
He will tipple at it solemnly, as long as it is stale.
And the rather I think it is he because of his talk,
For he said before his going that all the pots should walk.
      (*Here the Vice goeth out.*)
    (JUDAS *cometh in like a damned soul, in black, painted with flames of
fire and with a fearful vizard, and speaketh as followeth.*)
JUDAS: O, woe, woe, that ever on earth I lived!   1340
Woe be to that hour when I first was delivered!
My guilty conscience pricks me day by day.
Judas I was called, that did my master betray.
I did see Christ's miracles and hear his predication,   *preaching*
O that I had had grace to be with the rest in salvation!
I wanted God's grace and his especial favor,
Whereby I hanged myself and died in despair,
And now the time is past any mercy to crave.
One half hour to live I would desire but to have.
Well, it will not be; nothing will help me now;   1350
Wherever I do go Damnation doth me follow.
Woe worth that money, that ever it was made,
By which occasion my master was betrayed!
But had I had grace to have asked mercy therefore,
And repented my faults, as Peter did before,
I should have been pardoned as other sinners be,
And accounted no sinner. God will have mercy
So that they ask mercy so long as they do live,

All which time he is ready their sins to forgive.
Woe therefore to me, and to all that have so died,   1360
For without remedy now I am forever damned!
> (*Here cometh in* DIVES, *with suchlike apparell and vizard as*
> JUDAS *hath, who speaketh as followeth.*)

DIVES: O, what hath belly pleasure brought me unto?
To hell torments, to a place of everlasting woe!
Woe, woe and again woe to me forevermore,
That consumed so much on myself and nothing on the poor!
Poor Lazarus was at my door, whose hunger was so great
That he therewith soon died, not having for to eat;
When I with all fine fare like a glutton was served,
And like a greedy cormorant with belly full farced,
Not suffering one morsel to Lazarus to be given,   1370
And yet was there more spoiled than an hundred would
    eat, certain.
To feed the dogs therewith I was much better content,
Or else some relief to him I would have sent.
The silly and dumb dogs did him more good than I,
They licked his sores, O woe therefore to me!
And then he died full soon, whose death pleased God so well,
That in Abraham's bosom he aye shall rest and dwell.
And I then died also, without any repentance,
Whereby I have got God's wrath and heavy vengeance,
For I am a damned soul, forever in torment and pain,   1380
My pleasures on the earth hath brought me to this gain.
And though the torments be so vehement and the fiery flames
    so great,
Yet I cannot have a drop of water to quench and cool my
    heat.
I denied poor Lazarus to give him meat and food,
And now he denies me to help or do me good.
A woeful change to me, to him it is not so,
For he from pain to pleasure passed, and I from weal to woe;
For if I were on the earth as I was once before,
I would spare from myself and give it to the poor.
What am I the better now, for all my joy and pleasure?   1390

And what is he worse now, for all his pain and hunger?
If having all my pleasure at the last I had been saved,
My former pleasures had been vain; none doth them there
    regard.
And if in cruel torments all my life I had lain,
Yet in respect, they all are joys to this eternal pain.   *in comparison*
Damnation, Damnation is coming, woe to us therefore!
Alas, alas, that [   ] this sore scene before.[43]
      (*Here cometh in* DAMNATION.)
DAMNATION: Come, come, you woeful wight, 'tis folly now
    to pray,
To speak, complain, or else of matters to debate.
Away unto that doleful place whereas the devil lieth,   1400
The best cheer that you shall have there is groan and gnash
    of teeth.
      (*Here he speaketh to* JUDAS.)
Of money thou so greedy wast, thy master to betray,
And after in despair thou madest thy life away.
      (*Here he speaketh to* DIVES.)
And thou didst pamper up thy gorge and poor didst not
    regard,
Wherefore thy last assuréd hope is hell, for thy reward.
      (*Here he speaketh to* JUDAS.)
Where is now thy money wherefore soldest thou thy master?
      (*Here he speaketh to* DIVES.)
Where is now thy fare wherein thou hadst thy pleasure?
You would not take heed while that you were living,
Therefore you must pay for it in hell without ending.
I think if on the earth you were alive again   1410
You would not from your pleasure, for all this, refrain;
For the most part on the earth do live so wickedly
That they think there is no hell to punish sin, truly.
In money they have great love, in pride they do exceed,
In gluttony and lechery their lives they do still lead.
JUDAS: O, if I were on earth and were alive again

---

[43] Something was splashed across this leaf when the ink was perhaps still wet. This, however, is the only passage that cannot be read at all.

I would be a spectacle to all that remain.
O vain love of money, O most stinking pride,
The remembrance of such sins I cannot now abide!
DIVES: If I had but one hour in flesh and blood to live,   1420
I would a thousand turn from sin, I certainly believe.
Woe worth the pleasures past that works me now such care,
Whereby I am a damned soul, good folk of me beware!
DAMNATION: Away! Away you wretched souls, to hell you must
          needs go,
And such as die as you have done shall dwell with you also.
          (*Here* DAMNATION *drives them out before him, and they shall
          make a pitiful noise.*
          Here cometh in GODLY ADMONITION [VIRTUE, HUMILITY
          and CHARITY.])
GODLY ADMONITION: What heart but must lament
To hear the rueful dolor of those two damned wights?
What hard and stony heart but will hereat repent
And pray continually, yea, both days and nights?
Who dies without repentance, thus Damnation them dights.   1430
Therefore happy are they, what trouble soever they have,
Which trust and die in Jesus Christ, through whom God will
          them save.
Here have you had inordinate love,   (seen)
Which man hath to money, although it work his woe,
But such as have any grace, this will them stir and move,
To cast their love from money and other pleasures also,
For fear they dwell with the devil, their cruel and mortal foe.
Too late then to repent, as Judas and Dives did.
There is no help in hell, for then God's mercy is hid.
Therefore I am come, called Godly Admonition,   1440
Warning you to repent before your breath is gone,
For fear you bring yourself to endless damnation;
But then there is no hope, although you cry and groan.
Therefore how happy are they that have time to make their
          moan.
Now cast away your pride and also the love of money,
For fear you shall not when you would, as lately you did see.

VIRTUE: I am to the godly a precious jewel and virtue,
  Who can without me, Virtue, be in good favor?
HUMILITY: Humility, or Clemency, is my name truly.
  Blessed (saith Christ) are the meek, for they shall obtain
    mercy.   1450
  We may learn humility of Christ our master and head,
  Who bore his cross meekly, whereon he was killed.
CHARITY: Who can live, without charity, to God's honor and
    glory?
  Who, without me, can die in God's favor?
  Charity is enemy to all hatred and fury;
  I cause the rich to help the needy and the poor.
GODLY ADMONITION: For that you are all three the especial
    gifts of God,
  Without whom none can be a perfect and godly wight,
  Let us pray therefore the sins that God forbade
  We may cast away with speed, most wicked in his sight: 1460
  The inordinate love of money, and pride in which many
    delight,
  And all other sins which lead us to damnation,
  And that we repent and die in Christ, whereby we have
    salvation.
VIRTUE: Let us pray for the Queen's Majesty, our sovereign
    governor,
  That she may reign quietly according to God's will,
  Whereby she may suppress vice and set forth God's glory and
    honor,
  And as she hath begun godly, so to continue still.
HUMILITY: Let us not forget to pray for the honorable
    Council,
  That they maintain justice and all wrong to repel.
CHARITY: And all the high estates and commons of this
    region,   1470
  With all that be here present, to have everlasting salvation.

FINIS, quoth T. Lupton

✳ *THE CONFLICT OF CONSCIENCE*

(Nathaniel Woodes, 1581)

As the general Introduction implies, the title of this play might serve as the composite title for a whole group of moralities that experiment with tragic action and tragic feeling. It locates the tragic ground with some precision.

It is often stated that there can be no such thing as Christian tragedy because the Christian God is both omnipotent and good. However, a cluster of doctrines work together to define Christian tragedy. To begin with, the doctrine of free will, which is fundamental to the popular theology which gave birth to these plays, leaves man free to refuse to benefit from God's mercy and be saved. Second, there is the doctrine that God's mercy exceeds his justice, and its corollary that to despair of salvation is a grievous sin. The works of the popular tradition again and again tell us that this is what the Prodigal Son was saved from, but what Cain and Judas were not saved from, though they could have been, had they stopped despairing and started repenting. This tradition believes that it is a tragic waste to die unsaved ("unhousel'd" is the word Hamlet uses for the way he wants Claudius to die) because it is needless. Finally, the doctrine of repentance clearly gives the means by which fallen man may regain grace, through contrition, confession, penance, and absolution. To theology then, it is merely shameful to die unsaved. But in drama, the spectacle of someone doing this excites pity and fear (since the someone is usually the Mankind character, the audience's self) and through him or her, in a very few of the best plays of this kind, that kind of strange exultation that we associate with tragedy. Similarly, the sight of a potential penitent almost losing his chance, or of a person who is torn between sin and the desire for repentance still causing pain to others, arouses the painful feelings that we associate with tragicomedy.

Apart from the turgidity of the first two Acts, *The Conflict of Conscience* is the best of its type, after, of course, *Dr. Faustus*, which adds to the basic formula dimensions not dreamed of in Nathaniel Woodes' philosophy. The reader will surely feel the power of Philologus' mind in the trial scene, and thus be able to measure the horror of its collapse. The last Act speaks for itself, though we would call attention to the fact that the character Horror who attacks Philologus, is obviously invisible to the latter's children. This device had been used in the moralities on at least three other occasions,[1] but here the dramatic value of it seems particularly striking.

Worth pointing out also is the Prologue's argument for allegory as a didactic device, when he tells us that the hero is given an allegorical name so we will be able to identify with him and not think that this tragedy only happened to one specific individual.

We reprint the redemptive ending of the play from its second issue in 1581 to remind the reader once more of the experimental nature of these plays. Masterful tragedy and really affecting tragicomedy cannot of course depend upon a little change in what a Messenger reports. But the morality playwrights had not yet discovered that the secret is *inevitability*, that the whole play must lead inexorably to the only possible conclusion.

Our text is a modernized spelling reproduction of the Malone Society Reprint of the 1581 edition, Oxford, 1952.

---

[1] In *The Castle of Perseverance*, when Penitentia is invisible to Humanum Genus; in *Mankind*, when Titivillus works his evil upon Mankind while remaining invisible to him; and in *The Longer Thou Livest the More Fool Thou Art*, when Moros, after a career of folly, is struck down by the "invisible" Godly Admonition.

THE CONFLICT OF CONSCIENCE

[*Enter*] *The* PROLOGUE

When whirling winds which blow with blustering blasts
Shall cease their course, and not the air move,
But still unstirrèd it doth stand, it chanceth at the last
To be infect. The truth hereof even day by day we   *infected*
    prove,
For deep within the caves of earth, of force it doth
    behoove   *necessarily*
(Sith that no winds do come thereto) the air out to beat;   *since*
By standing still the closèd air doth breed infections great.
The stream or flood which runneth up and down
Is far more sweet than is the standing brook;
If long unworn you leave a cloak or gown,   10
Moths will it mar unless you thereto look;
Again, if that upon a shelf you place or set a book
And suffer it there still to stand, the worms will soon it eat;
A knife, likewise, in sheath laid up the rust will
    mar and fret.   *corrode*
The good road horse if still at rack he stand,   *in stall*
To resty jade will soon transformèd be;   *restless*
If long untilled you leave a fertile land,
From strick and weed no place will be left free.   *chaff*
By these examples and suchlike, approve then well may we   *prove*
That idleness more evils doth bring into the mind of man   20
Than labor great in long time again expell out can.
Which thing our Author marking well, when wearied was
    his mind
From reading grave and ancient works, yet loath his time
    to lose,
Bethought himself, to ease his heart, some recreance to find,
And as he musèd in his mind, immediately arose
An history, of late years done, which might, as he   *story*
    suppose [d]
Stir up their minds to godliness, which should it see or hear;
But while the treatise we do play I pray you with us bear.
The argument or ground whereon our Author chiefly stayed

Is Francis Spera's history, to most men fully known,   30
Who through the love of worldly wealth, and fear of death
    dismayed,
Because he would his life and goods have kept still as his own,
From state of grace wherein he stood, he is clean overthrown,
So that he had no power at all in heart firm faith to have,
Being urged to pray unto the Lord, His mercies for to crave.
But Spera's name for causes just, our Author doth omit,
And at this time imagine him Philologus to be;
First, for because a Comedy will hardly him permit
The vices of one private man to touch particularly,
Again, now shall it stir him more who shall it hear or see,   40
For if that Spera had been one, we would straight deem in
    mind
That all by Spera spoken were—ourselves we would not find.
But sith Philologus is nought else but "one that loves to talk"
And common of the Word of God, but hath no further   *commune*
    care,
According as it teacheth them in God's fear for to walk—
If that we practice this indeed, *philologi* we are,
And so by his deservèd fault we may in time beware.
Now if as Author first it meant, you hear it with this gain,
In good behalf he will esteem that he bestowed his pain.
And for because we see by proof that men do soon forget   50
Those things for which to call them by, no name at all they
    know,
Our Author, for to help short wits did think it very meet
Some name for this his Comedy in preface for to show.
Now names to natures must agree, as every man do know;
A fitter name he could in mind no where excogitate
Than *The Conflict of Conscience* the same to nominate.   *call*
A cruel conflict certainly, where Conscience takes the foils[1]
And is constrained by the flesh to yield to deadly sin,
Whereby the grace and love of God from him sin reaves and
    spoils;
Then (wretch accursed) no power hath, repentance to begin.   60

To "take the foil" is to hunt down the game.

Far happier if that unborn and lifeless he had been,
As in discourse before your eyes shall plainly provèd be,
If that with patience you abide, the end thereof to see.
And though the history, of itself, be too too dolorous,
And would constrain a man with tears of blood his cheeks to
    wet,
Yet to refresh the minds of them which be the auditors
Our Author intermixèd hath, in places fit and meet,
Some honest mirth, yet always ware *decorum*
    to exceed.   *lest he exceed*
But list, I hear the players prest in presence for to come!
I therefore cease and take my leave; my message I have
    done.   70
      [*Exit.*]

Act first, Scene one.

     [Enter] SATAN
SATAN: High time it is for me to stir about
  And do my best my kingdom to maintain,
  For why I see of enemies a rout   *because/crowd*
  Which all my laws and statutes do disdain,
  Against my state do fight and strive amain,
  Whom in time if I do not dissipate,
  I shall repent it when it is too late.

    My mortal foe, the carpenter's son,
  Against my children, the Pharisees I mean,
  Upbraiding them did use this comparison,   10
  As in the story of his life may be seen:
  There was a man which had a vineyard green,
  Who, letting it to husbandmen unkind,
  Instead of fruit, unthankfulness did find.

    So that his servants firstly they did beat,
  His son likewise they afterward did kill,
  And hereupon that man, in fury great,
  Did soldiers send, these husbandmen to spill;   *kill*
  Their town to burn he did them also will.

But out, alas, alas for woe I cry!   20
To use the same far juster cause have I,
  For where the kingdom of this world is mine,
And his on whom I will the same bestow,
As Prince hereof I did myself assign
My darling dear whose faithful love I know
Shall never fail from me but daily flow.
But who that is perhaps some man may doubt.
I will therefore in brief portray and paint him out.

  The mortal man by nature's rule is bound
That child to favor more than all the rest   30
Which to himself in face is likest found,
So that he shall with all his goods be blest;
Even so do I esteem and like him best
Which dost most near my dealings imitate
And doth pursue God's laws with deadly hate.

  As therefore I, when once in Angel's state,
So doth my son himself now elevate
Above man's nature, in rule and dignity,
So that *in terris Deus sum* saith he,
In earth I am a god, with sins for to dispense,   40
And for rewards I will forgive each manner of offence.[2]

  I said to Eve, "Tush, tush, thou shalt not die,
But rather shalt as God know everything."
My son likewise, to maintain idolatry,
Saith "Tush, what hurt can carvèd idols bring?
Despise this law of God the heavenly king
And set them in the Church for men thereon to look;
And idol doth much good, it is a layman's book."

  Nembroth, that tyrant, fearing God's hand,   (Nimrod)
By me was persuaded to build up high Babel,   50
Whereby he presumed God's wrath to withstand;
So hath my Boy devisèd very well,
Many pretty toys to keep men's soul from hell,
Live they never so evil here and wickedly,

---

[2] The outright purchase of indulgences seemed to the early Protestants the most obvious sign of the decadence of the Roman Church.

As masses, trentals, pardons and *scala coeli*.[3]
   I egged on Pharoah, of Egypt the King,
The Israelites to kill so soon as they were born;
My darling likewise doth the self same thing
And therefore cause [s] Kings and Princes to be sworn
That with might and main they shall
     keep up his horn,   *exalt him* 60
And shall destroy with fire, axe and sword
Such as against him shall speak but one word.

   And even as I was somewhat too slow,
So that, notwithstanding, the Israelites did augment,
So, for lack of murdering, God's people do grow
And daily increase, at this time present;
Which my son shall feel, incontinent.   *very soon*
Yet another practice, this evil to withstand,
He learned of me, which now he takes in hand.

   For whenas Moses I might not destroy   70
Because he was of the Lord appointed
To bring the people from thralldom to joy,
I did not cease, whilst I had invented   *until*
Another means to have him prevented—
By accounting himself the son of Pharoah—
To make him loath Egypt to forgo.

   The same advice I also attempted
Against the Son of God when he was incarnate,
Hoping thereby to have him relented
And for promotion's sake himself to prostrate   80
Before my feet when I did demonstrate
The whole world unto him, and all the glory,
As it is recorded in *Matheus'* history.   *(Matthew 4, 8—10)*

   So hath the Pope, who is my darling dear,
My eldest Boy, in whom I do delight,
Lest he should fall, which thing he greatly fear [s],
Out of his seat of honor, pomp and might,
Hath got to him, on his behalf to fight,

[3] *Scala coeli* were Masses for the dead, which were connected with certain altars and which carried indulgences with them.

Two Champions stout, of which the one is *Avarice*,
The other is callèd *Tyrannical Practice*.   90
   For, as I said, although I claim by right
The kingdom of this earthly world so round,
And in my stead to rule with force and might
I have assigned the Pope, whose match I nowhere found,
His heart with love to me so much abound[s];
Yet diverse men, of late, of malice most unkind,
Do study to displace my son some wayward means to find;
Wherefore I marvel much what cause of let there is   *hindrance*
That hitherto they have not their office put in use.[4]
I will go see, for why I fear that somewhat is amiss.   100
If not, to range abroad the world I will them straight
    procure.
But needs they must have one to help, men's hearts for to
    allure
Unto their train. Who that should be I cannot yet espy—
No meeter match I can find out than is *Hypocrisy!*
   Who can full well in time and place dissemble either's part;
No man shall easily perceive with which side he doth bear,
But when once favor he hath got, and credit in man's heart,
He will not slack in mine affairs, I do him nothing fear.
But time doth run too fast away for me to tarry here,
For none will be enamoured of my shape, I do know;   110
I will therefore mine imps send out from hell, their shapes
    to show.

Act first. Scene two.

[*Enter*] MATHETES, PHILOLOGUS
MATHETES: My mind doth thirst, dear friend Philologus,
   Of former talk to make a final end,
   And where before we 'gan for to discuss
   The cause why God doth such afflictions send
   Into his Church, you would some more time spend;

---

[4] "They" apparently refers to the "two champions stout," Avarice and Tyrannical Practice.

In the same cause that thereby you might learn
Betwixt the wrath and love of God aright for to discern.
PHILOLOGUS: With right good will to your request herein I do
        consent,
As well because, as I perceive, you take therein delight,   120
As also for because it is most chiefly pertinent
Unto mine office to instruct and teach each Christian wight
True godliness, and show to them the path that leadeth right
Unto God's kingdom, where we shall inherit our salvation,
Given unto us from God by Christ, our true propitiation.
    But that a better ordered course herein we may observe,
And may directly to the first apply that which ensue [s],
To speak that hath been said before, I will a time reserve,
And to proceed from whence we left, by course and order due,
Unto the end. At first, therefore, you did lament and rue   130
The misery of these our days, and great calamity
Which those sustain who dare gainsay the Romish hypocrisy.
MATHETES: I have great cause, as hath each Christian heart,
To wail and weep, to shed out tears of blood,
Whenas I call to mind the torments and the smart
Which those have born who honest be, and good,
For nought else but because their errors they withstood.
Yet joyed I much to see how patiently
They bore the cross of Christ with constancy.
PHILOLOGUS: So many of us as into one body be   140
Incorporate, whereof Christ is the lively head,   *living*
As members of our bodies, which we see
With joints of love together be conjoined,
And must needs suffer, unless that they be dead,
Some part of grief in mind which other feel
In body, though not so much by a great deal.
    Wherefore, by this it is most apparent
That those two into one body are not united,
Of the which the one doth suffer and the other doth torment
And in the wounds of his brother is delighted.   150
Now, which is Christ's body may easily be decided,

For the lamb is devourèd of the wolf alway,   *by*
Not the wolf of the lamb, as Chrysostom doth say.   *St. Chrysostom*
   Again, of unrighteous Cain murdered was Abel,
By whom the Church of God was figurèd;[5]   *represented*
Isaac, likewise, was persecuted of Ishmael,
As in the Book of Genesis is mentionèd;
Israel of Pharoah was also terrified,
David the Saint was afflicted by his son
And put from his kingdom—I mean by Absolon.   160
   Elias the Thesbite, for fear of Jezabel
Did fly to Horeb and hid him in a cave;
Micheas the Prophet, as the story doth tell,   *Micah*
Did hardly his life from Baal's priests save;
Jeremy of that sauce tasted have,   *Jeremiah*
So did Esay, Daniel and the Children three,   *Isaiah*
And thousands more which in stories we may see.

MATHETES: In the New Testament we may also read
That our Saviour Christ, even in His infancy
Of Herod the King might stand in great dread,   170
Who sought to destroy Him, such was his insolency.
Afterward, of the Pharisees He did with constancy
Suffer shameful death; His Apostles also,
For testimony of the truth did their crosses undergo.

PHILOLOGUS: James, under Herod, was headed with the   *beheaded*
   sword;
The rest of the Apostles did suffer much turmoil.
Good Paul was mudered by Nero his word,
Domitian divised a barrel full of oil,
The body of John the Evangelist to boil;
The Pope at this instant sundry torments procure [s]   180
For such as by God's holy word will endure.
   By these former stories two things we may learn
And profitably record in our remembrance:
The first is God's Church from the Devil's to discern,
The second to mark what manifest resistance

---

[5] Philologus is practicing *typology*, which was second nature to medieval and Renaissance Christians. It is the practice of interpreting the Old Testament as prefiguration or unwitting prophesying of the New.

The truth of God hath, and what encumbrance
It bringeth upon them that will it profess;
Wherefore, they must arm themselves to suffer distress.
MATHETES: It is no new thing, I do now perceive,
  That Christ's Church do suffer tribulation.   190
  But that the same cross I might better receive,
  I request you to show me, for my consolation,
  What is the cause, by your estimation,
  That God doth suffer His people [to] be in thrall,
  Yet help them so soon as they to Him call?
PHILOLOGUS: The chiefest thing which might us cause or move
  With constant minds Christ's cross for to sustain,
  Is to conceive of heaven a faithful love;
  Whereto we may not come, as Paul doth prove it plain,
  Unless with Christ we suffer, that with Him we may reign.   200
  Again, sith that it is our heavenly father's will
  By worldly woes our carnal lusts to kill.
    Moreover, we do use to loath that thing we alway have
  And do delight the more in that which mostly we do want,   *lack*
  Affliction urgeth us also more earnestly to crave;
  And when we once relievèd be, true faith in us it plant,
  So that to call in each distress on God we will not faint;
  For trouble brings forth patience, from patience doth ensue
  Experience, from experience hope, of health the anchor true.[6]
    Again, ofttimes God doth provide affliction for our gain,   210
  As Job, who after loss of goods had twice so much therefore;
  Sometime affliction is a means to honor to attain,
  As you may see if Joseph's life you set your eyes before;
  Continually it doth us warn from sinning any more,
  Whenas we see the judgments just, which God our heavenly
      king
  Upon offenders here in earth for their offences bring [s].
    Sometime God doth it us to prove if constant we will be,   *test*

[6] The fact that the author was a minister emerges in passages like these, which give the standard answers to the standard theological questions. What is striking is the way the play itself functions as a critique of all these "comforts" and all these instances from the Old and New Testaments. As Philologus sinks into despair Woodes reduces the materials of his own calling to mere words.

As he did unto Abraham; sometime his whole intent
Is to declare his heavenly might, as in John we may see,
When the Disciples did ask Christ why God the blindness sent   220
Unto that man that was born blind, to whom incontinent   *at once*
Christ said, "Neither for parents' sins, nor for his own offence
Was he born blind, but that God might show his magnificence."
MATHETES: This is the sum of all your talk, if that I guess
    aright:
That God doth punish His elect to keep their faith in ure,   *use*
Or lest that if continual ease and rest enjoy they might,
God to forget through hautiness frail nature should
    procure;
Or else, by feeling punishment our sins for to abjure;
Or else, to prove our constancy, or lastly that we may
Be instruments in whom His might God may abroad display.   230
    Now must I needs confess to you my former ignorance,
Which knew no cause at all why God should trouble His elect,
But thought afflictions all to be rewards for our offence,
And to proceed from wrathful Judge, did alway it suspect,
As do the common sort of men, who will straightway direct
And point their fingers at such men as God doth chastise
    here,
Esteeming them by just desert their punishment to bear.
PHILOLOGUS: Such is the nature of mankind, himself to
    justify
And to condemn all other men, whereas we ought, of right,
Accuse our selves especial, and God to magnify,   240
Who in His mercy doth us spare, whereas He also might,
Sith that we do the self same things, with like plagues us
    requite.
Which thing our Saviour Christ doth teach, as testifieth Luke,
The thirteenth Chapter, where He doth vainglorious men
    rebuke.
    But for this time let this suffice. Now let's homeward go,
And further talk in private place, if need be, we will have.
MATHETES: With right good will I will attend on you your
    house unto,

Or else go you with me to mine, the longer journey save,
For it is now high dinner time, my stomach meat doth crave.[7] 250
PHILOLOGUS: I am soon bidden to my friend. Come on, let us
    depart.
MATHETES: Go you before, and I will come behind, with all my
    heart.

Act second. Scene first.

    [*Enter*] HYPOCRISY
HYPOCRISY: God speed you all, that be of God's belief,
    The mighty Jehovah protect you from ill!
    I beseech to the living God that he would give
    To each of you present a hearty good will
    With flesh to contend, your lust for to kill,
    That by the aid of spiritual assistance,
    You may subdue your carnal concupiscence.

    God grant you all, for His mercy's sake,   260
    The light of His Word to your heart's joy.
    I humbly beseech him a confusion to make
    Of erroneous sects which might you annoy,
    Earnestly requiring each one to employ
    His whole endeavor God's word to maintain,
    And from strange doctrine your hearts to refrain.

    Grant, Lord, I pray thee, such preachers to be
    In thy congregation, thy people to learn,
    As may for conscience's sake, and of mere sincerity,
    Being able 'twixt corn and cockle to discern,   *teach* 270
    Apply their study to replenish the barn,
    That is, Thy Church by their doctrines increase,
    And make many heirs of thine eternal peace. Amen. Amen.

    But soft, let me see—how doth me aspect?[8]   *my horoscope*
    First, sluggish Saturn, of nature so cold,

---

[7] The text reads "high," but it is possible that "nigh" was intended.

[8] The text reads "who doth me aspect," which may be read as meaning "who is looking at me?" It is not impossible to read the passage that follows as an answer to this question, but the emendation, based on the occasional appearance of "who" for "how" and the rarity of "aspect" as a verb, seems to better serve as an introduction to the astrological material. It means, roughly, "Well, what's the outlook for me?"

Being placed in Tauro my beams do reject,
And Luna in Cancro in sextile he behold—
I will the effect hereafter unfold.
Now Jupiter the gentle, of temperature mean,
Poor Mercury the turncoat he forsook clean.   280
Now murdering Mars retrograde in Libra
With amiable trine, apply to my beam,
And 'splendent Sol, the ruler of the day,
After his eclipse to Jupiter will lean.
The goddess of pleasure, Dame Venus I mean,
To me her poor servant seems friendly to be,
So also doth Luna, otherwise called Phoebe.
But now I speak mischievous—I would say "in a
      mystery"—
Wherefore to interpret it I hold it best done,
For here be a good sort, I believe, in this company   290
That know not my meaning, as this man for one.
What, blush not at it, you are not alone!
Here is another that know[s] not my mind,
Nor he in my words great favor can find.
      The planet Mercurius is neither hot nor cold,
Neither good nor yet very bad, of his own nature,
But doth alter his quality with them which do hold
Any friendly aspect of him, even so I assure.
We Mercurialists—I mean hypocrites—cannot long endure
In one condition but do alter our mind   300
To theirs that talk with us, thereby friendship to find.
      The little chameleon by nature can change
Herself to that color the which she behold[s];
Why should it then to any seem strange
That we do thus alter? Why are we controlled,
Sith only the rule of nature we hold?
We seek to please all men, yet most do us hate,
And we are rewarded, for friendship, debate.
Saturnus is envious; how then can he love
Adulation, or Hypocrisy, to him most contrary?   310
The Jovists, being good, do look high above,

And do not regard the rest of the company.
Now Mars, being retrograde, foretelleth misery
To tyrannical practice, to happen eftsoon,   *very shortly*
As shall be apparent before all be done.

   Which tyranny with flattery is easily pacified,
Whereas Tom-Tell-Troth shall feel of his sword,
So that with such men is fully verified
That old said saw, and common byword:
Obsequium amicos, by flatteries friends are prepared,   320
But *veritas odium parit*, as commonly is seen,
For speaking the truth many hated have been.

   By Sol understand Popish principality,
With whom full highly I am entertained,
But being eclipsed shall show forth his quality;
Then shall Hypocrisy be utterly disdained,
Whose wretched exile, though greatly complained
And wept for of many, shall be without hope
That in such pomp shall ever be Pope.

   By Venus the riotous, by Luna the variable,   330
Betwixt whom and Mercury no variance can fall,
For they which in words be most unstable
Would be thought faithful, and the riotous liberal,
So that Hypocrisy their doings cloak shall.
But whist, not a word, for yonder come some,
While I know what they are I will be dumb.   *while = until*
    (*Step aside*).

Act second. Scene two.

    [*Enter*] TYRANNY, AVARICE
TYRANNY: Put me before, for I will shift for one,
    (*push* AVARICE *backward*)
So long as strength remaineth in this arm,
And pluck up thy heart, thou faint-hearted mome,   *fool*
As long as I live thou shalt take no harm.   340
Such as control us I will their tongues charm,
By fire or sword or other like torment,

So that ever they did it they shall it repent.

    Hast thou forgotten what Satan did say,

That the k[nave] Hypocrisy our doings should hide,

HYPOCRISY (*aside*): *Ambo!*[9]   *(Both* knaves!)

TYRANNY: So that under his cloak our parts we should play

And of the rude people should never be spied,   *simple*

Or, if the worst should hap or betide,

That I, by tyranny, would both you defend   350

Against such as mischief to you should pretend.

AVARICE: Indeed, such words our Belsire did speak   *dear father*

HYPOCRISY (*aside*):   *Tut, Father Jotsam!*

AVARICE: Which, being remembered doth make my heart glad.

But yet one thing my courage doth break,

And when I think of it it makes me full sad,

I mean the evil luck which Hypocrisy had

When he was expelled out of this land,

For then with me the matter evil did stand.

    For I by him so shadowed was from light   360

That almost no man could me out espy,

HYPOCRISY (*aside*):   *A little k[nave] to hide so great a lubber!*

AVARICE: But he being gone, to every man's sight

I was apparent. Each man did descry

My pilling and polling, so that glad was I   *plucking and shearing*

From my nature to cease, a thing most marvellous,

And live in secret, the time was so dangerous.

TYRANNY: Tush, Avarice, thou fearest a thing that is vain,

HYPOCRISY (*aside*):   *He feareth nothing. He thinketh the hangman is*
    dead.

TYRANNY: For by me alone both you shall be stayed,   370

And if thou mark well thou shalt perceive plain

That if I, Tyranny, my part had well played,

And from killing of heretics my hand had not stayed,

HYPOCRISY (*aside*):   *He can play two parts, the fool and the knave!*

TYRANNY: They had never grown to such a great rout,

Neither should have been able to banish him out.

---

[9] In the original, Hypocrisy's asides are printed in the right margin, in italic, in a type size much smaller than that of the main text. Here, they are also set in italics, but are printed as part of the dialogue.

But *sero sapiunt Phriges*, at length I will take heed,[10]
And with blood enough this evil will prevent,

HYPOCRISY (*aside*):   *A Popish policy!*

TYRANNY: For if I hear of any that in word or in deed,   380
Yea, if it be possible to know their intent,
If I can prove that in thought they it meant
To impair our estates—no prayer shall serve,
But will pay them their hire as each one deserve [s]!

HYPOCRISY (*aside*):   *Antichristian charity!*

AVARICE: The fish once taken, and 'scaped from bait,
Will ever hereafter beware of the hook.
Such as use hunting will spy the hare straight
Though others discern her not, yet on her shall look.
Again, the learned can read in a book,   390
Though the unskillful, seeing equal with them,   *unlearned*
Cannot discern an F from an M.
So those which have tasted the fruit that we bear
And find it so sour, will not us implant.

TYRANNY: Tush, Avarice, I warrant thee thou needst not fear.
In the clergy I know no friends we shall want,   *lack*
Which, for hope of gain, the truth will recant

HYPOCRISY (*aside*):   *Utilitas facit esse Deos.*[11]

TYRANNY: And give themselves wholly to set out Hypocrisy,
Being egged on with Avarice and defended by Tyranny.   400

AVARICE: Well may the clergy on our side hold,
For they by us no small gain did reap,
But all the temporality, I dare be bold   *laymen*
To venture in wager of gold a good heap,
At our preferments will mourn, wail and weep.

TYRANNY: Though indeed no just cause of joy they can find,
Yet for fear of my sword they will alter their mind!

HYPOCRISY (*aside*):   *This is sharp arguments!*

TYRANNY: But I marvel much where Hypocrisy is;
Methink it is long since from us he did go.   410

---

[10] The Latin tag is a proverb referring to the episode of the Trojan Horse in the *Iliad*. "The Phrygians [the Trojans] realized too late."

[11] "Advantage (gain) makes Gods of us," that is, for our own profit we become capable of doing anything.

AVARICE: I doubt that of his purpose he miss,   *fear that*
   And therefore hath hanged himself for woe.
HYPOCRISY (*aside*):   *Pray for yourself!*
AVARICE: How sayest thou, Tyranny, dost not think so?
   In faith, if I thought that he might be spared
   And we have our purpose, beshrew me if I cared!
HYPOCRISY (*aside*):   *Your kind heart shall cost me a couple of*
      rushes.   *reeds (i.e. nothing)*
TYRANNY: Saw you ever the like of this doubting dolt?
HYPOCRISY (*aside*):   *Not I, the like of such a cut-throat colt!*
TYRANNY: It grieves me to hear how faint-hearted he is.   420
   A little would cause me to kill thee, thou ass-colt.
   See, see, for woe he is like for to piss!
   To give an attempt, what a fellow were this!
   But this is the good that cometh of covetousness,
   He liveth alway in fear to lose his riches.
     Again, mark how he regardeth the death of his friend,
   So he hath his purpose he cares for no mo;
   A perfect pattern of a covetous mind
   Which neither esteemeth his friend nor his foe
   But rather Avarice, might I have said so,   430
   Who, if he were gone, myself could defend,
   Where thou, by his absence, wert soon at an end.

Act second. Scene three

HYPOCRISY, TYRANNY, AVARICE
HYPOCRISY: O loving father and merciful God,
   We through our sins thy punishment deserve,
   And have provoked to beat with thy rod
   Us stubborn children which from thee do swerve.
   We loathed thy word, but now we shall sterve,   *die*
   For Hypocrisy is placed again in this land
   And thy true Gospel as exile doth stand.
     This is thy just judgment for our offence   440
   Who, having the light, in darkness did stray.
   But now if thou wouldst, of thy fatherly benevolence,

Thy purposèd judgments in wrath for to stay,
The part of the Prodigal Son we would play
And with bitter tears before thee would fall
And in true repentance for mercy would call.
In our prosperity we would not regard
The words of the Preachers who threatened the same,
But flattering ourselves, thought thou wouldst have spared
Us in thy mercy and never us blame;   450
But so much provoked thee by blaspheming thy name,
Indeed to deny that in words we maintain,   *that which*
That from thy justice thou couldst not restrain.

   So that Romish Pharoah, a tyrant most cruel,
Hath brought us again into captivity,
And instead of the pure flood of thy Gospel
Hath poisoned our souls with devilish hypocrisy,
Unable to maintain it but by murdering tyranny,   *murderous*
Seeking rather the fleece than the health of the sheep
Which are appointed for him for to keep.   460

TYRANNY: Lo, Avarice, hark what a traitor is here,
Against our Holy Father this language to use!

HYPOC. (*aside to* AVAR.):   *He speaketh to you, sirra.*

TYRANNY: I might have heard more if I would him forbear,
But for grief my ears burn for to hear him abuse
His tongue in this manner. Wherefore no excuse
Shall purchase favor, but that with all speed
By sword I will render to him his due meed.

   Wherefore, thou miscreant, while thou hast time,
Pray to the Saints thy spokesmen to be,   470
That at God's hand from this thy great crime
By their intercession thou may be set free.

AVARICE: Nay, hearest thou Tyranny, be ruled by me.
First cut off his head and *then* let him pray,
So shall he be sure us not to bewray.   *betray*

HYPOCRISY: O wicked Tyranny, thou imp of the Devil,
Too joyful tidings to thee have I brought,
For now thou art emboldened to practice all evil—

TYRANNY: Marry, thou shalt not give me thy service for nought,

But for thy pains to please thee I thought.   480

HYPOCRISY: Thou art nothing so ready to do any good
As thou art to shed poor innocents' blood.

AVARICE: Nay, Tyranny, suffer this rascal to prate
Till some man come by, and then he is gone;
Then wilt thou repent it when it is too late.
Dispatch him, therefore, while we are alone.

HYPOCRISY *(aside)*: *On your face, sir.*

HYPOCRISY: Well may the covetous be likened to a drone,
Which of the bees' labors will spoil and waste make,
And yet to get honey no labor will take.   490

The covetous, likewise, from poor men extort,
Their games to increase they only do seek;
And so they may have it of them a great sort,
What means they use for it they care not a leek.
Yet will these misers scarce once a week
Have a good meal at their own table,
So, by avarice, to help themselves they are unable.

Avarice to a fire may well comparèd be,
To the which the more you add the more still it crave;
So, likewise, the covetous mind do we see,   500
Though riches abound, do wish still more to have,
And to be short, your reverences to save,
To a filthy swine such misers are comparable,
Which, while they be dead are nothing profitable.[12]

AVARICE: Nay, farewell Tyranny, I came hither too soon!
I perceive already I am too well known.
I were not best in their claws for to come,
Unless I were willing to be clean overthrown.

TYRANNY: By the preaching of God's word all this mischief is
grown,
Which, if Hypocrisy might haply expell,   510
All we in safety and pleasure might dwell.
Stay therefore, while from Hypocrisy we hear.

---

[12] Woodes goes much further than most morality playwrights in allowing his Vice to utter moral truths. Of course this makes Hypocrisy all the more alarming as a character (cf. Tartuffe) because he demonstrates that truths can be held verbally without affecting actions.

AVARICE: Dispatch then this merchant, lest our counsel he   *fellow*
    tell.

HYPOCRISY: I am content for God's cause this cross for to bear.

TYRANNY: It is best killing him now his mind is set well.

HYPOCRISY: Your scoffing and mocking God seeth,
    each deal.   *every bit of it*

TYRANNY: Yea, dost thou persist us still thus to check?
    Thy speech I will hinder by cutting of thy neck.[13]

HYPOCRISY: Nay, hold thy hand Cadby, thou has killed   *("fellow")*
    me enough!

    What, never the sooner for a merry word?   520

    I meant not good earnest, to your ma'ship I vow,   *mastership*

    I did but jest, and spake but in bourd;   *jest*

    Therefore, of friendship, put up again thy sword.

TYRANNY: Nay, caitiff, presume not that thou shalt go scot free.

    Therefore, hold still and I will soon dispatch thee!

HYPOCRISY: What, I pray thee, Tyranny, know first who I am.

    Ye purblind fools, do your lips blind your eyes?

    Why, I was in place long before you came,

    But you could not see the wood for the trees.

    But in faith, father Avarice, I will pay you your fees   530

    For the great goodwill which you to me bear

        (HYPOCRISY *fighteth*.)

    And in time will requite it again, do not fear.

AVARICE: Content yourself, good Master Hypocrisy.

    The words which I spake I spake unaware.

TYRANNY: Hold thy hand Hypocrisy, I pray thee heartily;

    So like a madman with thy friends do not fare!

HYPOCRISY: For neither of you both a pin do I care.

    Go shake your ears both, like slaves as you be,

    And look not in your need to be holpen of me!   *helped by*

TYRANNY: What, Master Hypocrisy, will you take snuff   *take offence*
    so soon?   540

    Marry, then, you had need to be kept very warm!

AVARICE: I swear to your mastership by the man in the moon

---

[13] Hazlitt emends to "cutting off thy neck." We let it stand, though "of" does frequently appear for "off" in contemporary writing.

That to your person I intended no harm.

HYPOCRISY: But that I am weary I would both your tongues
   charm.

See how to my face they do me deride?

I will not therefore in your companies abide.

AVARICE: Why Master Hypocrisy, what would you that I do?

For mine offence, of mercy I you pray.

HYPOCRISY: With you I am at one, but of that merchant too

I look for some amends, or else I will away.   550

TYRANNY: The presumptuous fool's part herein thou dost play.

What, of thy master dost thou look for obeisance?

I will not once entreat thee if thou wilt get thee hence!

HYPOCRISY: *Nimia familiaritas parit contemptum.*

The old proverb by me is verified:

By too much familiarity contemned be some.

Even so, at this present to me it betide,

For of long time Hypocrisy hath ruled as guide,

While now of later years, through heretics' resistance,

I retained Tyranny to yield me assistance,   560

   But through overmuch lenity he thinks himself checkmate

With me his good patron, Master Hypocrisy.

TYRANNY: List, I pray thee Avarice, how this rascal can prate,

And with me, Tyranny, doth challenge equality,

Where he, of himself, hath neither strength nor ability

But thou to him riches and I strength do give,   *But=unless*

So that I must be his master, though it doth him grieve.

HYPOCRISY: Two dogs oftentimes one bone would fain catch,

But yet the third do both them deceive;

Even so, Hypocrisy for the preeminence doth snatch,   570

Which Tyranny gapes for, ye may perceive.

But I must obtain it, for of me they retain

All kind of riches, their states to maintain.

To yield to me, therefore, they must be both fain.

HYPOCRISY: Was Judas Christ's master because he bore the
   purse?

Nay, rather of all he was least regarded.

Have not men of honor stewards, to disburse

All such sums of money wherewith they be charged?
Yet above their master their honor is not enlarged.
Even so, thee, Avarice, my steward I account,   580
To pay that whereto my charges amount.
   And to thee, Tyranny, this one word I object:
Whether was Joab or David the king?
When Joab was glad his ease to reject,
The Ammonites in Rabah to confusion to bring,
When David with Bethsaba at home was sleeping,
Was not Joab his servant, in warfare to fight?
And so art thou mine, mine enemies to quite.   *requite*
TYRANNY: Nay then, at the whole, God give you   ("if that's the case")
   goodnight!
Shall Tyranny to Hypocrisy in any point yield?   590
HYPOCRISY: With this one word I will vanquish thee quite,
   That thou shalt be glad to give me the field:
   The end to be preferred all learned men wield;   *say*
   Sith, therefore, hypocrisy of tyranny is end,
   I must have the preferment, for which I contend!
AVARICE (*aside*):   *Indeed, you say troth.*
TYRANNY: I will make you both grant that I am the chief,
   Or else with my sword your sides I will pierce.
HYPOCRISY: That were sharp reasoning indeed, with a mischief!
AVARICE: I will yield him my right, if that he be so fierce.   600
HYPOCRISY: The nature of hypocrites herein we rehearse,
   Which, being convinced by the text of God's Word,
   The end of their spouting is fire and sword!
     But if you will needs be chief, God speed well the plough!
   I will be none that shall follow your train,
   For if I should I know well enough
   That to fly the country we all should be fain.
   Then were my labor done but in vain;
   You know not so much as I do, Tyranny,
   Therefore I advise you be ruled by me.   610
TYRANNY: *Inter amicos omnia sunt communia,* they say:
   Among friends there is reckoned no property,
   But what the one hath of his own, the other may

Have the use of the same at his own liberty.

Even so among us it is, of a surety,

For what the one hath of his own proper right,

It is thine to use by day or by night!

AVARICE: Indeed, you say truth: the end is worth all

Such things as to get the end are referred,

And by this reason to you I prove shall   620

That I before Hypocrisy must be preferred.

HYPOCRISY (*aside*):   *He hath learned logetes!*   *logic*

AVARICE: The conclusion of my reason is thus inferred:[14]

Sith hypocrisy was invented to augment private gain,

I am the end of hypocrisy, this is plain.

HYPOCRISY: *Actum est de amicitia:* the bargain is dispatched

And we two in friendship are united as one.

AVARICE: In the same knot with you let me also be matched,

And of money I warrant you you shall want none.   *lack none*

HYPOCRISY: I agree. What say you, shall he be one?   630

TYRANNY: I judge him needful in our company to be,

HYPOCRISY (*aside*):   *Friendship for gain!*

TYRANNY: And therefore, for my part he is welcome to me.

Let us now on our business speedily attend,

And labor each one to bring it about.

HYPOCRISY: That is already by me brought to end,

So that of your preferment you need to doubt;

And my coming hither was to find you out,

That at my elbow you might be in readiness

To help, if need were, in this weighty business.   640

To tell you the story it were but too tedious,

How the Pope and I together have devised

Firstly to inveigle the people religious

For greediness of gain, who will be soon pressed,

And for fear lest hereafter they should be despised,

Of their own freewill will maintain hypocrisy,

So that avarice alone shall conquer the clergy.

---

[14] The marginal system does not make clear exactly where Hypocrisy's intrusion is supposed to come in Avarice's speech. "Logetes" is Hypocrisy's error, perhaps for *logices*. The passage is a nice little parody of the theological discussion between Philologus and Mathetes.

Now of the chiefest of his carnal Cardinals
He doth appoint certain, and give them authority
To ride abroad in their pontificals,   650
To see if with avarice they may win the laity;
If not, then to threaten them with open tyranny,
Whereby, doubt not but many will forsake
The truth of the Gospel and our parties take.   *our side*

TYRANNY: This device is praiseworthy. How sayest thou,
    Avarice?

AVARICE: I like it well if it were put in ure,
Yet little gain to me shall this whole practice
More than I had before time procure[d].

HYPOCRISY: The Legates are ready to ride, I am sure,
Wherefore we had need to make no small delay;   660
They stay for my coming alone, I dare say.
    Howbeit the laity would greatly mistake
If they should know all our purpose and intent,
Yea, and perhaps some means they would seek
Our foresaid business in time to prevent.

TYRANNY: Will you then be ruled by my arbitrament?
Lest the people should suddenly dissolve tranquillity,
For the Legates' defense let him use me, Tyranny.

HYPOCRISY: Herein your counsel is not much unwise,
Save that in one thing we had need to beware: 670
Lest you be known we will you disguise
And some grace apparrel for you will prepare.
But your name, Tyranny, I fear all will mar.
Let me alone and I will invent   *leave it to me*
A name to your nature which shall be convenient.
    Zeal shall your name be! How like you that?
And therefore in office you must deal zealously.

TYRANNY: Let me alone, I will pay them home pat.
Though they call me Zeal they shall feel me Tyranny.

HYPOCRISY: Lo, here is a garment, come dress you handsomely. 680
Aye, marry (quoth he), I like this very well.
Now to the Devil's Grace you may seem to give counsel!
    Now must I apply all my invention

That I may devise Avarice to hide.
Thy name shall be called Careful Provision,
And every man for his household may lawfully provide.
Thus shalt thou go cloaked and never be 'spied.
AVARICE: Thy counsel, Hypocrisy, I very well allow,
And will recompense thee, if ever I know how.
TYRANNY: Now, on a *bon voyage* let us depart,   690
For I well loath any time to delay.
HYPOCRISY: Nay, yet in sign of a merry heart
Let us sing before we go away.
AVARICE: I am content. Begin, I you pray.
But to sing the treble we must needs have one.
HYPOCRISY: If you say so, let it even alone.
      (*Exeunt.*)[15]

Act third. Scene one.

      [*Enter*] PHILOLOGUS
PHILOLOGUS: Too true alas, too true I say, was our divination,
The which Mathetes did foresee when last we were in place,
For now indeed we feel the smart and horrible vexation
Which Romish power unto us did threaten and menace;   700
Wherefore, great need we have to call to God alway for grace,
For feeble flesh is far too weak those pains to undergo,
The which all they that fear the Lord are now appointed to.
   The Legate from the Pope of Rome is come into our coasts
Who doth the Saints of God each where with tyranny oppress,
And in the same most gloriously himself he vaunt[s] and
      boast[s].
The more one mourneth unto him, he pitieth the less.
Out of his cruel tyranny the Lord of heaven me bless,
For hitherto in blessed state my whole life I have spent,
With health of body, wealth in goods and mind always
      content.   710

---

[15] If Hypocrisy's "let it alone" means "forget it," this is a nice mockery of the convention of the Vices' song. But it may mean "leave it to me."

Besides, of friends I have great store, who do me firmly
  love,
A faithful wife and children fair, of woods and pasture store,
And diverse other things which I have got for my behoof,
Which now to be depravèd of would grieve my heart full
  sore;
And if I come once in their claws I shall get out no more
Unless I will renounce my faith and so their mind fulfill,
Which, if I do, without all doubt, my soul for aye I spill.
  For sith I have receivèd once the first fruits of my faith
And have begun to run the course that leadeth to salvation,
If in the midst thereof I stay or cease, the Scripture saith   720
It booteth not that I began with so good preparation,
But rather maketh much the more unto my condemnation;
For he alone shall have the palm which to the end doth run,
And he which plucks his hand from plough in heaven shall
  never come.
  Those laborers which hired were, in vineyard for to
  moil,   *work*
And had their penny for their pain, they tarried all while night,
For if they ceasèd had, when sun their flesh with heat did broil,
And had departed from their work, they should have lost by
  right
Their wages penny. I likewise shall be deprivèd quite
Of that same crown the which I have in faith long lookèd for.   730
But for this time I will depart; I dare here say no more.
    (*Exit.*)

Act third. Scene two.

[*Enter*] HYPOCRISY
HYPOCRISY: Ha ha ha! Marry, now the game begin[s]!
  Hypocrisy throughout this realm is had in admiration,
  And by my means both Avarice and Tyranny crept in,
  Who in short space will make men run the way to desolation—
  What did I say? My tongue did trip. I should say
    "consolation"!

For now, forsooth, the clergy must into my bosom creep
Or else they know not by what means themselves alive to
    keep.
  On the other side, the laity, be they either rich or poor,
If rich, then Avarice strangles them because they will not lose 740
The worldly wealth, or else we have one subtle practice more,
That is that Sensual Suggestion their outward man shall pose,
Who can full finely in each cause his mind to them disclose.
But if neither of these twain can to my train them wind,
Then, at his cue to play his part doth Tyranny begin.
  As for the poor knaves, such a one as this is
We do not esteem him, but make short ado.
If he will not come on, we do him not miss.
But to the pot he is sure to go—[16]
Tyranny deals with him and no mo. 750
But I marvel what doth him from hence so long stay.
Sooner named, sooner come, as common proverbs say.
    (*Step aside.*)

Act third. Scene three.

      HYPOCRISY. [*Enter*] TYRANNY, AVARICE
TYRANNY: By His wounds, I fear not, but it is cock sure now!
HYPOCRISY (*aside*): *He hath a goodly grace in swearing.*
TYRANNY: Under the Legate's seal in office I am placed;
  Therefore whoso resist me I will make him to bow.
  Who can make Tyranny now disgraced?
HYPOCRISY (*aside*): *He is graceless already.*
TYRANNY: With a head of brass I will not be outfaced
  But will execute mine office with extreme cruelty, 760
  So that all men shall know me to be plain Tyranny.
AVARICE: Nay Master Zeal, be ruled by me,
  To such as resist, such rigor you may show—
TYRANNY: Zeal? Nay, no Zeal. My name is Tyranny!

---

[16] "Such a one as this is" refers to Philologus. "To the pot" surely does not here have the modern sense of "going to pot;" rather it may have the contemporary dialectal meaning of "pit," i.e. hell, or perhaps just "dungeon."

Neither am I ashamed who doth my name know,
HYPOCRISY (*aside*):   *He is Kit Careless.*
TYRANNY: For in my dealings the same I will show,
   None dare reprove me, of that I am sure,
   So long as authority on my side endure.
   But to thy words awhile I will list,   770
   Therefore in brief say on what you will.
AVARICE: I would have you show rigor to such as resist,
   And such as be obstinate spare not to kill,
   But those that be willing your 'hests to fulfill,
   If they offend, and not of obstinacy,
   For money excuse them, though they use villainy.
HYPOCRISY (*aside*):   *Hark, the practice of spiteful Summoners.*[17]
AVARICE: Thus shall you perform your office aright,
   For favor or money to spare the offendant.
TYRANNY: So may I also of malice or spite   780
   Or rancor of mind punish the innocent,[18]
   But I will be ruled by thine arbitrament
   And will favor such as will my hand grease.
   The Devil is a good fellow, if one can him please!
HYPOCRISY (*aside*):   *And you are one of his sons, methink, by your
         head!*
TYRANNY: But to follow our business great pains we do take,
   On a hasty message we were fit to be sent.
HYPOCRISY: When I lie a-dying I will you messengers make!
   You ply you so fast, you are too too diligent!
   Hoop ho, Master Zeal! Whither are ye bent?   790
AVARICE: Hark, methought one halloed and called you by name.
TYRANNY: I would it were Hypocrisy.
AVARICE: It is the very same.
   What, Master Hypocrisy, for you I have sought
   This hour or two but could you not find.
HYPOCRISY: That is no marvel. It is not for nought,
   For I am but little and you two are blind,

---

[17] Cf. Chaucer's Summoner, and the Pardoner; members of the semi-clerical army that grew up around the Indulgence system.
[18] Original reads "rancor of mine."

Neither have you eyes to see with behind;
Yet may the learned note here a mystery,
That neither Tyranny nor Avarice can find out Hypocrisy!   800
But what earnest business have you in charge,
That with so great speed must presently be finished?
TYRANNY: Marry, see here.
HYPOCRISY: What is it?
TYRANNY: A commission large
From my Lord Legate himself authorized,
The effect whereof must presently be practicèd.
HYPOCRISY: What is the tenor, I pray you let me know?
TYRANNY: Avarice hath read it, not I. Let him show.
AVARICE: He hath firstly in charge to make inquisition   810
Whether altars be re-edified, whether chalice and Book,
Vestments for Mass, sacraments and procession
Be prepared again: if not, he must look
And find out such fellows as these cannot brook,
And to my Lord Legate such merchants present,
That for their offence they may have condign punishment.
  If any we take tardy, Tyranny them threat
That for their negligence he will them present,
And I, desirous some money to get,
If aught they will give me, their evil will prevent.   *punishment* 820
Yea, sometime of purpose such shifts we invent.   *tricks*
HYPOCRISY: Peace! Yonder comes one, methink it is a priest,
By his gown, cap and tippet made of a   *scarf/strips of cloth,*
   list.   *i.e. patchwork (?)*

Act third. Scene four.

HYPOCRISY, TYRANNY, AVARICE. [*Enter*] CACONOS[19]
CACONOS: In gude feth sir, this newis de gar me lope,
Ay is as light as ay me wend, gif that yo wol me troth,

[19] Caconos is the comic relief spoken of by the Prologue, and is an early instance of ethnic humor. Like Sir Lawrence Livingless in *The Tide Tarrieth No Man*, Caconos is the ignorant priest figure, with the added opprobrium of being Scottish. Woodes' rendition of the Scottish dialect is not perfect, which makes it harder to read, but since it is impossible to gloss every line we offer a translation of part of his first speech, which will show the reader most of the important characteristics of the dialect. Because of the unevenness of

For new ayen within awer londs installèd is the Pope,
Whese Legate with authority tharawawt awr country goth,
And charge befar him far te com, us priests and layman
    bath,
Far te spay awt, gif that he may, these new sprang arataikes
Whilk de disturb awr hally Kirk like a sart of saysmataikes.   830

   Awr gilden gods ar brought ayen inta awr kirks ilk whare,
That unte tham awr parishioner ma affer thar gudewill,
Far hally Mass in ilke place new the auters de prepare,
Hally water, pax, cross, banner, censer and candle,
Cream, crismatory, hally bread, the rest omit ay will,
Whilt hally Fathers did invent fre awd antiquity,
Be new received inte awr kirks with great solemnity.

   Bay these though laymen bene apprest, the clargy sall het
    gean,
Far te awr sents theis affer yifts all whilk we sall receive.
Awr hally Masse thaw thea bay dere thea de it but in vayne,   840
Far thaw ther frends frea Purgatory te help thea dea beleve,
Yet af ther hope, gif nede rewhayre, it wawd theam all deceve.

---

the dialect we made no attempt to modernize his lines. His name, incidentally, is of Greek extraction and
means "evil."

Caconos. In good faith sir, this news [delights me?]
  I am as light as ever I was, if you want the truth from me,
  For now again within our land installed is the Pope,
  Whose Legate with authority thereabout our country goeth,
  And charges before him for to come, us priests and laymen both,
  For to spy out, if that he may, these new-sprung heretics
  Which do disturb our holy Church like a sort of schismatics.

   Our gilded gods are brought again into our churches everywhere,
  So that unto them our parishioner may offer their good will,
  For holy Mass in every place now the altars (they) do prepare,
  Holy water, pyx, cross, banner. censer and candle,
  Cream, chrism, holy bread—the rest omit I will,
  Which holy Fathers did invent from old antiquity,
  Be now received into our churches with great solemnity.
         *   *   *   *   *   *

   The sacraments if we might sell, were better than them all,
  For if the Jews gave thirty pence to hang Christ on a tree,
  Good Christian folk thrice thirty pence would count a price but small,
  So that to eat Him with their teeth delivered he might be.
  Now of this thing, deliverance, now man can make but we,
  So that the market, in this point, we priests should have at will,
  And with the money we should get, our pouches we should fill.

Sea wawde awr pilgrimage, reliques, trentals and pardons,
Whilk far war geyn inte awr Kirk ar braught in, far the nones.
  Far well a nere what war awr tenths & taythes that gro in
    sild,
What gif we han of glebed lond ene plawwark bay the yeare,
Awr affring deas de vara laytell ar nething te us yeld.
Awr beadroll geanes, awr chrisom clethes de laytle mend
  awr fare,
Gif awt af this we pea far vale, we laytle mare can spare,
Sawl Masses, Diriges, Monethmayndes and Buryinges,   850
Alsowlday, Kirkings, Baneasking and weddings.
  The sacraments gif we mowt sell war better then thea all,
Far gif the Jewes gave thratty pence te hang Chrayst on a tree,
Gude chrystian folk thrayse thratty pence wawd count a price
  but smal
Sea that te ete him with ther teeth delayvered he mawght be.
New of this thing delayverance ne man can mak but we,
Se that the market in this punt we preests sawd han at will,
And with the money we sowd yet, awr pooches we sowd
  fill.
HYPOCRISY: I will go and salute him. Good morrow, Sir John!
CACONOS: Naw, bay may preesthade, God give ye ten far ene. 860
HYPOCRISY: Do you, Master Parson, in this parish sing?
CACONOS: Yai sir, that ay de, gif yowll give me troothing.
HYPOCRISY: I have a commission your house and church to
  seek,
  To search if you any seditious books do keep.
CACONOS: Whe ay? Well a neare ay swer bay the sacrament,
  Ay had rather han a cup af nale then a Testament.
HYPOCRISY: How can you without it your office discharge?
CACONOS: It is the least thing ay car far bay may charge,
  Far se lang as thea han Images wharon te luke,
  What nede thea be distructed awt af a Buke?   870
HYPOCRISY: Tush, that will modify them all well enow![20]
  As well a dead image as a dumb idol, I make God a vow!

---

[20] Original reads "nodifie." We accept Hazlitt's emendation to "modify." although it may be that "noddify," that is "turn them into noddies (fools)," was intended.

CACONOS: Yai, ay my sen, bay experience thot con showe,
   Far in may portace the tongue ay de nat knowe,
   Yet when ay see the great gilded letter
   Ay ken it sea well as nea man ken better:
   As far example, on the day of Chraistes Nativity
   Ay see a Bab in a Manger and two Beastes standing by;
   The service whilk to Newyeares day is assaygned
   Bay the paicture of the Circumcision ay faynd;   880
   The service whilk on Twalfth Day mun be don,
   Ay seeke bay the marks of the three kynges of Colon;
   Bay the Devill tentyng Chraist ay faind Whadragesima;
   Bay Chraist on the Crosse ay serch out gude Frayday;
   Pasch for his marke hath the Resurrection;
   Ayenst Hally Thursday is pented Chraistes Assention.
   Thus in mayn owne buke ay is a gude Clarke,
   But gyf the Sents war gone, the cat had eate my mark.
   Se the sandry mairacles whilk ilk Sent have done
   Bay the pictures on the walles sal appeere to them soone,   890
   Bay the whilk thea ar lerned in every distresse
   What Sent thea mun prea te for succour, doubtles;
   Sea that all Lepers te Sylvester must prea,
   That he wawd free tham, ther disease take away;
   Laykwais, thea that han the fallying saicknes,
   Te be eased therfre thea mun prea to St. Cornelis;
   In contagious aier, as in plague or pestilence,
   Te hally Sent Ruke thea mun call for assistance;
   Fra parill of drawning, Sent Carp keepe the mariners,
   Fra dayng in warfare Sent George gard the soldiers;   900
   Sent Job heale the pore, the agew Sent Germayne,
   Far te ease the toothache call te Sent Appollyne;
   Gif that a woman be barren and childles,
   Te help her herein she must prea te Sent Nicolas;
   Far wemen in travayle call to Sent Magdalene,
   Far lawlynes of mind call te Sent Katheryne,
   Sent Loy save your horse, Sent Anthony your swyne.
TYRANNY: What, this parson seemeth cunning to be,   *learned*
   And, as far as I see, in a good uniformity.

Yea, he is well read in that Golden Legend.[21]   910

CACONOS: Bay may trooth, in readyng any other ne taym do I
          spend,

Far that, ay ken, bay general caunsell is canonized,

And bay the hely Pope hymselfe is authorized.

That buke, farther, is wholly permytted,

Wharas the Bayble in part is prohibited.

And therfore, gif it be lawfull to utter my conscience,

Before the New Testament ays give it credence.

HYPOCRISY: I allow his judgment before Ambrose
          and Austin,   (St. Augustine)

And for Hypocrisy a more convenient Chaplain.

AVARICE: It grieveth me much that no fault we can spy,   920

For now of some bribe disappointed am I.

Yet haply he may tell us of some heretics.

TYRANNY: Is there, M[aster] Parson, in your parish no
          schismatics?

CACONOS: Yai, mara, is ther a vara busy bodye

Whe will jest with me and call me fule and noddye,

And sets his lads te spowt Latin ayenst me,

But ay spose then with *Deparfundis Clam avi.*

And oftentimes he wil reson with me of the sacrament,

And say he can proove bay the new Tastament,

That Chraystes body is in heaven placed.   930

But ays not beleve him, ay woll not be awt faced!

He says besayd that the Pope is Antichraist,

Fugered of John bay the seven hedded beast,

And all awre religion is but mons invention,

And with Gods ward is at utter dissention,

And a plaguy deel mare af sayk layk talke

That ay dar not far may nars bay his yate walke,

But ay wawd he wer brunt, that ay mawght be whaiet!

TYRANNY: He must have a cooler; his tongue runs at riot.

AVARICE: What is his name, Sir John, canst thou tell us?   940

CACONOS: Yai sir, that ay ken. He is cleped *Phailelegoos.*

TYRANNY: Wilt thou go show his house where he dwell?

---

[21] *Legenda Aurea,* a large collection of lives of the Saints.

CACONOS: Yai, or els ay wawd may sawl war in hell.
  Te de him a plesure ay wawd gang a whole yeare,
  Gif it war but te make him a fadocke te beare!
TYRANNY: Go with us, Avarice, and bear us company.
AVARICE: Nay, if you go hence I will not here tarry.
HYPOCRISY: Away sirs! In your business in a corner do not
      lurk,
  That my Lord Legate, when he comes, may have work.
TYRANNY: Come on, let us go together Sir John.   950
CACONOS: Ay sall follow after. God boy you, good Gentleman.
HYPOCRISY: Farewell three false knaves as between this and
      London.
TYRANNY: What sayest thou?
HYPOCRISY: As honest men as the three Kings of Colon!
      (*Exeunt* TYR., AVAR., CACON.)
  This gear goes round, if that we had a fiddle!
  Nay, I must sing too. Hey, derry, derry, derry,
  I can do but laugh, my heart is so merry.
  I will be minstrel myself, hey diddle, diddle, diddle.
  But lay there a straw, I begin to be weary.[22]
  But hark, I hear a tramping of feet.   960
  It is my Lord Legate; I will him go meet.

Act fourth. Scene one.

  HYPOCRISY. [*Enter*] CARDINAL, AVARICE, TYRANNY,
    PHILOLOGUS
CARDINAL: Go to, Master Zeal, bring forth that heretic
  Which doth thus disturb our religion Catholic.
HYPOCRISY: Room, for My Lord's Grace! What, no manner
      reverence,
  But cap-on-head-Hodge, and that in a Lord's presence?
CARDINAL: What, Master Hypocrisy, I have stayed for you
      long!
HYPOCRISY: You were best crowd in and play us among.
CARDINAL: Where have you been from me so long absent?

---

[22] Original reads "began." "Lay there a straw" is apparently a colloquialism meaning "stop."

I appointed to have been here three hours ago,
In my consistory to have sat in judgment   970
Of that wretched schismatic that doth trouble us so.

HYPOCRISY: What, have you caught but one and no mo?
In faith, Father Avarice, you have plied your chaps well!

AVARICE: I must needs confess that I am paid for my travail.

TYRANNY: Room for the prisoner! What, room on each hand,
Or I shall make some out of the way for to stand!
Lo, here my lord, is that seditious schismatic
That we have laid wait for, an arrant heretic.

CARDINAL: Sit down Master Hypocrisy, to yield me assistance.

HYPOCRISY: I thank your Lordship for your courteous
      benevolence.   980
I will be the noddy—I should say the "notary"—
To write before my Lord Legate, which is commissary.   *commissioner*

CARDINAL: Ah sirra, be you he that doth thus disturb
The whole estate of our faith Catholic?
Art thou so expert in God's laws and word
That no man may learn thee? Thou arrant heretic—   *teach*
But this is the nature of every schismatic,
Be his errors never so false doctrine
He will say by God's word he dare it examine.

PHILOLOGUS: With humble submission to your authority   990
I pardon crave if aught amiss I say,
For being thus set in peril and extremity
To me unacquainted, my tongue soon trip may;
Wherefore, excuse me, I do your Lordship pray,
And I will answer to every demand
According to my conscience, God's word being my warrant.

CARDINAL: To begin therefore orderly, how sayest thou,
      Philologus,
Have I authority to call thee me before?
Or, to be short, I will object it thus:
Whether hath the Pope, which is Peter's successor,   1000
Than all other bishops preeminence more?
If not, then it follow[s] that neither he
Nor I which am his Legate, to accounts may call thee.

PHILOLOGUS: The question is perilous for me to determine,
Chiefly when the party is judge in the cause,[23]
Yet if the whole course of Scripture ye examine,
And will be tried by God's holy laws,
Small help shall you find to defend the same cause,
But the contrary may be proved manifestly,
As I, in short words, will prove to you briefly.   1010

The surest ground whereon your Pope doth stand
Is, of Peter's being at Rome a strong imagination;
And the same Peter, you do understand,
Of all the Disciples had the gubernation,
Surmising both without good approbation,   *proof*
Unless you will that by the name of "Babylon,"
From whence Peter wrote, is understanded "Rome;"

As indeed diverse of your writers have affirmed,
Reciting Jeremy, Austin, Primasius and Ambrose,
Who, by their several writings, have confirmed   1020
That Rome is new Babylon. I may it not glose,   *interpret*
But it were better for you they were dumb, I suppose,
For they labor to prove Rome by that acception   *interpretation*
The whore of Babylon spoke of in the *Revelation*.

But grant that Peter in Rome settled was,
Yet that he was chese, it remains you to prove,   *chosen*
For in my judgment it is a plain case
That if any amongst them to rule it did behoove
He should be chese whom Christ most did love,
To whom he bequeathed his Mother most dear,   1030
To whom in revelation Christ did also appear;
I mean John Evangelist, by birth cousin german   *first cousin*
To our Savior Christ, as stories do us tell,
From whose succession if that you should claim
Superiority, you should mend your cause well,
For then of some likelihood of truth it should smell;
Where none so often as Peter was reproved,   *while*

---

[23] Philologus is being slyly humorous and very bold here in noting that the Cardinal is both prosecutor and judge. The "trial" is a fairly high-powered scene, although the author loses something by giving the Cardinal no intelligence at all. Cf. the trial scene in Shaw's *St. Joan*.

Nor from steadfast faith so oftentimes removed.
   But grant all were true herein you do feign:
Mark one proper lesson of a Greek orator—   1040
As a good child of his father's wealth is inheritor,
So of a father's virtues he must be possessor.
Now Peter follows Christ and all worldly goods forsakes,
But the Pope leaveth Christ and himself to glory takes.
   And, to be short, Christ himself refused to be a King,
And the servant above the master may not be,
Which being both true, it is a strange thing
How the Pope can receive this pomp and dignity
And yet profess himself Christ's servant to be.
Christ will be no King, the Pope will be more;   1050
The Pope is Christ's master, not his servant therefore.
CARDINAL: Ah, thou arrant heretic, I will thee remember!
I am glad I know so much as I do.
I have weighed thy reasons and have found them so   *arguments*
    slender
That I think them not worthy to be answerèd.
How say you, Master Hypocrisy?
HYPOCRISY: I also think so,
But let him go forward and utter his conscience,
And we will awhile longer hear him with patience.
CARDINAL: Say on, thou heretic! Of the holy sacrament,   1060
Of the body and blood of Christ, what is thine opinion?
PHILOLOGUS: I have not yet finished my former argument.
CARDINAL: Say on, as I bid thee. Thou art a stout
    minion.   *bold fellow*
PHILOLOGUS: I shall then gladly. It is a sign of union,
The which should remain us Christians among,
That one should love another all our life long.
   For as the bread is of many kernels compounded,
And the wine from the juice of many grapes do[th]
    descend,
So we which into Christ our Rock are engrounded
As into one Temple, should cease to contend,   1070
Lest by our contention the Church we offend.

This was not the least cause, among many more
Which are now omitted, that this sacrament was given for.
　The chiefest cause why this sacrament was ordained
Was the infirmity of our outward man;
Whereas salvation to all men was proclaimed,
That with true faith apprehend the same can,
By the death of Jesus Christ that immaculate Lamb,
That the same might the rather of all men be believed,
To the Word to add a sacrament it Christ nothing grieved.　1080
　And as we the sooner believe that thing true
For the trial whereof more witnesses we find,
So by the means of the sacrament many grew
Believing creatures where before they were blind;
For our senses some savor of our faith now do find,
Because in the sacrament there is this analogy:
That Christ feeds our souls and the bread doth our body.
CARDINAL:　Ah, thou foul heretic, is there bread in the
　　　sacrament?
Where is Christ's body then, which He did us give?
PHILOLOGUS:　I know to the faithful receiver it is there present,　1090
　But yet the bread remaineth still, I steadfastly believe.
CARDINAL:　To hear these his errors it doth me greatly grieve,
　But that we may shortly to some issue come,
　In what sense said Christ, "*Hoc est corpus meum*"?　(This is my body)
PHILOLOGUS:　Even in the same sense that he said before
　Vos estis sal terris, vos estis lux mundi,
　Ego sum ostium, and a hundred such more,　(see below, ll. 1105—1108)
　If time would permit me to allege them severally;
　But that I may the simple sort edify,
　You ask me in what sense these words I verify　1100
　Where Christ of the bread said This is my body:
　　For answer herein I ask you this question—
Were Christ's Disciples into salt transformed
When he said, "Ye are the salt of the earth every one"?
Or when the light of the world He them affirmed,
Or himself to be a door when He confirmed,
Or to be a Vine did His body then change?

If not then, why now? This to me seemeth strange.

CARDINAL: Why, dost thou doubt of Christ His omnipotency,
But whatso He willeth doth so come to pass?   1110

PHILOLOGUS: God keep me and all men from such a
frenzy   *wild notion*
As to think anything Christ's power to surpass
When His will to his power joined was;
But where His will wanteth, His power is ineffectual;
As Christ can be no liar, God cannot be mortal.
Set down therefore some proof of His will
That He would be made bread, and then I recant.

CARDINAL: This caitiff mine ears with wind he doth fill.
His words both truth and reason doth want.
Christ's word is His will, this must thou needs grant.   1120

PHILOLOGUS: He spake the word likewise when He said "I am
the door."
Was His body transformed into timber therefore?

CARDINAL: Nay, if thou beest obstinate I will say no more.
Have him hence to prison and keep him full sure.
I will make him set by my friendship more store.
But hearest thou Zeal, go first and procure
Some kind of new torment which he may not endure.

TYRANNY: I am here in readiness to do your commandment,
And will return hither again incontinent.

HYPOCRISY: At thy return bring hither Sensual Suggestion,   1130
That if need be he may us assist,
Lest that both I and Careful Provision
The zeal of Philologus may not fully resist.
But he in his obstinacy doth still persist;
To put him to death would accuse us of tyranny,
But if we could win him, he should do us much honesty.

TYRANNY.   I hear you, and will fulfill your words speedily.
          (*Exit* TYRAN[NY].)

HYPOCRISY: Good Master Philologus, I pity your case,
To see you so foolish yourself to undo.
I durst yet promise to purchase you grace   1140
If you would at length your errors forgo.

Therefore I pray you be not your own foe.

PHILOLOGUS: Call you those errors which the Gospel defends?
I know not then whence true doctrine descends.

CARDINAL: Nay, Master Hypocrisy, you spend time in vain.
To reason with him; he will not be removed.

AVARICE: Had I so much to live by as he hath, certain,
I would not lose that which I so well loved.

CARDINAL: He stands in his reputation; he will not be reproved,
And that is the cause that he is so obstinate.   1150
But I shall well enough thy courage abate.

PHILOLOGUS: I humbly beseech you, of Christian charity,
You seek not of purpose my blood for to spill,
For if I have displeased your authority
In reasonable causes redress it I will.
But in this respect I fear I should kill
My soul forever, if against my conscience
I should to the Pope's laws acknowledge obedience.

HYPOCRISY: Cease from those words if your safety you love!
As though no man had a soul more than you!   1160
Such nips perchance my Lord's patience will move;
Then would you please him if that you wist how.
But if you will be ruled by my honesty, I vow[24]
I will do the best herein that I can,
Because you seem to be a good gentleman.

AVARICE: Were it not better for you to live at ease
And spend that merrily which erst you have got,
Than by your own folly yourself to disease
And bring you to trouble, which other men seek not?

HYPOCRISY: In faith, Philologus, your zeal is too hot,   1170
Which will not be quenched but with your heart blood.
If I were so zealous I would think myself wood.   *mad*

CARDINAL: Tush, it will not be. He thinks we do but jest;
Wherefore, that some trial of my mind he may have,
That Careful Provision should go, I think best,
Into the town, and there assistance crave
His house for to enter and his goods for me save,

---

[24] Original reads "But, if you will be ruled, (by my honesty) I vow."

Lest, when his wife know that they be confiscate,
Into other men's keeping the same she doth dissipate.

HYPOCRISY: You speak very wisely, in my simple judgment,   1180
Therefore you were best to send him away.

CARDINAL: Go to, Careful Provision, depart incontinent
And fulfill the words which I to you say.

AVARICE: Of pardon herein I do your Lordship pray.
You doubt not, I trust, of my willing mind
Which herein most ready you alway shall find;
For who is more ready by fraud to purloin
Other men's goods than I am each where?
But lest some man at me should chance to foin[25]
And kill me at once, I greatly do fear.   1190
I had rather persuade him his folly to forbear.

CARDINAL: Prove then if thou canst do him any good.   *Try*
He shall not say that we seek his blood.

AVARICE: Ah Master Philologus, you see your own case,
That both life and goods are in my Lord's will;
Therefore you were best to sue for some grace,
And be content his words to fulfill.
If you neglect this, hence straightway I will,
And all your goods I will sure confiscate;
Then will you repent it when it is too late.   1200

PHILOLOGUS: My case indeed I see most miserable,
As was Susanna betwixt two evils placed;
Either to consent to sin most abhominable[26]
Or else in the world's sight to be utterly disgraced.
But as she her chastity at that time embraced,
So will I now spiritual whoredom resist,
And keep me a true virgin to my loving spouse Christ.

AVARICE: Wilt thou then neglect the provision of thy household?
Thou art therefore worse than an infidel is.

PHILOLOGUS: That you abuse God's word, to say I dare be
     bold,   1210
And the saying of Paul you interpret amiss.

---

[25] Original reads "fain." "Foin," which means "thrust a weapon," is Hazlitt's emendation.
[26] Again, as in *The Tide Tarrieth No Man*, the supposed etymology *ab homine*.

CARDINAL: I never saw the like heretic that this is.
Away, Careful Provision, about your business.
AVARICE: Sith there is no remedy, I am here in readiness.
PHILOLOGUS: I beseech your Lordship, even from the heart root,
    (*Exit* AVA[RICE].)
That you would vouchsafe for my contentation   *peace of mind*
To approve unto me by God's holy Book   *prove*
Some one of the questions of our disputation,
For I will hear you with heart's delectation,
Because I would gladly to your doctrine consent   1220
If that I could so my conscience content.
    But my conscience crieth out and bids me take heed
To love my Lord God above all earthly gain,
Whereby all this while I stand in great dread
That if I should God's statutes disdain
In wretched state then I should remain.
Thus crieth my conscience to me continually,
Which if you can stay, I will yield to you gladly.
CARDINAL: I can say no more than I have done already.
Thou heardest that I called thee heretic and fool;   1230
If thou wilt not consent to me, and that speedily,
With a new master thou shalt go to school.
HYPOCRISY: Thou hast no more wit, I see, than this stool.
Far unfit to dispute or reason with my Lord;
He can subdue thee with fire and sword, quite with one word.
    [*Enter* TYRANNY *and* SENSUAL SUGGESTION.]
TYRANNY: Come, follow apace, Sensual Suggestion,
Or else I will leave you to come all alone.
SUGGESTION: You go in haste, you make expedition.
Nay, if you run so fast I will none!
This little journey will make me to groan.   1240
I use not to trouble myself in this wise,   *I am not used to*
And now to begin I do not advise.
TYRANNY: Have not I plied me, which am come again so soon
And yet have finished such sundry business?
I have caused many pretty toys to be done,   *tricks*
So that now I have each thing in readiness.

CARDINAL: What, Master Zeal, you are praiseworthy, doubtless.
  Art thou prepared this gentleman to receive?
  He will roast a fagot, or else he me deceive.
TYRANNY: In simple manner I will him entertain,   1250
  Yet must he take it all in good part,
  And though his diet be small, he may not disdain
  Nor yet contemn the kindness of my heart;
  For though I lack instruments to put him to smart,
  Yet shall he abide in a hellish black dungeon;
  As for blocks, stocks and irons, I warrant him want   *lack none*
    none.
HYPOCRISY: Well farewell Philologus, you hear of your lodging.
  I would yet do you good, if that I wist how.
CARDINAL: Let him go, Hypocrisy; stand not all day
    dodging.   *chatting*
  You have done too much for him, I make God a vow.   1260
HYPOCRISY: Stay, for Suggestion doth come yonder now.
  Come on, lazy lubber, you make but small haste;
  Had you stayed a while longer your coming had been waste.
SUGGESTION: You know of myself I am not very quick,
  Because that my body I do so much tender,
  For Sensual Suggestion will quickly be sick
  If that his own ease he should not remember;
  Thus one cause of my tarriance to you I do render.
  Another I had, as I came by the way,
  Which did me the longer from your company stay.   1270
HYPOCRISY: What was that, Suggestion, I pray thee to us utter,
  For I am with child, till that I do it hear.
SUGGESTION: A certain gentlewoman did murmur and mutter,
  And for grief of mind her hair she did tear;
  She will at last kill herself, I greatly do fear.
HYPOCRISY: What is the cause why this grief she did take?
SUGGESTION: Because her husband her company did forsake.
  Her children also about her did stand,
  Sobbing and sighing, and made lamentation,
  Knocking their breasts and wringing their hand,   1280
  Saying they are brought to utter desolation

By means of their father's willful protestation,
Whose goods, they say, are already confiscate,
Because he doth the Pope's laws violate;
And indeed I saw Avarice standing at the door
And a company of ruffians assisting him there.

PHILOLOGUS: Alas, alas! This pincheth my heart full sore.
Mine evils he doth declare, mine own woe I do hear,
Wherefore from tears I cannot forbear.

HYPOCRISY: Ha, ha! Doth this touch you, Master Philologus? 1290
You need not have had it, being ruled by us.

SUGGESTION: Why, what is he thus, Master Hypocrisy,
That taketh such sorrow at the words which I spake?

HYPOCRISY: One that is taken and convinced of heresy,   *convicted*
And I fear me much, will burn at the stake.
Yet to reclaim him much pains would I take,
And have done already, howbeit in vain.
I would crave thine assistance were it not to thy pain.

SUGGESTION: I will do the best herein that I can,
Yet go thou with me, to help at a need.   1300
With all my heart, God save you, good gentleman!
To see your great sorrow my heart doth well nigh bleed;
But what is the cause of your trouble and dread?
Disdain not to me your secrets to tell;
A wise man sometime of a fool may take counsel.

PHILOLOGUS: Mine estate, alas, is now most lamentable,
For I am but dead whichever side I take;
Neither to determine herein am I able
With good advice mine election to make,
The worse to refuse, and the best for to take.   1310
My spirit covets the one, but alas, since your presence
My flesh leads my spirit therefro by violence.
    For at this time, I being in great extremity,
Either my Lord God in heart to reject
Or else to be oppressed by the Legate's authority
And in this world to be counted an abject;
My lands, wife and children also to neglect,
This latter part to take, my spirit is in readiness,

But my flesh doth subdue my spirit, doubtless.

SUGGESTION: Your estate perhaps seemeth to you dangerous   1320
 The rather because you have not been used
 To incur beforetime such troubles perilous,   *before now*
 But to your power such evils have refused;   *by your power?*
 Howbeit, of two evils the least must be choosed;
 Now, which is the least evil we will shortly examine.
 That which part to take yourself may determine.
  On the right hand you say you see God's just judgment,
 His wrath and displeasure on you for to fall,
 And instead of the joys of heaven, ever permanent,
 You see for your stipend the torments infernal.   1330

PHILOLOGUS: That is it indeed, which I fear most of all,
 For Christ said, "Fear not them which the body can annoy,
 But fear him which the body and soul can destroy."

SUGGESTION: Well, let that lie aside awhile as it is,
 And on the other side make the like inquisition.
 If on the left side you fall, then shall you not miss
 But to bring your body to utter perdition,
 For at man's hand you know there is no remission;
 Beside, your children fatherless, your wife desolate,
 Your goods and possessions to other men confiscate. 1340

PHILOLOGUS: Saint Paul to the Romans hath this worthy
   sentence:
 "I account the afflictions of this world transitory.
 Be they never so many, in full equivalence
 Cannot countervail those heavenly glories
 Which we shall have through Christ his propitiatory.
 I also account the rebukes of our Savior
 Greater gains to me than this house full of treasure."

SUGGESTION: You have spoken reasonably, but yet, as they
   say,
 One bird in the hand is worth two in the bush;
 So, you now enjoying these worldly joys may   1350
 Esteem the other as light as a rush,
 Thus may you 'scape this perilous push—

PHILOLOGUS: Yea, but my salvation to me is most certain,

Neither doubt I that I shall suffer this in vain.   *fear I*

SUGGESTION: Is your death meritorious then, in God's
    sight?

That you are so sure to attain to salvation?

PHILOLOGUS: I do not think so, but my faith is full pight   *set*

In the mercies of God, by Christ's mediation,

By whom I am sure of my preservation.

SUGGESTION: Then to the faithful no hurt can accrue,   1360

But whatso he worketh, good end shall ensue.

PHILOLOGUS: Our Savior Christ did say to the tempter

When he did persuade Him from the pinnacle to fall

And said he might safely that danger adventure:

"Because that God's Angels from hurt him save shall,

See that thy Lord God thou tempt not at all."

So I, though persuaded of my sins' free remission,

May not commit sin upon this presumption.

CARDINAL: What, have you not yet done your foolish tattling?

With that froward heretic I will then away.   1370

If you will tarry to hear all his prattling

He would surely keep you most part of the day.

It is now high dinner time, my stomach doth say,

And I will not lose one meal of my diet

Though thereon did hang a hundred men's quiet.

SUGGESTION: By your Lordship's patience, one word with him
    more,

And then if he will not, I give him to Tyranny.

HYPOCRISY: I never saw my Lord so patient before,

To suffer one to speak for himself so quietly,

But you were not best to trust to his courtesy;   1380

It is evil waking of a dog that doth sleep,

While you have his friendship you were best it to keep.

CARDINAL: I promise thee, Philologus, by my vowèd chastity,

If thou wilt be ruled by thy friends that be here

Thou shalt abound in wealth and prosperity,

And in the country chief rule thou shalt bear

And a hundred pounds more thou shalt have in the year;

If thou will this courtesy refuse

Thou shalt die incontinent—the one of these choose!

SUGGESTION: Well, sith it is no time for us to debate   1390
In former manner what is in my mind,
I will at once to thee staight demonstrate
Those worldly joys which here thou shalt find,
And for because thou art partly blind
In this respect, look through this mirror,
And thou shalt behold an unspeakable pleasure.

PHILOLOGUS: Oh peerless pleasures! Oh joys unspeakable!
O worldly wealth! Oh palaces gorgeous!
Oh fair children, oh wife most amiable!
Oh pleasant pastime, oh pomp so glorious!   1400
Oh delicate diet, oh life lascivious!
Oh dolorous death which would me betray,
And my felicity from me take away!
  I am fully resolved without further demeanor,
In these delights to take my whole solace,
And what pain soever hereby I incur,
Whether heaven or hell, whether God's wrath or grace,
This glass of delight I will ever embrace;
But one thing most chiefly doth trouble me here—
My neighbors unconstant will count me, I fear.   *consider me* 1410

HYPOCRISY: He that will seek each man to content,
Shall prove himself at last most unwise.
Yourself to save harmless, think it sufficient,
And weigh not the people's clamorous outcries;
Yet their mouths to stop I can soon devise:
Say that the reading of the works of S[aint] Selflove
And Doctor Ambition did your errors remove.
  And hark in thine ear—delay no more time.[27]
The sooner the better, in the end you will say.
[*To Cardinal*] We have now caught him as bird is in lime.[28]   1420

TYRANNY: Come on sirs, have ye done! I would fain away.

HYPOCRISY: Go even when you will: we do you not stay.
Philologus hath drunk such a draught of Hypocrisy

[27] Original reads "in mine ear."
[28] Original reads "in line."

That he minds not to die yet; he will master this   *has decided*
    malady.

CARDINAL: Come on Master Philologus, are you grown to a
    stay?

I am glad to hear that you become tractable.

PHILOLOGUS: Let it please your Lordship, I say even what you
    say,

And confess your religion to be most allowable;

Neither will I gainsay your customs laudable.

My former follies I utterly renounce;   1430

That myself was a heretic I do here pronounce.

CARDINAL: Nay Master Philologus, go with me to my palace

And I shall set down the form of recantation

Which you shall read on Sunday next, in open place;

This done, you shall satisfy our expectation

And shall be set free from all molestation;

Into the bosom of the Church we will you take,

And some high officer therein will you make.

PHILOLOGUS: I must first request your Lordship's favor

That I may go home, my wife for to see,   1440

And I will attend on you within this hour.

CARDINAL: Nay, I may not suffer you alone to go free,

Unless one of these your surety will be.

SUGGESTION: I, Sensual Suggestion, for him will undertake.

CARDINAL: Very well. Take him to you; your prisoner I him
    make.

Come on Master Hypocrisy, and bear me company,

Or else I am sure no meat I should eat;

And go before, Zeal, to see each thing ready,

That when we once come we stay not for meat.   *wait*

HYPOCRISY: With small suit hereto you shall me entreat.   1450

        (*Exit* TYR [ANNY].)

CARDINAL: Farewell Philologus, and make small delay;

Perhaps of our dinners for you I will stay.

        (*Ex* [*eunt*] CAR [DINAL] *and* HYP [OCRISY].)

SUGGESTION: Had not you been a wise man, yourself to have
    lost

And brought your whole family to wretched estate;
Where now of your blessedness yourself you may boast,
And of all the country account yourself fortunate.
PHILOLOGUS: Such was the wit of my foolish pate.
But what do we stay so long in this place?
I shall not be well whilst I am with my Lord's grace.   *until*

Act fourth. Scene two.[29]

PHILOLOGUS, SUGGESTION, *[Enter]* SPIRIT
SPIRIT: Philologus, Philologus, Philologus I say!   1460
In time take heed; go not too far; look well thy steps unto!
Let not Suggestion of thy flesh thy conscience betray,[30]
Who doth conduct thee in the path that leadeth to all woe.
Weigh well this warning given from God before thou further
        go,
And sell not everlasting joys for pleasures temporal,
From which thou soon shalt go, or they from thee bereavèd
        shall.
PHILOLOGUS: Alas, what voice is this I hear so dolefully to
        sound
Into mine ears, and warneth me in time yet to beware?
Why, have not I the pleasant path of worldly pleasures found?
To walk there in for my delight no man shall me debar.   1470
SUGGESTION: Look in this glass Philologus; for nought else do
        thou care.
What dost thou see within the same? Is not the coast all clear?
PHILOLOGUS: Naught else but pleasure, pomp and wealth herein
        to me appear
SUGGESTION: Give me thy hand; I will be thy guide and lead
        thee in the way.
What dost thou think, Philologus, where I dare go before?
SPIRIT: Yea, think so still, Philologus! In time turn back, I say;[31]
In Sensual Suggestion's steps see that thou tread no more;

[29] Original reads "Scene 4."
[30] Original reads "thy conscience thee betray."
[31] Original reads "no time."

And though the frailty of the flesh hath made thee fall full
    sore,
And to deny with outward lips thy Lord and God most dear,
The same to 'stablish with consent of conscience, stand in
    fear.[32]   1480
    Thou art yet free Philologus, all torments thou mayest 'scape.
Only the pleasures of the world thou shalt awhile forbear.
Renounce thy crime, and sue for grace, and do not captivate
Thy conscience unto mortal sin; the yoke of Christ do bear.
Shut up these words within thy breast which sound so in thine
    ear;
The outward man hath causèd thee this enterprise to take;
Beware, lest wickedness of spirit the same do perfect make.
PHILOLOGUS: My heart doth tremble for distress, my
    conscience pricks me sore,
And bid[s] me cease that course in time which I would gladly
    run.
The wrath of God it doth me tell doth stand my face before; 1490
Wherefore I hold it best to cease that race I have begun.
SUGGESTIONS: These are but fancies, certainly, for this way thou
    shalt shun
All worldly woes. Look in thy glass and tell me what it show[s].
Thou wilt not credit other men before thyself, I trow.
PHILOLOGUS: Oh gladsome glass, O mirror bright, oh crystal
    clear as sun!
The joys cannot be utterèd which herein I behold,
Wherefore, I will not thee forsake what evil soever come.
SPIRIT: If needs thou wilt thyself undo, say not but thou art told.
    [*Exit* SPIRIT.]
PHILOLOGUS: Hap what hap will, I will not lose these pleasures
    manifold;
Wherefore, conduct me once again. Here, take me by the
    hand.   1500
SUGGESTION: That Sensual Suggestion doth lead him, understand.

---

[32] This is technical theology. The Spirit is referring to the doctrine that sin is committed in two phases, the actual act and the consent of the will to commit the act, and that these may occur in either order. Sin with consent, that is conscious sin, is of course the deeper and more difficult from which to recover.

Act fourth. Scene three.

PHILOLOGUS, SUGGESTION, [*Enter*] CONSCIENCE

CONSCIENCE: Alas, alas thou woefull wight, what fury doth thee move
So willingly to cast thyself into consuming fire?
What Circes hath bewitched thee thy worldly wealth to love
More than the blessed state of soul? This one thing I desire:
Weigh well the cause with sincere heart, thy conscience thee require;
Resist suggestions of the flesh, who seeks thee for to spoil,
And take from me, which God elect, true everlasting soil.[33]
See where confusion doth attend, to catch thee in his snare,
Whose hands, if that thou goest on still, thou shall no way eschew.   1510

PHILOLOGUS: What wight art thou which for my health doth take such earnest care?

CONSCIENCE: Thy crazed Conscience, which forsee[s] the plagues and torments due,
Which from just Judge whom thou deniest, shall by and by ensue.

SUGGESTION: Thou hast good trial of the faith which I to thee do bear;
Commit thy safety to my charge—there is no danger near.

CONSCIENCE: Such is the blindness of the flesh that it may not descry
Or see the perils which the soul is ready to incur,
And much the less our own estates we can ourselves espy,
Because Suggestion in our hearts such fancies often stir[s]
Whereby to worldly vanities we cleave as fast as burr,   1520
Esteeming them with heavenly joys in goodness comparable,
Yet be they mostly pricks to sin abhominable.   *spurs*
      For proof we need no further go than to this present man
Who, by the blessing of the Lord, of riches having store,   *plenty*
When with his heart to fancy them this worldling once began,

---

[33] "Soil" is apparently here in the metaphorical sense of a "ground" upon which to build the life of the spirit. Original reads "take from thee."

And had this glass of vanities espied his eyes before,
He God forsook, whereas he ought have lovèd him the more,
And chooseth rather with his good to be thrown down to
    hell
Than by resisting of the same with God in heaven to dwell.
SUGGESTION: Nay, hark Philologus, how thy Conscience can
    teach,   1530
And would detain thee with glosings untrue;   *false interpretations*
And hearest thou, Conscience—thou mayest long enough preach
Ere words, from whence reason or truth none ensue,
Shall make Philologus to bid me adieu.
What, shall there no rich man dwell in God's kingdom?
Where is then Abraham, Job and David become?
CONSCIENCE: I spake not largely of all them which have this
    worldly wealth,
For why I know that riches are the creatures of the Lord,
Which of themselves are good each one, as Solomon us telleth,
And are appointed to do good withal, by God's own word;   1540
But when they let us from the Lord, then ought they be
    abhorred,
Which caused Christ himself to say that with much lesser pain
Should camel pass through needle's eye than rich man heaven
    obtain.
  Here by rich man Christ did not mean each one which wealth
    enjoy[s],
But those which fastened have their love upon this worldly dust,
Wherefore another cries and saith "Oh death, how great annoy
Dost thou procure unto that man which in his goods doth
    trust!"
That thou dost this, Philologus, thou needs acknowledge must,
Whereby each one may easily see thou takest more delight
In mundane joys than thou esteemest to be with Angels
    bright.   1550
PHILOLOGUS: This toucheth the quick! I feel the wound which if
    thou canst not cure,
As maimed in limbs I must retire; I can no further go.
This is the grief which Conscience takes against thee, I am sure,

Because thou usest those delights which Conscience may not do,
And therefore he persuadeth thee to leave the same also,
As did the fox, which caught in snare and 'scaped with loss of
    tail,
To cut off theirs, as burdensome, did all the rest counsel.

CONSCIENCE: Indeed I cannot use those fond and foolish
    vanities
In which the outward part of man doth take so great delight,
No, neither would I, though to me were given that liberty,   1560
But rather would consume them all to nought, if that I might,
For if I should delight therein, it were as good a sight
As if a man of perfect age should ride upon a stick
Or play with counters in the street, which pastime children like.
    But all my joys in heaven remains, whereas I long to be,   *where*
And so wouldst thou if that on Christ thy faith full fastened
    were,
For that affection was in Paul the Apostle, we may see;
The First to the Phillipians doth witness herein bear.
His words be these: "Oh would to God dissolvèd that I were,
And were with Christ another place." His mind in those words
    tell[s]   1570
We are but strangers all from God while in this world we dwell.
Now mark how far from his request dissenting is thy mind;
He wished for death, but more than hell thou dost the same
    detest.

SUGGESTION: The cause why Paul did loath his life may easily
    be assigned—
Because the Jews in every place did seek him to molest.
But those which in this world obtain security and rest
Do take delight to live therein, yea, nature doth indue
Each living creature with a fear lest death should them
    accrue.
Yea, the same Paul, at Antioch, dissembled to be dead,
While they were gone who sought his life with stones for to
    destroy.   1580
Elias, for to save his life, to Horeb likewise fled,
So did King David flee when Saul did seek him to annoy;

Yea, Christ himself, whom in our deed to follow we may joy,
Did secretly convey himself from Jews so full of hate,
When they thought from the top of hill him to precipitate.
Wherefore it is no sin at all a man for to defend
And keep himself from death so long as nature gives him leave.

CONSCIENCE: The same whom you recited have, conceived a
    further end
Than to themselves to live alone, as each man may perceive,
For when that Paul had run his course he did at last receive 1590
With heart's consent, the final death which was him put unto;[34]
So when Christ had performed his work he did death undergo,
And would to God thou wouldst do that which these men
    were content,
For they despisèd worldly pomp, their flesh they did subdue,
And brought it under, that to spirit it mostly did consent;
Whereby they, seeking God to please, did bid the world
    adieu,
Wife, children and possessions forsaking, for they knew
That everlasting treasures were appointed them at last,
To which they, thirsting, did from them all worldly pleasures
    cast.
But thou, o wretch, dost life prolong, not that thou wouldst
    God's name,   1600
As duty binds us all to do, most chiefly glorify,
But rather by thy living still wilt God's renown defame,
And more and more dishonor him, this is thy drift, I spy.

PHILOLOGUS: I mean to live in worldly ways, I can it not deny.

CONSCIENCE: What are those joys which thou dost mean, but
    pleasures straying from God,
By using of the which thou shalt provoke his heavenly rod?

SUGGESTION: Tush, knowest thou what, Philologus? Be wise
    thyself unto,
And listen not to these fond words which Conscience to
    thee tell [s] ;
For thy defense I will allege one worthy lesson mo,
Unto which I am right sure he cannot answer well: 1610

---

[34] Original reads "smal death." "Final" is the conjecture of the Malone Society editor, Herbert Davis.

When David, by vain trust in men of war, from God sore fell,
And was appointed of three plagues the easiest for to choose,
He said God's mercy easier is to get than man's, as I suppose.
 Again, he saith among the Psalms, it better is to trust
In God than that our confidence we settle should in man;
Wherefore, to this which I now say of force consent thou
  must:
That when two evils before us placed no way avoid we can,
Into the hand of God to fall by choice is lawful then,
Because that God is merciful, when no man mercy show[s].
Thus have I pleaded in this cause sufficiently, I trow.   1620
CONSCIENCE: How can you say you trust in God whenas you
  him forsake,
And of the wicked Mammon here do make your feignèd friend?
No, no, these words which you recite against you mostly make,
For thus he thinks in his distress God cannot me defend,
And therefore, by suggestion frail, to man's help he hath
  leaned.
Mark who say truth of him or me, and do him best believe.
PHILOLOGUS: I like thy words, but that to lost these joys it
  would me grieve.
CONSCIENCE: And where Suggestion telleth thee that God in
  mercies flow[s].
Yet is He just, sins to correct, and true in that He speak [s],
Wherefore He saith "Whoso my name before men shall not
  know,   1630
I shall not know him when as Judge I shall sit in my seat."
This if you call to mind it will your proud presumption break.
Again He saith, "Whoso his life or goods will seek to save
Shall lose them all; but who for Christ will lose them, gain
  shall have.
SUGGESTION: What, did not Peter deny, yet mercy did obtain,
Where, if he had not, of the Jews he should have tasted death?
PHILOLOGUS: Even so shall I in tract of time with bitter tears
  complain.
SUGGESTION: Yea, time enough, though thou deferest until
  thy latest breath.

CONSCIENCE: So saith Suggestion unto thee, but Conscience it
    denieth,
And in the end whatso I say for truth thou shalt espy,   1640
And that most false which Conscience shall in secret heart deny.
PHILOLOGUS: Ah wretched man, what shall I do, which do so
    plainly see
My flesh and spirit to contend, and that in no small thing,
But as concerning the event, of extreme misery,
Which either study to avoid or else upon me bring,
And which of them I should best trust it is a doubtful thing.
My Conscience speaketh truth, methink, but yet because I fear
By his advice to suffer death, I do his words forbear.
And therefore pacify thyself, and do not so torment
Thyself in vain. I must seek some means for to eschew   1650
These gripping griefs which unto me I see now imminent,
And therefore will no longer stay, but bid thee now adieu.
CONSCIENCE: Oh stay I say, Philologus, or else thou wilt it rue!
PHILOLOGUS: It is lost labor that thou dost,
        I will be at a point,   *I declare*
And to enjoy these worldly joys I jeopard will a joint   *risk a limb*
        (*Exit* PHIL[OLOGUS] *and* SUG[GESTION].)
CONSCIENCE: Oh cursed creature! Oh frail flesh! O meat for
    worms! O dust!
O bladder puffèd full of wind, O vainer than these all,
What cause hast thou in thine own wit to have so great a
    trust,
Which of thyself canst not espy the evils which on thee fall?
The blindness of the outward man Philologus show shall   1660
At his return, unless I can at last make him relent,
For why the Lord him to correct, in furious wrath is bent.
        (*Exit* CONSCIENTIA.)

Act fifth. Scene one.[35]

        [*Enter*] HYPOCRISY
HYPOCRISY: Such chopping cheer as we have made the like hath
    not been seen!

[35] Original reads "Scene 3."

And who so pleasant with my Lord as is Philologus?
His recantation he hath made, and is dispatchèd clean
Of all the griefs which unto him did seem so dangerous,
Which thing, you know, was brought to pass especially by us,
So that Hypocrisy hath done that which Satan did intend,
That men for worldly wealth should cease the Gospel to defend.

    What shall become of Foolish Goose—I mean Philologus—   1670
In actual manner to your eyes shall represented be,
For though as now he seems to be in state most glorious,
He shall not long continue so, each one of you shall see.
But needs I must be packing hence; my fellows stay for me.
Shake hands before we do depart; you shall see me no more,
 And though Hypocrisy go away, of hypocrites here is good
    store.
       (*Exit* Hyp[OCRISY].)

Act fifth. Scene two.[36]

    [*Enter*] Philo[LOGUS], Gisbert[US], Paphi[NITIUS]
Philologus: Come on my children dear to me, and let us talk
    awhile
  Of worldly goods which I have got, and of my pleasant
    state
  Which Fortune hath installèd me, who on me cheerly smile[s],
  So that into the top of wheel she doth me elevate.   1680
  I have escaped all mishaps of which my Conscience did prate,
  And where before I rulèd was, as is the common sort,
  Now as a Judge within this land I bear a ruler's
    port.   *dignified position*
Gisbertus: Indeed, good father, we have cause to praise your
    gravity,
  Who did both save yourself from woe and us from begging
    state,
  Where, if you had perseverèd still, as we did fear greatly,
  Your goods from us, your children, should to Legate been
    confiscate.

---

[36] Original reads "Scene 4."

Our glorious pomps then should we have been glad for
    to abate.
PAPHINITIUS: But now, not only that you had for us, but also
    have
Such offices whereby more gains you year by year shall have. 1690
PHILOLOGUS: I was at point once, very near to have been
    quite forlorn,
Had not Suggestion-of-the-flesh from folly me reclaimed,
And set this glass of worldly joys my sight and eyes
    beforn,   *before*
The sight whereof did cause all things of me to be disdained.
I thought I had felicity when it I had obtained,
And, to say truth, I do not care what to my soul betide,
So long as this prosperity and wealth by me abide.
   But let us homeward go again, some pastime there
    to make;
My whole delight in sport and games of pleasure I repose.
    [*Enter* HORROR.]
HORROR: Nay, stay thy journey here awhile. I do thee
    prisoner take.   1700
I shall abate thy pleasures soon, yea, too soon, thou wilt
    suppose.
PHILOLOGUS: What is thy name? Whence comest thou?
    Wherefore, to me disclose?
HORROR: My name is called Confusion and Horror-of-the-
    mind,
  And to correct impenitents of God I am assigned.
   And for because thou dost despise God's mercy and his
    grace,
And wouldst not admonition take by them that did thee warn,
Neither, when Conscience counselled thee thou wouldst his
    words embrace
Who would have had thee unto God obedience true to
    learn;
Nor couldst between Suggestion's craft and Conscience['s]
    truth discern,
Behold, therefore, thou shalt of me another lesson hear,   1710

Which, will thou nil thou, with torment of conscience thou
  shalt bear.
  And where thou hast extinguishèd the Holy Spirit of God,
And made Him weary with thy sins which daily thou hast done,
He will no longer in thy soul and spirit make abode,
But with the graces which He gave to thee, now is He gone,
So that to God-ward, by Christ's death, rejoicing hast thou
  none.
The peace of Conscience faded is, instead whereof I bring
The spirit of Satan, blasphemy, confusion and cursing.
  The glass, likewise, of vanities, which is thine only joy,
I will transform into the glass of deadly desperation,   1720
By looking in the which thou shalt conceive a great annoy.
Thus have I caught thee in thy pride and brought thee to
  damnation,
So that thou art a pattern true of God's just indignation,
Whereby each man may warnèd be, the like sins to eschew,
Lest the same torments they incur which in thee they shall
  view.
        [*Exit* HORROR.]
PHILOLOGUS: O painful pain of deep disdain, oh gripping grief
  of hell!
  Oh horror huge, oh soul suppressed and staine [d] with
    desperation!
  Oh heap of sins the sum whereof no man can number well!
  Oh death, oh furious flames of hell, my just recompensation!
  Oh wretched wight, oh creature cursed, oh child of
    condemnation!   1730
  Oh angry God and merciless, most fearful to behold!
  Oh Christ thou art no Lamb to me but Lion fierce and bold!
GISBERTUS: Alas dear father, what doth move and cause you
  to lament?
PHILOLOGUS: My sins, alas, which in this glass appear
    innumerable,
  For which I shall no pardon get, for God is fully bent
  In fury for to punish me with pains intolerable.
  Neither to call to him for grace or pardon am I able;

My sin is unto death; I feel Christ's death doth me no good,
Neither for my behoof did Christ shed his most precious
    blood.

PAPHINITIUS: Alas dear father, alas say I, what sudden change
    is this?   1740

PHILOLOGUS: I am condemnèd into hell, these torments to
    sustain.

GISBERTUS: Oh say not so, my father dear! God's mercy
    mighty is.

PHILOLOGUS: The sentence of the righteous Judge cannot be
    called again,   *revoked*

Who hath already judgèd me to everlasting pain.
Oh that my body buried were, that it at rest might be,
Though soul were put in Judas' place, or Cain's extremity.

GISBERTUS: Oh brother, haste you to the town and tell
    Theologus

What sudden plague and punishment my father hath befell.

PAPHINITIUS: I run in haste, and will request him for to come
    with us.
      [*Exit* PAPHINITIUS.]

GISBERTUS: Oh father, rest yourself in God, and all thing shall
    be well.   1750

PHILOLOGUS: Ah dreadful name, which when I hear to sigh
    it me compel[s].

God is against me, I perceive. He is none of my God
Unless in this, that he will beat and plague me with his rod.
  And though his mercy doth surpass the sins of all the
    world,
Yet shall it not once profit me or pardon mine offence.
I am refusèd utterly; I quite from God am whirled;
My name within the Book of Life had never residence;
Christ prayed not, Christ suffered not my sins to
    recompence,
But only for the Lord's elect, of which sort I am none.
I feel his justice towards me, his mercy all is gone.   1760
  And to be short, within short space my final end shall be;
Then shall my soul incur the pains of utter desolation,

And I shall be a precedent most horrible to see,
To God's elect, that they may see the price of abjuration.
GISBERTUS: To hear my father's doleful plaints it bringeth
    perturbation
Unto my soul. But yonder comes that good Theologus.
Oh welcome sir, and welcome you, good Master Eusebius.

Act fifth. Scene three.[37]

    GISBERTUS, PHILOLOGUS. [*Enter*] PAPHINITIUS, THEOLOGUS,
    EUSEBIUS.

[EUSEBIUS] God save you, good Philologus! How do you, by
    God's grace?
PHILOLOGUS: You welcome are, but I, alas, vile wretch, am
    here evil found.
EUSEBIUS: What is the chiefest cause, tell us, of this your
    dolorous case?   1770
PHILOLOGUS: Oh, would my soul were sunk in hell, so body
    were in ground!
  That angry God now hath his fill, who sought me to
    confound.
THEOLOGUS: Oh say not so Philologus, for God is gracious,
  And to forgive the penitent his mercy is plenteous.
  Do you not know that all the earth with mercy doth abound,
  And though the sins of all the world upon one man were laid,
  If he one only spark of grace or mercy once had found,
  His wickedness could not him harm? Wherefore, be not
    dismayed;
  Christ's death alone for all your sins a perfect ransom paid.
  God doth not covet sinner's death, but rather that he may,   1780
  By living still, bewail his sins and so them put away.
  Consider Peter, who three times his Master did deny,
  Yea, with an oath, and that although Christ did him warning
    give,
  With whom beforetime he had lived so long familiarly,
  Of whom so many benefits of love he did receive,

---

[37] Original reads "Scene 2."

Yet, when once Peter his own fault did at the last perceive,
And did bewail his former crime with salt and bitter tears,
Christ by and by did pardon him, the Gospel witness   *at once*
     bears.
     The thief likewise, and murderer, which never had done good.
But had in mischief spent his days, yea, during all his life;   1790
With latest breath when he his sins and wickedness
     withstood,   *repudiated*
And with iniquities of flesh his spirit was at strife;
Through that one motion of his heart, and power of true
     belief,
He was receivèd into grace, and all his sins defaced,   *wiped away*
Christ saying, "Soon in Paradise with me thou shalt be
     placed."
     The hand of God is not abridged, but still he is of might
To pardon them that call to him unfeignedly for grace.
Again, it is God's property to pardon sinners quite;
Pray therefore with thy heart to God here in this open place,
And from the very root of heart bewail to him thy case,   1800
And I assure thee God will on thee his mercy show,
Through Jesus Christ who is with him our advocate, you
     know.
PHILOLOGUS: I have no faith. The words you speak my heart
     doth not believe.
I must confess that I for sin am justly thrown to hell.
EUSEBIUS: His monstrous incredulity my very heart doth grieve.
     Ah dear Philologus, I have known by face and visage well
A sort of men which have been vexed with devils and
     spirits fell,   *evil*
In far worse state than you are yet, brought into
     desperation,
Yet in the end have been reclaimed by godly exhortation.
     Such are the mercies of the Lord—He will throw down to
     hell   1810
And yet call back again from thence, as holy David writes.
What should then let your trust in God, I pray you to us tell,
Sith to forgive and do us good it chiefly Him delights.

What, would not you that of your sins He should you clean
    acquit?
How can He once deny to you one thing you do request,
Which hath already given to you His best beloved, Christ?
    Lift up your heart in hope, therefore; a while be of good
      cheer,
And make access unto His seat of grace by earnest prayer,
And God will surely you relieve with grace, stand not in fear.
PHILOLOGUS: I do believe that out from God proceed these
    comforts fair;   1820
So do the devils; yet of their health they always do despair.
They are not written unto me, for I would fain attain
The mercy and the love of God, but He doth me disdain.
How would you have that man to live, which hath no mouth
    to eat?
No more can I live in my soul, which have no faith at all;
And where you say that Peter did of Christ soon pardon get,
Who in the self-same sin with me from God did greatly fall,
Why I cannot obtain the same, to you I open shall:
God had respect to him always, and did me firmly love,[38]
But I, alas, am reprobate; God doth my soul reprove.   1830
    Moreover, I will say with tongue whatso you will require;
My heart, I feel, with blasphemy and cursing is replete.
THEOLOGUS: Then pray with us as Christ us taught, we do you
    all desire.
PHILOLOGUS: To pray with lips unto your God you shall me
    soon entreat;
My spirit to Satan is in thrall, I can it not thence get.
EUSEBIUS: God shall renew your spirit again; pray only as you
    can,
And to assist you in the same we pray each Christian man.
PHILOLOGUS: O God, which dwellest in the heavens and art
    our Father dear,
Thy holy name throughout the world be ever sanctified;
The kingdom of Thy Word and Spirit upon us rule might
    bear;   1840

[38] Hazlitt emends to "did him firmly love."

Thy will in earth, as by Thy Saints in heaven be ratified;
Our Daily bread we Thee beseech .O Lord, for us provide;
Our sins remit Lord unto us, as we each man forgive;
Let not temptation us assail, in all evil us relieve. Amen.

THEOLOGUS: The Lord be praised, who hath at length our
  spirits mollified.
These are not tokens unto us of your reprobation.
You mourn with tears and sue for grace, wherefore be
  certified   *sure*
That God in mercy giveth ear unto your supplication.
Wherefore despair not thou at all of thy soul's preservation,
And say not with a desperate heart that God against
  thee is;   1850
He will, no doubt, these pains once past, receive you into bliss.

PHILOLOGUS: No, no my friends, you only hear and see the
  outward part,
Which though you think they have done well, it booteth not
  at all;
My lips have spoke the words indeed, but yet I feel my heart
With cursing is replenished, with rancor, spite and gall;
Neither do I your Lord and God in heart my Father call,
But rather seek His holy name for to blaspheme and curse.
My state therefore doth not amend, but wax still worse and
  worse;
I am secluded clean from grace, my heart is hardened quite,
Wherefore you do your labor lose, and spend your breath in
  vain.   1860

EUSEBIUS: Oh say not so, Philologus, but let your heart be
  pight
Upon the mercies of the Lord, and I you ascertain *assure*
Remission of your former sins you shall at last obtain.
God hath it said, who cannot lie, at whatsoever time
A sinner shall from heart repent, I will remit his crime.

PHILOLOGUS: You cannot say so much to me as herein I do
  know,
That by the mercies of the Lord all sins are done away,
And unto them that have true faith abundantly it flow;

But whence do this true faith proceed to us, I do you pray?
It is the only gift of God, from Him it comes alway.   1870
I would therefore he would vouchsafe one spark of faith to
    plant
Within my breast; then of his grace I know I should not
    want.
    But it as easily may be done as you may with one spoon
Take up the water clean which in the seas abide
And at one draught then drink it up; this shall ye do as soon
As to my breast of true belief one sparkle shall betide.
Tush, you which are in prosperous state and my pains have
    not tried,
Do think it but an easy thing, a sinner to repent
Him of his sins, and by true faith damnation to prevent.
    The healthful need not physic's art, and ye which   *medicine*
        are all hale   *healthy* 1880
Can give good counsel to the sick, their sickness to eschew,
But here, alas, confusion and hell doth me assail
And that all grace from me is reft, I find it to be true.
My heart is steel, so that no faith can from the same ensue;
I can conceive no hope at all of pardon or of grace,
But out, alas, Confusion is alway before my face.
    And certainly, even at this time I do most plainly see[39]
The devils to be about me round, which make great
    preparation,
And keep a stir here in this place which only is for me.
Neither do I conceive these things by vain imagination,   1890
But even as truly as mine eyes behold your shape and fashion.
Wherefore, desired death dispatch, my body bring to rest,
Though that my soul in furious flames of fire be suppressed.
THEOLOGUS: Your mind corrupted doth present to you this
        false illusion,
But turn awhile unto the spirit of truth in your distress,
And it shall cast out from your eyes all horror and
    confusion,
And of this your affliction it will you soon redress.

[39] Original reads "at his time."

EUSEBIUS: We have good hope, Philologus, of your salvation,
    doubtless.

PHILOLOGUS: What your hope is concerning me, I utterly
    contemn;

My Conscience, which for thousands stand [s], as guilty me
    condemn [s].   1900

EUSEBIUS: When did this horror first you take? What think you
    is the cause?

PHILOLOGUS: Even shortly after I did make mine open abjuration,

For that I did prefer my goods before God's holy laws.

Therefore in wrath he did me send this horrible vexation,

And hath me wounded in the soul with grievous tribulation,

That I may be a precedent in whom all men may view

Those torments which to them that will forsake the Lord
    are due.

THEOLOGUS: Yet let me boldly ask one thing of you without
    offence:

What was your former faith in Christ which you before did
    hold?

For it is said of holy Paul in these same words in sense: 1910

It cannot be that utterly in faith he should be cold,

Whoso he be which perfectly true faith in heart once hold.   *held*

Wherefore, rehearse in short discourse the sum of your
    belief,

In those points chiefly which for health of soul are thought
    most chief.

PHILOLOGUS: I did believe in heart that Christ was that true
    sacrifice

Which did appease the Father's wrath, and that by Him alone

We were made just, and sanctified; I did believe likewise

That without Him heaven to attain sufficient means were
    none.

But to re-knowledge this again, alas, all grace was gone.

I never loved Him again with right and sincere heart,   1920

Neither was thankful for the same, as was each good man's part,

    But rather took the faith of Christ for liberty to sin,

And did abuse his graces great to further carnal lust.

What wickedness I did commit I carèd not a pin,
For that that Christ dischargèd had my ransom I did trust;
Wherefore the Lord doth now correct the same with torments
    just.
My sons, my sons, I speak to you. My counsel ponder well,
And practice that in deeds which I in words shall to you
    tell.
    I speak not this that I would aught the Gospel derogate
Which is most true in every part, I must it needs confess,   *1930*
But this I say, that of vain faith alone you should not prate,
But also by your holy life you should your faith express.
Believe me sirs, for by good proof these things I do express.
Peruse the writings of S[t]. James, and First of Peter's too,
Which all God's people holiness of life exhort unto,
    By sundry reasons; as for first, because we strangers are;
Again sin from the flesh proceed[s], but we are of the
    spirit;
The third, because the flesh alway against the spirit do
    war;
The fourth, that we may stop the mouths of such as would
    backbite;
The fifth, that other, by our lives, to God reduce we   *lead back*
    might;   *1940*
Again, they sing a pleasant song which sing in deed and word,
But where evil life ensue good words, there is a foul discord.
    But I, alas, most wretched wight, whereas I did presume
That I had got a perfect faith, did holy life disdain,
And though I did to other preach good life I did consume
My life in wickedness and sin, in sport and pleasures vain,
No, neither did I once contend from them flesh to restrain.
Behold therefore the judgments just, of God doth me annoy,
Not for amendment of my life but me for to destroy.
EUSEBIUS: We do not altogether like of this your
    exhortation,   *1950*
Whereas you want us not to trust so much unto our faith,
But that good works we should prepare unto our preservation.
There are two kinds of righteousness, as Paul to *Romans* saith;

The one dependeth of good works, the other hangs of
 faith.
The former, which the world allows, God counts it least of
 twain,
As by good proof it shall to you in words be provèd plain.
 For Socrates and Cato both did purchase great renown,
And Aristides, surnamed "Just," this righteousness fulfilled,
Wherefore he was, as justest man, expelled his native town.
Yet are their souls with infidels in hell forever spilled,   1960
Because they sought not righteousness that way that God them
 willed,
For other righteousness comes from faith, which God regards
 alone,
And makes us seem immaculate before his heavenly throne.
 Wherefore, there is no cause you should send us to outward
 act
As to the anchor or refuge of our preservation.
THEOLOGUS: The meaning of Philologus is not here so exact
 As do his words make it to seem by your allegation.
He doth not mean between good works and faith to make
 relation,
As though works were equivalent salvation to attain,
As is true faith. But what he meant I will set down more
 plain: 1970
He did exhort the young men here by him for to beware,
Lest, as he did, so they abuse God's Gospel pure,
And without good advice usurp of faith the gift so rare;
Whereby they think, whatso they do, themselves from torment
 free,
And by this proud presumption God's anger should procure,
And where they boast and vaunt themselves good faithful men
 to be,
Yet in their lives they do deny their faith, in each degree.
 Wherefore he saith, as Peter said, see that you do make
 known
Your own election by your works; again, S[t]. James doth
 say,

Show me thy faith, and by my works my faith shall thee be
    shown.   1980
And whereupon his own offence he doth to them bewray,   *betray*
Whereas he did vaingloriously upon a dead faith stay,
Which for the inward righteousness he alway did suspect,
And hereupon all godliness of life he did neglect.

PHILOLOGUS: That was the meaning of my words, how ever I
    them spake;
The truth, alas vile wretch, my soul and conscience too true
    feel.

THEOLOGUS: What, do you not, Philologus, with us no
    comfort take,
When all these things so godlyly to you I do reveal,
Especially sith that yourself in them are seen so well?
Some hope unto us of your health and safety yet is left;   1990
We do not think that all God's grace from you is wholly reft.

PHILOLOGUS: Alas, what comfort can betide unto a damnèd
    wretch?
Whatso I hear, see, feel, taste, speak, is turnèd all to woe.

EUSEBIUS: Ah dear Philologus, think not that aught can God's
    grace outreach.
Consider David, which did sin in lust and murder too,
Yet was he pardoned of his sins, and so shalt thou also.

PHILOLOGUS: King David always was elect, but I am
    reprobate,[40]
And therefore I can find small ease by weighing his estate.
    He also prayèd unto God, which I shall never do;
His prayer was that God would not his spirit take away,   2000
But it is gone from me long since, and shall be given no mo.
But what became of Cain, of Ham, of Saul, I do you pray?
Of Judas and Bar-Jesu, these must my conscience stay.
Of Julian Apostata, with other of that crew,
The same torments must I abide which these men did ensue.

THEOLOGUS: Alas my friend, take in good part the chastisement
    of the Lord,
Who doth correct you in this world that in the life to come

---

[40] Interestingly, Philologus has swung from acquiescence to Rome straight into Calvinism.

He might you save, for of the like the Scripture bears record.
PHILOLOGUS: That is not God's intent with me, though it be
   so with some
Who after bodies' punishment have into favor come.   2010
But I, alas, in spirit and in soul these grievous torments bear.
God hath condemend me conscience to perpetual grief and
   fear.
I would most gladly choose to live a thousand thousand year,
So that at length I might have ease, it would me greatly cheer.
But I, alas, shall in this life in torments still remain,
While God's just anger upon me shall be revealèd plain,
And I example made to all, of God's just indignation.
Oh that my body were at rest, and soul in condemnation.
EUSEBIUS: I pray you, answer me herein: where you by deep
   despair
Say you are worse here in this life than if you were in hell,   2020
And for because to have death come you alway make your
   prayer,
As though your soul and body both in torments great did
   dwell;
If that a man should give to you a sword, I pray you tell,
Would you destroy yourself therewith, as do the desperate,
Which hang, or kill, or into floods themselves precipitate?
PHILOLOGUS: Give me a sword—then shall you know what is
   in mine intent.
EUSEBIUS: Not so, my friend. I only ask what herein were
   your will.
PHILOLOGUS: I cannot, neither will I tell whereto I would be
   bent.
THEOLOGUS: These words do nothing edify, but rather fancies
   fill,
Which we would gladly, if we could, endeavor for to kill.   2030
Wherefore I once again request, together let us pray,
And so we will leave you to God, and send you hence away.
PHILOLOGUS: I cannot pray. My spirit is dead, no faith in me
   remain[s].
THEOLOGUS: Do as you can, no more than might we can ask at
   your hand.

PHILOLOGUS: My prayers turned is to sin, for God doth it
　　disdain.

EUSEBIUS: It is the falsehood of the spirit, which do your health
　　withstand,

　That teach you this. Wherefore, in time reject his filthy
　　　band.

THEOLOGUS: Come kneel by me, and let us pray the Lord of
　　heaven unto.

PHILOLOGUS: With as good will as did the devil out of the deaf
　　man go.

　O God, which dwellest in the heavens—　　　　　　　　2040

　Tush sirs, you do your labors lose. See, where Beelzebub doth
　　come,

　And doth invite me to a feast. You therefore speak in vain,

　Yea, if you ask aught more of me, in answer I will be dumb,

　I will not waste my tongue for naught. As soon shall one
　　　small grain

　Of mustardseed fill all the world, as I true faith attain.

THEOLOGUS: We will no longer stay you now, but let you
　　hence depart.

EUSEBIUS: Yet will we pray continually that God would you
　　convert.

THEOLOGUS: Gisbertus and Paphinitius, conduct him to his
　　place,

　But see he have good company—let him not be alone.

AMBO: We shall so do, God us assist with His most holy　*Both*
　　grace.　　　　　　　　　　　　　　　　　　　　　　　　2050

GISBERTUS: Come, father. Do you not think good that we from
　　hence be gone?

PHILOLOGUS: Let go my hands at liberty! Assistance I crave
　　none.

　Oh that I had a sword a while—I should soon easèd be.

AMBO: Alas, dear father, what do you?

EUSEBIUS: His will we may now see.

　　　　　(*Exeunt* PHIL[OLOGUS], GIS[BERTUS], PAPH[INITIUS].)

THEOLOGUS: O glorious God, how wonderful those judgments
　　are of Thine!

Thou dost behold the secret heart; naught doth Thy eyes
    beguile.
Oh what occasion is us given to fear Thy might divine,
And from our hearts to hate and loath iniquities so vile,
Lest for the same Thou in Thy wrath dost grace from us
    exile.   2060
The outward man doth Thee not please, nor yet the mind alone,
But Thou requirest both of us, or else regardest none.

EUSEBIUS: Here may the worldlings have a glass, their states
    for to behold,
And learn in time for to escape the judgments of the Lord,
Whilst they, by flattering of themselves, of faith both dead and
    cold,
Do sell their souls to wickedness, of all good men abhorred.
But godliness doth not depend in knowing of the word
But in fulfilling of the same, as in this man we see,
Who though he did to others preach, his life did not agree.

THEOLOGUS: Again, Philologus witnesseth which is the truth
    of Christ,   2070
For that, consenting to the Pope, he did the Lord abjure,
Whereby he teached the wavering faith on which side to
    persist,
And those which have the truth of God, that still they may
    endure
The tyrants which delight in blood, he likewise doth assure,
In whose affairs they spend their time. But let us homeward go.

EUSEBIUS: I am content that after meat we may resort him to.
    (*Exeunt* THEO[LOGUS] *and* EUSE[BIUS].)

Act six. Scene last.

      [*Enter*] NUNTIUS   *Messenger*
NUNTIUS: Oh doleful news which I report and bring into
    your ears!
Philologus by deep despair hath hanged himself with cord.
His wife for dolor and distress her yellow hair she tears,

His children sigh and weep for grief; life is of them
　　abhorred.　　　　　　　　　　　　　　　　　　　2080
But in this man we may descry the judgments of the Lord,
Who, though He spare His rod awhile, in hope we will amend,
If we persist in wickedness, He plagues us in the end.
　These thirty weeks Philologus hath had afflicted mind,
All which time we would take no meat, but that against his
　　will
A certain man, of courage stout, his hands with cords did
　　bind,
And with a feather or a spoon his mouth with broth did fill,
He, with his power laboring the same on ground to spill.
He did avoid no manner thing, no sleep he could attain,
And his own hand, now at the last hath wrought his endless
　　pain.　　　　　　　　　　　　　　　　　　　　　2090

Finis

From the Second Issue of the Play, Lines 29–42 and 57–70 of the
PROLOGUE, *and the Final Speech of the* NUNTIUS.

The argument, or ground, whereon our Author chiefly stayed
Is, sure, a History strange and true, to many men well known,
Of one, through love of worldly wealth and fear of death
　　dismayed,
Because he would his life and goods have kept still as his own,
From state of grace wherein he stood was almost overthrown,
So that he had no power at all in heart firm faith to have,
Till at the last God changed his mind, His mercies for to crave.
And here our Author thought it meet the true name to omit,
And at this time imagine him Philologus to be;
First, for because a Comedy will hardly him permit
The vices of one private man to touch particularly;
Again, now shall it stir them more who shall it hear or see,

For if this worldling had been named, we would straight deem
    in mind
That all by him then spoken were; ourselves we would not
    find.

    *   *   *   *   *   *   *   *

A cruel conflict certainly, where Conscience takes the foil,
And is contrainèd by the flesh to yield to deadly sin,
Whereby the grace and love of God from him his sin doth
    spoil.
Then wretch accursed small power hath, repentance to begin.
This History here example shows of one fast wrapped therein,
As in discourse before your eyes shall plainly provèd be.
Yet, at the last God him restored, even of His mercy free.
And though the History of itself be too too dolorous,
And would constrain a man with tears of blood his cheeks to
    wet,
Yet to refresh the minds of them that be the auditors
Our Author intermixèd hath, in places fit and meet,
Some honest mirth, yet always ware decorum to exceed.
But list, I hear the players prest in presence forth to come.
I therefore cease and take my leave; my message I have done.

Act six, Scene last

NUNTIUS: Oh joyful news which I report and being into your
    ears!
    Philologus, that would have hanged himself with cord,
    Is now converted unto God, with many bitter tears.
    By goodly counsel he was won, all praise be to the Lord.
    His errors all he did renounce, his blasphemies be abhorred,
    And being converted left his life exhorting foe and friend
    That do profess the faith of Christ to be constant to the end.
    Full thirty weeks in woeful wise afflicted he had been,
    All which long time he took no food but forced against his
        will,
    Even with a spoon to pour some broth his teeth between;

And though they sought this wise to feed him still,
He always strove with all his might the same on ground to
    spill,
So that no sustenance he received, ne sleep could he attain,
And now the Lord in mercy great hath eased him of his pain.

BIBLIOGRAPHY

Abbreviations

Adams: Joseph Quincy Adams. *Chief Pre-Shakespearean Dramas*. Boston, 1924.

Brandl: Alois Brandl. *Quellen des weltlichen Dramas in England vor Shakespeare*. Strassburg, 1898.

Dodsley: Robert Dodsley. *A Select Collection of Old English Plays*. 4th ed. by W. Carew Hazlitt. 15 vols. London, 1874–76.

E.E.T.S.: Publications of the Early English Text Society. London, to date.

Jahrbuch: *Jahrbuch der Deutschen Shakespeare, Gesellschaft*. Berlin, 1864 to date.

Materialien: *Materialien zur Kunde des alteren englischen Dramas*. W. Bang, general editor. Louvain, 1902–14. Continued as *Materials for the Study of Old English Drama*. Henry de Vocht, general editor.

M.S.R.: Malone Society Reprints. Walter Greg, general editor. London, to date.

T.F.T.: Tudor Facsimile Texts. Issued by John S. Farmer. London, 1907–14.

Plays

A list of morality plays not included in this volume, with references to facsimiles of the original editions, reliable reprints, and widely available modern editions. The list is not intended to be exhaustive.

Appius and Virginia, "by R.B.," 1575. Dodsley, IV. M.S.R., 1911.
Calisto and Melibea, J. Rastell(?), 1525(?). Dodsley, I. M.S.R., 1908.

Cambises, Thomas Preston, 1570(?). Dodsley, IV. Adams. Baskerville, Heltzel and Nethercott. *Elizabethan and Stuart Plays.* New York, 1934.

The Disobedient Child, Thomas Ingelend, 1570(?). Dodsley, II. T.F.T., 1908.

Godly Queen Hester, anonymous, 1561. *Materialien,* V, 1904. J. S. Farmer. *Anonymous Plays,* London, 1906.

Hickscorner, anonymous, 1513–19. Dodsley, I. J. S. Farmer. *Six Anonymous Plays.* London, 1905.

Horestes, J. Pickering, 1567. T.F.T., 1910. Brandl.

Impatient Poverty, anonymous, 1547–58. T.F.T., 1907. *Materialien,* XXXIII, 1911. J. S. Farmer. *"Lost" Tudor Plays.* London, 1907.

John the Evangelist, anonymous, 1520–57. T.F.T., 1907. M.S.R., 1907. J. S. Farmer, *"Lost" Tudor Plays.* London, 1907.

King John, John Bale, 1530–36. M.S.R., 1931. *Materialien,* XXV, 1909.

Liberality and Prodigality, anonymous, 1567. M.S.R., 1913. Dodsley, VIII.

Life and Repentance of Mary Magdalene, Lewis Wager, c.1550. F. I. Carpenter. Chicago, 1902.

Like Will to Like, Ulpian Fulwell, 1562–68. T.F.T., 1909. Dodsley, III.

The Longer Thou Livest, the More Fool Thou Art, W. Wager, 1560–68. T.F.T., 1910. Jahrbuch, XXXVI, 1900.

Lusty Juventus, R. Wever, 1547–53. T.F.T., 1907. Dodsley, II.

Magnificence, John Skelton, 1513–16. E.E.T.S., 1908, ed. R. L. Ramsay. P. Henderson. *Complete Poems of John Skelton.* London, 1931.

Mankind, anonymous, c.1460. F. J. Furnivall and Alfred Pollard. *The Macro Plays.* E.E.T.S., extra series, 91. London, 1904. Adams. Brandl.

The Marriage between Wit and Wisdom, Francis Merbury(?), c.1579. T.F.T., 1909. Shakespeare Society, 1846, ed. J. O. Halliwell.

The Marriage of Wit and Science, anonymous, 1568–70. T.F.T., 1909. Dodsley, II.

Misogonus, Laurentius Bariona(?), 1560–77. Brandl. J. S. Farmer. *Anonymous Plays.* London, 1906.

Nature, Henry Medwall, 1490–1501. T.F.T., 1908. Brandl. J. S. Farmer. *"Lost" Tudor Plays.* London, 1907.

The Nature of the Four Elements, John Rastell, 1517–18. T.F.T., 1908. Dodsley, I. J. S. Farmer. *Six Anonymous Plays.* London, 1905.

New Custom, anonymous, 1559–73. T.F.T., 1908. Dodsley, III. J. S. Farmer. *Anonymous Plays.* London, 1906.

Nice Wanton, anonymous, 1547–53. T.F.T., 1909. Dodsley, II.

Patient and Meek Grissell, John Phillip, 1561–65. M.S.R., 1909.

The Pride of Life, anonymous, c.1390. Brandl. E.E.T.S., 1909, ed. O. Waterhouse.

The Satire of the Three Estates, Sir David Lindsay, 1535–40. D. Hamer. *Works of Sir David Lindsay.* Edinburgh, 1931–36.

Three Ladies of London, Robert Wilson, 1581. Dodsley, VI.

Three Laws, John Bale, 1530–36. J. S. Farmer. *The Dramatic Writings of John Bale.* London, 1907. T.F.T., 1908.

Three Lords and Ladies of London, Robert Wilson, 1589. T.F.T., 1912. Dodsley, VI.

The Trial of Treasure, W. Wager(?), 1567. T.F.T., 1908. Dodsley, III. J. S. Farmer, *Anonymous Plays.* London, 1906.

Wealth and Health, anonymous, 1553–57. M.S.R., 1907. J. S. Farmer. *"Lost" Tudor Plays.* London, 1907.

Wisdom, Who is Christ, anonymous, c.1475. J. F. Furnivall and Alfred Pollard. *The Macro Plays.* E.E.T.S., extra series, 91. London, 1904.

Further Reading

A list of books and articles on the morality drama, its place in Medieval and Renaissance drama, and its influence on Elizabethan drama.

Adams, Henry Hitch. *English Domestic or Homiletic Tragedy.* New York, 1953.

Armstrong, William A. "The Authorship and Political Meaning of *Cambises,*" *English Studies,* XXXVI (December 1955).

————. "The Background and Sources of *Cambises,*" *English Studies,* XXXI (1950).

Bevington, David. *From Mankind to Marlowe.* Cambridge, Mass., 1962.

Bernard, J. E. "The Prosody of the Tudor Interlude," *Yale Studies in English,* XC (1939).

Boughner, D. C. "Vice, Braggart and Falstaff," *Anglia,* LXXII (1954–55).

Brown, A. "The Play of Wit and Science," *PQ,* XXVIII (1949).

Campbell, O. J. "The Salvation of King Lear," *ELH,* XV (1948).

Chambers, E. K. *The Elizabethan Stage.* 4 vols. Oxford, 1923.

————. *The Mediaeval Stage.* 2 vols. Oxford, 1903.

Craig, Hardin. "Morality Plays and Elizabethan Drama," *SQ,* I (1950).

Craik, T. W. *The Tudor Interlude.* London, 1962.

————. "The Tudor Interlude and Later Elizabethan Drama," *Elizabethan Theater,* Stratford Upon Avon Studies, IX. London, 1966.

Farnham, Willard. *The Medieval Heritage of Elizabethan Tragedy.* Berkeley, Calif., 1936.

Mackenzie, William Roy. *The English Moralities from the Point of View of Allegory.* Boston, 1914.

McCusker, Honor. *John Bale, Dramatist and Antiquary.* Bryn Mawr, 1942.

Owst, G. R. *Literature and the Pulpit in Medieval England.* Cambridge, 1933.

Reed, A. W. *Early Tudor Drama.* London, 1926.

Ribner, Irving. *The English History Play in the Age of Shakespeare.* Princeton, 1957.

————. "The Morality Roots of the Tudor History Play," *Tulane Studies in English,* IV (1954).

Righter, Anne. *Shakespeare and the Idea of the Play.* London, 1964.

Robinson, J. W. "Mediaeval English Acting," *Theater Notebook,* XIII (1959).

Rossiter, A. P. *English Drama from the Early Times to the Elizabethans.* London, 1950.

Schell, E. T. "On the Imitation of Life's Pilgrimage in *The Castle of Perseverance*," *JEGP,* LXVII (1968).

Southern, Richard. "The Contribution of the Interlude to Elizabethan Staging," *Essays on Shakespeare and Elizabethan Drama in Honor of Hardin Craig.* Columbia, Mo., 1962.

————. *The Medieval Theatre in the Round.* London, 1957.

Spivack, Bernard. *Shakespeare and the Allegory of Evil.* New York, 1958.

Thompson, E. N. S. "The English Moral Play," *Transactions of the Connecticut Academy of Arts and Sciences,* XIV (1910).

Tillyard, E. M. W. *Shakespeare's History Plays.* London, 1956.

Williams, Arnold. *The Drama of Medieval England.* East Lansing, Mich., 1961.

————. "The English Moral Play before 1500," *Annuale Mediaevale,* IX (1963).

Wilson, John Dover. *The Fortunes of Falstaff.* New York, 1944.

Wright, Louis B. "Social Aspects of Some Belated Moralities," *Anglia,* LIV (1930).

Rinehart Editions